A CRITICAL HISTORY OF WESTERN PHILOSOPHY

(Greek, Medieval and Modern)

D1028346

A CRITICAL HISTORY
OF
WESTERN PHILOSOPHY

(Greek, Medieval and Modern)

Y. MASIH, *Ph.D. (Edin.), D. Litt. (Pat.)*
Formerly University Professor of Philosophy,
Magadh University, Bodh Gaya

MOTILAL BANARSIDASS
Delhi Varanasi Patna Bangalore Madras

Fifth Revised & Enlarged Edition: Delhi, 1994

*Earlier edition printed as "A Critical History of
Modern Philosophy"*

© **MOTILAL BANARSIDASS**

Bungalow Road, Jawahar Nagar, Delhi 110 007
Chowk Varanasi 221 001
Ashok Rajpath, Patna 800 004
16, St. Mark's Road, Bangalore 560 001
120, Roypettah High Road, Maylapur, Madras 600 004

ISBN : 81-208-1241-1 (Cloth)
ISBN : 81-208-1242-x (Paper)

Price :   Rs. 150 (Cloth)
           Rs. 95 (Paper)

PRINTED IN INDIA
BY JAINENDRA PRAKSH JAIN AT SHRI JAINENDRA
PRESS, A-45 NARAINA, PHASE I, NEW DELHI 110 028
AND PUBLISHED BY NARENDRA PRAKASH JAIN
FOR MOTILAL BANARSIDASS, DELHI 110 007

Preface to the Fifth Revised and Enlarged Edition

The present book was first published in 1947. Since then many printings and revisions have taken place. The present edition shows that Plato has continued and developed Socratic thought. Again, a very intimate relationship has been shown between Platonism and Christianity, which is not emphasized for Indian students. Further, there is much in Greek and Medieval Philosophy which echoes the religious thought of India. It is not true

> East is east and West is west
> And the twain shall never meet.

They do meet and part, and will meet again and again, for the human spirit is one and the same.

Patna
November 1993   Y. MASIH

Preface

In the early days of Logical Positivism it was contended that metaphysics is pseudo-science and as such it had to be denounced wholesale. In this connection some of the essays of Moritz Schlick,[1] of Prof. R. Carnap[2] and Prof. A.J. Ayer's *Language, Truth and Logic* are worth-mentioning. However, even at this time it was suggested that after all metaphysics need not be science at all. It may be just a kind of poetry.[3] However, Prof. R. Carnap and Prof. A.J. Ayer reject this way of viewing metaphysics. Prof. R. Carnap remarks that the pages of metaphysics are full of arguments and polemics. But a poetry is never constituted of them.[4] Hence, he does not regard metaphysics as poetry. In the same strain Prof. A.J. Ayer holds that a poem is a conscious attempt at expressing and arousing emotions by means of nonsensical statements. As opposed to this, a metaphysician unknowingly lapses into linguistic confusion in the vain attempt of knowing the world by non-scientific means.[5]

Further, some positivists like Richard Von Mises do not accept the validity of the distinction between science and poetry. Mises holds that poetry does not indulge in nonsensical statements. Even poetry conveys, according to him, cognitive meaning. So metaphysics too, according to this writer is a sort of science. It is a form of science in its stage of beginning.[6] Now most probably the majority of empiricists would not regard metaphysics as a form of science even in its initial stage. For them metaphysical statements lack cognitive meaningfulness. However, they may hold that these statements are characterised by significant nonsense (Wittgenstein), or, that they may be helpful in 'seeing the world in a fresh and interesting way',[7] or that metaphysical statements are schizophrenic verbalism.[8] Here the views of M. Lazerowitz are interesting.

1. *The Turning Point in Philosophy* [1930] and *Positivism and Realism* (1932-33) have been reprinted in **Logical Positivism**, edited by A. J. Ayer [The Free Press, Glencoe, Illionis 1959].
2. *The Elimination of Metaphysics* (1932), reprinted in **Logical Positivism.**
3. C. A. Mace, *Representation and Expression* (1933-34) reprinted in Macdonald, **Philosophy and Analysis**, *Metaphysics and Emotive Language*, ANALYSIS 1934-35. 'A.J. Ayer, Demonstration of the impossibility of metaphysics', MIND, 1934, reprinted in **A Modern Introduction to Philosophy**, edited by Edwards and Pap (Free Press 1957). Similarly Prof. R. Carnap regards metaphysics as an expression of the general attitude of a person towards life, *Logical Positivism*, pp. 78ff.
4 *Ibid.*, p. 79.
5 *Language, Truth and Logic*, pp. 44-45.
6. *Positivism*, pp. 267-68.
7. A.J. Ayer, *Editor's Introduction*, p. 17 in **Logical Positivism**; J.O. Wisdom, *Metaphysics and Verification* in **Philosophy and Psycho-analysis** p. 100; F. Waismann, '*How I See Philosophy*' in 'Contemporary British Philosophy', reprinted in **Logical Positivism.**
8. S. Freud was not in the Vienna Circle of positivism, but his *A Philosophy of Life* leaves in no doubt about his leanings. He would regard metaphysics as schizophrenic verbalism, Collected Papers, Vol. IV, p. 136; Preface to T. Reik's *Ritual*, pp. 7-8.

> Like a dream, a metaphysical theory is a production of the unconscious and has both sense and motivation. We enjoy it or are repelled by it, it gives us pleasure or pain, a feeling of security or one of danger. . .A metaphysical theory, I shall try to show, is a verbal dream, the linguistic substructure of which has to be uncovered before we see what it comes to and how it produces its effect.[1]

Within the pages of this book, I have assumed that the empirical attack has conclusively shown that metaphysics is not a cognitive enterprise. But I also hold that it has not undermined the foundation of metaphysics. Only a few metaphysicians could have taken metaphysics as a *science* of the transcendental entities or of the supersensible. The empirical attack has at least removed that confusion about metaphysics. The perennial philosophy both in the west and east has its concern with self-knowledge. It is not an accident that Socrates heard the oracles of Delphi 'Man! know thyself'. The most important school in India has repeatedly held that the vocation of philosophy is embodied in आत्मानम् विद्धि (know thyself). Hence, we can say that metaphysical statements aim at expressing and arousing the state of being a complete self or whole.

But can an individual become a whole without being in commerce with his physical, social and cultural environment? The answer is beautifully conveyed to us in Bernard Bosanquet's *Individuality and Value,* and *The Value and Destiny of the Individual.* And if an individual has to live in an interactive relationship successfully, can he disregard the cognitive statements concerning empirical sciences relating to his environment? But as science has only an instrumental value for man, as Prof. John Macmurray has held in *The Boundaries of Science,* and as all the responses are in the service of restoring and preserving the psychical balance or equilibrium of an individual, according to Freud and C.G. Jung, so we can say that all cognitive statements remain subservient to the holistic tendency in man.

Any response which helps an individual to satisfy his sovereign and master drive of becoming a whole certainly will have a rhapsodical resonance. But this feeling is quite distinct from ordinary affective and emotional states. It is eudaemonistic or bliss which pertains to the whole being of an individual. Two things at once stand out in the holistic statements of metaphysics. First, arguments, mostly linguistic and logical, have to be carried out in order to have a genuine holistic state. Any holistic state felt in relation to a false world would be treated as misplaced and even illusory. Arguments and polemics do form an important part in any metaphysical discourse, whether it be Vedantic, Buddhistic or be Kantian and Hegelian. But cognitive statements determine the genuineness and appropriateness of our holistic state; the attainment of which remains the primary end of a metaphysician.

Secondly, the metaphysical language has to be skilfully used for evoking an holistic response. Theologians are now getting aware of convictional (W. Zuurdeeg)

---

1. *The Structure of Metaphysics*, p. 26.

language and of the language of myth and parables (L.S. Thorton, Austin, Farrer and other image-linguists), for inducing numinous experience. In the same strain we can say that metaphysical language is delicately balanced by metaphors and analogies. For this reason the metaphysical language only superficially will be called as 'linguistic confusion'. Let me illustrate this point.

Theological statements assert that God is omniscient, omnipotent and perfect. He has created the world out of Himself with a view to having creatures worthy of His fellowship. Such statements have the purpose of firmly establishing an individual in his endeavour of becoming and realising himself as a thing of value in that station of life in which he is placed. He is in effect assured that his endeavour is not going to be rebuffed for the world is so made that his endeavour of becoming a whole by incorporating the cultural values of mankind must succeed. God and Creation statements are non-cognitive, but they have holistic meaning.

But even this holistic purpose would not be achieved if we do not show that holistic emotion is well founded as something supervening over cognitive achievements. Arguments and the marshalling of scientific facts are necessary for this assurance. But can cognitive statements guarantee this? No, not at all, but philosophical endeavours can show that after all holistic emotions are not unworthy of conscious organisms who have developed reason by way of administering the satisfaction of man's need. All arguments and polemics are so many persuasive statements.

In the past myths and parables were adequate for the holistic striving in thinkers. As logical insight deepened, and as myths and parables began to show their insufficiencies of supporting convictional attitude to life, so they were exchanged for the employment of metaphorical and analogical employments of scientific terms. 'Life', 'entelechy', 'matter', 'evolution', 'theory' etc., are all terms which have become metaphorical in philosophy. On the other hand, 'God', 'Soul', 'eternity' etc., are terms which have become intellectualised to such an extent that they often lose their religious and mythical significance. Who would worship the God of Descartes, William James, Samuel Alexander and Ward? What religious emotion can be expected from the primordial and consequent nature of Whitehead's God? Logical Positivism stands for de-mythologising and de-analogising process in philosophy. Its logic is relentless. But can man cease to be a living organism? If he is going to be an *organism*, can he be stopped from becoming a whole? Now man by virtue of his becoming a conscious organism cannot refrain from forming symbolic ideal of himself as a complete whole. Can this symbolic concept of the self in relation to the universe in which he has been cast be exorcised of its charms?

I have assumed that Kant was essentially right in holding that man cannot totally shake off the *transcendental illusions*. Man has to create a world after his ideals that well up in him by way of fulfilling an holistic purpose, deeply implanted in him. But of course man cannot consciously allow himself to be duped by language of myths and metaphors who has to meet the demand of precise statements. However, my contention is that 'mere precision is not enough' for philosophy. The constant battle for creating effective metaphors and analogies will remain in philosophy. The ding-dong battle between myths and scientific concepts for being harmonised in metaphors will continue. If one chooses to call this metaphorical language as linguistic confusion, then the objector will be partly right. He would be wrong, however, if he would maintain that metaphorical language aims at giving us information about the supersensible world.

I have shown that modern philosophers were strongly motivated by metaphysical considerations. I have sought to show that their vision is unerring but their 'metaphors' have to undergo much modification as suitable vehicles of expressing and evoking holistic experiences. To a great extent it is true that Hume practised analytic philosophy, but all the rest, in my humble opinion, were primarily metaphysician.

The book does not claim any originality and certainly not any scholarship. It proposes to focalise certain issues in Western philosophy which are important for any student of philosophy. Much material has been taken from the most recent publications and journals.

Contents

PART II: MODERN PHILOSOPHY

✶ ✶ ✶ ✶ ✶

Introduction

0.01. The nature of Philosophy: The word 'philosophy' consists of two Greek words, namely, 'philos' and 'sophia'. Hence the etymological meaning of the term is 'the friendship or love of wisdom'. As such, a philosopher may be called a 'wise man'. However, this title is too pretentious. Therefore, Socrates defined a philosopher as 'a seeker after wisdom'. Even when so defined the term 'philosophy' does not become any more precise. The important thing is to note that philosophy seeks **wisdom,** and not **knowledge,** प्रज्ञा (wisdom) and not the empirical knowledge. Indian philosophers aimed at immortality and not a world of sentient happiness :

सर्वा पृथिवी वित्तेन पूर्णा स्यात्कथं तेनामृता स्यामिति[1]

Even if the world be full of wealth, how does this lead to immortality?
Again :

येनाहं नामृता स्यां किमहं तेन कुर्याम्[2]

This search after wisdom is a comprehensive undertaking and is directed to the solutions of such problems.

किं कारणं ब्रह्म कुत: स्म जाता, जीवाम केन क्व च संप्रतिष्ठा: ।

अधिष्ठिता: केन सुखेतरेषु, वर्त्तामहे ब्रह्मविदो व्यवस्थाम् ।[3]

In the Western Modern Philosophy Kant outlined the problems of philosopher thus:

1. What can I know?
2. What I ought to do?
3. What may I hope?

From the above considerations it follows that the subject-matter of philosopy is all-comprehensive. According to Whitehead it is descriptive "of the generalities which apply to all the details of experience". Similarly, Hoernle holds that to philosophise is 'to seek an attitude towards the universe as a whole'. Thus philosophy is both an *intellectual pursuit* and an *attitude* to the reality as a whole. Hence, we can define philosophy **as a resolute and persistent attempt to understand and appreciate the universe as a whole.**

0.02. Metaphysical construction : As a synoptic study metaphysics tries to offer us a scheme of generalities or an overall map of the universe. In its construction there are two steps at least, according to Whitehead[4].

1. A metaphysician is usually conversant with a number of concepts in any restricted field of enquiry.

---

1. Brih. Upanishad — 2. 4. 2. This is the question asked by Maitreyi.
2. *Ibid.* — 2. 4. 3. 3. Svet. Upanishad 1.
3. The author is obliged to Dr. P.B. Vidyarthi of Ranchi University for the three questions given here.
   कस्त्वं कोऽहं कुत आयात: — शंकराचार्य
4. A.N. Whitehead, *Process and Reality,* pp. 6, 17.

2. According to his range, depth and quality of experience and temperamental interests, he picks up one or some of these concepts and transforms them into a scheme of key-notions. This is effected by extending the concepts to cover all the facts. Of course, the concepts in order to become Key-notions must be 'applicable' and 'adequate' with regard to our total experience.[1]

The adequacy of metaphysics, according to Pepper[2] and Prof. D.M. Emmet,[3] lies in the 'comprehensiveness' and natural 'facilities', with which its creative notions can illumine our variegated experiences. By 'comprehensiveness' is meant the largeness of scope or the range of consistent description of facts. In the same way, 'natural facility' means the 'fittingness or appropriateness' with which the key-notions succeed in harmonising its data with ease and spontaneity.[4] In this way, Plato discovered his key-notion of 'horme' from his studies of mathematics, Aristotle found his metaphysical key of 'horme' in the concept of 'biological drive to completion.' Similarly *Descartes picked up* the key-concept of 'clearness and distinctness' from co-ordinate geometry. Leibnitz derived the theory of monadological harmony from algebraic model and Kant obtained the creative concepts of *a priori* forms from his moral experience. Even the modern demand of precision in expression has been actuated by a study of the formal language of science.

Of course, no scheme of generalities or any system of key-notions can exhaustively and in equal measure explain the whole range and variety of experience. It throws its searchlight most on those facts from the study of which creative notions have been derived. Facts far removed from the field of enquiry are left in comparative darkness. Thus, every scheme of key-notions illuminates certain facts and at the same time leaves other facts in obscurity. For this reason Prof. D.M. Emmet has compared key-notions to Fougasse cartoons.

> There is distortion; there is a high degree of selectivity; there is certainly the artist personal way of seeing; yet the result conveys an important character of the situation.[5]

The view outlined above concerning the nature of metaphysical construction has been approved of by H.H. Price.[6] Prof. W.H. Walsh,[7] Prof. Ian Ramsey[8] and by many others. But if this view be accepted then the following characteristics of metaphysics at once follow:

---

1. A.N. Whitehead, *Ibid.,* p. 4.
2. S.C. Pepper, The root-metaphor theory of metaphysics *Journal of Philosophy,* Vol. 32, 1935, World hypotheses 1942.
3. The Nature of Metaphysical Thinking.
4. S.C. Pepper, *Ibid.,* p. 368; D.M. Emmet, *Ibid.,* p.196.
5. D.M. Emmet, *Ibid.,* p.204.
6. H.H. Price 'Clarity is not enough' in Proceedings of Aristotelian Society, 1945, Supplementary Volume XIX, p. 21n.
7. Reason and Experience, pp. 241-47.
8. Possibility and purpose of metaphysical theology, in *Prospect of Metaphysics* (George Allen, 1961).

1. Metaphysical concepts, originally are cognitive, since they do describe facts in a certain field of scientific enquiry. But when they are extended to cover all facts coming under all kinds of experience, they become metaphors and analogies. Their meanings are transformed. Here *a priori* concepts may be used to cover even empirical facts. For this reason, metaphysics has been accused of creating linguistic confusion.

2. Creative concepts are selected on account of subjective interests of the metaphysician. These concepts bring to much illumination to the metaphysician that he takes them to be most real. In this sense that which appears to be most objective is also at the same time the most subjective.

0.03 Subjectivity in Metaphysical Construction: From the above account it is clear that metaphysics is a synoptic world-view. However, this enterprise is not scientific. The language of metaphysics of necessity becomes paradoxical, metaphorical, symbolical and analogical. No doubt metaphysics comes to be supported by cognitive statements of science, logic and commonsense, but the end to which these statements are directed is non-cognitive. Normally one would try to adjust oneself to reality and would not raise any problem concerning it. Psychologically speaking a problem concerning reality arises only when one's sense of value or meaning in relation to the world and fellow-beings becomes deficient. In metaphysics, the nature of reality is a problem to be solved. However, for normal persons reality is something to which they adjust and concerning which they do not raise any question. Psychologically speaking, we can raise a problem concerning reality only when our sense of value (concerning ourselves primarily and secondarily about our fellow-men and the larger world around us) has grown dim and deficient. Hence, the subjective need for obtaining self-esteem and meaning in life is a psychological affair. And it is this need which promotes metaphysical construction. Hence subjective impulses enter into metaphysics in some important respects.

1. First, a field of enquiry becomes favoured because of the subjective proclivities of the metaphysician. Here we are to be guided by the category of importance as Prof. Emmet reminds us of Whitehead's insight into the matter.[1] Bosanquet[2] too refers to this category. According to him there is the idea of proportion, centrality and sanity in the selection of experience and experience so selected determines our philosophy. For putting, therefore, central things in the centre, he recommends us to make use of our 'penetrative' imagination:

> Philosophy is the formal embodiment of the 'penetrative imagination'; it deals with the significance of things and transforms them, but only by intensified illumination.[3]

---

1. *Ibid.*, pp.196f.
2. *Individuality and Value*, p. 3.
3. *Ibid.*, p. 13; R. F. A.. Hoernle' states that philosophy requires an openness of mind which, whilst rejecting no evidence, relies on the significant and illuminating experiences (Quoted by C. J. Ducasse in *Philosophy as a Science*, pp. 16-17.)

Quite obviously 'penetrative imagination' and the category of 'importance' suggest a subjective way of evaluating our experiences.

2. At the creative moment of form-making, some concepts with regard to the 'important' experiences assume a dominant role. In relation to them "the thinker finds himself saying 'yes' freely with the whole being".[1] He is caught up with the spirit of totality. The absolute, total and non-tentative staking out of the whole personality with regard to some creative notions has its root in the unconscious depth of the thinker.

3. This 'click' or 'aha-experience' when gets elaborated into a comprehensive and harmonious metaphysical construction, then it brings 'peace and pistis' or the feeling of 'it is finished'.

From the nature of philosophical construction, it is clear that it is not a purely intellectual discipline, though certainly it is not bereft of it. The important thing is that in philosophy 'vision' counts. And this is what Waismann and Wisdom have found to be the most important thing about philosophy.[2] But a philosopher who has tasted the fruits of the tree of knowledge cannot remain content with dreams only. His poetry has to be intellectualised. Unless logic and scientific reaches of the time prove adequate to his vision, his philosophy would remain a fiction only. As such philosophers bring the full force of their arguments to bear upon their conclusion. However, there is hardly any metaphysical system which does not show serious gaps in reasoning and/or disagreements with scientific propositions. At the present time of anti-metaphysical thinking the subtleties of logical distinction and the immense development in science have made it difficult for philosophers to portray their vision with sufficient consistency. However, the important thing in philosophy is not precision but vision. And the 'truth' of vision does not lie in describing any actual state of affairs, nor in presenting knowledge or morality, but in evoking the whole man in relation to the values in which lie enshrined the history and prophecy of the whole human race.

True, all philosophers have not dealt with metaphysics in which axiological factors are found in a dominant way. But certainly all of them have busied themselves with elements which go to the construction of a system. For some philosophers, the theory of knowledge itself has acquired the status of full vision, as in Locke, Berkeley and Hume. In others, the final destiny of individuals assumes a dominating role 'as in Josiah Royce, Bernard Bosanquet, Pringe-Pattison and others. In the same way the ideal of a completed system of knowledge is itself a dominant key, as in Descartes, Spinoza and Leibnitz. The cry of precision in expression and the test of verifiability at the present time are epistemological problems. Even the anti-metaphysical conclusion based on the demand for verifiability implicitly supports the Bradleyan dictum.

1.   D.M. Emmet *Ibid.,* p.198.
2.   F. Waismann, How I see philosophy in Contemporary British Philosophy, 1956 p. 483; J. Wisdom, Metaphysics and Verification in Philosophy and Psychoanalysis, p. 100.

. . .that the object of metaphysics is to find a general view which will satisfy the intellect, and I have assumed that whatever succeeds in doing this is real and true and that whatever fails is neither.

Hence, the demand for consistency of vision with the propositions of science, logic and commonsense is necessary. But this demand is a demand for efficient craftmanship in philosophical construction, the core of which lies in vision which evokes the best in philosophers, which enhances his life and thought for creative enterprise and which aims at inducing in others and in them for holding fast the golden key which opens the gate to eternity. After reading the works of a philosopher the evaluative question should be : 'Oh reader ! have you felt uplifted, have you found the pearl of great price, have you been shaken from the very depth of your being?' Even sceptical writings stir us for they rouse us from our slumbers and complacency. Therefore, we shall treat the history of modern philosophy as a series of visions. Whatever may be the value of cognitive enterprise and of the analytic achievements, they all remain subsidiary to the vision of the philosophers. Philosophy so understood is not lyrical poetry, but is an intellectual poetry that is, in which poetry an intellectual needs are sought to be suitably matched.

0.04. Objections against philosophy: Seeing that there is no agreement about any statement in philosophy and seeing that there is no steady advance in the content of philosophical study, many critics have hazarded uncharitable remarks against it. At times it is pointed out that philosophers search for a black hat in a dark room where it is not. Again critics admit that people may think of many things which have never been dreamed of by philosophers to be under heaven and earth but like Lichtenberg, they add that philosophers dream about many things which are neither in heaven nor on earth.

Whatever may be the difficulty about the exact formulation of the theory of verifiability, at least it aims at distinguishing factual from non-cognitive propositions. If metaphysical propositions be taken as cognitive; then certainly the jokes of the critics are justified. But we have already held that philosophy is not a scientific enterprise. As such it does not describe anything under heaven and earth. Metaphysical entities like God or immortal soul, are neither to be found in heaven nor on earth. They are symbols of human aspirations.

Of course, a great deal of confusion has arisen concerning the congnitive nature of metaphysical propositions. The reason is that the vision of philosophers has always been supported by science and logic. A great many times, they very nature of scientific thinking has occupied a central place in their reflection. The present pre-occupation of philosophers with the grammar of language is itself a consequence of reflecting on the language of science. Similarly, a great deal of advance has been made in logic. Now linguistics and logic are certainly cognitive and they do come under philosophy. Hence the confusion has arisen concerning the cognitive status of metaphysics. However, it would be better to hold that metaphysics is an intellectual poetry whose language has to produce, induce and sustain conviction. Hence, metaphysical contention does include logic and the syntactics but their place remains subsidiary to philosophical vision. Again, since metaphysical entities cannot be cognitively established, therefore, they are dubbed as 'meaningless' or 'nonsense'. However, the contention of logical empiricists against metaphysics is based on a mistaken view about its nature.

Human beings have to live and for doing so they have to think. Philosophy at least in its metaphysical undertakings arises from reflection on the problems of living. In this sense philosophy is a biological process lifted up on the plane of reflection. One has to have an idea about what one is and about what one is going to be. Further the story of an individual is inextricably woven into the texture of society and the physical environment. Naturally one has to put question of 'wither', and 'whence' and 'why' concerning man and the universe. It is the holistic tendency in man as a biopsychical creature which will not allow him rest until he finds some moorings at least for some time for himself and for his fellowmen. As men have been differently brought up, and as they differ from one another in their mental constitution, so their philosophies too would be equally varied. We may, therefore, jot down the following point concerning the nature of philosophy.

1. This construction would vary from age to age and even with persons belonging to the same age. The relativity of metaphysical values depends on the psychological type to which the metaphysician belongs, on this repressed and suppressed impulses and on the statements of science, logic, and commonsense peculiar to his times.

2. The problem of metaphysical meaning is not one which can be cognitively settled. Any view of the universe which contributes to the expansiveness, enhancement and psychological health of the thinker is highly meaningful to him. Ultimately the meaning of metaphysical proposition has its cash value in the promotion of the holistic tendency of the process of self-realization of a metaphysician.

3. However, metaphysical proposition is cognitively supported and at times the argumentative aspect comes in heavily, but in the end it remains in the service of the holistic tendency in man. In comparison with metaphysics, religious construction is farless cognitively supported but is superior in being more completely total and holistic.

4. The language of metaphysics, not being primarily cognitive has to be transformed and changed into metaphors, paradoxes and symbols in order to convey and arouse the sense of being whole. Concepts, only in appearance are cognitive in metaphysics. The grammar of metaphysical language is geared to the purpose of evoking and inducing the sense of totality.

5. The lack of cognitive meaningfulness is no argument against metaphysics. The urge for metaphysical activity is deeply rooted in man and cannot be

eradicated without doing violence to man as a bio-psychological creature.

We may conclude then that if a bio-psychological standpoint has dethroned the primacy of intellect, it has done so to make room for a deeper purpose. Each individual from this point of view is urged to become a complete whole. He has to become a fully blossomed flower a thing of beauty. And a thing of beauty is a joy for ever, it would never pass into nothingness. The world is a veritable 'vale of soul-making'. Metaphysics aims at making men conscious of their final destiny as things of beauty. This mission of metaphysics cannot be treated as trite, superficial or nonsense.

Thus, the tirade against the unprogressiveness of philosophy made by Descartes, Kant and Schlick in our opinion is unfounded. If metaphysical entities were observable, then one could have brought the charge of fruitless controversies, needless battle of opinion and pre-occupation with pseudo-problems at the door of metaphysics. Seeing that the task of metaphysics lies in an evaluative enterprise in the service of bio-psychical function of man, the whole objection based on the unprogressiveness of metaphysics is misplaced.

Further, the charge of unprogressiveness is exaggerated. Philosophy has always been science-and-logic-supported. Advance in science and logic would certainly lead to a better and a more consistent and comprehensive construction in philosophy. The metaphysics of Spencer, Alexander and Whitehead is a great advance over Greek cosmogonies and over the systems of Modern philosophers. Again, only prejudiced critic would not notice any advance in logic and epistemology. Further, the very nature of metaphysics is becoming clearer now, which was not so in the past, not even in the recent past belonging to the first quarter of the 20th century.

If the nature of metaphysics is to be essentially vision-centred, then all arguments are mere pleas in the interest of some vision. If the defence of metaphysics has produced no conviction in the critics of philosophy, then we would recommend them to have no truck with metaphysics. But we know that no body can have a vigorous intellectual life without some metaphysics. Ordinary people remain satisfied just with the prevailing *Weltanschauung* of the age; its critics are those who begin to realise its inadequacy. However, the creative and constructive thinkers take a bold step and produce a system of sufficient depth and comprehensiveness so as to drown the criticisms of the anti-metaphysicians. The atmosphere is surcharged now for a bolder advance in metaphysics and perhaps a study of the past failures and success of the modern thinkers would contribute materially to this phase of philosophical development.

0.05. The history of Philosophy and its functions: Any history of thought is both instructive and interesting. It is instructive, since as a permanent record of thought it becomes corrective of and prescriptive for our present thoughtful enterprise. Even the failures of great minds, are important since they point out the direction in which success can be achieved. In the history of philosophy, great thinkers are they who have broken untrodden paths for humanity and have laid down new ways of thinking. In this sense, Plato-Aristotle, Descartes-Spinoza-Leibnitz, Locke-Berkeley-Hume, Kant-Hegel, Bradley-Bosanquet, Alexander-Whitehead, Moore-Russell-Ayer etc., would be remembered, for they have introduced new turnings in human thinking. Our grasp always falls short of our reach. So logic and cognitive statements on which they have tried to base their insight, have fallen short. In this sense, successive constructions of philosophers are so many attempts at overcoming the failures of the past. But the success of philosophers is not to be judged in terms of logic, logistics, linguistics, and scientific statements, but on the largeness, comprehensiveness and well-knitness of the vision portrayed. If a philosophy helps in deepening of consciousness, in the grasp of details and surenesses of direction hinting at illumination, in broadening and opening new dimensions of human experiences, then it is successful precisely in that proportion. As such the history of thought is also interesting.

It is interesting, since it contains the contributions of great minds down the ages to the solution of issues dear to all of us. It contains an articulate record of the strivings of the souls for 'peace and pistis'. In this sense, a history of thought is more important than a history of action, since an action is performed in the service of some thought. This is how Arnold Toynbee regards the history of the world. He is really a dull historian who chronicles the rise and fall of empires only, without understanding the conflicting ideologies at the basis of warring nations. Thrones have become dust, and, kings have become commoners, because a sense of dignity, inherent in the concept of individuality, has become the prevailing creed in the democratic countries of the world.

In the light of above observation, the following points of importance in the study of a history of philosophy can be made out.

1. A history of philosophy presents us a series of visions about the universe. Each vision, directly or indirectly, aims at establishing values after which our broken lives limp pitifully and miserably. Again, there are some persons who remain dissatisfied with the traditional and prevailing values of life. They have to win for themselves new insight into things. To such seekers a history of philosophy would prove unfailing stimulus and would provide helpful suggestion.

2. Much depends on the creative notions and a history of philosophy would make us acquainted with them.

3. Again, the adequacy and appropriateness of the key-notions are determined not only by their own possibilities, but also by being organised by certain pervasive ways of thinking. These have been variously called as principles, categories, postulates, conventions etc. Nobody can hope to proceed far in philosophising without getting himself acquainted with them.

4. True, philosophy comes out of life and very often it is a reflection of life. But philosophy may as well shape and determine future life. This is an important

consideration with regard to an evolutionary scheme of things. Nobody can deny that evolution involves physical and biological factors. But after social life has become fully established the great source of evolutionary changes have to be ascribed to human thought. Hence, there is an urgency to devise power-thinking for explaining evolutionary forces. This can be greatly aided by a study of a history of philosophy which provides us with the instances of such power-thinking. Works of Plato-Aristotle, Darwin, Hegel, Marx and Engels are eloquent examples to the point.

5. If a philosophy can change the course of direction, then it also indirectly points out the *importance of individuals,* in the evolution of civilization. Great minds, like Lord Buddha, Plato, Hegel, Marx have revolutionised human ways of living and thinking. Their thoughts have permanently either increased or decreased the possibilities of human happiness and misery.

6. Of course, no unanimity of opinion, or agreement in conclusion is possible in philosophy, since it is not a cognitive enterprise. But the vision with which philosophy deals may be either petty or great, superficial or deep. A study of a history of philosophy, with the success and failure of many a vision, makes as sensitive and responsive to the depth, comprehensiveness and richness of reality at the heart of things.

0.06. The stream of Philosophical thought: Currents of philosophical thought have been characterised by the three phases of *Creativity, Analysis* and *Scepticism.* The first phase is of creativity in which a thinker is gripped by his vision. He remains occupied with the working out of his vision through his logic, scientific statements and other cognitive statements of everyday life. He remains unaware of the gaps and of the refractory materials which cannot be brought under his system. This phase is followed by consolidation and analysis. The analysis of the entire system reveals the difficulty of the task and the limitation of the solution. An awareness of the limitation of the system and its failure in including many outstanding details of experience leads to the discarding of the whole of the prevailing system. This is known as scepticism in which the very possibility of knowledge is doubted. Scepticism is only a halt in the progress of philosophising. At most it offers a difficulty to be overcome. Its sole function lies in a deepening of consciousness. In the fullness of time it is sure to invite higher creativity, a more comprehensive vision worked out with greater craftmanship. However, no creativity in philosophy can be final. It is bound to be followed by deeper analysis and a more thorough-going scepticism. Let us illustrate these phases of philosophising in the baldest of outline.

The Western philosophy begins with the speculations of the Greeks. They seem to have been the first people to have freed themselves from religious philosophy of their country and age. In having a world-vision, they, like every philosopher had to support it with cognitive statements. These statements, in the beginnings, deal with the outer world, since it is this reality which has to be taken note of in the task of living. However, the important thing to notice is that these early thinkers tried to grapple with the whole of reality with their limited resources. The world-picture which they tried to convey was relatively unsatisfactory and primitive. But even the most primitive cosmology in terms of the key-notions of water, air and other elements brings intellectual at-homeness and emotional stability to the philosophers and to all participants in it. Dissatisfaction with other philosophers always begins with intellectual deepening. Whether it be the first phase of scepticism or the current state of anti-metaphysical thinking, it has its basis in intellectual dissatisfaction. Now this dissatisfaction can be dispelled not so much by intellectual probings as by a new world-vision. However, no world-vision can be owned, unless it is supported by arguments. In this sense Bradley's observation is correct that metaphysics must satisfy the intellect.But he has also noted that we give bad reason what we believe on instinct. No world-vision can be deductively demonstrated or inductively established. Intellect is necessary and it must remain a hand-maid of world-vision. But as intellect supports and as intellect announces the revolt against any philosophy so one is likely to misconceive philosophy as an intellectual discipline.

The early Greek cosmologists variously styled their key-notions as earth, air, and other elements. These notions were conflicting. Nobody could think that all these elements either separately or together would explain the reality as a whole. There was no intellectual standard in relation to which we could decide the matter either in favour of 'air' or 'water' or 'other elements' to be the real stuff of the cosmos. As wise men differed and no one appeared to find out an acceptable solution concerning the ultimate stuff of the cosmos, so dissatisfaction arose with these cosmologies. The first response to these conflicting views was that no one cosmology was right, and perhaps all were wrong. This is exactly what the sophists did. They denied the possibility of knowledge on the basis of *Homo Mensura*, i.e., each man is the measure of his knowledge.

But human spirit cannot remain in despair. The hope of gaining knowledge can be deferred, but cannot be irrevocably denounced. The period of sophism was followed by the golden age of Socrates-Plato-Aristotle. True, knowledge concerning the outer world may not be possible, but why should not philosopher turn inward? Why should he not pay heed to the Delphic oracle : 'Men ! know thyself? Most probably philosophers in the west as yet have not mastered the real meaning of this oracle. Philosophy does not consist in obtaining any knowledge, either of the outer or of the inner world. It is concerned with the improvement of one's own self and of the world around him insofar as the latter relates to the realisation of the self. The philosophy of Plato is an impressive monument in human thinking as far as it relates to a system which bases itself on the **meaningfulness** of human life. The correctness of such philosophy does not depend on the confirmation—disconfirmation with regard to the observable data. The value of such a kind of philosophy is sustained by appropriateness of feeling, by having 'peace and pistis' and by promoting meaningfulness, psychic health, inner freedom, and joy. This lesson is hard to learn.

Even the daring speculation of Plato-Aristotle could not satisfy the restless craving of the intellect. The later thinkers found Plato and his pupil Aristotle differing as much about the 'inner man' as the former cosmologists were found with regard to the outer reality. The second phase of scepticism, known as pyrrhonism was deeper than the revolt of the sophists. The intellect appeared to be paralysed. The wise Stoics and Epicureans took shelter in attaining a state of 'apathy' or 'indifference'.

However, scepticism is at most a halting stage. It was soon overtaken by another period of creativity. True, intellect has failed to penetrate the mysteries, but why should not feeling take us into the heart of reality? Plotinus, who was greatly influenced by Indian speculation, sought refuge in religious mysticism. In religion, it is claimed, we come face to face with the Absolute Reality called God. But unless we become as trusting as babes are, we cannot enter into the mystery of God.

Religious experience is shaking experience. For some time on its basis we can dispel the inopportune questionings by holding that heart has a language which the head cannot understand. But can we silence the intellect? Feeling may be warm and comforting, but its weakness is patent. It is fleeting, unstable and relative. At this stage appeared Christianity which combined the intellectual subtleties of the Greek, the institutionalisation and legalism of the Romans, the mysticism of the Alexandrian school and the righteousness of the Jews. It was a synthesis of philosophy, morality, religion and politics. A system so rich, so reasonable, so well organised was destined to reign for a long time.

Even though it be rebuffed and rebuked, reason cannot be subdued. Its feeble protests in the long run overwhelm feeling and sentiment. And yet we trust that reason remains an instrument only in promoting a life devoted to values. However, it can fulfil its mission only by assuming the role of a mistress of human soul. These are some of the factors which contributed to the rise of rationalism in Modern Philosophy.

1. In philosophy the distinction of believing and knowing has to be noted. Knowing is backed by evidence, at least in principle. Believing lacks sufficient evidence to be sure of its content. Scriptural truth for St. Augustine is a matter of faith or belief, but not the subject of knowing;

I confess ....that I believe rather than know that the things in those (scriptural) stories were true at that time as they have been written; and those whom we believe knew the difference between believing and knowing. . . . Therefore, what I understand I also believe, but I do not understand everything that I believe . . . ."

Believing was also considered to be the prerequisite of understanding deeper things. So Anselm held the formula **'credo ut intelligam'** (I believe in order to understand).

First the motto of **Credo ut intelligam** did not allow free hand to reason. But thinking was allowed an instrumental function to fulfil in the service of faith. Reason began to exploit this opportunity to the full. The church fathers began to advance conflicting arguments in support of their faith. If fathers differ, then who would be arbiter or judge? Naturally 'reason' came to be slowly recognized as an authority above the authority of the church.

2. Again, reason no doubt has a universal significance but it has its locus in an individual. Therefore, emphasis on reason is also at the same time a recognition of individuals at the expense of the Church. This individualism combined with the deepening of religious consciousness tended to pass into mysticism. Mysticism consists in the right of each individual to commune with God without mediation, without the authority of the Church. Hence, reason slowly undermined the authority of the church and prepared the way for modern philosophy. "The under-current, which for a thousand years had accompanied the main religious movement of the intellectual life among the Western peoples, swelling here and there to a stronger potency, now actually forced its way to the surface, and in the centuries of transition, its slowly wrested victory makes the essential characteristic for the beginning of modern times." (Windelband, *History of Philosophy*, p. 348). The whole characteristic of the modern Philosophy has been well observed by Thilly in the following way : "The history of the new era may be viewed as an awakening of the reflective spirit, as a quickening of criticism, as a revolt against authority and tradition, as a protest against absolutism and collectivism, as a demand for freedom of thought, feeling and action."

However, even this brilliant period, in which genius proved adequate to the opportunities offered, could not remain the final stage of human thinking. The modern philosophy has the opposing currents of empiricism and rationalism. both currents meet in the philosophical contemplation of Kant. Kant, by his deeper analysis and criticism of knowledge, tempered with extreme caution, became the water-shed of thought. His three critiques became the precursor of many new thoughts. But the most influential school of idealism fully flowered in the philosophy of Fichte, Schelling and Hegel. After Hegel we come to the present era of multitudinous details. We are too much in it to fully appreciate the revolution of thought but we trust that this period is not without a golden page in human thinking.

In conclusion we can say that no system can enclose in it the wealth of human strivings and aspiration. The deepest system of thought, profound and wide in extent is nothing but a chapter in the surging, struggling, unfolding drama of the spiritual urge in man.

0.07. Main Divisions of the History of Philosophy and the Characteristics

of Modern Philosophy: For our convenience we have divided the continuous river of thought into four periods.

1. Ancient Philosophy.
   (a) Greek Philosophy from Thales to Aristotle.
   (b) Greco-Roman Philosophy.
   (c) Neo-Platonism of the Alexandrian school.
2. Mediaeval Philosophy or Scholasticism from the fifth to the fifteenth century.
3. Modern Philosophy.
   (a) The renaissance from the 15th to the 17th century;
   (b) The Period of enlightenment from Locke to Kant;
   (c) German Philosophy from Kant to Hegel.
4. Contemporary Philosophy from 1860 to the present times.

0.08. Characteristics of Modern Philosophy: Medieval philosophy remained wedded to theology. In contrast, modern philosophy arose in the wake of science and remained subservient to scientific methodology. Modern philosophy developed three important ideas, namely, philosophical method, formation of philosophical systems and humanism. In contrast, contemporary philosophy may be said to begin with antimetaphysical tendencies due to excessive pre-occupation with linguistic analysis. Contemporary philosophy is also suspicious of system-building.

The spirit of modern philosophy is critical of the past. Bacon begins with an attack on Aristotelian Deduction and proposes to give a *Novum Organum* for the real progress of knowledge. Descartes also disparages the old philosophy and advises us to begin *de novo* for a sounder metaphysics. This revolt is not only confined to Bacon and Descartes but Locke and Kant are equally conscious of a need for a new method in philosophy.

This aggressiveness and individualism were the result of recapturing of faith in human capacity to known all things. Nothing could escape from the arbitration of reason. Religion cannot evade this criticism on the ground of its sanctity nor law can escape under the smoke-screen of its majesty. Thus the voice of reason which was smoothered by Christian dogmatism is once more restored to its rightful throne. This was the hearkening back to the free Greek spirit, which deeply inspired men of letters in this period of Renaissance. *Credo Ut Intelligam* of Augustine, Anselm, and other medieval theologians was rejected in favour of 'knowledge for the sake of knowledge'. This faith in the human capacity to know was partly the result of inner self-criticism of the dogmas of faith (for the difference of views of the church fathers had to be constantly referred to reason for arbitration which undermined the authority of the ancient authorities and indirectly paved the way for the supremacy of reason) and partly was the result of scientific advance. It was really the latter which inspired the moderners and in spite of the scepticism of Hume could not allow men to remain in despair.

This emphasis on reason led to several tendencies. First, everywhere there is an appeal to natural agencies in place of supernatural ones. However, this ideal was only partially realised, for God remains to be the centre of the moderners. After all we cannot change our entire legacies and mental legacy is the most difficult to give up. But then philosophy was brought down from heaven to earth. God is there but only as an *ex macbina* as we shall see for ourselves.

Another result of rationalism was the individualism of thinkers. The reason which is the arbiter cannot be our private reason, but universal and absolute reason. And this was not fully realised, though vague anticipation of this is found in Descartes, Berkeley and Leibnitz. The result was a series of ambitious systems which clashed with one another. This led to the warring of different schools and bred a spirit of scepticism. The inherent scepticism of both rationalism and empiricism could not take firm root in the moderners because of the progress of the sciences which kept alive the hope in the human capacity to know anything under heaven and earth. The result of scepticism led only to a deeper search for finding out the real elements of knowledge. This task was undertaken by Kant who at the outset took for granted that there was knowledge and therefore, the scepticism, he held, must have been due to a wrong analysis of knowledge.

The moderners impress us with the necessity of a new method of progress to be introduced in philosophy. This was to be devised mainly in the spirit of mathematics (with the exception of Bacon and Berkeley who undervalued mathematics). This emphasis on the clearness of knowledge like the demonstrativeness of mathematics led to far-reaching consequences in the history of modern philosophy. It was this spirit which led to the distinction between secondary and primary qualities of matter, the pantheism of Spinoza, and the critical philosophy of Kant.

The emphasis on reason and on the new method of discovery led to enquiries into the limit, nature, and function of knowledge. This study of knowledge for ascertaining nature and limit is called epistemology. The epistemology, then is the special contribution of the moderners. There is hardly any modern philosopher who does not discuss the theory of knowledge. The culmination is reached in Kant who gave a special and a prominent place to epistemology for which he is justly famous.

Thus modern philosophy begins with immense faith in the human capacity to know everything. It has this faith which made this period most productive and epochal in the history of thought.

0.09. Empiricism and Rationalism: We have raised problems concerning empiricism and rationalism and now we shall try to outline the issues involved in them.

Empiricism

Empiricism has a glorious tradition in the writings of Locke, Berkeley and Hume. It has been extended into a rich epistemological school by Bertrand Russell,

George Moore, Wittgenstein, Carnap and many other important philosophers of the present century. However, there is some distinction between classical empiricism of modern philosophers and of contemporary thinkers. The contemporary empiricism includes much of logico-mathematical elements in it. Besides, it is called 'Reductionism' by Prof. W.V. Quine.[1] The contemporary empiricism maintains that all cognitively meaningful statements can be reduced to two basic statements, called analytic and synthetic. Secondly, it holds that ultimately all synthetic statements can be reduced to sense-data or protocol statements or immediate sense-experience.

That all meaningful statements can be reduced to the two basic kinds of propositions namely, analytic and synthetic can be found in Descartes, Leibnitz and the modern empiricists. Leibnitz had correctly stated that a necessary or analytic statement is one whose predicate cannot be denied without involving self-contradiction. He had also stated that Geometrical propositions are the instances of necessary truths or analytic statements. Later on Kant, though not more precisely yet more emphatically dwelt upon the distinction between analytic and synthetic statements. However, the distinction was implicit in the epistemology of Descartes, according to which mathematical propositions follow from the 'light of reason alone' : and propositions concerning 'matters of facts' are based on 'a certain spontaneous inclination'.[2] In the same way, Locke had distinguished between trifling and instructive propositions.[3] But it was the empiricist Hume whose observation is taken to be the corner-stone of contemporary empiricism. According to Hume there are only two kinds of propositions, namely, concerning 'Relation of Ideas' and 'Matters of fact'.

> If we take in our hand any volume — of divinity or school metaphysics, for instancelet us ask, Does it contain any abstract reasoning concerning quantity or number? No. Does it contain any experimental reasoning concerning matter of fact and existence? No. Commit it then to the flames, for it can contain nothing but sophistry and illusion.[4]

The propositions concerning 'relations of ideas' are the same that deal with number or quantity and which are called 'analytic'.[5] In the same way propositions concerning 'matter of fact' are called 'synthetic'. Further, the propositions concerning number do not deal with actual states of affairs, but are necessary; propositions concerning matters of fact or sense-experience can never be necessary, but deal with the actual state of affairs. The contemporary empiricists on the whole accept that there is a fundamental distinction between these who

---

1. **Two dogmas of empiricism** in *Philosophical Review*, LX, 1951.
2. §. 203 **Criterion of truth** of this book.
3. §. 5.18 Instructiveness of knowledge (of this book).
4. David Hume, Edited by A. Flew, Collier Classics, 1962, p. 163.
5. *Ibid.*, pp. 47, 52, 54-55.

kinds of propositions and that necessary or *analytic* propositions can never be established by sense-experience. That 'two and two are together equal to four' has not been reached by observing a number of instances of two and two becoming four. The 'necessity' between the relationship between '2+2' and '4' is due to the consistent use of the stipulated definitions of 'two', 'plus' and 'four'. As these definitions are matters of convention, so analytic propositions concern conventional use of terms only.

That there is a fundamental cleavage between analytic and synthetic propositions has not been maintained by all empiricists and Mill later on did try to derive even analytic propositions from sense-experience. We may therefore distinguish between classical empiricism and contemporary empiricism. The former does not explicitly state that there is a fundamental cleavage between analytic and synthetic propositions; the contemporary does accept this.

Secondly, the most general thesis of empiricism is that 'all ideas are derived from experience'. Here all the three key-terms 'ideas', 'derived' and 'experience' are vague and the contemporary empiricism has done a lot to sharpen their precise meanings. 'Ideas' have been taken as sense-data, protocol-statements or basic propositions. At times these are taken to be 'propositions' and at other times their extra-linguistic referents are also emphasized. Attempts at making the meaning of the term 'derived from sense-experience, has given birth to the theory of verifiability with its whole host of intricate problems. However, the most generic notion of 'derived from' ultimately means 'reduced to' the most elementary propositions which may be wholly linguistic or extra-linguistic. Now a synthetic proposition is said to be reducible to propositions, either linguistic or extra-linguistic. Well, the classical or modern empiricists were not aware of the ambiguities of the terms 'ideas' and 'derived from'.

Besides, the classical empiricism of even Hume was not fully clear of its implications. If we admit that all cognitively, meaningful statements are either analytic or synthetic, then moral statements, in the language of Hume, had to be consigned to flames. Certainly all modern empiricists were not ready to go to this length.

The greatest trouble of the classical empiricism was that it could not explain the necessity involved in proposition concerning number and mathematical demonstrations. This therefore was a favourite point with the rationalist. According to him 'necessity' cannot be derived from experience, but follows directly from the 'light of reason' or the innate faculty or of reason. Later on, this necessity was derived from the *a priori* elements, which instead of being derived from experience, according to Kant, make experience itself intelligible or possible. This knotty problem was explained by contemporary empiricism by advancing the theory of conventionalism, to which we have already alluded with regard to mathematical necessity.

The distinction between classical and contemporary empiricism has been drawn so that the readers of this book might not be led to think that empiricism is as inherently incapable of solving philosophical problems as it proved in Modern Philosophy. Secondly, one must not commit the other error of thinking that the classical empiricism of Locke, Berkeley and Hume is as powerful as is contemporary empiricism. Hence, we are confining ourselves strictly to modern empiricism of Locke, Berkeley and Hume.

According to classical empiricism knowledge begins and ends with experience. Unfortunately the term 'experience' is too vague. It may include mystic intution, poetic vision and even the yogic perception. However, 'exerience' for the classical empiricists means 'sense-experience' or 'impressions'. Hence keeping this meaning of experience the aphorism of Locke is 'There is nothing in the intellect which is not previously given in the senses'. Every form of knowledge according to this statement, should ultimately be based on sense-experience, outer or inner. For instance, our knowledge of the table is fully analysed in terms of the sense qualities or sensory data of colour, weight, touch etc., and, according to this theory, apart from these nothing more is required for explaining knowledge.

The thesis of classical empiricism seems very plausible if it is stated in a negative way, namely, there is no factual knowledge of a thing if there is no sense-experience about it. For example, there is no possibility of knowing colour as sensation for a person who is born blind. Similarly, we can have no knowledge of music as auditory sensation if we are born deaf.

Therefore, the classical empiricists state their fundamental statement thus: "All these sublime thoughts which tower above the clouds, and reach as high as heaven itself, take their rise and footing here, in all the great extent wherein the mind wanders in those remote speculations it may seem to be elevated with, it stirs not one jot beyond those ideas which sense or reflection have offered for its contemplation."—Locke : *Essay on Human Understanding.*

Again, Berkeley restates this Lockean stand : ". . . . all these choirs of heaven and furniture of the earth, in a word all those bodies which compose the mighty frame of the world have not any subsistence without a mind, there being is to be perceived or known." Berkeley: *Treatise of Human Knowledge.*

Finally, Hume agrees with his predecessors on the fundamental issue of sense-experience:

> Let us chase our imagination to the heavens, or the utmost limits of the universe: we never really advance or step beyond ourselves, nor can conceive any kind of existence but the perceptions which have appeared in the narrow compass.[1]

This compass is exclusively composed of impressions and their ideas.

---

1. David Hume on *Human Nature and the Understanding*, edited by A. Flew, Collier Books, 1962, p. 186.

Fundamentals of Classical Empiricism

1. Mind at birth is a clean state or *tabula rasa*. All the characters of knowledge are *acquired* through sense-experience.

2. Sensation and reflection, the outer and inner sense-experience, are the only two windows through which the dark chamber of mind comes to be filled with light.

3. The elements of experience, for example, the sensations of light and heat, colour and smell etc., are all *simple* and *unrelated*.

4. Of course, knowledge can never be exhausted by *particulars* supplied by senses. It does not deal with *universals*. But, empiricism holds that universal propositions can satisfactorily be explained by particulars. In this context, the contribution of Hume and Mill is important.

5. We find that judging, relating and combining the discrete items of sense-impressions is the special function of intellect. Without these functions there can be no knowledge proper. Empiricists take various stand on the issue of intellectual elements involved in knowledge. Hume, whose opinion is highly valuable for empiricism holds that the work of connecting the separate data is brought about by the *association* of ideas and by *imagination*. Mill, whose contention has not found support by a majority of philosophers, holds that intellectual operations are fully explicable by sense-experience. Berkeley has given a very confused account of the connecting process. Here Locke's original stand is much more defensible. According to him, comparing, contrasting and compounding of simple ideas are different from sensing and may be called intellectual operations. They do account for the formation of complex ideas. However, the basic stand of Locke is that intellectual operations are secondary. Intellectual operations come only after simple ideas are imprinted by the senses. Hence, on the whole, according to empiricism sensation and introspection (reflection) are the *sole primary* sources of knowledge and the part of the intellect remains *subsidiary* to them.

Empiricism and mathematical propositions : Older empiricism had factual propositions of commonsense as its instances. At present logical positivism or empiricism, which is its most up-to-date version, mostly confines itself to the factual propositions of empirical sciences. The reason for this is that though empiricism looked plausible with regard of factual proposition of everyday life, yet it did not do so with regard to mathematical propositions. In mathematics propositions are universal and necessary. And strictly speaking, they cannot be obtained from experience. *Universal* propositions deal with *all* instances coming under them e.g., 'All men are mortal'. Obviously we cannot experience *all men* dying, since the experiencing man, a philosopher has to be alive to make this statement. And so 'all men' cannot be brought under experience. Secondly, experience can inform us that this *has been so*, but it cannot tell us that this *must be* so. For instance, on the basis of experience all that we can say is that the sun rises in the East, but we cannot say that it *must* rise in the East. The reason is that we can always conceive or imagine something contrary to it. There is no absurdity in imagining the sun to rise in the West. Similarly, we can imagine fire to give us cold, instead of heat. However, in mathematics we find necessary propositions like 2+2=4. If we understand the meaning of 'two', 'addition' and 'four', then we cannot even imagine that two and two can be anything else besides four.

Hume has an important statement concerning mathematical propositions, but on the whole classical empiricism failed to do full justice to them. The very failure of empiricism paved the way for rationalism which seemed to explain mathematical propositions very well.

0.10 Rationalism. According to rationalism intellect is an independent source of knowledge. This gives us innate or *a priori* ideas. Knowledge, according or it, consists in these innate ideas alone. These self-evident universal truths are given by our intellect, the best example of which is found in mathematics. For example, 'two and two are together equal to four'. The extreme form of rationalism denies the part which sense-experience plays in the formation of knowledge. However, generally rationalism does give a subordinate place to sense-experience. Therefore, according to it, experience does not *constitute* but serves an occasion for the exercise of intellect, whose innate ideas constitute knowledge. Hence, sense-experience serves only an opportunity for the play of intellect and its innate ideas. For instance, sense-experience according to Plato furnishes us an occasion for reminding us of the 'Ideas in Heavens'. Hence the following tenets of rationalism may be laid down :

(i) Intellect is an independent source of knowledge. This supplies us with self-evident innate ideas.

(ii) Knowledge is constituted by innate ideas alone. Knowledge so gained is *universal* and *necessary*.

(iii) Sense-experience is not totally disregarded. It serves an occasion for the exercise of intellect. Sense-experience illustrates a universal truth given by our intellect. Thus sense-experience can clarify but does not constitute knowledge.

(iv) Unlike empiricism, according to which mind is passive with regard to simple ideas, rationalism supposes mind to be active, both in obtaining self-evident innate ideas and in constituting knowledge.

(v) The theory of innate ideas was transformed into that of *a priori truths* by Kant. Now rationalism does explain universality and necessity involved in knowledge.

On the basis of rationalism we can say that in all cases two and two are together equal to four. *A priori* truths, according to Kant, are *universal,* because they follow from the common mental constitution of all human thinkers as thinkers. All human beings in thinking do take the help of the categories, according to Kant. Such categories are substance, casuality etc. Again, rationalism does explain *necessity*.

Mind according to Kant gives its own laws and without these laws it cannot think at all. Therefore, mind cannot help noting these very laws which it gives to things, whilst thinking about them.

Issues between empiricism and rationalism. As noted earlier philosophers use metaphorical and symbolical thinking. They take their model from a certain field of enquiry and according to the vision this model given them, they build their theories. The empiricists draw their model from empirical experience of everyday life. Similarly, the rationalists have their model from mathematics. Unfortunately, they did not pay heed to empirical sciences like physics and chemistry. In physics, as in other empirical sciences, knowledge is a happy marriage between sense-experience and mathematics. Therefore, Kant who occupied himself with physics tried to reconcile empiricism and rationalism.

The classical empiricists were aware of two kinds of propositions namely, *factual* propositions and propositions of logic and mathematics. Even Locke was aware of sensitive knowledge on one hand, and, intuitive and demonstrative knowledge on the other hand. But it was Hume who clearly laid down that there are two kinds of *meaningful* propositions namely: propositions of facts and propositions of mathematics. Propositions of facts, being based on sense-experience, can never be universal and certain. They can be at most *probable* in character. Again, propositions of mathematics are necessary. But they do not describe any actual state of affairs. For example, geometry does not deal with actually observed points, lines and surfaces. A point, according to it, has position but no magnitude. Similarly a line according to it has length but no breadth. However, no observed line can be found without breadth. Now Kant has posed a question which still remains highly debated namely the possibility of synthetic judgments *a priori*. Synthetic judgments roughly correspond to empirical propositions, and, *a priori* judgments to propositions of mathematics and logic. Now, Hume holds that propositions are either *a priori* or synthetic but not both. Against this, Kant holds that there is a possibility of synthetic judgments *a priori*.

PART I

Greek and Medieval Philosophy

1

The Nature of Greek Philosophy

What is philosophy?

According to Aristotle, philosophy arises from wonder. Man experiences rains and drought, storms, clouds, lightning. At times, he is greatly terrified. Then the events of life and death mystify him. He begins to reflect over the events. The sun, moon and the stars appear to him wonderful and beautiful. As a result of his reflections, he thinks that the events can be explained by powers akin to man. He proposes to control them by means of magical spells. This magic gives way to science, philosophy and religion in due course.

Magic gives way to science when natural events begin to be explained and controlled with the help of *natural causes*. Magic, again, becomes religion when the *powers* are taken to be *supernatural beings*. Manaism, animism and polytheism are so many kinds of early religions of man. The same magic flowers into philosophy when man makes an attempt to *explain the world as a whole*. Thales, Anaximenes and many others are both philosophers and scientists. They are philosophers inasmuch as they want to explain the world as a whole. They are scientists inasmuch as they try to explain the world with the help of natural stuffs. But religion too remains there. At times, the early Greek philosophers are sceptical about religion, and, at another times, they offer sublime view of religion.

Greek thinkers are praised for their scientific enquiry, but their philosophy, religion and morality too are important. Here we find that early vague concepts become precise and refined through their progress for about a thousand years. Western philosophy owes much of their development to the free Greek enquiry. In Greek thinking there is much which echoes in Indian thought. They are parallel and independent developments.

The earliest Greek religion is said to be Homeric. Homeric gods were anthropomorphic. In relation to man they were taken to be very powerful and immortal. Homeric religion was polytheistic and Zeus was taken to be the chief God. On the whole Homeric gods were not moral. They were also said to be bound by *fate* e.g., the Rigvedic gods were fully controlled by *rta*. Early Greek thinkers very often protested against this kind of polytheistic worship. But there was also another kind of religion known as Orphic religion.

Orphic Religion

Very little is known about Orpheus, but Orphism greatly influenced Socrates,

Plato and Christianity too. It has much in common with Indian religious thought. However, the two, the Greek Orphism and Indian thought are regarded as two independent and parallel development of religious consciousness. In any case it requires very brief treatment.

Orpheus is said to be a reformer of the religion of Dionysus. Later Pythagoras adopted some elements of Orphism in his philosophy. And Pythagoreanism greatly influenced Socrates and Plato.

1. Orphism relied on the doctrine of revelation which had been written in sacred books.

2. Secondly, this religion was *universal* for it was open to any member, irrespective of any tribe or race, provided he chose to be initiated into it and promised to obey the laws of Orphism.

Orphism assumed that men are in a fallen state, but in their pristined glory they are akin to gods. Man can attain to his original state by a system of purification. He might win redemption from sin and death and become immortal thereby. Orphic saints are stated to have pre-existed their birth and would exist after death.[1] They are immortal. Body is the tomb of the soul and imprisons the soul in the 'wheel of birth'.[2] Hence, Orphism subscribed to the doctrine of the transmigration of the soul.

Life for an Orphic is essentially suffering. Only by a method of purification and renunciation, an ascetic can escape from the wheel of endless rebirths.[3]

Most Orpheans abstained from animal meat, but on ritualistic occasions they used meat sacramentally. The Orpeans sought union with the god by means of mystic knowledge, which is quite different from ordinary knowledge. This mystic union means release from the wheel of rebirths.[4]

Characteristics of early Greek thought

1. We find that early Greek philosophers were *free* thinkers and indulged in free enquiry, untrammelled by any supernatural reference. Xenophanes (570-480 B.C.) denied polytheism in favour of monotheism. He rejected also the theory of the transmigration of souls. Heraclitus (525-475 B.C.) rejected the worship of gods current in his time. Democritus (460-360 B.C.) traced the worship of gods to fear. Again, Anaxagoras (500-428 B.C.), Protagoras (480-410 B.C.), Socrates (469-399 B.C.) and Aristotle (384-322 B.C.) were deemed anti-religious.

2. Freed from religious bias, the Greek thinkers supported science and are called as the founders of science in the west.

3. What is the meaning of science in early Greek contexts? Nobody can think that early thinkers could have fully understood the nature of science as the modern

---

1. Compare, *Gita* 2.20.
2. *Greek Philosophy*, John Burnet, London, 1968 (Print), pp. 24-25.
3. Compare, Indian religious thought of Buddhism, Sankhya.
4. Russell, *A History of Western Philosophy*, London, 1946, pp. 35-42.

scientists understand. For the early Greek thought science means an independent and free enquiry into natural events, systematically and methodologically without being burdened with religious requirement. The early Greek thinkers gave rational explanation of natural phenomena by taking recourse to hypothesis which according to them must harmonise with facts. The Greeks invented mathematics, wrote history (e.g., Aristotle), not annals and thought freely without being hampered by religious orthodoxy.

Man's first response is to the outer world and only afterwards he becomes reflective about his inner life of epistemology, morality and the nature of political conditions of life. The beginning of the Greek speculation is essentially cosmogonic. Here the principle was, 'Nature has to be explained according to natural stuff'. According to Thales (624-550 B.C.) the world arises from water and returns again into water. The next cosmogonist, Anaximander (611-547 B.C.) hazarded that the ultimate stuff of the universe is boundless *something,* an *undifferentiated mass.* Anaximenes (588-524 B.C.) held that *Air* is the fundamental thing underlying the whole universe; Pythagoras (588-500 B.C.) explained through number. For Heraclitus (535 -475 B.C.) everything is flux and everchanging and fire is the ultimate symbol. Again, Empedocles stated that (495-435 B.C.) fire, earth, water and air are the basic elements which can explain the universe and for Democritus (460-360 B.C.) the material atoms alone can account for the whole universe.

The early Greek cosmogonists laid down the basic structure of scientific explanation, namely, the universe has to be explained through natural causes, without reference to supernatural agencies and religion. The intellectual pursuits of the Greek were exceptional. They invented mathematics, science and philosophy. They were the first to write *history* in the place of annals.

4. We have stated that philosophy is the interplay of science and religion. Gone were the anthropomorphic and largely immoral gods, but religion refuses to be thrown out of human life. Throw it through the doors and it comes again through the windows. Socrates was guided by a voice (*daimon*) and was subject to ecstasy or trance akin to what Sri Ramakrishna experienced frequently. Then both Plato and Plotinus speak of meditation through which man can rise to great heights in his spiritual attainments. But the religion of mysticism was coupled with the idea-ism of Plato and advaitic kind of philosophy in Plotinus. However, Aristotle kept largely to science, and, Aristotelianism remained the most important philosophy for sustaining science both in the world of Arabs and Europe.

Later on both Plato and Aristotle were Christianised by Church fathers. St. Augustine and Anselm were Platonic, but St. Thomas Aquinas was Aristotelian. In medieval philosophy, religion dominated and science was largely kept in abeyance. When science began to rise, religion tried to oppose its advance. Even when science triumphed religion continued its conservative function. Only in the 20th century science and religion have made truce and both of them are working independently of each other.

Divisions of Western Philosophy

Historians of philosophy have divided Western Philosophy according to their convenience. In this book we shall deal with only a few thinkers who have largely moulded the thought in the west. We shall divide the Western philosophy into Greek, Medieval, Modern, Post-Kantian, Metaphysicians and the 20th Century philosophy.

I.   *Greek Philosophy*

It covers a period between 600-400 A.D. This period has three sections.

Section I. Pre-Socratic Philosophy.

Section II. Socrates, Plato and Aristotle.

Section III. Greco-Roman Philosophy.

II.   *Medieval Philosophy* 400-1500 A.D.

III. Modern Philosophy (Bacon to Kant) *Post-Kantian Philosophy*

IV.   *20th Century Philosophy.*

GREEK PHILOSOPHY (PRE-SOCRATIC)

Thales

The first Greek thinker is said to be Thales who belonged to Miletus in Asia Minor. This Miletus was an important trading centre. He is said to have flourished about 624-550 B.C.

The chief aim of Thales was to account for the fundamental stuff of which the universe is made. Hence according to him the universe is fundamentally water, because water admits of being vaporous, liquid and solid. When water is heated it assumes the form of vapour; when chilled it becomes solid and when it is allowed in its natural course then it is a flowing stream. Hence water succeeds in explaining all the possible states of being solid, liquid and vaporous. For this reason water can be said to be the fundamental stuff of the universe. Even the earth, according to Thales, is a disc floating on the water.

Aristotle the biologist conjectured that Thales chose water to be the ultimate stuff, for food is always wet and this liquid food nourishes the body. Even the generating seeds are wet.

The most important thing about Thales is that he gave birth to scientific way of thinking. It is said that he predicted the eclipse which took place in 585 B.C. According to Russell.[1] Thales discovered how to calculate the distance of a ship at sea with the help of observations taken at two points and how to calculate the height of a tree or pyramid from the length of its shadow.

No doubt the philosophy and science of Thales will appear to us to be very crude, but he laid down the foundation of scientific worldview in the sense that

---

1.   B. Russell, *Ibid.*, p. 44.

his speculation was wholly naturalistic. It was neither anthropomorphic nor theocentric.

However, he regarded magnet as something living for it attracts things towards itself. Again Thales is said to have said that all things are full of gods. Hence Windelband holds that the philosophy of Thales and of other Milesians to be hylozoistic.

Anaximander (611-547 B.C.)

Anaximander also belonged to Miletus. He was a man of daring venture of thought. He was a cosmologist like Thales. However for him the primary matter was 'boundless something',—a formless, infinite and eternal mass not yet parted into particular kinds of matter. In positing 'boundless mass' as the fundamental stuff of which the world is constituted, he indirectly lays down an important principle, namely, a formless general principle can account for the particulars, but not *vice-versa*. For example, formless earth mass can be converted into particularised things like pitchers, bricks, tiles etc. But the earthen pitchers cannot be directly shaped into tiles or goblets. In order to give rise to tiles or bricks, the earthen pitcher has to be reduced again to the formless mass of earth. This distinction of formless matters and particulars will be found again in the theory of Aristotle known as the doctrine of *matter and form*. Anaximander appears to have stated that the world is governed by the opposites like hot and cold, wet and dry. It is by the working of the opposites that the world goes on. In this context it can be said that the earth, air, water and fire cannot be the ultimate stuff of the universe, for they have opposite characters. For example, fire burns and water dampens. If any one of them be allowed to work unfetteredly then the world would become either dry or watery and the world as such would cease to be.

According to Anaximander the world has *evolved* in due course. At one time there was water everywhere. There were only watery creatures. By drying up of water, land appeared and creatures of the sea were left on the dry land. Those creatures from the sea which could adapt themselves to the dry land alone have survived. One can easily see the germ of the organic evolution in the speculative adventure of Anaximander.

Anaximander held that the earth is cylindrical in shape and moves freely in space. This positing of the earth moving freely in the space is once again a foreshadow of the theory of gravitation.

Anaximander calls his infinite, boundless matter 'God'. This is the first philosophical concept of God. This God no doubt is matter. But is not mythological or anthropomorphic. Clearly it remains monotheistic. Besides, the doctrine of *creation* of the universe by God has been completely ignored.

Anaximenes (588-524 B.C.)

Like Thales and Anaximander, Anaximenes belonged to Miletus. Like Thales, Anaximenes regards 'air' as the primary stuff of the universe. Why air, and, not water? It is only a matter of conjecture. Most probably Anaximenes paid more attention to the living than to any other things. Here breath, i.e., air is the predominant thing. Therefore for Anaximenes air is the fundamental stuff of which the world is composed.

Anaximenes chose air as the first thing because of its mobility, changeability, and inner vitality. As a matter of fact air was considered to be the breath of the universe. Hence this breathing universe was considered to be a living organism. For this reason Anaximenes is really a hylozoist.

For Anaximenes, this primary air is regulated by the opposed principles of *condensation* and *rarefaction*. Condensation simply means compression of the air in a narrow space and rarefaction means expansion of the air in the greater space. By rarefaction air assumes the form of fire, and, by successive condensation it gives rise to water, earth and stone.

Anaximenes accounts for all the important elements and states of material things through his fundamental stuff of air. And more. He tells us, *how* air accounts for the formation of water, fire and earth. It is the knowing-how which alone constitutes scientific explanation. Hence the two principles of condensation and rarefaction are important steps in developing the scientific thinking about the universe. There is also another point which must be noted.

The world is not only vaporous, liquid and solid, but is also sound, colour, rough-smooth etc. Now to explain this world of quality? The principles of condensation and rarefaction admit of *quantitative* differences. Hence, here is involved the principle that *quantity can explain the quality.* Later on Pythagoras laid down his famous statement 'what exists, exists in number'. In the modern times no scientific explanation is considered reliable unless it is put into quantitative formulae. Hence, the thinking of Anaximenes is a step forward towards the scientific world-view.

Pythagoras (580-500 B.C.)

Religion : Pythagoras is said to have travelled widely. He had been to Egypt, where he must have learnt the value of geometry which was used there for measuring the land. He is also credited to have travelled in the east. He was better known as the founder of a religious order which was the reformed kind of Orphic religion. As Orphism has much in common with Indian thought, so Pythago-reanism too is an echo of Indian thought.

For Pythagoras the soul is immortal. He believed in rebirths and even the transmigration of the soul. The whole wheel of rebirths is essentially painful and it is the duty of man that he should put an end to this wheel of rebirths.

The body is the tomb of the soul and the visible world in which man lives is false and illusive. How to get one's release from the round of endless reincarnations in this false world? By means of mystic meditation. This meditation is intellectual and not emotional. No doubt the Pythagoreans had ceremonies and rituals and a recommendation for an ascetic life. But the most important thing was the disinterested pursuit of science and the *contemplation* of the ultimate things of the universe. This sort of contemplation was considered most conducive towards release from the chain of endless rebirths.

Pythagoras had laid great stress on mathematics which was also the greatest science of the period. Hence the most devoted pursuit was also the greatest means of attaining the religious 'release'. Hence, scientific pursuit was also the religious duty of man.

Pythagoras founded an order in which men and women were regarded as equal. They led a common way of life. Even the mathematical discoveries were regarded as collective achievement.

Plato was greatly influenced by Pythagoras and he too regarded this world as mere appearance and a world of *becoming*, and, taught men to contemplate the realm of eternal ideas. He too emphasized the communistic state of affairs in the rulers of his ideal Republic. Something of Pythagoreanism lingered on in the Essene Sect in the times of Jesus Christ. The Essene Sect not only held all things in common, but also practised vegetarianism which was one of the tenets of Orphic religion. The mystical aspect of Pythagoreanism was fully practised by Plotinus who was certainly influenced by Indian thought.

Ethics : Pythagoras laid emphasis on asceticism and the purity of conduct. In later pythagoreanism vegetarianism was also accepted. Though life was deemed essentially full of miseries and the soul immortal, yet suicide was not deemed desirable. The reason is that suicide instead of putting an end to the wheel of transmigration, really strengthens it.[1]

The most important belief of Pythagoreanism lays stress on the doctrine of transmigration of the soul, and, the main prohibition on taboo was not to eat beans. Along with asceticism, Pythagoras mentioned some taboo-restrictions[2] :

1. To abstain from beans.
2. Not to touch a white cock.
3. Not to stir the fire with iron.
4. Not to eat the heart.
5. And many other such prohibitions.

Mathematics and Pythagoras

Like his previous cosmogonists, Pythagoras declared that whatever exists, exists in number. This is not a wild statement. Mathematics means proportion, order and harmony. For example, a woman is said to be beautiful when she has the right proportion of her legs, thighs, waist etc. And this proportion can be expressed in quantitative terms. Similarly, a colony is physically built of certain number of lanes with some definite number. Its streets and roads also can be

---

1. This is what is held in Buddhism.
2. B. Russell, *A History of Western Philosophy*, p. 50.

expressed as 12 ft and 20 ft wide etc. It is also found that music can be explained as *harmony* between the vibrations of sounding of different musical instruments. There is also an important aspect of mathematics which Pythagoras might have known.

Pythagoras was certainly a geometrician. He is credited to have discovered the theorem that in a right-angled triangle, the sum of the squares on the sides in equal to the square on the hypotenuse.

For example, if the sides be 3" and 4", then $3^2+4^2=5^2$. There is some difficulty of this theorem in relation to its expression in arithmetical terms. However, at this stage one has to note some very important features of geometry.

Theorems in geometry are very neatly proved if we accept the definitions, axioms of geometry. Further, with the help of geometry land can be very easily and exactly measured. Here geometry applies to the measurement of empirical things. But are lines, planes, triangles really found in the empirical world? Does not a point occupy some space? Has a line no breadth? Are all the angles of a triangle exactly equal to two right angles? None of these statements are exactly true. There are two questions with regard to this anomalous situation.

1. If the geometrical truths do not exactly correspond to observed points, lines and triangles, then how have they been obtained?
2. If the geometrical truths do not correspond to the actual states of affairs, then how do they apply to the empirical world?

The second question is certainly a weighty question, and, it has to be raised and clarified in its appropriate context, but let us apply ourselves to the first question.

The question of finding out the universal truth is not only found in geometry, but also in arithmetic. We are said that two things may be equal, or two and two are together equal to four. But are there any two *observed* things exactly equal? Not even two peas or two particles of sand are found to be exactly equal. Then how do we say that two things may be equal? Again, if take two drops of water and add another two drops, then we do not find four drops, but one drop only. Similarly two rats and two snakes put together will not be four, but only two. Hence, the arithmetical truths, though apply to the empirical world, yet they cannot be *derived from observation*. If they are not found through the senses, then how do we obtain them? Mathematical truths are found through *intellect*. What the senses reveal to us is illusory and false, but what the intellect discovers is alone true and eternally true. Thus thought was stated to obtain the ideal of knowledge as distinguished from knowledge supplied by the senses. Hence for Pythagoras, thought and contemplative knowledge of mathematics were alone true, and not the sensible things.

This relation between thought and the sensible has loomed large in Socrates, Plato, Descartes, Spinoza, Leibnitz and Kant.

However, the Pythagoreans tried to show that things are but number in some arbitrary manner. According to them the world is composed of the opposites. This formula was certainly laid down by Anaximenes too. But the Pythagoreans have ten opposites, namely, (1) Odd and even, (2) Limited and unlimited, (3) One and many, (4) Right and left, (5) Masculine and feminine, (6) Rest and motion, (7) Straight and crooked, (8) Light and darkness, (9) Good and evil, (10) Square and oblong.

Then again in the most arbitrary manner, the Pythagoreans called point 'one', line 'two', plane 'three', solid 'four', material qualities 'five', animal animation 'six' etc. Similarly justice is four or nine, because four is the square of equal number 2×2, and nine is of three $\times$ three.

Cosmogony: According to Pythagoras there is a central fire around which the earth, the sun, the moon and five planets move. In this speculation Pythagoras was nearer the truth in not regarding the earth as the centre of the universe. Aristotle rejected the Pythagorean speculation in favour of a geocentric theory which was accepted by the Western Christian theologians. However, Copernicus and Galileo conclusively showed that not the sun, but the earth moves round the sun.

Aristotle in his *metaphysics* has severely criticised the Pythagoreans. Of course, one thing has to be kept in mind that the Pythagoreans were not simple physicists. They were mystics and to explain the world, they, have often resorted to aphorisms. Hence, Aristotle the logician and the clear headed scientist has justly criticised the Pythagoreans. Aristotle's criticism follows from his philosophy of matter and form and the theory of causation.

First, Aristotle tells us that the *number-theory* has not been derived from the sensible. It is wholly abstract and a static principle. Yet the Pythagoreans have used their number-theory exclusively to explain the sensible. But how can a principle not derived from the sensible can explain the observable world, according to Aristotle? How can movement, change of the sensible world be explained? How can the principle of 'limited' and 'unlimited' explain the movement of stars? Again, how can the opposite of 'Odd and Even' explain the lightness and heaviness of things?

"Finally, how can we admit number and its modifications as the cause of all that has existed or happened from the beginning now, ...?"

Of course, the Pythagoreans have not tried to explain the physical world of earth, water, air and fire. Perhaps this physical world with its elements was taken for granted. But to explain the physical world number-theory was advanced.

The importance of Pythagoras

1. Pythagoras is important in the Western world both for science and religion which he tried to harmonise by holding that scientific pursuit is also the religious duty of man. Much of Pythagoreanism was kept alive in the Essene Sect of the Jews. The Essene ascetics abjured sex, held all things in common by the members of the order.

2. But in philosophy, Pythagoras is remembered for his mathematical pursuit. We have already alluded to the Pythagorean theorem, according to which the square on the sides of a right-angled triangle are together equal to the square on the hypotenuse. If we use this theorem with regard to an isosceles right-angled triangle, then this theorem need not be true. It gives rise to the discovery of incommensurables which engaged the brain of subsequent mathematicians.

3. That mathematics, being the product of intellect alone should apply to the empirical world gave rise to the transcendental Aesthetics of Kant and only in the modern times, this riddle has been solved.

4. Again the aphorism of Pythagoras that whatever exists, exists in number, is not only most true for any theoretical sciences, but in modern times it has been adopted in social science like psychology and economics. However, number for the moderners is not the stuff of the universe. It is only the language of science for predicting and controlling the events in nature, and, for the communicability of scientific information.

5. There is little doubt that Plato established the independent and eternal reality of ideas on the basis of mathematical truth. Mathematical truth is true independently of what the senses inform us. We have already explained the bifurcation of thought and perception, intellect and senses, respectively with regard to mathematical truths. So Plato also has bifurcated the realm of ideas from the world of Senses.

6. Not only Plato, but the modern thinkers like Descartes, Spinoza, Leibnitz, Kant, Russell were greatly influenced by the methodology of mathematics, but even the modern trend of linguistic analysis has developed from the scientific use of mathematics. Mathematics has been regarded as the language of science. Hence in order to know science, one must known the nature of this mathematical language.

7. According to Russell, Platonism is in essence Pythagoreanism and Plato has greatly influenced the whole of Western philosophy.[1] The mystic element of Platonism has influenced St. Augustine, and his rationalism had influenced St. Thomas Aquinas, Descartes, Spinoza and Leibnitz.

8. Lastly, Pythagoras in order to establish number as the stuff of the world has drawn our attention to the order and harmony amongst the world events. This has suggested the teleological proof for the existence of God. According to

---

1.   B. Russell, *Ibid.*, p. 56.

Russell, but for Pythagoras, Christians would not have sought logical proofs of God and immortality.[1]

9. Pythagoras as a religious founder of his order, paid emphasis on physical exercise, music and medicine. In other words, he wanted a harmonious development of mind and body. Plato too in his Academy introduced physical exercise, music and mathematics. Since then the prime aim of education has been 'a sound mind in a sound body'.

Xenophanes (About 570-480 B.C.)

Xenophanes is more of a religious reformer than a philosopher. His famous utterance is *All is one*; and, this statement has become the cardinal principle of the Eleatic School, best represented by Parmenides and Zeno.

Xenophanes begins his tirade against the prevailing polytheism of the Greeks. First, he takes Homer and Hesiod to task for promulgating immoral gods and goddesses, for they are pictured as deceitful and given to sex weaknesses. Secondly, Greek gods suffer from anthropomorphism.

'... if oxen and horses or lions had hands, and could paint with their hands, and produce works of art as men do, horses would point, the forms of gods like horses, and oxen like oxen .... The Ethiopians make their gods black and snobnosed; the Thracians say theirs have blue eyes and red hair.'[2]

Xenophanes also rejected the doctrine of transmigration of souls. But when one tries to know the real nature of one God, according to Xenophanes, then he experiences a great deal of obscurities. He appears to have identified his deity with the universe which may be described as a world-God. Is this conception of a world-God monotheistic or pantheistic? Looking out into the wide heaven he declared, 'The One is God'. This appears to be a pantheistic utterance. However, this world-God is said to be eternal and imperishable and is said to guide the universe rationally. Besides, He is an object of reverence. Most probably the question of Pantheism or monotheism is not legitimate, for at that time this distinction had not become articulate.

According to Xenophanes the world has originated from earth and water and into which again all things will enter. Xenophanes not only held 'All is one', but he also regarded world-God to be immovable and perfectly homogeneous. But in that case how can plurality, and change be explained? This formed the main problem for Parmenides and Zeno.

Xenophanes with a view to dedeifying the sun held that the sun every morning is formed out of the vapours of the sea and disappears again into the sea in the evening. This means that the sun is very ephemeral and cannot be an object of worship.

1. B.Russell, *Ibid.*, 56.
2. B. Russell, *Ibid.*, p. 59.

Parmenides (b. 514 B.C.)

Parmenides has written a poem *On Nature* which has two parts. His own philosophy has been presented in 'the way of truth'. The second part 'the way of opinion' is a polemic against prevailing views.

Xenophanes had declared 'All is one'. This was the starting-point of Parmenides. How could he establish this truth? He like the rest of the people found that the world of sensible things is always *becoming*. Things come into the world and the next moment they perish. They are as much *are* as also they *are not*. What can we say about this flux? Heraclitus declared that *flux alone is real.* To Parmenides it appeared impossible. For him, real is eternal, unchangeable and indestructible. Of course it was left for his pupil Zeno to give reason for regarding the real as one, unchangeable and eternal. For Parmenides it appeared self-contradictory to hold that a thing which is passing away to be real. What is the point involved in saying that the real is permanent and unchangeable?

Ordinarily when we say, that this is the *same* table which I saw yesterday and day before yesterday. Of course, all things keep on changing, then how can we say that it is the same table? We make a distinction between a substance and its changing qualities. We say that a substance *persists its changes,* i.e., only that is substantial and real which remains the same and changes remain comparatively unreal. According to B. Russell this concept of substance as the persistent subject of varying predicates played a very important part in Western philosophy.

For Parmenides, One alone is real, and, manyness and changes are unreal. This distinction is a matter of intuition and at most a postulate of his philosophy. But in real life changes and plurality of things are palpable. What can we say about them? For Parmenides plurality and changes are given by the senses. At most they can be called 'mere appearances'. But what is the reason for regarding them as 'appearances'. Quite obviously they are and yet they cease to be. They appeared to be shot through with self-contradiction, as H. Bradley said and which Zeno, the disciple of Parmenides tried to prove.

If the world of senses is illusory, then how do we know the One? Of course, through thought. Hence, Parmenides makes a distinction between *the appearance and reality*, sense and thought. He gives predominance to thought.

> "Thou cants not know what is not—that is impossible—nor utter it; for it is the same thing that can be thought and that can be."

Again,

> "The thing that can be thought and that for the sake of which the thought exists is the same; for you cannot find thought without something that is, as to which it is uttered."[1]

---

1. B. Russell, *Ibid.*, p. 68.

In order words, non-being or that which is not, cannot be and cannot be thought. At least many have interpreted the above remarks of Parmenides as holding the identity of *thought and being*. No content of thought without *being* and no Being which is not thought.

The above interpretation of Parmenides as the identity of thought and Being is essentially the tenet of Idealism. Again, here *thought* and *utterance* are also equated. 'Utterance' really means language. So indirectly thought and being, utterance and Being may also means that language is a key to the understanding of Reality. And this is the most important slogan of linguistic analysis.

If in one way Parmenides teaches the primacy of thought, then in another way he teaches that his 'One' is corporeal, a spherical Being with filling space or plenum. If plenum is being, then empty space alone is non-being or unreal. Hence there can be no empty space. What is the implication of holding that empty space is unreal or illusory?

The first implication is that manyness is an illusion. If there are many things like tables, chairs and books, then it means that there is some spatial distance or empty space between the things. But there is no empty space. Hence, there can be no plurality of separate things.

Further, there can be no motion. For example, a car moves from a point A to another point B. This means again there is an empty space between A and B. But empty space is illusory. Hence, movement or motion is unreal.

We shall find that Zeno has put forth many puzzles for us to solve, for he gives out reason for holding the unreality of motion and the plurality of things. But the value of Eleatic monism is important in the development of Western philosophy.

The Importance of Parmenides

Parmenides holds that reality is one, eternal and indestructible. But certainly senses reveal to us that the world consists of manyness and change. Hero to reconcile these two observations? Well, for Parmenides reality is permanent, eternal and unchangeable, and, the plurality and change are appearance and are illusory. Now this distinction of reality and appearance is found in Plato and in many idealist thinkers.

Again, for Parmenides reason and sense are opposed. This was maintained by Plato and many other thinkers. Leibnitz and Kant have tried to reconcile their mutual claims.

The problem of permanence and change not only is found in Heraclitus, but has been in some sense important even in modern times. Bergson has taken up 'flux' as the reality and the modern idealists have favoured permanence as the reality.

In some modified sense the successors of Eleatic school in the form of atomists (Leukippus, Deonocritus) have accepted the eternal and unchangeable atoms as the sole reality. Each atom is really the One of Parmenides broken into many. But

Plato regarded the ideas as eternal thought-forms.

We find that atomists are materialist and Plato is an idealist. And both of them have been influenced by Parmenides. Is Parmenides an idealist or a materialist?

Yes, there are certain elements in the philosophy of Parmenides which seem to support the view that he was an idealist. First, Parmenides teaches the identity of thought and thing. This is notable in Hegel. According to Hegel that which is rational is real and the real is rational. But rational means that which is in accordance with reason or thought. Hence, for Hegel thought and being are real. Secondly, Parmenides makes a distinction between appearance and reality. This distinction was further clarified by his disciple Zeno. For Zeno the principle of distinction lies in the maxim 'that which is self-contradictory is not real'. This again is the principle which was taken up by F. H. Bradley for whom that which is self-contradictory is unreal or is a mere appearance.

Thus the tenet of identity of thought and things, and, the distinction of reality and appearance support the idealistic trend in the philosophy of Parmenides. However, Parmenides also holds that the one is limited in space and is also spherical. Only a material entity is said to occupy space. Hence, the One of Parmenides is material. But materialism and idealism are supposed to be opposed. Then can we say that Parmenides holds a self-contradictory view about reality? Well, the distinction of materialism and idealism has emerged much later and Parmenides saw no distinction between them. He could picture reality both as thought and as spherical without noticing any contradiction in doing this. That way even the identity of thought and thing is not quite clear. Certainly we can think of the non-existence of ghosts. Does it mean that in some sense non-existent ghosts are also real? Even Russell at one time held this view and so did the Vaisesikas. But Wittgenstein showed conclusively the absurdity of this.

From our above-mentioned observations it is clear that Parmenides not only influenced the philosophy of his immediate successors, but somehow he is still alive in the Western modern thinkers today.

Zeno (489-430 B.C.)

The philosophy of Parmenides is an exercise in metaphysics and it is said that we give bad reason what we believe on instinct. It is a vision of reality as we find in the post-Kantian speculation, and, we as rational beings give out reasons in support of our metaphysics. This is the case with Zeno. For Parmenides one is the reality and this is just a postulate for him. Zeno accepts this ontology of Parmenides and supports this by presenting arguments. If reality is one, indestructible and unchangeable, then manyness and change (or motion) can only be illusory. What is an illusion? An illusion is that which is self-contradictory and that is exactly what manyness and motion are.

Many is Illusory

Zeno accepts the view of Parmenides that senses give a false view of things.

Only thought gives us the reality. No doubt the senses inform us that there are many things. But thought shows that manyness is false.

If the plurality of things be real, then we have to maintain that the reality is both infinitely small and again infinitely large. If reality is many, then each thing must be composed of units. But ultimately each unit must be indivisible, for an infinitely divisible unit is no unit at all. But if indivisible then it (the unit) can have no magnitude (extension), for where there is magnitude it become divisible. If each unit is without magnitudes then its aggregate too can have no magnitude. Therefore, reality is a collection of illusory units which have no magnitude.

On the other hand, if a unit is infinitely divisible then it is composed of parts which are themselves infinitely divisible. What is divisible is magnitude. Hence each unit has magnitude. And the reality, then becomes a collection of infinite magnitude. Therefore, reality, becomes infinitely large. The upshot?

If there is plurality, then the world is riddled with contradiction. It becomes both infinitely small and infinitely large. And this is self-contradictory. Therefore, plurality is an illusion.

Similarly, the world becomes at once limited and unlimited if we accept the reality of plurality. If the units are indivisible, then it must be *limited*, for each unit remains enclosed in its magnitude. But if each unit is limited, then the world as a whole as the sum-total of limited units, itself becomes limited. Again, each unit to be unit must have some magnitude[1] and magnitude is infinitely divisible. Hence the world as the sum-total of an infinitely divisible units, itself becomes *unlimited*, i.e. *infinitely* divisible.

Just as plurality is illusory, so movement or change is also illusory.

Now movement means covering a distance between *A* and *B*. This *A* and *B* can be represented by a line

A———————————————————— B

But each line is infinitely divisible into infinite parts and an infinite number of parts require an infinite time to traverse. Hence, any distance no matter however short will require infinite time, which no finite man can have. So no motion is possible between any distance whatsoever.

Similarly, Achilles can never overtake a tortoise in a handicap race.

A————————————————————B

Suppose a tortoise has been given a distance between *A* and *x* before Achilles is given a start. But the distance of *A-x* is again infinitely divisible into infinite number of parts. Once again this distance will require infinite time to be covered, which is not possible for any finite man.

In the same way Zeno proves that no arrow can ever move. If there be an arrow, then either it is at one moment of time *where it is* or *where it is not*. But quite obviously an arrow cannot be *where it is not*. So an arrow at any moment of time

---

1. As noted earlier, Parmenides regards empty space to be unreal. Hence in order to be real each unit must have magnitude.

remains *where it is*. But if the arrow is at any moment of time where it is, then it will be said to be stationary. Hence an arrow does not move.

Critical Comments

To say that there is no plurality or motion is a statement against the commonsense of mankind. But much later F. H. Bradley has argued exactly like Zeno that the categories of human thought are riddled with contradiction. In the same way, quite independently of Zeno, Nagarjuna (c.A.D. 150) showed that the categories of space, time, substance are shot through with contradiction. Hence the arguments of Zeno against motion or plurality are impressive. But in our times now we know the fallacious nature of Zeno's arguments.

1. Zeno confuses between the *Geometrical definition* of lines and points with the factual and observed points and lines. A geometrical line has length, but no breadth. Has anybody found any observed line either on the board or plain paper to be without breadth? Again, a geometrical point has no magnitude. But put any dot anywhere and this factual point will have some magnitude no matter however small. In the same manner a geometrical line is *infinitely* divisible, but no actual line or spatial distance is infinitely divisible. Now Zeno argues from the *geometrical line* to the *actual* or factual line. In everyday life the movement between any distance is *not* infinitely divisible. Nor is any observed time, the time which we live through as short or long, is infinitely divisible into moments. Hence Zeno's paradox is due to the confusion of two standpoints.

In modern times we will say that Zeno confuses between *analytic* and synthetic statements. A proposition is said to be analytic when its truth is due to a consistent use of the terms employed in their stipulated meanings. An analytic proposition does not require any observation to confirm-disconfirm its truth. If one accepts the definition of a line, he has to admit that a line is infinitely divisible. On the other hand, a *synthetic proposition* is true if it corresponds to an actual state of affairs. For example, 'it is a hot day' is true when actually the temperature is high. It requires an actual state of affairs either to confirm or disconfirm the truth of a synthetic proposition. Now a distance is *infinitely* divisible, or, time is *infinitely* divisible into moments is only an analytic statement. But *actual* distance traversed in some *observed time* is *not infinitely* divisible. Hence, Zeno has simply confused an analytic proposition with a synthetic proposition.

2. Again, in modern times space *and* time are not separated as two distinct entities. The actual entity is called *space-time continuum*. Hence, in our popular way of speaking we do say that this car covers 10 km. in 20 minutes. Here, space and time are separated. But in science a scientist talks of *events* or *space-time* continuum. But Zeno talks of space and time as if they are separate entities. So he thinks that infinite parts of space to be traversed will require *infinite moments* of time. Bergson too from his metaphysical standpoint criticizes the notion of *spatialized* time. For example, we say that an hour is that which a short hand of the watch covers a distance between the number 2 and 3 on the dial. For Bergson

real time is *duration* in which each moment of time melts into another without a break or gap. So in accordance with the philosophy of Bergson it can be said that Zeno has confused real *duration with* the unreal spatialized time.

3. According to linguistic convention 'movement' is always spoken of as that which is *related* with parts of a distance and moments of time. Hence, 'movement' cannot be reduced to *separate* parts of space or moments of time. In terms of the idealistic way of stating, it can be said that space and time can be *distinguished in thought*, but *cannot* be separated in reality. Hence Zeno has indefensibly confused between the legitimate distinction of space and time *in thought* with inseparable space-tine continuum.

Are then the paradoxes of Zeno useless? No. As long as language with regard to space, time, movement was not precise, the paradoxes of Zeno served as a powerful challenge to thinkers. They showed the contradictions involved with regard to our usual categories of thought. Secondly, the opposition between sense and reason had to be worked out. This was first taken up by Leibnitz and Kant who have tried to reconcile the rival claims of sense and reason, and, which reconciliation has been fully achieved in our own times. Meantime paradoxes of Zeno remind one of the *antinomies* of Kant and their synthesis in the dialectic method of Hegel. Hence, even the errors of Zeno have proved very fruitful in the history of Western philosophy.

Heraclitus (Heracleitus, 535 to 475 B.C.)

Heraclitus of Ephesus was a contemporary of Parmenides. But their philosophies were opposed. According to Parmenides reality is one, eternal and unchangeable being. For Heraclitus, reality is change, flux and *Becoming*. How has Heraclitus reached at this conclusion?

Well, Heraclitus was not a scientist. He was a religious thinker who indulged in aphorism. Fragments of his writing have been largely presented by B. Russell in *The History of Western Philosophy*. Socrates stated that he admired the writings of Heraclitus as much of it as he could understand, and, perhaps, what he could not understand was equally admirable. This means that Heraclitus indulged in obscure aphorisms.

Further, Heraclitus speaks ill of his predecessors, except of one Hermodorus. He holds that Homer should be whipped. Hesiod was considered to be an ignorant man and Pythagoras was taken to be a mischief-maker.

The main teaching of Heraclitus is that everything is in constant flux. Rivers and mountains and all seemingly permanent things are in constant flux. All is flow and becoming. No one can step into the same river twice, for when a man enters into a river, then he meets one stream of water and the next moment the first stream pases away, yielding to a newer stream of water. One can easily see that no man can ever remain the same for even two moments. Blood-stream changes and also the mental stream. Man keeps on changing form moment to moment. The doctrine of *flux* will remind the teaching of Lord Buddha relating to momentariness. How has Heraclitus reached this conclusion?

According to Heraclitus, every existent-thing is a *harmony of opposites*. The opposites of hot and cold, day and night. Thus was or strife of the opposites is the father of all things

> "We must know that war is common to all and strife is justice, and that all things come into being and pass way through strife."

Thus the world is becoming and Becoming is the unity of opposites.

For Heraclitus, not water or air is the primordial stuff. Process alone is reality and is best symbolized by fire. Hence, fire is the ever-changing entity which constitutes reality. Fire keeps on changing every moment, burning fuel into ash and that ash too changes. Ever the sun is not the same and with Xenophanes, Heraclitus maintains that everyday it is fed with vapour to be renewed. Then is there nothing abiding?

Yes, there is an abiding *order* in the everchanging fire. All things come from fire and return to fire. There is the *downward* way and also the *upward* way. According to the downward way, through *condensation* fire changes into water and earth. And again according to the upward way, through *rarefaction*, water and earth give way to fire. This order of succession produces the illusion of permanence. Here the reader is reminded of Hume who also accounted for permanence as an illusion, born of quick succession of resembling impressions.

There is fire in man too. The more of fire is in a man, the more intellectual he is, and, as this fire decreases there is darkness in man and sickness. This point again will remind one of *Sattva* and *Tamas* elements in man, according to Samkhya.

Comments

Is there then nothing abiding? Though there is no *permanent substance* which is abiding, yet there are abiding entities in the philosophy of Heraclitus.

1. The process of becoming is certainly abiding.
2. The harmony of opposites is also an abiding principle.
3. There is the abiding *Order* of downward and upward ways of fire.
4. Then again there is the permanent law of change which gives us the appearance of permanent things.

The influence of Heraclitus is noticeable even in the modern thinkers. Though Parmenides and Heraclitus differ with what is to be regarded as real, yet both of them appeal to reason. For Parmenides senses yield illusory knowledge and this lies in taking plurality and movement as real. For Heraclitus, senses give us wrong information about what is permanent. Men wrongly sense the mountain and river as abiding. Reason will convince them that all is *flux*. This distinction of sense and reason remains influential in Plato and other subsequent thinkers.

In the same manner, the distinction of change and permanence remains throughout Western philosophy. For Fichte action is considered to be *original* and Being is conceived to be secondary. Even God is conceived as 'the universal Ego or Self', who is always a free, world-creating entity. But Henri Bergson (1858-1941) has really revived the metaphysics of Heraclitus, inasmuch as he posits the ever-changing vital process as the supreme reality.

Again, Sigmund Freud (1856-1940) maintained that human life is the dance between death and love instincts. Present life is just an equilibrium between *Eros* and *Thanatos*. Does he not teach that life is a strife between two principles?

Again, what can we say about the abiding *order* of downward and upward ways of things. Of course, Heraclitus was not a scientist, nor had science become self-conscious amongst its devotees then. But it teaches the *uniformity of nature* which is at the basis of every scientific pursuit.

Even the morality of austerity not only was by the Stoics and Epicureans, but was preached by the Christian fathers.

It is important to note the comments of Aristotle.[1] The doctrine of Heraclitus is that everything is and is not. If everything is, then it means that all judgments are true, and, if everything is not, then all judgments are false. Therefore, to say that everything is and is not, simply means that all judgments are true and not true. And this is manifest contradiction in the statements of Heraclitus.

Again, if A says that everything is true, then he also implies that his opponent's view, *B*'s is true. Hence, *A*'s view is false because it is opposed to that of *B*. Here one is reminded of 'Liar's paradox' which plays an important part in Russell's philosophy.

Besides, for Heraclitus everything is in motion. But the very meaning of motion is that which changes must itself be something, for change is of something from some of its states to another.

Much of Heraclitean metaphysics was taken up by the Stoics.

Empedocles (490 B.C.-430 B.C.)

Empedocles was a statesman, physician and an orator. Later in life he became a priest and a prophet. He was also known as a miracle-worker. His religion was Orphism and Pythagoreanism. He ended his life by leaping into the crater of Etna to prove that he was a god. He was a philosopher and also a scientist.

In his philosophy, Empedocles was eclectic and worked out a philosophy of compromise between the conflicting claims of his predecessors. For Thales, water was the fundamental stuff, for Anaximenes, air, for Anaximander, 'boundless, undifferentiated matter' and for Heraclitus, fire. For Empedocles, fire, water, air and earth are the four equally fundamental stuff of which the world is constituted. Not one of them can be transformed into another. Though it is not clear, yet it is conjectured that the four fundamental entities are divisible into 'particles' or

---

1. *Aristotle's Metaphysics*, ed. John Warrington, London, 1946, Chap. VIII.

'elements'.

Again, Heraclitus maintained that all is flux, and, against this Parmenides held that there is only one reality, eternal and indestructible. Against these claims and counter-claims, Empedocles maintained that the fundamental reality is not one, but four. And these four do not remain static, but they keep on mixing and intermixing giving rise to the world of becoming. Hence, with the Eleatics, Empedocles maintained that the four material entities constituting the universe are permanent and eternal and yet they give rise to the world of Heraclitean flux.

Empedocles believed that the world is guided by the opposed principles of love and hate. However, these principles are not psychical in nature. They are better understood as the forces of 'attraction and repulsion'. Really 'love and hate' are akin to what Anaximenes called 'condensation and rarefaction'. Thus, Empedocles maintained a compromise between Anaximenes and Heraclitus.

According to empedocles, all the different states of nature are brought about by the mixture and inter-mixture of the elements of the four fundamental entities water, earth, fire and air.

1. First, there is a complete inter-mixture of the elements of the four fundamental entities, giving rise to a spherical order. Here love alone rules, and, there is perfect peace, Hate is excluded. Here is a blend of scientific thought combined with the Orphic view of *restoration* towards the end of the universe.

2. Again, hate enters into the sphere and separates the sphere into individual things. This is the state of worldly existence.

3. Again, hate completes the separation of all particles into their separate fundamental entities. This is the state of complete dissolution.

4. Then, again, love brings the elements together.

Neither in the case of complete mixture (1), nor in the case of complete separation of all the particles (3), there are individual things. Here Eleatic ideal is found in (1) and (3) and the Heraclitean state is found in (2). Hence, again, a balance is maintained by Empedocles with regard to Eleatism and Heracliteanism.

For Empedocles and the Atomists the world-creation and dissolution are a perpetual affair, as is also the case with Indian thinkers who also hold to the four stages of *Satya, Treta, Dvapara* and *Kaliyuga*. According to Anagoras, the world-creation takes place once for all. Again, for Empedocles and Heraclitus world-creation and dissolution is *periodic*. But for the Atomists, creation-dissolution of the world takes place in countless number.

Empedocles accepted his belief in reason. So he tries to show his interest in scientific experiment. He held that air is independent of water. If an empty glass, containing nothing but air, is immediately immersed in water, then water does not enter the glass. Why? Because the air in the glass does not allow the water to enter the glass. Hence, air too is an independent stuff.

According to his astronomy, Empedocles held that the moon shines by reflected light and also thought that perhaps this is also true of the sun. He is also credited to know the cause of lunar eclipse. He, learning from Anaxagoras, held that the solar eclipse takes place by the interposition of the moon.

In biology, Empedocles foreshadowed the Darwinian theory of the survival of the fittest. According to Empedocles, animals came into being in grotesque forms. There were bodies without heads, necks and shoulders. Creations came into being with the faces of men and heads of oxen; similarly, human bodies came into being with various kinds of heads and faces. The best forms alone could survive. Thus, Empedocles conjectures his speculation concerning the organic theory of Evolution.

Empedocles did not believe in the teleological explanation of creation-dissolution of the world. According to him the world is ruled by *chance and necessity.*

The religion of Empedocles was greatly influenced by Orphism and Pythagoreanism. Strangely enough Empedocles believed in the Zoroastrian doctrine of *restoration.* According to Empedocles there are some people who through purification in many incarnations become sinless and enjoy immortal bliss in the company of gods.

Thus Empedocles shares his belief in transmigration along with Orphism, Pythagoras, Plato and Plotinus.

Comments

Aristotle mentions that Empedocles no doubt has posited the four corporeal entities for explaining the world, but apart from corporeal entities, there are incorporeal entities too which have not been explained by Empedocles.

But apart from this, the principles of 'love and hate' are mythical and obscure. They cannot serve as the explanation of changes in the world.

Anaxagoras (500 B.C.-428 B.C.)

He was an Ionian and he made Athens the centre of philosophical activities. Anaxagoras continued the scientific and rationalistic tradition of Iona. But he was not interested in morality and religion. He was accused of atheism and even blasphemy. Why? Athenians regarded the sun and moon as divinities. Even much later Plato and Aristotle hold the stars to be deities. As against this, Anaxagoras held that the sun was constituted of red-hot stones and the moon of earth. This astronomical notion served to rob sun and moon of their deityhood. Hence, the Athenians accused Anaxagoras of blasphemy.

Empedocles had held that the four substances of fire, water, air and earth constituted the whole universe. Against this Anaxagoras maintained that there were countless elements differing from one another in form, colour and taste. Each element was found in *mixed* form and no matter how we divide each mixed form, each element still contained all other elements.[1] However, what we call gold

---

1. This was held by Ramanuja in his doctrine of *panchikarana.*

is that stuff in which the elements of gold predominate over all other elements. Similarly in the smallest particular something of everything is found.

These mixed elements could mix with one another. But mere mixing together of mixed elements would yield only chaos. But the world is a harmony. He looked at the starry heavens and he was struck with wonder at the beauty and harmonious movement of the stars. How could this beauty of the sky and the harmony of the starry movements be explained? Anaxagoras fell upon a new idea of *nous*, a quasi-psyche or mind. What is the nature of this nous?

Nous is quite different in kind and opposite of the countless materials or mixed elements, composing the universe. Nous is pure, thin and unmixed and simple. It is the lightest and most mobile entity. It alone is self-moved and can communicate motion to the mixed corporeal elements. In other words, all other corporeal elements are set in motion by nous. But nous has also some corporeal features, for it occupies space, is said to be thin and simple. Nous then is a stuff or substance, a corporeal entity, unproduced, imperishable and diffused throughout the whole universe.

Again, spontaneity of motion is most characteristic of animate beings. Hence, it can be said to be a living motive-force. Anaxagoras put forth the existence of nous to explain the beauty and perfection of the heavenly bodies. Hence, Anaxagoras regarded nous as working with design and plans. Hence, nous may be taken to be reason and 'thought-stuff'. In nous then mind?

Well, the distinction of mind and matter in clear form started with Descartes and not before. However, the reality of 'soul' was well admitted by Pythagoras and the Pythagoreans in their doctrine of transmigration. Previous to Pythagoreanism, Orphism recognized the distinction of soul and body, and, body was said to be the prison of the soul. But 'mind' for the moderners, means consciousness and even self-consciousness, endowed with personality and will. But Greek-philosophy-scholars deny that nous was regarded as a personal, self-conscious creator of the world. All that we can say that the obscure forces of 'love and hate' posited by Empedocles was made more articulate in the doctrine of *nous*. However, by virtue of its being spatial, simple, thin, it was considered corporeal as well. All that we can say that nous was taken to be quasi-mind and not mind as the term is understood by the moderners. It is also worthy of note that even Descartes who distinguished mind from matter, thought that the soul *occupied pineal gland as its seat*. Hence, even Descartes thought of the soul as a spatial entity needing a spatial seat in the pineal gland.

The beauty and harmony of the starry heavens struck Anaxagoras with wonder. He thought that this beauty could not be produced accidentally by the fortuitous movement of corporeal mixed elements. Hence, for him the universe appeared to be a product of design and a planning mind. But he could not have thought of this *nous* as a 'Personal God' who created the world out of his own resources. Why?

First, this conception of a personal God is not found even in Plato and Aristotle.

The Idea of the Good in Plato and the doctrine of a 'Prime Mover' in Aristotle are akin to the concept of 'Nous'. But they are not regarded as 'Person'. Hence, nous too cannot be regarded as personal. Further, the Stoics were influenced by Anaxagoras and they did not talk of a personal God, but they, did think of a 'world-logos or reason' as the designing principle of the universe. Hence, *nous* is not a personal God. Is nous then a creator God?

A creator God is one who *creates the stuff* and designs it according to His purpose. But for Anaxagoras the corporeal *mixed elements* are eternal and non-created. Nous can at most bring order, system and design into these elements. Hence *nous* at most can be an ordering entity, and not even an *architect*, for to be an architect means a fully conscious being who plans and designs.

Further, teleology to which Anaxagoras has drawn our attention, is limited to the starry heavens only and that also is limited to the starting of the world-process. He did not extend this presence of end or purpose in the biological world, which was very carefully worked out by Aristotle in his doctrine of entelechy. Of course, the further presence of the organic relation between the different orders of physical, biological and animal kingdom could not have been visualized even by Aristotle. But the teleological view of Anaxagoras was a great step in this direction.

As there is *one nous* which orders the whole world, so there can be no plurality of worlds. In the beginning the world was a chaos, due to the movement of countless elements. Then came nous, the 'Reason-stuff' which introduced into the chaos a vortex-motion, which separated and divided the mixed elements into smaller parts. Silver, gold and other countless elements emerged, even though each particle of silver or gold contains all other elements in lesser proportion. The world-reason planned the beauty and perfection of the starry bodies, but Anaxagoras explained the movements of the terrestrial bodies in the mechanical way like his predecessors and the Atomists.

For Anaxagoras, cognition in man is very important and he hardly made any mention of willing and feeling. We have already stated that for Anaxagoras, nous is diffused throughout the world, animating all living men and animals. Hence the moving force in each individual was a part of the world-reason. Nous no doubt is the moving force throughout the whole universe, but is found in different degrees. There is more of nous in man than in animals. Hence, knowing-stuff, called nous is more in man than in animals. Hence, the presence of more or less of cognitive power has been explained by Anaxagoras in a quantitative way. Again by virtue of his knowing, man participates in the world-reason. So men's knowing is universal reason. Hence there is one world-logos in man and in the universe at large. This conception of a common world-logos plays an important part in the Stoics.

Anaxagoras was essentially a scientist. As noted earlier, nous initiates the unmixing activity into the primordial chaos. As a result of this separating or unmixing movement, various element tend to get aggregated with the result that gold, silver, iron and many such entities come into being. With the stuff of relatively less unmixed elements, things of daily life is produced. Again, because of rotation-motion imparted into the primordial chaos, earth emerges. This earth, like other Greek predecessors, Anaxagoras holds is flat and floats in the air.

For the first time in Greek astronomy, Anaxagoras correctly explains the cause of lunar and solar eclipse. He has pointed out that by the coming of the moon between the sun and the earth, there is the solar eclipse, and by coming of the earth between the sun and moon, there is the lunar eclipse. Empedocles had followed Anaxagoras on this point, to which reference has already been made.

The importance of Anaxagoras

1. Anaxagoras continued the independent Greek scientific thinking alive. In his turn he correctly gave the real scientific explanation of lunar and solar eclipse.

2. Perhaps the most important contribution of Anaxagoras lay in holding that the world with its harmony and beauty could not have come into being without some rational element he called 'nous'. This nous is quite distinct from all other corporeal mixed elements posited by Anaxagoras. But nous is quasi-mind-stuff. But it soon became the starting-point of mind-body problem, specially for the moderners and the Western thinkers on the 20th century.

3. In due course, the concept of nous gave birth to the concept of a personal God and a *creator* God as distinct from God as an architect.

4. In the scientific world-view, Anaxagoras initiated the concept of teleology which was taken up by Aristotle and became important for Leibnitz and for the vitalists in the 19th-20th century.

5. It is also noted that Anaxagoras, laid the foundation of rhetorics, which become an important element in Greek democracy. It was developed by Gorgias and other sophists.

6. Again, Anaxagoras did not take the help of supernatural powers in explaining the world. Nay, he was condemned for his atheism and blasphemy.

In spite of his important contributions, Aristotle has severely criticised Anaxagoras.

According to Aristotle, the doctrine of mixed elements constituting the world is not correct. Anaxagoras should have realised that mixed things must have previously existed in an *unmixed* form. In the other words, the concept of 'mixed' implies the concept of the simple. There cannot be mixed without the simple. Hence, Anaxagoras should have posited the simple elements as his starting-point. Secondly, mixed elements cannot combine with one another. But, according to Aristotle, Anaxagoras should be given the credit of recognizing Mind which alone is said to be pure and unmixed. Reality is constituted both of sensibles and non-sensibles. And certainly *nous* is meant to be incorporeal and non-sensible.

The Atomists

Leukippus and Democritus have been jointly regarded as the atomists. It appears that the teaching of Leukippus was fully incorporated into the writings of Democritus. However, Theophrastos has distinguished the atomism of Leukippus from that of Democritus. Aristotle has also regarded Leukippus as the real founder of atomism and democritus is said to have popularised and extended the theory of atomism. Leukippus, Empedocles and Anaxagoras appear to be contemporaries. Leukippus appears to have flourished about 440 B.C. and it might also be held that Leukippus has simply extended and enriched the philosophies of Empedocles and Anaxagoras. It can also be stated that Leukippus has laid down the fundamentals of atomism and Democritus carried the message of atomism into ontological materialism and mechanical epistemology.

Leukippus

Leukippus really belonged to Miletus, but he was endocrinated in Eleatism. In contrast with Eleatism, Leukippus held

1. The reality of empty space or void.
2. The plurality of things and their motion.

Whilst Empedocles held that there are four fundamental elements with their distinctive qualities, and, Anaxagoras regarded that there are countless elements with their various qualities, Leukippus did not recognise the reality of *qualities*. According to him, qualities can be explained with the help of *quantity* alone.

Against the reality of One, Leukippus held that there are countless real entities, each one of them is eternal, indestructible, indivisible and invisible. Because each such entity is uncuttable or indivisible, so he called it 'atom', that is, what cannot be further cut or divided. Hence each atom was as real as the one of Parmenides. Leukippus simply shatters the One reality of Eleatism into infinite number and scatters them in the empty space. Because there are infinite number of atoms, so they move about in the empty space. Does Leukippus refute the One reality of Parmenides? No. He is moved by the experienced world of manyness and simply ignores the hair splitting and chopping of logic.

Atoms are stated to be inherently mobile and he grants that original motion will continue till it is retarded or stopped by the movement of other atoms. Aristotle could not believe in the teaching of continuous movement, but Galileo and above all Newton made this doctrine acceptable to the scientists in modern times. This doctrine of continuous movement is simply an extension of Empedocles and Anaxagoras. For Empedocles, love and hate are the mythical entities for accounting motion, and, for Anaxagoras it is the mind-like *nous* which explains motion. Leukippus substituted the scientific view of motion that is, atoms are inherently mobile. Further, Anaxagoras tried to introduce a teleological view of the universe, but Leukippus substituted a mechanistic explanation of movement. Here Leukippus has simply made Empedocles and Anaxagoras consistent. Both Empedocles and Anaxagoras had introduced their vague kind of forces for *initiating* movement for explaining movement in the universe. Now Leukippus substituted mechanical explanation, both for *initiating* and *sustaining* movement in the universe.

Again, for Empedocles the world comes into being and passes away perpetually. For Heraclitus the world-formation and dissolution takes place periodically. For Anaxagoras, the world has come into being once for all times. In contrast, for Leukippus the countless number of worlds come into being and pass away.

Besides, Leukippus appears to reconcile the rival claims of Heraclitus and Parmenides. For Heraclitus *becoming* or flux is real; for Parmenides the One eternal and motionless *Being* along is real with Heraclitus, Leukippus maintains that *becoming* is asmuch real as the One reality of Parmenides. The atoms keep on darting out in all directions in the limitless space, giving rise to becoming. Hence, for Leukippus both *being and becoming* are real.

All atoms are indivisible, invisible and countless in number. They differ from one another only in shape and size. What about their weight and lightness? For the atomists, weight is really a function of size. Later on, the Epicureans held that atoms are falling downward because of their weight through infinite space. This unscientific notion will not be able to explain the impact of atoms on one another. Against this the atomists did not hold that weight is the primary property of atoms. Further, Democritus pointed out that there is neither up nor down, middle or end of the infinite space. For Leukippus weight was not primary, but could be explained by size in the combinations of atoms.

Atoms keep on darting about because of their inherent motion in the infinite space. As a result of movements, atoms clash with one another and some fit together and form aggregations. These aggregations because of their whirling motions give rise to larger complexes and even the worlds. In these rotations, the finer and more volatile atoms are driven towards the periphery and the insert and more dense atoms remain at the centre. In this way, those atoms which fit into one another keep on forming bigger and bigger aggregations, through the law of pressure and impact. Such aggregates, even the worlds as a result of aggregations continue as long as they are not shattered into bits by collision with another world or complex of aggregates. Is the coming of the world, or, its passing away due to mere change?

The atomists were strict determinists, holding that all things come together or pass away in accordance with natural laws. Leukippus is said to have stated,

"Naught happens for nothing, but everything form a ground and of necessity."

Even perception and thinking are explained with the mechanical laws of impact of the atoms on one another. However, we come to Democritus who has given a fuller and richer view of epistemological explanation and of materialistic ontology.

Democritus (460-360 B.C.)

Democritus was the famous and gifted disciple of Leukippus Democritus accepted the theory of atoms and void and extended this theory to explain epistemology, ethics and metaphysics. The problem of Democritus was to establish the possibility of knowledge, consequently science which the sophists has denied. The second thing was the problem of morality which again was considered to be mere expediency and relative by the sophists. Democritus tried to explain scientific knowledge and absolute morality with the help of his thoroughgoing mechanism and materialism.

Epistemology

For Democritus even the soul is nothing but an aggregate of atoms. However, the soul consists of those atoms which have the essence of *fire*. These fiery atoms are the finest, smoothest and most mobile. These atoms are distributed throughout the whole universe including animals, plants and other things, but these fiery atoms are found in the largest number in man.

Democritus explains his epistemology on the basis of mechanism and materialism. But he makes a sharp distinction between perception and thought. They do not differ in *kind* but only in *degree*. But even then the two are sharply distinguished. For Democritus, perception gives us the information about the world of *becoming*; but thought gives us the knowledge of being. Indeed knowledge given by sense perception is relative and transitory. The same honey tastes sweet to a healthy man, but in fever it may taste bitter. Besides, thought gives us universal and objectively valid knowledge. In contrast, perception gives us knowledge of what is fleeting and transitory. As the sophists had maintained that *knowledge is perception,* and as perception is relative and transitory, so they denied the possibility of scientific knowledge which is universally valid for all the scientists. Hence, by upholding the claim of *thought over senses*, Democritus defended science against the epistemological scepticism of the sophists.

Further, the knowledge given by the senses concerning colour, sound, smell and taste are in the changing things of the world, and wholly dependent on the senses. In contrast, thought gives us knowledge of the true atom-forms which consist of shape, size and position. This is the famous distinction between secondary qualities of colour, taste etc. and primary qualities of shape, size and position. The distinction is found in Descartes, Locke and other moderners. However, the atomists explained the secondary qualities with the help of quantity alone. But can a scientist ignore the world of experience and perception?

No doubt the scientist explains the perceptual experience through conceptions of the true reality. Hence, the scientist must win the truth 'preserved' in perception. Therefore, Democritus held that thought has to seek the truth which inheres in perception. Unfortunately Democritus has not worked out the relation between perception and thought, which relationship was left for his successors right up to the present time.

However, it will be soon shown that Democritus held that perception and thought differ only *in degree*. This was the position of Leibnitz. Of course, Plato put *ideas* into a realm of its own as quite opposed to the phenomenal world of perception. But Plato was not a scientist, and so he could ignore the claims of sense-impressions. Aristotle on the other hand, held that ideas must be instantiated in percepts. Nominalists denied the reality of universal thought. Kant has given a very penetrating relationship between perception and thought. Since then an intimate relationship has been worked out between perception and thought.

In explaining perception and thought, Democritus takes the help of *images (eidolas)*. Idolas or images are the infinitely small copies. These images are continually shed off by the things end they are received by the senses attuned to them. Since impact and presence are the only means through which the atoms exert their influence, so *touch* in the wide sense can explain both perception and thought.

The images of things can pass both through the sense-organs which are simply passages to let in the images. In thought too the images impress directly on the fire-atoms of the body, which fire-atoms are distributed all over the body. But these images are not the *exact copies* of things external to the soul. In perception these images are distorted by air and possibly by the senses. But perception is certainly due to impressions. For example, colour is due to roughness and smoothness of the images. Sound also is a stream of atoms which cause motion in the air and this motion is communicated to the ear.

Thought also is due to the pressure of images. But in this case the fire-atoms are distributed all over the body, and, in thought there is the direct contact between the images and fire-atoms of the body, without the intervening senses. Again, in perception the images are coarse images of atom-complexes. Whereas in thought the finest images, representing the atomic structure impinge on the fire-atoms of the soul. Besides, in perception coarse images make impact on the fire atoms through the senses *violently*. In thought, however, the *finest images* directly impinge on the fire-atoms of the soul in a gentle, fire motion, yielding genuine insight into the atomic structure.

In this connection one has to note that perception and thought differ in degree and not in kind. Further, the materialism of Democritus has no room for consciousness which characterizes the soul and forms the essential features of perception and thought. Besides, if men is confined to mere *images of things*, then how can one decide whether the perceived image is a true copy of the things perceived?

Ethics

Democritus laid emphasis on happiness which in general means the surplus of pleasure over pain. This sounds headonistic, but it is more Socratic than hedonistic. According to Democritus, pleasures of the senses are not true pleasures. First, pleasures of the senses depend on external things. Secondly, they are fleeting, and very often pleasures turn into their opposites. Besides, pleasures differ with men; but happiness is what is true end of all men; hence it is universal. But most importantly pleasures depending on the senses give obscure images. And obscure images are as fatal for obtaining happiness, as they are for obtaining true knowledge. Then what is happiness?

First, happiness lies in cheerfulness which is the state *of the soul*, and, not of the body or of the senses. Hence, happiness is gaining calm body and calm soul. Calm body can be obtained by promoting health, and, calm soul can be gained only by cheerfulness by having true insight into pleasure and pain.

"He who chooses the goods of the soul chooses what is divine; he who chooses the calm of the body chooses what is human."

True happiness follows the gentle movement of the fiery atoms, which happiness results from the right insight into fiery atoms. This insight alone secures peace, guards the soul from emotional disturbance and yields mastery over passions through knowledge. This is really Socratic inasmuch as the aphorism of Socrates is 'Virtue is knowledge, and Vice is ignorance'. Democritus does not favour sex-pleasure, for it is disturbing, fleeting and follows from crude images. Democritus teaches the cultivation of true friendship. The ideal of Democritus resting as it does on materialism teaches the steadfastness and tranquillity of the inward soul, which ideal has been taught by the *Gita* also.

The Materialism of the Atomists

Materialism is that doctrine of ontology according to which matter alone is the fundamental stuff of the universe. Further, thought, feelings and any movement can be explained only through the mechanical and quantitative laws.

1. According to the atomists even the soul of man consists of atoms alone. The distinctive feature of soul is that it is constituted of fire-atoms. The difference between man and all other animate objects is that the soul of man is constituted of fire-atoms in for greater *quantity* than what they are in all other animate objects. Hence the difference between man and all other animals, plants and animate objects is one of *number* of fire-atoms.

2. Even thought and sensation are explained through the impact of one atom on another. In sensation the *coarse* images are thrown out by the things on the fire-atoms of the soul through the disturbing air and intervening passages of sense-organs. In contrast, in *thought* fine images of things directly come in contact with the fire-atoms of the soul. Again, in thought the impact of the images of things

is most delicate, very fine and gentlest. In contrast, in sensation the impression is violent, produced by the obscure images. Hence, the difference between sensation and thought is only one of *degree* and not of kind, and can be measured quantitatively in terms of force and impact.

3. Even the ethical considerations defend on the same sort of mechanical laws. The chief ethical end of man is found in attaining cheerfulness or calm of the soul in distinction from pleasure or the calm of the body. In other words, the ethical goal of men lies in attaining to emotional quietiem and mental tranquillity.

4. If the soul of man consists of smooth, spherical and fine fire-atoms, then it consists in the aggregation of such atoms. Once the aggregation is broken up at the time of death, there is no possibility of life after death. Here one is reminded again of Charvaka according to whom soul is nothing but body, and, once the body is consigned to flame there is no possibility of its coming back to life.

In the atomists the scientific worldview of the Greek has become fully articulate. Its insistence on mechanism was fully rewarded by the pursuit of the scientists in the West. But it must not be maintained that Anaxagorean view of teleology was useless when it was adopted by Plato, Aristotle and the utilitarians.

Again, the materialism of the atomists has not explained the nature of consciousness. It never occurred to them that the psychical aspect of life is very different from lifeless atoms. This is a problem which is still very much alive in modern times in the form of values and current ideologies, and in the problem concerning mind-body relationship.

2

Greek System

THE SOPHISTS

Introduction

The word 'sophist' has been derived from the word 'sophia' which means wisdom. Hence, literally 'sophist' means a wise man. But it is a tall claim for anybody to call himself 'wise'. This was shown to be a false claim through what is known as Socratic irony. Socratic held that the oracle of Delphi declared him to be the wisest man. But in what was he wise? Yes, he found that really he knew nothing. 'He was an ignorant man.' But the sophist claimed to know. When Socrates questioned the sophists then he found that they knew as little as he. Hence, according to the circle of Socrates' friends the claim of the Sophist rested on mere *pretension of being wise*, when he really was not. Secondly, Aristotle looked at the Sophist with contempt, for he took fees for teaching. This charge of Aristotle was not fair. But most probably Aristotle felt that the sophist not only had no knowledge, and, on the other hand gave a false account of knowledge proper, morality and political life. In other words, the sophist received money for subverting the truth. Thirdly, 'wisdom' cannot be imparted externally. Socrates held that knowledge proper is found in each man and it has to be drawn out from him by skilful questioning. A real teacher is one who helps his pupil to be aware of real knowledge, lying dormant in him. Hence, for the critics of the sophists, the sophists were not clear at all about 'teaching'. How could they claim to *know and teach.*

Hence, for reasons outlined above, the Sophists were ridiculed.

The second question about the sophist is that he did not continue to extend scientific knowledge. Instead he concerned himself about man himself. His questions are not about the *object or content* of knowledge, but about *knowledge* itself. He asked questions about the origin, nature and the kind of certainty which human knowledge can yield. This kind of question is not about knowing any object, but about knowing itself. This will be called 'the first level of language', according to the *theory of types.* This is the type of question which was raised by John Locke, who may be called the originator of 'modern empiricism'. But why did the sophist ask the question which he did?

It is a matter of guess. The sophist asked this question because most probably he felt that the cosmologists or the scientists of his day had reached an impasse.

The scientists had come to conflicting conclusions. The Eleatics held that reality is One, eternal and undifferentiated. On the other hand, Heraclitus concluded that reality is in constant flux. Both of them claimed to rest their conflicting conclusions on the basis of reason in opposition to deceiving senses. Under the circumstances, can one hold that reason alone can deliver the good? Can one lay aside the claim of senses?

Further, the cosmologists reached the conflicting conclusions with regard to the fundamental stuff, constituting the universe. Some said water, some said air, some stated the undifferentiated matter as the fundamental stuff. Again, some held that the fundamental stuff is one, others as four and Anaxagoras held that there are an infinite number of elements, and finally the atomists held that there are an infinite number of atoms, which constitute the universe. Whom should we accept and whom should we reject?

Why have the scientists failed? Can we say with Kant that knowledge is only an instrument. Should we, therefore, first of all examine this instrument to ascertain as to what it is and what we can know with its help?

After the inquisitive Greek must raise questions about what man can know. Should he not turn towards the inner man himself to make his object of enquiry, seeing that Nature, external to man, is difficult to know with certainty?

There is also another reason, why the sophist turned to known man himself instead of Nature. If one cannot know the world outside, why should not the philosopher turn towards himself? This became a necessity for him. First, there was the demand of law-suits. In Athenian court there was no provision for lawyers, nor were the judges themselves were supposed to be the knowers of the laws. The plaintiff and defendant had to appear in person and not through their professional lawyers. But the concerned man could make his own case or he was allowed to read out his case prepared by another man. Naturally the speech required rhetoric and persuasive arguments. This necessity was favourable for the rise of the sophists who could teach men in the art of rhetorics and argumentation for either persecution or defence.

Besides, Greece was ruled by a democratic tradition spread out in different small states. Each state was either an oligarchy ruled by noblemen, or, a plutocracy ruled by rich men. Hence, to be elected as a member of the then democracy required much rhetoric and skill in the art of persuaion and argumentation. Hence, the prevailing democracy in the city States of Greece helped the rise of the Sophists for imparting education to the youths who could pay the required fee to the sophists.

In this context the names of Protagoras and Gorgias are most important. Protagoras was interested in political movement and political philosophy, and, Gorgias was interested in rhetoric and language.

PROTAGORAS (480-410 B.C.)

The Sophist Epistemology

It appears that Protagoras was much influenced by Democritus in propounding his epistemology and Gorgias was indebted to Zeno in expounding his thesis of nihilism.

According to Democritus, knowledge is due to the motion of the atoms, specially impinging on fire-atoms. There is only a difference in degree between perception and thought. In perception, motion is coarse and rough, and, in contrast in thought the motion is fine and gentle. But in principle both perception and thought are mere motion. So really there is no real distinction between sense and reason. Hence for Protagoras *knowledge is perception.* But what is perception?

In perception there is the motion from the external object towards the sense-organ. And yet again there is also a corresponding motion of the sense-organ towards the motion of the external object. Hence there is a double motion, one from the external thing and another from the sense-organ of the percipient. But quite obviously perceiving is not the object perceived, and, yet again perceiving is quite different from the perceiving subject. Thus perception is the product of both the object moving towards the subject, and the subject moving towards the object. This perception alone is knowledge. Thus *Man is the measure of all things, of what is, that it is; of what is not, that it is not.* (152 *Thaetetus*, Plato) But what is meant by knowledge?

Knowledge means that which is true for all and for all the moments of human life. Is perception knowledge in that sense? No. But it is nonetheless knowledge of the object as it appears to a percipient at a particular *moment* and true for him at that moment alone. Is it true for another? No, for perception of one is true to him alone at one particular moment of time, and, a thing is what appears to another at another moment of time. It appears then no two perceptions of the same man are the same, and not two perceptions of two men are quite the same. And yet for all practical purpose perception alone is knowledge. This knowledge is *relative* to different men at different times. Hence the famous saying of Protagoras *Homo Mensura,* i.e., man is the measure of all things. In other words, what appears to me is true for me and what appears to you is true for you. Is there no knowledge which is valid and acceptable to all men universally? No. Then the conclusion of *homo mensura* not only shows the relativism, of knowledge, but also its universality as impossibility. This is known as scepticism. In others respects, it also means all statements are true and none are false. Is it not self-contradictory to say that the same object is *x* as it appears to me, and, is not *x* as it appears to you? No, because I may be talking about one object and you might be speaking about a different object. But from this very statement, it appears that there is not *anyone object* about which two persons can communicate. And this is what Gorgias holds that no knowledge is possible, and even if knowledge be available it cannot be communicated to others.

The very momentariness of perception really rests on the Heraclitean theory of flux. Everything is fleeting. No object remains the same for two moments. Consequently there is no object to know.

Thus relativism of knowledge couched in the phrase *homo mensura* leads to scepticism and even *nihilism* of Gorgias. There are other consequences which follow in Ethics and public morality belonging to the State. But we shall refer to them a little later.

Of course, there is another sense of 'man' in 'Man is the measure of all things'. 'Man' may mean not individual men who differ from one another, but the *universal* man, the rational man. It is reason which is one and the same in all, and what reason tells us is universal and valid for all. In this sense, 'man' taken as a 'rational being' is certainly the measure of all things. This interpretation of man as a rational being will not admit relativism in knowledge which ultimately leads to scepticism and nihilism. But the 'man' of *homo mensura* of Protagoras is not the rational man. Protagoras does not uphold the claims of thought or reason in constituting knowledge. For him knowledge is perception. Against this view, Socrates maintained that *knowledge is thought*. Hence the Protagorean aphorism of *homo mensura* necessarily leads to scepticism and nihilism. Here 'man' really means 'men' for Protagoras. The full consequences of *homo mensura* are seen in Gorgias.

Gorgias (483-375 B.C.)

Gorgias was a master of rhetoric and has developed the art of persuasion by means of artistic prose. For this reason he was not interested in the search for truth. For him any weapon is good enough to beat his adversary. Hence his philosophy is eclectic. But for explaining his tenets he took the help of Zeno's arguments, the epistemology of Protagoras with its sceptical conclusion. Gorgias has written a book *On Nature or the Non-existent*. In this book he laid down three of his tenets, namely,

1. There is nothing.
2. Even if there be anything, it cannot be known.
3. Even if there be any knowledge of anything, it cannot be communicated.

In explaining the first tenet, Gorgias is said to have borrowed Zeno's arguments leading to the falsity of *motion and plurality*. If there be anything then it can be known only through perception. But perception tells us that things are many and that they are in motion. But Zeno has shown that plurality and motion are shot through with self-contradiction. So they do not exist. Hence, there is nothing.

Of course, Zeno had not established a nihilistic conclusion. For Zeno there is One Reality. Against this, Gorgias had drawn a nihilistic conclusion partially to prove his tenet. For him any stick is good enough to kill the dog. But let us proceed further.

Perception is the only knowledge. And perception tells us that everything has come into being from its earlier state. But this arising of things can be either from Being or non-Being. But quite obviously a world of *becoming* [1] cannot come from an unchanging Being. Again, nothing can arise from non-Being. Hence, there is nothing in the world.

The second tenet of Gorgias is, 'Even if there is anything, we cannot know it'. First, Protagoras has informed us that perception is a joint product of the object perceived and percipient. But a perceived object is not the external object in itself (as Kant would say), nor is it the *perceiving act* (as G.E. Moore would say). Hence, we do not know what the real object is.

The sophists were interested in the refutation of the statements of their opponents. Naturally they concentrated on the logic of proof and contradiction. Most probably, following Eleatism, Protagoras had developed the theory of refutation.

Even Gorgias seems to have supported the opinion that all statements are false, upon the assumption that it is incorrect to predicate of any subject anything also than just this subject itself. [2]

That is, any judgment can really be a tautology. For example,

This table is black.

Either, the predicate 'black' is the same as 'this table' or not. Quite obviously the predicate is quite different from its subject term. Hence. it tells us something of the subject term (this table) which it is not. So it is false. Similarly, whatever synthetic judgment we frame it becomes false. [3] Hence, we are permitted to say.

This table is this table

which is really a tautology and really says nothing at all. Therefore, we cannot know at all. Let us come to the third tenet.

Even if we could know anything, we cannot communicate our knowledge to anyone else.

First, things and knowledge are quite separate. [4] Hence, whatever our knowledge be, it cannot be about things (as shown in the first tenet). Hence, what kind of knowledge can be obtained to be communicated at all? Further, we have already seen that according to Protagoras, knowledge is perception, and, perception is true

---

1. Perception is the only means of knowledge. But perception is nothing but motion, as the Atomists had shown. Hence, perception can yield nothing but a realm of *Becoming*. And both Plato and Aristotle had accepted this conclusion.
2. W. Windelband, *A History of Philosophy,* pp. 89-90.
3. This was really the view of T.H. Bradley who adopted this logic to show that our thought is shot through with self-contradiction.
4. This is quite opposite of what idealism maintains. For Plato things are ideas, which has been developed out of the Socratic teaching 'knowledge is through concepts or thought'. The identity of things and thoughts was explicitly stated and developed by Hegel.

for the perceiver alone and that also at the moment of its occurrence. It cannot be shared with anybody at all, 'My perception is mine, and yours is yours'. There is nothing which two persons can perceive alike. Hence each man is shut up in his cocoon-like existence from which nothing can go out and into which nothing can enter. Hence, no knowledge can ever be communicated. Here the theory of Gorgias refuted his practice, for he was teaching and communicating his knowledge to his pupils. However, one can see the influence of Gorgias with regard to incommunicableness of knowledge in Plato's allegory of 'the cave' and in Leibnitz's theory of monads.

The Sophist Theory of Morality

For the later sophists, not only perception but feeling and desires were relative. As feeling was taken to be the seat of morality, so the sophists held that morality consists in pleasure. What is pleasant, agreeable and desirable feeling for one is morally right for him, and, what is agreeable and desirable for another is morally right for him. Here in morality the individual state becomes the measure of morality. As these states are relative to individuals, so morality differs from persons to persons. Therefore, the sophists were pragmatist and utilitarian in moral philosophy.

In later developments of Greek philosophy Aristippus accepted the hedonistic ideal in morality and this hedonism was modified by Epircureanism. In modern times John Sturart Mill was the famous utilitarian and Bentham a hedonist. Of course, Socrates disputed the very foundation of the sophist theory of morality. For Socrates true morality consists in having insight into the Good. For him *Virtue is knowledge* and not the fleeting, subjective and relative feeling of what is right and wrong. But let us proceed further.

What is true of individuals is true also for justice, law and goodness of the State. For the sophists the State law is based on customs and convention. The law of one State is not the same as the law of other States. Even in the same State the law framed by one ruling party is changed by the next ruling party. Under the circumstances goodness and justice are relative. It is really based on the principle of 'might is right'. The brute majority of the ruling party in the State frames the laws for the weaker ones. Hence justice is the right of the strong.

This doctrine of hero-worship was accepted by Carlyle and in a big way was the doctrine of 'superman' promulgated by Nietzsche and was actually practised by Hitler. Of course, the doctrine of 'might is right' was opposed by Plato who taught *right is might*. There is little doubt that the doctrine of 'might is right' does. away with the distinction between right and wrong.

In religion too the sophists were non-committal. Protagoras is supposed to have written a book called *On the Gods* in which he has jotted down:

With regard to the gods, I cannot feel sure either that they are or that they are not, not what they are like in figure; for there are many things that hinder sure knowledge, the obscurity of the subject and the shortness of human life.

Thus, Protagoras was really, sceptical about the existence of God. But he advised the traditional worship of gods, perhaps as a measure of prudence. Protagoras is said to have been charged for his impiety because of his scepticism about the existence of gods.

Socrates (ABOUT 469-399 B.C.)

Socrates is a great Athenian figure who completely gave himself to philosophical enquiry, and, as a result of this embraced martyrdom haroically. Socrates has not written anything, yet three accounts have been left about him. Plato is the chief exponent of the life and teachings of Socrates. Plato's dialogues from a masterpiece of philosophical literature. The condemnation and defence of Socrates have been most beautifully portrayed in *Apology*. Xenophon was also a follower of Socrates, but he has rather emphasized the coarser aspect of Socratic teaching in his work *Memorabilia*. The third writer Aristophanes caricatured Socrates in *The Clouds*. The works of Plato and Xenophon together give a better account of the Master.

The Man Socrates

We must know the man, Socrates, if we want to understand his teaching properly. First, Socrates was a religious man. He believed in the immortality of the soul, after-life, in rebirth and the doctrine of reminiscence (Phaedo 72). To some extent he also accepted some of the tenets of Orphism, for he regarded the body as the tomb in which the soul lies buried.

Socrates used to hear voices from what he called his 'Daemon'. Jesus is also said to hear 'voices' and so did Joan of Arc. Socrates called this voice divine, which counselled him in difficult situations. Very often it served as premonition and dissuaded him from doing wrong (*Apology* 31d, 40a). It is also mentioned that Socrates experienced deep trance for hours together. Are the hearing of voices and cataleptic-like trance symptoms of insanity? Adjustment to social demands, loyalty to friends and consistency of the highest order with regard to philosophical thinking give lie to his being regarded as an insane person. It was a case of supernormality and divine restlessness (Phaedrus 249d, as Plato termed it) as was the similar case with Sri Ramakrishna and Swami Vivekananda. Gandhiji is also reported to be hearing divine voice. The *voice* of Socrates is at times taken to be the voice of one's conscience and also at times the voice of one's guardian angel. In any case the 'voice' and trance of Socrates shows that he was a mystic.

Divine Mission: One day Socrates paid a visit to the temple of god Delphi. There the oracle came that Socrates was the wisest man (*Apology*, 21). Socrates on hearing this oracle was greatly surprised and wanted to test the truth of this cracle. He questioned many people who claimed to know, but on careful questioning, Socrates found them not knowing at all.

> Whereas I am quite conscious of my ignorance. At any rate it seems that I am
> wiser than he is to this small extent, that I do not think that I know that I do
> not know (*Apology* 21d)

But it became his divine mission to question every so-called wise man.

> This duty I have accepted, as I said, in obedience to God's commands given in
> oracles and dreams. (*Apology* 33c)

But this divine mission to search for knowledge by questioning wise men brought
him into trouble, and, he was condemned to death on three counts:

(a) For denying the national gods.
(b) For setting up of new gods.
(c) For corrupting the youths.

Socrates in his defence denied all these three charges. But what could be the
meaning of first and second charges?

It appears that Socrates along with the other gods accepted the existence of one
supreme God. Further, according to *The Clouds*, Socrates is represented to have
denied the existence of Zeus. But certainly according to the *Apology* (29d), Socrates
believed in one God.

> Gentlemen, I am your very grateful and devoted servant, but I owe a greater
> obedience to God.[1]

Certainly Socrates took *daemon* to be his guardian god. Socrates used to hear this
voice ever since his childhood, which dissuaded him from doing what was wrong
(*Apology*, 31d). This 'daemon' might have been interpreted as a new god.

As to the charge of corrupting the youths, Socrates flatly denies by adducing
the verdict of his many pupils (*Apology* 33 c, d). He was condemned to death
because his teaching and popularity among the rich Athenian youths were not in
the interest of the ruling party. The saints are too good for this world. Socrates took
the cup of poison. According to Socrates, it is easier to escape death, but the real
difficulty is to escape from doing wrong. (*Apology*, 39f) The last words of the
Master were:

> Now it is time that we were going, I to die and you to live, but which of us has
> the happier prospect is unknown to anyone but God.

The General Problem of Socrates[2]

The problem of Socrates was suggested by his immediate predecessors and

---

1. This plea has been accepted by the Christians, See Act 5.29.
2. The source of the philosophy of Socrates and Plato is 'The dialogues of Plato'. Each para of each
   dialogue has been numbered for easy reference. Here we have used 'The Collected Dialogues',
   ed. E. Hamilton/H. Cairns, Princeton, sixth printing, 1971.

contemporaries, namely, the Sophists. Socrates was far more committed to know the inner man than the Sophists. He was concerned to find the truth involved about the universal validity of moral laws, which were connected with the chief problem "Man! know thyself", ignoring the scientific enquiry into the external world.

> I can't as yet 'know myself', as the inscription at Delphi enjoins, and so long as that ignorance remains it seems to me ridiculous to inquire into extraneous matters. Consequently I don't bother about such things, but accept the current beliefs about them, and direct my inquiries, as I have just said, rather to myself
> .....   (*Phaedrus* 230a)

Of course, 'knowing one's own self' meant for Socrates, the analysis of knowledge for determining the universal validity of moral principles, laws of the State and the nature of religious faith. In other words, the problem of Socrates was the same which was clearly laid down by Kant:

1. What can one know?
2. What ought one should do?
3. What can one believe?

Why were these enquiries forced on Socrates?

1. First, the problem of knowledge forced itself on Socrates, for he found that sophists laid down the maximum 'knowledge is perception'. Further, they concluded that perception can give only *relative* knowledge of things, for perception differs from persons to persons, and even with the same person at different moments. Hence the maxim of the sophists was *homo mensura*. Protagoras not only held that knowledge is relative, but Gorgias maintained that no knowledge of anything is possible, leading to scepticism and nihilism as the logical consequence of *homo mensura*.

2. In the same way the sophists maintained that morality is based on *feeling and desires*. But feelings and desires of men are not only relative with what is agreeable or disagreeable, and also fleeting. Hence, the sophists denied the *universality* of moral laws. They regarded moral laws as subserving individuals' interest and are at most mere convention.

3. The conclusion relating to the laws of the State was of the same nature. The Sophists held that the laws of the State are made in the interest of the ruling party, the underlying principle of which is 'might is right'.

Socrates did not accept the conclusions of the Sophists. They disturbed his deep conviction. Socrates believed in truth and morality and universal validity of knowledge, social and political laws. What was wrong with the Sophists, according to Socrates?

The one fundamental mistake of the Sophists, according to Socrates was that they denied the role which *reason* plays in the formation of knowledge and morality. The Sophists did not distinguish between reason and perception, and, reason and feeling. Hence, the Sophists came to support the claims of scepticism and nihilism in their epistemology and conventionalism in morality and politics.

The distinction between perception and reason was drawn up by Parmenides and Heraclitus. Socrates accepted this distinction. Consequently for Socrates, perception can yield only what is *relative* with regard to the realm of becoming. Reason alone can give to us what is universal and valid for all persons. Why? Because reason is *one and the same* in all persons. But perception depends on senses in which all persons differ. Perception can never give us knowledge of what a thing *is,* but how a thing appears to us in the form of constantly changing images which a thing keeps on shedding from itself (according to the psychology of the Sophists).

The case of *feeling* is much worse than that of perception. Hence, morality and political laws, being based on feeling can only be relative and conventional. As against this, Socrates maintained that virtue is *knowledge of the good through concepts,* and, concepts are formed by reason, and, reason is one and the same for all. Hence, if virtue is knowledge through concepts which are given by reason, then there will be universal knowledge and moral and political laws. But how did Socrates go about his task of controverting the Sophists' doctrine and establishing his own?

The Method of Socrates

The Method of enquiry of Socrates was *conversational.* Conversation invariably was limited to ethical subject-matter, for Socrates was trying to know his ownself. This self for him was essentially ethical. Naturally the subject-matter of conversation included the nature of justice, virtue, knowledge, temperance etc. By skilful questionings, he drew out the views of others with regard to virtue, justice, and so on. Then Socrates showed the inadequacies of their views. Hence, Socrates came to the conclusion that those who claim to know really do not know. Further, he concluded that he was wiser than others inasmuch as he knew that he did not know. At least he knew his own ignorance, which others did not. So of a truth he was wiser than others. From this irony he laid down the important starting insight into one's ignorance as the beginning of any knowledge.[1] This method of questioning and answering is known as dialectic method. So let us explain this.

The dialectic Method of Socrates

The conversational method of Socrates took the form of what is known as 'dialectic'. The dialectic method is an art of argument by skilful questions and answer (*Meno 85 d*). The answer to the question has to be answered in the fewest possible words which should be precise and to the point. Usually the philosophical

---

1. One can compare this starting-point of Socrates with the method of doubt of St. Augustine and Descartes.

investigation used to start with the generally accepted statements with regard to the subject-matter. For example, with the enquiry about the nature of justice, one could start with the statement that justice is in the interest of the strong against the weak, expressed in the aphorism 'might is right'. This may be called 'hypothesis', as the term is used in geometry (which has been stated in *Meno* 86a), i.e., that which has to be proved. At the first stage of elaboration or explication of the thesis, no adverse question is allowed. Next, by way of anti-thesis, absurd consequences are shown to follow, leading to contradiction of the thesis and its possible rejection. For example, Is wealth good? It is not because sometimes it is good and at some other time it is not. Hence, it leads to contradiction. Therefore, wealth is not the absolute good. (*Meno* 88d)

The rejection of one hypothesis, may lead to the acceptance of another hypothesis with less of contradiction e.g. 'Right is might'. Hence, by the process of dialectic enquiry, the investigation is led on to newer hypotheses with fewer and fewer contradiction. But Socrates never finds any absolutely correct notion of virtues idea, justice. Is it a fruitless search of a philosopher who seeks a black hat in a dark room? No. It shows passionate love of the philosopher of reaching absolute knowledge. But absolute knowledge lies in constant search and not in reaching and grasping it. In this sense, philosopjy is search after wisdom. For Socrates, as also for Indian sages true knowledge leads to *the release of the soul from bondage to the senses.*

A very brief account of the dialectic method of Socrates will show that it was this method of thesis and anti-thesis without any final termination of the enquiry was confirmed by Kant in his *Transcendental Dialectic*. Again the presence of thesis and anti-thesis led to the higher truth of synthesis, in Hegel and then again by Karl Marx. Therefore, the dialectic method of Socrates is still living in 'dialectic materialism'. But it is not all of the Socratic method. It has another side as *maieutic method.*

Maieutic or Midwifery Method

Socrates's mother was a midwife and helped in the delivery of the child which was already there in the womb of the mother. So Socrates claimed that real knowledge of justice, virtue, eternal ideas are already present in man. This knowledge is dormant, wating to be recollected by skilful questioning. Socrates had in his mind, the immortality of individual souls, their perfect knowledge of ideas in their previous births and in their pristine glory. Socrates regards the soul to be immortal.

. . . . it (soul) is immortal and has been born many times, and has seen all things both here and in the other world, has learned everything that is. So we need not be surprised if it can recall the knowledge of virtue or anything else which, as we see, it once possessed. (*Meno* 81c; See also *Phaedo* 72-76)

Therefore, for Socrates, we have already knowledge of absolute beauty, goodness, uprightness, holiness and so on (*Phaedo* 75d). This point will help us in understanding the epistemology of Socrates, and, also what Aristotle said about the method of Socrates. Aristotle said that the method of Socrates was one of definition and induction.

True, Socrates sought the definition of the concept of virtue, justice etc. We also know that definition means the explicit statement of the essence of a thing. And this is what Socrates sought.

> . . . and it seems we must inquire into a single property of something about whose essential nature we are still in the dark.   (*Meno* 86a)

But what does 'induction' mean?

It *does not mean* the kind of inductive method which was very roughly described by Francis Bacon and later more elaborately John Stuart Mill. Here John Burnet in his book *Greek Philosophy* has very correctly described the nature of induction as was understood by Socrates.

Socrates makes a sharp distinction between perception and conception. By conception is meant universal idea of a class. Now for Socrates there is an absolute gulf between perception and conception. So the observation of a number of particular things *cannot yield* the conception of cowness or horseness. Then how do we get the concept, for Socrates accepted that knowledge is through concept? And certainly there is true knowledge for Socrates. Then how do we reach concepts? Perceptions of things simply *suggest* concepts which are already sleeping in each man. *The promptings of perceptions simply serve to excite our previous knowledge of eternal verieties by recollection.* This point now will be elaborated in the epistemology of Socrates.

The Epistemology of Socrates

We have already seen that the Sophists held that knowledge is a mere matter of motion and that thought too stands on par with sensation. Hence for the Sophists, knowledge is perception.

But if knowledge is perception, then it is but movement from the objects to the senses, and, a corresponding movement of the senses towards the objects. Hence, perception is a joint product of the movement from the objects to the senses, and from the senses towards the objects. The result? Perception does not reveal the real object nor is it the subjective state of the percipient. We somehow know that there are objects, but we cannot have their true knowledge of objects. This state is known as *agnosticism*. But Protagoras does not emphasize this.

For him in perception there is true knowledge. Only this is true at the moment it occurs and that for the perceiver alone. Hence, knowledge is *relative* to each person and that also at the moment it occurs. But knowledge proper for Socrates is *universal* and *even eternal*. How can this kind of knowledge be possible?

Even on the theory of the Sophists, perception is momentary and of that which is a matter of *becoming*. In contrast, the universals deal with *Being*. Hence, for Socrates *knowledge is through* concept.

A concept *now* means the idea of a class of particulars. The notion of the class is obtained by comparing a number of particulars under that class and by abstracting from such comparison that which is common and essential attribute by neglecting the variable and accidental features of the particulars. For example, the colour of whiteness or size is an accidental attribute of the cow, but its *cowness* is its essential feature present in all cows. But does Socrates mean the formation of a concept outlined here, by comparison and abstraction?

No. Why? Because he makes a sharp distinction between the universals obtained by conceptual reasoning and perceptual process. Perception can yield only what is momentary and merely *becoming*; concept alone can take us to *being*. This distinction of being and becoming was introduced by the Pythagoreans.

For example, in geometry we have the notion of equality. But do we get this notion from the observation of two equal sticks, two equal pieces of stones, or, even of two peas? No. Because observed equality of things does not always appear to be so.

Is it not true that equal stones and sticks sometimes, without changing in themselves, appear equal to one person and unequal to another? (*Phaedo* 74b)

Then how do we get the concept of absolute equality? They *suggest,* i.e. the observed equal sticks and stones suggest the notion of absolute equality. How can the bastard observed equality suggest absolute equality? Here we do not know how much Socrates really held the idea of the immortality of soul and its pristine knowledge of the true knowledge of absolute equality, absolute justice, goodness and so forth, and how much of this doctrine really belonged to Socrates. Socrates is said to have held the notion of the immortality of the soul, the fall of human beings into the world of their ignorance, cycle of rebirths and of faint recollection of absolute knowledge in their pristine glory. In *Phaedo* 74 and *Meno* 81 and 82, Socrates is said to have held the view about the soul just outlined above.

Now observed equal things suggest to us idea of absolute equality, for the observed particulars *poorly imitate* absolute equality. Persons have knowledge of absolute equality, justice, virtue, goodness etc., but they become dim and dormant in them because of the deception of senses. But in their pristine glory they had knowledge of absolute equality, goodness etc., and they always remain in them in their dormant form, waiting to be resurrected by the promptings of observed equality, actual examples of goodness or beauty. Hence, conceptual knowledge is more *recollection.*

. . . what we call learning is really just recollection? (*Phaedo* 72e)

Thus the soul, since it is immortal and has been born many times, and has seen all things both here and in the other world, has learned everything that is. So we need not be surprised if it can recall the knowledge of virtue or anything else which, as we see, it once possessed. (*Meno* 81c)

Here two things require a little elaboration. First, how do we know that learning is mere recollection? Well, Socrates brought a slave boy and by skilful questionings made him know of the 29th theory of Euclidean Geometry. This shows that all knowledge is dormant and teaching simply means the recollection or recovery of the forgotten knowledge (*Meno* 81, 82). But how do the observed particulars *suggest* their corresponding universals?

Well, observed particulars imitate the universals. There is some similarity and dissimilarity with the universals. And on account the law of Association by similarity or contrast, observed particulars remind one of the universals based on the points of similarity, and these universals human being knew well in their pristine glory.

Does it not follow from all this that recollection may be caused either by similar or dissimilar objects? Yes, it does.

When you are reminded by similarity, surely you must also be conscious whether the similarity is perfect or partial. (*Phaedo* 74a)

Of course, the similarity is very imperfect, for things are poor copies. The problem of bridging the gulf between the observed particulars and universals remains a very serious problem which Plato tried to bridge through his doctrine of *participation*. To this solution Aristotle objects in his criticism of Plato's doctrine of ideas. But really Plato himself was conscious of the weakness of the theory of participation in his dialogue known as *Parmenides*.

From the above account of the universals a few things are very clear. First, the distinction between the universals and their corresponding particulars was derived from the Pythagoreans, but Socrates extended this distinction between the particulars and universals into the fields of morals and aesthetics. Universals cannot be found in particulars because universals can never be found there. No doubt particulars poorly imitate or are poor copies of the universals. They can however prompt and suggest the corresponding universals on the basis of similarity and contrast.

No doubt the distinction between the universals and particulars was drived from the Pythagorean theory of number. But the doctrine of concept was examplified by the Pythagoreans in a few universals of justice, marriage etc., and that also arbitrarily. Socrates substituted a systematic enquiry into the fields of morals and aesthetics. This enquiry took the form of the dialectic method of skilful questions and answers. But is Socratic method really inductive in the sense of Mill?

No. For the simple reason that particulars only imitate their corresponding universals. Really the universals are *not in the particulars*. To explain our knowledge of absolute ideas or universals, Socrates takes recourse to this theory of recollection or reminiscence. And the recollection takes place by the promptings of their observed instances.

> Then if we obtained it before our birth, and possessed it when we were born, we had knowledge, both before and at the moment of birth, not only of equality and relative magnitudes, but of all absolute standards. Our present argument applies no more to equality then it does to absolute beauty, goodness, uprightness, holiness, and, as I maintain, all those characteristics which we designate in our discussion by the term 'absolute'. (*Phaedo* 75c, d)

Then *Phaedo* 73c suggests that this recollection takes place as if of a long-forgotten entity rather suddenly. Hence, concept is really formed by a glimpse or intuition of the universals. The midwifery-method of Socrates clearly states that the concept of the universal is really *in the mind* of the enquirer and this is not to be found in the observed particulars. Socrates makes a sharp distinction between sense and reason. There is the confused manifold of sense and against this there is the colourless, shapeless, intangible realm of thought which can be grasped by reason alone (*Phaedrus* 247 c). Again, there is a class of perceptual things which can be seen but not thought, while the ideas can be thought but not seen (*Republic* 507b). Hence, the perceptual things passionately strive to become the corresponding real ideas. But they never can be true ideas. Again, Socrates points out that knowledge is not in the *impressions* of the sense, but by reflection on them (*Theaetetus*, 186d). Socrates was really a mystic and knowledge is to be found in mystic intuition of universals. As a matter of fact, Socrates tells us that senses are really more of hindrance than help in the realisation of universal ideas.

> Surely the soul can best reflect when it is free of all distractions such as hearing or sight or pain or pleasure of any kind—that is, when it ignores the body and becomes as far as possible independent, avoiding all contacts and associations as much as it can, in its search for reality. (*Phaedo* 65c)

Again,

> Don't you think that the person who is likely to succeed in this attempt (of knowing the reality) most perfectly is the one who approaches each object, as far as possible, with the unaided intellect, without taking account of any sense of sight in his thinking, or dragging any other sense into his reckoning—the man who pursues the truth by applying his pure and unadulterated thought to the pure and unadulterated object, cutting himself off as much as possible from his eyes and ears and virtually all the rest of his body, as an impediment which by its

presence prevents the soul from attaining to truth and clear thinking?

(*Phaedo* 66 a; also 67a)

Again, only after leaving the body, a philosopher will have wisdom in purity (*Phaedo* 68b) and even in this life by the mortification of the body, a philosopher will get the glimpse of eternal verieties. (*Phaedo* 67c)

Therefore, the concepts of Socrates are not obtained by the inductive method of Mill, but *only by intuition*, by *glimpse or sudden illumination through meditation.* This interpretation of 'knowledge or concept' will be also found in Socratic theory of morals, for the real aim of Socrates was to find the solution of an ethical problem. For Socrates *Virtue is knowledge.* So his epistemolongy is only a preparation for his ethical theory.

The Ethical Theory of Socrates

Before the rise of the Sophists, an Athenian observed the laws of the State and subscribed to moral laws. It was considered advantageous for the individuals to observe the laws and disadvantageous for the breaker of the laws. The Athenians made no enquiries into the origin and the validity of the laws. But with the rise of the city States and frequent changes of the State laws in different States and even in the same State by the ruling parties, made the Athenian think about the origin and basis of the state laws. They not only found the *relativity* of the State laws, but also found moral laws too to be relative for different races and the peoples. The Sophists made enquiries about the origin and basis of the laws of morality and States.

Just as the Sophists had explained perception on the basis of *private sensation,* so they also based morality on primary ethical *feeling* and *desires.* Feeling is extremely subjective and differs from person to person. What is agreeable to one is not so to another. So the Sophists concluded that morality is what is agreeable, useful and desirable to the majority of the people. Hence morality is based on *convention.* In the same vein, the Sophists concluded that the basis of the State laws is *might is right.* A law is backed by the majority. Hence, it is the right of the strong man to rule over the weaker ones. Is it also not in accordance with what is found in Nature? It is writ large in Nature that the strong rules over the weak. Hence the State laws have the principle 'might is right'.

Against the teaching of the Sophists, Socrates maintained that morality is knowledge of the Good through concepts. Morality issues forth from *rational insight* into the good. As reason is one and the same for all, so moral laws are universally valid. Hence, moral laws are not based on feeling and desires, but on rational thought. In relation to Ethics, Socrates laid down three propositions:

1. Virtue is knowledge through concepts. So nobody does wrong knowingly. Therefore, vice is ignorance.
2. As virtue is knowledge, *so virtue can be taught.*
3. Virtue is *one.*

Virtue is Knowledge Through Concept

For Socrates, virtue is the chief business of life (*Laws* 7.807c) and the greatest good (*Laws* 2.661b). But this virtue must be universal consistent and the same for all. And this virtue must be equally binding on all if it were knowledge. How can this be established?

> . . . if there exists any good thing different from, and not associated with knowledge, virtue will not necessarily be any form of knowledge. If on the other hand knowledge embraces everything that is good, we shall be right to suspect that virtue is knowledge. (*Meno* 87d)

Now Socrates grants that health, wealth and good looks are all good, but in the absence of knowledge proper they all can be misused.[1] Courage and temperance are all good and would lead to happiness when they are guided by wisdom, and, evil if they are controlled by folly. (*Meno* 88a, b, c,)

> If then virtue is an attribute of the spirit, and one which cannot fail to be beneficial, it must be wisdom, for all spiritual qualities in and by themselves are neither advantageous nor harmful, but become advantageous or harmful by the presence with them of wisdom or folly. If we accept this argument, then virtue, to be something advantageous, must be a sort of wisdom. (*Meno* 88d)

Finally the right knowledge is the *mind* of the wise man, and wrong user is the mind of the foolish (*Meno* 88e). Similarly in *Euthydemus*, it is printed out unless it is guided by wisdom, and, nothing is bad unless it is backed by ignorance (281d, e).

Both Socrates and the Sophists agreed that morality is guided by knowledge. But difference lies in the *kind* of knowledge and the *kind of goodness*. For the Sophists knowledge is perception; for Socrates knowledge is through concept. For the Sophists goodness is a matter of *habit* (*Republic* 7.518d) i.e., by habit and practice, without the help of philosophy and reason (*Phaedrus* 82b). But obviously habit cannot be always reliable specially in novel situations and in predicaments. In such circumstances, customary goodness becomes variable, inconsistent and relative. Similarly, *true opinion* may lead to the good accidentally, but not always.

> . . . the man with knowledge will always be successful, and the man with right opinion only sometimes. (*Meno* 97c)

Further, for the Sophists goodness is a kind of art or skill for managing the affairs of the State and the family (*Republic* I. 332). But if goodness is an art, then it becomes relative, for what is good for the ruling party is not so for the *opposition*. Besides, art is always of the *opposites*. For example, a man who can guard the

---

1. One is reminded of Kant who held that without good will health, wealth etc., can be used for evil ends. For Socrates however good will is one which has been moulded by the knowledge of the good.

treasury best, is the man who knows all the ways of committing theft. So he is also a kind of thief. This was seen in the case of Gorgias who disclaimed any responsibility of his pupils if they used the art of rhetoric for evil purpose. But what is the kind of knowledge through concept?

We have already seen that concepts are given by reason and is not given by the perceptions of the particulars. Concepts are always in the mind of everyone and they have to be *enkindled* by skilful questionings. But if virtue is knowledge, then certainly it can be taught (*Meno* 89e). But certainly it can be taught by one who knows what is virtue or the good. However, where are the teachers of the concept of the good? (*Meno* 89d, e)

Socrates does not accept that the Sophists are the real teachers of the good, for they believe in customary morality, based on opinion which is based on feeling and tempting desires. Can Socrates claim to be a teacher? No. For he knows that he does not know. Then should we give up theory that knowledge is the concept of the good?

Indirectly by his assumed ignorance, Socrates has guided us towards the direction in which the seeker can have the kind of knowledge of the concept of the good. The real concept is always a matter of recollection of and by meditation on the idea of the good. In this way one can get a glimpse of the good. The process, says Socrates,

> . . . .is recollection, as we agreed earlier. Once they (all sorts of good) are tied down, they become knowledge, and are stable. That is why knowledge is something more valuable than right opinion. What distinguishes one (the real seeker) from the other (men of right opinion) is the tether (the idea of the good).
>
> (*Meno* 98a)

The conclusion of Socrates is:
> Our present reasoning then, whoever has virtue gets it by divine dispensation. (*Meno* 100b)

In our Indian language the intuition of the good is a matter of enlightenment (*bodhi*) which metaphorically can be said to be the gift of God.

One part of the whole discussion has been left out, i.e., virtue is knowledge and vice is ignorance. No man *knowingly does* wrong. This follows from another tenet of Socrates, namely, virtue is one.

Virtue is One
The kind of knowledge to which Socrates is pointing is not mere intellectual achievement. It is the kind of knowledge which *controls the will* and necessarily issues in action. Some sort of this thing is contained in what is known as Ideo-motor theory. The theory means that if one concentrates on an idea with sufficient intensity and frequency then it issues into an appropriate action. For Socrates, however, the idea of the good controls all other ideas and ultimately guides the whole man, his will and feelings too, and necessarily issues into good acts. Hence,

it lies in the culture of the soul which ultimately leads the soul, in a virtuous man, towards regaining its pure, pristine glory. This is the real interpretation of 'no one does wrong knowingly', and that 'knowledge is virtue, and virtue is true knowledge'. This is the eudaemonistic theory of Socratic ethics, which was taught by Aristotle. But in Plato the knowledge of the good has soteriological end, which one finds in the philosophy of Samkhya and Advaitism.

There is also another sense in which Socrates says that virtue or goodness is one. For example, cowness is one but many cows poorly imitate it. Similarly, wisdom, temperance, courage, justice and holiness are five kinds of virtue, but there is one single reality which underlies them all (*Protagoras* 349a). Again in *Meno* 74a, Socrates was looking for one virtue which permeates all other virtues named above. In the same way, Socrates speaks of one form of excellence only (*Republic* 4.445c). But how to explain this?

In *Gorgias*, Socrates points out that all kinds of bodily excellence follow from one single health of the body. Similarly, all kinds of virtue follow from the *health of the soul*. And what is meant by 'health of the soul'? The health of the soul follows from the order and arrangement between the different functions of the soul (*Gorgias*, 504d). Socrates speaks of reasoning, temper and desires as the three parts of the soul. The function of reasoning is *wisdom,* of temper is courage, and of desire is soberness or temperance. Now the health of the soul follows from the discipline among these parts. Wisdom commands, whilst temper assists in the execution of these commands, and, desire furnishes the material basis of action.[1] This is in harmony with the teachings of modern psychology. Conation (desire of Socrates) drives the individual towards all kinds of action for food, mate etc.; cognition controls these activities. A successful functioning of the harmonious activities under the regulation of reason (cognition) yields happiness. Hence, Socrates means that virtue is one in the sense that the *self of a good man is an organic unity of all its functions.*

Lastly, Socrates, as also Plato is supposed to hold that there is one Idea of the Good which underlies all that is right and beautiful.

> . . . in the region of the known the last thing to be seen and hardly seen is the idea of good, and that when seen must needs point us to the conclusion that this is indeed the cause for all things of all that is right and beautiful, giving birth in the visible world to light, and author of light and itself in the intelligible world being the authentic source of truth and reason, and that anyone who is to act wisely in private or public must have caught sight of this.

Republic 7.517c

---

1. John Burnet, *Greek Philosophy,* pp. 144-45.

Hence, the Idea of the Good is one single reality which underlies all that is called virtue or good. Once one gets this knowledge of the good or its glimpse, one cannot do wrong. Only in this sense, virtue is knowledge, and, the knowledge of the good is virtue. An Indian reader can note in this interpretation that there is an echo of the advaitic teaching that the knower of Brahman himself becomes Brahaman, and goes beyond both good and evil. Aristotle himself was a biologist and for him knowledge meant ordinary knowledge of subject-object type. From his standpoint certainly a *mere knowledge* of what is *conventionally* regarded as good or evil, does not issue into its corresponding action. But for Socrates knowledge meant the glimpse of the Supreme Source of good and this changes, moulds and transforms the total personality of the seeker.

The Importance of Socrates
The most important thing about Socrates is that he gave a new turn to Greek thought. He influenced Plato and Plato in turn influenced Aristotle with the result that European philosophy still hovers around Platonism and Aristotelianism. Thus Socrates wrote nothing but his thought still echoes and re-echoes in Western philosophy.

The most significant enquiry of Socrates was spelled out by him in the oracle of Delphi "Man! know thyself". In one sense, he diverted scientific investigation from physics and Nature to Man. Does this investigation mean the science of psychology? Yes, it was understood as such by the Sophists. But the Sophists reduced knowledge into scepticism and even nihilism. But Socrates believed in truth and knowledge, and, his enquiry turned towards knowing one's own self. In knowing one's own self, Socrates first laid down that knowledge is *through concept.* Now what is a concept?

There are three theories which have resulted in determining the nature of concept. These three are known as *realism, conceptualism* and *nominalism.* Plato is supposed to have held realism, Aristotle some sort of conceptualism, put really in its pure form it is associated with British Empiricism and also in Thomism. But *nomination* is the most dominant theory in the modern western thought, though it was most clearly held by *Rescelin* and *Ockham* in the middle ages. All these theories relate to the place of *universals* in relation to particulars. Whatever may be the best view concerning the place of universals in relation to particulars, all the views relate to be problem initiated by Socrates. Therefore, Socrates is very much alive even today.

Secondly, Socrates is said to be primarily an ethical thinker and here it is held that Socrates maintained that moralit{ is through the *concept of the Good.* Negatively, he held that morality is not based on *feeling and desires.* Moral laws are universal, because a concept is universal. Therefore, for Socrates, morality is universal knowledge of the Good. The Good is advantageous for man and contributes to his *happiness.* But what is happiness? Is it that which we call as *pleasure?* It is significant that Socrates could never say anything definite about Good. Naturally it led to various interpretations. The doctrine of the Good as happiness led to the theory of cyrenaicism and hedonism of *Aristoppus and Epicureanism* respectively. On the other hand, Antisthenes (444-368 B.C.) who was the disciple of Socrates held that his master taught about attaining virtue. And virtue is one in which a man becomes independent in the midst of the course of nature. This means the doctrine of *cynicism*, according to which man should suppress his desires, and, restricts his wants to the minimum. Hence a man, pursuing virtue becomes independent of the course of life by ridding himself from the wants of life, as far as possible. Thus the ethical theory of Socrates not only influenced Greco-Roman moral theory, but even in the modern times has influenced modern theories of utilitarianism and hedonism.

However, the Good of Socrates and Plato goes even beyond God. A mere glimpse of the Good leads to the transformation of the personality of the seeker. Contemplation of and meditation on the Idea of the Good, finally lead to the release of the soul from the bondage of senses and restore to the seeker his pristine glory. Hence, the concept of the Good is not an ordinary concept, but a concept which *controls the will* of the seeker. The Western man has not learned this aspect of philosophy, but was upheld by Plotinus and has been retained in the Christian doctrine of becoming of *a new Being*, a new creation in Christ. Thus, the mystical aspect of the knowledge of the Good still lingers on in Western thought.

PLATO (428-27—347 B.C.)

Introduction

Plato was a poet at heart and his philosophical writings form a masterpiece of literature. He had to take recourse to myths, allegories, metaphors in order to express what could not be stated in prose with precision. He wrote in delightful dialogues with Socrates at the centre, but the philosophies of the previous period were all taken into account.

Plato has given a system of thought to the Western philosophy. It was through Pythagoras that Plato owned respect for mathematics and also this mathematical thought paved the way, for *Ideal realism* known as the doctrine of ideas. Further, Pythagoras was also a religious thinker. Hence, Plato derived from Pythagoras belief in the immortality of soul, the doctrine of the transmigration of the soul, its pre-existence and the theory of reminiscence and mysticism concerning bondage and release of the soul. From Parmenides, Plato derived the doctrine of the eternity and changelessness of idea. From Heraclitus, Plato accepted the doctrine of the flux of sensible things. This realm was the realm of ceaseless *Becoming*. But the influence of Socrates remained with him as an abiding element of thought. Plato took the thought of Socrates, specially his own doctrine of the idea of the Good as the crowning of his thought under the influence of the Socratic teaching of virtue as knowledge through the concept of Good.

Plato lived with his Master Socrates in his last eight years of Socrates and was drunk with the thought and life of the Master and his martyrdom on the altar of philosophy. To the end of his life, Plato was stirred up by his philosopher master, friend and guide.

Of course, without Plato, Aristotle could not have arisen whose encyclopaedic genius and the most complete system of Greek thought never ceased to influence Western thought. But the Dialogues of Plato has so many hints about the many fibres of philosophical thought that he has never ceased to influence Western philosophy. Up to the thirteenth century, Plato influenced Christian theology almost exclusively and even in the modern thought Platonic tradition is fully alive. For this reason, J.H. Muirhead has noted that the whole of Western philosophy is nothing more than 'the series of footnotes to Plato'.[1]

At this stage we must not ignore the starting-point of Plato's philosophical search. We can now remember that Socrates was dissatisfied with the teaching of the Sophists, and with the difficulties involved in the theory of 'knowledge is perception'. Socrates laid down that 'knowledge is through concept'. Plato also started his investigation with opposition to the Sophists. Plato characterised the nature of reality of the Sophists as belonging to the realm of darkness. His own teaching about the Ideas as the realm of brightness (*The Sophist* 254a). Hence, the first part of the thesis of Plato is negative, namely, knowledge is *not perception*. After demolishing the stand of the Sophists, Plato advances his own theory of Ideas. So let us begin with the negative theory of Plato.

Knowledge is Not Perception

Protagoras is said to be the best exponent of the theory that knowledge is perception. According to him, what appears to me is true for me, and, what appears to you in perception is true for you. Hence, man is the measure of all things. Plato criticizes this doctrine most thoroughly in *Theaetetus* and we shall largely confine ourselves to this dialogue of Plato. For Protagoras sensation is due to continuous motion of the atoms, and, what is in continuous flux cannot be known, for there is nothing which remains the same for two moments. There is no *being*, not something which can be known. The conclusion is

> that nothing is one thing just by itself, but is always in process of becoming for someone, and being is to be ruled out altogether . . . .   (*Theaet.* 157a)

Nay, something more.

---

1.   J.H. Muirhead, *The Platonic Tradition in Anglo-Saxon Philosophy*, p. 15. The author has used "Plato", tr. by E. Hamilton/Huntington Cairns Princeton, 1971. Here every dialogue has been paragraphed and numbered which is also the case with Jowett's translation.

Perception results from double movements; one from the side of objects and another from the side of the percipient. Take the taste of wine.

> The sensation, on the patient's side, makes the tongue percipient, while, on the side of the wine, the sweetness, moving in the region of the wine, causes it both to be and to appear sweet to the healthy tongue. (*Theaet.* 159d)

The result is that perception is a joint product of the perceived object and percipient. So nobody knows what the perceived object is in itself. The conclusion is that in perception there is no object in itself to be known at all. For example, the eye which catches the motion and the motion from the object, but the perceived object is something between the two (*Theaet.* 154). Hence each perception is relative to the percipient. Nobody is sure that what appears to you is the same which appears to another. Nay, even what appears to me is not the same to me in the next moment because I never remain in the same condition in the two moments. (*Theaet.* 154a, 160a)

> "Accordingly, whether we speak of something 'being' or is its 'becoming', we must speak of it as being or becoming for someone, or of *something,* or *toward something.* . . ." (*Theaet.* 160b)

The result? Perception yields self-contradictory conclusion. What appears sour to a sick man is sweet to the healthy. Thus, the same thing becomes sour and sweet, which is opposed to each other. (*Theaet.* 166e, 167b)

Further, if knowledge is perception then there will be no distinction between truth and falsity. If what appears to one is true for him, and, what appears to another is true for him, then when a dreamer dreans that he is flying in the air and that a madman thinks that he is a god, then what appears to them is true for them (*Theaet.* 158b). But quite obviously what a madman imagines and what a dreemer dreams are considered false. Hence the doctrine of *homo mensura* blurs the distinction between truth and falsity. Of what a madman imagines, and, what a new born child sees and what a brute perceives and what a healthy man senses are all equally true, then quite obviously there can be no distinction between truth and falsity (*Theaet.* 161d and 162e). Other more absurd things follow.

If perception is knowledge and memory is not, then see the absurdity. If a man shuts his eyes after seeing something, but remembers it, then he has no knowledge of what he remembers (*Theaet.* 164). Again, suppose a man sees a thing with one eye, but shuts his other eye, then with one eye he knows and with the closed eye he does not know. Thus, a man knows and at the same moment does not know (*Theaet.* 165). Is it not self-contradictory? Hence, knowledge is perception is an absurd doctrine.

Further, if every man is the measure of what appears to be true, then the statement of *Homo Mensura* appears false to me. So it becomes false for me. This is a grand conclusion.

Protagoras, for his part, admitting as he does that everybody's opinion is true, must acknowledge the truth of his opponents' belief, about his (Protagoras's) own belief, where they (opponents) think he is wrong. (*Theaet.* 171a)

Thus Protagoras has to admit that his own theory of *homo mensura* is false as his opponents see it.

The Ideal Theory of Plato

We have already referred to the three theories concerning universals and we have to make them clear for our purpose here.

We meet a large number of objects which we can call as 'particulars' for our convenience. For example, cows, dogs, tables etc., are so many particulars. Each class of particulars has some common qualities. Some of these qualities are called essential and some others as accidental. For instance, the colour, shape and size of cows may be deemed as accidental. The smallness and largeness are not the essential qualities. Similarly some cows may not be black but white, and some others may be black but not white or piebald. Hence, the colour of the cows is its accidental quality. In contrast, cowness is an essential quality of the whole class of cows, for without the quality of cowness, no animal can be called a cow. Hence, cowness is said to be *universal* and cows comprising the class cow are said to be *particulars*. Now what is the status of a universal like cowness, dogness, beauty, justice and so on?

Ordinarily we do not think that universals have their own independent existence as trees or flowers and other particular objects have. *Realism* is the doctrine that universals have their own independent existence in their own rights. This is the view of Plato. Aristotle criticized the realistic theory of universals accepted by Plato. According to Aristotle, universals do exist but only in *individual* things. For example, beauty does exist but only in beautiful things viz., beautiful flowers or birds, butterflies etc. Hence, Aristotles's views are somewhat like Platonic realism, even though he admits that universals do not exist apart from particulars. In other words, according to Aristotle, a universal must be *instantiated.* But what about *unicornness*? It is certainly a universal even though it cannot be instantiated. But let us leave aside this difficulty with the Aristotelian view of universals. Another important view about universals is known as conceptualism.

Conceptualism is the doctrine that universals are constructed by the human mind after the observation of particular instances. This is the view largely held by the British empiricists. According to conceptualism, universals have their locus *in the mind.* We find that Plato rejects the subjectivity of universals. (*Parmenides* 132b)

There is the third theory of *nominalism* concerning the status of universals, which was first propounded by *Roscelin and Ockham* (1290-1350). According to nominalism, universals are mere words to think about the class of objects, and, they have no independent existence, nor even their existence in the mind. But 'dogness' is no quality, then how do we think about dogs as soon as the word 'dog' is uttered? Nominalism was defended by resorting to the principle of *resemblance* exemplified by an eminent member of a class. This obviously is putting the cart before the horse. How do we select an eminent member of the class known as 'Type'? In recent years Wittgenstein has propounded the theory of 'family resemblance'. We need not go into further detail. We are concerned with the realistic theory of univerals propounded by Plato called *Ideas or forms*, by contrasting this from conceptualism and nominalism. But how and why Plato has held the theory of Realism?

Parmenides and Heraclitus have made very sharp distinction between the worlds of *Being* and *Becoming*. According to them, reality is to be known through reason and not through the senses. Of course, Parmenides and Heraclitus differed with regard to the nature of reality, but they kept to the absolute distinction of reason and senses. Again, we have already seen that for Socrates knowledge is not perception, but through concepts which again are quite different from sensation (*Phaedrus* 247c). Socrates did not clearly establish the status of concepts, but for him too concepts are not perception and are not to be found in perception. Perceptible objects *imitate* the real ideas just as the many copies of *Mona Lisa* do today. But no copy can be taken for the original. It was Plato who made a sharp distinction between intellect and senses, universals and perceptibles. Ideas as universals are the real originals which can be copied by the perceptible, but no perceptible can even be the original idea. Ideas can be thought but not sensed, and, percepts can be sensed but not thought

> And the one class of things (perceptibles) we say can be seen but not thought, while the ideas can be thought but not seen. (*Republic* 507b)

But why should we make such a sharp distinction between Ideas and perceptibles? This point was suggested by the Pythagorean concepts in mathematics.

Take the notion of equality. It is not to be found in objects, given by senses. No two lines, two sticks and two stones are *exactly equal*.

> Is it not true that equal stones and sticks sometimes, without changing in themselves, appear equal to one person and unequal to another? (*Phaedo* 74b)

Then from where have we got the idea of equality or beauty? Well, both Socrates and Plato hold that the ideas are hinted at by the perceptibles on account of recollection or the theory of *reminiscence* which we will soon describe.

There is another reason which has to be kept in mind. The Greek mind in general accepted the pure receptivity of mind in receiving the objects of knowledge. Senses reveal becoming or the objects in constant flux (becoming), and Intellect reveals the ideas. Knowledge is always *of something* (*Theaetetus* 167b). But cannot thought be *in the mind* as subjective, of the knower of ideas? Socrates suggests this and yet at once rejects this

> No, that is impossible. So it is a thought of something?
> Yes.
> Of something that is, or of something that is not?
> Of something that is. (*Parmenides* 132b)

If ideas cannot be found in *becoming*, then where else it can be? Ideas are to be found in their own being in the realm of reality. In order to explain this realm of reality Plato takes the help of a myth. But from the above account it is quite clear that Plato would reject conceptualism and even nominalism.

The Myth Concerning Ideas

Ideas are not to be found in empirical things. Then how are they to be found? What is their origin? Here Plato takes the help of a myth, which once again was greatly influenced by Socrates, Pythagoras and which ultimately has to be traced to Orphism.

According to Plato, the soul is immortal (*Phaedo* 85e sq, 92 sq) and in its pristine existence it enjoyed the pure experience (*Phaedo* 75c, d). But at present the soul is in bondage to senses, and continues in bondage till it regains its pristine glorious existence through proper philosophical knowledge through meditation on the Idea of the Good. As long as the soul does not regain its release it passes through endless cycle of rebirths. Thus learning of ideas is really *recollection.*

> Thus the soul, since it is immortal and has been born many times, and has seen all things both here and in the other world, has learned everything that is. So we need not be surprised if it can recall the knowledge of virtue or any thing else which, as we see, it once possessed. (*Meno* 81c)

Therefore, learning of ideas is really recollection. (*Phaedo* 72e, 76a, 81c) Myths are not precise concepts and no logical conclusion can really be drawn from them. Hence, Plato could not really explain the real relation between eternal ideas and the percepts. But it is the world of seeming things or perceptibles that a philosopher has to explain. So what does Plato do?

Plato takes the help of metaphors to explain percepts through his theory of ideas or forms. According to him, ideas are the patterns, and things simply imitate them, or, the ideas are the original entities, and, things are their copies. At times, he tells us, that sensible things simply *partake* or *participate* in their corresponding ideas.

On other occasions, Plato tells us that things *remind* us of ideas by being similar or dissimilar of ideas (*Phaedo* 74a). One can see that the relationship between the Ideas and perceptible things is merely metaphorical. Hence, this relationship has been subject to just criticism by Aristotle. Nonetheless Plato himself was aware of the difficulties concering his ideal theory and he clearly states them in *Parmenides*.

Parmenides asks Socrates, 'Does an Idea participate in the perceptibles in whole or parts?' If one and the same idea as a whole covers (e.g., sail over a number of passengers) a number of separate things, then the idea itself will get divided. Again, if the same idea is found in parts in number of sensible things then again the idea is divided. Thus one and the same idea gets divided. Then how can an idea be called one, as Plato maintains? *(Parmenides* 131)

Further, if the sensible is like an idea, then the idea too will be like the sensible. In that case, another idea of likeness will be required to explain the first idea of likeness with the likeness in *like* things, participating in the idea. In other words, there is a third standard likeness with which to judge the two likenesses. Further, this second pattern of likeness, will be required to explain the likeness of the second order. This will land us into *regressus ad infinitum.*

Besides, the *participation-theory* is open to the fallacy of the *third man.* An idea is the common element which is found in many particulars e.g., the idea of man is found in many men. But there is an element which is common to the individual men and to the Idea of man. This may be called a 'third man'. Again, between this third man and the Ideas of man will require another idea to explain the common element. This will finally lead to infinite *regress.* (*Parm.* 132)

There is another interesting point. Perfect knowledge is not to be found in our sensible world of things. It is to be in the ideal realm, say, gods' heaven. But gods cannot know the world of sensible things, for their knowledge is of heavenly realm of alone.

Just as we do not rule over them by virtue of rule as it exists in our world and we know nothing that is divine by our knowledge, so they, on the same principle, being gods, are not masters nor do they know anything of human concerns. But surely, said Socrates, an argument which would deprive the gods of knowledge would be too strong. (*Parm* 134d, e)

When Plato was aware of the difficulties of his Ideal Theory, then why did he still continue it? Well, the reason appears to be this. No person can jump over his own shadow, and, hardly anybody over the intellectual climate of one's age. In order to revise his Ideal Theory, Plato would have to give up the absolute dualism of sense and reason, the universal and the percept. Mind again would have to be taken as an active and creative principle for explaining knowledge, as people believe now ever since the time of Kant. But, perhaps Plato was not in a position to revise his theory wholesale.

The Characteristics of Ideas

We have followed John Burnet in the interpretation of Socratic view of concepts and Platonic theory of Ideas. The view of John Burnet given in *Greek Philosophy* is very different from that of W.T. Stace. Everywhere documentary evidence has been given to justify the Socratic theory of *concepts* and Platonic Ideas. Both in Socrates and Plato, concepts and ideas are quite *separate* and *distinct* from percepts. Naturally the most important point is to establish a real relation between Ideas and Percepts in the Ideal theory of Plato. As for Plato, the realm of Ideas is the region of reality, of *Being* and that of percepts is the region of *Becoming*. Therefore, keeping this view of Ideas, we can outline the characteristics of Ideas.

1. Ideas are said to be *substances*. A substance is that which is in itself and for itself and does not require the existence of anything else for its reality. For Plato the Idea is *in and of itself* (*Rep.* X. 597c).

2. Ideas are *universal*. For example, cowness or beauty. The beautiful things only imitate and copy the idea of beauty. But beauty is not to be found in beautiful flowers, beautiful birds, beautiful forms of women. These beautiful sensible things simply remind one of the idea of beauty. No doubt a concept is formed by comparing and contrasting the beautiful things and by *abstracting* the common features found in them. But this is not the Idea. The Idea of beauty and all other Ideas are already there in the intellect of men in their dormant stage. Sensible things simply *remind* men of these dormant Ideas. In this sense a concept of beauty is not the Idea of Beauty. The Ideas are said to be universal in the sense that all their corresponding sensible things *participate* in Ideas and serve as provocative agencies for evoking the reminiscence of Ideas which men once experienced them in their pristine glorious existence before their fall in this earthly bondage.

   Concepts are in our common usage in sensible things and are drawn or *abstracted* from them by the knower and are *in his mind*. Platonic Ideas, on the other hand, are *not* in the mind either of human beings or God. They exist in their own rights as objective entities.

3. Hence Ideas are *eternal*. Now eternity may mean that which *endures*, throughout the whole duration of time, past, present and the future. But Plato's Ideas are said to be eternal in the sense that they are *timeless*. According to Plato time was created by God along with the world, but Ideas pre-exist the creation of the world and would remain even when the world is destroyed.

4. If Ideas are eternal in the sense that they are timeless, then they are not perishable or mutable. They are *immutable*. Again, if sensible things as mutable are corporeal, then Ideas may be called incorporeal. Plato advises

us to reflect on the Ideas without the distractions of hearing, seeing or bodily pleasures, in search of reality with unaided intellect and unadultered thought (*Phaedo* 65c, 66a). Hence, the Ideas are nonsensible and incorporeal. They can be only thought and not sensed. (*Rep.* VI.507b)

5. Each Idea is *one* and *unique* (*Rep.* X.597c, d). In his mythic way, Plato declares that God has created each Idea as one and yet again each in its unique nature. Of course, the Idea of beauty is *one,* but it is imitated or copied by many beautiful things.

6. Ideas are absolute, for they are eternal verities and form the very *standard* of knowledge (*Phaedo* 76d). Plato speaks through Socrates,
   I am assuming the existence of absolute beauty and goodness and magnitude and all the rest of them (Ideas). (*Phaedo* 100 b; also see *Phaedo* 75d)

7. As the Ideas are absolute, so they are *invariable and constant.*
   Does absolute equality or beauty or any other independent entity which really exists ever admit change of any kind? Or does each one of these uniform and independent entries remain always constant and invariable . . . .? They must be constant and invariable. (*Phaedo*, 78d)

8. Idea are the *essence* of things, not in the sense in which the common and important qualities abstracted from the observed things are said to be the essential qualities of things e.g., animality and rationality form the essential qualities of man. Ideas are the essence of things in the sense that Ideas are real and sensible things are their poor imitation.

9. In a way Ideas are the causes in the sense that they attract things towards them, just as Sita attracted the princes in her *Svayambara*. They are the unmoved and unmoving causes of things. This is best illustrated in the case of the Idea of Good (*Rep.* VI.509b), for it causes an upward urge in men and in all things. (*Rep.* VII.517c)

The System of Ideas

One of the objections of Aristotle against Plato is that Ideas are just the duplication of percepts or objects of sense-experience. Yes, in many respects it appears that Ideas form a plurality without any principle of co-ordinating arrangement. This would mean chaos and no system. However, Plato was quite conscious of introducing co-ordination and arrangement of Ideas in a system. For example, Plato does not favour the confusing plurality of Ideas, but wants to combine them in a system. He first attempts to combine the five ideas of existence, motion, rest, sameness and difference with the help of an Idea of greater generality (*Sophist* 254 ff). However, he does not mention any principle of combination.

However, Plato aims at organic unity and harmony in the working of various faculties of the soul as rational, high spirit (temper, will) and appetites. The health of the soul follows from the harmonious functioning of reasoning, temper and the appetites (e.g., hunger and thirst). The function of the rational part is *wisdom*, that of high spirits (temper) is courage and that of appetites is soberness or temperance. The health of the soul follows from the discipline amongst the various parts of it. Wisdom commands, whilst the temper assists in carrying out the command to order the materials supplied by the appetites (*Republic* IV.441-42).

The same kind of harmony is suggested in the three classes manning the State, namely, money-makers (traders, artisans etc.), the helpers (soldiers, officials) and rulers (counsellers, philosophers). The rulers have to administer the law for the benefit of the whole State, and the officials have to carry out their duty for the sake of duty in administering the law and the workers have to observe the rule of law. The harmonious functions of the three classes alone ensure the good of the State as a whole.

Besides, Plato suggests that the unity amongst Ideas may be a pyramidal system. For example, in searching the Idea of Beauty, one has to ascend a ladder like height, step by step, till he reaches the highest goal of the sphere of Beauty itself.

> Starting from individual beauties, the quest for the universal beauty must find him (the seeker) ever mounting the heavenly ladder, stepping from rung to rung —that is, from one to two, and from two to every lovely body, from bodily beauty to the body of institutions, from institutions to learning, and from learning in general to the special lore that pertains to nothing but the beautiful itself until at last he comes to know what beauty is.   (*Symposium* 211c)

Here no doubt the quest starts from the particular concrete examples of beauty to the ever-rising levels of the study of the Idea of Beauty. But even here, the principle of the pyramidal system has not been mentioned.

However, Plato tells us that the Idea of the Good alone rules and regulates the order of all Ideas. Plato compares the Idea of the Good to that of the sun. The sun is not the vision, but is the cause of vision. Similarly, the Idea of the Good is the highest reality and is the cause of truth and knowledge (*Republic* VI. 509). The sun not only furnishes to visibles the power of visibility but it also provides for their generation and growth and nurture, though it is not itself generation (*Republic* VI. 509b). Similarly, the Good is not itself the essence but transcends essence in dignity and surpassing power. Thus the Good is beyond all Ideas and rules and regulates them all. Again, Plato states the following:

> ... my dream as it appears to me is that in the region of the known the last thing to be seen and hardly seen is the idea of good, and that when seen it must needs point us to the conclusion that this is indeed the cause for all things of all that is right and beautiful, giving birth in the visible world to light and the author of light and itself in the intelligible world being the authentic source of truth

and reason, and that anyone who is to act wisely in private or public must have caught sight of this. (*Republic* VII.517c)

But the Idea of Good is the supreme and towards which the whole corporeal and incorporeal entities move. This point will be clearer still in relation to the bondage and release of the soul. Hence, no doubt the Good controls, guides and overrules the whole hierarchy of Ideas but this organising principle is certainly *teleological*, and not logical. Is it a great blemish?

No, for the supreme purpose of philosophy for Plato is to enable souls to gain their pristine glory. This soteriological purpose cannot but be teleological.

THE ETHICS OF PLATO

Plato simply cultivated the seeds of Socrates in his Ideal philosophy. Plato accepted along with his Master that Ethics is the highest and greatest study for the philosopher (*Republic* 6.504, 505, 509a, b). Nay more, one should study ethics for all the hours of his life (*Laws* 7.807). No doubt knowledge and truth are great things. But it is the Idea of the Good which is 'the source of knowledge and truth', and yet itself surpasses them in beauty. For surely you cannot mean that it is pleasure'. (*Republic*, 6.509a) Why is pleasure not the good? Because pleasure is momentary, being based on feeling and desire, but the Good is eternal and timeless. Secondly, if pleasure be the good, then the good will become *relative*, for what is agreeable to one may not be so to the other. If again what is relative has no absolute standard. What is right for one may not be so for others. Hence, by accepting the thesis that pleasure is the good, one will have to accept that there is no valid distinction between the good and bad. This will lead to moral chaos. But the greatest criticism of the doctrine 'pleasure is the good' is that it leads to the bondage of the soul. The soul for Plato is purely incorporeal in its pristine existence and its being chained to the body is bondage. Pleasure or pain leads to the imprisonment of the soul by being chained to the body (*Phaedo* 82, 83).

> . . . every pleasure or pain has a sort of rivet with which it fastens the soul to the body and pins it down and makes it corporeal, accepting as true whatever the body certifies. (*Phaedo* 83d)

But in spite of general agreement between Plato and Socrates about ethics, there is a good deal of development of Socratic doctrine in the system of Plato.

1. Socrates did say that nobody does wrong knowingly. But he did not clarify the notion of 'knowing' when he declared that virtue is knowledge. Plato clarified this notion of 'knowing' by holding that ethical knowledge meant rational will, — a will which obeys the command of reason by conquering feeling and desire.

2. Secondly, Socrates held that virtue is advantageous, beneficial and useful to the virtuous man. Nay, he also held that virtue gives *happiness*. But he did not

analyse the concept of happiness. We find that lack of precision of the conception of happiness, led to the two misguided doctrines of hedonism (by Aristippus) and cynicism. For Plato happiness is the consequence of the harmonious working of all the faculties of the soul e.g., the working of desires and appetites under reason of the soul. A *just* man alone will get happiness in whom the will has been under the control of reason. Health, beauty and wealth are all good for the just, but evil for the unjust.

> But what you and I maintain is that though all these endowments (health, beauty, wealth) are great goods to men of justice and religion, one and all of them, from health down, are great evils to the unjust.   (*Laws* 2.661b)

Thus, we find the clarification of happiness in the ethical theory of Plato.

3. We have already seen that Plato transformed the concept of Socrates into *Idea*. In like manner, Plato has transformed the *concept* of the Good into the *Idea* of the Good. By saying that ethics is concerned with the Good means that the Idea of the Good is wholly non-sensuous and incorporeal and should be sharply contrasted with any satisfaction of desire and appetite which are considered bodily functions. Hence, *happiness* should not be *confused with pleasure.*

4. No doubt Socrates did hold that nobody does wrong knowingly. Here knowing does not mean *ordinary knowing* as is known in daily life or science. Aristotle being a scientist (a biologist) understood by 'knowing', the kind of knowing which is found in science. But by 'knowing', Plato meant that knowing which follows from *meditating on the Idea of Good, transforming the will of man towards release from his mundane* bondage. It means *becoming* good, fit for the intelligible world. By meditating on the Idea of the Good, the soul feels the upward. urge towards sojourn to the higher region of the Intelligible world (*Republic* 517b, c; 518c). Thus, Plato has clarified the meaning of 'nobody does wrong knowingly' by explaining the meaning of *knowing* which for Socrates and much more for Plato means transformed or purified will under the influence of contemplating on the Idea of the Good. A soul meditating on the Idea of the Good

> secures immunity from its desires by following reason and abiding always in her company, and by contemplating the true and divine. . . .   (*Phaedo* 84a)

gets rid of all human ills and gets restored to its pristine glory. Thus, for Plato the true end of morality is the perfection of the soul. Hence, it is an Eudaemonistic theory of morality which Plato supports and which can never be confused with hedonism or utilitarianism.

5. Lastly, Plato enlarges the picture of an individual ethics into that of the working of the State, so that the moral life of an individual may be correctly appraised. Plato has tried to study moral justice in an individual man in its magnified form called the State or the city (*Republic*, 434c). This no doubt is an innovation

of Plato, but in many aspects justice in the State throws light on the nature of the soul and its real pursuit for reaching the highest excellence.

With the thought of Plato on morals presented above, let us further elaborate his ethical teaching. According to Plato, the final end of Ethics is the culture of the soul. But what is the nature of soul?

For Plato the soul can be viewed from two aspects. The ordinary soul in the world is in bondage of the body. But the real nature of the soul in its pristine glory before its fall in bondage is pure, contemplating the Idea of the Good. Hence, the culture of the soul means working out the release of the soul from its bondage. Therefore, we have to know the nature of the embodied soul in its worldly existence.

An individual has three aspects in the worldly existence, namely, reason, high spirits and appetites (*Republic* 4, 439-42). In this aspect soul alone is responsible for moral good and evil.

> Hence we are driven, are we not, to agree in the consequence that soul is the cause of good and evil, fair and faul, right and wrong. . . .
>
> (*Laws* X. 869d; *Charmenides* 156e; *Epistles* 7.335a)

How?

Well, soul in the world has the three parts of reason, high spirits and appetites (of hunger, thirst etc.). When man is moved by the guidance of reason, then soul becomes the author of good (*Phaedrus* 253c). If the parts do not work harmoniously and do not work in accordance with the knowledge of the Good, then the soul falls into evil. Hence, it is the knowledge of the Idea of the Good, which determines moral goodness. But knowledge is due to reason and the rational part of the soul belongs to the world of the Intelligibles. Therefore, moral excellence lies in the effort of the soul in realising the purification of the soul by the knowledge of the Idea of the Good. But do we have the knowledge of the Idea of the Good?

The knowledge of the Good is hard to get (*Cratylus,* 384b),

> . . . it appears to me is that in the region of the known the last thing to be seen and hardly seen is the idea of good, and when seen it must needs point us to the conclusion that this is indeed the cause for all things of all that is right and beautiful, giving birth in the visible world to light, and the author of light and itself in the intelligible world being the authentic source of truth and reason, and that anyone who is to act wisely in private or public must have caught sight of this. (*Rep.* 517c)

Indeed Good is light and ethical life has to be seen in this light. Like the sun which is not vision, but helps visibility, Good causes knowledge and truth and even more than these (*Rep.* 509a). It is inconceivable beauty and is the source of truth and knowledge "and yet itself surpasses them in beauty". Good is not essence but still transcends essence in dignity and surpassing power. (*Rep.* 409b)

Good is beyond 'essence' or Idea, for all Ideas are drawn by it and shines by its light. Good is beyond 'knowledge and truth' because it alone works out that change in the seeker of Good which makes the seeker immortal by enabling him to regain his pristine glory. Here whatever the highest instruction philosophy might have given to the seeker, he at/most gets a glimpse of the Good. This glimpse is enough to draw the seeker towards it and makes him *contemplate* and *meditate* on it. By contemplation of and meditation on the Good, the soul feels the upward urge and yearning for the brightest region. (*Rep.* 517d)

> . . . . Soul secures immunity from its desires by following reason and abiding always in her company, and by contemplating the true and divine and unconjecturable, and drawing from it, because such a soul believes that this is the right way to live while life endures, and that after death it reaches a place which is kindred and similar to its own nature, and there is rid forever of human ills. (*Phaedo* 84a)

The philosophy of Plato teaches that man should not lose the opportunity of release from its bondage of bodily desires and appetites.

> . . . the true philosopher feels that it must not reject this opportunity for release, and so it abstains as far as possible from pleasures and desires and griefs because it reflects that the result of giving way to pleasure or fear or desire is not as might be supposed the trivial misfortune . . . (*Phaedo* 83b)

Giving way to pleasure or desire would mean bondage and enchainment of the body for endless cycle of rebirths (*Ibid.* 83d). Hence, for Plato contemplation of the brightest region of being is called Good (*Rep.* 518c).

Therefore for Plato the *summum bonum* of ethical life is not pleasure of the senses, but is wholly reason, for it comes from the rational part of the soul which is eternal. Not even *good opinion* is wholly good, for Plato contrasts opinion and intellect (*Rep.* 7.534a). True opinion sometimes is right and sometimes not, because it is not based on knowledge (*Meno* 97c). It is not even art of living successfully. It will reduce good to be relative, for what is good for the ruler, is not so for the opposition. Besides, an art means the capacity of doing the opposites. But good is good for its own sake and cannot be a *means* (*Gorgias*, 499c).

> Do you too share our opinion, that the good is the end of all actions and that everything else should be done for its sake, not the good for the sake of everything else. (*Gorgias*, 449e)

Hence pleasure is for the sake of good and good is not for the sake of pleasure.

The *summum bonum* of an ethical life is release from its bondage, but even preparing the soul for contemplating the Good, some moral principles have to be laid down.

We have already stated that soul has three parts of reason, high spirits (temper) and appetites. A soul is healthy if there is orderliness and discipline in the functioning of these parts. Bodily quality of functioning in an ordered and disciplined manner is called health (*Gorgias* 504b, c). Similarly, regular and disciplined working of different parts of the soul results in temperance (*Gorgias*, 504d), and the temperate soul is good and the intemperate is evil (*Gorgias* 507a). But before further elaborating the notion of 'happiness', let us very briefly state the meaning or orderliness in the functioning of the three parts of the soul.

Orderliness of the soul means that reason ought to rule over desires and appetites (*Rep.* 439d, 411e, 442d). Similarly, indiscipline and disorderliness in the three parts leads to evil and unhappiness. In other words, a man is just and good if his desires and appetites are controlled and guided by reason. And a good soul alone is happy (*Symposium* 204e). Again, a righteous man is certainly happy and the most righteous man is the happiest and he is a king over himself (*Rep.* IX. 580c). And a wise man (good, righteous and just) alone savours the delight that contemplation of true being and reality gives (*Ibid.* 582c). Not only a wise man contemplating on the Good gets happiness in this life, but enjoys bliss after his death (*Phaedo* 81a, *Epin* 973c). Thus, happiness results from the harmonious functioning of all the three parts of the soul and this harmony means a rational life by regulating desires and appetites, and by being able to contemplate the Idea of the Good. This constant contemplation gives a glimpse and an insight into the Idea of the Good which generates an upward urge towards regaining one's pristine existence belonging to the realm of the Intelligible. Such a seeker enjoys happiness in this life and bliss in life hereafter in the state of his release.[1] Hence, for Plato the true well-being of the soul is the ultimate standard of morality. However, one question still remains, 'How can we understand the reasonableness of this eudaemonistic and soteriological account of morality?' Of course, much of the whole account of Plato follows from 'the myth of Ideas and of soul'. But within this frame of reference, Plato thinks that the view about morality can be seen clearly if the individual morality is magnified into the Ideal of the ideal Republic. This larger form is the city government

> and so we constructed the best city in our power, well knowing that in the good city it would of course be found (the ideal form of justice). What, then, we thought we saw there we must refer back to the individual and, if it is confirmed, all will be well. (*Republic* 4.434e)

We find in the ideal republic of Plato three classes corresponding to the three parts of the soul, namely the rulers or wisemen corresponding to the rational part, soldiers corresponding to the high spirit of the soul and the money-makers, traders, artisans

---

1. This will remind the Indian reader of *jivanmukti* and *Videhamukti* in the Vedanta.

corresponding to the appetites of the soul. Each class has its own distinctive functions. The wise rulers have to lay down laws for the benefit of all classes of citizens; the soldiers or the administrators have to enforce these laws without fear or favour; and lastly the artisans, money-makers, traders, skilled workers have to carry out their functions with utmost soberness. (*Republic* 439d, 440d and 441, 442). When all the classes work in orderly and disciplined manner, then justice is the inevitable result (*Gorgias* 504). Justice is more valuable than gold (*Rep.* 1.336c; 9.589d). When any class does not work its own proper function, then injustice results and injustice is not profitable for the State (*Rep.* 4.334d, b, c).

Here we find that the harmonious relation between parts of the soul corresponds to the justice in the State when all the classes mind their own proper jobs and functions. This requirement means that every class has to be properly educated. And education means the culture of the whole man, i.e., his mind, body and soul have to be trained to shoulder the task. Here the responsibility of the rulers is the greatest. Hence Plato lays down,

> Unless philosophers become kings or our kings and rulers take to the pursuit of philosophy seriously and adequately there can be no cessation of our trouble.
> (*Rep.* V. 473; VI. 484)

By 'philosophy', Plato understands spiritual training and discipline, along with full physical culture. Secondly, philosophers have to work for the whole community. Thirdly the ideal State is a blue print for the whole humanity.

As noted earlier, the ethical end of an individual has to be measured by the perfection of the State and the perfection of the State determines the moral excellence of each individual (*Rep.* 4434c). Hence, now we have to detail the outline of the ideal republic of Plato.

The Ideal State of Plato

The ideal Republic of Plato has its purpose of promoting justice through the rulers who have the vision of the Good. Plato at first draws the blue print of the republic in *Republic* and *Laws* which are the longest dialogues. *Laws* is the last work of Plato representing his mature thoughts concerning this subject. In the *Laws*, Plato keeps to the original Socratic doctrine, according to which no one does wrong knowingly. Plato in the *Laws* maintains that men commit crimes on account of passion, ignorance and concupiscence. We shall see this in his description of Timocracy and Oligarchy. Besides, later on Plato gives up the idea of the government by philosophers. He becomes more religious and proves the existence of gods and their concern over human beings. Further, in the *Laws*, Plato favours monogamy (*Laws* 11.930), but in the *Republic* (5.457d) he writes that there can be

> no denial that the community of women and children would be the greatest good, supposing it possible.

We shall follow the *Republic* in presenting the account of the ideal State.

Plato admits that his account of the ideal State is only artistic construction like the painting of a perfect man by a painter (*Rep.* 5. 472d). Again, Plato states that the *Republic* is nowhere found on earth, but its pattern is found in heaven (*Rep.* 10.592a). But it is not altogether a day-dream (*Rep.* 540d).

There are three classes of citizens in the State corresponding to three parts in an individual, namely, reason, high spirits and appetites. Corresponding to reason, there is the class of wise men who form the rulers or the guardians of the State. Likewise corresponding to the high spirits there are soldiers (helpers), and to the appetites are traders, money-makers and artisans. Counsellors or guardians are characterized by wisdom, soldiers by courage and bravery and money-makers by sobriety (*Rep.* 442). The most important class is of the counsellors.

> They have to set their vision on their souls and fix their gaze on the Good which sheds light on all things.

They have to use the pattern of the ideal republic throughout their lives, and have to study philosophy.

> They have to toil hard in the service of the state and to educate others to become like themselves. And the women as rulers too have the same task and vision. Their chief task will be the promotion of justice in the State. (*Rep.* 8.540)

> They have to acquire the knowledge of the Good (*Rep.* 6.506d, c). They have to be watched 'to see whether their nature is capable of enduring the greatest and most difficult studies ..." (*Rep.* 6.504a).

> They have to remain servants and the ministers of law. (*Laws* 4.715c)

There is also a danger for the rulers of lingering on the meditation of the good. Plato tells us that one need not be surprised that those who have attained to the vision of the Good are not willing to return to the affairs of men (*Rep.* 517c). But it is the duty of other brother rulers to compel those who have already reached the Island of the Blessed to return to the affairs of men (*Rep.* 7.519c, d).[1]

As noted earlier, the reason guides and high tempers working under the law of reason controls the appetite. By working in harmony, the individual soul gets happiness. In the same way the three classes of guardians or rulers (corresponding to the rational part of the soul) lay down law for the good of all classes, *warriors* (corresponding to high spirits) administer the laws for regulating the function of money-makers, *artisans* (corresponding to the appetites of the soul). The three classes are at first, perhaps determined by the legislators and later on they breed according to their nature in the future. In principle these classes are not hereditary

---

1. Here one finds the echo of the picture of *jivanmukta* described in *Advaitism*. This is most vividly stated in the life of Ramakrishna Ashrama under the guidance of Swami Vivekananda, when there was the conflict between a life of meditation and the demand of social service.

and some children born of the educated rulers fall short of the requirements of wise men, and, in the same way some children of warriors and traders may rise up to the talents of the rulers. This selection is made on the basis of education and constant tests. Thus it is accepted that men and women by nature are different and are fit to carry out their specific function according to their specific nature (*Rep.* 5.453b). Hence, it is expected that in an ideal Republice very class will work according to its assigned task (*Rep.* 5.453b; 5.415c). And the state will promote the sons and daughters even of inferior class if they are fit.

> . . . if from these (inferior class) there are born sons with unexpected gold or silver in their composition they (the authorities of the State) shall honour such and bid them go up higher, some to the office of guardian, some to the assistantship (helpers, soldiers), alleging that there is an oracle that the State shall then be overthrown when the man of iron of brass is its guardian. (*Rep.* 3.415c)

Thus each man must perform his social service in the state for which his nature was best adapted (*Rep.* 4.433a). If one does one's business, then justice in the state results[1] (*Rep.* 4.433b). Hence, justice in the state is the outcome of working according to one's capacity

> . . . this principle that it is right for the cobbler by nature to cobble and occupy himself with nothing else, and the carpenter to practise carpentry, and similarly all others. (*Rep.* IV. 443c; see also *Rep.* 4.442d)

If everyone does his duty, then justice, consequently the greatest possible happiness of the city as a whole will result (*Rep.* 420b). And what is injustice and injury to the state?

> The interference with one another's business, then, of three classes, and the substitution of the one for the other, is the greatest injury to a State . . .
> (*Rep.* 4.434b; also *vide* 9.489d)

Therefore, confusion of functions should be avoided (*Rep.* 4.434a). Naturally, each class has to be educated to perform the task assigned to it, according to its nature.

Education

The aim of education is that the child may be educated on the right lines concerning pleasure, pain and dislike so that a correct habit may be formed with regard to what he will learn to abhor and, relish, when he grows up (*Laws* 2.653b). What a child has to be taught has to be determined by judge who is truly a judge (*Laws* 2.659a). Again,

---

1. This is again according to the *Gita* 18:45.

... that education is in fact, the drawing and leading of children to the rule which has been pronounced right by the voice of the law, and approved as truly right by the concordant experience of the best and oldest men.   (*Laws* 2.659d)

Therefore, education has to be conducted by experts, for Plato regards education to be the highest blessings for mankind (*Laws* 1.644a). Hence education has to be made compulsory for every child (*Laws* 7.804d).

Education is supposed to start even when the child is in the womb, specially with regard to the health of the would-be child (*Laws* 7.789b). It is really a lifelong process (*Protagoras* 325c), for it alone makes a perfect man (*Timaeus* 44c). Much ahead of his time in matters of education, Plato recommends the same education both for the male and female children (*Rep.* 5.451e).

And in stating my doctrine I intend no reservation on any point of horsemanship or physical training, as appropriate for men but not for women.

(*Laws* 7.504e)

Plato recommends the partnership of men and women not only in education, but also in the guardianship of the state and in the conduction of war (*Rep.* 5.466c).

The principle of education is 'a sound mind in a sound body'. So early education begins with the exercises of body and the discipline of mind (*Laws* 7.807d), or, as Plato put it through rhythmic dance and melody, i.e., the Muses and Apollo (*Laws* 2.654a). He also recommends education through gymnastics for the body and music for the soul (*Rep.* 2.376e). Early education to children has to be given through play, and, Plato here gives an outline of this method which strangely enough reminds one of Watsonian method through *conditioning*. By means of play a child has to be trained into a farmer or a carpenter through the means of play-tools.

We should seek to use—games as a means of directing children's tastes and inclinations towards the station they are themselves to fill when adult. ... the sum and substance of education is the right training which effectually leads the soul of the child at play on to the love of the calling in which he will have to be perfect, after its kind, when he is a man.   (*Laws* 1.643c,d)

Along with gymnastics and music, arithmetic too has to be added in the game of children. According to Plato by incorporating elementary arithmetic in the children's game useful preparation is made for military life and domestic management,

and makes them more alert and more serviceable to themselves in every way.

(*Laws* 7.819c)

Afterwards they learn the measurements of length, surface and cubical content. Again, Plato recommends the incorporation of arithmetic (*Rep.* 5.747a, 7.809c,

819c) and geometry (*Rep.* 7.525c sq and 7.536d).

At every step tests for higher education has been recommended by Plato. For the select few, ciphering and arithmetic as one paper, as we would say today; mensuration, linear and solid, will form the second paper; and; the third paper will comprise the true relations of the planetary orbits to one another (*Laws* 7.817e sq.).

In the first five years of life the bodily development of the child is very great and so it has to be disciplined through adequate exercise (*Laws* 7.789a). But Plato as a true educationist reminds us that education should not be conducted through compulsion, but by play. And whilst at play they show their attainments in physical growth and studies for being selected for higher studies (*Rep.* 7.536e; 537a). Again, there will be further selection of youths about the age of twenty (20) for still higher studies. Finally at the age of thirty there will be the selection of youngmen for the still higher honours. They will be deemed 'in company with truth' (*Rep.* 7.537d). They are expected to devote themselves to the continuous study of dialectic and bodily exercise, for another five years. After this they are in a position to command, other officers to do their duty according to their disciplined character and intellect.

After all kinds of taste and trials in the office and becoming successful in all of them, the seasoned men will be permitted to fulfil their final goal. They will be required to turn their gaze upward, fix it on what is their highest study, i.e., the study of the good (*Rep.* 6.540a, 6.503e, 504b and 505). They have to devote the greater part of their time to the study of philosophy, and, when their turn comes for toiling in the service of the State and specially the education of the younger generation, they have to come back for performing their duty. Doing all these thing, at the end they will depart to the Island of the Blessed. For such men memorials will be set up and sacrifices will be offered (*Rep.* 6.640b). Such persons regard justice and the State as their chief end.

Strange it may sound that Plato himself the greatest poet of philosophy has no room for poetry in his curriculum for studies (*Rep.* 3.398a; 8.568b, 595sq, 605b, 607a). But one thing is to be noted that the last attainment of the wise ruler is the attainment of a place in the Island of the Blessed, i.e., he is deified. This is the same as getting release from bondage as a result of the ethical attainment of the good (*Phaedo* 84a).

Theories of the Government

Plato backed communistic form of Government, both in *Republic* and *Laws*. *Laws* 5.739c is very clear with regard to common ownership of property, women and children.

1. First, 'friends' peroperty is indeed common property. In respect to women and children the possessions of friends will be in common (*Rep.* 5.449c). In fact there should be no individual ownership of anything (*Rep.* 5.464d).

Thus, Plato notes that 'girls and gold' are the two things which individuals are tempted to own exclusively and this was also accepted by Indian thinkers[1]. So in his communistic state, he has made them the property of the whole community. Above all Plato recommended the principle of egalitarianism. Men and women have the same education and the same tests for all types of responsibilities. Only at the appointed time heterosexual activities were allowed for the procreation of children. Here all children will have common mothers and fathers. Children will be taken away at their birth so that no children will know their parents. And only a minimum of private possession was allowed. Of course, in such a state, the rulers had to be philosophers. But what is the meaning of 'philosophers'?

A philosopher was one who through his long physical, moral and spiritual discipline looks at worldly honours with scorn and cherishes heavenly riches and regards justice as the chief end of this worldly existence (*Rep.* 8.540d). Keeping these attainments of a philosopher in view, Plato has observed,

> unless the philosophers become kings and kings and rulers become philoso-phers, there can be no cessation of troubles for the mankind. (*Rep.* 5.473d)[2]

But Plato afterwards realised that this sort of communism was too utopian and he regarded several other forms of government.

Plato mentions five forms of government along with their respective kinds of rulers (*Rep.* 545). These are Aristocracy (monarchy or royalty and even aristocracy), giving way to *Timocracy* which deteriorates into *Oligarchy* and Oligarchy gives way to *Democracy* and ultimately democracy ends in *Tyranny*.

According to Plato that government is best in which the aristocrats of educational excellence rule for the good of all classes and in which the officials of warriors support the enforcement of the laws laid down by the best educated (called 'Philosopher') and in which the workers observe the rules with sobriety. This form of government promotes *happiness* and *justice* for all (*Rep.* 4.445d). This form of government may be called *aristocracy* which is governed by the just men truly. This is the best form of government (*Rep.* 8.544e).

> If one man of surpassing merit rose among the rulers, it would be denominated royalty (monarchy) if more than one, aristocracy. (*Rep.* 84.448d)

But in the case of royalty, let the autocrat be young, of good memory, quick to learn and temperamentally high-souled. He must have all the parts of goodness (*Laws* 709c).

---

1. Buddhism in its monastery allowed only the celibates and held all things in common. In West, the essenes at the time of Christ, upheld the same ideology.
2. In other words, king Janaka was such a philosopher king.

Deterioration in the form of government results from dissension in the ruling class itself. When from among the ruling class rulers give themselves to the love of honours, then Aristocracy deteriorates into *timocracy* or timarchy (*Rep.* 8.545b). In timocracy itself there is the principle of avidity of wealth. One group will try to turn to virtue and original constitution in spite or their secret avidity for silver and gold and the other group will have the greed for wealth, land and property (*Rep.* 8.547b). This rivalry paves the ground for *Oligarchy* which is based on property qualifications. The rich hold office and the poor get ruled (*Rep.* 8.550d). First, in this oligarchical rule of the propertied class wealth and the wealthy are honoured and virtue and the good are less respected (*Rep.* 551a). Besides, this state of affairs invites the revolution of the poor get and the have nots against the rich. Here in oligarchy the poor despised. This state of oligarchical order belongs to busybodies, — traders, farmers and soldiers, all rolled into one. Hence this is just the opposite of the ideal state in which all the three classes work harmoniously (*Rep.* 8.552a). In oligarchy the rich and the poor keep on plotting against one another. This results in revolution and paves the way for democracy.

Both in democracy and tyranny, justice is of the advantage of the stronger. Laws are enacted in democracy for the advantage of the democrats, and, autocratic laws in tyranny. Those who deviate from the law are dubbed as law-breakers and wrong-doers (*Rep.* 1338e). In democracy money is taken to the only good. Here everybody has license to do what he likes (*Rep.* 8.557b). It is anarchic and mostly form of government 'assigning a kind of equality indiscriminately to equals and unequals' (*Rep.* 8.558c). When constitutions are lawful and ordered, democracy is least desirable (*Statesman* 302b). When in democracy avidity becomes the criterion of good, then dictatorship steps in (*Rep.* 8.562c).

Along with democracy, Plato denounces most strongly any form of dictatorship as tyranny.

And this is tyranny, which both by stealth and by force takes away what belong to others, both sacred and profane, both private and public, not little by little but at one sweep. (*Rep.* 1.344a)

It is injustice on a grand scale and doing wrong is the greatest evil (*Gorgias* 469b). Tyranny surpassing democracy is the final malady of a state (*Rep.* 8.544c). Tyranny is maintained by violence.

Tendance of human herds by violent control is the tyrant's art.
(*Statesman* 276c)

The tyrant is faithless and unjust to the last degree. Such a tyrant is really most miserable, and, the whole city is most wretched (*Rep.* 9.576). In a word in tyranny the whole soul is enslaved (*Rep.* 9.577d). Therefore, Plato did not favour either democracy or tyranny.

THE IMMORTALITY OF SOUL

We have already referred to Plato's notion of soul in his explanation of Ideal theory and ethics. There Plato regards the soul as immortal; in this embodied life in bondage to the body, transmigrating into countless rebirths and ultimately its release by contemplating on the Idea of the Good. Now we can describe these notions about the soul.

Plato does say that the soul is immortal and it never perishes (*Rep.* 10.608c).

> They say that the soul of man is immortal. At one time it comes to an end—that which is called death—and at another is born again, but is never finally exterminated. (*Meno* 81b)

He further adds here that the soul has been born many times. But what is the proof? In his own way Plato adduces several proofs.

1. First, soul is the only *entity which moves by itself and moves all other things.* Plato mentions ten kinds of motion. The ninth kind of motion is that which moves some other objects other than itself, and is itself induced by another object. The tenth kind is that which moves itself as well as other things. This tenth kind of motion is infinitely most effective (*Laws* 10.894c, d). This self-movement belongs to soul alone (*Laws* 10.896a). Why and how?

> All soul is immortal, for that which is ever in motion is immortal. But that which is while imparting motion is itself moved by something else can cease to be in motion, and therefore can cease to live; it is only, that which moves itself. . . this self-mover is the source and first principle of motion for all other things that are moved. (*Phaedrus* 245c)

> And if this last assertion is correct, namely 'that which moves itself' is precisely identifiable with soul, it must follow that soul is not born and does not die. (*Ibid* 245e-246a)

2. From Incorporeality and Simplicity

The argument of Plato is that the compound or composite alone can break into its elements, both that which is simple and incorporeal cannot be traced to any of its elements, for it has no parts (*Phaedo* 78c, 85e-86). Therefore, the soul as simple and incorporeal is eternal.

3. From the nature of relative terms or opposites

Everything is generated in the pair of opposites, e.g., separating from combining, cooling and heating, and so on. Therefore, from life comes death, and from death comes life. If living things came from living beings alone, and the living things died, then life itself will extinguish one day after life was exhausted by death (*Phaedo* 71-72).

4. Proof from recollection
Plato maintained that learning is really relearning or recollection:

> If that is true, then surely what we recollect now we must have learned at some
> time before, which is impossible unless our souls existed somewhere before
> they entered this human shape. So in that way too it seems likely that the soul
> is immortal. (*Phaedo* 72e)

Plato has at length showed that our ideas of universals (e.g., beauty, equality,
goodness, holiness etc.) cannot be explained unless we bring in the notion of our
knowledge from previous births (*Phaedo* 72-76, 85e, 86b).

Transmigration
We have already seen that the soul of man is immortal, but man is an embodied
spirit. Man therefore keeps on transmigrating from one body to another, till the soul
gets the vision of the good and learns to shed off the elements of the body by
contemplating on the Idea of the good (*Meno* 81c). Exactly like the *Gita* (2.20, 22),
Plato maintains that the soul keep on changing its body in its countless rebirths:

> . . . soul is a long lived thing whereas body is relatively feeble and short-lived.
> But while we may admit that each soul (i.e., embodied and imprisoned soul)
> wears out a number of bodies . . . the soul never stops replacing what is worn
> away . . . (*Phaedo* 87d)

Soul persists through its visions incarnations (*Phaedo* 88a).
As long as the soul, keeps to the vision of the good, man remains happy. But
when the vision of the good fades, man sinks deeper and deeper into lower births,
even births into animals (*Phaedrus* 248).

> And seeing that a soul in successive conjuctions first with one body and then
> with another, runs the whole gamut of change through its own action . . . .
> (*Laws* 903d)

Here no God is responsible for the acts of men. As they sow, so they reap in their
successive rebirths. If they learn to have the vision of good, then they rise in upward
births, till they regain their former pristine glory (*Laws* 903d; See also *Rep.*
10.617e). Plato speaks of following justice, most probably of rulers (*Tim* 41c).
Hence, a ruler doing justice also realises the state of release (*Rep.* 7.519c) called
as dwelling in the Island of Bliss or the blessed.

Bondage and Release
God himself is good and wise, and, in creating man, His motive was to create a
creature who should be as good and wise as He is himself (*Timaeus* 30).

God desired that all things should be good and nothing bad, so far as this was attainable . . . . On this wise . . . a living creature truly endowed with soul and intelligence by the providence of God came into being. (*Timaeus* 30a, b)

At another place Plato informs us that God mingled the soul with elements of earth, water, fire and air, (*Tim* 41d) Again, love in man was mixed with pleasure and pain, fear and anger. If he could conquer his feelings of pleasure and pain, then he would get back to his original abode with gods. Otherwise falling into the snare of pleasure and pain, man will get enchained by his desires (*Tim.* 42).

Again, Plato proclaims the ordinance of necessity. Whatsoever soul has followed in the train of a god and discerned something of truth, shall be kept away from sorrow (*Phaedrus* 248c). Hence, man alone is responsible for his bondage and also release (*Rep.* 10.617c). Two reasons which are in principle one, have been mentioned.

First of all, at the time of death, there is the *craving for the body*. At the time of death when the soul has not learnt to dissociate itself from body through the practice of philosophy, then after death the soul in the form of a ghost seeks a body (*Phaedo* 81b, d). Hence, the embodied soul remains in bondage. Secondly, instead of working out the release, the soul gives itself to the enjoyment of pleasure and pain.

Because every pleasure or pain has a sort of rivet with which it fastens the soul to the body and pins it down and makes it corporeal accepting as true whatever the body certified. (*Phaedo* 83d)

Release can be won if the soul gets wholly preoccupied with one's release from the body (*Phaedo* 67d). Secondly, the soul must get itself purified from every taint of the body (*Phedo* 82d). No release is possible of impure body is used for its release (*Phaedo* 79).

But no soul which has not practised philosophy, and is not absolutely pure when it leaves the body, may attain to the divine nature; that is only for the lover of wisdom. (*Phaedo* 82c)

In other words, philosophical enquiry should be conducted "with the unaided intellect, without taking account of any sense of sight in his thinking or dragging any other sense into his unadulterated thought to the pure and unadulterated object, cutting himself off as much as possible from his eyes and ears and virtually the rest of his body, as an impediment . . ." (*Phaedo* 65e-66a). But what is philosophy?

1. First, philosophy means taking the help of reason, for the rational part belongs to the soul alone. It also means abandoning the path of pleasure—pain and griefs, for this path leads to the imprisonment of the soul (*Phaedo* 82c).

2. Secondly, it means eagerness for release (*Phedo* 83b).

3. The contemplation of the Good. No doubt the idea of good is the final and last stage of philosophical knowledge. But those who reach this height 'are not willing to occupy themselves with the affairs of men, but their souls feel the upward urge and yearning for their sojourn above." (*Rept.* 7.517c). By constantly contemplating the true and divine in the right way in this life, after death they reach a place where their all human ills are left behind (*Phaedo* 84a, b). In the case of philosopher rulers, they reach the Island of Bliss (*Rep* 7.519c).

The whole purpose of philosophy for Plato is wholly soteriological;

And the desire to free the soul is found chiefly, or rather only, in the true philosopher. In fact the philosopher's occupation consists precisely in the freeing and separation of soul from body. (*Phaedo* 67d)

Soul and Body Relationship

We have already seen that soul is immortal. It exists before being embodied in this world and exists after death and undergoes the cycle of rebirths till it succeeds in releasing itself by purifying itself. Plato speaks of two things about the soul. First thing is its dateless anteriority to all things generable and the second thing is its immortality and sovereignty over the world of bodies (*Laws* 967d). Again, soul is utterly superior to body, and, the body is nothing else but its shadow. But the soul is responsible for its deeds after its death (*Laws* 959a, b). Further, Plato tells us that soul is immortal and imperishable and will certainly live after death (*Phaedo* 106e). Each soul has to face judgment. The wicked ones who have cultivated gluttony or selfishness will assume the form of donkeys and other animals (*Phaedo* 81e). However, those who have lived in purity will enjoy the company of gods (*Phaedo* 108c).

Plato has separated the soul from body and this has led to the dualism of soul and body, but he has not clarified the relationship between them. Their nature is quite opposed. The soul is immortal; the body is perishable. The soul is simple; the body is composite of the four elements of fire, air, earth and water (*Tim* 43a). In a crude way, Plato has explained the interaction between the body and the soul (*Tim* 67a, b). We also know that the embodied soul has three parts of *reason, high spirits* and *appetites*. Reason is near the soul and appetites largely belong to the body.

All that we can say now that Plato has raised the important issue of soul-body relationship without any clear solution.

The Notion of God

Plato appeared to be a devout man, for according to him, ministry to God is the highest post of man on this earth (*Laws* 4.475c). Ontologically speaking God can never cease to be (*Phaedo* 106e). He is eternal and does not change (*Rep.* 2.282e). From the moral point of view God is altogether good and righteous.

God is altogether simple and true in deed and word, and neither changes himself nor deceives others by visions or words or the sending of signs in waking or in dreams. (*Rep.* 2.382e)

Again in *Theaetetus* (176a, b), Plato tells us that in God there is no shadow of unrighteousness; there is perfection in Him. There is no evil in Him (*Rep.* 2.379c). He is the source of all good things and He provides food and the means of enjoyment for man (*Epinomis* 977a).

God is a creator of the whole world (*Rep* 10.597d). In the beginning there was nothing but chaos. God created the world by introducing order into it according to the original in the heaven. He created the world out of the four elements of water, air, fire and the earth (*Timaeus* 31a, b; 53b). God has created time which is the moving image of eternity. The created time has come into being along with the creation of the world. But in eternity there is no past, present and future. But the distinctions of time we wrongly transfer to eternal being. We wrongly say of eternal time that

it 'was', or 'is', or 'will be', but the truth is that 'is' alone is properly attributed to it, and that 'was' and will be' are only to be spoken of becoming in time, for they are notions, but that which is immovably the same forever cannot become older or younger by time. (*Timaeus* 38a; for detail see *Tim* 37d-39e)

Thus God is said to be an architect and not a Creator God, for God created the world not out of himself, but according to the original pattern in heaven. Secondly, God has created the world with the four elements and out of chaos. Thus, the materials have not been created by God, but for a creator God the materials too should have been created by Himself. But still the question arises, 'Why has God created this world?'

God is perfect and He does not require anything for Himself. He is good and He desired that all things be as good as He is.

This is in the truest sense the origin of creation and of the world ... on the testimony of wise men. God desired that all things should be good and nothing bad, so far as this was attainable. (*Timaeus* 30a)

Plato also hints that God created soul with intelligence so that man may have fellowship with Him. But what is the proof that this world has been planned and created by a wise and a good God? Could not this world be due to mere chance or some spontaneous causes? (*Sophist* 265c). Plato holds that the world has been designed as a work of art by God, and, presents a teleological proof in favour of his thesis.

There is orderliness in the movements of planets and other bodies. By an observation of this one believes that there is a wise maker of this world.

No man who has once turned a careful and practised gaze on this spectacle has ever been so ungodly at heart that its effect has not been the very reverse of that currently   expected.   (*Laws* 12.966e; *Vide* 967)

Again, earlier in *Laws* 897c, Plato repeats the teleological argument. The whole path and movements of heaven and all its contents, with their revolution, and calculation of wisdom show that there is the supremely good soul which controls and guides the universe. In the same manner along with the argument called *consensus gentium,* Plato repeats the teleological argument.

. . . think of the earth, and sun and planets, and everything! And the wonderful and beautiful order of the seasons with its distinctions of years and months! Besides, there is the fact that all mankind, Greeks and non-Greeks alike, believe in the existence of gods. (*Laws* 886a)

The same argument of *consensus gentium* (Universal consent) is repeated by Plato, stating that all mankind, Greeks and non-Greeks alike, without the remotest shadow of doubt believe that gods are real (*Laws* 887e).

Plato also suggests cosmological arguments stating that which moves itself and never ceases in its motion is the source and first principle of motion (*Phaedrus* 245d). Again, Plato tells us that the first principle of motion is that which moves itself as well as all other things (*Laws* 894c). Thus, Plato concludes that chance and circumstances are all under God (*Laws* 709b). Even 'if there be God', what is His place for man? (*Laws* 709b).

For Plato, the study of God pertains to what is sublime, true and beneficial to society (*Laws* 821b).

. . . of all rules, to my mind, the grandest and truest is this. For the good men 'tis' most glorious and good and profitable to happiness of life, age, and most excellently fit, to do sacrife and be ever in communion with heaven through prayer and offerings and all manner of worship . . . . (*Laws* 4.716d)

God and the Good

It appears that there are two parts in Plato's philosophy. At the beginning Plato was much more pre-occupied with his ontology and ethics, we find that the idea of the Good was the highest and all things were ruled and guided by it. Even in Ethics there the seeker was required to purify himself from the pursuit of pleasure and the snare of senses and the body. He was at last required to meditate and contemplate the Good with a view to getting a glimpse of that. In his ontology and ethics, the seeker of his liberation did not require the help of God. However, towards the later part of his philosophy Plato appeared to have given himself to the play of his imagination in theology. In theology he abounds in myths and for supporting the notion of God leans on the verdict of wise men, ancient thinkers and so on. Naturally there is really no knowledge of God, but mere *opinion* about God. Under the circumstances there is a conflict between Plato's ontology and ethics and his theology. Can therefore be any logical relation between theology and ontology of the Ideas; between the Idea of the Good and God?

God is a person with a will and purpose who has designed the world so that all men may be as good as He is Himself. Here 'good' appears to be moral concept and not the Good of his ontology of Ideas. In contrast, the idea of the Good is non-personal, but it controls and guides all other ideas towards itself, exactly as insects are attracted towards the light. Three relations may be imagined to exist between God and the Good.

God may be the cause of the whole system of Ideas, including the Good. This will not do because ideas are eternal and substantial and do not exist as ideas in any mind whatsoever. If God cannot be the creator of Good, can the Good be the basis of God? This does violence to the nature of God himself, who must be thought as absolutely real and not dependent on anything else. Can we imagine that both God and the Good, both are equally real? But this is not possible, for instead of one there will be two absolute realities which will do violence to the unity and orderliness of the whole system of thought. Then what is our conclusion with regard to the relation between God and Good? All that we can say that there is no harmony between the ontology and theology of Plato. However, there are a few places where Plato drops a hint of some relationship between the two with relation to the soteriological search of man. In his ethics, specially in *Phaedo* it appears that man by his unaided divine help can win his freedom (*Phaedo* 81a; *Rep.* 7.517b, 518). But in *Phaedo* 67a, God is said to help the deliverance of man. Later on, Plotinus tried to show through his theory of emanations to show the relation between the system of Ideas and God.

On the whole Plato maintains monotheism. Of course, Plato does refer to gods, but they are said to remain subordinate to God. Further, God is said to be absolutely righteous and He made the embodied soul so that they become as good and righteous as He is. Then why has evil sprung up?

Plato admits that there is one absolute God who is righteous, who moves all things in the universe (*Laws* 10.896; 898a). But it is not certain that he thinks that there is *one* evil soul called Satan. However, Plato also maintains that God is not the author of evil *Rep.* 2.279. Then whence is the evil? Man is certainly responsible for evil. Man in this world is always found with his body and it is this body which is responsible for evil. First body in its primary nature was disorderly and it is due to this disorderly nature that man falls into bodily desires and creates evil. (*Statesman* 273b). Once evil is in the world, it corrupts all things (*Rep* 10.608e). Secondly, man gives himself into momentary pleasures and gives rise to evil (*Phaedrus* 240a; *Prota* 353c). Further, Plato tells us that contraries will be there; good presupposes evil for one cannot exist without the other (*Theaetetus* 176a).

Most probably creation of an embodied soul means bondage and man cannot be created without the limitation of his body. If he guides himself rationally with the contemplation of Good, then he succeeds in regaining his pristine glory, or else, he keeps on moving in the circle of countless rebirths. But althrough man is responsible for evil.

The World

With regard to the world, Plato takes recourse to myths allthrough. For Plato God is the creator of the world (*Statesman* 269c). In this connection, Plato mentions that God has created the world out of chaos, but of what was absolutely disorderly (*Tim* 30a, 53b). By 'disorderly' is meant that the matrix out of which the world was created was without any shape, without any form and without any laws. It was without any quality, without colour, sound, without heat or temperature. If things with shape or form or weight etc., be called to be existing in some sense, then the world did not exist before creation. Secondly, Ideas are said to have being and these Ideas alone shape the chaos or that which was utterly disorderly. So the two are opposed. Hence if Ideas have being, then the chaos or the non-existing world before creation had non-*being* (*Sophist* 265c). Elements like fire, water, air and earth have some forms, for each of them has quality of their own. So elements were created later on.

God no doubt is wise and good, but this world has been created out of disorderly matter, according to the original pattern belonging to the world of the Intelligible. But the world is a sensible world and belongs to the realm of becoming. Hence it is not perfect. It can never be as perfect as the heavenly original of which it is a copy (*Tim* 28b; 29a). The reason is obvious that the so-called formless matter has tendency to be disorderly even when formed by God according to eternal Ideas. Secondly, all produced things are found to be destructible. Ant the copy can never be as the original (*Tim* 29a), in spite of the fact that the intelligent creator has created the world and guides its motion (*Laws* 10.897c).

God has created time along with the world, according to its original pattern which is eternity. Hence, the created time is only 'a moving image of eternity'. By eternity is meant that all the parts like the past, present and future are all simultaneously one everlasting 'now' (Time 37c). By saying that time was created along with the world means that question cannot be asked, 'What was God doing before the creation of the world'. This point was emphasized by St. Augustine.

But apart from time, there is space. It is a receptacle and nurse of all things. This has been called a 'matrix':

And there is a third nature, which is space and is eternal, and admits not of destruction and provides a home for all created things, and is apprehended, when all sense is absent, by a kind of spurious reason, and is hardly real . . .

(*Tim* 52b)

Therefore, in explaining the world, three-things are formed, the form (the Idea), the recipient (matrix) and the corporeal entity which is the mixture of form and matrix.

Finally, one has to admit that the boundary line between the intelligible and sensible is not fixed. The sensibles are made to realise the intelligible progressively. Hence, according to John Burnet (*Ibid.,* p. 280) there is no absolute dualism in Plato's philosophy.

The Importance of Plato

The towering figure of Plato stands out amongst the world philosophers. Plato has influenced Western thought in all its ramifications. Philosophy, religion, Ethics and theology, all has been influenced by Plato, Till the 13th century, Plato was the main religious philosopher of Christianity and even now he has not ceased to influence it.

True, Plato is not considered to have influenced the thinking of India. But there is remarkable resemblance between Plato and Indian thought. Like Indian thought, Plato's philosophy is soteriological. Plato too thinks that human beings are in bondage and they continue in this state in their countless rebirths, transmigration till they gain their pristine pure existence through meditation and completion of the Idea of Good. He even hints that God may help the real seeker after liberation. Like Indian thinkers (*Nyaya, Samkhya, Jainism* and the *Gita*), Plato accepts the doctrine of the immortality of soul. This is hardly emphasized by Western, scholars of Plato. But this is a remarkable coincidence between Plato and some prominent, ancient Indian thinkers. Only in neo-Platonism, the mysticism and the doctrine of liberation of Plato has been taken up in the philosophy of Plotinus. Of course, Plotinus was also influenced by Indian thought.

Plato, like his master Socrates, was not interested in the philosophy of nature. But his interest in psychology is quite deep and penetrating. Plato has noted the tripartite division of human psyche, namely, reason—high spirits—appetites which has been a little more precisely described as cognition, conation and affection in current psychology.

Plato's importance can be thus a little more detailed.

1. *Mysticism* : As has already been stated that Plato maintained the soteriological view of Ethics and religion. He regards the present human life in bondage to sense and pleasure, which means misery. Man cannot overcome this bondage unless he becomes good by meditation and contemplation of the Idea of Good. By strenuous efforts, man can get riddance of the body, senses and pleasure. But if man does not get release, then he will keep on transmigrating in many kinds of life in his countless rebirths. Here Plato was greatly influenced, largely through Socrates, by Orphicism and Pythagoreanism with the belief in rebirth, transmigration and the immortality of soul. In turn Plato was followed by Plotinus and the whole host of mystics down to the present in the philosophy of Underhill and W.R. Inge.

2. *Idealism* : Plato is certainly justly famous of being the founder of Western idealism. 'Idealism' means *Ideaism* and at the same time the priority and supremacy of ideals or values. In the philosophy of Plato, both the meanings of idealism have been intermixed. Plato maintains that ideas alone constitute true knowledge and reality. The *ideaism* of Plato also means that all the ideas are hierarchically arranged, dominated by and regulated by the Idea of the Good. Plato has not clearly defined 'Good', but it certainly is a more valuative term than a mere abstraction. Plato's illustrious follower Aristotle also regards *actus purus* at the top of all things in the ascending order of greater actuality or finer forms, less mixed with matter. 'Purity' and 'actuality' have also axiological overtone. Hence in the subsequent development of idealism, both the meanings have been inextrically mixed up. *'Ideaism'* is more epistemological and 'Idealism' is more ontological. Berkeley first establishes epistemological idealism and then finally ontological idealism. In Hegel, Bradley, Bosanquet, Pingle-Pattison, Royce, both the forms of Idealism are found inextricably, as R.B. Percy finds it.

3. *Dualism* : Most probably Plato did not uphold dualism. But whilst establishing idealism, Plato has given birth to the dualism of sense and reason, the *intelligible* world and the world of *becoming,* Good and God. In due course, emphasis on sense contribution in knowledge gave birth to empiricism, and, a similar emphasis on reason as the constitutive of knowledge led to rationalism. In further development of thought, empiricism and rationalism paved the way for the *criticism* of Kant. And the criticism of Kant has generated the present epistemology of Russell and others.

Again, the distinction of soul and Body in the soteriology of Plato has given rise to the dualism of matter and mind, which even now defies solution.

Further, the Idea of Good cannot be said to be the God of religion. However, the Idea of the Good has been established by philosophy and *God* has been dragged into philosophy as a popular measure. Since the time of Plato, this conflict continues in the monadology and theodicy of Leibnitz and even now at the present time between analytic school and theology.

4. *Theory of reminiscence* : If the ideas are not derived from perception, then how have they been acquired? To explain the origin of ideas, Plato takes the help of the myth of the immortality of soul, its fall into this world of rebirths and transmigration of soul. All ideas therefore have been experienced at the stage of pristine existence before the fall and during its sojourn in different rebirths. Hence, learning is really *recollection* of the past. Everything is really in the soul. This has given rise to the doctrine of innate ideas of Descartes, Leibnitz and the doctrine of a *priori* elements in knowledge.

5. Plato not only introduced tripartite elements of the psyche, but has given the most essential aim of education i.e., a sound mind in a sound body. His insistence on gymnastics, Music and Mathematics from the very beginning has influenced the philosophy of education. He even suggested some tests of selection for higher teaching.

6. Plato was as much against hedonism as the standard of moral judgment as Socrates was. His standard of moral judgment was really the well-being or happiness of the soul. Till now this is the standard of moral judgment in the idealist school.

7. Plato whilst trying to solve some problems of his idealism has left unsolved some other problems. Plato has left a gulf between *Ideas* and the world of *Becoming*. Aristotle, the successor of Plato has tried to solve the problem through his own theory of ideas. This theory meant to find a real relationship between perception and universal. This problem even now has not been completely solved.

No double Plato tried to present a hierarchical system in ideas, but he has not explicitly laid down any principle of his system. The principle hinted at in the *symposium* concerning movement of ascending order suggest the principle of abstraction concerning *beauty*. But it was left for Aristotle to introduce the principle of potentiality and actuality. This again was converted into the dialectic method of Hegel.

The doctrine of a Creator God has not allowed the Western theologian to rest, for the very concept of God is riddled with paradoxes and specially with regard to the problem of evil.

In conclusion we can say that Plato has become the legislator of Western philosophy for he has presented a number of problems to solve for posterity. But it was a fortunate thing that Plato has left Aristotle to give a logical and a scientific direction to his thought and now we can turn to Aristotle.

Aristotle (384-322 B.C.)

Introduction : Aristotle was born in 384 B.C. at Stagirus which was a Grecian colony. At the age of seventeen he entered the Academy of Plato and lived with Plato for the next twenty years till the death of Plato. Because of his brilliance, Plato called him 'the mind of the Academy'. Of course, Aristotle has criticized the ideal theory of Plato. He was not really a foe of Plato, but his friend. True, he criticized his master, for he loved truth much more than his master. As a matter of fact, Aristotle may be called a real successor of Plato, for he has elaborated and elucidated the ideal theory. All along the influence of Plato overshadowed Aristotle.

Aristotle was quite different from Plato in his mental constitution and orientation. Plato was a poet, mystic and an ethico-religious thinker. In contrast Aristotle was a scientist, a logician and an austere thinker. He has written almost on every subject and that also as an authoritative writer. Hence, he is known as an encyclopaedic genius. He is certainly the father of Logic and Biology and these two studies have largely influenced his thinking, specially in contrast to Plato the mathematician.

The works of Aristotle have been placed as early and late, according to the influence of Plato on his works. In the earlier part, the influence of Plato is most marked, and, in the later part, this influence seems to be least. The first part includes *Organon* (Logic), *the Physics, De Anima, Eudemian, Ethics* and the oldest parts of *Metaphysics* and of Politics. The second and the later part includes *Nichomechaen Ethics, The Politics* and *The Rhetorics.*

The Metaphysics is important for, it not only describes the nature of his philosophy, but also the first written history of philosophy. The history shows that Aristotle was the most synthetic thinker of his time. Towards his final conviction he held that the 'Form' and meaning of nature and history are to be found *not apart*, but embedded in 'matter'. In a way Aristotle was the first philosopher who realised the importance of precise technological language. He has invented a large number of technical words. Here the austere thinker Aristotle can be easily distinguished from Plato who has copiously used myths, metaphors and allegories to express his ideas.

Logic

Before undertaking the exposition of Aristotle's philosophy, a passing reference to his logic is necessary. Logic of Aristotle is a work of a great genius and till the 19th century, Aristotle's Deductive logic came to be regarded as the most standard work on the subject. As Aristotle is regarded as a scientist and also a philosopher of science, so it is expected that he must have been a logical thinker, and, that he was. His work on logic is known as *Organon,* i.e., an instrument of acquiring knowledge. Logic of Aristotle deals with inference, fallacies, division, definition, and also Induction. His Deductive logic is far more complete than Induction. Aristotle regarded that both deduction and induction are necessary in acquiring knowledge. In his times, and even much after, mathematics was considered the most important science, and, the mathematical thinking is largely deductive. Aristotle paid far greater attention to deduction than to induction.

Aristotle regarded induction as *Complete Induction* which consists in enumerating *all* the instances coming under it. This is not the best form of induction, for scientific induction proceeds from *some* cases observed *to all* cases on the basis of leap. Besides, Aristotle did not dwell on the importance of hypothesis and the method of testing hypothesis. However, Aristotle maintained that deduction and induction go together.

Logic is regarded in modern times as purely formal. For Aristotle, form and things go together. Concepts do delineate the nature of reality. In this sense, Aristotle was a conceptual realist. Here the doctrine of categories is important, for a category is a way of *thinking about things*. Aristotle mentions *ten* and also at times eight categories. Here Aristotle also mentions *Predicables* which are the possible predicates with which we describe a subject. They are *genus, species, differentia, property* and *accident.* With the help of predicables, Aristotle gives an exposition of definition, division etc.

As noted just now, Aristotle was a realist in the sense that concepts or universals *are in things.* Hence there can be no universals without percepts. Therefore, there is redness in all red particulars given by the sense. Therefore, percepts need not be variable and relative. For this reason, Aristotle has not accepted Protagoreanism. But he does not accept the theory of Ideas, as was advanced by Plato. For Aristotle, Ideas cannot be separated from the perceptual things. There can be no redness apart from and independently of red things. Redness is real, but only in red things. But the relation of Aristotle with Plato is complex and requires a separate treatment.

Plato and Aristotle

As noted before, Aristotle remained in the Academy of Plato for twenty years. Naturally he remained under the influence of Plato to the end. As Aristotle was a genius himself, so he has elaborated the implicit thought of Plato, specially with regard to Plato's theory of Ideas. From the Aristotelian criticism of Ideas, one must not infer that Aristotle was an unfriendly critic of Plato. There is deeper resemblance between the two than difference, which can be thus stated.

1. Both Plato and Aristotle accept idealism and this means the acceptance of the same view of the universe. Idealism means the priority and supremacy of spirit over matter, of the higher over the lower, of thoughts over things and matter. Plato holds that the Idea of the Good is most real and guides the whole world of hierarchical ideas. In the same vein, Aristotle maintains that *actus purus* or the Prime Mover moves the whole world without itself being moved at all. *Actus purus* has been styled as the form of forms, or, the Idea of Ideas. Aristotle maintains that all things are moved by *actus purus* as the object of love or desire on the parts of things. This is the same thing as saying with Plato that the world of *becoming* strives towards ideas to participate or become as perfect as their corresponding ideas are. All ideas are thoughts. So all things by striving to become ideas are potentially thought. And this is the central teaching of idealism. Hence, the acceptance of idealism both by Plato and Aristotle means the sharing of the most fundamental stand in philosophy.

2. Again, both Plato and Aristotle reject *Mechanism* and accept the *teleological* explanation of the world. According to Plato, Good is the supreme end or purpose of the world. He also maintains that God has created the world so that all things be as good as He is. Further, Plato states that the purpose of becoming a philosopher is that the philosopher be released from bondage to senses and pleasure.

Aristotle was the first important biologist and he accepts teleology by holding that form is implanted in each embryo so that it may become a whole, a member of the species to which it belongs. For example, there is a holistic tendency in each incubated egg so that in due course it may become a chick. Thus in the whole biological world there is an unconscious teleology. Again, as stated above, the whole universe is controlled and regulated by the Prime Mover.

3. Again, both Plato and Aristotle teach the sole purpose of the universe is to create souls. Plato holds that the release from bondage is the supreme purpose of the universe, and Aristotle holds that the perfection of the self is the supreme end of the universe. Thus both Plato and Aristotle hold that the ethical end is the sole end of the universe. For this purpose, both reject that pleasure is good and accept that happiness is the real end of moral life. In order to uphold their end of individual morality, they both regard that the state is nothing but a magnified view of individuals.

Thus there is far greater similarity than difference between Aristotle and Plato. But certainly there is difference between the two with regard to their orientation to the world. Aristotle is a scientist and a logician. He therefore pays very great attention to facts, which in his poetic flight, Plato tends to ignore or depreciate. Plato in the poetic fancy, indulges in myths, metaphors and allegories. In contrast, Aristotle uses sober and austere prose. In science and logic he uses precise language and has created technical terms and scientific terminology. In another respect, Plato is also nearer science, for he has emphasized the importance of mathematics, which Aristotle could not fully make his own. Instead, Aristotle remained a great biologist and the marked dynamism in the growth and decay in life. In other words, Plato's line, triangles etc., do not grow, do not propagate. A mathematical view of the world tends to be a static world as in Spinoza. In contrast, keeping to a vitalist world, Aristotle held to a dynamic world view like Henri Bargson.

The static view and dynamic stand (of Plato and Aristotle respectively) have given rise to two different theologies. Plato, indulging in myths and metaphors has ended his theology in the concept of a *personal God*. This might have succeeded in influencing Christian theology. But this remains unreconciled with his Ideal metaphysics. Aristotle has consistently held to 'Prime Mover' who remains in his lonely sublime object of love and beauty, unconcerned with prayers of his worshipper. The prime mover is loved, but remains the vision of unrequited love. It is the love of the moth for the flame, which love greatly attracted Goethe and Spinoza What a paradox? Plato the mystic and the mythologist has given to the world a personal God and worshippers, — a dualistic theology. And Aristotle, the austere thinker has given birth to 'the God intoxicated' Spinoza. But for that Aristotle is not to blame. He remained committed to his 'sublime thinker, thinking its thought'.

Lastly, the myth-maker Plato has made philosophy subordinate to the soteriological purpose of religion. But Aristotle has kept philosophy as the pursuit of knowledge for its own sake. But even Aristotle could not wholly outgrow the shadow of his master Plato, for Aristotle thinks that philosophy deals with wisdom and not with ordinary knowledge, and, wisdom goes beyond scientific knowledge.

Aristotle's criticism of Protagoreanism and Plato's theory of Ideas

In this book we are presenting the view that Aristotle is really Plato made consistent with regard to his theory of knowledge. In the first instance, Aristotle, like Plato, rejects the theory that knowledge is perception, and, in doing so he goes beyond his master.

The most important principle of Aristotle view is the principle of contradiction, according to which some thing cannot be predicated of the same subject at the same time in the same sense and in the same respect.[1] As the Sophist theory of knowledge has been best propounded by Protagoras, so Aristotle criticizes the Protagorean theory of *homo mensura*. *Homo Mensura* means that each man is the measure of truth, and that every appearance is true to the person who accepts it as true.

1. If all opinions and appearances are true, then every statement must be at once true and false. This doctrine of *homo mensura* means that the same thing, at the same time *be* and *not be,* which are contradictory conclusions.

2. What has been stated from the side of the knower can be stated again from the aspect of the known or the object. If every statement is equally true of a certain state of affairs, then it means that everything *is* and at the same time *is not* and in the same sense and in the same respects.

But contradictory statements cannot be accepted as equally true. Hence, the Protagorean doctrine of *homo mensura* cannot be accepted. However, what is the reason behind this absurd conclusion? Thinkers have maintained that objects themselves are riddled with contradictions. For instance, Anaxagoras holds that everything is *mixed* in everything. For Democritus, Void and Full are alike in every part, though the full *is* and void *is not.*[2] Further, Heraclitus holds that everything is in constant flux. So nothing remains for two moments. How can we know at all?

Refuting Heraclitus, Aristotle observes,

> . . . if a thing is perishing, there must be present something which exists; and if a thing is coming to be, that form which it comes and by which it is generated must exist".[3]

But the most important thing about the doctrine of *homo mensura* is that the doctrine is based on insufficient analysis. The apparent self-contradiction of sensation disappears if we make sufficient analysis of the whole perception. The same thing does not appear different to the sense, in the same respect, at the same time, under the same conditions.

> No sense contradicts itself at the same moment about the same object, nor at different moments with regard to that object's quality. . ."[4]

---

1. Many excellent treatises are available with regard to the philosophy of Aristotle. Here we will be following. David Ross, *Aristotle,* Methuen, 1964.
   John Warrington, Aristotle's Metaphysics, Edited by J. Warrington, London, 1956. (It is a translation by D. Ross).
2. J. Warrington, *Metaphysics,* p. 134.
3. *Ibid.,* p. 135.
4. *Ibid.,* p. 138.

In order there may be some sensation at all, it must be so to some percipient

> For the apparent is always apparent to *someone* . . . . . that an appearance is true not in itself, but for him *to whom* it appears, at the time when, to the sense which, and *under the conditions* which it appears".[1]

Hence, no perception is of flux.

> But since things *have* happened, and will continue to do so, without someone first thinking so, everything cannot be relative to opinion"[2]

If every perception is properly analysed, then it is based both on the thing and also on the percipient. For example, the thing must be conveniently near the percipient, and the percipient must be in his normal health, in his waking state and with the sound condition of his senses involved. Later on the view of Aristotle developed into the theory that *sensa* do not err, but our judgment with regard to them does. David Ross appears to state this as the real meaning of Aristotle's analysis of perception. If this be true, then Aristotle would retort the Protagoreans that no *sensa* err. Perception requires proper analysis. Things are and so are the individuals. Independent of sensation, a substrate which causes the sensation remains. Similarly, there must be a percipient to perceive. If both continue in the same conditions, then perception too remains the same. Hence really there is *no relativity* of perception. Neither the things are *sensations*, nor are the individuals. Hence, Aristotle refutes the doctrine of subjective idealism. He also protests that percipient or *percipere* can be reduced to mere sensation.

Therefore, Aristotle totally agrees with his master in refuting the doctrine of *homo mensura* and in doing so he has presented certainly a truer account of perception. The same thing can be said that Aristotle does not simply criticize the Platonic Ideal theory, but submits a truer account of the *universals*.

But Aristotle's reason for rejecting the theory of 'knowledge is perception' is different from that of Plato. Plato rejects the view that knowledge is perception, because perception is relative, illusory and is shot through with contradiction. He appears to have accepted the reason for the depreciatory character of perception in the light of the views of Anaxagoras, Democritus and Heraclitus. In contrast, Aristotle thinks that perception appears to be shot through with contribution, because it has not been satisfactorily analysed. In perception there are two elements, one of which is *sensum* and the other element is of meaning or interpretation which we put on the *sensum*. The meaning of a *sensum* depends on memory and the total experience of the percipient. So far as *sensum* is concerned there can be no error.

---

1. *Ibid.*, pp. 139-40.
2. *Ibid.*, p. 140.

If the meaning is correctly put, then also there can be no error. Only when there are no favourable conditions in the percipient or the outer world that confused perception may arise. But Aristotle does not think that perception is inherently erroneous. He would favour better analysis of perception and its standardisation. If all the conditions of outer world and the percipient be standardised then there is fairly reliable perception. For Aristotle, if all the conditions of a perception be the same, then the same perception will follow.

Plato thinks that perception is inherently erroneous and unreliable, so he rejects the claim of perception as knowledge. This outright rejection of perception, for Plato does not pave the way of scepticism and nihilism. He believed in the possibility of knowledge. For him knowledge in constituted of *universals* called ideas. His reason is that universals are the common characters to many individuals. For example, cowness remains the same in all cows. No matter in whatever manner they differ in other respects. Because a universal remains the same, unchangeable and constant for all percipients and knowers, so knowledge must consist of universals alone. Therefore, Plato to *emphasize* the place of universals, seemed to have *separated* the universals from the particulars. Besides, Plato was a poet and to *distinguish* between variable perceptions and constant universals he has used allegorical and pictorial language. In accordance with this pictorial language, Plato without meaning the actual *separation* of universals from particulars, spoke of universals as belonging to a different realm. But this pictorial language has certainly bewitched him much more than Aristotle. Aristotle saw that perception and universals are *distinct but not separate.* For Aristotle, a universal cannot exist anywhere except in particulars. Cowness does not exist anywhere except in individual cows. Hence, *ideas* of Plato are found in individuals alone and *never apart from them.* But Plato in order to explain ideas took the help of myths and fell into the bewitchment of language. Plato himself saw the difficulty of relating ideas and the world of *becoming* consisting of individual things, and, he himself has raised objections about his theory of Ideas in *Parmenides*. Therefore, Aristotle has tried to correct the language of his master by criticizing the Ideal theory of Plato. Thus, Aristotle is really Plato made consistent and precise.

There is the fact that Plato has been himself misled by his own poetic language. His myth of the immortality of soul, reminiscence, theory of endless rebirths, transmigration etc., has given rise to the contrasted views of Plato and Aristotle.

For Aristotle real universals are as objective to the perceiver as individuals are. For example, cowness is as objective to the perceiver in the same way in which cows are. But they have no existence apart from the individual things in which they reside. In other words universals must be *instantiated.* As contrasted with this, Plato gives rise to the impressions that universals exist in their own rights irrespective of their being instantiated. In other words, Plato's ideas have their own reality and they exist even before instantiated and even when their instances cease to exist. Such a view certainly stands in needs of further elucidation. But even Aristotle

admits the existence of three non-sensibles, namely
1. God, the unmoved mover of the universe,
2. Gods or intelligences, themselves being moved by the Prime Mover, and which move the planetary spheres, and
3. Human reason which is supposed to exist even after the death of individual men.

Criticism of the Ideal Theory

We have already observed that Plato himself has raised objections against his theory of Ideas, specially the fallacy of the third man and that an Idea is not a unity in explaining one-and-many particulars. Aristotle comes to criticise the ideal theory again and again in his writings. He has jotted down twenty-three objects in Chapter IX of *Metaphysics* which we will summarise. In his criticism, Aristotle has developed his own view of philosophy. Hence, by criticizing the ideal theory, Aristotle tries to present a more consistent view of Plato's idealism. Let us now summarise the objections of Aristotle against the ideal theory of Plato.

1. Aristotle very pertinently points out that Plato's ideal theory cannot establish any logical relationship between ideas and particular things. No doubt Plato takes the help of metaphors. He says that particular things *participate* in the ideas, or, are the copies of ideas as their pattern. But Plato himself sees the difficulty with regard to his *theory of participating*.

If the sensible is like the non-sensible idea, then the idea too will be like the sensible. In that case we require another pattern which will explain the likeness between both of them. In order to explain likeness between A and B we need C. And in order to explain the likeness between C and Idea, we will require a fourth pattern D, to explain the likeness between D and the Idea. Hence in the long run we fall into the fallacy of *regressus ad infinitum* (*Parmenides* 132b). This has developed into the fallacy of the *third man*.

An idea is the common element which is found in many particulars, e.g., the Idea of man is found in many individual men. But there is also an element which is common to individual men and the Idea man. This requires a 'third man' to illustrate the common element in individual men and Idea man. This again will require another idea to show the common element between it and Idea man. Hence this will land us into *regressus ad infinitum*.

2. Again, Plato held that each Idea is one and indivisible, being non-sensuous. But he himself saw the difficulty of this view in *Parmenides*. Do individual horses participate in *one*, indivisible horseness, or, in the *whole* of horseness Idea? If so, then the Idea will be in as many places as are the individual horses and the Idea Horseness gets divided. If only a part of Idea horseness participates in each one of them, then again the Idea gets divided. Hence there can be no Idea as *one* and *indivisible*.

3. For Plato, Idea is a substance, which can exist in the intelligible world

without being instantiated. For Aristotle, an Idea must exist only in particulars, i.e., individuals. Hence substance, is a concrete individual. A substance, for Aristotle has three elements :

(a) A universal,

(b) Qualities, relations etc.

(c) An unknown substratum called matter by itself.

An universal without qualities and substratum does not exist, for Aristotle. Therefore, for Aristotle, the Idea of Plato is not a substance, for Idea exists apart from individuals without *b* and *c*.

4. Aristotle's next objection is that Ideas as causes are mere doubles of the things to be explained. Ideas are as many as are the particulars which they want to explain.

5. Aristotle observes that there are Ideas of negation according to Plato. Again, Aristotle objects to there being Ideas of relative terms.

6. How can Ideas explain the world of particular things? How can the Idea of whiteness explain the particular white things? If we could show that white cows, white flowers etc., logically follow from whiteness, then alone we would say that Idea whiteness explains the white things of the world. But there is really no logical relation between them.

7. Even if we say that white is the common element in all things called white, the change or movement in white things does not get explained thereby. For Aristotle change or movement is an important thing, for as a biologist he was interested in the change and growth in the embryo and even in adolescents, adults and their decay.

Here there is a difference of two stands. Plato's view is static, as we find later on in Spinoza. In contrast, Aristotle's standpoint is dynamic, as we find in Leibnitz.

8. Again, according to Plato's view of Idea is the pattern which for individual things copy. This leads to contradiction. The species will be the pattern for individuals, but the genus will be the pattern of the species. Hence, one and the same thing will become both pattern and copy. For example, man is the pattern for men, but becomes itself a copy in relation to its genus called 'animal'.

9. Aristotle also criticises Plato's theory of reminiscence. He observes, while a student learning geometry may have some knowledge of other things, but he has no knowledge of the principles of geometry. Again, when we are told that all-embracing knowledge is innate, it seems incredible that we should have this supreme science all along without our knowing it.

Later on Locke has repeated this objection against innate ideas.

10. The important objection of Aristotle against regarding Ideas as the essence of things is this. No essence of anything can be outside of it. But for Plato Ideas are in the Intelligible world, away from the things which belong to the world of *becoming*. For example, Idea cow is in the Intelligible world which is outside of and external to the cows in the sensible world. This is absurd for the Idea as essence

must be *in the thing* of which it is the essence. It *can never be external* to the things of which it is the essence.

Further, Ideas are static and immobile. How can they effect any change in the things belonging to the realm of becoming? Aristotle is most earnestly concerned with the explanation of change and movement.

THE PHILOSOPHY OF ARISTOTLE

For Aristotle philosophy has its source in the sense of wonder and it is the function of philosophy to satisfy that wonder or curiosity. The problem of wonder was felt in relation to the contrasted worldviews of Heraclitus and Eleatics, of Becoming and the static reality of Plato's Ideas. Aristotle's fundamental problem was to solve this problem of Being and Becoming. Again, Democritus had developed the theory of atoms and through their mechanical impact, he tried to solve the world process and becoming. Plato on the other hand advanced the doctrine of Ideas which the becoming in the form of particulars kept on striving to realise the perfecting of stationary ideas. In both cases we have to know the real relation between Being and Becoming. But what is the nature of knowing?

To know a thing is to know its cause. But what kind of cause will put an end to our human wonder finally?

1. First, knowing means knowing through causes. Science is considered to be the highest knowledge, which is the highest achievement of human civilization. It is called the highest knowledge because it is the purest knowledge of causes, for its own sake, without any ulterior end.

2. But metaphysical knowledge is much more than scientific knowledge. It is called 'wisdom'. It is concerned with the first and most universal cause. It wants to know the *final* cause of all things. A final cause is the end and purpose for which a thing is. Hence, Aristotle from the very beginning aimed at the teleological explanation of the universe. In contrast is the mechanical view taught by science which deals with the world of facts and becoming. But Aristotle reconciles mechanism and teleology. In its own way this also was the problem of Plato; only the view expressed by Plato was mythological, metaphorical and poetic. For Plato, there is the Idea of Good which draws all things towards itself, and, all things too 'imitate', 'copy' or participate in the Idea. Hence, the end of all things is to become as perfect as Ideas are. For Aristotle, the whole cosmos realises a supreme end, embodied in it. This is best seen in the working of an organism, and, also in the producing of a work of art. Hence, the end is *in the universe* and is not outside of the universe or even any existing fact. Here too this final teleology in the form of *actus purus* as the object of supreme love works in all things and the world as a whole. Here Aristotle reconciles mechanism and teleology through his conception of matter and form, and, this concept of matter and form has been deduced from the analysis of causation. So let us try to explain the meaning of 'cause', according to Aristotle.

Four Kinds of Causes : Aristotle starts with facts and never loses his sight from them. He takes his cue from human production of a building or a chair, and, analyses the factors constituting a cause. Here his assumption is that human and cosmic production is of the same nature, and, human causation at work is an exemplar of the cosmic becoming. Aristotle finds that in human production, e.g., of a chair there are four kinds of causes at work simultaneously, namely, *material, efficient, formal* and *final* causes. For example, in making a chair there is the wood which may be called the *material* cause. Again, there is the skill and instruments through which a carpenter builds a chair. This may be called the *efficient* cause. Here energy, skill, instrument and the power are all included. Then comes the *formal* cause which means the shape, the design and the kind of chair which has to be made. Lastly, there is *final* purpose for which the chair has to be made. For example, the chair has to be made either to serve the purpose of office, or dinner or an arm-chair.

Here one or two remarks will be helpful. All that can be said here is that this concept of causation is not scientific in the modern sense. The very meaning of 'material' cause is not the same as physical matter. We shall explain the nature of 'matter' a little later. Secondly, scientific causation refers to the succession of events, and, a cause is said to be an invariable *antecedent* of the effect. But for Aristotle all the four kinds of causes are *simultaneously* present together. Thirdly, the *efficient cause* really means for scientific purpose, the how of working out into effect. This part of science is said to be the nature of scientific explanation. The 'how' really means the mechanical view of causation. This bars out *formal and final* causation. Hence. science does not admit the *teleological* explanation of factual events. Thus, Aristotle's view of causation is metaphysical, for he is in search of the first and final cause of the universe. Lastly, modern science does not seek explanation of the world as a whole, but only of particular kinds of events. The point is that Aristotle was a philosopher and his wonderment referred to the world as a whole. He is trying to solve the problem raised by Heraclitus, Eleatics and Plato. And only in that context his philosophy has to be adjudged.

Philosophers previous to Aristotle had accepted material cause of the universe. The Ionics has admitted one or the other kind of matter as the cosmic reality e.g., water, air etc. Even Heraclitus had accepted fire as the world-ground, Empedocles admitted four elements and Anaxagoras some indefinite kind of matter. Efficient cause was admitted by Empedocles in the form of *love and hate* as the moving force in all things. Anaxagoras called *nous* as the moving force. Plato had admitted Ideas as the moving force in the world of becoming. Further, Plato accepted not only *formal* cause in the form of Ideas, but also *final* cause in the form of the *Idea of the Good*. Of course, Anaxagoras too had called *nous* as the world-forming force. But it was Aristotle who combined all the four kinds of cause into a consistent form of philosophical explanation of the world. Not only this, but he reduced the four kinds into *Form and Matter* for conveniently explaining the whole world.

Matter and Form : First, formal and final causes are really identical. Formal cause means what a thing is in its essence, it is what it is, or, what Plato called its real Idea. The final cause is the becoming of what it is, or, the end of what it is after the essence of the thing has been actualised or realised. For example, what a dining chair is in its essence is the formal cause of the dining chair, and, when it has been actually made, then this was the very end towards which the wood was being shaped. Again, the *efficient* cause means movement, or, becoming by means of the skill and energy put into it. But why is the wood cut and chiselled in a skilful way? Because the final end of a dining chair has to be realised. Hence, it is the final cause or end which guides and regulates the efficient cause. Hence, it is the end or final cause which is the real cause behind the efficient cause. Hence, the final cause is the real cause of becoming and movement in the world. Therefore, we can say that final cause is really the efficient and formal cause too. Thus, the end is the real beginning. The first act in a play is really the beginning of the drama and last scene is the real cause towards which all Acts are driven. Thus, the real cause is the *end* or teleology for which mechanism is used. This point is clearly seen in the human production of an art, as in painting or sculpture or carpentry. But this is also seen in the functioning of an organism or Nature. An egg has to become a chick. Hence, chick is the end towards which the egg-movement is directed. In the same way, there is the end of becoming an oak by virtue of which all the movement in an acorn is directed. Of course in an organism the *end is in* the organism and this teleology is unconscious. However, the end in the production of a work of art is more or less conscious. Again, this teleology is also found in Nature. Both Plato and Aristotle hold that the perfection of Nature is directed. The Final End is the Idea of the Good for Plato and *Actus Purus* or the Prime Mover for Aristotle. Hence in the final analysis both Plato and Aristotle agree that the world is guided by some Supreme End, and, this is the real message of Idealism. But what is the final upshot of reducing efficient, formal causes into final causes?

The conclusion of Aristotle is that all the three causes, efficient, formal and final, are really one, and, Aristotle calls this as the *Form* of the thing. But the material cause cannot be reduced to any kind of cause. So ultimately there are only two things, namely, *Form and matter* which can explain all movements, becoming and development in the whole world in man, organism and Nature.

By 'matter' is understood ordinarily physical matter like iron, gold, bronze, earth etc. But Aristotle's meaning of matter is much deeper than that. By 'matter', Aristotle understands, that which has no shape, no quality of any type and kind. It is neither red nor green, neither heavy nor light, neither rough nor smooth. Then what is it? It appears to be as good as *Nothing*. But it cannot be nothing nor 'non-Being', for after all it is something which has to be moulded by the *form* into Nature, organism and man, i.e., physical matter, life and Conscious Being. Ordinarily we think that a lump of clay in the hands of a potter is without any form. But it is not so. All that one can say, of this lump of clay is that it has no definite form. But because it has no definite form, so it can be formed into a plate or a goblet or a cooking pot. Similarly, primal matter has no form, but it gives way to all things by the form. All that we can say here is that matter without form does not exist, even when it is not non-Being. But it has the potentiality of becoming anything. Similarly, form is the most important aspect of any existing thing. For example, we value a chair not because it has wood, but because it has the form either of a dining chair or of an office-chair. Hence, the form is the real thing about anything in the world. But form by itself is nothing or we can say that it does not exist. Hence neither matter nor form by itself exists. What exists is *formed matter,* i.e., matter and form together inseparably. A form is the universal. For example, redness or greenness is a universal. But by itself it does not exist, what exists is a green leaf or green grass or green book. But greenness apart from the green things does not exist. Hence neither matter by itself without the form exists, nor the form without matter exists. What exists is an individual thing e.g., a green book or green grass. Greenness is no doubt a universal because it is a common quality in green grass or green things like a green book, or green leaf or green flag. A universal is the 'Idea' of Plato. But Plato failed to see that a universal or an Idea by itself does not exist. Only individuals exist, like green grass or green leaves in which universal greenness resides. Hence, matter and form are *inseparable.* No doubt we can *distinguish* them in our thought, but we *cannot separate* them in any actual state of affairs. This is a very important truth one has to grasp, according to Aristotle.

The second reason why 'matter' cannot mean physical matter is that matter is *relative* to form. A physical matter remains the same e.g., iron remains iron no matter in whichever, shape or size into which it is put. The same thing is true of gold, silver or bronze. Again, by 'form' is not meant mere physical shape. For example, a rectangle remains the same shape, no matter in how many things it is found. But form means much more than shape or size. The reason is that form and matter are relative terms. What is matter in one relation becomes form in another relation. For instance, wood is matter in relation to a chair which may be said to be its form. But the same chair becomes matter, in relation to furniture. Thus the terms 'matter' and 'form' are fluid, just as illustrated in the case of chair. What changes or operates is the form, and, that which is made to change is matter. Matter is what becomes, and, that towards which the movement is made is its form. In the language of W.T. Stace,

What becomes is matter, and, what it becomes is form.

What is form in one aspect is matter in a changed situation. For example, wood is matter in relation to the chair, which is its form. But 'wood' is again form in relation to a growing tree. From another stand one can say that matter is bare possibility of becoming its 'various form'. For example, 'wood' is the possibility which can be actualised into chair, table, doors or windows. In the same manner, 'form' may mean *physical shape* e.g., shaping the wood into planks. Again, it may mean thought, or, even *an object* of *thought* as distinct from sense. It also may mean the *plan of the structure* of a thing which can be put in the form of a mathematical formula. 'Form' also may mean the inner holistic organization e.g., the tendency within a fertilized egg to become a chick. It also may mean the *function* for which a thing is made e.g., the form of a knife means the function of cutting a thing. It also at times means merely the efficient and final causes together, e.g., the final cause in the production of an art.

Thus the concepts of 'matter and form' are fluid and relative.

Potentiality and Actuality

Matter by itself has no form. It is absolutely formless, lawless and purposeless. But it is not non-Being for it becomes anything by the generating principle of form. For example, clay by itself is nothing. But it has the potentiality of becoming either a brick or a goblet or a cooking utensil and so on. Hence, it is something. Aristotle calls it 'potentiality' for it has the capacity of becoming something actual. What makes matter actual? It is the form. The potter by his skill with the idea of a brick and shaping it, forms the indeterminate clay into actual bricks. The illustration of clay and bricks has described the form (as the efficient, formal and final cause). Hence, the form is the principle of actualisation.

Take another example. Greenness is certainly an idea as objective as any quality is, but greenness does not exist. It can be, however, actualized in a green leaf, green books and other green things. What is greenness? Greenness is a universal which is also a form. So a form is the principle of actualisation. Now one can mention the view of Aristotle's predecessors with regard to the explanation of becoming or change or movement.

According to Democritus, change is brought about by *mechanical* impact of atoms on one another. Plato too held that the Idea of the Good draws all things towards itself and that all things strive after the Ideas which they long to become. This Platonic explanation of striving or becoming is teleological. But the whole Platonic explanation is mythological and unclear. Against his predecessors, Aristotle advances the doctrine of *unfoldment*. All things are caught up in development, from less developed form to higher developed form. It is the form which leads to unfoldment. Aristotle supported his doctrine of unfoldment by the presence of form in organisms and the working of a man in an artistic or even ordinary production.

In the case of an organism, matter and form potentiality and actuality, work together inseparably. They can be *distinguished* only in thought but not in actuality. For example, the end of becoming a chick is in a fertilized egg. The fertilized egg has a potentiality of becoming a chick, but it is actualized only when the form of a chick actualizes itself in the egg. Here matter is being shaped into an actual chick. The unfoldment is wholly teleological.

In human production the matter and the actualizing form can be seen by somewhat distinguishing and separating them. For example, a potter has the end of making a brick, which impels him to turn potential clay into the actual brick. But it is always the form which is prior to actualization of implicit potentiality.

Actuality is prior to potentiality even in time. For example, an actual member of a species precedes any potential member. This is seen in begetting of one man by another man; in training a musician by another musician. An actual man as an actualized individual man begets another man who previously to his birth was only potentially an individual man. An individual Dasrath alone could produce Rama. Similarly, only an actual musician can train a man to become a musician who before starting his career as a pupil was at first only potentially a musician. In both cases an actual man or an accomplished musician is prior to a potential man or potential musician as a learner.

Again, everything that comes to be, moves towards a principle, e.g., an end. Now actuality is the end. Therefore, actuality is prior to potency.

All things in this world, which exist can be arranged in a hierarchical order. For example, individual men come under the species 'man'. Again, the species man comes under the higher class 'animal'. This again is further subsumed under 'creature'. Let us put the order thus :

Creature
↓
Animal
↓
Man
↓
Individual men

In this graded order, one class may be called matter in relation to the higher order which is its form. But, this higher order itself becomes matter in relation to a still higher order. For example, species 'man' is the form in relation to individual men, and, species 'man' becomes matter in relation to 'animal'. Of course, the existing things in graded classes are all materialised forms, or, formed matter. But they are called higher or lower according to the principle of all-pervasiveness. 'Animal' is said to be higher than 'man', because 'animal' includes not only man, but also cow, horse etc. If we arrange all the classes in a hierarchical order, then we find that at the top is matterless form, *Actus purus* (pure activity) without any matter or potentiality. At times, Aristotle calls this *actus purus* God. Now God is all perfect and has nothing which He wishes to realize or desire. It is said to be its own end. It is also called Prime Mover in the sense that it moves everything, but Itself remains unmoved. But at the bottom there is pure potentiality; for it is nothing definite. It is simply wholly indeterminate. It is called primordial matter, formless matter. It is pure potentiality which under the influence of Prime Mover progressively gets actualized from the lower order to higher order, till it reaches the highest order.

Theology of Aristotle

For Aristotle, theology is the highest science which deals with substantial, self-dependent Being, which moves everything without itself being moved, i.e., *Unmoved Prime Mover*. Why is Aristotle so much thrilled about this unmoved mover?

Aristotle believed that the Universe is eternal with its hierarchical order, and each rung of the ladder is characterized by its own form actualizing itself in its individuals. Hence, all the rungs of this ladder-like order are in movement. Hence, the teleological movement of each rung and again the whole hierarchical order is caught up by an all-pervasive movement by this unmoved mover. We have already seen that at all rungs of the ladder, forms are actualizing themselves. Some rungs are higher than others. Higher rungs have lower rungs as their matter or potentiality. At the top of this hierarchical order, there is actuality, but no potentiality. At the base of the graded scale; there is potentiality, there is no actuality, but potentiality waits for being actualized into individual objects belonging to higher and lower levels. But even bare potentiality is not non-Being, but is a substratum and support and stuff of all things in the process of being from the lowest to the highest. At the top there is actualized *matterless form* and at the bottom of this graded system is pure matter without form.

The second thing is that the Unmoved Prime Mover, called matterless form is pure *activity* (*actus purus*). Why? Because the whole universe exists because it is characterized by never ending activity and is substained by activity. As the universe is eternal, so unmoved mover, called God is also eternal.

Here Aristotle is concerned to hold that what is eternal is prior logically to what is perishable. Further, no potentiality can ever be maintained to be eternal and actual, for, whatever is potential may not become actual. For example, a potential artist may not paint a picture of *Urvasi*. Again, eternal is that which by its own nature cannot fail to be. Hence, God is by His own nature an actual Being, for there is nothing of potentiality in Him. He is all perfect and nothing is lacking in Him.

As God is eternal, and exists of His own necessity, so He alone sustains Himself and the whole universe without anything outside of Him to sustain Him. All other things are moved by Him, but He alone remains unmoved. *A* is moved by *B*, and *A* in its turn moves *C*, and *C* moves *D* and so on. But if this series continues *ad infinitum,* then no moving thing will contain the cause of itself. Everything moved by another comes to an end. But the universe is eternal. It must have a mover which keeps on moving by itself without being by anything else.

Ordinarily form by itself does not exist. It exists in something individual. God is form of forms; its own thought of thought. Because God thinks its own thought, so God is said to be self-conscious. Therefore God is mind,

God also must have life; for the actuality of thought is life, and God is that actuality. His essential actuality is life most good and eternal. God therefore is a living being, eternal, and most good; to Him belong—rather He is—life and duration, continuous and eternal. (Warrington, *Metaphysics*, p. 346)

Aristotle also maintains that God thinking His own thought and goodness enjoys perfect blessedness. It is difficult to imagine God's mind, life, blessedness literally as we human beings are said to experience and know them. These terms appear to us figuratively used. So Aristotle appears to be as metaphorical, even mythical as Plato was. Indeed the pure form or the prime mover in Aristotle is the same as the Idea of the Good in Plato. Aristotle uses all the words of Platonic Idea of the Good for the unmoved mover. It is eternal, unchangeable, immovable, incorporeal, at the same time the final cause of generation.

As God is without matter, potentiality and body, so He is wholly immaterial. Nay, God's thought is without body, without senses, so He is said to be pure Spirit. He is again stated to be spiritual because He is pure rationality and the rational end for tne whole universe. Aristotle's thought has provided the idea of spiritual monotheism to the West.[1] A question crops up at this stage. True, God is transcendent to the whole universe, for He is at the top of the hierarchical order in which this universe is found. As a transcendent God, He does not respond to the prayers of His worshippers, for He is absorbed in His own thought.[2] But God is also said to be the final cause of the world. Does the world love God without being loved? Is there also an inner teleology in the universe which sustains the graded order or hierarchical system of the universe? David Ross, a great authority on Aristotle thinks that Aristotle does imply some sort of God's immanence.

Yet he (Aristotle) speaks of the order as due to God, so that his God may truly he said to be at work in the world, and in *this* sense immanent.[3]

However, it will be too much to state that God works in the world immanently, or, even on the world providentially. So far we human beings are concerned, we become self-conscious by knowing an object external to us. For example, when we perceive a tree, we become aware of ourselves as 'I am perceiving the tree'. But it has been suggested by some Christian scholars that this self-consciousness on the part of God is reversed. He knows Himself *directly* and the world *indirectly*. The reason for this is that God alone has direct knowledge of Himself, but all things depend on Him. So by knowing Himself, He knows all things indirectly, by knowing Himself as a Being on which all other things depend. Against this interpretation

---

1. God is spirit and those who worship Him must worship Him in spirit, St. John 4.24.
2. A *jin* who has won his own primordial nature, remains absorbed in Himself. He is loved, but He loves none.
3. D. Ross, Aristotle, p. 185.

Ross states that Aristotle denies any relation of God with evil, and, so his God cannot have knowledge of the world which is infected with evil. Therefore, Ross concludes,

> God, as conceived by Aristotle, has a knowledge which is not knowledge of the universe, and an influence on the universe which does not flow from His knowledge;. . .[1]

Further, Ross adds that God's influence on the world is of the same sort which a statue has on its admirers. Certainly, Aristotle will not hold any theory of divine creativity and His providential care for the world.[2]

God's creativity and providential care are not allowed by Aristotle on the ground that Aristotle maintains that God is not moved by desire, but by thought. Aristotle grants the primacy of thought over desire, even when he thinks that both desire and thought can move without themselves being moved.

> Now desire depends on thought rather than thought on desire, for thought is the starting-point[3]

But this is against Aristotle's criticism of Socrates, and, is against the findings of modern philosophy. How does the world move by God then?

> The final cause (God), then, moves by being loved, while all other things that move do so by being moved.[4]

Hence, man has to be attracted by God who is good and pure spirit, but he cannot expect any responsive love of God. Like Platonism, one can meditate on God and by meditating on Him can be slowly and gradually transformed, or, as Aristotle himself has observed that one can be influenced by a statue, so God can influence the world by being loved. It is a case of unrequited love, which Spinoza and Goethe understood to be the highest king of love.

Ross asks, 'Is this concept of final cause defensible'?

Of course, the doctrine that the whole universe is being drawn towards the unmoved mover or God means that the grand End called God is moving the world, as its culminating end. The whole world is realising God, but it can do so only unconsciously. Hence, there is the doctrine of unconscious teleology. Is it a defensible doctrine?

The term 'teleology' implies purpose, and, purpose means some *conscious* purpose in the mind of a person. However, we have seen that for Aristotle, God

---

1. D. Ross, *Ibid.*, p.183.
2. D. Ross, *Ibid.*, p. 184, 186.
3. Warrington, John, *Aristotle's Metaphysics*, p. 345.
4. Warrington, J., *Ibid.*, p. 345.

is not a person who responds to the prayers of His devotee. He remains absorbed in His own thought and enjoys His own blessedness. In other words, 'purpose' means *conscious end*. Therefore, unconscious purpose or teleology will be deemed self-contradictory phrase. Besides, Aristotle denies God's providential activity, for it would mean that God lacks something which he would like to attain through this universe. But God is perfect and has no potentiality in Him. He is complete *actus purus* lacking nothing. Again, there is a tricky question. God is said to be unmoved Mover. How does He move all things?

Of course, God is matterless form; He is form of form, or, thought. Hence, He is wholly incorporeal and acts non-physically. He is said to act like desire and as an object of supreme love, or as a statue on its admirers. But God is the final cause which moves the world by also becoming its efficient cause. Aristotle maintains that God moves the first heaven *directly* and all other things through it indirectly. Here 'the first heaven' is said to be a god, living and eternally moving in a circle. Of course, the heavens are regarded as near-perfect gods who exercise their influence on things lower than what they are as their objects of desire and love. Can the inanimate worldly objects have desire and love? The truth is that the final incorporeal God cannot initiate material and physical movement.

In conclusion, it can be said that God moves the first heaven *directly*. What does it mean? It is obscure and we have already seen that unconscious teleology is only an *analogical* expression. The very concept of God as thought thinking its own thought cannot explain the universe. God as life, mind and even self-conscious spirit remains obscure and the whole description is figurative. Hence, St. Thomas and Duns Scotus have tried to give a more theistic interpretation of Unmoved Mover. St. Thomas has been said to be Aristotelian and his 'five ways of knowing God' has its roots in Aristotle's proofs of God. So let us briefly mention *proofs* of God's existence.

Proofs for God's Existence : Some sort of Cosmological argument has been thus presented by Aristotle. All existing things are perishable substances. But there are two imperishable existing things, namely *time* and *change*. Time is actually experienced thing. If it is not eternal, then it will have either beginning or end. But if we say that time began. It means it began at *some point of time*, which means that to think of time as having a beginning means that time was already there in which it had a beginning. In the same way if we say that time ceased to be, then it means once again at some point of time it ceased to be. Hence there must be time when it ceases to be. Hence, time cannot have any beginning or ending without presupposing time at both ends. Hence, time is eternal. Again, either time and change are identical, or, change is one continuous change as heavenly bodies have. Both Plato and Aristotle supposed that planets have been moving in their circular movement since eternity.

Therefore, to account for eternal time and change there must be an eternal self-moved mover. This self-moved mover not only must have the potential power to move, but must be necessarily everlastingly actual. Mere potentiality for eternal actuality will not do, for potentiality may possibly not be.

Again, Aristotle suggests that men beholding the beauty of earth and see and the majesty of starry heavens cannot but conclude that these wonderful things are works of gods. This may be called teleological argument for the existence of God.

Of course, the contention that matterless form is of its very nature must exist if necessity speaks of ontological argument. But apart from this Aristotle proves the existence of God, from graded things in nature. His argument is:

> Where there is better, there is the best. Now among existing things one is better than another; therefore, there is the best, which must be divine.

This proof has been called argument from gradation of things in nature by St. Thomas. But it has been used by Descartes in relation to his ontological argument. According to Descartes, *God in mere thought* is inferior to God who is both in thought and existence. Similarly, Anselm proves the existence of God by the idea of God than which greater and higher cannot be thought.

Hence, Aristotle has advanced certain proofs for God which have proved important later in Christian and Western philosophy.

Aristotle's Philosophy of Nature

Aristotle along with Plato regarded the sun and moon and stars as divine with superior Intelligences. They were supposed to have been created by God and were regarded as eternal. Being perfect they moved in the sky with perfect circular motion. The earth was the centre of this universe. They were also supposed to influence the life and conduct of men. This belief of Aristotle appears to be quite popular in his time, but quite apparently does not have any rational basis. The only effect it had was to encourage astrology. But why did Aristotle think that the heavenly entities moved by the Will of superior Intelligences?

The moderners find that animals, plants and men move in a way quite differently from the lifeless, inanimate things of the world. The movement of inanimate things can be best styled as mechanistic like motor cars, aeroplanes and hosts of things in daily life of the moderners. Whereas the movements of men and animals are supposed to be guided by some ends or purpose. These movements are known as teleology.

In modern science, every effort is made to assimilate teleological explanation to mechanical one. Much of human education is supposed to be explained by conditioning and by mathematical statistical laws which at bottom are mechanistic. In contrast, the Greeks tended to assimilate mechanical movement to teleological explanation. For this reason Aristotle tried to explain the movement of the heavenly entities by the will of superior intelligences. Nay more. This explains as to why Aristotle tries to give a teleological explanation of Natural movements. For example, for Aristotle there is the form of an Oak which is at work in the acorn to move it in the direction of becoming a full-fledged oak tree. Similarly, in every embryo there is the appropriate form of the species in order that the embryo may grow into a proper member of that species. In the fertilized egg, there is the form of the kind of fowl (species) to transform it into a proper chick of its kind. In the same way Aristotle thinks that there is an unconscious end or teleology in the natural workings. In every case there is the form which actualizes the potential matter into its appropriate kind. Therefore, Russell thinks that the concept of teleology may work somewhat in explaining the world of plants, animals and man. But even in these things, teleological explanation will bar scientific advance. However, for understanding Aristotle's philosophy of Nature, we have to keep in view that for Aristotle, Nature is a thing of growth towards its ends. There is always an *internal principle* of movement towards some implanted ends.

Like a botanist which Aristotle was, he has arranged all things into a pyramidal scheme which can be thus schematically represented.

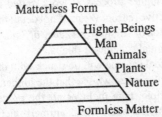

No doubt the tapering ladder is suggesting higher and lower entities. At the bottom there is the formless matter, pure potentiality. Of course, for Aristotle formless matter does not exist, —it is not actual. In contrast, at the apex of this pyramidal scheme, there is the matterless form, called God or Prime Mover. This Prime Mover exists, is wholly actual. Here we may note that Aristotle's system is a type of idealism like that of Plato. 'Form' corresponds to the essence or Idea of Plato. So Aristotle not only holds the primacy of form or Idea, but its greatest reality. In other words, for Aristotle as also for all forms of idealism, the highest Idea is the most real of all things. This is reflected well in the Ontological Argument for the existence of God, and in the Idealistic systems of Plato, Hegel and the whole Hegelian movement.

If we now reflect on the suggested pyramidal scheme of things of Aristotle's system, then we find that here things have been arranged in higher and lower forms. The principle is one of form and activity. It appears that the whole universe has been so constructed that matter may be purified and transformed into higher and higher reality. This again may be put by saying that the matter may be spiritualized. Of course, up to man, matter continues largely untransformed and so a source of evil.

At the level of inanimate things of nature, man by his rational activities, tries to unearth laws embedded into all inanimate things. But by means of rational activities, called as scientific investigation, man has not been able to pierce into the dead nature very far. But even the inanimate nature works according to ends planted into it. It works according to unconscious teleology.

At the next rung of the pyramidal ladder there are plants characterized by nutritional activities pertaining to growth and propagation. Animals stand higher in the ladder. They include all that plants have, i.e. physico-chemical excitation, nutrition and propagation. But in addition to all these, animals have spontaneity of locomotion. They have sensation and are guided by pleasure and pain. Further still higher stands man. He not only includes that plants have and animals too, he has *reason*, or, we can say that man has a soul, with higher and lower faculties, but with no parts. Further, though man has vegetative functions of plants and sensation along with pleasure and pain, they all get transformed at the level of man.

In man there is not only sensation, but the life of sensation is transformed by past memories stored into apperception, which includes the process of comparison and contrast. Further, there is the higher process at work called imagination, memory, recollection, passive and active reason. We need not detail them here, for we shall mention them again in relation of Aristotle's *Theory of Soul*. But we have to reflect a little more on this pyramidal scheme of things.

Anyone who looks at the pyramidal scheme will be struck with the idea of an evolutionary order of things, especially when we see that the higher includes all the stages lower to them. For example, man includes all the processes which characterize animals and plants. In the same way, animals include all the characteristic features of plants. Hence, this graded arrangement would suggest that lower has given birth to its next higher stage, and, the higher not only includes all the processes characteristics just lower to them, but something more supervening the lower features. Hence, the pyramidal scheme really represents an evolutionary arrangement of things. One should not be surprised at it.

Earlier than Aristotle, Anaximander had hinted at the process of evolution in the organic world. Better explanation was presented by Empedocles. But their hints were mere adumbration of organic evolution. Plato did mention the stages of development of one's graded insight into the Idea of love. But in Aristotle these hints were worked up into a very definite pyramidal scheme which reminds one of Llyod Morgan and Samuel Alexander who flourished towards the first half of the 20th century. But there are significant differences between Aristotle's pyramidal scheme and the evolutionary philosophy based on. Darwin's theory of Organic Evolution.

1. The first important difference is that for the moderners, time is real. On the face of it, Aristotle also takes time to be eternal. But for Aristotle time makes no difference so far the different species and genera are concerned, for Aristotle, they are eternal, and, animals are not said to have evolved from plants, or, man from animal. Hence, time, though eternal, the pyramidal scheme of Aristotle is eternal and all the different stages of the order have remained ever since in the same way.

For the organic Evolution of Darwin and the wider picture of Bergson, Llyod Morgan, Alexander, the orders have emerged through temporal processes in the midst of failures. For example, many beings between higher apex and man, have become extinct. So species and genera, for Aristotle, are eternal and fixed. But modern evolutionists believe that at one time the present species and genera were not in existence, and in due course they have evolved.

2. Can we say that the modern theory of evolution is a dynamic theory, and, Aristotle's theory is not? This requires some elucidation. For Aristotle too there is movement within each species and genus. For example, there is the form of Oak in an acorn which helps it (acorn) to grow into an oak. Again, there is the form of a chick in a fertilized egg, which under proper conditions grows into a chick. So there is dynamism at each stage of the evolutionary scheme. But between one stage to another there is no real evolution.

Further, modern evolutionists not only take recourse to teleological causation, but very often prefer mechanistic explanation of the evolution of species and genera. Hence, from the viewpoint of science, Aristotle's explanation of evolution is speculative, for it does not take recourse to the *mechanism* of evolution, i.e., the *how* of explanation of evolution. Hence, Aristotle's theory of evolution is a painted, static picture of evolution just like the graded skeletons of living things in Calcutta museum. But how do we say that one species is higher than others? How do we say that man is higher than apes, or, that apes stand higher than dogs?

3. Spencer has suggested a criterion. For him, evolution has been moving from homogeneous states to heterogeneous stage of development. For example, gaseous matter has given birth to physico-chemical state of development. Gaseous stage is supposed to be homogeneous and the physico-chemical state is really from chaos to orderly evolution and other regular processes. In the same way, living processes are supposed to be more complex than physico-chemical processes, for the living beings are not only physico-chemical, but in addition they have powers of spontaneous movements, propagation and holism. Hence, the greater the complexity of organisation and the higher is its position in the hierarchical scheme of things.

In contrast, for Aristotle, the higher form (activity, actuality) is the criterion for placing a species in the higher rung of the ladderlike scheme of things. When we look at man, then we find that Aristotle takes recourse to the elements of reason by virtue of which man is higher than all other animals, plants and other things. Hence, in explaining higher and lower, Aristotle really keeps to the criterion of rationality. However, is this criterion satisfactory?

There is hardly any reason in animals and insects. How can we say that animals are higher than plants? Criterion of form is also highly vague.

Therefore, Aristotle's pyramidal scheme of things is far more clear than of his predecessors like Anaximander, Empedocles and Plato. In due course, this scheme helped in grasping the organic evolutionary of Darwin and the speculative philosophy of modern times.

Aristotle's Teaching About Soul

In accordance with the teaching of Aristotle, neither matter exists without the form, nor does form without matter. In this context, 'soul' is the form of the body and they are always found inseparably together in man. We can say that together they form one higher organism in the pyramidal scheme of Aristotle. Further, the higher includes the lower, and, the higher transforms all that is grand at the lower level. Human beings include the vegetative processes within themselves, namely, growing nutritional activities, propagation and the rest. They have also the animal processes of sense preception and some memory. But the most distinctive feature of man is his reason. By virtue of this reason, the whole of sense-perception and memory is greatly changed and transformed in man. Man does not merely sense. His sensation is greatly overlaid with his past experience. What a man senses, by virtue of the enmassed past experiences, he interprets into an object. Object-perception includes comparison—contrast and assimilation in the light of past experiences and creative imagination. One can analyse even the simple process of sense—perception into the elements of sensation, apperception, memory, imagination, recollection and recognition. These are all found together inseparably. Further, the processes of recollection and recognition involve much of self-reference, as *Kant* pointed out later. For example, we not only remember to have seen Rama in the past, but also 'Oh! I now recognise that he is the same Rama whom I saw in the library'. Thus, man has sensation, memory-imagination and reason.

'Reason' means for Aristotle, *passive* and active reason. Passive reason simply means registering the experiences of objects, as on a clean piece of paper. We now know that even this kind of passive reason requires much of activity. For Aristotle, active reason is the capacity to know mathematics and philosophy. Like Plato, active reason consists in *contemplating* on God, or, what Plato called the Idea of the Good. This contemplative life itself is the most rational thing for man and this contributes to his happiness. This fully rational life is rarely realised in man and that also for a very short time. This contemplative life is the most divine element in man. In the spirit of Plato, Aristotle writes,

> . . . we must not follow those who advise us, being men, to think of human beings, and being mortal, of mortal things, but must, so far as we can, make ourselves immortal, and strain every nerve to live in accordance with the best thing in us; for even even if it be small in bulk, much more does it in power and worth surpass everything.[1]

However, Aristotle rejects the views of his Master Plato with regard to the final destiny of human soul. First of all, Aristotle regards soul as the *function* of the body, just as walking is the function of legs and seeing is the function of eyes. As soon

---

1. Quoted by Russell, B. *Ibid.*, p. 194.

as legs are amputated, walking ceases. Similarly, if eyes are destroyed there can be no seeing. In like manner when the body dies, its function in the form of the soul disappears. Hence, Aristotle does not accept the Platonic teaching of the immortality of soul. But does nothing of soul survive the dissolution of body?

We have already noted that the active or contemplative reason in man is most divine. And the divine is immortal. So on death, this active reason returns to God. Does it some truncated part of man is personal and immortal? Of course, reason in some form does survive, but this is what is found in all men and there is nothing distinctive in Rama's reason as different from Shyam's reason. Reason is one and the same in all members of human beings. Hence, it is personal. Therefore, for Aristotle, there is no case of personal immortality.

Besides, sensation, perception and memory; all belong to the body. So with the dissolution of the body memory is lost. But without memory, there can be no personality. Therefore, for Aristotle, there is neither personal immortality, nor transmigration of the soul. However, reason in man is eternal and on death mingles with the world-reason and becomes one with it.

The Nicomachean Ethics of Aristotle

Like all other things of the world, man is a combination of matter and form. What is the matter of man? Man's matter includes what is in the corporeal region, living things and specially animals. Hence, the form of man moulds and transforms in man his physics-chemical activities, vegetative, sex, and, the senses in man. This form is reason, for the reason in man is his distinctive feature. Hence, the highest end of man is the becoming his highest being or the attainment of goodness or a life of virtue which Socrates and Plato could not articulate clearly as the *content of goodness*. Nor does Aristotle. He vaguely tells us that the highest thing which a man can attain is a life of contemplation of God's goodness. This life of contemplation is also the highest end of man. So if we are asked, 'what is the highest end which man can attain', then our answer would be the same as of Socrates and of Plato, namely, happiness.

This is the life of passion and appetites *regulated by reason*. Is not pleasure the satisfaction of passion and appetites? Yes, it is. Then is pleasure the highest end which man seeks to attain? No, Why?

First, appetites and passion are the matter of ethical life and they have to be regulated by the *form* which for man is his reason. Hence, pleasure cannot be the end of man. Besides, form everywhere is the activity which actualizes matter towards its highest becoming or end. But appetites and passion are said to be passive potentiality or *feeling*. So feeling cannot be the highest end of the rational man. Therefore, pleasure cannot be the end of man's moral life. Aristotle, therefore, rejects *hedonism*. But does he reject the claim of appetites and passion? No, Aristotle rejects *asceticism*. Man is a living body and he must live with his appetites for food, mate, and fear, etc. Hence, man has to include them in his rational activity.

Here Aristotle makes a very pregnant statement. According to him, feeling cannot be the guide of life, but it follows of necessity as *a necessary consequence* or *accompaniment* of man's rational life. Therefore, pleasure comes in his moral pursuits.

The pursuit of the highest rational end of man means the control of passion and appetites by reason, and, this is known as diagnostic. Again, Aristotle does not deny the place of personal good as riches, friends, good fortune, health etc. For they are auxiliary means for a moral life. Therefore, Aristotle, denies *cynicism*. However, external good fortune is not constitutive, but merely a help for moral life.

The essential of a moral life is the control of appetites and passion by reason and this has to be constantly exercised. This habitual control of appetites and passion by reason is known as virtue. In due course, virtue creates a good disposition and character. This character is an inward organisation of a settled habit of will which pertains to a good moral life. Hence, neither appetites have to be extirpated, as asceticism wrongly maintains, nor, appetites have to be satisfied, as hedonism holds. But appetites have to be regulated by reason. This regulation of appetites by reason has to be carried out by moderation and tact. In other words, moderation means an insight into the reasonable desires. It means neither the excess nor the denial of appetites has to be allowed. This is known as the principle of Golden Mean. Of course this arithmetical term 'mean' that in each case there is some *quantitative* mean. In each case one has to decide for oneself the mean of rational choice. For example, courage is a mean between cowardice and rashness, liberality between prodigality and meanness ; modesty is a mean between bashfulness and shamelessness, and so on. This regulation by a rule of adopting a mean is greatly assisted by the cultivation of virtue, i.e., by the settled habit of will in the choice of the mean by a rule which a wise man in his practical life would adopt.

In this context, Aristotle speaks of *justice* which for him does not come under individual ethics, but under the activity of the State. Justice is achieved by means of two processes called distributive and corrective. Distributive justice means reward for right activity and corrective justice is attained by punishing wrong actions.

For Aristotle, morality is an activity, but what kind of activity is to be called moral? It is voluntary action alone for which men are praised or blamed, rewarded or punished. Hence, voluntary actions alone may be called moral. But an involuntary or non-voluntary actions are not the object of moral judgment. An action is said to be involuntary when it is performed by the external circumstances beyond the control of the doer. For example, if a man falls on a child as a result of being pushed from behind, then his action is involuntary and for his fall he is not morally responsible. Hence an action is said to be involuntary when it is a compelled action from an external agency, or, performed under ignorance. For the time being we can ignore non-voluntary action which may be treated as the involuntary one. On the contrary, an action is voluntary when it originates from within the agent himself, and the doer has to choose the course of action with his free will. The choice is deliberate desire of things in our power. Hence, it is a reasonable desire, the origin of which is in the man himself. Hence, for Aristotle, freedom of will means freedom of choice. This choice may mean either the *choice of means* or the choice of *an end* for which the action is performed. Aristotle, according to Ross, limits the choice to means and not of ends.[1] Does Aristotle make a significant omission? In our opinion not, for choice has to be rational and reason in man is one and the same, and, it has one ultimate end. The chief end of man is the attainment of goodness which is the goodness of God. Hence, for a human being there is one and one ultimate end. Therefore, 'choice' means the choice of 'means' for the attainment of the highest end in man.

Aristotle is a great supporter of the freedom of will. For his virtuous actions are not only voluntary, but also in accordance with rational choice. Hence, virtue and vice are within the power of man. No man can be said to perform a moral action or virtuous *action of necessity.* For this reason Aristotle censures Socrates for maintaining that nobody does wrong voluntarily. For Aristotle, both virtue and vice follow from free choice. Secondly, Aristotle criticizes Socrates for holding that man is wholly rational. However, man is not only rational, but also an animal driven by appetites and passion. Naturally at times knowing the right course of action a man is overpowered by his passion and appetites. Hence, only by the settled habit of will man has to control his lower passions by means of his rational choice. But even if we grant that choice is limited to the free choice of means, is this choice itself wholly free, or, is it determined by man's psychological determinants? This is a very modern analysis of free actions, but even in passing to other topics related to ethics of Aristotle, we should note this as a very knotty problem.

Happiness is said to be the end of moral life. This happiness is attained by the performance of virtuous activities, and, perfect happiness lies in the best activity which is contemplative. This follows from the fact that virtuous activities aim at the goodness of God.

> The activity of God, which surpasses all others in blessedness, must be contemplative.

This contemplative activity is found in philosophers who are most godlike in this state of contemplation, and therefore the happiest and the best. This is what Plato has held. Therefore, with all his professed differences, Aristotle has not been able to free himself from the shadow of his master.

The State

Plato's State is the individual magnified. Aristotle has a similar view about the State. But for him the relation between individuals and the state is much more

---

1. D. Ross, *Aristotle*, p. 200.

intimate and closer. The formation of a State, for Aristotle is natural, for Aristotle regards man by nature, a social and a political being. Politics for Aristotle has an ethical end. The individual finds his ethical completion in the life of state. By introducing the mechanism of compulsion, in the form of reward and punishment, state makes passion and appetites subservient to the rule of reason. It does so by the education of its citizens for attaining virtue and happiness. Here the body has to be cultured for the soul of man, and his appetites have to be taught to be regulated by reason. The reason for this is that the ethical conduct is social and political. What does honesty and truthfulness mean, if not in a social context? Again, what does 'justice' mean if not in the context of a State? Hence, the State offers wider and deeper opportunities for the unfoldment of individuals' character, virtue and happiness.

Of course, in this realationship of the State and individuals, State is the form and the individuals are its matter. State, therefore, moulds the ethical life of individuals. But this picture has to be a little modified. For Aristotle, not the individual, but the family is the real unit of the State. The individual without its mate does not exist. But the individual with its mate is called a family. A number of families form a village, and a number of villages together form community and a number of such communities form a State.

However, the relation between the families and the State is not mere mechanical. This relation is of the nature of parts and the whole in a living organism. A hand is a living part which upholds and supports the life of the whole body, and, the vitality and health of the body keeps the hand healthy and strong. A hand cut off from the body is dead and useless. Both must be there in a close relationship. But the State is said to be the *end* and the family as its real unit is said to be its *matter*. No doubt in order of time, family comes first, but the end is logically prior to the family. It is the end which controls and guides the activities of the family. By making *family* as the unit of the State, Aristotle criticizes his master's conception of collective parental life. This, according to Aristotle, cuts the natural feeling between the parents and their children.

Again, by holding on to the organic relationship between individuals and the State, Aristotle is clear about the later Rousseau's contract-theory of the State. Aristotle denies outright the reality of individuals *as the units* of the State. So there can be no real contract between individuals for their mutual co-operative and defensive end in view. In the contract-theory the State becomes an *external* mechanism for sustaining the life of individuals. But for Aristotle, individuals and the State form *one living organism*, and the State is the real meaning and end of individuals.

Aristotle also does not favour the absolute reality of the State by denying the right of the families and the individuals. Did Plato teach this? In our opinion, Plato did believe in a structured constitution of the State into workers, soldiers and rulers.

But his Utopian State did not have an organic view of the State. But Aristotle's view has very great relevance in relation to a totalitarian fascist state in which individuals live for the State alone, and where the individuals are merely a canon-fodder for the glorification of the State.

Thus, by insisting on the ethical function of the State, Aristotle has sounded a very healthy view about the State. It is so unfortunate that Aristotle accepts the institution of slavery. He also tells us that some men are born free and some are slaves. This view of Aristotle teaches that every philosophy is dated and a product of its time.

Aristotle has not elaborately discussed the nature of different kinds of State-government. According to the ethical function of the State, a government is good when it upholds the good of the whole State. There are three kinds of government which are good and their opposite bad. *Monarchy* is the rule by one wise man, superior to all his compeers in virtue and wisdom. Its opposite is *Tyranny* where there is the rule of one man based on force, and not on virtue and wisdom. Next is *Aristocracy*, the rule by a few wise rulers. Its opposite is *Oligarchy*, the rule of the few rich and powerful men who do not consider the good of the poor. Constitutional Republic is that where citizens are of equal stature and a few of them rule the State. Here it is the rule of the needy who ignore the interest of the rich. Democracy is the opposite of Timocracy, where the poor few rule over the rest. Oligarchy is the rule of the rich and democracy is the rule of the poor.

It is significant to note that Aristotle judges a government good and bad, according to the ethical qualities of the rulers. For this reason *monarchy and aristocracy* are said to be good forms of government. But for the moderners a government is said to be good or bad, according to the constitution it adopts.

A Critical Estimate of Aristotle's Philosophy

Aristotle has been regarded as an encyclopaedic genius. There is nothing even in the modern world which Aristotle has not touched and in relation to which he has not presented his masterful insight. Hegel, Spencer and others have in vain tried to emulate Aristotle in presenting a system of thought in all fulness. Only in Leibnitz and A.N. Whitehead we get a glimpse of the encyclopaedic grasp of Aristotle, of the universe as a whole. Naturally, Aristotle has influenced Western thought throughout all ages, down to the present time.

1. First, it will be wrong to think that Aristotle was unfriendly to Plato. We have held that Aristotle is Plato made consistent. Nay, more, Aristotle has included all that was best in all his past predecessors and has presented them in his own system of thought. In this respect he not only reconciles the rival claims of Heraclitus and Eleaticism, but also the Sophists and Socrates. Being and Becoming, Sense and Reason, Hedonism and Ethical Good have been reconciled by Aristotle, and, in harmonizing them Aristotle has gone beyond all these one-sided systems of thought.

2. Aristotle is regarded as the founder of science inasmuch as he has influenced the rise of modern science by his insistence on *facts*. According to him, universals and ideas are found objectively only in individual things. Arabs and the Scholastic European world were awakened into scientific search by the contributions of Aristotle.

Aristotle not only showed the importance of the observance of particular facts for science, but he himself was a great biologist. Not only he insisted on teleology for explaining life, but he also created scientific terminology for the sake of precision and clarity of thought.

3. Aristotle has presented his whole philosophy in a pyramidal scheme of things. This has not only suggested an evolutionary trend in the universe, but has laid down the foundation of Logical division, Classification and Definition.

4. One should not ignore the fact that Aristotle has become the legislator of Western Logic, Ethics and Science. Not only Deductive Logic, but also his Induction is important which unfortunately was not paid so much attention as it actually deserved.

5. The whole pyramidal scheme is based on the distinction of higher and lower orders of things. But what is the criterion of higher and lower. For Aristotle an order is higher according to the criterion of more inclusiveness, complexity and integration: for example, human beings are said to higher than other animals, because they include all that animals have. In addition they have greater integrity and complexity of elements in composition with those found in animals. For example, men and animals, both have sensation, but in men a sensation along with the memory-mass means greater understanding and interpretation of a sensation.

6. Aristotle's contributions to ethical thought till now has remained unsurpassed. In his teaching of Nicomachean Ethics, Aristotle gives a very clear solution of hedonism, rationalism. Aristotle tells us that morality is the habitual control of passion and appetites by reason, and, in doing this pleasure and happiness necessarily result as necessary consequences. Thus, Aristotle successfully reconciles the partial claims of Sophists, Socrates and Plato.

7. In his theory about the State, Aristotle has not presented an Utopian state as does Plato. But he holds that the State has an ethical purpose to serve; for social ethics can be fulfilled only in a State. He also shows that the happiness of the citizens depends not so much on the constitutional structure of the State, as on the moral education of the rulers.

8. Nobody can leap beyond his own shadow, so nobody can leap beyond the intellectual world view of his times and of his upbringing. Socrates and Plato, without deliberately accepting dualism have really supported dualism'. Socrates accepted the dualism of sense and reason which he could not successfully reconcile. Plato not only accepted the dualism of sense and reason, but he accepted the dualism of Ideas and matter. Aristotle too accepted the dualism of matter and form, of

potentiality and actuality, of mechanism and teleology, of God and Good. Nay more, though Aristotle meant that a delicate dualism be maintained, he has given weightage to 'form'. A formless matter does not exist, but for Aristotle, there is matterless Form, or, God or *Actus purus*. This doctrine of matterless form or thought teaches the primacy and priority of thought. And this is essentially the teaching of idealism. Hence, Aristotle has maintained idealism.

Aristotle not only wrote the first history of Greek Philosophy, but also has chartered the advance of Western philosophy as a whole.

3

Semi-Socratic and Greco-Roman Ethics

Cynicism

As against the Sophists, Socrates taught the doctrine of universal morality. His main ethical teachings were:

1. Virtue is knowledge and vice is ignorance. No man does wrong knowingly.
2. If Virtue is knowledge, then it is teachable.
3. Virtue is One.

What is the meaning of saying that virtue is knowledge? It means the concept of Good. This concept of Good is of the nature of insight into, or intuition or illumination of Good. But what more is the content of Good? Here Socrates is delightfully vague. Sometimes it meant that which is advantageous for man, and, at other times he said that Good is happiness. But he was not clear either about 'What is advantageous for man', or 'What happiness is'. Consequently 'Good' could be interpreted variously by his disciples. Aristippus interpreted 'happiness' as pleasure of the senses. He did not fully understand the meaning of Good, which Socrates did not and could not clearly define. Naturally, 'Good' could not be momentary, variable and subjective state called pleasure. But Socrates did say that the virtue is not only the highest, but is the sole good. What is virtue then? Most probably it meant 'the intelligent conduct of life' which makes a virtuous man happy. This intelligent conduct is good, not because of any consequence, but because it is *good in itself*, for it is the sole end of man. Virtue results from contemplation on the good, as more or less permanent disposition of man. Hence, by contemplation on the good, the virtuous man becomes good. Thus a virtuous man is a wise man. This was the main thrust of Socratic ethical teaching which is found in Plato and even in the Greco-Roman ethical thought.

But the followers of Socrates were not only influenced by the teaching, but also by the exemplary life of Socrates. They saw in him the kind of wise man as the ideal good man. And what did they find the most characteristic feature of his life? Antithesnes (444-368 B.C.), the disciple of Socrates found that the master did not care for the conventional moral opinions, nor the opinions of men. He remained steadfast even in hunger and thirst. Therefore, for Antisthesnes virtue lies in becoming independent as far as possible of the courses of events. In one dialogue, Socrates is said to have given his consent to a life of few wants. "You, Antiphon, would seem to suggest that happiness consists in luxury and extravagance; I hold a different creed. To have no wants at all is, to my mind, an attitude of godhead; to have a few wants as possible the nearest approach to godhead." But how can one achieve this?

Well, fate and fortune remain external to the man. He can have no control over natural events, nor over socio-political events. But he certainly can control his own self. He is a bundle of appetites and passion which can be called 'desire' as was called even in Buddhism (*trsna*). Therefore, a virtuous man is he who not only controls his desires, but even overcomes them. A wise man must be freed from everything that does not lie wholly within the power of mind itself. He has to suppress his desires. He becomes an *ascetic*. In Indian system of thought this is known as the state of *sannyasa* (renunciation). This attitude in morality is known as *cynicism*. Cynicism was really founded by Antisthenes (444-368 B.C.) and was popularized by Diogenes of Sinope.

For the cynics even a good fortune has to be more dreaded than welcomed, for it is precarious in the first instance, and, secondly it is not the reward of our virtuous efforts. Therefore, a virtuous man is he who limits his wants to a minimum. A virtuous man tries to be a king in himself by the conquest of his desires. He has to remain unperturbed by hunger and thirst, cold and heat. A cynic still could live by begging as an 'Indian fakir', as Russell has put it. He despised the very civilization which supported and maintained him by giving him food by begging.

Everything for the cynics was 'indifferent'. Pleasure, riches, honour, poverty, misery, even death were regarded as indifferent events. If a man has conquered, himself, his desires, he is a wise man. Otherwise a man is a fool. Virtue is one. Hence, men are either wise or fools. A wise man has all virtue and happiness, and a fool has all misery, imperfection and evil.

The attitude of the cynic has been called purely *negative*. The cynic taught the theory of 'back to Nature'. They derided honours and wealth, art and science and showed utter indifference to the presence of Generals and Kings. But even a cynic like Diogenes prized mental training, and, was an ardent seeker after virtue. Diogenes called himself 'a cosmopolitan citizen'. True, it was not the teaching of becoming a world-citizen, but only the negative denial that he did not belong to any one community. One cynic denied the existence of the plurality of gods, as due to the opinion of men; but according to nature he stated that there is only one God. However, this does not mean that the cynic really believed in monotheism. He really meant the denunciation of any religion whatsoever.

Cynicism was later taken over by Stoicism in Greco-Roman ethical thought.

Aristippus of Cyrene (435-366 B.C.)

Socrates was not interested in metaphysics. So was the case with his disciples, Antisthenes and Aristippus. Aristippus ignored metaphysics and was interested with ethical problems alone. Socrates had suggested that the end of ethical life is happiness. But Socrates did not define happiness. He however did state that virtue is the knowledge of Good. But one would like to be more clear about Good and would ask, Good for what? Socrates did not say like G.E. Moore, that Good is good and is indefinable. So if one wants to know, 'Good for what', then naturally the immediate answer would be 'pleasure'. People have the most direct acquaintance with sensation and feeling. So they would like their satisfaction which means pleasure. So Aristippus held that 'happiness' of his master is really pleasure. So Aristippus, laying down the hedonistic standard stated that the end of ethical striving is pleasure. This is also known as *Cyrenaicism*.

This cyrenaicism had its earlier roots both in Atomism and the Sophist. Atomists laid down that pleasure lies in the subtle atoms, and in their soft and gentle movements. In the same vein the Sophists maintained that morality lies in the satisfaction of feeling. That alone is ethically good which is agreeable to one. So Aristippus simply simplified and systematized this ethical doctrine of hedonism. Hedonism passed through three phases. In the first instance, it was held that the pleasure of the moment is the sole end of ethical life. But it was soon realized that heedless satisfaction of momentary feeling brings more pain in the long run than pleasure. Hence, in the second phase it was held that prudent and thoughtful pleasure is the real end of ethical life. Finally, it was held that not only pleasure has to be pursued, but pain too has to be avoided. Hence, in the final phase of cyrenaicism, the avoidance of pain rather than the pursuit of pleasure was emphasized. Later on Cyrenaicism was taken our by Epicureanism and in this post-Aristotelian ethical thought hedonism was greatly modified and systematically presented. Let us begin now with the first phase.

Aristippus stated that feeling is most palpably felt by us, and, we immediately enjoy the satisfaction of pleasure. So without any hesitation we can say that the chief end of life is pleasure. Hence for Aristippus men do desire pleasure and they should desire pleasure. One should give oneself to pleasure as it comes along one's way. It is momentary and fleeting. So one should not lose time in thinking about its *pros and cons*, for by the time we think, the bird of pleasure will be on her wings. So one should plunge heedless and headstrong into the river of pleasure. No doubt, pleasure means satisfaction of desire and feeling, and, this feeling is felt only by *me* and that also *now*. Hence, this pleasure is most subjective and cannot be directly shared. No doubt we can share sweets with other friends, but I alone experience their taste, and the sweet pleasure in the mouth of others cannot be shared. Hence, it is useless to promote the benevolent feeling of pleasure for the community.

In the first phase, there were no *kinds* of pleasure. All pleasures were equally alike, the pleasure of senses and of the intellect, of the body and of the mind. But the bodily pleasure was to be preferred, for it was more intense. However, it was soon discovered that heedless enjoyment of sensual pleasure is more often gives rise to greater pains. One cannot disregard the past and future because they are not at the moment. For pain will be the inevitable consequence. Hence, in the second phase it was stated that a wise man will use his reason and would prudently choose even lesser pleasure to avoid pain; for not only pleasure has to be sought, but pain too has to be avoided. Here mental pleasures have to be preferred to bodily ones on account of their greater duration and chances of getting no pain at all. Hence, sensual pleasure has to be checked and moderated in favour of safer pleasure. As pleasure was regarded as the sole end of morality, so conventional laws should be disregard. Theodorus is reported to have recommended even stealing and committing adultery if they could go undetected. Laws of the land are conventional, but morality is to live according to nature, which is universal and binding on all.

Finally, the Cyrenaics had to admit the place of finer feeling in friendship and family life. But even here the life of prudence, foresight and intelligence was encouraged for the sake of egoistic pleasure. Certainly a wise man should not work for the State for it entails much fruitless work and hard labour. But a cyrenaic would like to enjoy all the fruits of civilized existence. Hence, Theodorus stated,

> It is not reasonable that a wise man should hazard himself for his country, and endanger wisdom for a set of fools.

Thus, the cyrenaics were rather parasites who enjoyed at the table of Grecian beauty without either creating it or working for it. At last Aristippus found that one should weigh pleasure with a view to avoiding pain. Even Thodorus found that a wise man would rather cultivate a cheerful frame of mind than run after fugitive pleasures. Annicersis found that the spiritual pleasure in the intercourse with friends was much better than bodily pleasure. At last, Hegesias declared that one should try to avoid pain in preference to any pursuit of pleasure. Perhaps time was not ripe for cyrenaics to realise that pleasure is not the end of life, but is the *consequential* result of a good life. This was already shown by the Eudaemonism of Aristotle.

Aristippus clearly shows what hedonism is in its clearest form. It shows, if hedonism is the right, then it should not be the right, for even the short history of cyrenaicism showed that ultimately it gives rise to pessimism and negative approach to life. Cyrenaicism shows that it has no room for the sanctity of duty and no room for robust faith in the creation and maintenance of social refinement and culture. Search for pleasure is vain, for ultimately it leads to a flight from life. Hegesias became a philosopher of suicide, for he advocated painless death rather than enjoyment of life. Hence, Cyrenaicism was further taken up by Epicureanism in its fulness.

THE SCHOOL OF MEGARA

The school of Megara requires only a passing reference. It was founded by Euclides (450-374 B.C.). Euclides was as much an Eleatic as also a follower of Socrates and his ethical teaching. Eleatism taught that reality is One. It is Being, without plurality and becoming. Socrates taught that there is Good whose knowledge alone makes one virtuous. By combining these two teachings, Euclides held that Being alone is Good. Hence, the empty Eleatic concept of Being got an ethical content of Good. Consequently plurality, becoming is evil.

It was more a metaphysical school than an ethical system. The Megarics delighted in using the dialectic arguments of Zeno to establish the illusory character of multiplicity and motion. Therefore, the Megarians were opposed to the senses and the pursuit of pleasure. For them virtue consisted in the *contemplation* of One Good or One Being called Good, as was taught by Plato and was also adumbrated by Socrates.

STOICS AND STOICISM

Introduction : *Cynicism and Stoicism*

Cynicism was taken over by Stoicism and in many ways the stoics completed cynicism in many respects. Stoicism not only took over cynicism, but to some extent Heraclitus, Socrates, Plato and Aristotle. Cynicism had become a negative philosophy of life. It denies the place of passion and emotion, which to a great extent even stoicism does the same. Again, cynicism has no place for the achievements of Greek science, art and culture. But Stoicism welcomes them and instead of flight from social and political participation, it welcomes them and has room for them. By its insistence on 'Duty', Stoicism reached the highest ethical achievement of Greek thought. Both cynicism and Stoicism accept the phrase 'Go back to Nature', but nature means quite differently for them. For the cynics, nature is not rational, but man alone is. The reason in man is opposed to the appetites and passion. For the Stoics, however, the universe itself is rational and man a part of world reason is rational. Hence, for the Stoics, living with nature, means living in *harmony with nature.* Again, both cynicism and Stoicism teach 'world citizenship'. But they mean differently. For the cynics, cosmopolitanism is a *negative* concept, meaning not the belonging to any one community. However, for Stoicism *cosmopolitanism* means *one world-brotherhood*, belonging to one rational realm. Hence, Stoicism completes cynicism and corrects its many tenets of narrowness.

Stoicism was founded by Zeno (336-264 B.C.) in Athens about 314 B.C. He was simple, upright and of friendly disposition. He was full of moral earnestness. Afterwards the school was looked after by Cleanthes (264-232 B.C.). But Chrysippus (280-207 B.C.) was the ablest stoic who defended stoicism against the attacks of Epicureans and Sceptics. Later on some Roman thinkers accepted stoicism, namely, Seneca (3-65 A.D.), Epictetus (c. 60-100 A.D.) and the emperor Marcus Aurelius (121-180 A.D.).

Logic and Epistemology

Stoicism is essentially an ethical philosophy which is based on reason. Naturally this ethics is based on Logic and a theory of knowledge. We shall also find that Stoicism has its own metaphysics. Thilly has put the matter thus:

> The Stoics compared philosophy to a field, of which logic is the fence, physics the soil, and ethics the fruit. (p. 131)

This means that Stoic Ethics is based on logic and metaphysics.

Logic accepted by the Stoics is essentially Aristotelian with their emphasis on Syllogism. They could not add much to it. At most they clarified and classified the categories and added the hypothetical-categorical and Disjunctive-Categorical syllogism. But the Stoic theory of knowledge is important, since much of it was taken over by Locke and other modern empiricist.

According to Stoicism, the soul at birth is a clean slate, a *tabula rasa*. There are no Platonic innate ideas. Knowledge begins with perception and leaves its trace on the soul. The impression persists to form memory-images. Out of sense-impressions and images born of a number of particular cases, concepts are formed. These concepts have no independent existence of their own. They are in the mind. But a judgment is formed by means of reflection through the faculty of thought and speech, which is the same as the faculty of reason. Here the metaphysics of stoicism comes in. Human reason is only a spark of the world-reason which is the supreme reality. This world-reason has given rise to the whole universal order. Naturally human reason as long as it resorts to its judgment knows the laws imbedded in all things.

Again a sense-image is true if it corresponds to its sense-object. But how do we know whether this correspondence is true or false? Here the Stoics become wholly subjective. When the sense-impressions carries *our full conviction,* then we know it is true. In practice it means that when our perception is clear, distinct and vivid, and, gets repeatedly verified and perhaps also by other observers, then it may be taken to be true knowledge.

However, the Sceptics successfully refuted this subjective theory of conviction. Again, the doctrine of repeated observation by oneself and by others has been adopted by the moderners with their own elaboration and refinement. But at this juncture, the stoics added the element of *assent* which has important implication for their central ethical theory, and, which was also taken up by Descartes to explain his theory of truth and error.

According to the Stoics, there can be no judgment without our giving assent. If we give assent to confused and indistinct impressions, then we fall into error. If however assent is given to vivid, clear and distinct impressions, then there is no possibility of error. This giving or withholding our assent is due to our free will.

Thus, knowledge no doubt begins with perception, but without rational judgment there can be no knowledge. Hence, the soul is passive with regard to impression coming from external objects, but afterwards *active reason* begins to play its most important role. Afterwards, Locke accepts much of Stoic epistemology.

The epistemology remains subordinate to Stoic ethics, for it is only one element in stoic ethics. This ethics largely has been deduced from Stoics Metaphysics which includes physics, cosmology, psychology and theology. We, therefore, proceed now to Stoic Metaphysics.

Stoic Metaphysics

The Stoics maintained complete materialism, but stoic materialism is quite different from the atomistic materialism of the Epicureans. The Epicurean materialism was mechanistic and referred to the plurality of material atoms. In contrast, the Stoic materialism arose from a critical consideration of the dualism of Plato and Aristotle's dualism of matter and form. The stoics found that the universe is one unitary organic whole. If it is an organic whole, then Ideas and things cannot be separate, and, the dualism of form and matter must give way to either form or matter. But form cannot exist without matter as Aristotle maintained. Besides, form apart from matter is too transcendental an entity. As empiricists, the Stoics denied the reality of transcendetal *form*. Hence, for the Stoics that alone is real which can be known through the senses. Hence, matter alone exists. For the Stoics *nothing incorporeal exists*. But the Stoics maintained that there are only two principles, one entity is active and another is passive. That which acts is a finer material stuff, and, in comparison with it that which is acted upon, which is moved is a coarse kind of matter. But everything is matter. The whole of Nature, God and even the soul of man are all material, for only that which acts and that which is acted upon or moved can only be material. Even emotion is material for it makes man moves. To make materialism simple and clear, the Stoics held that Fire (of Heraclitus) is the primordial matter. God is fire, and, so is the soul of man. Fire permeates and pervades the whole universe. Just as the soul permeates the whole body, and, moved the body, so material God pervades the whole world and brings about the whole, harmonious cosmos. But how can material God can give rise to a harmonious world?

For the Stoics God is material, but He is also the *reason* of the universe, for matter is living and pulsating with life. God for the Stoics is endowed with Will and Intellect. He is the reason and the *logos* of the universe. As a rational will God determines everything. Similarly, man is essentially rational and the *pneuma*, the active and activising spirit and breath of the whole body. Again, God being the rational will has brought about a well-ordered, good and beautiful universe.

This has formed the kernel of the teleological proof for the existence of God.

Further, God is a benevolent, good father of all things, who punishes the evil and rewards the good. Thus, the Stoics accept much of theism. At the same time, the concept of a God as the all-pervading and all-permeating principle of the universe, and, governing it with iron laws, gives rise to pantheism. But how pantheistic metaphysics and theism can go together? This problem was never seriously taken up by the stoics. We shall further find that pantheism supports deterministic will and theism supports free will. How can these two opposite thoughts be reconciled? This has posed a problem not only for the Stoics, but is still a problem in modern theology.

There is another question about matter which is called rational and endowed with intellect and will. Is this not a self-contradictory concept? But the stoics unmindful of the logical knot have built up their cosmology and psychology and their central theme of Ethics on this principle of material reason.

Cosmology: The world follows from divine fire in order of gradual condensation. Fire first gets transformed into air, then water and lastly earth. One can see that is due to gradual lessening of activity and motion. But divine fire permeates all elements, even earth.

In terms of evolutionary scheme reminding one of later idealism, it is said that the divine fire differentiates itself in inorganic nature where laws of nature work blindly. In due course it (inorganic nature) gives rise to vegetable world, where purposiveness can be dimly discerned. In animal kingdom this purposiveness becomes more articulate till we find that in man this purposiveness becomes clear in man's rational purpose and will.

The Stoics believed that the whole cosmos was floating in empty space, moved and animated by the divine fire by which the whole cosmos was permeated. The world undergoes dissolution and periodical recreation in endless cycle. Readers here can mark that it is what has been taught in some Indian systems. But in each recreation, according to the Stoics, the same rational order is repeated with the same detail. The whole process in the universe is strictly determined, even though it is *teleological*. Even human will is strictly determined. But man is said to be free in giving his *assent* to his action. However, whether a man guided by his thought and reasoning assents or not, his action will be the same. In one case, with rational choice, the wise man becomes aware of the divine dispensation and bows his head with resignation to it cheerfully. If one rebels, his action is not going to be different, but he will perish like a fool with grumbling. This teaching of resignation to the sovereign will of God was accepted by Spinoza and Freud, and, is also accepted in Islam. But when a wise man assents to the divine will, then he is said to be working in harmony with Nature or God. Hence, Fate and the *providence* of God are one and the same thing.

True, in Stoicism there is no clear theism, but it held that God has will and intellect, and, that He is good and benevolent. If so, then why there are *natural evils* and also *moral falls.* Here Stoics' solutions appear to be quite penetrating for they have been adopted even in modern philosophy. First, it is pointed out that there are no evils at all. It is only the partial view which looks upon some parts as evil, but from the viewpoint of the whole what appears as evil will be seen as necessary in the perfection of the whole. For example, in any masterful painting shadows are as necessary as light, or, as Kalidas has pointed out that even the shadows in the moon enhance the beauty of the full moon. Here the Stoics hold that the whole is superior to the part. Man as a part of the organic whole will rationally endure every evil as contributing to the larger whole of which he is a willing partner. Secondly, in achieving moral excellence, trials and temptations are necessary so that a life of reason may emerge. As a matter of fact, man's morality lies in remaining steadfast by conquering appetites and passion.

The first negative answer to the presence of evil was taken up by Leibnitz and the modern British idealists. The second affirmative reply has been partly adopted both by A. Flew and J.L. Mackie in their course of discussion.

Psychology: The Stoic psychology is really metaphysical. According to it, man is a composite or a unity of body and soul. This soul isasmuch material as body is; only soul is finer and a spark of the divine fire. The soul pervades the body in the same way in which the divine soul pervades the whole universe. The soul is situated in the heart and guides perception-inference, feeling and will. However, man is essentially rational insofar as he acquires the power of conceptual or logical thought, and, *not* by images or feelings. In other words when he deliberates, weighs the various alternatives and chooses with full awareness of the total situation. Again, a man is said to be free when knowing the laws of nature, acts according to this knowledge. In other words, man is rational when he is under the control of his own reason and in accordance with the reason of the world. A man is said to be free when he acts in accordance with his rational nature or thoughtful choice and assent. A man is free only in the sense of rational self-determination.

According to Stoicism, necessity is completely compatible with human freedom. No doubt man's actions are determined, but they are not determined by something external to them, but by the law of his own being. This view is completely opposed to the view that freedom means indeterminism, or, doing what one wishes, according to one's whims. As against this the Stoics maintain that one should learn to say,' everything may happen as it does'. No doubt we are born dependent subjects, but to obey God is perfect liberty. This is what a Christian says, and, Ramanuja proudly holds.

Stoicism is the ethical philosophy of self-possession and of self-steadfastness, of becoming a willing partner in a rational cosmic drama.

Ethics

The Stoic ethics follows from Stoic metaphysics and psychology. In their ethics, the stoics mention three things, namely *Nature, Virtue* and *Duty*. By 'nature', the Stoics mean that it is working according to laws and all the processes within it are fully determined. Hence, nature means 'necessity'. Secondly, this nature is the *logos* of the world and is fully rational. Man is a part of world-reason to which he is bound by necessity (and he has no option but) to obey the natural laws. Man is said to be rational, when he submits himself to his own rational nature. However, the Stoic psychology tells him that man is not only rational, but there is something external to him, namely,

(a) Appetites, passion and emotions which disturb the rational working of man.

(b) Fortune, riches, poverty, disease, health etc., over which man has no control.

What did Aristotle say about the morality of a good man?

According to Aristotle, man *has not to extirpate* feeling, impulses and appetites, but he has to control and regulate them by means of his reason. For Aristotle, man has not to pursue pleasure and avoid pain, for feeling is *not* the direct object of moral pursuits. Feeling is a necessary consequence or accompaniment of an action.

Secondly, Aristotle also did not set aside fortune or health or friends, for they are helpful means in the pursuit of a good life. Stoic ethics is opposed to Aristotle's views.

Stoicism has two phases. The first phase is nearer cynicism, and, the second form lies in its moderation or softened modification. The first phase may be called rigorous. Hence, in its first rigorous form the Stoics maintained the following:

Asceticism: Since appetites and emotions are external to the rational nature of man, and, they serve as difficulties and disturbances in the exercise of rational morality, so they have to be annihilated. Therefore, a truly wise man has to be an *ascetic*. Should we help a man or our friend out of pity? Stoics would say 'no', not out of pity, for 'pity' is feeling which is external to the rational nature of man.

The second key word of the Stoics is *Virtue*. Virtue means working according to conceptual thought through deliberation. Of course, Aristotle gave a very important theory here. According to Aristotle, impulses and appetites have to be regulated and controlled by reason. By this he meant that *the will* of man gets fully educated and becomes fully rational. But in *contrast*, for the Stoics, impulses and emotions have to be annihilated and a wise man has to work with the help of reason alone. Nature or God is the *logos* of the universe. So a wise man is he who acts according to his reason alone. By habitual exercise of will with the help of reason alone man becomes a part of the rational Nature or world-reason. Hence, a wise man alone is virtuous and all others are fools. Therefore, there is absolute chasm between wise men and fools. And there is no intermediate class between the wise and the fool.

However, in the modified form later on, the rigour of morality was softened.

On being questioned about the examples of wise men, they could mention only a few names of Socrates and Diogenes the cynic. But are you Mr. Stoic wise or foolish? He could not say that he was either the one or the other. Here again the Stoics had to retreat to a moderate view. The Stoics were only seekers after wisdom and virtue. They formed an intermediate class of proficient men on the way to *improvement.*

Further, the Stoics maintained that *virtue is really one*, for it is a matter of mental disposition and character of being guided by reason alone. This doctrine strengthens the rigorous division of men in the two absolute compartments of virtuous and fools. However, soon the doctrine of virtue led to another key-word 'duty'.

'Duty' really means the same thing as virtue. However, it means moral act in accordance with rational, all-embracing Nature in which the rational man lives in full harmony with Nature. Here in his performance of duty a wise man is not only in his own rational nature and in his full command by annihilating his impulses, but he feels that in his moral 'ought', he is experiencing a command and an imperative from his higher self called God. Thus, the Stoics in their ethical emphasis on 'duty' contained the essential of Kantian rigorism.

Here again the Stoics later on modified their opinion. They found that along with primary good or duty there are cases of secondary good. Virtue or duty in itself is the primary good, but in relation to this there are secondary goods or duties. They drew a distinction between three kinds of *indifferents*. At the first rigorous phase, the stoics had maintained that, that alone is virtue which is in accordance with world-reason is to be called duty. Further that which is against nature and human reason, or, that which hinders virtue is *vice*. But in the modified, mild phase, the Stoics held that out of the three kinds of indifferents, that kind of indifferents has to be allowed which is helpful in the acquisition of virtue. For example, fortune, riches can be allowed as *secondary* good. However, the immoderate impulses, namely, pleasure, desire, grief and fear are harmful indifferents, and, they have to be eradicated. All else, besides secondary good and avoidable indifferents, are absolutely indifferents. To the end, the Stoics maintained the primacy of freedom from disturbing passions. But in modified form, the stoics permitted courageous and temperate life.

Society and Politics

For the Stoics there is one logos or reason which has brought about one well organized, well-ordered whole in which each part is well adapted to function for the health of this one world. This world follows from one God and one Law which governs the whole system called the universe. In this world, man has come into being so that he may co-operate with the functioning of this world and society. The society is not an accidental product, but it has come into being to serve God's rational purpose, and, men in this world are in essence rational. Each man becomes rational by remaining in self-possession, unruffled by appetites, emotions and irrational impulses. All men are essentially rational and they have to become and realize their rational nature by becoming fully conscious of the rational principles in nature and society. As essentially rational, men form so many units of one rational State. Nay, all men as essentially rational form one brotherhood.

As the society is divinely established, so as stoic has not only to preserve himself, but to preserve the whole human species. So he has to carry out his family life, and, help his fellow-men. As a rational being a man will perform his duties in the society, but this duty should not be prompted and vitiated by any desire or impulses. A rational man who has become aware of the higher principle following from God, will perform his duties towards society, but without any sense of patriotism e.g., for the sake of duty alone. He will maintain a family, but without affection for children and wife. He will perform his duties conscientiously as so many imperatives of God, without being influenced by any emotion. Quoting the words of Seneca, A.K. Rogers states thus :

> I will bear in mind that the world is my native city, that its governors are the gods, and that they stand above and around me criticising whatever I do or say.[1]

The whole thing is a grand precursor of Kant's rigorous ethics of duty for duty's sake, of universal brotherhood of men, all belonging not to kingdom of means, but of ends. Recognizing that each man is equally rational in essence, there will be justice to all, even the slaves.

Thus the Stoics could reach the highest and ripest conception of the ethical life. As society was taken as the institution set by the world-reason, and as all men were brothers, so this society is the One State, and all men are citizens on equal footing of this world of universal reason. So the stoics taught the doctrine of one world-citizenship and cosmopolitanism. But this cosmopolitanism was an ethical concept for the Greeks. This has been well put in by Emperor Aurelius :

> My nature is rational and social, and my city and my country, so far as I am Antonius, is Rome, but so far as I am a man, it is the world.[2]

Later on, with rise in power and might, the Roman became aware of their historical mission to establish one rational and civilized State of the world as a whole. Later on Alexander, Napoleon, Britishers and Hitler, were all influenced by the idea of the Stoics, to establish one kingdom of values, according to their mission. We must not forget the proud words of W. Churchill, 'It is the burden of the white men to civilize the native states.'

---

1   A.K. Rogers, *A Student's History of Philosophy*, p. 147.

2. *Ibid.*, p. 145.

Religion

It has already been stated that the universe is the expression of the world-reason, and, as such it is a beautiful and well-ordered world. Man is also a part to fulfil the purpose of this world-reason which may be also called world-will and Intellect. As such man has to know God and pattern his will accordingly by making his will divine, by surrounding his will to Divine Will.

Though the Stoics accept the existence of God because of the design in the world and His providence, yet they reject the superstitious and anthropological view of God. For the first time in the history of religious philosophy, they try to treat the superstitious view of God as purely allegorical. However, this shows that mankind in general believe in the existence of God. Hence His existence rests on *consensum gentium*.

For the Stoics God is a necessary support of morality and in this respect too they are the precursor of modern theology according to which religion is the fulfilment of moral demands. God Himself is moral, and, so a rational man subordinating his will to God cannot but be moral. Hence, morality becomes resignation to the divine will, or, to the inevitable rational order.

EPICURUS AND EPICUREANISM

Introduction: Epicurus (c.341 B.C.-270) was the founder of Epicureanism. He combined his ethical philosophy with the atomic materialsim of Democritus and with the Cyrenaicism of Aristippus. The term 'Epicureanism' has been greatly misunderstood as a philosophy of licentiousness, which certainly it is *not*. On the face of it, many tenets and aphorisms of Epicureanism are verbally the same as those of Stoicism. For example,

(1) The ethical ideal is happiness which is reduced ultimately to having a serene and calm mind.
(2) Live according to nature.
(3) Virtue is One.
(4) Materialism.
(5) World-citizenship.
(6) A life of few desires and wants.
(7) An insistence on the necessity of a group of friends.

Of course, the *interpretations of these tenets and aphorisms are* entirely different from those of Stoicism. Why? Because the metaphysics and epistemology and their ethical theories are entirely different. Therefore, 'Stoicism' is, popularly interpreted as a philosophy of stern rigorism, behoving a brave and courageous man who stifles emotions and lives a life of dutifulness. As opposed to this, Epicureanism is understood as a philosophy of ethical licentiousness, which it is not. Hence, we have to start with Epicurean epistemology which is as empirical in theory as Stoic epistemology is.

Semi-Socratic and Greco-Roman Ethics

Epistemology: The Epicureans admitted that knowledge is based on perception, which in this context, is as evident as pain or pleasure is in our felt experience. As the Epicureans accepted atomic materialism, so they also admitted, that in perception, the images of external things are received. For the Epicureans perception at times may yield illusory knowledge, but this is due either to judgment or weak images or distorted images or some defect in the sense-organs. But in general our perception is reliable. In order to be sure we have to repeat the observation of things by ourselves as well. No doubt without concepts, there can be no knowledge. The Epicureans also believe, like Democritus, that empirical knowledge is possible. But against Plato, the Epicureans think that universal ideas or concepts refer to a class of similar objects or concrete particular things, but the universal ideas are neither independent of these concrete particulars, nor are they in things. They are merely verbal marks to enable us to think about the class of particular things. Hence, the Epicureans of foreshadowed medieval *nominalism* and also modern empiricism.

As the Epicureans held that knowledge is true of sensible things alone, they may be said to be the forerunners of modern positivism. But in their metaphysics, on Epicureans accepted the reality of invisible, indivisible atoms. Are they based and they aces? No. The reason is that the Epicureans were not really scientists, because it was convenientomistic materialism of Democritus and Leukippus, was the pupil of Nausiphanes the at.. Here we must also keep in mind that Epicurus simply a matter of his education and was not a ....er of his own scientific investigation. For this reason, Epicurus introduced unscientific matter in the atomism of Democritus.

Metaphysics: Adopting the atomistic materialism, Epicurus assumed that the world is constituted of indestructible, indivisible, unchangeable atoms.

Atoms are eternally self-moved mobile units. They move freely in empty space, but there is no space in the body of the atoms themselves. For this reason they are said to be indivisible, or uncuttable. They have however shape and size. But the Epicureans added another characteristic of *weight*. According to the Epicureans, atoms keep on falling in a straight line. But if they continue to fall in the same straight and parallel lines, then there cannot be any collision of them, and, without collision they cannot combine in various combinations, giving rise to various things. But there are various combinations constituting various things. So in order to explain collision between the atoms, Epicurus assumed two things. First, as atoms have various weight, so the heavier atoms fall with greater speed than the lighter ones and so the heavier atoms overrun the lighter ones and collide. But this was an unscientific assumption, since in a vacuum all things fall with the same speed. Epicurus again added that atoms 'swerve' in their vertical fall and so they come in clash with other atoms. Hence atoms now become endowed with spontaneity and their movements come to be endowed with chance. Man too being endowed with finer and more mobile atoms having swerving and spontaneous movement give rise to possible human free will. Hence, human beings are not fully determined by mechanical forces, but in moral actions they are *free*.

The atomistic materialism accepts mechanical necessity and so for it is certainly scientific. But in morality, unless man is free, he cannot be punished for moral lapses or rewarded for the performance of duty. Hence, there is a clash in Epicureanism between its atomistic metaphysics and ethical theory.

The Epicureans were also the forerunners of organic evolution like their predecessors Anaximander and Empedocles. According to the Epicureans, living organisms first arose from earth, and, were of various shapes with their limbs not adapted either to the body or the environment. Only those organisms have survived which have become adapted to the environment. Men too have emerged in the same way. They have not been created by any gods or God.

No doubt men have souls constituted of fine, minute, round and speedy atoms. The soul having its seat in the heart rules the will and desires of men. The gentle impact of clear images of things give rise to true knowledge and coarser ones, with violent impacts of images give rise to disturbing impulses. Here, the Epicureans largely follow the psychological origin of knowledge and impulses on the basis of the atomistic theory.

On the basis of their metaphysics, briefly mentioned here, we the ethical philosophy of the Epicureans.

Ethics

The Epicureans developed the Cyrenaicism of Aristippus. For Aristippus, pleasure of the body and of the moment is what man should seek. Epicureans accepted that man seeks pleasure and avoids pain, almost instinctively. So the good of man lies in the pursuit of pleasure and the avoidance of pain. So for, the Epicureans are one with Aristippus. But they began to differ from Cyrenaicism and even went beyond it.

For the Epicureans the pleasure of the moment, transitory pleasure should be set aside in favour of more enduring pleasure for life as a whole. As such the pleasure of the *present now* should be sacrificed if it is going to be followed by greater pain. Again the pain of the moment should be endured if it is likely to be followed by greater pleasure. Further, Epicurus found that there is no distinction between higher and lower pleasures, but the pleasure of mind is to be preferred to bodily pleasure, for

1. Mental pleasure is more enduring than bodily pleasure. The bodily pleasure lasts only at the moment it is enjoyed. In contrast, mental pleasure lasts much longer. Here through memory, the past pleasure can be ruminated upon, and, pleasure of the future can be anticipated. Thus, by memory and anticipation, mental pleasure becomes far more enduring than transitory bodily, pleasure.

2. Besides, bodily pleasure is likely to be followed by pain more frequently than mental pleasure. For example, the pleasure of food and drink, and of lust is likely to be followed by bodily suffering and even by lasting pain.
3. Further, without the participation of mind, even the bodily pleasure cannot be enjoyed.

Again, Epicurus found that perhaps a life of positive pleasure is not possible, but negative pleasure is more desirable. Instead of trying to attain positive pleasure, it is more desirable to avoid pain. A wise man for the Epicureans is one who enjoys imperturbability (*ataraxia*). One should try independence of the world, for the external world cannot be controlled. But happiness within one's own self can be attained. He can become master of his own self by the control of his emotions or passions, i.e., by attaining to *apathy*. This is the state of painless rest, of mental equipoise and serenity. Now there are three kinds of wants and a wise man requires an insight into them. Some wants are indispensable even for a wise man. They are natural and inevitable, e.g., appetite for food, rest and sleep. And even a wise man cannot avoid them. Again, some wants are merely conventional and artificial, e.g., cosmetics for women, television set or even electricity. A wise man can afford to get away from them. In between the two there are a great many things which may add to the happiness of a wise man. A wise man can enjoy some of them, if their satisfaction does not disturb the equanimity of his mind.

Above all Epicurus prized mental joys much more than bodily pleasure. A wise man is he whose wants are few, Epicurus was satisfied with bread and water alone. The Epicureans loved the aesthetic refinement of life. This life meant refined conversation between friends, but this did not mean strenuous scientific pursuits. Mathematics, logic, rhetoric; the theories of music and art, the researches of historians and philologists, and all such pursuits, were disparaged by the Epicureans. What they cared for was peace of mind, undisturbed by any fear of death, fate and gods.

People are afraid of what will happen to them after they die. They imagine that they will be punished in the future for their misdeeds in the present life. Epicurus calmed their minds by denying the survival of men after their death. Man and his soul are formed by the combination of atoms. At the time of death, all atoms are dissolved and so there can be no survival. So there can be no fear of death and the vicissitudes of after-life.

When we are, death is not yet; and where death comes, there we are not.

Yes, there are gods. They are like human beings. They eat and drink without bothering about men. Hence they neither reward nor punish men. Every god is really a projection of what a thinker thinks of being an ideal man, so the gods of the Epicureans are just what they themselves desire to be.

Lastly, men think that they are working under some fate from which they cannot run away. Against this, the Epicureans taught the doctrine of free will. Man is not working under any Fate, for the Epicureans; man by virtue of his own free will can become the master of his own fate and can make his life happy.

Social and Public Life

Epicurus has explicitly accepted pleasure as the end of morality. But pleasure is a matter of feeling, and, feeling can be subjective only. Rama can feel pleasure and pain all by himself, and, his wife, children and friends, no matter however much they may sympathise with him, they *cannot share* his pleasure or pain. At most they can have only intellectual understanding of Rama's pleasure or pain. As such any insistence on making hedonistic standard of morality is bound to be a subjective standard. Therefore, Epicurus could have consistently upheld that *egoistic* pleasure alone can be the standard of morality. For this reason, consistently Epicurus could not have maintained any commitment to social or public life. And indeed this is the case.

The Ecpicureans seemed to have accepted the Sophist's maxim of *homo mensura*. For the Sophist society is not a social structure, but it has come into being as a result of a *social contract* between the individuals for their mutual advantage and protection. This was later on held by Rousseu. But there is nothing sacred about the social convention. Some Epicureans held that there is nothing wrong if a wise man commits a social crime for some advantage, with the prospect of not being discovered and punished. If he desists at all then he does so because of his likely uneasy conscience. Hence, for the Epicureans there is no logical basis for social and political moral rectitude.

But inconsistently enough, the Epicureans held the importance of friendship. It could be maintained on the utilitarian ground of self-protection and mutual helpfulness. Their *atomistic materialism and hedonistic ethics could have supported only individualism.*

The Epicurean theory stands in sharp contrast of Aristotle and Plato with regard to social and political morality. For Aristotle one's moral life becomes complete only by participating in the performance of duty in the State. In contrast, for the Epicurean social and political life is based on expediency and utility. Except for a cheerful frame of mind without any pain, and, aesthetic friendship, the Epicureans have no place for heroism and sacrifice for the well-being of society and State. They have no place for virtue, patriotism and duty for duty's Sake. Their typical statement is :

It is not our business to work for crowns by saving the Greeks, but to enjoy ourselves in good eating and drinking.

Their sickly way of life is contained in the following instructions :

Eat little, for fear of indigestion : drink little, for fear of next morning; eschew politics and love and all violently passionate activities; . . . .

Though Stoicism and Epicureanism use more or less kindred statements, yet their inner interpretation is almost opposed and different, so let us try to elucidates their famous statements.

Epicureanism and Stoicism (A Comparative Study)

1. Both the Epicureans and the Stoics are materialistic. The Epicureans favour atomistic materialism of Democritus, and the Stoics favour rational materialism. But the Epicureans become inconsistent by allowing spontaneity to atoms and freedom of will to man on account of the spontaneity in atoms constituting man. Again, the Stoics also become inconsistent in endowing matter with rationality and material God with intellect and will, benevolence and providential care for men.

2. Again, both the Epicureans and the Stoics come to regard the serene mind as the end of ethical life. Both of them disregard the claims of desires, and the ataraxia of Epicureanism and asceticism of the other are very similar. But the different interpretations of 'the disregard of pleasures' are also remarkable. The *ataraxia* or *apathy* of the Epicureans follows from the fact that in the end, they realised that the positive pleasure is difficult to obtain, but the negative principle of the absence of pain is more feasible. They cared for painless rest which comes from having fewer wants and avoiding pursuits of pleasure.

The Stoics disregarded the claims of pleasure and avoidance of pain, for both desires are external to the essentially rational nature of man. Hence, they tried to live by annihilating desires. For them virtue means living according to reason, by knowing the rational laws of nature, of God, and even of man. Hence, they insisted on becoming *ascetic* by extirpating passion, and, emotionlessness by discarding emotion. But by adhering fast to duty for the sake of duty, they could consistently maintain strict rigorism.

3. Both give the call to *live according to Nature*. But their meaning of nature is poles apart. With the Epicureans 'nature' has only metaphysical and theological use. They used atomistic materialism to show that the world has not been created by gods or God, and that in after-life there is not going to be any judgment, for atoms constituting man utterly dissolve, and, there is no possibility of man's survival. In order to show that the world has not been created by God, they took an anti-teleological stand. But the Epicureans were not interested in the scientific investigation of nature, which meant for them mental disturbance. Instead of establishing that in nature there is a reign of law, they taught the spurious doctrine of the spontaneity of atoms and free will of man.

On the contrary, the Stoics taught that Nature is rational through and through. And Nature is an organized world as a whole. Man and things of nature in their essence are rational. So Nature and God have produced this well-ordered world.

Hence Nature works teleologically.

Of course, the Stoics were also inconsistent inasmuch as in their metaphysics they maintained that fire permeated all things. So their metaphysics was pantheistic. But their theistic pro~~~ ~~~ endowed God with intellect, will and purposiveness in opposition to metaphysical determinism and mechanism.

The metaphysics of the Epicureans is mechanistic and deterministic. But in ethics they accept that men are free. Hence, here metaphysics and ethics did not go well together. Therefore, the consequences of the aphorism 'live according to Nature' meant very different stands for them with regard to 'Society and Politics'.

4. The Epicureans accepted *egoistic* hedonism and atomistic individualism. For them, society is just a conventional development out of contract by the individuals for their self-protection and individualistic advantages. Hence, the Epicureans had no moral obligation towards society and the State.

In contrast, the Stoics found that man and Nature are both rational and men are the inseparable parts of the same organism called Nature. It is nature which has given rise to man, well-ordered universe and the society. Hence, it is the duty of man to fulfil his obligation to society and the world. Consistently with their stand, the Stoics maintained their doctrine of world-brotherhood and world-citizenship.

5. Yes, both the Stoics and Epicureans taught the doctrine of world-citizenship. But in the case of Epicureans, they supported the doctrine of world-citizenship because they did not like to belong to any one community. Hence, their doctrine of world-citizenship is a negative principle.

In contrast, for the Stoics it is a rational thing to promote world-citizenship, for the world and man are created by world-reason and which is the same in man and the world. Hence, it is a rational thing for a Stoic to become a member of the rational world.

6. Both stress the *need of few wants*. But their reasons are quite different for this statement. Epicurus is said to have lived on simple bread and water. The reason for having few wants was that by multiplying one's wants, one is likely to lose one's peace of mind. The end of living, for the Epicureans, is to live without fear and pain. He favours a life of *apathy* and ataraxia. For the Epicureans any desires for wealth and honour are futile. Marriage and children cause more pain than pleasure.

In contrast, for the Stoics, appetites and pain are external to the essential nature of man which is reason. So desires have to be annihilated. Again, fortune, wealth and honours are not within the control of men. So the Stoics recommended a life of withdrawal from these good things of life. So man of reason has to stifle desires in order to lead a life of self-possession.

The Sceptics and Scepticism

Scepticism is the philosophy which doubts and denies the possibility of knowledge, and despairs of attaining truth. The germs of scepticism are clearly discernible in the Sophists' epistemology, ethics and religion. For example, Gorgias laid down three of his sceptical tenets:

1. There is nothing.
2. Even if there be anything, it cannot be known.
3. Whatever knowledge be there it cannot be communicated.

Similarly, the Sophists hold that knowledge is perception and, this knowledge is relative and variable from person to person, ending in the doctrine of *homo mensura*. Besides in ontology, Heraclitus emphasized 'Becoming' and denied possibility of Being. As against this, Parmenides emphasized that human beings Becoming. Hence, these opposed views gave way. *Parmenides* could not define the are entitled to 'Opinions' only. Further, lead to the doctrine that no morality is concepts of Justice and Good and Epicureans had come finally to the doctrine possible. Nay, both and emotionlessness.

of *ataraxis* not of all these ontological, epistemological and ethical teachings leads to scepticism.

The founder of scepticism as a form of philosophy is said to be Pyrrho (c. 365-270 B.C.). Even the *Academics* of Plato accepted scepticism best represented by Arcesilaus (315-341 B.C.) and Carneades (213-129 B.C.) and Aenesidemus (perhaps first century B.C.).

Pyrrho asked and other sceptics believed that scepticism will lead to happiness. Hence scepticism was used as a means to ethical end. Pyrrho asked three questions :

1. What things are, end, how are they constituted?
2. How are we related to these things?
3. And what should be our attitude to these things?

Those questions are directed to the philosophy of stoicism and its epistemological tenets. We have already seen that the Stoics were empiricists. For them knowledge begins with perceptions, and, even the Epicureans accepted empirical theory of knowledge. But can we know things through sensation? This is the first question to be answered.

But by this time the criticism of sensationism was quite clear. Sensations vary with persons, which was made clear by the Sophist doctrine of *homo mensura*. So we can have only opinion, and not knowledge of things.

Besides, if we are confined to sensations alone and can never go out of our sensations to compare them with the eternal things of which they are the sensations, then how can we know whether these sensations are true or not? Of course, it has been held by the Stoics that true perceptions are intense, clear and vivid. As against this subjective conviction about the true sensation, the sceptics replied that even the deceptive perceptions are as clear, vivid and intense as are the so-called true perceptions. So human beings cannot know the true nature of things (Carneades).

But why not knowledge based on inference be counted as proved and valid? Well, the only form of inference, known to the sceptics was syllogism. Here the conclusion is based on premises, and, these premises on further wider premises. But this way of syllogistic proving will ultimately lead to *regressus ad infinitum.* Secondly, the sceptics brought another objection against syllogism, which was later on pressed forward by John S. Mill. It was pointed by the sceptics that the conclusion is proved with the help of the premises, but the premise itself is proved by the

      All men e.g.,

      Rama is a man,

    ∴ Rama is mortal.

Here the major premise is necessary to prove is mortal', we cannot say '*All* men are mortal'. Therefore mortal'. But unless 'Rama 'arguing in a circle'.   suffers from

Therefore, the net conclusion is, that we cannot have knowledge of anything either through sensation or inference. All that we can claim is that we can have only *opinion.* At most, we can say a particular *appears* to me as *X* or *Y.* But we cannot say that this thing *is* either *x* or *y. Probability* alone is our guide. Here we cannot have knowledge which can be our guide. Should we suspend our judgment? And as without ideas, impinging on our will, we cannot act, then should we suspend our action and remain in *ataraxia*?

Some of the sceptics found that *suspense* of judgment and consequently complete *ataraxia* cannot be maintained. Life demands action and a principle of conduct. Hence, they maintained that *probability* can be accepted as a guide to action. Carneades worked out a theory of probability. The lowest form of probability is based on unclear clearness and that also on a single perception. A higher degree of probability is attained when it is based on perceptions which can be harmoniously connected with previous ideas. Lastly the highest probability is reached when the perception agrees with a whole system of ideas, reached through constant verification. Thus, probability rises from isolated perception to the logical system of sciences. This is the forerunner of the harmony theory of truth advanced by Joachim and other idealists belonging to the 20th century. However, for the sceptics, the highest degree of probability can be the guide of life, even though probability falls short of certainty and truth.

In support of Scepticism, Aenesidemus, a very late sceptic, has advanced ten arguments, which can be really reduced to 2-3 arguments only. They are as follow:

1.   Feelings and perceptions of men differ.
2.   Men have physical and mental differences, which make things appear different to them.
3.   The different senses give different impressions of things.
4.   Our perceptions depend on our physical and intellectual conditions at the

time of perception.

5. Things appear different in different positions, and at different distances.
6. Perception is never direct, but always through a medium. For example, we see things through the air (and certainly through the light in the case of vision).
7. Things appear different according to variations in their quantity, colour, motion, and temperature.
8. A thing impresses us differently when it is familiar and when it is unfamiliar.
9. All supposed knowledge is predication. All predicates give us only the relation of things to other things or to ourselves ; they never tell us what the thing in itself is.

   (Bergson tells us that knowledge is through universal concepts. Concepts tell us what a thing has in common with others, but never what a thing is in itself.)
10. The opinions and customs of men are different in different countries.

Windelband, has thus summarised (the arguments)[1]:

Perceptions differ with different men, according to their customs and development at different stages of their lives, and in relation to their different relation to various things and individuals. *Objects* too differ in their internal changes, and, in relation to different media through which they appear to men. Hence, men can have no true and direct knowledge of things.

Even the opinions which men form with regard to objects vary and are but relative. At most these opinions can be *probable* only. Even inference is shot through with contradiction. The best form of inference then known was syllogism, and, syllogism suffers from

1. *Regressus ad infinitum* (as already explained).
2. *Petio principii* or arguing in a circle (as already explained).
3. As most hypothetically true, i.e., if the premises are true, then the conclusion is true. But quite obviously hypothetical truth can never be regarded as categorically true.

From their epistemological scepticism, the sceptics drew the ethical conclusion of *ataraxia*. For them, moral opinions are based on customs and convention, and, none of them are reliable. The best thing for them, therefore, was to suspend their judgments, and, without judgments there can be no movement of will and action. Hence, by not taking any action, they will be able to enjoy their peace of mind. Hence, their *attitude to things* will be of withdrawal from the events of life, and, an attitude of indifference and resignation to the inevitable flow of things.

Attack on the Stoic view of Religion

Carneades attacked the Stoic view of God, which in the first instance was based

---

1. W. Windelband, *A History of Philosophy*, pp. 220-21.

teleologically as following from the well-ordered universe. Carneades rejected the rational on-goings of the world and did not accept that the world was beautiful and well-ordered. Further, even if it be taken for granted that the world is well-ordered, it does not follow that it has been created by God. Hume and others maintained later on that the world has evolved through chance adaptation of parts to the whole.

Again, if there be a god without sensation and feeling, then he is of no concern to human beings. But if He has, then He will be as changeable as *feelings are*. So He fails to be eternal.

Further if God is corporeal, as the Stoics maintain, then like all other corporeal things, He will be perishable. On the other hand, if God is incorporeal, then He will be without feeling and will, and, so there can be no God at all (as was maintained by the Epicureans) for human beings. If, however, God is incorporeal and is endowed with moral values, then He will become finite by being limited by moral limits. If not moral, then He will be inferior to men. Some of these arguments have been adopted and adapted by the scoffers of God.

NEO-PLATONISM

Neoplatonism and Greek Philosophy

Neoplatonism is the name given to a religious mystic philosophy in which sense-perception, human discursive thought pave the way for *feeling*. We are said to know the absolute reality, the ineffable being by *becoming what it is* by means of contemplation, meditation and ecstasy. This will appear to remind the Indian reader of advaitic *nididhyasana* (meditation). The mystic philosophy of religion never appeared in a systematic form before the rise of neo-Platonism. But is it totally un-Greek and un-European? It may appear so in the eyes of Europeans today for whom scientism is the only form of accredited philosophy, but it is neither un-Greek nor un-European for the following reasons:

1. We have already made mention of Orphism which made deep influence on Pythagoras, Socrates and Plato. Much of Orphism is found in neo-Platonism. If Pythagoras and Plato are Greek, then neo-Platonism is.

2. Socrates experienced ecstasy and used to hear the voice of *daimon*. These elements of mysticism are found in neo-Platonism. If Socrates is Greek, so is neo-Platonism.

3. Plato is certainly most Greek and most European and the very name neo-*Platonism* has been borrowed from his philosophy. Plato talks of bondage and release. Plato teaches to depreciate the senses and recommends the human intellect to get a glimpse of 'the Good' (*Phaedo* 66) and even the mortification of the body with a view to attaining truth (*Rep.* 7.517 c). Plato also states the need of purification of the body for the release of imprisoned soul (*Phaedo*, 82c,d). And what does neo-Platonism does? It systematises these thoughts into a system. Why

should it be called un-Greek?

4. Neo-Platonism includes within its system the doctrine of 'world-soul' of Stoicism, Being of Eleaticism, 'Nous' of Anaxagoras and 'matter' of Plato-Aristotle. Neo-Platonism is certainly Greek, but it also includes much of oriental Judaism and even Indian advaitism.

For us, neo-Platonism is a bridge between East and West. Instead of dividing East from West, neo-Platonism brings them together to take a plunge into a new creative venture to become more than what a world-bound human spirit is, at the present time.

Neo-Platonism came to be established by Plotinus (c. 205-270 A.D.) after it was prepared for its reception by Philo, the Jew theologian (30 B.C.-50 A.D.).

Philo (30 B.C.-50 A.D.)

Philo was a Jew who came of a priestly class and who fully utilized the Greek thought into his system. He introduced a three-tiered *Ontology* matched with a three-levelled *epistemology*.

Ontology: I. Absolutely transcendent God.

II. World-logos.

III. Matter.

Epistemology: 1. Pure thought, Intelligence. We know God through inner illumination and revelation.

2. Through the *logos* within each man.

3. Sense-perception, for knowing plurality of particular things.

For Philo, God is the absolute, beyond ordinary thought, above human knowledge and virtue. Is He a human being that man should argue with Him? God is essentially unknowable.

Can you search out the deep things of God?

Can you find out the limits of the Almighty? (*Job.* 11.7)

But through his highest Intelligence man knows this much that *He* is, but *not what He is,* reminding one of Exodus 3.14 (Yahwe declared, 'I am that I am'). Thus, the absolute God of Philo is just his belief in his pure monotheism.

But God, the Absolute is so pure that He cannot be contaminated by the world. He is not the Creator God. How can there be any establishment of a relation between the Absolute God and the world? Philo makes use of the angels and demons of Judaism and mixes it with the Stoic notion of a world-soul and Platonic Ideas to serve as the intermediary between the Absolute God and the world. The intermediary is known as the Logos, the Divine Reason or wisdom. Human beings know through the logos in them. Here too one is reminded of the Stoic doctrine of the co-substantiality between man and the world-logos. This logos is also known as 'the first-born son of God, the image of God'. Here Philo expresses the relationship of the Absolute with the world, through the metaphor of 'radiation'. Just as the Sun radiates itself through its rays, so the world is the radiation of the Absolute God. This term 'radiation' was transformed into the doctrine of *emanation* of Plotinus.

This intermediary as the world-soul and Ideas requires a third thing called matter into which the ideas may take shape. Hence, this world is the creation of the visible things. Time has been created along with the world, but the relation between the Absolute and the world-soul is eternal.

The world-soul is good. Hence, matter is the source of evil. In man, his body is the cause of evil in him. Hence, man can release himself from his body by the annihilation of his appetites and passion, as was taught by the Stoics. But can man by his own effort get rid of his bodily desires? Man requires divine help. God must illumine the seeker. In the hour of ecstasy, the seeker apprehends the divine. Thus, through ascetic practices man prepares himself for the divine vision, and, in his ecstasy, he apprehends him. Thus, asceticism and mysticism were the two ways of apprehending God.

Philo prepared the ground for Plotinus by laying down the path to ecstasy, first by withdrawal into oneself, then by the flight of the ego and the total negation of senses, human reason and his being. These steps were taken up by Plotinus.

Plotinus (c. 205-270 A.D.)

Plotinus was born in Lycopolis, Egypt and studied philosophy in Alexandria under Ammonius Saecas. Alexandra was a big cosmopolitan city where Greek, Roman and Hebrew thought intermingled. Here was a scientific museum with its celebrated library which contained 700,000 volumes.

The religious philosophy of neo-Platonism is a systemised philosophy of Philo, the Jew. This neoplatonism is largely based on the teachings of Plato. Hence, the name of neoplatonism. Further, it contained the Greco-Jewish philosophy of Philo. Besides, the doctrine of neo-Phythagoreanism also entered into neo-Platonism with regard to the transmigration of soul. Plotinus also accompanied Emperor Gordian III in his expedition against the Persians, with a view to meeting the Indian saints and mystics. Unfortunately the Emperor was assassinated by his own army and so Plotinus had to return. But it is noted that he met the Indian mystics in Persia and most probably learnt their doctrine of indescribable Brahman and the pathway to Brahma-realization. Certainly there is a great deal of kinship between advaitism and neoplatonism.

Plotinus returned to Rome about 243 A.D. and established his school there. He wrote his philosophy at the age of 50. After the death of Plotinus, his pupil Porphyry (232-304 A.D.) revised and systematised his philosophy in six Enneads.

Philosophy

Plotinus established the Trinity consisting of *One* absolute God, *Nous* (thought, mind and reason), and world-soul.

The absolute God is One, a unity beyond multiplicity, discursive thought, will and is absolutely indeterminate. No predicate can describe Him, for every predicate will finitize Him.[1] No category of 'unity' or 'existence', strictly speaking, can be applied to Him. We can say *What He is not;* we cannot say *what He is.* The whole litany of 'Noes' can be applied to Him[2]. Being immutable, God cannot be described as *creator.* Every description of God can be only 'analogical'.[3]

Though 'creation' cannot be attributed to God, yet an analogous expression can be used here, which is known as *emanation.* Just as fragrance is emitted by the rose, so other entities emanate from God. God is super-perfect. There is an abundance of His goodness and perfection which *overflows* or radiates from Him. Just as the rays of the Sun radiate from it the Sun without any diminution of its energy, so Nous and world-soul emanate from God without losing his perfection. God, Nous and world-soul are One in essence, but fading-out of light begins after the creation of the world of particular things and human beings,[4] from the world-soul.

The universe is an overflow of God's infinite power, without any loss of his perfection. On the contrary 'creation' means intention and will on the part of the creator. But for Plotinus, God is absolute, constant and eternally the same. Hence, Plotinus advances the doctrine of *emanation* in the place of *creation.* If God be the emanational cause, then the universe, the effect does not limit the cause. But as the light fades off in the distance, so by the time and distance from the world-soul explains the darkness into which matter falls.

From God or the One there is the emanation of Nous, which means thought, mind and reason. Only this thought is not discursive. The One is beyond thought and thought emanates from the One. However, the thought which characterizes *Nous*, is not discursive. It is intuitive. Nous looks upward towards the One and has an intuitive grasp of Him. But it also thinks itself as its object of thought. In other words, it is thought of thought, as the *actus purus* of Aristotle has been called.

From *Nous* emanates world-soul from where the fading out of divine light starts. This world-soul is not in time. It is incorporeal and indivisible. It has twofold nature. In one phase it looks upward towards *nous*, and, also downward towards Nature. The world-soul requires matter on which to act and which is to be formed. This *matter* has neither form nor any quality. It is darkness, farthest away from God and so matter stands as the fading out of the divine light. However,

---

1. Here one is reminded of Spinoza's aphorism 'every determination is negation'.
2. Romain Rolland, *The Life of Vivekananda*, p. 353. Here again one is reminded of, *neti* in the Upanishads.
3. Here one is reminded of St. Thomas Aquinas 's *A analogia entis.*

there are individual souls in the world-soul and they impress their ideas ultimately derived from Ideas in divine Intelligence, upon matter to create sensible objects. The spatial arrangement of things is due to matter; but beauty, order and unity of things in the universe are due to the reflected Intelligence of the world-soul.

The world-soul creates *Nature* and also Time in the creative act. Hence, Time and the world come together, which view was later on, held by St. Augustine. The whole process of emanation from One to the world-soul through Nous is regarded as logical and not temporal. Hence, at times, like Aristotle, Plotinus regards the world eternal. But at time he subscribes to the periodical *recurrence* of the world, which was also taught by the Stoics. However, this recurrence simply repeats the same order. Hence, recurrence means no change. This eternity and recurrence could be maintained in the same breath. Hence, the world has been and will always be.

Man and his destiny: We find that the world-soul has two-fold aspect. It may look-up at One and nous, or, it may look-down towards Nature of matter. Similarly, man has both the part of the eternal *nous* and also of the material body with the lure of the senses. The more the individual soul remains under the lure of bodily desires, the more enduring will be his bondage to the body. As Plotinus accepts the doctrine of rebirths and incarnation, so according to this theory after the death of an individual, he will keep on transmigrating into men or animals. Only when this lure of the bodily desires, ceases, he gets his release, that is, his return to God.

The Pathway to God: How can the finite man know the Infinite? The finite must *become* the infinite. But how?

First, matter is the source of evil and an instrument of finitizing the human spirit. Hence, man must be purified. He must learn to overgrow the life of senses, his bodily desires and even the ordinary, prevalent ethical code. Man has to become one with the One. So matter, the source of plurality has to be eradicated.

But all men are not born with the same temperament. They belong to different types. Some are ravished by the vision of beauty, as we find in the poets. Others are given to finding unity and system of orderly laws in Nature. They are the scientists and philosophers. Then there are devout souls who seek the divine through prayers. Music, poetry, dialectics (philosophy) and prayers are all the different means of purifying and elevating thought, reason and philosophy.

However, withdrawal from the senses and transcending the human intellect are preparatory for the ascent of the human soul to the One or the Absolute God. The last step is *ecstasy*. It is not a faculty, but a leap from every form of cognitive process. It is the *revelation* of God, and *becoming* Him. Here God is not the object to be known. But one is one with God, and, he becomes God. Here an Indian reader is reminded of advaitism, according to which 'a knower of Brahman *becomes* Brahman'.

4

Medieval Philosophy

The period of A.D. 400-1400 is counted as the era of medieval philosophy. During this period philosophy was used as a handmaid to theology. Greek philosophy of Plato-Aristotle, Stoicism and neo-Platonism was used to elucidate theology, to defend it against attacks and to further the interest of religion. Christianity itself had arisen as a protest against Judaism and many complicated issues were raised. This made the task of theology extremely difficult and even now the issues raised in Christian theology remain unsolved. Such issues may not be of much interest to the Indian readers and only a few of the religious thinkers will be taken up for our study. St. Augustine, Anselm and St. Thomas Aquinas are certainly important thinkers, but a few others also cannot be ignored, for their contributions prepared the ground for the rise of modern philosophy. Now we shall take up St. Augustine whose writings set the plan for the whole Christian philosophy.

Aurelius Augustine (353-430 A.D.)
St. Augustine was born in Tagaste, North Africa in 353. His father was a pagon, but his mother Monica was a devout Christian. Because of his mother, Augustine was converted to Christianity in 387 and died finally as a bishop of Hippo in Africa in 430 A.D. The most important and popular writings of St. Augustine are *The Confessions of St. Augustine* and *The City of God*.

St. Augustine was largely Platonic in his philosophy, and at times took the help of Aristotle also. He was also greatly influenced by Manichaeism between 373-82 and even after his rejection of Manichaeism, he could not shake off its influence. St. Augustine was greatly involved in Trinitarian controversy and he took his stand in favour of Athanasian creed against Arianism. He was also against Pelagian teaching. These religious involvements show that St. Augustine was very much occupied with religious problems. But readers will also find that there is much in St. Augustine which may be deemed as real academic philosophy. This will be clear from his theory of knowledge.

Theory of Knowledge: St. Augustine has advanced his theory of knowledge, for not mere academic purpose, but for the true happiness and true beautitude. This, for the saint means 'possession and vision of God'. The theory of knowledge must lead to the contemplation of eternal things, bereft of sensation, as Plato had held. Hence, the theory of knowledge, according to St. Augustine is very much mixed up with faith and knowledge. According to him, 'faith seeks, understanding finds'.

Again, 'understand in order that you may believe, believe in order that you may understand'. Intellect is needed for elucidating what faith believes. But what to believe and what not to believe? This depends on revelation. This is for the Church in general or in any particular case to decide whether revelation has or has not been made, in general or in any particular case. Hence, Church is the final authority in matters of faith. The church has been regarded as the viceregent of God on earth.

St. Augustine was very much occupied in his life with the nature of Trinity, comprising father, son and the Holy Ghost. He appears to have adopted trinitarian divisions in his major philosophical subject.

(I) Knowledge has three stages of development, namely, sensation, empirical knowledge i.e. judgments with the help of Ideas, and finally contemplation on the divine essence. In other words, sensation, judgment and contemplation are inseparably found in his epistemology.

(II) Philosophy of the world has the three aspects of creation out of Nothing, according to the Ideas, and God. This nothing at times is called Matter.

(III) Soul has three inseparable aspects of Being, knowledge and Will. These three aspects are also held to comprise all reality.

Let us begin with the account of sensation, empirical knowledge and contemplation of eternal things.

St. Augustine, following Plato, makes soul superior to the body. Soul uses organs of sense as its instrument. No doubt soul pervades the whole body and but at the time of sensation, soul intensifies its activities in a particular sense-organ concerned. Sensation therefore arises both from sense-organ and the outer object. Consequently difficulties in sensation may be due to both the defect of the sense-organ and the object. St. Augustine accepts that there are cases of deceptive sensations and that they are relative and private. But from these deficiencies it does not follow that sensations cannot be used as our starting-points for finding out God. Besides, sensations are indispensable for practical life. This may be called the stage of empirical knowledge which is only rationalised sensation. In judging sensation of a beautiful or ugly corporeal objects we have to take the help of eternal and incorporeal ideas. Such corporeal objects become thereby the copies of eternal ideas, as Plato held. But this empirical knowledge ultimately must lead finally to the contemplation of eternal ideas. Plato does not think that eternal ideas are in a *personal God*, but St. Augustine thinks that these eternal ideas are in the mind of a *personal God*. In the highest stage of contemplation, we strive after wisdom, whereas empirical knowledge is only practical knowledge for the guidance of life. Do we know God after we know the eternal ideas in the mind of a personal God? St. Augustine would say that in knowing the eternal ideas we see only *darkly*. Only in the next life, after our purification and reception of God's Grace in the present life, we will have clearer vision of God. But even now we are talking about true knowledge or certainty in knowledge. Do we know anything as true or certain?

Yes. When there is perception, there is also a perceiving being. Can I doubt that

I, the perceiver exist ? If I doubt, then it means that *I am* there to doubt. Doubt at once leads to the existence of doubting and the reality of consciousness.

1. Doubting means that the doubting consciousness lives and exists. Living means that the person who doubts, perceives, remembers and *knows*. But more, he *wills*. For St. Augustine, in his epistemology, 'will' is an important function of soul. But let us proceed, doubt implies another thing.

2. 'Doubt' means that there is the standard of 'truth' for finding which a person doubts. Doubt and certainty are correlative terms. And in doubting we know the standard of certainty by implication. For St. Augustine we do not have the logical truths only, but also the norms of the good and the beautiful.

Such norms of logical truths, mathematical truths, of the good and the beautiful are found in all persons, and, are purely incorporeal. They are the Ideas in the mind of God. Thus, the inner certainty in the process of one's doubting, not only of the self but the certainty of God too is implied. But in the certainty of God we know only this much that *He is, but not what He is*. The method of doubt was not only taken up by Descartes, but the nature of agnostic knowledge of God held by St. Augustine leads to the theory of *analogia entis* of St. Thomas Aquinas. Further, doubting implies that the doubter *lives* (exists), knows but above all *wills*.

St. Augustine shows that without active will on the part of man, he will not be able to sense, know and rise to the final vision of God. St. Augustine shows that sensation is a passive affair. It is not due to the external impression on the senses, but is a case of consciousness which can be induced by attention to sensation. For example, we get the sensation of a red rose. But if we do not attend to the rose, we will not see its redness. But attention is an interest in action. When we are interested in the rose and its colour, then we sense its redness and smell its fragrance. *Attention* for St. Augustine is a matter of active will. The case of remembering and imagining is certainly possible when we recall the past voluntarily. In the case of rational judgment and reasoning (e.g., mathematical reasoning or syllogistic thinking), the presence of active will becomes all the more clear. But how we know the eternal ideas in the mind of God, which knowing is certainly, knowing something of God, for eternal ideas are nowhere to be found except in God ?

First, for St. Augustine, we do not fully know God. We at most can apprehend that God *is*, but *not what He is*. This position is not difficult to understand. The more active will is superior in relation to less active will. God is the most active will. So in relation to God, man remains passive. Man can know God even partly only when God chooses to will this for man. Not only man cannot know God by his own efforts, but even his receptivity with regard to God's knowledge is not possible without the Grace of God. Hence, the theological doctrine of Grace contradicts the epistemological theory of the importance of free will in man. According to the theological doctrine of Grace only when God chooses to reveal Himself then by His illumination alone man knows Him and the intelligible truths. This theological teaching has important implications for St. Augustine's explanation of evil and the theories of two cities, heavenly and earthly. But before embarking on further, we must explain the theology of St. Augustine.

Theology

God, for St. Augustine, is for worship and adoration. God has absolute majesty, power and untrammelled free activity. He is eternal, transcendent, absolutely good. He creates out of His will, but even then all laws of nature are absolute and unchangeable and His creation is continuous through which He sustains the whole universe. The important thing is to maintain that God creates matter too. So there is no lingering dualism in the theology of St. Augustine. But we shall have something more to say with regard to God's creation of the world. For St. Augustine man and the whole world point upwards to the living God. Only in this form of devout attitude to God, St. Augustine mentions some proofs for His existence, which have their basis in Plato's theology.

1. From the *effects*, God's existence as the cause of this world may be maintained.

From the very order, beauty, change and motion of the world and of the visible things, God's existence can be inferred. This may be called the teleological argument for the existence of God.

2. Again, we human beings are aware of eternal truths or ideas. They cannot be due to finite human beings, for these eternal truths for transcend any finite creature. Here, they must be in the supreme ground of our Being in whom, by whom and through whom all things are true which are true in every respect. This proof is again Platonic.

3. Again, God is the cause of the continued existence of the world and God is the necessary conservative ground of the world. This may be called the cosmological proof.

4. Further, reminding one of Plato, St. Augustine mentions the proof from universal consent (*Consensus gentium*) of the whole mankind. All human beings concur in believing God to be the author of the whole universe.

The World: For St. Augustine, God is a creator God. This concept has to be distinguished from neoplatonistic theory of emanation. According to this neoplatonistic theory, the world emanates from God as the overflow from His abundance. This diffusion in the form of the world means no decrease in God or diminution. Again, creator God is different from an architect. An architect God creates the world out of pre-existing matter or chaos or any such material. *A creator God* creates everything from His own self. So there is no matter independent of God even in attenuated form, as in Plato and Aristotle.

If there is matter, then St. Augustine holds that either it is absolutely formless or with the bare capacity of receiving form. But there can be no *absolutely* formless matter, for then it means that it is utterly without any quality of hardness or softness, colour, taste, smell etc. In this state, it means that absolutely formless matter is really as good as *Nothing*. Hence creation out of absolutely formless matter really means creating out of Nothing. If, however, matter means *relatively* formless in comparison with other formed or qualified things like a tree or an animal, then it means 'matter with indefinite form, or, matter with the potentiality of receiving form'. But God becomes the creator of matter with the potentiality of having form or *germinal potentiality*. Thus, God is the absolute creator of all things, even of matter.

The world as the creation of God *depends* on God, but the world and God are not one and the same, as is held in pantheism. God *transcends* the world, and from the world as the *effect*, one cannot fully know God. All that one can say that he *apprehends* God, but cannot *comprehend* Him.

God has created the world with everything in it, including man, not all at once and together, but with their future potentiality and evolution also, or, what may be called *germinal* potentiality. Seminal or germinal potentiality is not absolutely passive, but tends to self-development when the requisite conditions ripen in due course. This recourse to germinal potentiality may remind one of Darwin's reconciling God's creation with the evolutionary scheme of things. However in the case of St. Augustine the theory of germinal potentiality was brought forward to reconcile the exegetic problem concerning the two contrasted statements in the Biblical books of *Genesis* and *Ecclesiastes*. This doctrine of germinal potentiality is more Aristotelian than Platonic.

Finally, the world was not created at any point of time. The time and space were created with all other things of the world. Hence, it is nonsense to say, why the world was created at one point of time, not earlier or later? Or, what was God doing before the creation of the world? For St. Augustine, God is eternal and for Him, past and present and future are all in one given *now*. In this sense God has foreknowledge of everything, even of the free action or choice of a man in any particular situation.

The doctrine of man

Man is the crown and roof of things, created by God. Man has a soul and body, as one unitary entity. Of course, soul is immaterial and far superior to body. As a matter of fact, soul uses the body as its instrument. It is the soul which moves any part of the body, but not *vice-versa*, for the soul is superior to the body. The question is, 'Is the soul immortal?'

St. Augustine teaches the immortality of soul, but is not soul a created entity? Can a created entity be immortal? St. Augustine grants that God can create man who endures for all time. But he does not grant the pre-existence of soul. St. Augustine, more or less, repeats the proofs for the immortality of the soul, as were given by Plato in *Phaedo* (71-72). Plato observes that everything is created in opposites like heating and cooling. Similarly, there is life and death. If life is extinguished in death, then in due course, all lives, even souls will cease to exist.

But life is a continuous creation of God. So we have to admit that death of man implies his birth too in some other forms. So the soul of man is immortal.

Besides, man is aware of the eternal truths. These eternal truths cannot have their abode in finite beings. So they can be entertained only by an equally indestructible soul of man.

These proofs cannot clinch the issue. For St. Augustine another problem concerning the soul appears to be more important. Is an individual soul created each time it comes into the world, or, is it transmitted from parents to children? The problem appears very simple, but for a theologian like St. Augustine, it is important. St. Augustine does not admit that each soul is created at the time a child is born, for man is born a sinner. If a sinner is created by God, then God becomes the creator of evil. This is not possible, for God is good. And if God be the author of evil, then evil can never be removed, even by His Grace, Hence, the soul is transmitted from parents to children. Is it not then a materialistic conception? St. Augustine favours this transmission-theory because of his theological belief in the original sin of man and his acceptance of the theory of pre-destination. We shall soon take up St. Augustine's theory of evil. However, we can pass on one remark in this context. In the background, St. Augustine implicitly accepts the dualism of mind *and* body, of the incorporeal soul and corporeal body.

The problem of Evil: A theist has to justify the ways of God to man. God is omnipotent, benevolent and good and omniscient. Then how evil is to be explained? Evil is a fact of life, physical and moral. Physical evil can be allowed under the theory of seminal good. The whole universe has been created by God that a good man may emerge by wrestling with the presence of physical evil. But then moral evil be explained in this way? Now as a metaphysician, St. Augustine advances three views about Evil, which have been followed subsequently, namely,

1. Evil is necessary for the enhancement of the greater good, in the same manner in which the shadow in the moon enhances the beauty of the full moon.

2. Evil is not a positive, but privative good, e.g., simply deficiency of goodness.

3. Not God but man is responsible for his moral fall. However, it is the third kind of expedient which looms large in the theological explanation of evil and this is really important in the theology of St. Augustine. Let us very briefly mention the metaphysical explanation of evil before undertaking the theological explanation of moral evil.

Though St. Augustine was largely a Platonist, yet he could not have accepted matter as the reason of evil, which was suggested by Plato. The reason is that for St. Augustine even matter was created by God. Hence, if matter be the cause of evil, then God will directly become the cause of evil. Secondly, God is omnipotent and so He could not be imagined to be limited by pre-existing matter. Then how to explain evil? Evil is not good, but *it is good that there is evil*. Firstly, what appears as evil is not really evil. It is only to enhance the excellence of good. For example, in explaining the birth of a man born blind, Jesus said that this man was born blind so that the glory of God may be made manifest. Secondly, evil is the privation of good, that is, *present absence* of the *expected good*. For example, there is the evil of blindness, but it is simple the present absence of the power of vision. But in due course, this vision (or good) can be restored. In the same way, God has created germinal potentialities. At present they appear as evil, but in due course in the fulness of time, they may be transformed into good. For example, Sahara was just a desert, but a part of it has become the source of petrol. Hence, God does not *create evil*, but has to *permit* evil. This is an important formula to explain moral evil, which was the real problem of St. Augustine. This requires some background to fully appreciate the theological explanation of moral evil.

The explanation of moral evil, for St. Augustine, is wholly religious and this is also of a particular type of thinking in Christian dogma. St. Augustine accepted the doctrine of Trinity according to which *father, son and Holy Ghost* are *three persons in One*. Jesus Christ is not created, but is the *begotten son* of God, that is, Christ and God are one in essence and Christ's ministry on earth did not prevent Him from remaining in one substance with Him. Without faith in holy trinity one cannot be saved, and, without being saved one cannot regain free Will.

Further, the first man Adam had free will, but with his fall by disobedience to God, Adam lost his free will. This condemnation of Adam being a sinner has been transmitted to the whole mankind. This is the doctrine of *Original Sin*.

'In Adam's fall, we sinned all'.

By one's efforts no man can save himself. He can be saved through God's Grace alone. This is a free gift to man, and cannot be won by one's own efforts or good deeds. God gives His grace to whomsoever He wishes. As for God, past, present and future are all given in one everlasting 'now', so God's Grace is pre-destined from the very beginning. Thus, men are divided into elect and damned.

Arius (256-336) disputed the co-substantiality of Jesus and God. Arianism laid down the following:

1. There is One and only One God, eternal and solitary from eternity. He became father only after creating the Son.

2. There are powers in God, but not persons in God.

3. God created *independent* substances, like wisdom, son, word.

4. The son is a separate substance, independent of the Father, different from Him in substance and nature.

5. The Son, truly speaking, is not God, but is the Word or wisdom. He has no absolute, but relative knowledge of the Father.

6. By special creation, Jesus has become 'begotten son'. His essence is similar to that of God, but he is subordinate to God.

7. Christ took a real body and suffered.

8. Holy Spirit, the third person of Holy Trinity, can be placed beside the Son; he might have been created by the Son.

Thus, Arianism denied the Unity of Father, son and Holy Ghost in one God.

St. Augustine regarded it as 'heresy' and worked against it, because Arianism denied the co-substantiality of father, Son and Holy Ghost. In comparison, Pelagius, a contemporary of St. Augustine, denied the doctrine of Original Sin, pre-destination and Grace. Pelagianism maintains the following:

1. God is above all just and good, and, His creation is good. Consequently human nature remains indestructibly good and indefeasibly free.

(St. Augustine taught the doctrine of Original Sin, with the loss of free will)

2. Man has reason, and, free will which is absolute in him.

3. Desire in itself is not bad, but its excess due to free choice of each individual becomes bad. Marriage is not sinful.

4. Every man at birth is innocent and free.

5. Physical death is not the consequence of sin, but spiritual death is, for which sin, every individual man is responsible.

6. The idea of inherited sinfulness (original sin) is unthinkable. Sin is always due to perverted exercise of free will.

7. Grace of God means the aid which God gives to the faithful, or by creating a good natural constitution for some men, or, by the law of God revealed to man with regard to what he ought or ought not to do, or, may mean in clearing the reason of some men which reason gets darkened by sin. Pelagius grants that some heathen like Plato, Buddha and others have become redeemed soul because God had given them a good constitution of soul.

8. Grace is given according to one's merits; it would not be consistent with God's justice to give it to all sinners.

(This is what Ramanuja also maintained with regard to the doctrine of Grace in Vaisnavism.)

We have already noted that St. Agustine was very much influenced by *Manichaeism*, which admitted the dualism of good and evil, light and darkness, Elect and Heares. This dualism is supposed to have been derived from Parsiism where there is the dualism of Ahura Mazda and Ahriman (Devil or Satan). St. Augustine rejected manichaeism but could not fully outgrow it. He continued to hold the dualism of the elect and the damned, the city of Heaven and the city of this earth. With these points, noted above, let us deal with the problem of Moral Evil.

Moral Evil

For St. Augustine, God is omnipotent and good and yet moral evil has to be admitted and satisfactorily explained. Secondly, the supreme end of moral life is happiness which can be found only in God.

'God has made us for Himself, and our heart finds no rest till it finds in Him.'

But it is a fact that men do evil, run for the worldly good. Has God left man to perish for ever? No. God has revealed His way through Jesus Christ and has established a Church to establish God's Kingdom on earth. Does it lie in the power of man, to get rid of his sin and enter the Church on his way to contemplate in the blessedness of the Heaven? No. Man by his own nature is utterly corrupt and by himself cannot be saved. He can only be damned for the eternal hell-fire. But God and a good and omnipotent God has created man. How is it that he has become so corrupt that he deserves hell? Here St. Augustine explains the origin of moral evil.

The first man called Adam was given free will. He misused free will by his disobedience. He ate the forbidden fruit. He became a fallen man. A fallen man can produce only a fallen being. All the descendants of Adam have become fallen disobedient persons. They all are sinners. They all love the world. *They have lost free will.* Hence for the sin of one man, all have sinned. This is known as the doctrine of *Original Sin*. All have earned eternal hell-fire. Are they no longer free to rise? No.

A sinner cannot do real good, for real good means free act. Free will means free choice or decision for assent to a definite course of action. St. Augustine who taught the doctrine of indefeasible free will in man in his epistemology, now teaches its absolute denial in his theology. In his theory of knowledge, St. Augustine taught that not even sensation is possible without free will. In theology he restricts this free will only to one man Adam and denies this to all subsequent human beings. This doctrine can no longer be accepted by the moderners. But in medieval times, even learned and wise men could do so. This is what religion is capable of doing in its believers. But is there no way of salvation?

God by His Grace can *redeem* some men. Instead of being given to corruptible things, God by His Grace turns some men towards, Himself, preparing them for communion with God. It is God's doing and God's doing alone. Man cannot earn his Godward tendency. God's grace cannot be earned. Here one is reminded of *Pelagian* heresy. One can further ask. 'Is not the act of God arbitrary in choosing *some* men to be saved by His Grace, from hell-fire?' St. Augustine maintains the absolute freedom of God and as such cannot be questioned because of His absolute Goodness. No damned person can question this Grace, for he is absolutely corrupt and deserves no salvation but ultimate condemnation. But how do we know that a particular individual has been saved by His Grace? By receiving the baptism, sacrament (holy communion), fasting and prayer. Does this mean that all persons belonging to the Church can be deemed as saved?

St. Augustine admits that if a Christian belonging to the Church indulges in self-love and has not divine intoxication in him, he belongs to the earthly kingdom, to the corporeal world, to the City of Babylon. Granted, but did not God know that all men will sin, then why did He create them at all. Is He not responsible for creating moral evil?

There is no past, present and future for God. They are all there all at once. Just as the present cannot undo the past, so it cannot create the future. They are all in the creative act of God with His unsearchable decree. Some are eternally damned because of the disobedience of one man Adam, and, *some are saved* because of the one saviour Christ. It is the substantial oneness of the human race, damned in one group and save in another. It is the doctrine of *predestination* which makes the picture so gloomy.

According to St. Augustine, God has so decreed all things, according to His law of predestination, either to be deemed elect or to be damned. This worldly belonging to the city of Satan, called Babylon, cannot choose to be good, for all good comes from God, and, God has chosen that a sinner in question be damned forever. Hence, all wills, either of the redeemed by His Grace or, damned by His decree, are forever determined forever. All works good (of the saved) or bad (of the damned) are mere shadows and puppet-plays. Such is the unbelievable contradiction in St. Augustine's philosophy. In his epistemology man was deemed indefeasibly free, and, now in his theology, man has become just a puppet. In this doctrine of predestination of man into saved and sinner, Manichaenism of his youthful years returns with all its horrors.

The Tale of Two Cities
In the theology of St. Augustine, God becomes the creator of the saved and the sinner at least because of His decree. They belong to two cities. The elect, the saved belong to the kingdom of God and the sinner and the damned belong to the kingdom of Satan or Devil, the city is called Babylon. The elect are the chosen people for living in communion with Him, and, the sinner is left to be condemned to the hell-torment forever. On this earth there is nothing to distinguish the one from the other, but internally in their inner spiritual constitution, they are two kinds of people far apart. The community of the elect does not belong to this earth.

Thus the kingdom of God and that of Devil are sharply divided. To the kingdom of God belong the faithful angels and the elect chosen to be so by His Grace. To the kingdom of Devil belong the devils and the damned, not predestined to redemption. The community of the elect has no home on this earth, but they remain united through His Grace, giving fight against the kingdom of the devil. In contrast, the damned people keep on fighting amongst themselves. For St. Augustine, the human world belongs to this worldly state, belonging to the kingdom of Devil. However, in the worldly history is born the saviour of the world called Jesus. Again, on this earth stands the Church, which may be called the semblance of the heavenly kingdom on this earth. The worst comment of this sharply divided world is that God, the omnipotent, most benevolent Being has created this world and the hell.

Further, the glory of the indefeasible will in man is subordinated again to the contemplative life of the blessed in the kingdom of God. In this world the elect are engaged in the purification of the head and heart by means of strict morality. The elect also have to fight a relentless fight against the devils and the damned, in favour of the heavenly kingdom. But the elect after the day of Judgment enter into the heavenly bliss in the life of contemplation with the intoxication of God's love. Thus becoming absorbed in the divine truth is the reward of the elect. They have the primacy of will, restored by divine grace, and, at the end, this Will is reduced in the life of contemplation. Here the influence both of Plato and neo-Platonism becomes clear. In contrast, the damned on this earth keep on fighting for ephemeral earthly gains till in the day of Judgment they are condemned to hell fire.

In Duns Scotus the primacy of will over intellect is most clearly upheld and this primacy is said to be Augustinian. This Augustinian primacy comes from his epistemology and not from his theological doctrine of 'Original Sin'.

JOHN SCOTUS ERIGENA (c. 810-877)

Erigena was an Irishman. He was a scholar of Greek language. He translated the works of Pseudo-Dionysius from Greek into Latin. Again, he translated the works of St. Gregory of Nyssa. In his own work, it was natural for him to be influenced by Dionysius and St. Gregory. But he was also influenced by the philosophy of St. Augustine. But above all he was greatly influenced by the Ideal Theory of Plato, and, also somewhat by Aristotle. But it was Neo-Platonism which Erigena appears to have adopted for explaining Christian tenets. However, Erigena has not been considered to be an orthodox theologian. He gave weightage to *reason* over the Christian emphasis on *faith*; he adopted pantheism in preference to theism under the influence of neo-Platonism; Erigena appears to give preference to *emanation* over creation. His explanation of Trinity is largely neo-Platonic rather than orthodox Augustinian.

Erigena believed in reason much more than in faith. According to him reason and revelation, both are sources of religious truth. In case of any conflict between them, reason is to be preferred. For him true philosophy is true religion. Again, for Erigena, reason is prior to authority, and, the true authority is the power of reason. This is not in accordance with the clear statement of St. Paul:

> . . . the righteousness of God is revealed from faith to faith; as it is written, 'The just shall live by faith'. (*Romans* 1.17)

Erigena's philosophy is Platonic in *content*, but Neo-Platonic *in expression*. According to the Ideal Theory, the Idea is real; the idea of Plato is universal. Hence, a universal is real and the highest universal is most real. By 'real' was meant not only that which is most valuable object of contemplation, but also that which is existent. For example, for Aristotle, the idea 'redness' is as objectively existent as the sensation of red. Only Aristotle did not admit that any universal can *exist* without the particulars or individuals in which it inheres. By 'existent' is meant is that which is given to us in the spatio-temporal frame of reference. Now from the reality of universal idea, Erigena proceeds in accordance with Neo-Platonic philosophy of pantheism. According to Platonic realism, individuals are mere reminders of the Idea. Naturally the highest Idea, God is the sole reality of the world and individuals. Hence, for Erigena, 'God is everything that truly is'.

Apart from his translations and commentaries, Erigena wrote a book called *De divisione naturae* i.e. *On the division of Nature*. Nature for Erigena meant an all-inclusive, all-comprehensive whole, as a Hegelian would say. This all-inclusive whole *diffuses* itself in the following steps, reminding one of the graded hierarchy of Being, as was outlined by Plotinus:

1. Nature which creates, but itself remains uncreated.
2. Nature which is created and also creates.
3. Nature which is created and remains uncreative.
4. Nature which is neither created nor creates.

Here the first three phases are also to be traced to Plato and Aristotle. Plato mentions ten types of motion of which IX and X are more to the point here. Aristotle mentions three kinds of phases, namely,

(*a*) unmoved mover

(*b*) moving and moved,

(*c*) moved, but not moving.

Put in the form of Christian theology, Nature in the first phase of being 'uncreated and creative' means God. How can we describe God who is ineffable and incomprehensible? We can say that He is super Truth, super-wisdom and super-Essence. Why are we not saying that God is Truth or Wisdom? Of course, by saying that God is wise, we are trying to describe God *affirmatively*. But can we describe God affirmatively? No. Only an entity of equal universality or reality can *know* a thing affirmatively. But human beings are mere creatures. They cannot describe God affirmatively. Then are we not saying that God is super-wise? Yes, this may sound to be affirmative, but really this is only a *negative* way of describing God. 'Wisdom' is only metaphorically (or analogically) attributed to God. After all what does super-wisdom mean? It means that God's wisdom is not the wisdom of Socrates or of Plato or of Aristotle or even of any man at all. Hence, 'super-wisdom' is really a negative way of describing God. Is it all negation without affirmation? In a way, it is, but it means God's wisdom is infinitely more than human wisdom. How is it that we cannot describe God at all?

The reason is the principle that the higher can know the lower, but the lower cannot know the higher. Through His effects, the creatures that we are, all we can say that God *is*, but not *what* He is. The categories of human thinking can legitimately apply to created things, but not to their creator who forever *transcends them*. Indeed this part of his philosophy is in accordance with the Biblical text and dogma, namely, God is transcendent to all created things, for He is much more than the created things. Again, the agnostic aphorism is contained in Exodus 3.14 (I am who I am). But let us come to the other three phases of Nature which includes God and everything else.

II. Phase 2. *Word or the Son*

Erigena keeps on repeating that God created the world out of nothing. What does 'out of nothing' mean? It means the absence of any material formed or unformed. It also means the negation of all things. It also means that God made all things out of Himself. But what does 'making' mean? Of course, literally making involves motion as it is the case with painting a picture or a potter making a pot. Thus 'motion' means, change. However, God cannot change. Therefore 'making' means that God is eternally in all things and is the essence of all things. The interpretation is clearly pantheistic, even with regard to the second phase of Nature.

The second phase of Erigena's Nature is Word or the Son. That 'Word' and 'the Son' are one and the same follows from St. John 1.1.4,10. When it is said that the Son created all that there is, it means that primordial, causes or all prototypes of all created things are in the word or the Son. This creation, like making is not a temporal process, but is an eternal procession from the Son. Hence, the Son is logically prior to the created world. Thus it (creation) means that nothing is there except what is eternally pre-ordained in their eternal prototypes. Hence all things are in word or the Son. Now how do the Son and the third phase of Nature, called creatures stand?

Exactly like neo-Platonism Erigena holds that the primordial causes as Prototypes look upwards *towards* God, and again, *down wards* towards the world of plurality. Hence, creation *participates* in the son as diffusion from Him. The world, the creation of God is eternal in the sense that its essence is in eternal primordial causes. Erigena also holds that the world is eternal and also *created as was foreseen and willed by God*. But the world remains within God. Hence, creatures and God are one and the same. In other words, God is substantially all that has been created.

But this pantheistic, eternal diffusion of God into the Son and then again His diffusion into the world of creatures, raises one serious difficulty. What about evil? If God is all, and, all is God, then evil is God too. Here like St. Augustine, Erigena maintains that not God, but man is responsible for evil. But in this pantheistic explanation, where is the room for shadow when God is simply unmixed goodness and eternal light ? Erigena once again like St. Augustine holds that evil is not *positive* but *privative*. By calling evil 'privative', the sting of evil does not become less painful. No real remedy is possible for a persistent malady, by coining words.

Lastly, Nature's last phase is that which is not created and does not create. This again simply means that all things come from God, and all things return to Him. In that state God remains what He has been all through, the same eternally. In this last phase, the Absolutely real is not creative, for all His creations have returned into Him. This is what was verbally stated by St. Paul himself,

And when all things shall be subdued into Him, then the Son also himself shall be subject into him that put all things under him, that God may be all in all.

(1 cor. 15.28)

However, religious effusion should not be taken as a philosophical statement. To say the least Erigena is not at all an orthodox theologian for the following reasons:

1. There can be no theology without philosophy. But there are various kinds of philosophy, and, the neo-Platonism is least suited to explain the tenets of Christianity. Neo-Platonism is essentially *pantheistic*, and, Christianity accepts the reality of a *transcendent* God. It is not enough to say that God transcends human intellect and categories. Christianity puts God as a transcendent creator of the world, analogically as a potter is in relation to the pot he makes.

2. True, Christianity accepts the doctrine of creation by God out of nothing. This is a difficult concept. But to substitute for creation, emanation or diffusion of God into His creatures is not in accordance with Christian orthodoxy.

3. Christianity accepts the doctrine of Trinity, i.e. the unity of father, son and the Holy Ghost into one Person. In contrast, Erigena accepts the reality of three Persons into what is known as *triadism* or tritheism.

4. Erigena teaches the *mergence* of individuals into God at the end. But Christianity teaches the independence of individuals to the end. They as faithful believers live in heaven, or, as rebels and sinners remain in hell.

5. As noted at the beginning, Christianity emphasizes faith at the expense of reason. But Erigena teaches the priority and primacy of reason over faith.

Is it any wonder then that the writings of Erigena were condemned in 855 and 859 and in 1225 and were declared heretical?

ROSCELIN (C. 1050-1120) AND ANSELM (1035-1109)

The significance of Universals in Christian theology

Universals were variously held in medieval philosophy. The most important theory was that universals (or ideas or forms) had an independent status of all things. This is known as Platonic realism. As against this Aristotle held that universals are as objective as individual things are. For examples, redness is as real as the red colour is. But he held that universals have no reality independently of the individual things in which they are found. As against this, *conceptualism* holds that universals are concepts which are abstracted from the class of objects as their essential common attributes in the form of a similarity or identity of qualities. Concepts are stated to be in the human minds, though they are also in objects. This was the view of Abelard (1079-1142). There is the fourth theory of *nominalism*, associated here in this context with the name of Roscelin. Nominalism denies the objectivity of universals, as is associated with the Ideal Theory of Plato. For it universals are mere names, *flatus voci* to indicate a number of things. A universal is really a human designation to comprehend many individuals bearing a common name. Only individuals are real, and are true substances. Universals are neither in things (as Aristotle supposed) nor in any mind whatsoever.

Christian theology had adopted Platonic realism. Trinity is an *idea*, not a mere name standing for three gods. Father, Sons and Holy Ghost. As an idea, Trinity means one substantial Being as Father, Son and Holy Ghost. Nominalism on the other hand would regard Father, Son, and Holy Ghost as three separate persons. This is known as *tritheism* or triadism. Hence, nominalism denied the co-substantiality of God and Jesus. Naturally nominalism was opposed to the traditional Christian theology.

Secondly, Platonic realism holds that ideas only are constitutive of the world. Hence, the idea being rational would show that the world is rational and knowable. Therefore, the world can be explained with the help of ideas which are sought through concepts.

Besides, ideas are eternal in relation to particulars which pass away. Hence, Trinity or Christian theism holds the eternity of God who outlasts all the passing particulars.

Further, there is one universal idea of man which holds together all men together. Hence, in Adam all men sinned, as was taught by St. Augustine in his theory of Original Sin. Again, in the vicarions death or redemptive death of Jesus, all believers have been redeemed. For substantiality of all sinners and believers remains eternally real. Hence, the doctrine of original sin and also that of redemption remain embedded in the reality of universals.

Finally, Church universal is an abiding entity over and above the particular members which compose it. Hence, Roman Catholic Church alone has the authority to save mankind and interpret the ways of God to men.

As against Platonic Realism, nominalism of Roscelin had sinister implications for the Church theology.

1. As there is no universal idea called God, so Father, Son and Holy Ghost do not form Trinity. Father, Son and Holy Ghost are three individual gods. So there is tritheism or triadism. Hence, nominalism denies trinity.

2. As individual men alone are real and the universal man is unreal, so the *solidarity* or co-substantiality of the human race stands refuted. With this refutation, stands denied the doctrine of original sin through Adam, and, the redemption of all men through faith in Jesus Christ.

3. For nominalism, only the particulars are real and particular facts are searched by science. Hence, nominalism purported to support science in the place of ecclesiastical pursuits. This was only an indirect result of nominalism.

4. The dogma of the church was established in the long past, when newer and fresh facts of experience had not been there. But since the formation of Christian dogma (about 450 A.D.), newer facts demanded their fresh review. So nominalism demanded a fresh review of the authority of the church and its dogma.

5. Again, as particulars alone are real, so particular churches and their views were considered real and the claim of one universal Roman Catholic Church came to be denied. Further, as particulars alone were regarded real, so nominalism served to exalt private judgment as higher than that of one universal church. Hence,

nominalism tended to undermine the authority of Holy Roman Catholic Church.

For the reasons outlined above, Anselm opposed nominalism in defence of Trinity and Atonement. For this reason, Anselm accepted Platonic Realism.

Anselm (1033-1109)

Anselm was a devout Christian and made sincere efforts to understand his Christian faith. In his theology Anselm followed St. Augustine who was a pronounced Platonist. Anselm accepted the priority and primacy of faith over reason. His slogan which was Augustinian was 'credo, ut intelligam', i.e., let me believe that I may understand. Without faith a man is blind to understand God who is light. But he also held that one should try to understand as much as possible the tenets of one's faith. His remarkable words are :

> For I do not seek to understand, in order that I may believe; but I believe, that I may understand. For I believe this too, that unless I believed, I should not understand.

Anselm died as Archbishop of Canterbury in 1109.

Anselm followed St. Augustine in explaining Trinity and the doctrine of Original Sin and Redemption on the basis of Platonic realism. For philosophy, St. Anselm's Ontological proof for the existence of God is important and we shall explain this now.

Ontological Argument: No doubt in *Monologion*, Anselm offers Platonic argument for the existence of God on the basis of the Good, cosmological argument and the argument on the basis of the gradation of entities. But the Ontological argument was presented systematically by him in *Proslogium.* It is known as ontological argument, for it shows that the very essence of the Idea of Perfect God implies His existence. In other words, the non-existence of God cannot be entertained even in thought if one understands the meaning of 'God'. In *Proslogium* the ontological argument has been thus stated.

There is an idea of an absolutely perfect being, i.e. the idea of God than whom none greater can be thought. If follows from this that the idea of God as absolute perfection is necessarily an idea of an existent Being. If it is supposed that the corresponding to the idea of a Perfect Being, God need not exist, then it means that the idea of a non-existing perfect being is not that of a being greater than whom nothing can be thought. For in this case, a Perfect existing being in reality (extramentally) is greater than of a perfect being as *mere idea.* Therefore a perfect being greater than which nothing can be thought must necessarily be of an *existing being*, and, in comparison an idea of a perfect being not existing is inferior.

Here by a 'perfect' being is meant a being which has a number of excellent attributes each in perfection. 'Existence' is also an attribute. Hence, a perfect being cannot lack existence. Everything depends on regarding 'existence' as an attribute. Since the time of Kant, *existence* is not regarded as an attribute. Therefore, one can entertain the idea of a perfect being without any actual entity corresponding to it. However, the whole proof of Anselm depends on the reality of Platonic Idea. An Idea exists independently on its own account. In this sense of Idea of a Perfect Being implies existence. As Anselm accepts Platonic realism, against conceptualism and nominalism, so for him this is a neat, fool-proof argument for the existence of God.

Gaunilo, a monk, objected to this ontological argument of Anselm. According to Gaunilo, in this argument the idea of God and the idea of existence have been put together. But even the idea of existence is only an idea, a mere thought. By thinking of a perfect island one cannot bring about an *actual* perfect island, Was Anselm convinced?

No, Anselm replied. The idea of a perfect thing, having a beginning or end, or being composed of parts, does not imply its existence.

But the only being that cannot be thought of as non-existent is that in which no thought finds beginning or end or composition of parts.

This ontological argument was rephrased by Descartes and Leibnitz and was severely criticized by Kant. But in spite of Kant, the argument has been retained by the Hegelians. For the Hegelians, thought and thing are identical. Caird and Bradley have given powerful support to this argument. Bradley holds 'What may be and must be, is'. The point is, when a believer worships, he cannot do so without taking God to be real for him. When a worshipper worships his deity, then his deity is recognized by him as the highest, the most perfect and most real. Hence, the ontological argument is not so much rational as it is an expression of one's faith. It is therefore for nothing that Anselm notes faith higher than reason.

PETER ABELARD (c. 1079-1142)

Peter Abelard was a Frenchman. He was a keen mind and a great teacher. He wrote a book *Sic et Non* (Yes and No). According to this book, apart from the scripture, dialectic is the sole source of truth. In other words, he gave weightage to reason, but not at the cost of faith. For him, one should not remain in blind faith. So reason is a must to make one's faith intelligible, but reason should *not supersede faith*. One should make serious enquiries into one's faith. Even when he does not make his faith intelligible, at the end he *must accept it.*

Abelard's sharp intellect made him make critical of Platonic ideal realism. His argument is quite simple but incisive. We cannot predicate a thing of a thing. Yet we predicate a universal of many things. Hence a universal is not a thing i.e., an idea has no independent existence of its own. Then what is an idea? Should we accept *nominalism?* No. Because a universal is much more than vocal sound. How? Things resemble one another and by mental abstraction of common resembling points we form a concept. But resemblance between two or more things is *not itself a thing*. Again, according to Platonic realism, men differ, not substantially but only accidentally. Against this, Abelard observed. If the human species is substantially and therefore wholly, present in both Socrates and Plato at the same time, then Socrates must be Plato and he must be present in two places at once. This is absurd. Further, Platonic realism leads to pantheism, as we see in Erigena, since God is substance and this will be identical with all substances. So it means 'God is all'. More. The general concepts are not in things alone. They are also in the mind in the form of confused images of many things. Ultimately Platonic ideas are in divine mind as patterns of things for creation. By stating that universals are concepts in human mind as confused images and many things, Abelard favours Aristotle. But by saying that Platonic ideas are patterns in divine mind according to which God creates, Abelard favours Plato. But his predominant view was that thoughts (universals) must conform to things.

Hence, Abelard is against ultra-realism of Platonic ideas, but supports 'moderate realism', because after all common resembling points are *in things*. This moderate realism was accepted by St. Thomas Aquinas. But ideas are *in human minds as well*, and they must conform to things. This stand may be called *conceptualism*, which is quite different both from nominalism and ultra-Platonic realism.

Abelard's views about Trinity aroused much opposition, for he reduced Trinity to three attributes. Father is stated to be One or Goodness, Son is the logos or mind of God; and the Holy Ghost is the world-soul. The three persons are taken to be goodness, wisdom and power of God.

However, the ethics of Abelard is really important and much of it characterizes the inwardness of morality. Abelard emphasizes intention as the real object of moral judgment. Intention is not the feeling or thought or desire but is the assent or *decision of the will*. If intention is sinful, then sin has already been committed. Hence, Abelard does not stress external bodily action or the consequences of actions. Therefore, moral judgment is related to the individual's will and his conscience. And what is conscience?

Conscience is the Natural Law, which in spite of some variation is the same in all men. Christian teaching wakes up the conscience of man which has been obscured or darkened through human sin. Further, this natural law is identical with the will of God. If one follows one's own conscience, then he obeys God, and, if he acts against it then he commits sin. This doctrine of conscience is really a clarification of St. Augustine's principle of inner experience. A goodwill, for Abelard, is prompted by the love of God and leads to the obedience of divine commands.

St. Thomas Aquinas (c. 1225-74)

Introduction

St. Thomas Aquinas is the greatest schoolman who most comprehensively systematized Christian theology. He is known as an angelic doctor, for in writing his theology he would frequently kneel down and pray for revelation.

As against St. Augustine and Anselm, St. Thomas is an Aristotelian. As against Platonic realism, St. Thomas accepted the conceptualism of Aristotle. St. Thomas was an empiricist, since for him there is nothing in intellect which was not previously given by the senses. He starts with the world of facts, the existent world and from this starting-point tries to reach the Highest Being. For Aristotle, metaphysics deals with the first principle and Being. And so does St. Thomas. St. Thomas throughout his religious philosophy uses Aristotelian technical terms like *actus purus*, form and matter, actuality and potentiality, four kinds of cause and some such technical terms.

All through his rather short life, St. Thomas wrote many commentaries. His most famous works are *Summa Contra Gentiles*, and *Summa Theologiae*. In *Contra* he tries to establish Christian articles of faith by arguments, and in *Summa Theologiae*, he uses reason to support his already accepted faith. Even today, St. Thomas is the official philosopher of the Roman Catholic World. All the time, St. Thomas assumed that religious truths can be supported rationally. But can they? St. Thomas himself made a distinction between Philosophy and Religion, Natural theology and Revealed theology.

Philosophy and Theology

Sciences depend on the workings of natural light of reason. Theology on the other hand, takes recourse to revelation. The philosopher starts from the world of facts or the created things and may reach the conclusion about the existence of God. However, a theologian starts from revelation and deduces the world of objects from revealed truths. In the long run, reason and revelation are not opposed. Faith is not opposed to reason, but is higher than reason. Very often reason may be employed to defend faith by destroying objections against the articles of faith. Reason working by itself may not fully understand the deep things of religion, and, even what they understand may be mixed with error. Hence, St. Thomas took revelation to be higher than reason, and, made a demarcation between the field of reason and revelation.

For the angelic doctor creatorship of God (i.e., creation out of nothing), Trinity, Incarnation of Jesus Christ, the doctrine of original sin, Last judgment are such articles of faith which come under revealed theology. These articles are not contrary to reason, but are above reason and can be grasped through the Grace of God. That a man has been created by God for perfect happiness by attaining the vision of God in the next life. It is not attainable by reason alone in this life. Reason can at most show that man is born for an *imperfect* happiness in this life. But how can reason rising from empirical experience say and state clearly about the supernatural vision of God relating to man's supreme happiness?

But the separation of faith and reason is not possible. Both are part of the same

man. St. Thomas upheld the primacy of revelation over reason. But this itself is
mere faith of an epoch. With the rise of science and its progressive march, reason
became more and more reliable mistress of the soul. And revelation has remained
confined within its narrow compass. Faith cannot remain secure in its ivory tower.
Faith has to be questioned, refined and its myths have to be demythologised. But
even when reason does its worst to faith, it itself must be propped by a different
myth. The myth of lasting progress of science and technology brought the two wars
in Europe. Reason and faith have to go together and must not be sundered. At least
this is the lesson of the conflict of religion and science for a long time in Europe.
Let us be heir to the wisdom which should dawn on mankind as a result of conflict
between reason and faith.

THEORY OF KNOWLEDGE

We have already stated that St. Thomas was an Aristotelian in his approach to his
religious philosophy. This is well illustrated in his theory of knowledge, on which
his proofs of God are based.

St. Thomas succinctly states: There can be nothing in intellect which was not
previously given in the senses. But what is a sensation? A corporeal object acting
upon a particular sense-organ gives rise to a sensation. This sensation is possible
only in an embodied soul, or, a body-soul complex. But by itself sensation is only
the starting point of knowledge, and, by itself it is no knowledge at all. Only when
it is thought then it becomes an object for human beings. But what is it to be thought?
Only when a universal is cognised imbedded in a material object, then it is said
to be known. And a universal is the essential elements or qualities inhering in a
number of particular things.

Without the starting-point of sensation, no knowledge is possible. But intellect
which deals with the universals or ideas cannot directly deal with the sensation,
being incorporeal, spiritual and rational. First, sensation has to be preserved in the
form of images (phantasms) through imagination. But the active intellect illumines
the image and enables the intellect to detect and isolate the universal elements
embedded in the image or images. Thus, Aquinas maintains that there can be no
imageless thinking[1] which meant for him no universal is possible without being
instantiated in particulars. Hence, it is important to note that no abstract universal
(idea) can be cognised apart from being materialised. Again, no particular things
are possible without being universalised, or in the language of Aristotle without its
forms. Hence, there can be knowledge only when the universal is isolated or
abstracted from an image, which is a product of imagination. In the language of
Kant, knowledge is the joint product of percept and concept. Of course, the meaning
of Kant is quite different from what St. Aquinas means.

---

1. Though as a psychological fact this has been refuted by the Wurzburg School.

Hence, the primary object of knowledge (intellect) is universal as it is found *in* and taken out from particular objects. Secondly, the universal is known as the universal on the reflexive level. In other words, a universal (idea) is in the mind of the human subjects and it cannot exist apart from the particular instances in which it inheres. This is pure Aristotelianism. The mind without sensation is a *tabula rasa* and sensation in the form of image arouses the active intellect. Only by the illumination of the image that intellect can find a universal. Hence, St. Thomas denies Platonic realism. But another difficulty arises.

If there be no sensation, then there can be no knowledge. God is nonsensible, so He cannot be an object of knowledge. Yes, even angels being purely spiritual cannot be cognised by human intellect. How can we rise above the objects of sense? Here St. Aquinas makes a sharp turning. He holds that human *intellect* as intellect has *being* as its proper object. Only those things can be known which partake of being. As a *human* being, man must start with senses, but as human *intellect* he can go beyond the sense.

> . . . the intellect does not and cannot by its own power apprehend God directly; but sensible objects, as finite and contingent, reveal their relation to God, so that the intellect can known that God exists.[1]

Moreover sensible objects, as effects from God as their cause manifest God. So far as sensible objects manifest God, human intellect can know God, imperfectly, very dimly. This knowledge of God, for St. Aquinas is known as *analogical*.

PROOFS FOR THE EXISTENCE OF GOD

Most probably St. Thomas's proofs for the existence of God are most famous and even now they are hotly discussed. St. Thomas has various reasons for advancing these proofs. First, he thinks that faith has a rational basis, even though faith cannot be fully understood. As St. Thomas believed that mind at first is a clean state and all knowledge is acquired through experience, so he rejects the doctrine of the innateness of God's knowledge. Even if there be some innate disposition for knowing God, this remains confused and vague.[2] Besides, it is a fact that there are atheists in the world. Though the times of St. Aquinas were not the times when atheism was rampant, yet St. Thomas felt that God's existence requires proofs. St. Thomas, being an Aristotelian rejects the primacy and priority of ideas. He therefore rejects the Ontological proof for the existence of God. St. Thomas does not think that a fact or an actuality can follow from an idea. In simple language, by having a thought of food, actual food cannot be found. Further, St. Thomas holds that by 'God' everyone does not mean God 'that than which no greater can be

---

1. F.C.S. Copleston, Vol. II, 1976, p.393.
2. St. Thomas grants that the idea of God is implanted in us by nature. This however does not mean that man knows absolutely that God exists (J. Hick, *The Existence of God*, p. 32, Paperback, 1964).

thought'. No doubt St. Thomas does grant that God alone is the source of all knowledge, however for him God is not the object of direct intuition, but is known through reflection. Hence, proofs for the existence of God strengthen the reflection of men on God.

Though St. Thomas denied that one can go from an idea to fact, yet he accepts *a posterioc* proof for God's existence. His starting-point is the experienced fact of the world. He presents five proofs and the first three proofs proceed directly from the given facts of experience.

1. First, proof is from motion.
2. Second, the series of efficient causes.
3. Thirdly, from the series of contingent causes.

But all the three arguments are really borrowed from Aristotle. However, for Aristotle the world is eternal. Therefore, ultimately the world has an eternal basis. For St. Thomas, the world was created. So the world can cease to be. For this reason, the three arguments of St. Thomas, following the proofs of Aristotle are not conclusive. These three arguments are called *cosmological* for they proceed from the experienced things of the cosmos.

Again, these arguments are not offered to the people who do not believe in God, but only for those persons who have vague and confused idea of God. Besides, all the proofs have to be taken together. There is nothing new about these proofs; they had been advanced by the predecessors of St. Thomas.

(I) From *motion*. It is an experienced fact that there is motion in the world. Now whatever is moved, is moved by another. Thus *A* moves *B*, *B* in turn moves *C* and so the series continues *ad infinitum*. But this cannot go on foreover. There must be a First Mover which moves without being moved by anything else. 'And this everyone understand to be God'.

(II) From *efficient cause*. Every cause is supposed to be caused by another. There is nothing which is known to be the efficient cause of itself. For a thing to be the cause of itself is to be prior to itself. This is absurd. But if every efficient cause has a prior cause of it, then in the long run, this will lead to infinite *regress*. In order to escape from this infinite regress one has to admit a *first efficient cause*, to which everyone gives the name of God.

(III) From *contingency*. By contingency is meant that a thing which exists now, may not exist at another time, i.e., a thing which has no ground of itself to exist. Now we find that a thing which is possible to exist now may not exist. Hence things may and may not exist. Therefore, if everything cannot exist, then at one time there was nothing in existence:

> Therefore, if at one time nothing was in existence, it would have been impossible for anything to have begun to exist.

But things are. Hence all things are not contingent. Therefore, there is a Being which keeps all contingent things in existence, and which by itself has its own ground of existence. For this reason one has to grant that there is *necessary being* which exists by its own necessity. This all men speak of as God.

This argument from contingency has been regarded by Thomists to be very important. It relies on the assumption that there can be no infinite series. In other words, the world as a whole requires an explanation. For Russell and A.J. Ayer, this is a pseudo-question. The world is and is a fact. It does not stand in need of any explanation. A series by itself cannot be explained either by a member in the series, nor by anything *outside* of the series. *The world as a whole* standing in need of an explanation is a metaphysical problem, and, a metaphysical problem is nonsense.[1]

(IV) *From graded excellence.* Things of the world are found *more or less* good, true, noble etc. But *more and less* point to a Being in which the perfection of goodness, truth and nobleness etc., are found. Therefore, there must be a Being which is the ground of all kinds of perfection in which things of the world participate. This perfect Being we call God.

That there is supreme perfection of the Good in which all things *participate* is essentially Platonic, and Plato refers to this proof.

(V) *The teleological argument.* Indeed as Kant observes that this proof is the oldest, clearest and most accordant with human reason. This proof is clearly presented by Plato. But let us briefly state it as St. Thomas does it.

We find that natural bodies, without consciousness and knowledge briefly work for an end. This end, therefore, is achieved by such bodies not fortuitously, but by being designed. Hence the end is pursued by some being endowed with knowledge and intelligence. This being we call God.

The argument is in favour of an architect and not a creator God. This teleological proof means only this that there is an intelligent Being who *designs* the end into pre-existing things. But a creator-God has to produce things as much as the design in them. Further, these proofs show the existence of God, but religion requires that this God is a Person, is Trinity and a Judge. As noted earlier this is what reason is not competent to establish. It is the work of revelation and rests on faith. After all, St. Thomas accepts agnosticism, according to which we know only this much that God exists, but not His essence or attributes. Whatever attributes are said to belong to God are held by us only analogically. Hence, let us state the analogical knowledge of what God is.

KNOWLEDGE OF GOD

There is a fundamental difference between man and God.

1.   Man is body soul complex, formed matter, potentiality-actuality. In God

---

1. A.J. Ayer and F.C.S. Copleston, *Logical Positivism*, ed. A.J. Ayer, p. 336; B. Russell and F.C.S. Copleston, *The Existence of God,* ed. John Hick, p. 175.

there is no matter, no corporeality. He is *actus purus*, pure activity or actuality. There is no poetentiality in Him which He has to actualise.

2.   Man is finite and God is infinite.
3.   Man is a creature and God is his creator.
4.   God is transcendent to the world and man.

Hence, man cannot know God. But through his reasoning he knows this much that God exists, but not what He is. Human intellect can know God through sensible objects, insofar as these objects manifest God, mirror Him and participate in His Being. After all finite things are the effects produced by God as their First cause, and, there is some similarity between cause and effect.

Since the creation of the world His invisible attributes are clearly seen ... by the things that are made. (*Romans* 1.20)

But finite things at most can tell us that *God is*, but not what He is, for there are fundamental points of difference between God and man. Hence, St. Thomas resorts to agnosticism, i.e., nothing beyond the bare existence of God can be validly stated.

We human beings know things through the categories of thought which are adequate for knowing sensible objects. For example, we know goodness, love, creativity in our finite experience. Hence, when we say that God is love or good, we cannot mean human love or human acts of goodness. All that we can say is the negative way. We can say that God loves us, but not the way human fathers love their children, or, husbands love their wives. We can in this way deny a great many attributes of God. He cannot have corporeality, for He is pure spirit, pure activity without potentiality which matter is. He cannot commit sin or undo the past for there is no past for him. He cannot commit suicide, and so on.

Negative way is the only way for knowing God, for men are quite different from God. So no term can be applied *univocally* to both God and men alike. For example, we say that God loves and we also say that men love. But the love of God is pre-eminent, super, infinite and transcendent. But the negative way leaves men stupefied and beclouded by ignorance. However, it has to be admitted too that men are really related to God and have some similarity with God. So to the extent men are really related and similar. We have to apply the affirmative way too. We have to say that God is wise with the proviso that His wisdom surpasses human wisdom. But certainly God's love or God's wisdom or goodness is not less than human wisdom or goodness. The affirmative way shows that God has human attributes, but even the most perfect human attributes merely trivialise Him who has love, wisdom and goodness infinitely more than what human intellect can understand. This concept is found in the advaitic doctrine of Purna Brahma, maintained by Kabir. This is the affirmative way of understanding the attributes predicated of God. As God is both quite different and infinite, so human attributes cannot be applied to God literally. And yet because men are really related and similar to some extent to God, so that our attributes do in some sense apply to God. This similar and yet different way of predicating attributes to God is said to be *analogical*.

There are two kinds of analogical predications, namely, the analogy of attribution and the analogy of proportionately. The analogy of attribution requires that one of the terms be *Prime analogate* to which the analogous property can be said to apply properly; while the other analogate has it only secondarily or improperly by virtue of its relation to the prime analogate. For example, 'healthy' is properly applied to man primarily, but derivatively it also applies to medicine or human complexion, because of the real relation between the analogates. Medicine is said to be healthy in the sense that is promotes or *causes* health, and, complexion of man is said to be healthy in the sense that it is an indication or effect of good health. Hence on account of real relation or causal relation terms are analogously applied to widely dissimilar analogates.

In the analogy of *proportionatly* the attributes are used in proportion of dissimilar essence belonging to the two analogates. For example, both 'dog' and 'man' are said to be intelligent. The term 'intelligent' *appears to be* univocally applied. But it is not so. The intelligence of a dog is in proportion to his essence or being, and, the intelligence of man is in proportion to his essence. As two essences of 'dog' and 'man' are different, so the term 'intelligent' is only analogically and not univocally applied.

As human beings do not know the essence of God, so by saying that God's wisdom is in proportion to His essence is really nonsensical. Hence, the analogy of proportion leads to complete agnosticism. But the analogy of attributes appears to throw some light, though dim concerning our knowledge of God. Hence the analogy of attribution is the more important form of analogical statement.

GOD AND EVIL

God is good and only good, then whence is evil in the world. This is a difficult question which every theist has to face. But before we tackle this question of evil, let us try to understand the meaning of creation, according to St. Thomas.

We have already seen that St. Thomas regards the world as an effect and God as its *First Cause*. How does this first cause create this world as its effect? St. Thomas states that God has created the world *out of nothing*. What does 'out of nothing' mean? First, the phrase means that God is a real creator and not an architect. An architect God fashions the pre-existing matter into the form of the world, for achieving an end. Hence 'out of nothing' means that there is no pre-existing matter out of which this world has been brought into being. In other words, the phrase means that God has created this world not out of any pre-existing *something*. There is nothing besides God.

God is good and out of His goodness, He has communicated. His goodness to this world. Is this creation necessary for God? For St. Thomas, the world is not necessary for God, but God is necessary for the world. The reason is that all things in the world and the world itself as a series of contingent things are contingent. They have no ground of their existence at all. God alone is their necessary ground. In other words, the world depends on God, but God does not depend for anything on this world. The reason is that God is perfect from eternity to eternity, and, there is no change in Him. Hence, the sole end of creation of the world is the communication of God's goodness to the world. Though God gains nothing from His creation, yet there is real relation between God and the world. There is creaturely dependence of the world and man on God.

Further, if God is eternal, then His creation ought to be eternal. St. Thomas accepts this. But says that the scripture, i.e., revelation tells us that the world was created in time. God willed freely form eternity that the world should come into being from eternity. Copleston puts the matter thus:

> There is no contradiction between being brought into existence and existing from eternity; if God is eternal, God could have created from eternity.[1]

Most probably it is contradictory to hold that God *acts* freely and that He is eternally unchangeable. Action implies change, and the word 'creation' specially according to the scripture, means a real bringing about after there being nothing. Hence, creation may mean the sportive act, as is maintained in Indian theism, or it may mean emanation as we find in Plotinus, or it may mean progressive unfoldment of the inexhaustible storehouse of potentialities in God, as the Absolist maintains. But St. Thomas does not accept any of these possibilities.

But our main question is, How can evil be explained if the world has been created by a good and omnipotent God?

According to St. Thomas, evil is not a positive, but a privative entity. Only a positive entity requires some explanation. A privative entity is there, but in due course it is likely to disappear. But this is really no explanation at all, since for St. Thomas evil is real, and, a source of further evil in the form of misery. Why is it at all? This man is blind, 'Blindness' no doubt is the deprivation of eyesight, and, the 'blindness' may be removed in due course, but why this man should suffer at all? Let us now explain evil in a general way.

Moral and non-moral evil : For example, cyclone, earthquake, pestilence etc., may be termed non-moral or natural evil. God is omniscient and before creation, He must have foreseen both kinds of evil. Why did He create evil at all?

St. Thomas would not admit that God, who is Good, could have created evil. But how is that evil has come about? Well, as far as natural evils are concerned, they are inevitable in a world of hierarchical order. The world is a work of an artist and in an art some imperfection is inevitable. Hence, there is corruption and decay. God, therefore, did not directly will evil, but willed a universe, good on the whole.

---

1.   Frederick Copleston, *A History of Philosophy,* 1976, p. 367.

In this working out a good universe on the whole, God has not created evil but has *permitted it*. But what about moral evil?

Moral evil arises from the perversity of human will. God has created man with free will, and, the gift of the free will is the greatest glory and gift of God. But it has to be admitted that free will has no meaning unless a real possibility of doing perversely be also permitted. But God foresaw everything. He foresaw the moral fall of man, his possible disobedience to the commandments of God. Why then God created a free man? God could not have created a free man without granting him *free choice* of good and bad, right and wrong. The abuse of free choice is as much a possibility as its right and proper choice. God could not have created a free man without the possibility of permitting sin and disobedience. But moral evil has not been willed by God, but has been permitted by Him. The grant of free will was given so that a few men will completely obey God and would voluntarily and assiduously will surrender their will to God for perfecting their own will. This perfection of will, through the Grace of God is called a *holy will*. Now the emergence of holy wills is the sole purpose of creation, as human intellect sees it. Once a holy will emerges in course of time, then this supreme end outwieghs all other considerations, even the sorrow and sin of the disobedient souls.

Thus God created the world and granted man free will. But free will means the possibility of sin and disobedience by the misuse of a perverted free will. This possibility of moral evil had to be permitted by God. But the real purpose of creating a free will is the possibility of the emergence of holy wills. Once a holy will emerges, then the supreme end of creation is fulfilled. Holy wills are higher than even the angels of heaven. Inevitably the problem of holy wills leads to the ethical view of St. Thomas.

The Ethics

St. Thomas follows Aristotle in his philosophy of morality. But his ethics has been greatly influenced by his theological considerations.

The first point to note in this context is that Aristotle was an intellectualist like Plato and Socrates. For instance, we should remember that for Socrates virtue is *knowledge*, and, for Plato the greatest end of man is contemplation of the Idea of the Good. Hence, for Aristotle, the highest end for man is the contemplation of the prime mover or God. This contemplation gives the highest happiness to man in this earthly life. Naturally the ethical view of Aristotle is intellectualistic. And St. Thomas in following Aristotle, gives priority to intellect over will. In contrast of Thomistic view John Duns Scotus and William of Occam favoured the primacy and priority of will over Intellect. Without comparing and contrasting the views of Intellectualist and voluntarist, we can state the intellectualistic view of St. Thomas with regard to his Ethics.

1. The will necessarily strives for good, and it is intellect which apprehends the idea of the good. Thus, intellect by determining the good which will has to

follow, is *superior to will, as a general rule.*

2. For St. Thomas the good (*verum*, truth) which intellect aims at is higher than the good (*bonum*) which will aims at. The reason is that intellect discerns the pure idea of the good. In contrast, will can find that good which is empirically possible instance of the good.

3. Again, St. Thomas regards divine intellect superior to divine will. The divine will follows necessarily from divine wisdom or intellect. This convention is based on the next point.

4. Is good in its own right, or, that alone is good which God wills in His free action? In other words, Does God will because good is good in itself, or, good is that which God determines by His will? According to St. Thomas, God commands the good, because it is good. That is, good is rational, good is good in its own right irrespective of its being willed by God.

5. For St. Thomas, the contemplation of the divine majesty, free from will, is the highest goal of human morality. The vision of God in His essence is the beatitude of human existence.

Thus, following Aristotle, St. Thomas accepts the primacy of intellect over will. Though St. Thomas follows Aristotle as far as possible, yet he also adds to it much which comes out of his Christian theology.

According to Aristotle, there is an intelechly in each man which drives him towards his perfection and his happiness. This development means the regulation of the appetites in each man by his reason. Only by a habitual control of passions by reason makes man virtuous. By remaining at the level of hedonistic satisfaction of senses, man becomes evil. But Aristotle also grants that friendship and fortune are also good. On the whole, Aristotle teaches the doctrine of *golden mean*. Aristotle's morality was essentially teleological, for the purpose of moral life is the attainment of happiness. It was also intellectualist, since for Aristotle, contemplation on the Prime Mover was the highest good. This contemplation really meant philosophical contemplation.

St. Thomas agrees with Aristotle's eudaemonistic ethics. But he added two points under the influence of his Christian theology. For St. Thomas, Aristotle's doctrine of happiness meant happiness of this earthly existence. For St. Thomas, this worldly existence extends into the next life. Hence, the complete happiness of man consists in the vision of God as He is in Himself. Further, this vision of God requires His Grace. Thus St. Thomas transforms the Aristotelian Ethics of a *wise* man into the morality of a *saintly* or holy man. Let us slightly elaborate this.

For St. Thomas, there is a natural desire in each man to realise happiness. This good is universal good. This universal good is not to be found in good fortune or even in sensual pleasure. As a matter of fact this universal good is not to be found in any created thing; but in God alone who is Himself the greatest good and most perfect good. Hence, the greatest good of man lies in having the vision of God. But man cannot attain this vision of God in his earthly existence. The vision of God as He is in Himself is possible in the next life alone. It is doubtful whether Aristotle ever believed in personal immortality. Hence, this was an addition of St. Thomas alone.

Secondly, it is doubtful whether Aristotle's *actus purus* was personal at all. But for St. Thomas *actus purus* is a personal God of the Christians. Now St. Thomas brings in another Christian doctrine of Grace. For St. Thomas no man by his own efforts can have the vision of God in His essence, unless he receives it by the Grace of God. This Grace is said to be a free gift of God. But like his Indian counterpart Ramanuja, St. Thomas states that God's Grace works only with the co-operation of human will. He who receives the Grace of God becomes a saintly man. This co-operation of will means that the recipient of God's Grace must abandon the pursuits of earthly gains and must be desirous of things eternal and heavenly. In other words, the aspirant of having God's vision must live a monastic life with the vows of celibacy, poverty and obedience to God's commandments. Naturally there are few who will tread this narrow path. Now we are in a position to compare the view of Aristotle with that of St. Thomas with regard to moral good.

1. Aristotle's ethic is confined to the love of man on this earth. For St. Thomas, this love must be love of God.

2. The happiness of which Aristotle talks is of this earth in the concrete existence of man. For St. Thomas, this earthly life is only a pilgrimage for the next life to come, where not happiness, but blessedness is found in the vision of God.

3. Aristotle's moral man is a philosopher, a *wise* man. In contrast, for St. Thomas a real moral man is a *saint* or holy man.

4. Lastly, in terms of Aristotle's technical terms, man becoming holy under the influence of God's Grace is the actualization of what is potential in a wise man. In other words, for St. Thomas, the wise men are the *matter* and *holy men* are the *form* of what wise men have to become.

St. Thomas and Aristotle

From the moral theory of St. Thomas, it is clear that he has not used Aristotle uncritically. He was fully aware of the fact that the philosophy of Aristotle existed much before the rise of Christianity. But he wanted to make Christian belief as much reasonable as possible and in order to make Christian faith intelligible, he used the philosophy of Aristotle. But he clearly made a distnction between philosophy and theology. Theology for him had a higher status than philosophy. Theology was based on revelation and was made to supplement the teaching of Aristotle. Nonetheless, philosophy and Theology formed a synthesis which lasted for the whole of the 13th century. However, St. Thomas disagreed wherever Aristotelianism seemed to be not in harmony with Christian theology. For examples,

1. Aristotle taught the eternity of the world and the unchangeable number and

the kinds of animal species. Against this, St. Thomas accepted the doctrine of creation of the world out of nothing, according to Christian revelation.

2. The highest reality of the cosmos, for Aristotle was *actus purus.* But this was not taught to be a person. Against this St. Thomas regard *personal God* as the highest reality.

3. For Aristotle, stars were gods which for St. Thomas was not acceptable. There is only one God and there are no gods at all.

4. For St. Thomas philosophy deals with the phenomenal or natural orders of things. In contrast, theology refers to the supernatural and heavenly orders of things.

5. For Aristotle, universals do not exist apart from individual things, but perhaps they exist in human minds, abstracted common and essential attributes of individuals forming a class. As against this, St. Thomas thinks that universals exist in the divine mind *before* the creation of individual things, and *in* things and in the human mind. As against this Aristotle denies the reality of Ideas *before* the creation of individual things in the divine Minds.

Thus, philosophy was made independent of theology. By demarcating the regions of natural and supernatural, a truce was made successfully between them. Underlying this truce was the principle that theology is supreme. Secondly, philosophy cannot contradict divine revelation, for theology extended the scope of knowledge and supplemented the findings of philosophy.

For St. Thomas, the synthesis of philosophy and religion worked well. But could faith be made wholly non-rational? Could philosophy be limited to things earthly? Did not the Church make claim to have some say in the earthly State power? Did not the Church made Galileo recant (in 1633) the theory of the rotation of the earth? Once we make reason independent of religion, it is bound to create upheaval in the religious philosophy of the people concerned. True, Roger Bacon, Scotus and Occam were priests and they wanted to continue the synthesis of St. Thomas. However, instead of maintaining the synthesis, they created the further conditions of Christian theology of mediaeval thinking very precarious.

ROGER BACON (c. 1214-94)

The exact dates of birth and death of Roger Bacon are not yet known. He was a British Franciscan monk. He was a brilliant and yet an independent thinker. Because of independent thought he was forced to leave his teaching job at Oxford and, later on, for the same reason of independence, he was imprisoned at Paris by the chief monk of the Franciscan Order. He wrote a lot, but the important work is known as *Opum Majus* (Maius). Contributions of Roger Bacon may be thus listed.

1. He separated science and philosophy from theology. But he allotted a superior place to theology. However, Roger Bacon insisted on the experimental investigation of science. True, theology is superior to science, but theology should not interfere with scientific method and growth. Roger Bacon knew the principles conditions of vision, conditions of reflection and refraction and the practical

importance of the science of Optics. He also recommended the use of mirrors for knowing things at a distance and used the laws of refraction for magnifying objects. But the time was not ripe for him for inventing a telescope.

Roger Bacon also dwelt on the need of studying nature for the use of medicine, for making explosives and believed that baser metals could be turned into gold by the laws of alchemy. He along with his insistence on astronomy, accepted astrology. For him, stars do influence the conduct of men.

2. Roger Bacon followed Aristotle in the sense that for Aristotle the universal is found in particulars alone, and, Bacon stressed the need for *observed particulars*. For Roger Bacon there are two kinds of experience. One kind depends on senses, either with or without instruments, along with trustworthy evidence of reliable persons. This kind of experience is used in science. Nay, more, he laid emphasis on experiments. As noted earlier he followed, lauded and praised experimental science, The *second* kind of experience relates itself to spiritual things and for deserving the grace of God. The spiritual experience, step by step leads to the mystical rapture. For Roger Bacon theology pursuing spiritual experience, depends on faith. But he does not disregard reason, sense for him, reason is of God. And it is necessary to discern the truth of pagan scriptures.

3. Even though theology is regarded as superior to science and philosophy, he yet advises the knowledge of Greek, Hebrew, and Arabic language, essential for finding the truth of Christian theology. Certainly this is a sound principle, which is acceptable in Christian seminaries.

4. Mathematics was very important for Roger Bacon. For him logic and grammar were dependent on mathematics[1] and, astronomy would not advance without mathematics. Roger Bacon following Arabian scientists, urged the quantitative treatment of observed data. Here Roger Bacon was wholly correct, for now what exists, exists in number.

Thus Roger Bacon will be remembered as an initiator of British empiricism because of his emphasis on mathematics and experiments. But he also mixed science with superstitions. For example, along with astronomy he credited astrology, and, accepted alchemy along with chemistry.

Hence, Bacon headed a new era in which men will be weaned away from books to the observation, from dialectics to actual experience, from authorities to fresh investigation. Roger Bacon stressed the importance of Mathematics and experimental science, Mathematical study of astronomy and the practical use of science. Considering his times, Roger Bacon can be excused for his acceptance of astrology and alchemy. As a matter of fact Roger Bacon fell into trouble for accepting astrology which was not acceptable to Christianity. His disregard of the Church authorities also earned the disfavour of his superiors.

---

1.   B. Russell has reduced mathematics into logic. Now mathematical precision also means linguistic clarity and precision.

JOHN DUNS SCOUTS (c. 1274-1308)

The date and place of birth of John Duns Scotus are not certain. He belonged to Franciscan order. This most probably accounts for his difference with Thomism. In a book like the present one, it is advisable to mention only those elements which are important philosophically. Duns Scotus advances his philosophy along the following points:

1. Separation of Theology for philosophy
2. The primacy of will over intellect
3. The doctrine of individuals.

Philosophy and Theology

As noted before, St. Thomas had made a distinction between natural theology (i.e., really philosophy based on *reason*) and revealed theology (based on *faith*). A clearer distinction was made between the two disciplines by Roger Bacon. But the final distinction between philosophy and theology was made by Scotus. The separation of philosophy from theology was made to safeguard faith from the unwelcome intrusion of philosophical objection against faith.

1. Formerly, the distinction was made with a view to supplementation of reason by faith. Faith went farther than reason as is clear in the Thomist doctrine of Ethics. Again, faith was regarded as superior to philosophy. The view of Scotus means the same, but in the place of supplementation of reason by faith, Scotus *separates* the one from another.

For Scotus reason is incapable of dealing with the mysteries of religion. For example, the divine nature and purpose, predestination, immortality of souls, doctrine of creation, God's Person and the doctrine of beatitude etc., all come within the domain of theology. Reason, for Scotus, can neither prove nor disprove the dogmas of religion.

2. Certainly the existence of God has to be proved by reason, and, Scotus does mention proof which were presented before, both by St. Thomas and by Anselm. But he considers that these proofs are imperfect. These proofs can at most show that there *is* God. But reason cannot show that God is a living God and a Person. This is certainly true with regard to the philosophy of Plato and Aristotle. Neither the Idea of the God (Plato) nor the Prime Mover can be said to be personal.

3. Even the doctrine of creation is not fully intelligible by reason. Creation is by the free will of God out of Nothing and willed eternally with the purpose of human beings reaching the final end of beatitude. Much of it has to be understood by faith and faith alone. Nay more.

4. Reason works first with the sensibles and later with the abstraction of the universals embedded in them. But theology ultimately rests on divine revelation and grace.

5. For Scotus, both theology and science are certain and both of them yield *certainty* of knowledge. But the certainty found in geometry is quite different from

that of theology. The certainty of geometry or of science in general is *theoretical,* but that of theology is *practical.* But one point of confusion has to be avoided. In Kant also ethics is known as *practical.* But for Kant, practical reason dealing with God, world and Soul cannot yield scientific knowledge proper. For Scotus, however, theology has *certain* (indubitable) knowledge given by revelation with regard to human conduct.

No doubt, Scotus separated faith from reason, theology from philosophy with a view to keeping the authority of revelation, safeguarded in an a 'ivory tower'. This was also later attempted by Karl Barth (1886-1968). But once philosophy is separated form theology, it becomes free, and slowly and gradually reason becomes the mistress of the soul. And this is what has happened in the further development of Western philosophy. Hence, the philosophy of Scotus has served the purpose of transition to what is known as Modern Philosophy.

The Doctrine of Universals

According to Scotus universals exist before instantiated in *the mind of God,* also in particular things as their essence, and, afterwards as abstracted concepts from observed particulars. But the universals do exist objectively.For example, redness abstracted as a concept from the observed red roses does exist objectively. This doctrine of universals differs from Platonic realism, since for Plato universals exist eternally in their own rights, whether there be any divine mind or not. For Scotus, universals exist as something mental in the divine mind. Secondly, universals even when abstracted from particulars exist objectively. Hence, universals are moderately real for Scotus, and not absolutely real as in the theory of Plato. Therefore, the doctrine of universals, according to Scotus, is more realistic than what is held in conceptualism. Conceptualism also accepts the *objective existence of universals in particulars,* but it does not admit the objective existence of universals apart from particulars in the divine mind. Hence, the objectivity of universals is most extreme in Platonic reality of universals, less in conceptualism and moderately so in Scotus's theory of universals.

As universals are said to be objectively real in individuals, so individuals are also said to be objectively real. Further, as science proceeds from observed individual things, so individual things have to be conceded for holding onto the objectivity of science. But in what does the individuality of particular things reside? According to St. Thomas, the individuality of a thing is accounted by matter and not by form. What does this mean?

Rama and Shyam are two individual men. It is said that they have the same essence (of humanity) in them, but they differ in their accidental qualities of colour, shape, age, height etc. This is what St. Thomas would allow. Against this, Scotus would say that there is *always difference of essence* too between two individuals. The reason? After death all souls become incorporeal. In that case, all will be alike and so one soul cannot be distinguished from another. This is the doctrine of the identity of indiscernibles in the philosophy of Leibnitz. Not only there will be indistinguishable souls in their immaterial existence after death, but there is some epistemological difficulty too.

Senses perceive the individuals and the intellect knows the universal embedded in the individuals. But the intellect must also be conceded to know the individuals even though darkly. Intellect must take note of the individuals as individuals from which universals have to be extracted. In that case individual must have the characteristics of *differentiating essence*, if individuals have to be known by intellect (for the intellect knows *essence* only).

Will and Intellect

Scotus differs from St. Thomas with regard to the superiority of will over intellect. For St. Thomas intellect is superior to will. If there is choice between intellect without will, then St. Thomas would go for it. On the other hand, if there is will without intellect then Scotus would choose it. Of course, both will admit that intellect and will work together, but in this cooperative enterprise, for Scotus will is superior to intellect on the following grounds:

1. For St. Thomas, man is a rational creature, and, intellect is his crowning glory. Intellect is superior to will, for intellect determines the functioning of will

As against this, Scotus regards will to be superior to intellect, for it is freer than intellect. Its freedom lies in the choice of one between two or more alternative which intellect presents to the will. Will will cease to be will, if it were determined by intellect to give assent to the good presented by intellect. The will has full freedom either to give assent or its denial in each particular case of choice. No doubt sense, imagination and intellectual apprehensions are indispensable preconditions for determining the will. But throughout intellect remains subservient to the activity of will.

According to St. Thomas intellect cannot withhold its assent to the truth which it apprehends. For example,

All men are mortal
Ram is a man
∴ Ram is mortal.

The intellect is not free in rejecting the truth of the conclusion if it apprehends the premises. According to Scotus, on the contrary, will is always free. Even God cannot create a rational will to choose the right alternative presented by intellect at all times. Hence, will is indefeasibly free. Scotus rejects the Thomist view that will *necessarily* chooses the good once it is clearly presented by intellect. Socrates too will agree with St. Thomas. But Scotus holds that even in heavenly abode the saints are *free* to revolt and rebel against the commandments of God. Of course they cannot do so because of their habitual choice of obedience to God. Habit is only a second nature. Hence, there is only a secondary necessity of will in the saint not to choose the evil, but this is not intellectual necessity. Hence, there is psychological *indispensability* but *not logical necessity* in the conduct of angels.

2. The will is more perfect, and, its corruption is much more deplorable than that of intellect. For example, a perverse will is much worse than the intellectual ignorance of God. Rebellion against God is much worse than remaining unconcerned about God.

3. Thinking about evil is less sinful than *committing the evil act.* Wish of adultery is not as bad as actual adultery.

4. Love of God is higher than contemplation of God. Love, which is a product of will, unites a saint with God. But knowledge of good can sustain at most contemplation of God. But contemplation can never overcome the dualism of the worshipper and God. But love can overcome. Love leads to the mystic union with God, i.e., becoming one with God.

Both Scotus and St. Thomas hold that man must go beyond the natural development of will and intellect in him. God's grace is necessary before will and intellect are perfected. Scotus holds that faith, hope and love are the real gifts of divine grace. Love as the final fruition of will, will get the saint united with God. On the other hand, for St. Thomas, intellect offers eternal blessedness in the contemplation of God. But Scotus would say that contemplation, no matter however deep, cannot bridge the gulf between God and the worshipper. The Indian reader can very easily see that this is the same controversy which he finds in the controversy between *jnanayoga* and *bhaktiyoga.*

Hence, for Scotus, knowledge and contemplation are mere means for love, and, love of God is an end for its own sake.

There is also some difference with regard to the ethical thought, between St. Thomas and Scotus. Scotus teaches the full and unfettered will of God. God could have created all things with quite a different order in nature. An act is morally good, because God prescribes it, according to Scotus. And if God were not fully free, He will not be so morally. It is the essence of morality, that the act be fully free. For St. Thomas, a moral act is good, because God sees it to be good and intellectual clearness has to be accepted necessarily.

Does Scotus mean that God can prescribe moral laws arbitrarily? Can He prescribe adultery or telling his as morally good? Scotus does not mean this. According to him, God cannot prescribe anything morally evil, for He is good, and, anything coming out of His nature cannot be evil, for He is eternally good. But God is eternally free and He cannot be bound ever by His intellectual necessity. This Scotus illustrates by his example of the first commandment. God as God could not have allowed to worship any other god besides Him. For the same reason God could not have commanded the worship of an idol, for the worship of an idol is not any worship of God at all. For 'worship' means intense love of God and the worship of any other god or idol cannot be the love of God which is the highest good of man. Hence, God prescribes laws because of His free, but good will.

But it must he conceded that Scotus has allowed far greater degree of prominence of will over intellect than what St. Thomas would allow.

WILLIAM OF OCCAM OR OCKHAM (c. 1280-1347)

Occam or Ockham was an English Franciscan priest. He was born about 1280 and died in 1347. He is credited with the foundation of nominalism and a principle known as 'Occam's Razor'. He is another important empiricist, nearer Aristotle and rather for removed from Plato.

For Occam only particulars exist and all our knowledge begins with the perception of them. We do abstract common qualities found in many objects to form universal concepts. Theses concepts are merely signs which designate many *similar* objects or particulars. But what about the reality of these universals?

Universals certainly do not exist separately from and independently of the objects, as Plato believed. They are not found even in the particulars, as is the case with conceptualism and Aristotle. They are not in human minds or even in the divine mind. Universals are mere conventional signs to designate particular things and their existence must not be hypostatized and multiplied besides the existence of particulars. This is known as 'Occam's Razor'. Popularly Occam's razor means *entities are not to be multiplied without necessity.* His own words are, "It is vain to do with more what can be done with fewer."

For Occam only the particulars exist which are known by perception. Besides, the particulars in the external world, human beings know their acts of will, joy and sorrow with the help of their introspection. But we do not know our souls, exactly as Hume has informed us.

Knowledge may be deductive and inductive. Deductive reasoning, as is illustrated in syllogism, is necessarily true. However, the basis of our knowledge is derived from experience with the help of induction. Beyond experience we have no knowledge of the transcendent entities. What about God?

We have no *demonstrative* knowledge of God, opposed to which what Anselm and St. Thomas supposed. We can have only *probable* knowledge of God from the world as His effects. In causal and cosmological arguments based on contingency, we take recourse to *infinite regress,* which is not an accepted principle of logic. What about dogmas like Trinity, Creation etc. According to Occam, they *cannot be made intelligible by reason.* But should we cease to believe in the Christian dogmas? No. Here we depend on revelation for our belief in dogmas.

Thus by the separation of philosophy and theology, ultimately a situation was reached in which the whole scholastic philosophy came to be rejected. No longer, in Occam, philosophy and theology cooperate with one another and that theology could be said to supplement philosophy. No longer theology could be called a science at all. The doctrine of universals on which the religious philosophy of St. Thomas (largely Aristotelian) and that of St. Augustine (largely Platonic) was based, was totally wrecked by the nominalism of Occam.

Again, like Scotus, Occam also maintains the thesis that Will is superior to Intellect. God has absolutely free will. He could have created a world with quite different natural laws, and, could have prescribed quite a different moral order. It appears that Occam was more extreme in holding voluntarism than Scotus.

Transition to Modern Philosophy

Greek thinkers were essentially free thinker Many of the early Greek philosophers were critics of religion (Xenophanes, Heraclitus, Democritus, Anaxagoras, Protagoras, Epicureans). But popular religion continued Socratico-Platonic thought was essentially ethical and religious.. But even in Plato, the Phythagorean emphasis on mathematics continued Aristotle was a biological scientist and he emphasized the importance of observation of facts.

In the same way Democritus and Leukippus were atomists and the atomistic theory was accepted by the Epicureans.

Lastly, the tradition of Pythagoras and Plato with regard to religious interest was fully upheld by Plotinus.

When Christianity occupied the centre of thought, then it built its foundation on Plato, Aristotle and the Stoics. In mediaeval philosophy a synthesis of theology and philosophy was worked out very well by St. Augustine, St. Anselm and St. Thomas Aquinas. But the delicate balance could not last long. Philosophy refused to be 'the handmaid of theology'. In Thomism, philosophy was given the task of preparing the 'preambles of faith'. But in Scotus and Occam, philosophy and theology fell apart. Meantime a third movement appeared.

Largely due to the rise of Arabic influence, Aristotelianism began to be studied in full detail. But apart from his philosophy of matter and form, his emphasis on observation of facts was greatly patronised by the Arabs. And the Christian people were convinced of the importance of patient observation

Of course, observation is not enough. Formation of hypothesis, building up of theories, public testing of hypothesis and mathematizing of the result are some of the basic tenets of modern science. But observation occupies the starting-point of science. Copernians (1473-1543), Kepler (1571-1630), Galileo (1564-1642) and finally Newton (1642-1727) largely by patient observation not only established science and set a new era for all times to come, but in due course have profoundly influenced philosophy and religion. Science could establish itself only when Christendom itself grew weak and allowed secular forces to dominate.

Two things contributed to the weakening of the authority the church First, there was the controversy between the Dominicans (followers of Thomism) and Franciscans (followers of St. Augustine) concerning the doctrine of divine grace and free will. Secondly, powerful kings of different States challenged the authority of the Church to interfere with their government. Papacy between 1305-77 and later because of the great schism was greatly weakened. Thirdly, for all practical purposes, Occam reduced theology to be a matter of faith But faith was beyond reason. Indirectly by putting the articles of Christian faith in the domain of theology, allowed full freedom to reason, and, reason in due course, flowered in the development of science.

Copernicus (1473-1543) was a Polish priest. He got interested in astronomy and as a result of his observations he came to realise that the sun was the centre and the earth went round the sun. The earth moves diurnally (giving rise to day and night) on its axis, and, annually in elliptical rotation round the sun. This heretical findings of Copernican heliocentric theory did not create much agitation for the Churchmen at the time of Copernicus. But when Galileo, proved experimentally the movement of the earth, then the Church realised the gravity of the situation, and, in 1633 made Galileo recant the theory of earth's movement round the sun. What was involved in this heliocentric theory ?

First, the ancient tradition which was accepted by the Church, had held that the earth was the centre of the universe. The Church further held that in this geocentric world, man was created by God for His special purpose. But what was the intellectual world view of the heliocentric theory ? The earth was the smallest planet. More.

From ancient times even Plato and Aristotle regarded the stars and planets as perfect and circular motion was the most perfect circular motion. But Kepler (1571-1630), along with Galileo held that the earth went round the sun in an elliptical orbit. But what about the divine purpose in the creation of man ?

Science showed however primarily through Galileo, Kepler and celebrated Newton (1642-1727) that mechanical laws prevailed everywhere. This mechanistic world view was further strengthened by Harvey (1578-1657) who discovered the mechanical circulation of blood. In the same manner, Robert Boyle (1627-91) taught the mechanical laws of Chemistry. The further use of telescope in 1608, thermometer and barometer strengthened this mechanistic world view of the universe Gone was the special divine purpose in the creation of the world.

The European world till now is guided by the scientific outlook of the universe Science can predict, control and guide the destiny of man. As yet Indians have not overcome their religious world view though they enjoy the fruits of Western science and technology.

Mediaeval Christian philosophy fully confirms the stages of development of Compte. At first there was the period of theology where philosophy was the handmaid of theology. Finally, religious philosophy has given birth to science, largely through Roger Bacon, Scotus and Occam. In modern times, philosophy is just the after-effect of science, its method and language. This is what we will discover about modern and contemporary philosophy.

5

Summary of Some Important Topics in Greek and Medieval Philosophy

1. Evolution

It will be an anachromism to suppose that Darwin's Organic theory of evolution could be seen as Greek thinkers. But there was an adumbration of it in its most primitive form.

Anaximander (611-577 B.C.) speculated that in the beginning there was only water everywhere and first creatures lived in waters alone. In due course, however water dried up. Only those creatures could survive which could adapt themselves to the conditions of dry land.

Of course, this kind of evolution is not scientific as it has not been proved by means of detailed observed data, in different kinds of living beings. But it is an adumbration of the Darwin's theory of adaptation and slow changes of organs in living creatures, according to the varying conditions of life.

Next thinker was Empedocles (c. 490-430 B.C.) According to Empedocles, living creatures occurred in all kinds of grotesque forms. There were bodies without heads, necks and shoulders. Some animals had human bodies with heads of oxen. Only the best formed animals alone could survive. Here is emphasis on the co-ordination and mutual adaptation of the various limbs of animals and men. This is certainly again a foreshadowing of organic evolution in its most primitive form.

Aristotle (384-322 B.C.) does talk of evolution and gives a static picture of animals in a graded scheme of things. But for Aristotle in the real sense there was no evolution from one species into another. For him all the species and the different kinds of genera were eternal. Really Aristotle spoke more of unfoldment than evolution. Each embryo simply unfolded its potentiality embedded in it into actuality. But species never evolved from one into another. Why could not the biologist Aristotle hint at the theory of organic evolution?

The real reason appears to be this. Aristotle denied the reality of real time where new things are thrown out in the creative drive of Nature. For him eternity was true and like his master Plato, thought that time is only a *passing image* of eternity. Hence, by denying the historicity of time, Aristotle could not develop the modern theory of evolution.

2. Freedom of Will

Freedom of will has relevance for morality. Unless man is morally free, he cannot be said to be responsible for his action. He is rewarded or punished because he is supposed to have acted differently from what he did. This question can be raised in a general way too. For the existentialist Sartre man is indefeasibly is free. In Greek and medieval philosophy, 'freedom of will' is discussed both in a general way and in the context of morality. For Aristotle, the topic of free will is important in moral Judgment.

For *Aristotle*, only a voluntary action is an object of moral judgment. An involuntary or a non-voluntary action is not an object of moral judgment. An action is involuntary when it takes place as a result of an external agency. On the contrary, a voluntary action is one which originates from the agent himself, and the door has to choose his course of action freely. Free will is regulated and sustained by reason. Hence rational and deliberate choice is free will. As reason is essentially the inner man, hence rational choice is self-determined action. Even now it is the most popular view of free will.

This choice may be of *means* or of ends. In general, 'end' may be proximate end or it may mean an ultimate end. For Aristotle, the ultimate end is same for all men. This end lies in the attainment of divine blessedness by contemplating on the goodness of God. Hence, *choice* really means choice of means, conducive to the attainment of the highest good of man.

Aristotle was a great supporter of free will. He opposed Socrates, for Socrates held that no man does wrong knowingly. For Aristotle man is not only rational, but he has appetites and passion too. They always tend to tempt a man towards wrong choice by overpowering his reason. Hence, no man in his virtuous action is wholly determined by his reason. Therefore, no action can be done by *rational necessity*. It is only by the settled habit of rational choice by regulating one's passions and appetites that man can be virtuous.

The problem of free will become important in Christian theology. The first great Christian theologian is St. Augustine. In his epistemology, St. Augustine maintains the theory of free will, but in his theological doctrine of Original Sin, he denies free will to a sinful man.

According *to St. Augustine*, without an active will man can neither have sensation nor knowledge and cannot rise towards the final vision of God. For him, sensation is a passive affair due to external impression. Hence unless a man attends to a sensation, he will not be aware of its happening. We can pass through the whole road without noticing the flowers growing on the tree if we are obsorbed in our own throught. Only by attending to the trees we become aware of the flowers on the trees. This necessity of the active will is all the more clear when we carry out syllogistic or mathematical reasoning.

Again, in knowledge proper we become aware of ideas, and, ideas are in the mind of God. So by knowing ideas, we apprehend God to some extent. Hence, can we know God through our own efforts and free will? No. Why?

According to St. Augustine we know only this much that God *is*, but *not what He is*. The reason? The reason is that the more active will is superior to less active will. In relation to God, man remains passive, and, God alone remains active. So man can know God only when God by His grace chooses men to apprehend Him.

Thus, St. Augustine maintains the doctine of free will in his epistemology. But he appears to deny free will to man according to his theological teaching of original sin. In his theology, St. Augustine holds that the first man called Adam alone had free will. After his disobedience in eating the forbidden fruit, he became a fallen man. His descendents too have become fallen men, and, no fallen men can have free will. Only by the grace of God can a fallen sinner be restored to have free will.

However, in later Western philosophy, St. Augustine is regarded as the upholder of free will, according to his theory in his epistemology.

St. Thomas grants that human beings are free in their moral choice. However, it is the intellect which decides what is good for a man, and the man has to choose the good freely. But at times by the violence of appetites and passions, a man may be overpowered, and his intellect may be befogged. In such conditions he might fall into vice.

St. Thomas follows to a large extent Aristotle in explaining moral act. A moral act is a self-determined act. In every self-determined or voluntary act, it is the will which gives it assent. But before doing so, the will has to be presented with the alternatives of what is good and what is not. This determination of the good is done by intellect. But the will is not coerced to do what is good, as ascertained by the intellect. There is no intellectual necessity. One like Socrates cannot say that no one does wrong knowingly. Under the overwhelming power of appetites and passion, a man may see what is good, and, finally choose the evil, A drunkard knows that drinking is bad, and, yet he falls a prey to it. But St. Thomas accepts the reality of free will. However, for him, *intellect is superior to will,* for the ascertainment of the true good has to be determined by intellect.

Later Christian theologians accepted the reality of free will. Nay more. Both Scotus and Occam held the superiority of will over intellect. This view is opposed to both Aristotelian and the Thomist view (see the index of 'intellect and will')

3. Early Greek thinkers and their Criticism of religion

Early Greek thinkers were free thinkers. They tried to explain things according to natural causes like earth, water, fire and air. They were not very respectful about their supernatural gods. They criticised their religions on account of

1. Anthropomorphism of gods and goddesses.
2. Also because of their immoral conduct.
3. Also on account of polytheism.

Xenophanes (570-480 B.C.) rejected polytheism in favour of monotheism and the Orphic theory of the transmigration of the soul. Heraclitus (525-475 B.C.) rejected the gods as taught by Homer and Hesiod. Democritus (460-360 B.C.) traced the worship of gods due to fear. Anaxagoras, Protagoras, Socrates and Aristotle were deemed anti-religious. The Epicureans denied the concern of gods of men and the religious belief in post-mortem existence. Let us elaborate the points raised here.

Xenophanes protested against polytheism and the immorality of gods and goddesses, as was taught by Homer and Hesiod. He accused the religious worshippers as anthropomorphic thinkers.

If oxen and horses could worship and paint their gods, then they would do so as oxen and horses. The Ethiopians make their gods black and snub-nosed; the Thracians say theirs have blue eyes and red hair.

Most probably Xenophanes conceived his God monotheistically as a world-God. His religion might have been pantheistic.

Heraclitus did not accept Homeric and Hesiodic gods and goddesses. Such deities, according to him, were due to ignorance.

Athenians regarded the sun and moon as divinites. Even Plato and Aristotle did not cease from thinking so. Anaxagoras held that the sun was constituted of red-hot stones and the moon of earth. Hence, he de-deified the sun and moon.

Protagoras was really sceptical about the existence of gods. He considered the subject-matter of gods as obscure and no sure knowledge could be claimed about divine existence. However, he recommended the acceptance of popular religious beliefs as a measure of prudence.

The Epicureans taught that there are gods like human beings, but they are not concerned about human beings. They eat, drink and enjoy themselves. Besides, the Epicureans being atomists, denied the possibility of post-mortem existence of human beings. Men come into being by the suitable combination of atoms and die because of their dissolution. Hence, there is no question of survival of human beings in their next life. Their aphorism is:

When we are, death is not yet; and where death comes, there we are not.

4. Knowledge is perception

In Greek thinking, 'knowledge is perception' was held by the atomists and the sophists. Protagoras and Gorgias are important for holding this theory. In the same way Socrates, Plato and Aristotle are the chief critics of the theory that knowledge is perception.

According to Democritus, knowledge is due to the motion of atoms. Perception and thought, both are due to the collision of atoms. In perception the atomic motion is *coarse and rough*. In thought this motion is *fine and gentle*. Hence, perception and thought do not differ *in kind*, but only *in degree*. Hence, thought and perception are of one kind. Therefore, one can say that knowledge *is perception.* But what kind of motion is perception?

In perception there is the motion from external objects to the sense-organs of the percipient. Hence, perception is due to the joint action of external objects and perceiving, sense-organs of the percipient. First, perception is not *of* the external object, nor of the percipient. But it is what *appears* to the perceiving subject, and, for him alone, at the moment it appears. As such each man is the measure of what appears to him true at the moment of its occurrence. This is known as the doctrine of *homo measura.*

> Man is the measure of all things, of what is, that is; of what is not, that it is not.

Consequences?

No two persons perceive alike, not even the same person at different moments of time. Hence, perception is momentary and relative. This interpretation of *homo measura* leads to scepticism *and nihilism* in the writings of Gorgias. Gorgias maintains three statements.

1. There is nothing.
2. Even if there be anything, it cannot be known.
3. Whatever is known, cannot be communicated.

By 'a thing' is meant a plurality of things, moved and moving one another. But Zeno has already shown that plurality and motion are illusory. Hence there is *nothing* which can be perceived.

Again, whatever we perceive is not the external object in itself, nor is it due to the perceiving subject. Hence, we do not know what the perceived object is.

Further, when we speak or communicate, then we use some predicate about a subject. For example,

> 'This table is black.'

But 'table' and 'black' are not the same thing. Hence whatever we say about the perceived table, then we say something about it what it is not.

Hence, there is *nihilism,* for there is nothing to know. Whatever we know is not the real thing, but its momentary perception. Finally, we cannot really communicate our knowledge. Hence, there is complete scepticism.

Criciticism

For Socrates and Plato, knowledge means what is universal and valid, that is, consistent and free from contradiction. But knowledge cannot be perception according to the definition of knowledge. Perception is momentary and *relative* to different persons. What is sweet in health is not so in sickness and fever. But knowledge is always of *something for someone.* But as elaborated by Gorgias, there is *nothing* to perceive and there is no knower who remains the same for all moments of time.

The doctrine of 'knowledge is perception' blurs the distinction between truth and falsity. If what a mad man imagines, and, what a new born child sees and what a brute perceives and what a healthy man senses be equally true, then quite obviously there can be no distinction between what is true and what is false.

' Further, if we open one eye and close the other, then we know with one eye and do not know through the other eye. Hence, the same man knows and does not know at the same time.

Finally, what appears to one be true, then what appears to the opponent of the Sophist as false becomes false. Hence, the teaching of *homo mensura* appears false to others. So it is false. Indirectly here there is the 'liar's paradox' which looms large in the philosophy of Russell.

Aristotle's Criticism

If all opinions and appearances be equally true, then it would lead to self-contradicting statements.

If objects exist at one moment and cease to be at the next, then it means that everything *is* and *is not*. If a thing is perishing, there must be *something* which perishes. Against the Sophists, Aristotle observes that no *sense* contradicts itself at the same moment about the same object. Further, the apparent is always apparent to *someone*, at the time when, to the sense, under the conditions in which it appears.

5. The Problem of Evil

'Evil' becomes a problem when some sort of theism is maintained. If God be infinitely Omnipotent and good, then why should be any evil at all. As Plato and Aristotle did not have explicit theism in their philosophy, so this problem was not very serious for them. For Plato, there was the intractable matter which accounts for evil in the universe. For Aistotle, moral evil is due to the overpowering of the intellect by appetites and passion. But this is a human problem when a man fails to have a settled habit of will in controlling passions through the regulative power of reason. The first serious problem arises with Stoicism.

The Stoics believed in God who is the world-reason endowed with intellect and will. Thus God is the creator of the world. So the question is; 'Why has God created evil, when He is the reason of the world?' He is also to be taken as good and benevolent; then why is there evil at all? There are natural evils and also moral falls. The Stoics give the following answer.

First, the Stoics deny that there is any evil at all. Only from a partial viewpoint, a thing may appear evil, but from the view of the whole thing, there is no evil at all. Natural evils, in the form of earthquakes and cyclones, disease and old age, have served as a challenge for men to understand and conquer them. Without such evils man would not have made any advance at all. Secondly, evil is a foil to the good. Even a shadow in the moon, enhances the beauty of the full moon. In any work of art, dark points are as necessary as the beautiful parts. Even moral excellence is not possible with the conquest of trials and temptations.

As a general observation, the Stoic solution is healthy, but the problem gets deeper in the Christian theism of St. Augustine and St. Thomas.

St. Augustine admits that God is omnipotent and infinitely beneficent. Then why is there evil at all? St. Augustine's solution and philosophy is wholly theological. According to him, god has established the church which teaches the way to find rest and happiness in God. But can man by his *own* efforts follow the way to secure his ultimate good? No. Because in Adam all have sinned, and, only through the grace of God, men will regain their lost free will. With the restored free will men can overcome their worldly nature.

The solution of St. Augustine concerning the original sin is wholly unacceptable to the moderners. Again, the loss of free will to the vast majority of unchristian men in their unrepentent state is too narrow and a sectarian view. Finally, the view of St. Augustine is wholly theological and of not much concern for philosophy. In contrast the view of St. Thomas is of far greater importance.

St. Augustine was a Platonist, but he rejected the Platonic explanation of evil due to matter. For St. Augustine, everything has been created by God, even matter. So if evil is due to matter, then God, becomes directly responsible for evil. Hence, for St. Augustine, evil is *not really positive but privative*, for in due course, through the grace of God it (evil) disappears. But pain is not less painful and less miserable by calling it 'privative.' As long as it lasts, it continues to be evil. Erigena (c. 810-77) does not see this point.

John Scotus Erigena adopts the Plotinian philosophy of pantheism. According to four phases of the universe, the world emanates from God and Ultimately returns to him. So *all is God*, and *God is all*. Hence, evil also is God. Erigena contents himself by calling evil as *privative* and not positive. But mere verbal solution does not take away the real pain. However, this pantheistic solution teaches the resignation of man to the inevitable, as was taught and practised by Spinoza and Sigmund Freud.

According to *St. Thomas*, God is good and He had created this world to communicate His goodness to it. Of course, the goodness of God means His Omnipotence, omniscience and benevolence. Naturally, why this kind of God has created evil? St. Thomas denies that a good God can create evil. Man is responsible. St. Thomas gives the following explanation of evil.

First, for St. Thomas, evil is not a positive but a privative entity. Hence, God is not responsible for the mere absence of good. But St. Thomas fails to recognise that even a privative evil is evil. If a painter paints a woman without the eyes, then is it not a significant omission? Is it not an ugly thing in the painting? Hence, the doctrine of privative evil is no explanation at all.

2. Secondly, St. Thomas observes that natural evils are inevitable in a world of hierarchical order, where the lower has to serve the higher.

3. Besides, the world is just like a work of art, and, in such a work some imperfection is necessary to enhance the excellence of the whole e.g., the presence of a villain in a tragedy. Hence in working out a good universe on the whole, some evil *has to be* permitted, even when God *does not will it.* This point is more relevant in relation to moral evil.

4. For St. Thomas, moral evil is due to the perversity of human will. God in creating man has given him the greatest gift of free will. But free choice has no meaning unless the possibility of choosing wrong be also allowed. However God's purpose in granting free will is that man should perfect his will by voluntarily surrendering it to the will of God.

Our will are ours, so that by surrendering it to the will of God, human wills may become deeper and perfect. But few become holy by submitting themselves to God. Their achievement far outweighs the failure of many who fall into moral lapses. Thus, God does not will, nor does He create moral evil, but He has *to permit moral* evil in the hope of the emergence of hóly wills.

6. Philosophy and Theology

The problem relating to the relationship between philosophy and theology has arisen in medieval philosophy. The relationship was first hinted at by St. Augustine and afterwards was detailed by St. Thomas and was refined by Scotus and Occam.

For St. Augustine, reason and faith, understanding and belief are supplementary. But belief is more important than understanding. His formula was *creds ut intelligam* (I believe that I may understand).

Some things we do not believe unless we understand them, others we do not understand unless we believe.

Thus, for St. Augustine, reason and faith may co-operate with one another. This was elaborated by St. Thomas and others.

For St. Thomas, reason and faith supplement one another and they are in no way opposed. But they are distinguishable.

1. Philosophy comes under the domain of *natural light of reason.* Whereas, theology dealing with Christian faith rests on *revelation.*

2. Philosophy, being constituted by human reason, starts its enquiry with created things which are the effects due to God as their cause. In contrast, the theologian has his starting-point in *revealed truths* and he deduces the world of things from these revealed truths.

3. Philosophy (reason) and theology (faith) do not oppose one another. The objections against revealed truths and their defence are carried out by philosophy. On the other hand, philosophical knowledge of earthly things is supplemented by the deeper knowledge of higher spiritual things. For example, philosophy can tell us how to reach happiness, but theology tells us how to expect *blessedness* in the

vision of God. Philosophy is the domain of *wise* men, but theology is pursued by the *saints*.

4. For St. Thomas, the creatorship of God, the doctrine of Trinity, incarnation of Jesus, the doctrine of original sin, Last Judgment and such articles of faith come under theology. They are fully understood only by the grace of God. These theological teachings are not contrary to reason. Further, theology based on revelation is *higher than philosophy*.

The synthesis of philosophy and theology worked out by St. Thomas was short-lived. Roger Bacon (c. 1214-94) separated science and philosophy from theology, even though he regarded theology to be superior to philosophy. However, he also maintained that theology should not interfere with the investigation of nature by science and philosophy. Further, Scotus (1274-1308) *separated* philosophy from theology. For him, philosophy confined to reason, is incapable of knowing and understanding the articles of faith. But he also upheld the superiority of theology over philosophy. For Scotus philosophy cannot establish that God is a *living* God, nor the mystery of creation. Both are certain within their own domain of faith and revelation. But the certainty of philosophy is *theoretical*, and that of theology is practical (i.e. with regard to one's conduct). But the separation of philosophy and theology made them opposed to one another, and, this paved the way of conflict between science and religion. Occam even criticised the attempt of reason to establish the existence of God. Thus, philosophy and theology really came in conflict and the synthesis between them of Thomist philosophy was destroyed.

7. Greek Philosophy and Indian Thought

If we date the beginning of Greek philosophy with Thales (624-550 B.C.) and Anaximander (611-547 B.C.), then they can be declared as free thinkers. They tried to explain natural phenomena with the help of natural causes. They did not take the help of supernatural gods. Hence Greek philosophy is called scientific in spirit. But man can hardly do without religion. Hence, there was also a strong undercurrent of religion in Greek life and thought.

There were two kinds of religion in the 6th century B.C. First, there were Olympian gods who were concerned with human beings, but were pictured with human passions and weaknesses. This kind of Olympian gods pictured by Homer was mixed with Hesiodic gods. Hesiod is supposed to have flourished about eighth century B.C. Hesiod provided his religious mythology with *cosmogony* and *theogony*. For the Greeks, Homeric and Hesiodic gods were quite popular. But along with the *anthropomophic gods*, there was the mystery cult of Dionysùs. The Dionysian religion practised rituals through which the initiated sought unity with their god of worship. This mystery ritual is the basis of Christian sacrament. Later on, this Dionysian cult of mystery was reformed by Orpheus. Orphism influenced Pythagoras and through him Socrates, Plato and Plotinus. The essentials of Orphism have marked kinship with Indian thought.

1. Orphism rests its case on revelation, contained in some sacred book. We know nothing of this book. But Indian thought very frequently refers to the sacred books called the Vedas.

2. Orphism also maintains that man in his pristine existence was glorious, but now in this world, he is in a fallen state.
   This is also maintained in Indian thought specially, in Jainism, Nyaya and Vedanta.

3. Orphism advises purificatory rites and ascetic practices as a means of release from the cycle of rebirths.
   This is also in common with Indian thought, specially Jainism, Buddhism and Vedanta.

4. The above-mentioned point means that Orphism maintains the doctrine of the wheel of rebirths and perhaps also of transmigration of the soul into animals.
   Indian thought strongly favours the doctrine of rebirth and also the majority of thinkers belief in transmigration.

5. Plato and Plotinus believe in the efficacy of contemplation (on the good, Plato) as a means of becoming good and even release from the wheel or bondage of rebirths.
   This doctrine of contemplation (specially *Dhyana, Samadhi* and *nididhyasana*) leads to release from the cycle of rebirths in Indian thought.

6. Plotinus was greatly influenced by Indian sages whom he met in Persia. Naturally, Plotinus maintains even the ontology of advaitism.

Orphians were vegetarians. This is also in harmony with the dominant Indian thought. However, Greek and Indian thought are expected to be independent and parallel developments of thought. In due course, the Greek thought favoured science and mysticism ceased to be the popular cult in the West. In contrast, religious thought occupied the major segment in Indian speculation, though it was never bereft of logic and science.

8. The doctrine of Universals and Christian Theology

In Greek and medieval philosophy, the doctrine of universals has been variously held. The most important doctrine is of Plato. According to Plato, universals (or ideas or forms) exist independently of particulars or any mind whatsoever (whether divine or individual mind). They are real in themselves and are eternal entities. This doctrine of universals is known as *Platonic realism*. As against this Aristotle held that universals are as objective as individual things are. He preferred to call them 'forms'. For example, cowness is as objective to the observer as the individual cows are. But where did he differ from Plato? Aristotle held that *universals do not exist apart from the individual things*, e.g. redness does not exist apart from the red roses. Take away the red things, and, no redness will be found anywhere. It is doubtful that Aristotle held that universals are found in human minds. However, St. Thomas held:

1. Universals exist in divine mind eternally.
2. Universals exist objectively in particular things.
3. They exist in human minds as abstracted common and essential attributes.

But the third important doctrine, called *conceptualism* holds that universals are found as class concepts which are formed by the human mind by comparing the attributes of particular things. For example, cowness is a concept which is formed by observing a number of cows and by abstracting from them the essential and common attributes found in them. Thus, a universal is a concept formed by *abstracting* the common and essential attributed found in particular things coming under a class. A concept is formed in the human mind but the attributes are in the particulars. Apart from the particulars, universals *do not* exist. Thus conceptualism is very much akin to the view of Aristotle. Conceptualism is first associated with the view of Abelard (1079-1142).

The fourth theory is of Roscelin (1050-1120) known as *nominalism* which denies that universals have any existence apart from any individual objects, or, that they are objective like individual things. Hence, nominalism refutes both Plato, Aristotle and conceptualism. Nominalism is supposed to have been first profounded by Roscelin, but it was powerfully defended by Occam (1280-1347). For nominalism, universals are mere names, *flatus voci* to indicate a number of things. A universal is really a linguistic device by human beings to designate many individuals bearing a common name. Universals are not *in* individuals (as Aristotle supposed) nor in any mind whatsoever as conceptualism supposes. Of course, any independent existence of universals, in their own rights, apart from individual things, is an absurdity for nominalism.

The different views about universals have very great bearing on Christian theology. Christian theology initially adopted Platonism, i.e. Platonic realism, according to which ideas are eternally real. Now God is eternally real, and, therefore, the idea of a perfect being is also eternally real. For this reason, St. Anselm deduced the actual existence of God from the Idea of a perfect being called God. Similarly, trinity is an idea, and the three, father-son-Holy Ghost are not separate, but one reality. For nominalism 'trinity' is only a word and father-son-Holy Ghost are three separate persons. This is known as *tritheism* or triadism. Hence, nominalism denies the co-substantiality of God and Jesus. This remains opposed to traditional Christian theology even now.

Secondly, Platonic realism holds that ideas are rational. The world is constituted of ideas. So the world is rational Hence, faith can be reasoned out.

The doctrine of original sin is based on the teaching of one common substantiality of man, because the idea of man is real, substantial and eternal. Hence in one man Adam, all men have sinned. Adam disobeyed God and so through his disobedience the one common humanity, which runs through all men, has sinned. Hence the reality of original sin follows from the one substantiality of all men. Similarly, through the vicarious death of Jesus all men can expect redemption of their sin through the grace of God.

Finally, there is one church universal which particular churches try to follow, copy or in which they all participate. This one church universal is Roman Catholic Church which alone is empowered to save all mankind. Hence, the sole authority of Roman Catholic Church came to be established.

Nominalism and Medieval Christianity

1. For nominalism there is no Platonic realism. Universals do not exist in individual things, nor in any mind. Universals are mere names, verbal sounds. Hence, according to nominalism. There is no trinity and really means tritheism.

2. Similarly, there is *no universal man.* Individual men alone exist. Hence, there is no co-substantiality of all men. Hence, there is no original sin, for by the sin of one man Adam, other men cannot be called sinners. Similarly by the redemptive death of one man called Jesus, all believers cannot be said to have been redeemed. Only individual believers can be redeemed by the grace of God.

3. As particulars alone are real, so there can be no one Universal Roman Catholic Church.

Thus universals and their denials have a good deal importance for Christianity.

PART II

Modern Philosophy

1

Francis Bacon (1561-1626)

1.01 General Outline of Bacon's Philosophy

Francis Bacon, in the words of Benn, was by profession a lawyer, by taste a scientific enquirer, by character a seeker after wealth and power; by natural genius an immortal master of words. For these conflicting tendencies he has been called by Pope "The greatest, bright test, meanest of mankind".

In other words his genius was great but his character was low. By virtue of the prostitution of his intellect he secured the exalted rank of the keeper of the Great Seal. In this capacity he was discovered to be accepting bribes for the perversion of justice. He was tried and was found guilty.

Bacon will be remembered for having given expression to the prevailing tendency of his age. He lived at a time when the world was alive to great hopes in the future of mankind. Magnet was discovered by Hilbert, Harvey had discovered the law of the circulation of blood, the new world was discovered with the help of Mariner's compass. With these discoveries as also of gun powder and printing, he thought that man at last through many failures in the past has succeeded in mastering the planet. An exotic excitement seized upon man's fancy and with the rest of his contemporaries Bacon shared the belief that nothing was impossible any longer. This unbounded faith in human development, he freely indulged in his Utopian work known as *Novum Atlantis*. In this he referred to the following noteworthy achievements: the prolongation of human life; the planned and improved production of new species of animal and vegetable life by artificial selection and breeding, and also by vivisectional surgery; he recommended the wholesale vivisection of animals, in order to throw light on what may be done with the bodies of men, the manufacture of cannon of enormous power of flying machines, and of submarine boats.

Thus Bacon was fired by two ideas. First, he wanted to understand nature by discovering its laws. Secondly, he wanted to understand nature and man for the sake of securing practical result. He believed that knowledge is power and this knowledge to be real can be attained by sober investigation of nature. By this insistence on the usefulness of knowledge, he may be considered as the father of pragmatism.[1] But the name of Bacon will rest on his method of discovery known

---

1. This claim may not be acceptable. See. 1.05.

as Induction. He saw that the moderners must begin with a new method for disclosing the secrets of Nature. The method, however, prevalent at his time was purely deductive, known as Aristotle's syllogism. Bacon opposed this method and to a certain extent he was justified. Syllogism no doubt makes the argument clear and convincing about laws already known to us. However, this is quite useless in discovering something new. Hence it was barren of any fruitful result. Besides, at the time of Bacon the universal premise in any syllogism could be got from the Bible, Aristotle or other Authorities. This led to hopeless muddle for anything could be proved or disproved. Therefore, Bacon discarded syllogism by comparing it to a consecrated virgin, bearing no fruit. Bacon attributed the hopelessness of philosophy to the following causes:

1. The prejudice against experiments and matters of actual facts.
2. The blind prejudice and fanaticism of religion which distort and warp judgment.
3. The exclusive attention to morals, politics and theology.
4. Too much veneration for antiquity.
5. Failure to overcome the difficulties arising in the actual investigation of nature.

1.02. Idolas

As opposed to syllogism Bacon hoped to give a method of *investigation, a novum organum.* The former philosophy proved hopeless for it based itself on conceptions derived from untested knowledge, merely based on authority. The new method then must be based on experience of fresh facts. Instead of anticipating nature we should interrogate nature in order to wrest from her the secrets known as the laws of nature. But before we hope to get facts from experience, our mind should be free from bias and prejudice. The initial need for a dispassionate enquiry of nature consists in getting rid of illusions or Idols which warp and distort our judgment. Bacon points out that there are four kinds of phantoms or idols which prejudice us in getting the particular fact leading to the discovery of laws. These four idols may be thus enumerated.

1. *Idola Tribus.* This illusion is the most common one for it is predisposition which more or less besets everyone. For example, we read our own ends or purpose in the things of nature and usually judge them in terms of final causes. We look upon trees, flowers and animals from human standpoint, as if they are created for human needs. Thus Bacon anticipates Spinoza in rejecting the teleological explanation of nature.

2. *Idola Specus.* In addition to general bias, everybody has some specialised cave or den of his own, called idola specus. These idolas take their rise in the peculiarities of mental or bodily structure, in education, habit or accident. For example, to the jaundiced eye everything appears yellow. This also includes all

those prejudices which arise from one-sided devotion to one's own method, profession or society.

3. *Idola Fori.* This arises from the connection of words and names. We think that we guide the words, but really in many cases words guide our thoughts. Very many false words arise from their association with false theory. For example, we still say that the sun sets or rises though we do not now believe that the sun moves round the earth.

4. *Idola Theatri.* Are those false notions which arise from the dogmas of philosophers like the dogmas of the Sophistical, Empirical and Superstitious systems, according to Bacon.

(a) In Sophistical system the dialectic subtleties are used about common experience.

(b) Empirical generalisation is one which is based on rash and chance observation.

(c) In Superstitious system the theories of nature are built on mystical traditions; e.g. stars move in circles.

After preparing ourselves subjectively we can get ready for the objective investigation of nature. This objective method is also known as Inductive Method. The end of the inductive method consists in the discovery of the *forms* of things. However, it is not clear to us what Bacon meant by *forms*. First, form means the deeper hidden basis of *self-manifesting phenomena* and their properties. Hence, 'form' means the true difference or essential property. Secondly, it may mean the generative nature of things; and thirdly, it may mean the laws which underlie phenomena. He who knows the form also can know how the secondary qualities are caused (Erdmann, *History of Philosophy* p. 680). Similarly, Hoffding (*History of Modern Philosophy* p. 202) thinks that form means those qualities which justify the presence of all other qualities. He thinks that the 'form' also means the hidden essence which may be taken as the atoms. Whatever may be the real meaning of 'form', it does not mean

1. The outward appearance or shape of things.
2. The ideas of Plato.
3. The law of nature as we understand by the term 'Scientific Law'.

1.03. Induction

Thus, really the form of Bacon means something hidden like the imperceptible atoms, the changes of which explain all variations in things. His form is intermediate between Aristotle's universals and modern 'laws'. The method of the discovery of the forms is called *Induction*. Corresponding to the three of the five inductive methods of Mill, Bacon mentions three ways of discovering the forms. First of all we should collect all the instances in which a certain phenomenon is present. This is known as *Tabula Presentiae,* roughly corresponding to Mill's method of Agreement. For example, in order to find out the forms of heat we should gather all cases where it is present like fire, sun, candle flame, burning glass etc. Bacon pointed out that mere affirmative instances would not yield the real form. We should take help of the table of negative instances to confirm the result of the tabula presentiae. We should gather other similar instances in which the required phenomenon is absent like the stones, the earth, the moon etc. This *Tabula absentiae* roughly corresponds to Mill's Joint Method. To the above two methods, Bacon adds a third, called *Tabula Graduum* or the table of comparison in which instances of varying intensities of the phenomenon are recorded. For example; we have to gather instances in which the phenomenon of heat is formed in different degrees. This roughly corresponds to Mill's method of Concomitant Variations. To these three methods, Bacon adds eleven other ways, but explains only three, namely exclusion, first vintage, and crucial instance.

These three methods and half-developed ways are to be subordinated to the supreme method of Exclusion. By observation and careful analysis we have to draw up exhaustive tables of the phenomena and forms under investigation. Afterwards we have to eliminate all those analysed factors which cannot invariable co-exist with the phenomenon of which the *form* is sought. This method takes the form of disjunctive-categorical syllogistic reasoning. Thus the tabula presentiae, and graduum should give rise to the following forms:

The form of heat is either A or B or C or D or E and so on.

But A or B or C or D (for they do not co-exist with heat, as given by the tables) cannot be the form.

Therefore "E" alone can be the form of heat.

1.04. Critical Evaluation

Bacon distinguished his method from earlier methods, especially from syllogism in these respects.

(a) In its end, i.e., it seeks fresh knowledge by discovering the form of things.

(b) By its means which avoids syllogism as well as hasty and chance observation.

(c) Lastly it enjoins on everyone to make enquiry with an unprejudiced mind.

According to Bacon complete observation, gradual elimination with exhaustive analysis constituted an ideal method. Negatively, he disparaged the formation of hypothesis for he held that we should not *anticipate nature*. He pointed out that mathematics is important but shows nowhere how it could be given a place in his induction. If Bacon will be remembered then he will be remembered for his method. However, we agree with Schiller in his estimate of Bacon's method. "Formally his method appears to be neither new nor strictly valid, scientifically it is certainly neither adequate nor workable" (*Formal Logic,* p. 258). Let us analyse the major defects of Bacon's method.

(A) Bacon begins with a strong protest against Aristotelian Logic but he falls into its fascination. Instead of finding out the cause or the law of things he tries to find out the mysterious forms; instead of drawing instances from actual observation and experience, he prefers to illustrate his method from bookish examples. Thus we agree with Windelband in his estimate of Bacon's method, "What Bacon presents accordingly as Induction is certainly no simple enumeration but an involved process of abstraction, which rests upon the metaphysical assumption of the scholastic Formation; the presage of the new is still quite embedded in the old habits of thought" (Windelband, *History of Philosophy*, p. 385)

(B) Bacon tells us to make an exhaustive table of phenomena, then alone by excluding all the inessential factors we can find out the real form. However, he does not see that it is materially impossible to collect *all* instances of any phenomenon. Besides, even if we could materially succeed we can never be logically certain that the instances gathered are *all the possible ones*. Again Bacon fails to see that even observation to be scientific has to be selective and this will make it dependent on some sort of hypothesis. For example, a doctor no doubt examines his patient but he does not examine everything. He selectively observes only those parts which he considers to be important. Similarly the scientist has to observe only those things which he considers to be important in establishing a cause or a law. This is another defect of Bacon's method.

(C) No doubt Bacon rejected Simple Enumeration for one single instance to the contrary is fatal to it. However, no scientific discovery is made by counting the instances but by connecting them. Any law is established not by the *number* but by the *nature* of instances. This requires not mere experience but insight based on experiment. But any experiment requires ample exercise of hypothesis. He lived in the midst of discoveries but does not seem to have gained any insight into the scientific method of his day.

(D) Besides, being mistaken in his inductive search, he wrongly tried to advance the cause of science by stressing its practical value. Instead of understanding nature, he wanted to subject nature to the will of man for serving his needs. Healthy no doubt has been his rejection of teleology in physics but just the reverse of it is his insistence on making knowledge as the lasting power. Great discoveries have been made by scientists in their disinterested search of knowledge for its own sake.

Again, instead of the sober investigation of nature he entertains phantastic hopes in his *Novum Atlantis*. But his utopian imageries are not born of any insight into the scientific discoveries of his day but they are the result of the mythical thinking under the mediaeval influence.

1.05. Was Bacon the Father of Modern Philosophy?

Macaulay accords the highest place to Bacon, not for his inductive method but for the new purpose and direction in which Bacon initiated the philosophical discipline. But even this claim is hard to establish. First, the movement of modern science started at least 50 years before the birth of Bacon and continued long after him without reference to his work. Secondly, no discovery can ever be made with the help of induction of Bacon, for reasons mentioned before. Lastly, the scientific advance really would have been stifled if the scientists had put their eyes on the practical fruit of knowledge.

Then the historians wrongly read a great many anticipations in the writings of Bacon. It is said that the doctrine of the Idolas is an anticipation of Kant, for like Kant it implies that the nature of the mind determines the nature of knowledge. However, we must not forget that mind for Bacon is a passive thing, for he points out that our mind should be as receptive as that of a child. Besides, the doctrine of the idolas is only a subjective condition for knowledge and unlike the view of Kant, mind is not regarded as constitutive and regulative of knowledge.

Some, again, look upon Bacon as the father of Pragmatism for he emphasizes the usefulness of knowledge. However, it is one thing to say that knowledge should be used for achieving practical ends and quite another thing to hold that knowledge is precisely what it does.

Therefore, we must not exaggerate the services of Bacon to mankind. He called himself the trumpeter of his times and that he was. He gathered the major thoughts and tendencies of his age and has given a systematic expression to them in masterly English. He is the aura of the dawn of Modern Philosophy and like a harbinger gave forth the signs of its greatness. In him we do not see the father or initiator of modern philosophy but rather the close of the middle ages. Measured by the standard of the mediaeval he sounds modern, but judged by the standard of the modern he is just mediaeval. No doubt Bacon tries to emerge from the mediaeval doctrines amongst which he feels insecure but he relapses into them. The more he struggles to be free, the more entangled he becomes in the shackles of the past. "No man can leap beyond his own shadow, hardly one beyond the shadow of his age" (Eradmann, *History of Philosophy* pp. 682-83). His philosophy, therefore, is just marginal.

Bacon's philosophy is full of vaguely unrealised promises. It is simply sound and fury signifying nothing. He made a propaganda to conquer the kingdom of Alexander but battered none of its defences. His philosophy can hardly be called a system for he has nothing to say about God, the world or the soul. As such he left no followers. But then it will be told that his emphasis on experience, in acquiring knowledge should entitled him to be the father of British Empiricism. To some extent this may be allowed. However, we must not forget that Locke hardly makes reference to Bacon. Lockean empiricism really derived a greater impetus from Descartes and the Cartesians than from Bacon.

2

Rene Descartes (1596-1650)

Descartes, a Frenchman, was born in Touraine in 1596. He came of a wealthy family. Throughout his life he remained a bachelor and his inheritance enabled him to dedicate himself to philosophical meditation. Apart from being an epoch-making philosopher, Descartes was a creative mathematician. His great fame induced Queen Christiana of Sweden. At her invitation he went to Stockholm in October, 1649 but the following year in February, 1650 he died of pneumonia.

2.01. The Method of Descartes

Descartes was very much worried by the uncertain state of philosophy in his times. He saw that philosophy was cultivated for many centuries by the best minds that had ever lived and there was yet not a single proposition in it which was not under dispute.[1] However, Descartes did not despair of knowledge, and knowledge for him, must attain a certitude equal to that of the demonstrations of Arithmetic and Geometry.[2] This knowledge, he thought, could be attained if we use an appropriate method of enquiry. Seeing that knowledge proper has already been attained in Arithmetic and Geometry, he was surprised to find that philosophers had not reared a lofty edifice on such a firm and solid foundation. However, it was the method and not the subject-matter so much which had enabled mathematics to attain certitude. So Descartes attempted to understand the method of mathematics which could be utilised for advancing knowledge in any subject. He called his own enquiry as 'Universal Mathematics' in Rule IV of his *Regulae*. This will be called 'meta-mathematics' today. "Such a science", according to Descartes, "should contain the primary rudiments of human reason, and its province ought to extend to the eliciting of true results in every subject".[3]

[Descartes has noted that deduction alone could yield *certain results* and experiential inference could not yield errorless results.[4] But he did not see that these methods dealt with two different kinds of propositions. Further, only now we are beginning to realise that philosophy does not deal with cognitive but with non-cognitive propositions concerning self-realisation. Such distinctions would show

---

1. "Discourse on the method" in *Philosophical Works of Descartes,* Translated by E.S. Haldane & G.R.T. Ross (Dover Edition 1931) pp. 85-86.
2. Rules for Directions, *Ibid.,* p. 5.
3. *Ibid.,* p. 11.
4. *Ibid.,* p. 4.

200   *A Critical History of Western Philosophy*

that the criterion of mathematics cannot be applied to the understanding of
philosophical problems.]

Descartes therefore was very much concerned with the enquiry into the method
of philosophising. He had proposed to lay down thirtysix rules of which he
mentioned thirtyone in the *Regulae*. The object of Cartesian methodology was to
apply mathematical method of philosophy with a view to obtaining certitude in
knowledge. As a result of his enquiry, he laid down four broad rules for his self-
guidance.[1]

1. Never to accept anything as true unless I clearly know it as such.[2]

Descartes believes that errors arise from poorly comprehended experiences or
from hasty, groundless and preconceived notions. The only remedy, therefore, he
thinks, lies in resolute refusal to believe in what is not clearly and distinctly
perceived.

2. Divide up each of the difficulties, under examination into as many parts as
possible.

We begin with something vague and indefinite and later on, step by step, attain
clearness and distinctness.

3. Commence with the simplest objects and ascend, step by step to the more
complex.

The explanation must be ordered and systematic. Here Descartes is in favour
of deductive use in philosophical thinking, for he implies that later steps, should
be clearly deducible from earlier ones.

4. In every case make the enumeration so complete that I might be assured that
nothing was omitted.

The complex thing can be understood when we know its (*i*) several constituent
factors separately, clearly and distinctly, and when we (*ii*) know the order or system
in which they are found.

Descartes, being himself a great mathematician, was struck by the excellence
of mathematics. Therefore, in order to make philosophy truly scientific he hoped
to make its method patterned on mathematics. Now in Geometry we first of all start
with a few self-evident axioms and then reach the whole body of its conclusions
by means of simple elaborative deduction. Now in the same way in philosophy too,
he tells us, to find out "by an inductive enumeration and a critical sifting of all ideas.
. . . a single certain point to deduce all further truths. The first task of philosophy
is *analytic*, the second *synthetic*." (Windelband, *Ibid.*, p. 390)

Now how can we find something which is sure and certain? Descartes believes
that the single, certain truth can be systematically sought by deliberate doubt. When
doubt is pushed to its farthest limit then it will reveal something which is
indubitable, which is clearly perceived. Now in order to discover the indubitable

1. "Discourse on method", *Philosophical Works of Descartes*, Vol. I, p. 92.
2. This he also states in rule IX of the *Regulae*.

intuition, let us doubt all that can be doubted.

(i) *Sense-testimony can be doubted*. Things of our daily life like tables, chairs, etc., we know through the senses. But the senses deceive us as is clear from illusions, hallucinations etc. Now prudence demands that we should not rely on things which deceive us even once.

We are deceived not only by distant and minute objects but also by other things. However, some may think that it is impossible to doubt that we are seated here, in a certain place at a certain time. but similar certainty is also found in our dreams, who knows that we may be dreaming and the things of the present sense-experience may be deceiving us?

Thus some sense-beliefs are more probable than others. All of them, again appear convincing, as long as they last. But, then, whether even one of them is certain, past doubt we have no grounds of believing; on the contrary have ample grounds for doubting.

(ii) *Even the truths of science can be doubted*. At this stage, it might be objects that the truths of sciences like 2+2=4 cannot be doubted, even in dreams. However, the case does not seem to be quite clear. We cannot know whether any truth of knowledge is at all intended for us finite beings; whether God has not created us rather for mere opinion and error. Besides, who knows there might be no God at all. There might be a demon at once potent and malignant who tricks us to believe in falsehood.

That I doubt cannot be doubted. When the doubt has done its worst it finds a fact of completely unassailable certainty. I may doubt anything but I cannot doubt that I am doubting. Whether it be a dream or a real consciousness, I must exist as a doubting or thinking being. Let there be a demon to deceive me, but then I must exist as a thinking being to be deceived. Hence, I doubt or think, therefore, I exist, i.e., *cogito ergo sum* is the one certain truth which may be taken as the foundation of philosophy.

The doubt of Descartes should not be confused with psychological doubt. For example, in darkness, when a small creature crosses our path, we may doubt whether it was a mouse or a mole. The two may be thus contrasted:

Descartes' Doubt	*Psychological Doubt*
1. It is not a thing of direct feeling and experience but is a deliberate and dispassionate attitude towards human experience in general.	1. This is directly felt and experienced by us as such, as in the previous example.
2. It is not directly determined by the nature of objects.	2. It is caused by the nature of object about which we want to know.
3. The logical doubt of Descartes is deliberate, depending on the will.	3. It is independent of our will. However, hard we my will, the doubt continues.

| 4. This is concerned with attitude towards total things or ultimate things. | 4. It is concerned with particular things of daily life. |

Again, the doubt of Descartes should not be confused with Scepticism. Descartes is not asserting that whatever can be doubted is false, but he is only supposing it to be false. Again, the scepticism is the finished conclusion about knowledge which professes the denial of any certain knowledge whatsoever. However, the Cartesian doubt is only a starting point to find out that which cannot be further doubted.[1]

2.02. Cogito Ergo Sum

This *cogito ergo sum* is the first final certainty and as such we have to be careful in its interpretation as well as in deciding its position in the Cartesian philosophy.

First, what Descartes tried to establish is not an inference but a simple fact of primitive knowledge or a self-evident axiom. Had it been an inference, then it would be merely dependent on premises for its certainty and then again these premises on other premises for their certainty. This would lead to infinite regress without reaching the indubitable truth. However, the certainty of the *cogito* is clear and distinct, and, that nothing else could be perceived or intuited with the same certainty. *Cogito ergo sum* means that my consciousness is the means of revealing myself as something existing. Here is the indubitable truth of the inseparability of thought and thing. My being implied in my being conscious is the first principle both logically and psychologically. Of course the use of the term 'therefore' was unfortunate for it led to the interpretation of the *cogito* as an inference. However, 'therefore' primarily means a step in inference but secondarily it means a relation of necessary connection. Descartes uses the term 'therefore' in the secondary sense.

Again, 'I think therefore I am' should not be emphasized to hold that thinking alone guarantees self-existence. The important thing is to show that it is my consciousness which carries with it the existence of myself. No other function apart from conscious function can guarantee the existence of the self. Therefore it would be wrong to say because 'I walk therefore I am', for walking without being conscious cannot imply self-existence.

Further, in Cogito I know that I am, but I don't know that I am, i.e., the content or that which constitutes the self is not known. All that we can say that the thinking this is that which doubts, imagines, senses etc. But beyond these, we cannot say that my *body* is myself or not.

Lastly, we can say that which thinks is a *substance*. "It is certain that thinking cannot exist without a thing which thinks or generally that any accident or activity cannot be without a substance of which it is the activity."

---

1. Discourse on the method, *Ibid.,* p. 99.

2.02A. Critical Comment on Cogito Ergo Sum

Descartes was of the opinion that the permanent self or Ego can be *known* with certainty. Even Locke believed that one's self can be known by intuition. However, Hume and Kant reject the contention of Descartes. They hold that the permanent self can never be known empirically. We shall find this in relation to Hume's refutation of spiritual substance and in relation to Kant's *paralogism of reason.* The contention of Kant that the transcendental subject can never be an object of knowledge is also maintained with a great deal of logical rigour by the Vedantins.

Descartes however was greatly influenced by his assumption with regard to the doctrine of 'substance' and its unchangeable attribute.[1] For this reason he concluded that there is a permanent self, since there is its unchangeable attribute of 'thinking'. Now-a-days this kind of reasoning will be called *a priorism.* Once we grant that there is a permanent substance which must have its unchanging attribute, we have to conclude that the self is a permanent substance, since we have found out its essence called 'thinking' which even the worst of doubt cannot demolish. But this is bad metaphysics. We cannot bring anything into existence by defining it. All that we are permitted to conclude is that from a given idea taken on our assumption, we can deduce another from it. This would mean that *not* that a permanent self is a *fact*, but simply from that from a certain *idea* we can deductively infer another *idea* of a permanent self. We shall find this point again with regard to the ontological proof for the existence of God. From an *a priori* idea, we can never pass to an actual fact.

The root of the trouble lies in the faulty use of the verb 'to be'. 'To be', properly speaking can be used only in conjunction with a predicate. For example, a proper proposition is, 'I am a poet', and not simply 'I am', — certainly not in conjunction with a proper name.[2] The verb 'to be' by itself cannot be a predicate.

Secondly, there can be no logical transition from 'I think' to 'I exist'. 'Existence' can be maintained not with regard to the subject, but regard to the predicate. When we say: 'I am a poet', it does not say with anything about my existence. It, however, points out that poets exist. Similarly, from 'I think' all that can be established is that there is thinking or that there is a state of thinking consciousness.

2.02B. Importance of the Cogito

Cogito occupies a strategic position in the philosophy of Descartes for the following reasons:

---

1. N.K. Smith, *New Studies in the Philosophy of Descartes*, pp. 328-29.
2. R. Carnap, 'The elimination of metaphysics', and M. Schilck, 'Positivism and Realism' in *Logical Positivism*, edited by A.J. Ayer, pp. 73f, 96, 98f.

(*i*) *Cogito* supplies its own evidence of clearness and distinctness which none of the things doubted had. This characteristics of clearness and distinctness which serves as the criterion of all other truths not deduced, but is *intuitively induced* from a single instance.[1]

(*ii*) *Cogito*, strictly speaking, is neither a first principle nor a premise. It is simply a sufficient answer to any future agnosticism which may hinder us from attaining certain knowledge.

(*iii*) Again, *cogito* is the first existential proposition which points out something actual existing, namely myself as the doubter or the thinking being.

(*iv*) Here we come in contact with a very important quality of consciousness which will serve as the distinguishing mark of mind in relation to material bodies.

The method of Descartes is deductive-inductive analytic-synthetic. It is inductive for it is based on the discovery of a certain truth. Again, it establishes a first clear and distinct perception or intuition. It is deductive for Descartes, as all other elements of his philosophy gradually follow from this one single certain truth, i.e., cogito. Of course, the deduction of Descartes is not syllogistic. In Descartes' words his deduction is unilateral, proceeding from one previously established point to the next and from this to others till we reach some hitherto unknown result. "Passing little by little from one to the other, we may acquire in time a perfect knowledge of the whole of philosophy."

Descartes seems to make three assumptions in his method carried on through doubting.

(*a*) That there is some certain knowledge about the actual world.

This seems to be the most important assumption. It is difficult to believe the possibility of any philosophy without this assumption. Any way the certain knowledge must be such as can be believed by all and such as can never be doubted by anybody. Its 'necessity' must be self-evident.

(*b*) Again, 'what is clear and distinct is true' can be proved to be true.

(*c*) The deductive knowledge involving memory can have the same certainty as intuitive knowledge.

2.03. Criterion of Truth

Now let us try to determine that in cogito (*Philosophy*, Vol. XVII, No. 69, April 43, Gewirth *'Clearness and Distinctness in Descartes'*) which makes it true. This something by virtue of which cogito becomes indubitable will serve as the criterion or touchstone of all further knowledge. Now cogito is true because it is clear and distinct. Hence, clearness and distinctness may be regarded as the criterion of any true knowledge.

Anything which is as clear and distinct as is *cogito* must be regarded as true. This criterion of clearness and distinctness has been regarded by Leibnitz,

---

1. *Philosophical Works*, vol. I, pp. 7, 33 for intuition.

Gassendi and Hoffding as purely subjective, for psychologically what is clear and distinct to me may not be so to others. Hence, Leibnitz demanded a proof of clearness and distinctness which should be palpable, mechanical and lacking the least difficulty in its understanding. No doubt Descartes required a certain psychological discipline to perceive something clearly and distinctly but he also supplied a certain logical standard about his criterion.

Idea has usually three elments, namely (*a*) Perceptive act, (*b*) a modification of the mind, a mental content and (*c*) a representative of something external to the mind. Now Descartes uses clearness and distinctness primarily for the first two functions of the mind and also determines later how it is to be attained in the third case. Now he defines his criterion of clearness and distinctness thus.

"A clear perception I call that which is present and open to the attending mind, just as we say that those things are clearly seen by us which, being present to the regarding eye, move it sufficiently strongly and openly. But that perception is distinct which is not only clear but is so precise and so separated from all others that it plainly contains in itself nothing other than which is clear."

Hence to be clear an idea must be *present* to the mind, *open* to the mind and the mind also must *attend* to it. Similarly, distinct is that which is precisely determined so that it may not be confused with anything else.

Again, Descartes uses clearness and distinctness in relation to the representative functions of ideas also. Now an idea is clear when the mind includes in it that content, which is 'integral and complete' in relation to the mind's interpretation of it, and it is distinct when the content of the idea includes nothing other than this. For example, the idea of God is clear when it includes all that which goes to constitute the idea of God, and distinct when it includes nothing else.

It is true, as Prof. N.K. Smith has pointed out[1] that Descartes has not been able to lay down any logical criterion of clearness and distinctness. But it is worthy of note that Descartes illustrates his meaning with regard to mathematical propositions and points out that they follow from the 'light of reason alone'. Whereas with regard to propositions of matters of facts, he points out, that they are obtained not by natural light, but by 'a certain spontaneous inclination'.[2] He also notes that intuition and deduction are the only certain routes to knowledge and no other routes should be admitted.[3] And inference based on experience can never be certain,[4] according to him. Hence, Descartes was classifying propositions into two kinds, namely, propositions of mathematics which are true by definition only and factual propositions which can be proved indirectly only, through the veracity of God. If he had thought sufficiently enough on the distinction between his knowledge of self or Geometrical axiom given by *intuition* and his knowledge of matters of fact based

1. *Ibid.,* p. 319f.
2. Meditation III.
3. Rules for direction III, *Philosophical Works,* p. 8.
4. Rules for direction, *Ibid.,* p. 4.

on 'confused ideas' given by 'spontaneous inclination', then he would have defined the criterion of truth more precisely.

However, Descartes, does not use the term clearness and distinctness for truth. Truth or falsity is found in judgments which are the product of intellect as well as will. This topic we shall take up later.

2.04. The existence of God

Let us try to rehabiliate the world which the doubt had destroyed. Now with the criterion of clearness and distinctness let us see which ideas are true or false. Now ideas are either innate or those derived from outside or are pure inventions. But of all the ideas there is one innate idea of Being who is 'eternal, omniscient, omnipotent, source of all goodness and truth, creator of all things and in sum having in himself all those things in which we can clearly note some perfection which is infinite, or tainted by no imperfection." Now what can be the cause of this idea? At least the cause must be equal to the effect. I cannot be the cause for I know myself to be finite being. Hence this idea must have been caused by an equally perfect cause, namely, the infinitely perfect being called God.

The casual proof of the existence of God is based on two assumptions, namely (i) Individual consciousness knows itself to be finite, and, (ii) This conciousness of 'God' is derived only from the conception of an absolutely perfect being. Of course, some may object that the infinite being may be a negative idea, i.e., that which is not finite. Now Descartes points out that the idea of the infinite being is the most positive idea for in comparison with the fullness of the Perfect Being we realise our finitude.

Ontological Proof: No doubt Descartes also adds to this causal proof, the cosmological proof for the existence of God. He asks, what can be the cause of myself, my parents and all other finite beings? This he concludes, can be proved only with the help of the idea of a Perfect Being who has created everything else in the world. But the most important proof of the existence of God is *Ontological*. According to this, the existence of God follows from the very idea of the perfect being just as the equality of 3 angles of a triangle = 2 right angles follows from the very idea of a triangle. The most perfect being cannot be thought without at the same time thinking of Him as actually existing. Of course, the idea and the actual finite thing are not inseparable. One can think of a winged horse though there may be none in reality. But this idea of a perfect being, according to Descartes, cannot be thought apart from His existence.

Descartes has been accused of copying Anselm's proof for the existence of God which runs thus : 'Consideration demonstrates the word God to mean that which must be thought as what is greatest; but to be in actuality as well as in thought, is greater than to be in thought alone; therefore, God exists not only in thought, but in fact.' This proof makes God's existence dependent on the thought of it. God exists, because we think of a perfect idea, namely, God. Descartes points out that his proof is different from that of Anselm for Descartes makes the thought of God dependent on His Being. 'Whatever we clearly and distinctly preceive to belong to the true and unalterable nature of any thing, to its essence, its form, that may be predicated of it. Now we find, on investigating God, that existence belongs to his true and unalterable nature, and therefore, we may legitimately predicate existence of God.

2.05. Critical Comments

Ontological proof is based on the assumption that 'existence' is a predicate or a quality like colour, taste, weight etc. Unfortunately, fictional entities do not form a class distinguishable from other object by virtue of their having 'non-existence'. For instance, chimeras and gold mountains do not form a class of non-existence. A non-existent mango has all those qualities which an existent mango has. A non-existent God no wise differs from an existent God. "A hundred real thalers do not contain the least coin more than a hundred possible thalers."

The content of both must be one and the same, otherwise the concept would not truly represent the actual coin. Hence, the question is not whether God exists or not. The real problem would be, 'Is God love or personal or responsive to human prayers?" If God could be shown to be 'love' or 'personal', then his actuality follows from this. If I could show that there is yellow, fragrant mango on the table, then its existence automatically follows from this.

One thing is certain that concepts are not things. 'If wishes were things, beggar would ride cars', and, certainly nobody would suffer from any want. Unfortunately, from no amount of thinking intensely we can produce an actual thing. At most from a concept we can deduce another concept as a result of entailment. Descartes himself points ou. that properties of a triangle follow from its definition. But we know that a proposition of mathematics is independent of any actual state of affairs. Here, as a result of deduction we can proceed from one proposition to another. But these propositions do not become *empirical* propositions as a result of deduction. Similarly, we can proceed from a perfect idea to another idea of 'an existent perfect Being'. But the idea of an existent Being is an idea and not an actuality.

The ontological proof is based on self-contradictory terms, viz., 'necessary Being'. If God is 'necessary', then it can be expressed in analytic propositions only, as in Logic and Mathematics. But as noted earlier, such propositions do not deal with actual state of affairs. Again, if God is an existing Being, then He can be given by experience only, as Kant had pointed out long ago. But we know that an empirical proposition, no matter how many times verified, can be *probably* only. The predicate of any synthetic proposition can be denied without involving us in self-contradiction. So if there is loving God, then His existence can always be questioned. So He cannot be conceived to be necessary. Thus, any, 'Being' is probable. So the concept of a 'necessary Being' is self-contradictory.

Kant's criticism of the ontological argument is unanswerable and at the present time its validity is accepted by a majority of philosophers. But the idealists had tried to rehabilitate this argument on the basis of their doctrine of inseparability of 'knowing and being'. However, in the present context, the identity of the idea of a perfect Being and the existence of such a Being can no longer be maintained.

2.06. God and the Criterion of Clearness and Distinctness

If there is God, then He is a perfect and truthful God and therefore, the hypothesis of a deceiving demon must be given up. This veracity of God is the ultimate guarantee of all knowledge, for He cannot have created us to err. All that we clearly and distinctly perceive must be true, otherwise God will become a deceiver. Thus the existence of God is a sufficient guarantee against any doubt and agnosticism. Hence the modern rationalism is introduced by Descartes by the circuitous route of scholasticism. In modern language the veracity of God simply means that the universe is rational through and through and we can hope to make enquiries about it without the fear of being baffled in our search. In making God the ultimate ground of all knowledge Descartes has been accused of arguing in a circle. From the criterion of *clearness and distinctness* of ideas he proves the existence of the veracious God and; again, from the veracity of God he proves the ultimate truth of the criterion of clearness and distinctness. However, the charge of arguing in a circle is more apparent than real. In the order of *knowledge*, the criterion comes first, but in the order of *existence* God comes first. The criterion is suggested as soon as we begin to apply the method, but the method itself it based on some metaphysical assumption. The veracity of God is the ontological assumption of the methodological criterion.

Descartes seems to be vague and indefinite in his use of the term God. His God is partly the Absolute of metaphysics on which everything depends, but which depends on nothing else; partly he is the personal creative Being of Christian theology. The Christian concept of a creator God is not adequate to support a rationalistic system. Here Spinoza has tried to make Descartes consistent.

2.07. The External World

Besides the ideas of God and self we experience many ideas of colour, taste, smell, extension etc. We believe that they are caused by bodies external to us. But how can we prove their existence? We cannot rely on their existence through our senses for they deceive us. However, in general we know that our ideas about the external world are caused by bodies outsides of us. At least in general it appears quite clear and distinct to us and we have a strong inclination to believe that really there is an external world of material bodies. If these ideas do not come from external bodies then either they are caused by our own selves or by God. But if these ideas be caused by either of them then God would be deceiver, for we clearly and distinctly perceive them to originate from external bodies. Thus corresponding to this clear perception there must be an external world for the veracious God cannot allow us to have a strong inclination to believe in delusion.

The clear and distinct perception of the external world shows that it is extended. But extension is known only through our ideas of it. The perception of the external world may be thus described after Descartes. There are firstly, the impressions made on the organs which lead to the excitation of the animal spirits in the nerves. Then there is the termination of the animal spirits in the brain, usually in pineal gland which gives rise to the sensation. Now the processes leading to the sensation are all non-conscious or non-mental. But somehow the conscious perception or ideas represent the objective material bodies. This correspondence of the ideas to the external bodies is guaranteed by the veracity of God.

The whole proof of the existence of the external world appears highly artificial. The account of perception shows that the ideas are highly indirect and non-representative so far as the material bodies are concerned. It is too much to expect that the ideas be true copies of the material bodies. This logical absurdity must not be laid in relation to the idea of God at least. Besides, how can we know that our ideas are the copies of their original, the external bodies which *ex hypothesis* are shut out from our verification? The representative function of ideas is unfortunate in explaining knowledge and this was clearly criticised by Berkeley.

Descartes was a naive realist in practice for he believed that there are bodies existing in their own rights like tables or chairs. They will continue to exist even if there be no human mind to perceive them. But what do we mean by bodies? Well, we understand by bodies to be independent *substances*. By a substance we understand that which so exists that it needs no other thing in order to exist. Strictly speaking then there is only one substance namely God for He alone exists in Himself and through Himself and does not involve the existence of anything else. However, besides God there are two relative substances, namely, mind and body. Each can exist without the other, though both of them depend on God for their existence. This essential property or characteristic of the substance is known as *attribute*. Now the attribute of mind is consciousness and that of the body is extension. The attribute manifests itself in many ways. This modification of the attribute is known as the mode. Figure or motion is the mode of extension, as sensation or imagination is the mode of thought. The mode cannot exist without the substance and its attribute, but substance and attribute can exist without the modes.

Material bodies then are substances with their attributes of extension. However, the things are perceived to have the other qualities also of colour, taste, smell etc. Do they also belong to the things? Here Descartes points out that there are two kinds of qualities, namely, *Primary and Secondary*. Primary qualities are those which are clearly perceived by us. This simply meant those qualities which can be put into mathematical form. As such they are extension, figure, motion, rest, duration and number. The primary qualities do belong to the material bodies. The secondary qualities are the confused ideas. They are heat, cold, colour, sound, taste etc. We cannot clearly and distinctly perceive them. They are in the mind of the perceiver.

The conception of matter as consisting of extension alone has had far reaching influence on the philosophy of nature. Where there is space, there must be extension. As such there is no such this as Vacuum. As, again, matter being extension is infinitely divisible, so there can be no atom. Besides, matter being purely extension is entirely passive. The activity or motion in material things is due to their mechanical impact, God imparted the first motion and thence it is being continued.

Much of Descartes' physics is obsolete but in certain observation he is delightfully modern. Specially his observation of motion as purely relative reminds us of the theory of relativity of Einstein. The same steamer is static in relation to the man on the board, but, says Descartes, it is moving in relation to the man on the shore.

Descartes reduces the whole world to mechanism. The so-called living organisms, are really machines, only they are more complex and refined. This doctrine led to the dissection of the animals and to the discovery of the reflexes. The automation theory, however, was mixed blessing for it led to cruelty to the animals as well as powerful tendency towards materialism. In his doctrine of the universe as a vast machine he anticipates the 19th century materialism and his insistence on reflexes is an anticipation of Behaviourism.

2.08. Truth and Error

The criterion of knowledge is that all that is clear and distinct must be true. If one asks, why should the clear and distinct be regarded as true? The answer is that it follows from the divine veracity. But, then, it is also a fact that we are deceived and commit mistakes and then we have to answer the question: "How could a veracious God give us faculties that so easily lead us astray?"

Now truth or falsity lies in judgements and not in ideas or perceptions. A judgement is a joint product of intellect and will. We perceive something and then we give assent to it either by affirmation or denial, leading to a judgement. If the ideas be clear and distinct, then their affirmation or denial leads to truth. The human intellect is finite inasmuch as it cannot hope to receive clear and distinct ideas of all things. But the will of its very nature is infinite for it has unlimited choice to make before it. If we could give our assent or dissent only to clear ideas, then there could be no room for error, but we give our will to confused and indistinct ideas also. And this gives rise to error.

Thus error is due to the joint product of intellect and will together. By itself intellect does not lead to error for every idea in itself is a psychical existence. Besides every "idea must have a really existing cause of its objective reality." By itself there is nothing wrong in the will to be infinite.

Though in general, Descartes holds that the part of intellect in producing error is very small, yet it cannot be totally absolved. The intellect supplies confused and indistinct ideas and to which the assent or dissent constitutes error. Specially this is true in relation to the secondary qualities of colour, heat, smell etc. These ideas do not represent anything objective in things but have their sole function in directing us to that which is beneficial or harmful for us. Thus errors arise due to its being finite and limited in giving us clear and distinct ideas and for making the intellect finite God is responsible. As such, to some extent at least, God is responsible for our errors.

Descartes answers by way of reply to the above observation firstly, by saying that we have no right to enquire into the how and why of what God does. Besides, God is the creator of the whole universe; and for the perfection and harmony of the universe it is better to have fallible rather than infallible intellect. Again, the created intellect of its very nature must be limited and the existence of even the finite intellect is undoubtedly good. Lastly, the will could not have been created in such a manner as to be limited to clear and distinct ideas. This would have made man a machine rather than a free spirit. Thus the gift of infinitely free will is necessary for spiritual growth and as such for its misuse we are to be blamed rather than the creator God. The positive causes of our errors are—

(a) Haste, without waiting for the adequate evidence.
(b) Prejudice and the early preconceived opinions that have never been tested.
(c) Too much reliance on memory which should be checked and refreshed by continual perceptions.

2.09. Mind and Body

The method of Descartes in reaching *Cogito ergo sum* is one of abstraction. One by one he takes all that is not essential in thinking and discards them till he comes to consciousness. Now in order to know consciousness one need not refer to extension. Similarly, in knowing extension one need not refer to consciousness. Consciousness and extension, mind and body, then are independent of one another and do not involve each other's existence. As such there are two independent substances called mind and body.

This dualism of mind and body is important, for human beings have both body and soul. The human body like all other organic bodies is a mere machine. The moving principle of this machine is the heat in the heart. The death is due to the destruction of some important parts of the body machine. In human beings alone God by a special creation adds soul. There can be no real relation between body and soul for they are diametrically opposed. The relation of the soul to the body is of the nature of the pilot to his machine.

However, this vague formulation of the mind and body relationship is very inadequate. We intuitively know that there is *some* relation between M and B, but we must decide the precise nature of it. Descartes wavers between interactionism which he seems to suggest and parallelism which follows logically from his absolute dualism. A great many bodily activities can be explained in terms of reflexes and his acute observation in this connection makes him the precursor of modern behaviourism. But bodily activities are to some extent influenced by the mind, and the mind is also influenced by the body. He regards sensing, imagining, remembering as mental acts but the objects referred to are not mental. But can the mental ideas tell us anything of the material bodies? No, for the sole function of the ideas is to guide us to what is harmful or beneficial to us and not to represent things external to us. However, Descartes believes that there are real material bodies. This general belief in material bodies is based on divine veracity. If we want to know definitely about the particular material bodies, then we can know only their primary qualities but the so-called secondary non-quantitative qualities are nothing but confused ideas. The confused ideas, however, are caused by external objects as is clear from his explanation of perception. In perception the material bodies effect the mental states through the human body.

(i)   Firstly, the exciting body affects the sense-organs of the percipient's own body.

(ii) This bodily affection moves the subtle animal spirits in the nerves. The movement of the animal spirits terminates in the pineal gland which he considers to be the seat of the soul. The soul is indivisible substance and therefore occupies the pineal gland which is the only undivided portion of the brain.

(iii) Lastly, a physical impress or seal is left on the pineal gland which serves as the occasion of the origin of consciousness.

Descartes seems to have explained away the mechanical pressure of the body on the mind by the mediating services of the animal spirits terminating in the pineal gland. Similarly, the mind acts on the body by moving the animal spirits in the pineal gland which coursing through the muscles leads to bodily movement. This direct interactionism he tries to conceal with the help of the analogy of the rider and the horse. Just as the rider spurs on the horse to run fast with his own energy, so the mind only excites the bodily movement without imparting its own energy into the material series. However, the artificial nature of the relation between M and B is open to various criticisms.

1. Even the above analogy of the rider and the horse does not totally exclude the possibility of interactionism. The analogy is false for both the rider and the horse are essentially of the same nature but M and B are quite opposed having nothing in common. Besides, even if the direct contact between M and B be excluded, still it remains true that they influence each other through the animal spirits. Again, grudgingly the interaction is admitted as soon as we grant that the soul is excited to activity by the animal spirits or that the soul moves the animal spirits. The animal spirits is material though it is subtle; and if it can move the soul, then there is no

bar in believing that the body can act on the mind and also *vice-versa*.

2. Descartes tried to soften the rigour of the absolute dualism of *M* and *B* by pointing out at least one place of pineal gland as their meeting ground. Not only the choice is purely arbitrary but also at the same time metaphorical. The soul being a spirit does not need a seat like any material body. And if the soul can occupy space in the pineal gland, there seems to be no reason why it should not occupy the whole body. Although Descartes limits the direct inter-action of soul and body to the pineal gland, he makes a departure in the case of memory. The memory appears to him more physical than mental and he conjectures it to be diffuse through the whole brain.

3. Descartes himself seems to be aware of the many difficulties raised and waves in his conviction of dualism when he comes to explain 'passions' like love, hatred, anger, fear etc. He is obliged to treat them as modes of thinking and yet believes them to be caused by the action of the body. They are treated to be complex and confused states. The so-called passions are perceptions, feelings and emotions of the soul. . . . which are caused, maintained and strengthened by some movement of the animal spirits. However, apart from the special difficulty of *M* and *B* in relation to passions, this observation of Descartes reminds one of the famous James-Lange theory of emotion, according to which an emotion is a sensation-mass caused by the stirred-up states of the body.

4. The difficulty of *M* and *B* dualism arises from an artificial division of a concrete reality. We never experience ourselves as mind *and* body but always as embodied mind or spiritualised body. The whole method of vicious abstraction led to the existence of consciousness apart from any relation to the body. This led Descartes to define mind as that which is not extended, and extension as that which is not conscious. But if we define *M* and *B* in such a way that they cannot be bridged then there can be no real relation between them. There can be no real remedy of a fancied malady. Here we can say that we ourselves have raised the dust and complain that we cannot see.

2.10. The Estimate of Descartes

Bacon and Descartes are rivals in being called the father of Modern Philosophy. However, we have seen that Bacon cannot be called the father of modern philosophy. It was really Descartes who not only establishes a new critical method but also propounds an original system of philosophy with far reaching development. He is justly called the prophet of the new era of his revolution proved most radical and influential in the history of thought between Aristotle and Kant. For this reason of creating an epoch in man's thinking he has been called the legislator of modern thought. We may now briefly summaries the important tendencies of his philosophy.

2.10A. Method

Descartes postulated the free enquiry into the philosophical domain. Instead of submitting to the authorities, he tells us, to bring everything to the bar of reason. Reason, after years of bondage, comes to her own. Faith in religion and moral goodness, he does not discard but he supplies them the better and more stable ground of reason. In this acceptance of the true of Magna Charta of thought he was followed by all the moderners. Later on the same necessity of free thought was clearly laid down by Kant.

In this method Descartes laid down that knowledge to be obtained must be certain, necessary and universal. This model of knowledge is clearly found in mathematics. Thus the real philosophical method should be cast in the form of mathematics, especially Geometry. This emphasis on mathematics led to Geometrical method of Spinoza and influenced the methodology of Leibnitz and Kant. Even the empiricists Locke, Berkeley and Hume could not ignore the claim of mathematics to be the model of knowledge. However, the method of Descartes was carried on through abstraction. It established the cogito by rejecting what cannot be sure and certain. This successive negation of the inessential factors was considered to be most important by Spinoza who laid down that every determination is negation with frightful result. Besides, the deductive aspect of mathematical reasoning was emphasized by Spinoza and Leibnitz and even Locke could not reject this part of reasoning.

2.10B. Rationalism

Descartes has been a real initiator of modern rationalism. First, as mentioned before he laid down that reason is the sole arbiter of philosophical dispute. In this he was followed not only by Spinoza, Leibnitz and Kant but also by the empiricists Locke, Berkeley and Hume.

However, Descartes is the founder of rationalism in its distinguishing feature by pointing out that real, universal and necessary knowledge is found in innate ideas alone. This doctrine of innate ideas was greatly opposed by Locke and then it was modified by Leibnitz, and, Kant finally shaped the whole controversy into sharper lines. Hence a brief reference to the Descartes' view will not be out of place.

Innate ideas: No amount of sense-experience can give us universal knowledge for necessity the former is particular. As such the universal principle is supplied by the mind to the sense data. Now divested of the inadequate and mediaeval expression, the doctrine of innate ideas really means that mind is not totally receptive but is also active. It supplies the active formative principles of knowledge. In this broad and sympathetic interpretation of innate ideas, Descartes seems to be essentially correct. At least Kant in the most characteristic ways points that general principles and concepts are inherent contribution of the mind to the sense-data. However, even the most sympathetic interpretation would point out that Descartes was rather vague in his doctrine of innate ideas. Descartes at least recognised the dual role of innate ideas.

(i) Since the essence of the mind is consciousness or thought so there are certain ideas which belong to the mind alone. Specially the innate ideas are characterised by clearness and distinctness. In this sense innate ideas meant pure and abstract thoughts. The best example of this is the innate idea of God defining His characters as infinite, perfect etc.

(ii) However, Descartes was also obliged to extend the innateness to sense ideas as well. First, he could not find their place in the mental series as they seemed to be caused by something external to the mind. But afterwards, he had to yield. The sense experience of colour, taste, etc. are not in objects and therefore, they belong to the psychical existence. The external stimulus at most serves the function of release mechanism, exciting the sense-organs and consequently through the pineal gland the soul to form sense-experience. Accordingly, Descartes had to concede even though reluctantly that the ideas of sense must be natural to the mind, i.e. innate. Upon the second view, then instead of the innate ideas forming a special class, innateness becomes characteristic of every idea. At least this was developed in the philosophy of Leibnitz, as the former interpretation of innate ideas as the formative principle of knowledge was developed by Kant.

In any case the doctrine of innate ideas was suggestive of future development in the modern stream of thought. There is yet another element in the Cartesian rationalism of modern development. This element consists in showing that certain knowledge is found in the analysis of self-consciousness. In simple language it amounts to this that the reality can be best interpreted on the analogy of the reality of self. The *Cogito ergo sum* of Descartes led Leibnitz to define the monads in terms of the self. This finally led in Kant and the subsequent idealists to the statement that the mind is the legislator to things. As a matter of fact in-spite of dualism Descartes really had an idealistic leaning inasmuch as he laid down that the mind alone can be known with certainty and the matter can be known only indirectly through the veracity of God. Concerning this point Russell in his *History of Philosophy* writes, "There is thus, in all philosophy derived from Descartes, a tendency to subjectivism, and to regarding matter as something only knowable, if at all, by inference from what is known of mind." (p. 586)

2.10C. Dualism

Descartes has been called a typical dualist and that he was as a metaphysician, psychologist and physicist. Descartes laid down that mind and body are two independent substances. This led to many subsequent theories concerning the relation between the two, like occasionalism, parallelism of Spinoza, Pre-established Harmony of Leibnitz and subjective idealism of Berkeley. Even in contemporary times the problem cannot be said to have been solved. Hence he supplied an important problem for the posterity to solve.

In other respect, the dualism of Descartes led to materialism. His insistence on human body as a complex automation led to the materialistic tendency towards explaining everything in terms of matter. The recent rise of behaviourism is simply a hearkening back to the Cartesian tendency.

Even in the theory of knowledge Descartes was a dualist. He believes that we have the ideas through which we know the external world. Here also he divides knowledge into ideas and the things of which we have the ideas. This epistemological dualism was held by Locke and was severely criticised by Berkeley.

It seemed that the dualistic tendency was rather strong in Descartes for he also divides the qualities of the external world into primary and secondary ones. In this he was followed by Locke but was severely attacked by Berkeley.

Lastly, Descartes divides the mental qualities into the two attributes of thought and will. In this he was followed by all up to the time of Kant who introduced the tripartite division of the mind instead of the bipartite.

2.10D. System Builder

Descartes believed in the capacity of reason to know all things. From the *cogito* he gets the criterion and from the criterion he establishes the existence and veracity of God. From the veracity of God he establishes the reality of the external world, the permanent self and knowledge. Thus with the proof and the veracity of God he closes the circle of his thought. In this ambitious attempt to build a system of thought he was followed by Spinoza, Leibnitz, Berkeley and Kant. Not only he makes a system but he builds a God-centred system and here also he was follow by Leibnitz and Berkeley.

Thus, many streams of thought have followed from the writings of Descartes. However, he himself looked upon his principles as merely preparatory to his system. But the principles and not the content of his system have proved momentous in the history of philosophy. Thus, Falckenberg observes:

The vestibule has brought the builder more fame, and has proved more enduring than the temple; of the latter only the ruins remain; the former has remained undestroyed through the centuries.

But, is the observation of Falckenberg sound? Well we have already noted in §0.02 that no key concepts can explain all the details of a world scheme of things. Similarly, the vision of mathematical philosophy could not be fully carried out in all the details. If Descartes and his successors could have seen the inherent weakness of such a vision, then they would have been helped into a deeper and more adequate vision. Unfortunately, the real weakness of mathematical key notions in philosophy could not be fully realised till very recently. Mathematics does yield necessary propositions. But the propositions of mathematics, as Hume noted, have nothing to do with actual state of affairs. but in philosophy we pick up a notion from a field of factual enquiry and apply it to all other data of all other fields. The propositions of mathematics and logic are important in connecting and organising the *relation* between facts with a view to obtaining a synoptic worldview. As such in general mathematical notions are not always very suitable for working out a philosophical system.[1]

But the real difficulty lay in selecting the characteristic of *necessity* involved in mathematical propositions. This can be obtained only in *a priori* propositions. But philosophy has to take into account actual state of affairs. But no propositions of empirical import can be *necessary*. Hence, the introduction of the key-notion of mathematical *necessity* raised an absurd ideal of philosophical knowledge, and created a false impression concerning philosophical propositions. They wrongly came to be regarded as cognitive statements. From this unfortunate impression concerning philosophy thinkers have not been as yet fully weaned. Further, the introduction of mathematical ideal in philosophy tended to prove philosophy an *a priori* system, as in Spinoza and in other idealistic thoughts.

2.10E. Concluding Remarks

From the preceding discussion another observation follows. If we keep the tradition of perennial philosophy in our account, then we find that philosophy aims at not giving us *knowledge but wisdom*. Wisdom implies not only sufficient knowledge of actual states of affair but also a high state of development in the wise man himself. In other words, philosophy aims at self-realization through the help of knowledge in science or in other walks of everyday life. Scientific knowledge remains subordinate, even when some important key-notions have to be borrowed from it. Descartes that way has changed this Platonic view of philosophy. He has introduced a new tradition into philosophy. He wants to make philosophy wholly cognitive enterprise like mathematics. This is a misconception of the task of philosophy. Many philosophers in the present twentieth century have come to the conclusion that systematic philosophy called metaphysics cannot fulfil the demand of scientific knowledge. From this inability of philosophy, they conclude that philosophy is nonsense. Is it so?

The reality as a whole has been the traditional subject-matter of philosophy. Now science deals with the observable either directly or indirectly. But 'reality as a whole' cannot be the object of any one's observation. It remains super-sensible. Naturally God or the immortality of soul cannot be known in the scientific way. But the perennial philosophers have not claimed any scientific knowledge of their subject-matter. They all the while were dealing *not with facts* but with the realm of *values*. Their language has always been mostly symbolical, metaphorical and analogical. If we try to understand and faithfully keep this end of philosophy in view, then philosophy need not be science. Though science is the only way of

---

1. This guarded statement becomes necessary in view of the philosophical system of Whitehead.

attaining knowledge, but is not the only *rational* discipline of man. The attainment of values is as much the serious concern of man. The task of philosophy is the determination of values.

Now Descartes should be remembered for introducing this misconception into the nature of philosophy. Here he has been followed by a number of philosophers. The anti-metaphysicians of the present era in their misguided way are simply carrying out this Cartesian tradition of philosophy. Fortunately Descartes was followed by Spinoza and in him we find the vindication of metaphysics in its true sense.

3

Benedict de Spinoza (1632-77)

3.01. Introduction

In the life and teaching of Spinoza we find embodied the harmony of the intellectual and moral excellence. This essentially Hellenic ideal, however, was achieved by an Oriental, for Spinoza was a Jew. Thus he is the symbol of what is best in the East and West. He laid down the most uncompromising monotheism in the west which essentially reminds one of the Vedanta philosophy. Hence Schwegler suggests that his system is a consequence of his nationality, an echo of the East.

Baruch Spinoza, as he was named originally, was born on the 24th November, 1632 in Amsterdam. He was well educated by his trader parent. However, his genius led him to have a different doctrine about God and he was, therefore, excommunicated from the Jewish synagogue about 1656. Spinoza dedicated his life to his lonely musing, living on the meagre pittance derived from the grinding of scientific glasses. He lived a life of frugal independence which he did not exchange for anything, in spite of many tempting offers. In 1673 he was offered a chair of philosophy at Heidelberg with full freedom to teach the subject. However, Spinoza wisely declined the offer. In early January, 1677 he fell ill and succumbed to it at an early age of 44.

The most celebrated work of the philosopher is *Ethica*. His other writings are: *The Principles of the Philosophy of Descartes* (1670), *Tractatus Theologico-Politicus* (1670), *Tractatus de Intellectus Emendatione*, *Epistolae*, and the recently discovered but important *Treatise Concerning God and Man*. No philosopher in the history of philosophy has been as variously interpreted as Spinoza. The conflicting systems of pantheism and atheism, idealism and empiricism, nominalism and realism, naturalism and acosmism have been attributed to him. He was known as a 'hideous atheist' in his time but Novalis prefers to call him 'God-intoxicated mystic'. Such diverse accounts of his philosophy follow because he has been more criticised than understood. Besides, the forbidding nature of the scholastic terminology and the geometrical nature of the presentation are also contributory factors towards the misconception of his thought. In order to estimate the just appreciation of Spinoza we have to find out the relation in which he stood to his predecessor Descartes.

3.02. Descartes and Spinoza

For a long time Spinoza was considered to be Descartes made consistent. This estimate of Spinoza was greatly facilitated by the remark of Leibnitz that Spinoza 'only cultivated certain seeds of Descartes' philosophy.' In spite of the fact that Pollock, after a learned commentary, showed that Spinoza was never a cartesian at all, we find Caird repeating the old view. "In the Spinozistic philosophy there are few differences from Descartes which cannot be traced to the necessary development of Cartesian principles."[1] Well Descartes greatly influenced Spinoza, but then the latter did not follow Descartes. The philosophy of Descartes ended in pluralistic scepticism and Spinoza's philosophy is a protest against it. Leon Roth, in a learned article in Mind of 1923, sums up the philosophy of Descartes in the three fundamentals of (i) the doctrine of discrete ideas, for in order to be true they must be clear and distinct, (ii) Creational Deity, for ultimately the essence of God consists in His power of creating and conserving the order of things, and (iii) the Voluntaristic metaphysics, for in the last resort, both in man and God, will supervenes over the intellect. But these fundamentals can lead only to scepticism in the following manner.

Cogito ergo sum showed two things. First, the ultimate guarantee of any truth is *lumen naturale,* i.e., the natural light of clear intuition. But if intuition be taken as the source of ideas, then it can supply only disconnected ideas. Secondly, the *cogito* led to the criterion of clearness and distinctness but this test can furnish us with only discrete ideas. Now if the idea be discrete and unconnected, then there can be no true intrinsic connexions in them. As such there can be no real and rational system of knowledge. Descartes saw that there could be no passage from one idea to another and yet he demanded that his method should lead to the construction of a system in such a way that one idea should lead to the next, in a chain of necessary connection. At this stage Descartes looked upon God for supplying the necessary principle for connecting and conserving the system of thoughts.

Cartesian philosophy ends in scepticism. The veracity of God, said Descartes, is the only touchstone of knowledge, the only valid guarantee against any doubt and scepticism. 'To one who pays attention to God's immensity, it is clear that nothing at all can exist which does not depend on him. This is true, not only of every thing that subsists, but of all order, of every law, and of every reason of truth and goodness. In the last resort the fundamental truths of mathematics, the laws of science and the fundamental principles of thought are valid because God wills them to be eternally true. But the arbitrary will of a transcendent God cannot explain the validity of the first principles, for Descartes points out that God can change them if He so desires. The validity of first principles could have been safeguarded if he had laid down that first truths are true, therefore, God willed them. In other words

---

1. Even B. Russell in 1946 in *History of Philosophy* writes that 'the metaphysics (of Spinoza) is a modification of Descartes'.

he ought to have like Spinoza, subordinated the will to the intellect. But Descartes by voluntarising the intellect of God has taken away the only plank on which he had fixed the safety board of knowledge.

When in the light of the veracity of God Descartes strives to explain error in human knowledge, he shows the same bankruptcy of his metaphysics. First, the powers of man are so feeble that he is incapable of understanding the works of God. Rather inconsistently Descartes also writes, "We ought to submit to divine authority rather than to our own judgment, even though the light of reason may seem to us to suggest with the utmost clearness and evidence something opposite." Secondly, all things depend on God who works according to ways inscrutable to us. Thus God becomes for us an asylum of ignorance. Lastly, the intellect is subordinate to the will in man. The man wills almost infinitely even when the intellect is highly limited. Hence man can hardly hope to have any knowledge.

The philosophy of Spinoza, then, is a vehement protest against these fundamentals of Descartes. His teaching is for a system of interlocking ideas and for a true rational system in which intellect is the sole mistress. Only in this light it will be possible to do justice to the contribution of Spinoza.

Two fundamentals of Spinoza's philosophy. According to Descartes an idea is true if it is clear and distinct. But even if an idea is so, we can affirm its existence but we cannot trace out its 'connection' with other ideas. However, without any connection between ideas there can be no real knowledge. Spinoza starts with a different assumption altogether. He begins with the unity of all that exists. A thing apart from its connections with any other thing is an abstraction and unreal on that account. In order, therefore, that a thing be true it must follow from the whole reality. God is considered to be the sole conserving cause of the universe but then the God of Spinoza is infinite, immutable and eternal intellect. A principle is eternal not because God wills it but He understands it and by understanding He creates it. Thus the universe remains thoroughly rational and intellectual. God Himself being logical or rational allows things to follow from him with intellectual necessity. Hence his well-known language is that everything follows form God with the same necessity as three angles of a triangle =2 rt. angles follows from the definition of a triangle. This insistence on the rational nature of the reality alone justifies the possibility of real connextion in things and in knowledge. Thus the two assumptions of the rationality of God and the reality of every idea so far as it follows from God, give rise to an absolute monotheism or pantheism.

Even when Spinoza is not to be regarded as Cartesian, we cannot forget that Descartes supplied a powerful impulse for the philosophy of Spinoza. We find that the important weapons in the armoury of Spinoza were forged in the philosophy of Descartes but he used them to establish a system with an opposed conclusion. With these observations let us try to interpret his philosophy systematically.

3.03. Method of Spinoza

Spinoza has cast the whole world in the form of a geometrical theorem. He treats human passions and actions as if they were lines, planes and solids. He seems to have directly derived from Descartes this use of the geometrical method. In one of the correspondences of Descartes, we find the following passage: "In order that it may be profitable for each and all to read your meditations containing as they do so much subtlety, and in our opinion, so much truth . . . . it would be well worth the doing if, hard upon your solution of the difficulties, you advanced as premises certain definitions, postulates, and axioms and thence drew conclusions conducting the whole proof by the geometrical method in the use of which you are so highly expert. Thus would you cause each reader to have everything in his mind, as it were, at a single glance, and to be penetrated throughout with a sense of the Divine being." Descartes himself seems to have approved of the geometrical method but he thought it to be unnecessary. However, Spinoza owned it as the method of reaching the truth as well as a convenient order of presenting his philosophy.

After the manner of Euclid, Spinoza in his *Ethica*, gives 27 definitions, 20 axioms and 8 postulates. However Spinoza was more than his method and the most important contributions are given in the appendices and longer scholia. This geometrical method is responsible for many unfortunate conclusions but the most objectionable feature of it is that it gives dogmatic colour to his philosophy. First, he does not tell us why there should be just these 27 definitions or 20 axioms and no other. Besides, his axioms are not self-evident. Again, we find other difficulties of the geometrical method, but at this stage let us trace the influence of the method on his philosophy.

1. First, the geometrical metaphor is indirectly responsible for his pantheism. In geometry there is only one presupposition of the single reality, namely, space and all other lines, planes and solids are but modifications of that all-embracing space. Similarly, according to Spinoza, there is only one reality, namely, God and all other things are but modifications of that reality.

Not only in geometry there is only one reality but that reality of space follows from the negation of its modification like squares, triangles etc. A square by itself is not real, but its reality is precisely that which it will have by cutting off or removing its periphery. In the same way the infinite space can be reached only by removing all the figures, lines and planes. In other words, the pure space is unlimited and any square or triangle only determines it or makes it limited. Thus runs the famous maxim of Spinoza that every determination is negation. The supreme reality of spinoza has no qualities or determination. It is the indeterminate ground of all that exists just in the same way in which the formless clay is the material ground of all pitchers and pots.

2. Again, in geometry there is no movement. The triangle once formed remains in that state. The relation which the angles bear to one another, or to the sides of

the triangle remains constant. Now Spinoza having cast the world in geometrical form has made it static. Thus he denies any freedom of will as a consequence of geometrical reasoning. If we grant that there is a triangle with certain properties, one has to further grant that all angles of a triangle =2 rt. angles The conclusion follows of necessity. Spinoza hopes to deduce everything following necessarily from the nature of the substance. Of course, man seems to be free but, according to him, it is the result of illusory pictorial thinking. Man is conscious of his desires and actions, but not of the conditions that determine them. A man, in states of intoxication, does a great many things and in that state he *Feels free*. Later on he realises that it was not he but the liquor which was working out into those actions. Similarly, when a man sees with the eye of reason then he will find that he can no more think himself acting otherwise than he has acted. His action is determined and is not free.

If there be no real movement, then there could be no real causes. Everything follows in the same way in which conclusions follow in geometry. However, the truth of geometry is eternal or timeless e.g. the angles of a triangle =2 rt. angles is true for all times. Hence everything in the philosophy of Spinoza is eternal or should be viewed *Sub specie aeternitatis*. Instead of causes we can find only the eternal reason of all things in substance or God.

3. Just as it is illusory to maintain that man has free will to do anything, so in like manner God has no end or purpose for which He can work. The teleogical conception of God makes Him finite. "If God works for the sake of an end, He necessarily seeks something of which he stands in need." This necessarily makes God imperfect. The teleological conception according to Spinoza, follows from anthropomorphism. Man thinks God to be a superman. Just as a man seems to run after an end so he thinks that God also has some unfulfilled desires. Thus the use of geometrical method led to the denial of personality to God.

Spinoza started with the unity of all things. This also presupposed a method in which everything may be shown to follow orderly. For this reason probably Spinoza chose the geometrical method. There is little doubt that he also considered the geometrical method as the best method of presentation for we find that he explains the intricacies of Hebrew Grammar in the same fashion. But the best reason seems to be the impersonal, exact and disinterested nature of mathematics which strongly appealed to him. Mathematics does not allow personal views to distort the truth. Human beings following their prejudices to prevail, would have remained in eternal ignorance "had not mathematics, which deals not with ends, but only with the essences and properties of figures, pointed out to them another standard of truth."

3.04. Comments on the Geometrical Method

Whatever might have been the reason which prompted Spinoza to adopt the geometrical method, we cannot justify its use in philosophy.

1. Any philosophy must explain all the varied experience of life. Nothing can be omitted from the thought compass of philosophers. However, mathematics of its very nature is partial and abstract. In geometry we ignore the size, area, colour etc. of the figure and concentrate on its extension alone. But why should we isolate some features? Yes, it becomes necessary in any science for the convenience of study, but then its limitation should be well kept in view. The truth of geometry is universal for it ignores actual state of affairs. But what gives it universality, for the same reason makes it utterly limited. The *a priori* nature of geometry cannot disclose empirical truths. But in philosophy we cannot ignore concrete reality. Hence the geometrical method with its inevitable abstraction cannot be thrust upon in philosophy. If we, without caring for the limitation of mathematics, use the geometrical method then of its very nature we will get partial and one-sided conclusion. Spinoza treats man as if he were pure intellect without any feeling. Like geometry he starts with a few thoughts and travels in their direction without digression. This vertical consistency prevents him from giving his system horizontal consistency as well. Thus in his thought-calculus a large sphere of life remains neglected and unexplored. He begins with grand unity, but misses the multiplicity.

2. Mathematics no doubt gives exactness of conclusion but then it has certain presuppositions. Like every science it is not only abstract but it has certain assumption, e.g., in geometry we assume that there is space. But who is going to evaluate its assumption? Mathematics cannot do it but is left for philosophy to find out the validity of its assumption. At least we need meta-mathematics to understand the philosophical implication of its statements. For this reason mathematics cannot be equated with philosophy. By using the geometrical method in philosophy, Spinoza has identified a part with the whole, something abstract with the concrete. In current language we say that Spinoza has confused the analytic statements of geometry with synthetic statements of science and commonsense.

3. Again, we have seen that no facts of experience can be excluded. Actions, movements and ends are the most glaring facts of experience. We cannot explain them away by declaring them to be illusory. Even if they are illusory, at best they as such still need explanation. However, Spinoza by his logico-mathematical considerations was led to deny the reality of human actions. But deny movement and we cannot explain anything. Spinoza uses the frequent metaphor of geometry. He says that all angles of a triangle =2 rt. angles follows from the definition of a triangle. But does it follow from a triangle? No, it is the human intellect with its moving and pulsating interest which moves the definition of a triangle to yield the conclusion. Yet this moving interest is denied by Spinoza.

The use of the geometrical method unnecessarily committed him to determinism. We find that he has to admit a certain freedom, movement and feeling in man, when he comes to teach human bondage and freedom. Thus if the geometrical method was the legacy of Descartes it was an unfortunate legacy.

3.05. The Doctrine of Substance, Attributes and Modes

According to Spinoza all our objects of knowledge fall into any of the three categories of substance, attributes and modes. So we shall explain each one of them.

Substance: Spinoza had the vision of the unity of all things. As such he starts with something from which everything can be shown to follow necessarily. This something he calls substance which following Descartes he defines "that which is in itself and is conceived through itself, i.e., the conception of which does not need the conception of another thin in order to its formation." Of course, Descartes had called mind and body also dependent substances on God but Spinoza points out that the phrase 'dependent substances' is contradiction in terms. A substance cannot depend on anything else. As such there can be only one substance. If there were more than one substance then they would limit each other and thus would take away their self-sufficiency. This one substance, he also calls God whom he defines as a "Being absolutely infinite; that is, substance consisting in infinite attributes each of which express eternal and infinite essence". Thus the substance is infinite or unlimited. By infinite, firstly he understands that which is uniquely individual for the substance can be conceived only 'in itself'. Ordinarily we conceive or understand a thing by comparing it with other things. For example, when we say that the orange is yellow, then we mean that orange has a quality of yellow colour which is found in other things as well. But Spinoza tells us that substance can be understood only by referring to itself. This insistence on the uniqueness of the substance prevents it from having any qualification. We cannot say that the substance is moral or intellectual for these terms limit Him. If God is moral, then He cannot be immoral. Thus Spinoza points out that *every determination is negation.* Hence his substance becomes most positive without any limitation. The actual table is not real for it is finite. It is finite for it is limited on all sides by other bodies. Its pure reality is reached when all qualities of colour, weight and so on are abstracted from it. Hence, the substance can only be negatively described. Here the famous maxim of Spinoza is: *Every determination is negation.* As soon as we determine or qualify substance by describing it we limit it. For instance, as soon as we say that substance is love, we at once deny cruelty to it. Similarly, any description of what substance is, indirectly tells us what it is not.[1] Later on, we shall find that Spinoza supplements this maxim with regard to his teaching concerning 'Infinite attributes'. Nevertheless, in this context, Spinoza points out that substance can be described as what it is not. But this is also true that every negation implies some affirmation. For instance, when we say this brown thing is not a book, then it, indirectly points out that it is some object to which the name 'book' cannot be applied. We shall soon see, therefore, that Spinoza held that substance is the most

---

1. Hegel and the Hegelians have raised this maxim to an important logical principle of their system. The simple converse of this lies at the basis of Hegel's dialectic method, 'concrete universal' and dialectical advance.

positive entity. Thus, it is both true that substance can be described only by negations and also that it is the most positive entity. Most probably we shall be better helped if we follow his own account of the substance.

Spinoza has so defined substance that it cannot but be *infinite*, since if it were finite it would mean that it is limited by something else. However, the substance is self-determined and self-contained and nothing can affect or modify it. He also calls it *causa sui*. To begin with 'cause' means for us an invariable relation between two successive events. Spinoza is not using the term for temporal connections at all. He is trying to find out non-temporal rational connection. A cause, according to him, *explains* phenomena and does not simply *describe* them. By 'explanation' is meant the showing of necessary connexion between phenomena which means, the establishment of a logical relationship between them. For example, a conclusion is said to be necessarily connected with its premises. Similarly, by saying that the substance is the cause of the universe, Spinoza wants to hold that it follows necessarily from the substance. This kind of casual explanation for Spinoza is best seen in the purely deductive system of Euclid's geometry. Hence, the oft-repeated statement of Spinoza is that everything follows from substance in the same way in which all the angles of a tringle are together equal to two right angles follows from the definition of a tringle. Hence, by describing substance as *Causa sui*, Spinoza means that the reality is a self-explanatory, all-inclusive, inter-related whole.

As Spinoza is picturing reality through geometrical metaphors, so he conceives of reality as a logical system in which time has no place. Therefore, he defines substance as *eternal*.

> By eternity, I mean existence itself, so far as it is conceived necessarily to follow solely from the definition of that is eternal.

In other words, eternity follows from the very essence of the substance. The very essence of the substance is that it is. Hence, the substance is non-temporal and duration-less. It cannot be described as ever-lasting. In other words, no terms pertaining to time can be meaningfully applied to it. This is important to note, since 'eternal' means:

(*i*)   either that which endures through all times. This is the sense in which the God of religion is described as eternal. He is said to persist through all times. Hence, Yahwe described himself: 'I am that I am'.

(*ii*) or, eternal may mean non-temporal. This is best seen in logical relationship of implication. For example, given the premises in a syllogism, the conclusion follows. The relation is not one of temporal priority in which premises appear first and the conclusion follows next. The premises and conclusion are found together and one cannot be without the other. In the same way, the substance and its essence are timelessly interlocked.

There is also another characteristic of substance, according to Spinoza, namely, it is *one* or simple. This does not require elaborate explanation here. If there were more than one substance, then they would limit one another, and none of them, therefore, would be infinite in the sense of being unaffected by another. However, if we argue that there are a number of substances which yet do not interact, as Leibnitz assumed in his *monadology*, then the difficulty would arise with regard to the unity and harmony of the universe. If one has to trust his experience, then this world certainly presents a multiplicity. Even if there is no complete harmony, certainly objects do appear in mutual interaction. How can a Leibnitz, assuming a number of independent monads, explain this interaction? Leibnitz had to assume the doctrine of *Pre-established Harmony* to account for the unity and inter-action in the multiplicity. But we shall also see that this doctrine of pre-established harmony has failed to explain the unity. Hence, Spinoza, consistently adhering to the definition of substance and its infiniteness rightly held that there could be one substance only.

3.06. Implications of the Doctrine of Substance

So far we have seen that Spinoza regards substance as one, infinite, self-caused and eternal reality from which all things follow necessarily. Apparently, this is also the description of God in theology. For this reason Spinoza calls substances as God. This created trouble for Spinoza in his life-time with the result that he was despised, decried and denounced by his contemporaries. Its real implication has not been fully realised even now. We shall comment on this a little later. Again, as God or substance is an all-inclusive whole, outside of which nothing can lie, so Nature conceived as a whole is identical with God. Hence, God and Nature are one. This is known as pantheism, according to which the reality of a single God permeates and indwells all things.

Again, as substance is infinite and whatever there is follows from God or substance, so God is said to be *causa sui* or self-creative. This at once makes clear what Spinoza meant by God. In Western theology God is taken to be a personal Being, having will, intellect and feeling. He is also said to be the creator of the universe. Spinoza denies this concept of God. According to him, God can create only out of some pre-existing matter. This would make matter co-eternal with God and ultimately would lead to dualism and not to monism. Later on, Kant in his own way has shown that a creator God at most can be an architect or a designer, but not an infinite God. For this reason, Spinoza consistently maintaining monism, denied the concept of a creator God. Further, the concept of a creator God would lead us to suppose the reality of the temporal order. It would mean that there was a time when there was no world and there would be a time when there would be no world. But we have already seen that nature or substance is eternal or non-temporal.

Further God and Nature are identical and nature is governed by eternal laws, i.e., by logical interrelationship. Under this rational order there is no room for chaos or arbitrariness. Everything is strictly determined. Everything follows necessarily in the same way in which implicates follow from a proposition. Given 'All S is P', it follows

I.   No not-P is S.
II.   Some P is S.
III. Some not-S is not-P etc.

Again, nature being *causa sui* is self-creating. Hence, it means that Nature is fully intelligible by itself alone, and, there is no necessity for appealing to a transcendent God. This is known as Spinoza's materialism. The important thing is to note that logical determinism has no room for voluntary freedom. The two things have different contexts altogether. 'Determinism' of Spinoza has nothing to say about the freedom of will in man which pertains to voluntary action. However, if we follow Spinoza and his doctrine of determinism, then the freedom of will also comes to be denied. God, being *causa sui* is said to be a *free* cause. But by 'free cause' is meant that there is nothing outside of him by which this action will be determined. But God cannot be said to have any will or feeling at all. God as nature is simply an all-inclusive, interrelated logical system. A logical system has no room for will. Similarly, a mathematical theorem has no room for will, activity or enjoyment. So God has no will or feeling. Hence, by equating God with Nature, Spinoza speaks of an impersonal God. Hence, from a theological standpoint the system of Spinoza is pantheism.

Pantheism is not quite popular in the West and evidence shows that Western pantheism, having its root in Plotinus was Indian in origin. Christianity, having its foundation in Judaism was anti-pantheistic. When Jesus said that he and his father were one, then, the Bible says, Jews sought to kill him because of this blasphemy. As pantheism maintains that all is God so trees, rivers and inanimate objects too are God. Hence, God in pantheism tends to impersonal. But the God of Jews and Christians hearkens to the prayers, alleviates the suffering of devotees and rewards and punishes each man according to his works. Therefore, he is personal. Now by denying the concept of a creator, and a personal God who works according to his inscrutable ways, Spinoza denied the only type of religion which was real to the Westerners. For this reason Spinoza was branded as a 'hideous atheist'.

As there is nothing over and above God, so all is God and everything follows from God. For this reason God is said to be the indwelling and pervading principle of the universe. So God, according to Spinoza, instead of being regarded as transcendent is really an immanent ground of all that is God or nature as a self-creating reality is known as *Natura Naturans* according to Spinoza. Again, in its static aspect, in its aspect of a creative product, nature is known as *natura naturata*, i.e., sum-total of all that exists. Hence, nature is a self-explanatory and self-contained system. Now if we emphasize the role of nature as a self-explanatory reality and if we emphasize the statement that God is *nature*, then this will be tantamount to *atheism*. Here nature is conceived as one inter connected system, one intelligible and self-contained cosmos, inclusive of all phenomena, physical and psychical, past, present and future.[1] In such a generalisation there is nor room for God. But, there are occasions where nature is suppressed. We shall find that things of human experience have been called by Spinoza as *modes*. And modes are like the ever-vanishing waves that never are. In this phenomenal aspect, the world appeared to him unreal and God as fully real. God alone is All. In this phase he becomes God intoxicated mystic and denies the reality of the cosmos. Here Hegel observes:

> Spinozism might really just as well or even better have been termed Acosmism (than atheism), since according to its teaching it is not to the world, finite existence, the universe, that reality and permanency are to the ascribed, but rather to God alone as the substantial.

One wonders as to why God should have been brought in an all-inclusive, self-explanatory system of nature. And if God does matter, then why should he be equated with nature which instead of fanning religious fire tends to obliterate it. We shall find that Spinoza is trying to teach about God certain things which were never taught about him. If Spinoza is teaching a religion, then this religion is not only anti-Jewish but is also anti-theistic. This new teaching could be better understood, according to Spinoza, by equating God with nature. We shall learn more about it if we follow Spinoza's doctrine concerning attributes and modes.

3.07. Attributes

There can be no substance without attributes. However, they may be either *essential or accidental*. The essential attributes define a substance, i.e., without which the substance would cease to be substance. The accidental attributes are those variable characters which a substance can lose without ceasing to be what it is.

> By 'attribute' I mean that which intellect perceives as constituting the essence of substance.

Are the attributes subjective? Are they what the *human intellect* perceives ? This is an interpretation which can be put on the definition of 'attributes' if we accent the first part of the sentence. However, subjectivism is foreign to Spinoza's thinking. He was brought up in scholastic logic, according to which there could be no substance without the attributes. Hence, attributes do be long to the substance as its essence. As the substance is self-contained and is infinite, so it has an infinite number of attributes. Hence, the substance of Spinoza has an infinite number of attributes, each of which expresses the essence of the substance infinitely. At this

---

1. Copleston, F.C., 'Pantheism in Spinoza and the German Idealists'—*Philosophy*, April, 1946. Also see Hampshire, S., *Spinoza*, A Pelican Book, pp. 46f.

stage one is reminded of the dictum 'every determination is negation' and according to this dictum the substance was interpreted as an empty Being without any content. Now it appears that like a juggler out an empty hat, Spinoza has filled the colourless, blank substance at a single stroke with an infinite number of attributes. But this criticism is unjust, since we have already remarked earlier that substance has no finite attributes which limits the substance. But an infinite number of attributes, each of which boundlessly or infinitely expresses the essence of substance cannot make the substance limited. In other words, under two conditions an attribute can limit the substance, namely,

1. If an attribute excludes the possibility of other attributes, i.e. if one determination negates other determinations, and,
2. If an attribute by itself is finite. Now God has infinite attributes which neither limit one another, nor the substance. They are co-existent properties each of which equally manifests the essence of the substance. Thus the infinite number of attributes, each infinite in itself leaves the substance indeterminate. Further, each attribute taken by itself does not limit the substance, but manifests its nature infinitely and boundlessly.

One wonders whether an infinite number of attributes can co-exist without mutual exclusion. By way of illustration his point on this score, Spinoza holds that out of an infinite number of attributes, human intellect can perceive only two, namely, extension and thought. Here thought and extension, as Descartes had made familiar, are quite independent of each other. As such these two attributes do not limit each other. Further, each of them is infinite in its own kind. Thus, there is possibility of an infinite number of attributes, coexisting together which neither limit one another nor the substance.

3.08. Parallelism of Thought and Extension

The doctrine of infinite attributes follows deductively from the definition of substance. But Spinoza might have been additionally satisfied about it because of its adequacy in solving the problem of mind-body relationship. Descartes had held mind and body to be *relative* substances which were quite independent of each other. In spite of its usefulness in evading conflict between science and religion, mechanism and Grace, the dualism of Descartes did not work well. First, there could be only one substance and if there were more than one, they would limit each other and would destroy their mutual substantiality. In the eye of Spinoza the phrase 'relative substances' seemed self-contradictory. Secondly, Descartes himself could not help noting their mutual interaction which went against his dualism. This position further deteriorated in later Cartesians who upheld the theory of *occasionalism*. According to this theory extension is not the cause of thought and *vice-versa*, but one is the *occasion* of the other. However, it was maintained that God intervened at such occasions in causing changes in mind and body. Spinoza did not favour this perpetual appeal to the inscrutable will of a mythical God. For this reason Spinoza rejected cartesian dualism and rejected the substantiality of mind and body. He regarded mind and body, extension and thought as two of the many inseparable aspects of a single, all-inclusive reality. Being co-existent attributes of the substance, thought and extension cannot interact.

How are they related? Well, only like can cause the like. The two, therefore, cannot interact, but they run parallel to each other. They are infinite but independent of one-another, each capable of expressing God infinitely in its own way. God is extended as well as thinking. These two are but two inseparable aspect of the same thing, like the convex and concave of the same lens. From one viewpoint God appears as infinite extension, as from another angle, he appears as infinite intellect in the same way in which the same person is known as Jacob as well as Israel. No one aspect can exist without the other. Substance thinking and substance extended are one and the same substance, apprehended now through one Attribute, now through the other. To every mode of extension corresponds a mode of thought, in the same order or series. A circle and an idea of a circle are one and the same thing, looked at from the angle of extension and thought respectively. But this parallelism excludes materialism as well as idealism, for matter cannot explain mind, nor mind can explain matter.

This parallelism, with the doctrine of infinite attributes, shows that not only God but everything has an aspect of infinite viewpoints but we human beings can know only two, namely, extension and thought. But we may legitimately ask, why are we condemned to two attributes alone? If thought can know extension, why can it not know the other attributes as well? Both these questions Spinoza could not answer satisfactorily. He pointed out that human beings can know only two for they are embodied spirits. But then everything is endowed with infinite viewpoints and so human beings too have many more aspects than two. Besides, if intellect can know something other than itself, extension, than how can it not know other attributes as well? Once grant that thought can overstep its boundary, there is nothing which can be excluded from its grasp. Again, in strict parallelism, this concession to intellect shows something corresponding to which there is nothing in extension. Hence, in spite of parallelism Spinoza has his idealistic leaning.

There are certain inconsistent points in the doctrine of attributes. First, there seems to be no logical reason why the indeterminate substance which has no determination should have any attribute at all. The solution of filling the empty substance with attributes appears to be highly *a priori* and verbal. Secondly, there is no principle underlying the attributes. They are infinite but they are independent of one another. Hence, the substance is simply an *aggregate* and not an organised whole of the attributes. Such an aggregate can never give us the true unity which is the real aim of Spinoza to establish. Besides, to call such an aggregate of attributes infinite is to confound the term. The 'infinite attributes' simply means numerical infinite or false infinite of endlessness or indefiniteness. Lastly, his definition of attributes is so ambiguous that ultimately it amounts to saying attributes really qualify nothing, since the very nature of an attribute is that it should be consistent with some state of affairs and inconsistent with others. But an attribute which continues to qualify under infinite number of circumstances is vacuous. Hence, the infinite number of attributes leaves the substance as indeterminate as before. The illustration of thought and extension as infinite does not help the case. What is the meaning of infinite thought? Is it the pure consciousness of the Vedantins or the pure thought of Aristotle which has no content? A consciousness which is not the consciousness of any object is nothing. The same trouble lies about infinite extension. The very nature of extension in the concrete is that it should be limited.

Further, can a substance be both extended and inextended (thought)? As long as we picture thought and extension as two parallel lines, we can go on with their co-existence. But this pictorial thinking should not blind us to their identity. According to Spinoza, mind and body are one and the same. Later on, Samuel Alexander,[1] elaborated this theory of Spinoza and he held that mind and body are identical. The object *contemplated* is the brain and the same thing lived through and *enjoyed* is the mind. Strangely enough, but quite consistently with Spinozism, Alexander held that thought is extended. It was this difficulty which led Leibnitz to deny extension in favour of the reality of spiritual inextended monads alone.

3.09. Modes

The attributes, even when they do belong to the substance, do not explain the finite things of human experience for they are infinite. In his doctrine of modes, Spinoza hopes to explain the world of finite and individual things. However, at the outset, we wonder whether the finite modes can ever be derived from the substance and attributes in the light of his saying that "only the infinite can follow from the infinite, the finite can follow only from the finite". Hence we find that modes keep the nature of the substance as much indeterminate as the possession of the attributes did. Into this seeming contradiction we shall enquire later. So now let us follow what he has to say about the modes.

"By mode", says Spinoza, "I understand affections of substance, or that which is in another, through which it is also conceived". The modes are individual things of finite experience. They are to the substance what the waves are to the sea, shapes that perpetually die away that never are. They can never exist without the substance though the substance can exist without them. He seems to hold that they are either in another or in God. Every mode is in God for nothing can exist without God. But then again says Spinoza, "That which is finite and has a determinate existence cannot be produced by the absolute nature of any attribute of God; for whatever follows from the absolute nature of any attribute of God is infinite and eternal. It

---

1. Space, Time and Deity, Vol. I, pp. 101, 103, 105.

   J.V. Bateman, *Professor's Alexander's proofs of the spatiotemporal nature of mind*, The **Philosophical Review** 1940, pp. 316-17.

must, therefore, follow from God or from some attribute of God, in so far as He is considered as affected by some mode, . . .∴(or) in so far as *He is modified by modification* which is finite and has a determinate existence."[1] To these two ways of looking at modes, he returns again and again. Modes are said to be *actual* in so far as they exist at a certain time and place. Viewed in this way they do not follow from God but from the interminable series or connection of finite things. But modes are said to *real* when we conceive them under the form of eternity. As such they are to be viewed as they are in God. Every mode is rot lost for every idea of an individual thing actually existing necessarily involves the idea of the eternal and infinite essence of God . . . for the force by which individual *thing perseveres* in its own existence follows from the eternal necessity of the divine nature."[1] Thus Spinoza sometimes regards the modes to be real affections actually existing in God and sometimes looks upon them as mere illusions created by abstract imagination which views things as separated and unrelated. We shall soon see that both these views can be reconciled but then they would leave the substance as indeterminate as before. However, before we conclude that the system of Spinoza is really acosmic nihilism let us see what he has to say about the other kind of mode which he calls infinite.

3.10. The Infinite Mode

Most probably Spinoza at this stage sought to reconcile the finite and the infinite for in the last resort the world of finite things has to be explained in terms of the absolute reality. He hopes to bridge this gulf between the infinite substance, and finite things with the help of theory of infinite modes. As modes they belong to the finite world and as infinite they belong to the order of substance as well. "Every mode which exists both necessarily and as infinite, must necessarily follow, either from the absolute nature of some attribute of God, or from an attribute modified by a modification which exists necessarily and as infinite." Thus infinite modes (i) follow immediately from attributes like the infinite intellect following immediately from thought, and motion and rest from the attribute of extension or (ii) they follow from the attribute already modified like the whole universe which though contains fleeting and finite thing is as a whole infinite and permanent. The infinite intellect following immediately from the absolute attribute of thought is that which while it remains one with itself, is yet the ground of all ideas. Thus this infinite mode of infinite intellect really means a consciousness which containing all other finite thoughts and ideas continues to be the same. Hence it means an all-embracing self-consciousness. However, Spinoza never clearly lays down its nature. Again, he says that motion and rest immediately follow from extension. This means that Spinoza does not regard extension as purely passive, but according to him extension is essentially endowed with activity.

But the infinite mode also follows from the attribute already modified by a modification. In this sense the whole universe is itself regarded as infinite mode. The things in the universe are no doubt finite but the universe as a whole, as the

---

1. Italics ours.

sum-total of all finite things is said to be infinite. This can be explained by saying that men as individual beings come and go but man as the species remains forever. In the same way the individual things are finite but together they are infinite.

Before we discuss the relation of the substance and modes, it would not be out of place to point out that the term 'infinite mode' does not give any meaning to the world of finites for the endless chain of finite things fails to give the finite in the same way in which the summation of zeroes cannot give a positive number or the addition of points cannot yield a line. His indefinite chain of modes should not be falsely called infinite.

3.11. Monism and Pantheism

Reverting to the earlier question we have to decide whether Spinoza is to be regarded as a pantheist or not. Pantheism is the doctrine according to which the things or modes have no existence of their own. They are mere illusion or abstractions drawn by imagination. In the last analysis pantheism lays down that God alone is real and all other finite things are suppressed or annulled in the existence of God. This question has to be answered for Spinoza regards modes sometimes as fictitious and at times he regards them as real. As held before the modes are said to be in God and as such they are eternal and real. But he also holds that the modes to be modes are determined not directly by God but by other modes and as such the modes being temporal and finite cannot follow from the infinite substance and therefore are unreal. In the light of these conflicting tendencies let us try to explain his philosophy with the help of his own illustration.

Though the modes cannot exist without the substance yet there are passages in Spinoza which show that really nothing exists except the substance and its ever-perishing modes. This relationship of the substance with the modes is of the same nature as of the plane of its various figures inscribed in it. In order to simplify the illustration let us liken the substance to the infinitely extended plane and the modes may be like-wise compared to the many squares on it as in a graph paper. Now the position, extent and area of each square are determined by surrounding squares. They also in turn are determined by other surrounding squares and there seems to be no limit to the chain. Hence any one square is determined by other squares and not by the infinite plane itself. In the same way each mode is in other things and through which it is conceived and determined. Interpreted in this way the mode is unreal and does not follow from the substance.

However, there is another sense in which a mode is in God and by virtue of this positive nature it perseveres in its existence. This eternal nature of the mode follows from the following considerations:

(*a*) Each finite thing, as in the graph each square, results from the infinite totality or multiplicity. However, this totality or *natura naturata* as infinite mode is directly caused by God. Therefore, each mode follows from God.

(*b*) Again, the modes cannot be conceived to be existent without the substance.

Thus the being of the substance is the necessary ground for the understanding and existence of the modes.

(c) Lastly, the substance is the pure being or the positive essence. Now even the finite mode must have some being, even though it may be momentary in the same way in which a square in the plane must have some extension at least.

Thus each mode is *real* when it participates in the nature of God and is *unreal* though actual, when it is seen to be determined by the infinite multiplicity of all other finite things. But still the question remains, why has Spinoza given apparently contradictory statements about the modes? now Spinoza had to talk of the modes for he had to explain the individual things of the world. But he seems to suggest that modes as modes really do not exist. Their sole reality, as of the square in the graph, lies when it is pure being. The square is said to be real by virtue of its being extended. But mere extension, which is said to constitute the reality of the square, really annuls it. A square is a square because of its area, extent and position, but these qualities do not follow from the plane. The real qualities by virtue of which a square becomes an actual thing are determined by the multiplicity of things and not by the substance.[1] Thus Spinoza is really pantheistic for he negates the actuality of things. The same trend is to be detected in his theory of Infinite modes.

The doctrine of infinite modes aims at reconciling the multiplicity of things with the infinite substance. But here as elsewhere what Spinoza gives with one hand he takes away with the other. There are places where Spinoza says that the nature is God and God is nature. He himself points out that God is *natura naturata* looked as the total aggregate of the finite things. This infinite mode in the form of the whole universes he says, is the first in the descent from the substance and the last in ascent of finite things. But then, *natura naturata* does not mean the sum-total of the modes as *actual* things for the following reason:

1. Finite things, like squares on the graph, come much later. The substance, as the infinitely extended plane, remains the only eternal reality. As such the sum total of the squares cannot be said to constitute the original plane.

2. Besides, the original infinitely extended plane can be reached, not by adding the squares but by removing them away. The *natura naturata* to be merged in *natura naturans* means the negation of all finite things.

This pantheistic tendency in negating the world of finite things is further seen in Ethics and his theory of knowledge. A point as point cannot be understood as long as it is not viewed in a line; a line as line does not exist as long as it is not viewed in relation to a surface and the upward urge for the completion of knowledge continues. However, though a point cannot exist without a line yet it ceases to be a point when merged in a line. Similarly, the finite things as finite cannot exist without the substance but being merged in the substance they cease to be.

---

1. A thing is said to be *actual* when it can be known through sense-organs in spatiotemporal frame. But a thing is *real* when it is permanent and eternal.

3.12. Criticism of Spinoza's Pantheism

Thus Spinozism is pantheistic and nihilistic and we doubt whether any monistic system can be anything else. It remains a vast structure of logical consistency but for that very reason it has proved vastly unconvincing. It has proved repellent for it is purely rationalistic. But is man purely rational? No, he remains a seething, surging sea of emotion and feeling. Yet Spinoza, like the vadantins in India, has completely ignored them. Trust Spinoza and his logic and we are promised a sublime height from which to view things *sub specie aeternitatis.* But the higher we ascend, we to our utmost dismay, instead of the promised sunshine find ourselves enveloped on all sides by the chilly wind.

The rationalist Spinoza is 'saturated with the strong confidence in the omnipotence of the reason and the rational constitution of true reality.' This rationalism leads him to abstractionism for he lays down that that alone is true which is clear to reason. All other things which cannot be clearly demonstrated as belonging to the total structure of thought must be regarded as illusory. The multiplicity of finite things as finite cannot follow from the infinite. As such they are set aside. This gives him an abstract unity from which multiplicity has disappeared. But abstractionism is a vicious method. The abstract man means a rational being. It is certainly more clear and simpler than a concrete man with a large number of other qualities besides animality and rationality. But we doubt whether the abstract man is more real than the concrete man.

Again, grant to Spinoza that the substance alone is real and it follows that everything temporal is illusory created by imagination. But then the question still remains, how has illusion arisen? What is the locus of this fictitious world of finite things? By calling the world imaginary created by human intellect does not explain it. When everything is eternal, how has temporal emerged; when all is light, how has shadow come?

Spinozism does not satisfy the intellect in spite of its intellectualism for it explains away the finite things. However, the finite things are our data or facts which, as philosophers, we want to explain. By declaring them to be non-existent we do not understand them. It simply means that there are no data for philosophy. But deny the data and we deny the conclusion which is philosophy itself. Thus Spinozism when, it is most true, is most self-contradictory. No conscious being can court self-contradiction and much less Spinoza. However, self-contradiction begins to show itself when the inner man rebels against his philosophy. Spinoza was greater than his philosophy and in his Ethics he tries to impart certain amount of freedom and eternity even to finite individuals. So let us try to understand his Ethics which is the final aim of his philosophy.

3.13. Ethics of Spinoza

Spinoza's philosophy no doubt is highly intellectual but his aim is practical.

His primary aim is to find out spiritual rest. We are miserable for the objects of our love, according to Spinoza, are finite and illusory. If somehow we could succeed in setting our heart on something that is eternal, permanent and steadfast, then it would be possible for us to attain our true blessedness. "Our happiness", says he, "depends entirely on the quality of the objects to which we are attached by love for, on account of that which is not loved, no strife will ever arise, no sorrow if it perishes . . . But love to a thing which is eternal and infinite feeds the mind only with joy—a joy that is unmingled with any sorrow; that therefore we should eagerly desire and with all our strength seek to obtain." In order to put our hearts on the infinite and eternal, we must be able to discover it. This requires, as such, intellectual pursuit and his philosophy is a prelude to attain to the knowledge of such an object. Besides, like Socrates and Indian philosophers, Spinoza believes that virtue is knowledge. No one knowingly does wrong. If we could know the right thing, then our conduct also will be good. Hence the important question is, how can we reach the knowledge of the infinite and eternal? In Spinoza, as later on in Kant, we find that the need of the heart overpowers the limitation of the intellect. Unlike his metaphysics Spinoza grants that human mind is not purely finite and illusory but is capable of raising itself to the highest state of knowledge. Then, again, he grants a certain amount of freedom for he points out that the lot of man can be bettered. Now we have to find out how mind can reach the infinite. So let us try to follow what Spinoza has to say about the human mind.

The Human mind: Spinoza calls the human mind as 'the Idea of the body' and then again, 'the idea of the idea'. Now the first phrase 'the idea of the body' follows from the parallelism of Spinoza. Thought and extension run parallel and the order and system of one corresponds to the order and system of the other. The actual circle must correspond to the idea of a circle. In the same way the actual body must have, in the corresponding series, the idea of the body or the mind. Once more to repeat, this parallelism excludes the possibility of both materialism and idealism. Matter cannot be caused by the mind, nor can mind be reduced to matter. Both are independent series and yet one and the same thing is both.

Mind as the idea of the body : Secondly, the idea of the body means that thought is never empty. It has always some object. A knowledge is always a definite knowledge of definite things. As things are found in a series, so corresponding to them there are ideal series. He does not seem to believe in permanent self which survives body for there can be no self without a corresponding body. Then, again, the term 'idea' has been rather used ambiguously. The idea here may mean the mental correlate of a certain modification of the body and then again it may mean the *concept* or general impression of that modification. Spinoza very often writes as if the mind as the idea of the body knows the body as its object. If so then the mind transcends it series and owns the series of extension as well. Thus the parallelism of Spinoza breaks down. Let us see whether the other description of the human mind as the idea fares any better.

Mind as the idea of the idea : First, the idea or the idea of the idea follows from the fact that the mind is a part of the infinite intellect of God. As such "the idea of the mind and the mind itself exist in God by the same necessity and the same power of thinking. As every mode must exist in God so the human mind or a mode is in God. As again God as an infinite intellect must be thinking of everything, so He must have a thought or an idea of human mind itself. Thus human mind is an idea of the idea. Secondly *idea ideae* means the mind's capacity of thinking about itself without any other object. "For one who knows anything, in the very act of doing so knows that he knows it, and so on *ad infinitum*.'' Here also there is an emphasis on the ideal side. In the series of ideas there is something of which there is no correlate on the material side. The mind can return to itself. This self-activity has no parallel in the material series. Besides, as noted before, the idea can over-reach itself in the sense that it can make matter its object, i.e., it can bring matter under it. Further, we shall find that intellect can also influence and modify the body and its affections. Thus in his doctrine of the human mind he was virtually become an idealist in spite of his parallelism.

3.14. Degrees of Knowledge

(i) *imagination.* The essence of mind consists in having ideas or intelligence. Thus he subordinates will, emotion and feeling to intellectual achievement. But even knowledge is found in ascending order of imagination, reason and intuition according to the degree of the adequate ideas. First, there is the stage of *imagination* in which we view things separately and individually. It is essentially pictorial thinking in which we invent language and the divisions of time to view things in their individuality.[1] The fragmentariness and confusion of imagination follow from the nature of the mind regarded as the idea of the body. Remembering the analogy of the squares in a graph, we can know the square only when we view it fully in the endless chain of cause and effect. However, this is possible only for the infinite intellect. Thus imagination remains condemned to a limited knowledge. Besides, we get ideas of other objects as they affect *our own* bodies. But any object has many more relations to other objects. The ideas of other objects, then, are thus partial and very incomplete. Further, the idea about our own selves too, largely contributed by the external objects cannot but be fragmentary.

But human mind can rise above the illusory knowledge of imagination. Imagination fails to give adequate ideas because it separates them. However, everything is unified in one whole, participating in the eternal nature of the substance. Real knowledge must be able to see things *sub specie aeternitatis*, in their real connection. By virtue of reason human mind can 'escape from the narrowness and confusion, the arbitrariness and contingency of its own subjective feelings or affections'.

---

1. This observation of Spinoza has been elaborated by Bergson in his explanation of *Matter and Intellect.*

(ii) *Ratio or reason.* Reason consists in having true *communes notiones,* i.e., ideas of what a totality of things has in common, and what is alike in the part and the whole. Thus it supplies the fundamental base or starting ground of reasoning in the form of primary definitions in Physics and Geometry. Similarly it supplies the laws or principles which are common to all particular things. By virtue of seeing things in relations which are true for all, at all places and times, ratio has the characteristics of eternity. Thus by reasoning we have 'knowledge of the eternal and infinite essence of God'.

Reason no doubt is adequate as far as it goes, but then it stops short of the highest kind of knowledge known *as Intuition.* No doubt reason by means of its principles introduces unity amongst things by finding out their essence but the principles themselves stand in need of further unification. Besides, it still views things in their separateness. Again, by virtue of the common points on which it insists, it leaves out other particularising details. But these details make a particular thing what it is. Hence reason fails to point out the necessary relations of any one particular thing.

Intuition. "Intuitive knowledge", says Spinoza is "that kind of knowing which proceeds from an adequate idea of the formal essence of certain attributes of God to the adequate knowledge of the essence of things". It is at once immediate and direct and the objects appear as if in a single flash, following from God. Instead of proceeding from the parts to the whole, we start with the whole and proceed to the parts. Just as we know the particular spaces from the idea of the all-embracing space, so in intuition we know the particular things by seeing them in God. Truths which reason had taken years to discover, intuition finds them in a momentary flash. The past, present and the future take the form of the everlasting now. In comparison with ratio, the intuition has the following characteristics:

1. The objects of reason are *communes notiones,* i.e., those factors which are common to the things. As such it *abstracts* the common properties by ignoring the factors which vary with different objects. The intuitive knowledge is of the *concrete* things for through it we know them in their fullness, as they are related to the whole scheme of things. Ideally we should be able to see the why and how of the table in relation to the universe as a whole. Thus intuition views each thing in its concrete fullness.

2. Reason is discursive and indirect. We know the equality of *A* and *C* by virtue of their connection with *B*. But intuition is a happy flash of insight. For example, two triangles having their three sides correspondingly equal are proved to be equal. Intuition *sees* them so at once without proof. Or, in order to know what is happening in Calcutta by remaining in Patna we take the help of newspapers, radio etc. However, intuition sees everything taking place in Calcutta as if they were occurring before us.

3. No doubt reason sees things 'under a *certain* form of eternity', but this viewing of things *sub specie aeternitatis* is fully achieved in intuition. As everything in intuition is viewed in substance who is the eternal ground of

everything, so all things are viewed under the form of eternity.

From this third kind of knowledge proceeds the highest blessedness of man, as we will see soon in the doctrine of Bondage and Freedom.

3.15. Human Bondage

In Ethics Spinoza emphasizes the self-determining tendency in everything by virtue of which a thing perseveres in its being. Now if the self-preservation depends on us wholly then it is said to be action and when it depends on something external to us, then it is said to be *passion*. Pleasure, pain and desire are the three primary emotions. "By pleasure", says Spinoza, "I mean a *passive* state by which it passes to a greater, by pain a *passive* state by which it passes to a lesser perfection. By perfection is meant the enhancement of bodily or mental power in the struggle of self-preservation. Thus in passion or emotion a man is acted upon from without by external objects and as such he is said to be in bondage. Thus passion is nothing but confused idea caused by the external objects in impact with the body and as such a man cannot but be in the bondage of passions. Man is found in bondage for being a part of nature he is influenced by an infinite chain of causes and effects. Of course, he wrongly thinks to be free. This is caused by the separateness of things as given by imagination. Imagination creates the illusion of man apart from other things and man under such and illusion imagines himself to be free, quite oblivious of the conditions of his action. But a man is no more free than a stone moving through the air.

3.16. Human Freedom

At first it seems that there is no freedom anywhere in Spinozism, for everything is governed by absolute necessity. Everything that happens follows from the nature of God and it is impossible that events should be otherwise than what they are. But an activity is said to be free when it follows from the very nature of our being. In other words a completely self-determined action is free action. A free action "is nothing but the essence of a thing itself . . . its power of doing those things which follow necessarily from its nature. But the essence of reason is nothing but our mind in so far as it clearly and distinctly understands." Again, Spinoza writes, "Man acts absolutely according to the laws of his own nature when he lives under the guidance of reason . . . we know assuredly nothing to be good save what helps, nothing to be evil save what hinders, understanding". Man is said to be free, then, when he acts according to the law of reason. This means the same thing as saying that man should act from the viewpoint of the whole in which things are inter-connected. Passion keeps us in bondage for it divides and separates us from the vision of the whole, unified reality. The objects, in passion, affect the individuals in infinite varieties of ways. As such by virtue of passions one individual differs from another. However, the essence of the mind is reason and this 'points out those factors which are common to all men. This alone frees us from the tyranny of accidental and ever-changing relation by raising us to the viewpoint in which all things appear *sub specie aeternitatis* to all.

In order to be free, then, we should always be rational and the role of passions should be reduced to zero. "An emotion which is a passion ceases to be a passion as soon as we form a clear and distinct idea of it." This follows from the fact that a passion is only a confused idea and as soon as we frame a clear idea of it, it vanishes. 'Error is extinguished, and its power over the mind ceases when we know it as error.' As soon as the passion becomes clear it comes under reason and therefore is transferred from passivity to activity or free action. When the confused idea in emotion becomes clear, then it is viewed in the universal setting. So viewed our sorrow ceases for it would be seen to promote the greater good of the universe. It would be seen to follow clearly from the very essence of the reality and it could not be otherwise. A perfectly wise man, therefore, will 'hate no man, envy no man, be angry with no man.' For this reason the distinction of good and bad cannot be obliterated. A good man participates more in the divine perfection but a bad man lacks the divine love which follows from the knowledge of God. "The wicked, knowing not God, are but as instruments in the hands of a workman, serving unconsciously, and perishing in the using; the good, on the other hand, serve consciously and in serving become more perfect."

Again, passions of pleasure or pain arise because they are caused by illusory objects. We set our hearts on perishing things, or else we remain in the illusory belief of external object. But as soon as we raise ourselves to the intuitive glance, then "all things speak of God, or are seen only as they exist in God, all passions that relate only to things finite and transient are quelled and every other emotion is absorbed in that 'intellectual love' which is only another aspect of the intuitive knowledge of God." This supreme state of freedom, which is also the stage of the highest knowledge, Spinoza calls *Amor intellectualis dei* or the intellectual love of God. This is the supreme emotion which subdues all lower passions for it is the complete satisfaction of the mind. When we see all things in God, then this vision fills the mind with the same love with which God loves Himself, not so far He is infinite but so far He is finitely expressed in man. "The man who lives according to reason will, therefore, strive to rise above pity and vain regrets. He will help his neighbour, but he will do it from reason, not from impulse. He will consider nothing worthy of hatred, mockery or contempt. He will look at life dispassionately fearlessly, obeying no one but himself, doing that only which he knows to be best conquered neither by human miseries nor his own mistakes."

However, it seems very hard for human mortals to act only from reason and Spinoza himself seems to realise this. In the last portion of his Ethics he gives vent to his feeling which reminds one of the dignity of Kantian morality or else the deep pathos of the last words of Socrates. "If the way which I have pointed out as leading to this result seem very hard, it can nevertheless be found. Needs must be hard since it is so seldom discovered. If salvation were ready to our hand, and could without great labour be discovered, how could it be by almost all men neglected? But all things excellent are as difficult as they are rare."

One very obvious criticism of the Ethics of Spinoza is that it is too intellectualistic. We may know that it is bad to smoke and yet may continue to smoke. However, in Spinoza's sense this knowledge is not complete. If he could know the badness of smoking in relation to the totality of all things, then the smoker will cease to smoke. Hence the knowledge of Spinoza is nothing less than the mystic's vision or simply mysticism. The *amor intellectualis dei* asks for no fatherly response from God. It is but a portion of the infinite love with which God loves Himself. Man loses himself in the divine. The complete subjection to God is the most perfect freedom . . . the emptying of oneself in God is the very fulness of the human mind. This love is neither selfish nor unselfish. This is selfless. This is like the consuming passion of the moth for the flame. A Spinoza would utter; "I love thee, what's that to thee." This is the highest and purest love which ask for no recompense and it was this love which recommended itself to Goethe.

In spite of the defects of Spinoza's Ethics the following uses may be attributed to the doctrine:

1. It teaches us that by virtue of intellectual love we can be participant in the divine nature. As such it fills the mind with the dignity of human life and knowledge and puts the heart at rest. As soon as we realise that we are greater than what we take ourselves to be, then we will rise above the petty needs and smallness of the world.

2. Again, the doctrine teaches us fortitude in misfortunes. Knowing that nothing can happen which does not serve the greater good of the universe, and that nothing could be otherwise than what it is, we will instead of bewailing our lot would like to reconcile ourselves to our fate.

3. This will also have beneficial social values. We will not think of revenge or hatred or pity or blame for everything follows from the divine necessity.

4. Lastly, it enjoins upon us to act from reason and not from passions. By virtue of our reason we do that which is good for all and as such the clamouring demands of emotions are set aside.

3.17. The Estimate of Spinoza

Few people care to read Spinoza for as he well says all excellent things are difficult as they are rare. He is an arch-rationalist for he shows what the world would be if it were purely rational. If Spinoza fails in his method and philosophy, it is due to the fact that the world is not purely rational. Reason itself demands certain dynamic principles of feeling and impulses in order that we may get the energy to sustain our thinking. As the world is not purely rational so the reality as a whole cannot be demonstrated mathematically. For this reason the geometrical method of Spinoza is inadequate for constructing a philosophical system. Again, Spinoza starts with the definition of substance as a self-existent and a self-conceived reality. He has followed this definition with full logical rigour.

As a result of this he has given us a deductive system. This is open to various charges which philosophers have brought against it in the past and present.

We have already seen that Spinoza by following the definition of substance to its logical consequence has established an abstract monism. He leaves no room for finite objects and things which he calls illusory modes which have no existence of their own.

But we human beings are ourselves modes. We, therefore, in consequence become as illusory as any finite objects and things. Our thoughts also, therefore, will share the same fate. Our philosophical speculations in turn would turn out to be equally illusory. Spinozism cannot escape from this charge of being a fictitious system.

This self-contradictory nature of abstract monism has invited the protest, revolt and reconsideration of the nature of monism.

Hegel, Bradley, Bosanquet and other idealists, therefore, have taken up the thread of Spinozistic thinking and have evolved the system of a concrete monism, which is based on the theory of concrete universals.

At the present time it is pointed out that Spinoza has developed a single deductive system on the basis of his definitions of substance, cause, freedom, attributes etc. Such a system is but a system of tautologies. As such it can have no relevance for actual state of affairs which can be known by observation and experiment and not by arm-chair, *a priori* definitions.

We shall discuss the nature and the possibility of metaphysics towards the end of the book. But we have maintained that metaphysics deals with the reality as a whole. And reality in this aspect cannot be scientifically investigated and known. Spinoza too, as all other great metaphysicians, has not given us a scientific treatise on the reality or God. However, it must be conceded that Spinoza never thought that he was developing tautologies which have no bearing on our own empirical world. All the while he thought that he was saying something which has a great deal of practical importance for man. Here he thought that he was saying something about the real world in which we live. But whatever he had to say about the real world had relevance for the man himself.

His metaphysics remains subordinate to his ethics. He was aiming at perfection for himself and for his fellowmen. He was recommending a life of intellectual love of God.

This is the highest kind of love for any being. This love asks for no recompense and remains undisturbed by the vicissitudes of life. Hence his metaphysics is for the sake of culturing the spirit in man.

Spinoza knew, as everyone knows, that a mind remains in a body and a spirit has its dwelling in nature. Hence we can convince sceptics and agnostics about the urgency of spiritual culture only with reference to life and matter, the world of our everyday existence. Hence according to Spinoza metaphysics dealing with this world is a prior necessity and a preparation for eventual culture.

But how can we know about the actual state of affairs? Now we know that empirical sciences can tell us about the real world of our everyday existence. We are quite clear that mathematics and logic deal with the relations between ideas. But they do not deal with facts. However, in the days of Spinoza the distinction between propositions of mathematics and logic on the one hand and empirical propositions on the other hand, was not clear. It was imagined that mathematics dealt with the actual state of affairs in the same way in which observation and experiment deal with empirical facts. Hence Spinoza thought that the geometrical method would be quite adequate to deal with the empirical world. As we see it now the supposition of Spinoza with regard to the geometrical method was mistaken.

Is his metaphysics mistaken? No. Because in metaphysics the vision counts and the propositions of science and commonsense which support it remains subordinate to it. The vision of Spinoza of seeing all things *sub specie aeternitatis* is as important today as it was in his time. A philosophy which helped Spinoza to remain calm and steadfast in spite of his being despised by his contemporaries and denounced by his own people is as important today as ever. The metaphysician, as Spinoza certainly was, helps us to see the world in a different perspective and to enjoy it, in the same way in which a great poem or a great drama helps us to undergo new experiences for the richness of our soul.

4

Gottfried Wilhelm Leibnitz (1646-1716)

4.01. Introduction

After Aristotle no man could be styled as an encyclopaedic genius except Leibnitz. We are staggered by his wide reading of the ancients and moderns, and are amazed by his deep grasp of the fundamentals of the issues raised in his own time. He was not a philosophical recluse like Spinoza but was an impulsive spirit like Descartes. He was at once a mathematician, a physicist, a historian, a metaphysician and a diplomat. In a literal sense he made the whole world his study and enriched everything he touched. He was really a man of universal attainments and genius.

He was a courtier and fully appreciated the value of reconciling differences. In a very special sense his philosophy has been called a philosophy of compromise. To understand me, he says, one should go back to Democritus, Plato and Aristotle. To this we can add that to fully evaluate him one should view him as a fore-runner of Kant immediate the contrasting claims of Descartes and Locke, and also of Frege, Russell, Carnap and other contemporary meta-mathematicians. He himself says, 'I agree with the greater part of what I have read . . . Most parties or schools are right in the greater part of what they affirm, but not in the greater part of what they deny.' This tendency in him has made his philosophy peculiarly eclectic but this eclecticism far from being a mere summary of views has focused the conflicting issues and has given them the most stimulating push. In his philosophy we find an attempted union of mechanical and teleological views, of inductive and deductive processes of observation and theory, of final and efficient causes, of reason and faith. However, in the sequel we shall see whether it is just to say with Alexander that "he delights in bringing together opposite views but he never succeeds in reconciling them. He abounds in ingenious distinctions, but never attains to a higer unity in which the differences disappear." Even when his philosophy is a compromise rather than a solution of the problems, it never fails to be highly suggestive of deeper solution.

Leibnitz was born in 1646 but his father who was a professor of Moral philosophy in Leipzig died in 1652. However, he left a rich legacy of books and intelligence to his son who showed unusual talents even in his boyhood. He secured the degree of the Doctor of Laws in 1666 and was offered a chair of philosophy, which he declined. In 1667 he entered the political service for the next forty years.

However, Leibnitz never forgot his mathematics, philosophy and science. His diplomatic profession made him visit Berlin, Paris, London, Venice and Amsterdam and gave him opportunities of mixing with the most learned societies of the time. Near about 1676 he met Spinoza and his whole philosophy was greatly influenced by him, though Leibnitz always tried to conceal his indebtedness to Spinoza. But we shall find that his philosophy was more Spinozistic than what at any time he was willing to concede.

Leibnitz has not left any finished treatise of his system. He gave expression to his views in the learned journals of the time in the form of essays. Even here we find that he published only the popular parts of his philosophy which could be accepted by the princes and princesses and withheld throughout his life-time his profound but highly Spinozistic philosophy. In 1684 he wrote in defence of the ontological proof of God and in 1694 he advanced a new doctrine of substance in terms of force. In 1695 in *Systeme Nouveau de la Nature* he clearly stated his monadology. In addition to many essays he wrote three treatises dwelling on the different aspects of his philosophy. In his very important treatise which remained for many years in oblivion he gave the first and lasting criticism of the doctrine of Locke. This is known as *nouveaux Essais* which he wrote in 1703. In 1710 he wrote *Theodicee* at the request of queen Sophie Charlotte. There he sought to prove that God has so arranged things that they work together for good. To this doctrine of the possible world Leibnitz wrote *La Monadologie* in 1714 for Prince Eugene of Savoy in which he gives an outline of his philosophy.

His last years were harassed by controversies and tormented by neglect. The end came in 1716 when none but his secretary to mourn his loss.

4.02. Fundamental Principles of the Philosophy of Leibnitz

Leibnitz had a very difficult task at hand and that he described himself by saying that he tried "to reconcile Plato with Democritus, Aristotle with Descartes, the Scholastics with the moderns, theology and morals with the dictates of reason." He tried to achieve this highly critical aim with the help of a few leading principles. Leibnitz was a great mathematician and along with Newton shared the credit of inventing infinitesimal calculus. Naturally like Descartes and Spinoza he was biased for a mathematical method in philosophy and as such he intended to give geometrical proof in metaphysics. Though he has not patterned his philosophy like a book on geometry, yet he could hardly escape from its peculiar charm.

Law of continuity: Following his mathematical bent he believed in the *law of continuity*. "It was originally a generalisation of the property of numbers—viz., that they can be continued without end, and divided without limit,—and referred, in this respect, to the infinitely large, in which everything is contained, and to the infinitely small of which everything is made up." This observation coupled with the infinitesimal calculus showed that there is no abrupt change but every change is followed by another, through an infinite number of infinitely imperceptible changes. This law of continuity from the highest to the lowest was firmly established in his thought and he was credited to believe that lines were generated by the movements of points, surfaces by the movements of lines and solids by the movements of surfaces. There is little doubt that the law of continuity helped him to bridge the gulf between the animate and inanimate, empiricism and rationalism, mind and matter, Descartes and Locke, Plato and Democritus.

Law of individuality: There is yet another principle which he draws from his mathematical discipline. In mathematics a lengthy chain of reasoning can be compressed in extremely abbreviated formulae. He who knows them can at once draw out much invaluable information and can achieve logical and intellectual satisfaction. This led him to establish the principle of individuality. Everything is real. To the course eye of imagination the connection between things is one of causal nexus. But everything is real and as such no external influence can change it. Leibnitz, in spite of his opposition to Descartes and Spinoza, looks upon the real in terms of self-containedness. However, this principle of individuality gives his system the appearance of great contrast to Spinoza. Spinoza gives us the whole or the *blank* universal from which parts have disappeared; but Leibnitz begins with the reality of parts, the extreme multiplicity of finite experience and tries to determine their nature in order to discover the real parts of the real whole. Now parts in order to be real parts must be as real as the whole of which they are parts. Each part somehow must be the whole and contains the whole. The insistence on the reality of individual things made him believe in pluralism. Thus we find that the substance of Spinoza has been broken into bits and each bit becomes as eternal and real as the one-substance of Spinoza. "In the smallest particle of matter there is a world of creatures, living beings, animals, entelechies, souls. Each portion of matter may be conceived as like a garden full of plants, and like a pond full of fishes. But each branch of every plant, each member of every animal, each drop of its liquid parts; is also some such garden or pond. Thus there is nothing fallow, nothing sterile, nothing dead in the universe; no chaos, no confusion save in appearance." By this doctrine of spiritual atomism he tries to reconcile Democritus and Plato.

Principle of harmony: To the above two principles may be added a third *principle of harmony* which partly arises from his mathematical discipline and partly from the desire to concede the Spinozistic truth of unity and partly from the necessity of reconciling the first two laws of continuity and extreme individuality. In order to explain the variety and richness of finite things he took the help of the law of individuality and held the plurality of real things. Further he maintained that everything is real for it contains the whole and in some sense is a whole, i.e., a unity within itself. Now this unity in plurality is called harmony. The law of harmony plays the some role in Leibnitz which the abstract unity played in the philosophy of Spinoza. For this reason his philosophy has been called the philosophy of pre-established harmony.

God the creator of harmony: With the law of harmony the inner circle of the thought of Leibnitz is closed but it seems certain that he believed also in God. He further held that individual things no doubt are real but they are knitted together in a grand harmony. This presupposes that some giant intellect has brought about the harmony. This giant intellect is called God. Hence Leibnitz, like Descartes and Spinoza, chooses to make his system *Theocentric,* i.e. *God-centred.*

4.03. The Doctrine of Substance

Leibnitz was greatly impressed by the unity which Spinoza had emphasized in his philosophy. But unfortunately Spinoza did so at the cost of variety and the individuality of things. Leibnitz begins with the opposite thesis of pluralism. His problem is, "what must be the nature of parts which can in some way contain or express the whole within itself?" In order to account for the reality in which individual things are real he begins with the notion of substance. However, Descartes had defined it as that which is in itself and conceived through itself, i.e. the existence of which does not involve the existence of anything else. this definition, if followed to the extreme logical consequence, says Leibnitz, leads to the dangerous pantheism of Spinoza. Besides, even in Descartes it leads to dualism and to true unity. Descartes had rightly established the importance of the self and should have established a reality on the pattern of the self. But apart from mind he believes also in the existence of matter which is taken to be mere extension.

Extension is not real: But how can extension be real? It is always divisible and cannot lead to something which is simple, elementary and really indivisible. Further, the composite nature of extension can give only an aggregate of individual things but not true unity. Lastly, extension by itself is purely passive and the world is dynamic. No doubt Descartes assumed that God imparted the first motion to extension. But even if this miracle is to be believed it becomes difficult to explain inertia or rest in things. And the law of continuity demands that there should be no abrupt change from motion to rest.

Hence Leibnitz concludes that extension cannot be real. Extension presupposes force which seems to be more ultimate. Extension can be explained in terms of impenetrability or resistance but resistance means some force. Hence force is real and extension and all other changes can be explained with the help of force.

Cartesian notion of mind amplified: Leibnitz rejects matter and retains the 'mind' of Descartes, but then the Cartesian notion of mind has to be further modified in order that it may serve to explain the variety of experience. According to Descartes the essence of mind is consciousness. But if consciousness be the essence of mind, then we have to say that our mind ceases to be when we fall unconscious or when we are in dreamless sleep. However, nobody will accept it. Besides, there are mental states which in themselves are so vague and indistinct that they never rise in full consciousness. For example, take a big sea-wave composed of many small ripples. Each ripple may not be heard but their combination gives rise to the mighty roar of the sea. Thus there are cases of vague, indistinct and subconscious mental processes. Hence mind's concept should be widened to include them as well. "Below the threshold of our clear consciousness there is a dark background of obscurer consciousness, *petites perceptiones,* unconscious states."

Leibnitz, thus defined the ultimate substance in terms of mind which includes the unconscious states as well. By extending mind to include the unconscious, he hoped to reconcile the animate and inanimate, mind and body which were left in hopeless muddle by Descartes. No doubt Spinoza had tried to reconcile them by reducing them to two parallel attributes of the same ultimate substance. But to say that the same substance is both conscious and extended is tantamount to saying that the two contradictory qualities of extended and inextended are true of the same thing. Thus the reality can be immaterial or spiritual only.

But Leibnitz believed in the principle of individuality. The reality cannot be one but many though each is eternal and real. The real whole can be explained only terms of the real parts. But there were the atomists who believed that reality is the sum-total of minute, eternal, qualitatively alike hard and indivisible atoms. As matter of fact Leibnitz was drawn first towards Democritus, but he soon saw that atoms cannot be real for the following reasons:

1. Atoms being extended can never be theoretically indivisible. However small they may be they can be divisible with the help of powerful, minute and delicate instruments.

2. Besides, the other quality of hardness is equally objectionable. It is purely relative. What is hard to one, may not be so to another.

3. Again, the atoms are qualitatively alike. Any difference between them is one of quantity. One atom is different from another only in mass, shape and size. However, quantity cannot explain the qualitative variety of the universe.

4. Lastly, the atoms are dead particles of matter. But reality should be on the analogy of that of which we are most sure. And that is our own self which is living and spiritual.

Thus Leibnitz concludes that the real elements must be spiritual. He calls these indivisible, self-active and spiritual units as monads. They are the true metaphysical points which though indivisible are non-existent. They are, again, different from atoms which though existent are not indivisible. Only a spiritual unit is indivisible like our own self-conscious existence, and yet is real. Hence the monads alone are real.

4.04. The Nature of Monads

There are infinite monads but each of them is as real as the single substance of Spinoza. The monads are eternal and can be destroyed only by miracle on the part of God.[1] No monad has any part and therefore is truly indivisible, but then like any

---

1. No doubt Leibnitz contradicts himself by saying that the monads have been created. If they are created, then they cease to be eternal and self-contained units.

ultimate reality is self-contained and exclusive of every thing else. Being a real unit, each monad contains the whole infinity of existence. It is the whole universe itself potentially. Each monad is a world in miniature . . . . a macrocosm in microcosm. It contains within itself the possibility of everything which happens to it. We can say, then, that it is 'freighted with the past and big with the future.' As an all-inclusive whole it mirrors the world. Every activity is reflected, either in vague or clear form, according to the nature of the monad. Again, being a self-contained unit, it excludes all other monads. Each monad is a world apart, all by itself. It has no windows through which anything might come in or go out.

The infinite number of monads are qualitatively unlike, so that no two monads are alike. They are found in a hierarchical order of existence. Each monad imperceptibly leads to others. There is no abrupt change anywhere in the *connexion graduelle*. Only with the help of the absolute continuity between the monads we can explain every variety of experience. Besides, with the help of the law of continuous series we can bridge the gulf between mind and matter, men and animals, conscious and unconscious states.

Monads being spiritual have two important characteristics of perception and appetition. By virtue of its *perception* each monad mirrors the whole infinity of existence. The more developed monad in the series has clear perception and the less developed monad has confused perception. The infinite gradations in the monads correspond to their infinite series of perceptions. Even in the same monad, according to its own stages of development, there are different degrees of perception. Because each monad is a force, therefore, it has *appetition* by virtue of which it tends to become the whole. Again, by virtue of its appetition each monad tends to pass from obscure to clear perception. If an action is done from very obscure perception then it is known as impulse and if it is done from clear perception, then it is known as will. Thus the activity of the low monads is purely random and impulsive, but in the higher monads the activity is prompted by will and desire. However the distinction between impulse and desire is one of degree and, not of kind.

The monads are found in a continuous series, one imperceptibly passing into the other. However, in this series we can note the main types of monads. The lowest or *bare monads* are those in which the perception is most obscure. They go to make the inorganic bodies. They are scarcely more than centres of forces and they express themselves in the form of motion which appears to us purely mechanical. They may be said to be in profound stupor or deep sleep. Then there are conscious monads endowed with memory. This may be called *souls*. They go to make the plant and animal world. However, the highest monads are called *spirits* having reason and universal, necessary knowledge. They are raised to the knowledge of the self as well as of God.

The Cartesians called spirits alone as souls but called the former two namely, bare monads and animals, automata. However, the difference between the monads is one of degree. In the bare monads the force appears only in the form of mechanical movement; in the animal the appetition is expressed in the form of instincts; and in the spirits the force is found in the form of self-conscious desire and will. In this hierarchical order the higher includes the lower. The self-consciousness emerges out of consciousness and includes certain perceptions which remain obscure. Only in this way Leibnitz hopes to reconcile necessity with freedom.

4.05 Pre-established Harmony

Spinoza established the unity but he explained away the variety. Leibnitz begins with the variety. Let us see whether he succeeds in introducing the ultimate unity. In order that there may be any unity the monads must be related, yet being windowless they cannot be related. "Each spirit being like a world apart, sufficient to itself, independent of every other created thing, involving the infinite, expressing the universe, is as lasting as continuous in its existence, and as absolute as the very universe of created beings." But in spite of the monads being independent, working according to their inner urge, the world is a harmony and a cosmos. The monads are not separate stories and events beginning and ending at odd intervals. But we have to explain this harmony between self-contained and exclusive monads. Leibnitz assumed that the harmony between the monads has been pre-established by God. He has so arranged the series of monads in their hierarchical order that the change in one is preceded and followed in other monads harmoniously. To the beholder it appears that the change in *A* is the cause of the change in *B*, but really the monads being windowless cannot interact on one another. What appears to us as inter-action is really concomitant relation. For example, we press the button and the fan moves. According to Leibnitz a change in the button-monad takes place as a result of its own preceding movement but a corresponding and correlative change takes place in the fan-monad. We wrongly interpret the independent but concomitant changes between the fan and button due to interaction. God has arranged the order and the working of all the monads in such a way that a grand plan in His mind may be fulfilled. The monads, no doubt, work independently of all other monads according to their own inner urge, but this inner plan coincides with the realisation of the one master plan in the mind of the creator. Because each monad tries to realise in the same final end in the mind of the creator, therefore, a harmony is reached in their working. "This combination of independence and harmony may be compared to different chairs of musicians playing their parts separately, and so situated that they do not see or even hear one another. Nevertheless they keep perfectly together, by each following their own notes, in such a way that one who hears them all finds in them a harmony that is wonderful and much more perfect than if there had been any connection between them."

This doctrine of the pre-established harmony is nothing but the extension of the parallelism of Spinoza. However, the Spinozistic parallelism was confined to the relation between mind and body only, but Leibnitz went to the very fundamental question regarding the relation between any two or more things. The relation between any things or monads, according to Leibnitz, is to be conceived in terms of concomitant variations between them with reference to the pre-established harmony.

We shall soon see that Leibnitz explains his reconciling tendency between mind and matter, mechanism and teleology, freedom and necessity with the help of pre-established harmony. Hence a short criticism of this doctrine will show the central weakness of the Leibnitzian system.

1. The doctrine of pre-established harmony is only an assumption to explain order in the world. However, this assumption is such that it will remain unverified for it is unverifiable. No monad can go beyond itself and cannot perceive the whole of infinite number of monads in their mutual relation. This is possible only for a perceiver outside the series of the monads. But by a monad, like Leibnitz himself, no harmony running in all the monads, can be perceived. Consistently a monadologist can be a subjectivist only. He can say what he perceives to be is real to him, but beyond this solipsistic world he has no right to posit a trans-subjective reality.

2. Besides, the harmony does not follow from the nature of the monads themselves. Leibnitz seeing the necessity of a common plan invented the assumption of a divine plan which every monad in its own way tries to realise. The plan, therefore, though internal to each monad is a plan introduction in them by an external mind or God. Hence the harmony of the monads is external to their real nature as monads.

3. At this stage Leibnitz comes in conflict with his desire to establish the supremacy of God and regards him as the creator of the monads. If God is the creator of monads, then monads become finite and created and cease to be self-contained units. If the monads are allowed to be eternal, independent and self-contained units, then God as a creator becomes unnecessary. Leibnitz chooses to be inconsistent by taking God as the creator of the pre-established harmony.

4. Later on we shall see that Leibnitz ends in the same blankness as that of Spinoza. Even at this stage it can be said that each monad is a series of reflection. But reflections of what? Leibnitz would say that the ultimate reality reflected in each monad is the clear and distinct thought in the mind of God. Each monad, then, is an emanation of God. God, then, becomes the only reality and all other monads become either an imperfect appearance or a modification of God.

The other difficulties of the Leibnitzian philosophy will be noted later. Now let us see how Leibnitz tries to bring together harmony in the conflicting trends of his time.

4.06. Mind and Matter

The doctrine of the pre-established harmony aimed at introducing unity in variety. It also hoped to solve the problem concerning mind and body. In strict sense there is no body or matter for there is nothing dead in the system of Leibnitz. What is called body is only an aggregate of bare monads. In this sense the human body is a machine of infinite complexity. Unlike ordinary machine, its every part is itself a complete machine. In other words it is an organism of which every part is a living force. Now in this aggregate of bare monads, there is a queen monad which in the first instance mirrors the activity of the surrounding monads and secondly, through the aggregate mirrors the changes of all other monads of the universe, more clearly than others. This queen monad by virtue of its superiority in the aggregate may be termed as soul. This ruling monad or soul by virtue of its more developed perception knows what is going to happen to the other monads. Besides God has subordinated the workings of the lower monads to those of the higher. Hence the lower monads appear as means and conditions for the realisation of the ends of the higher Monads. Thus as soon as a conscious desire for the movement of the hand occurs, there take place muscular changes concomitantly in the body, according to the pre-established plan. To the beholder it will appear as if the desire has caused the movement of the arm, but it is due to concomitant variation. ".... the laws by which the motions of the body follow each other are likewise so coincident with the thoughts of the soul as to give to our *volitions* and *actions* the very same appearance as if the latter were really the natural and the necessary consequence of the former." This relation between mind and body may be illustrated with the help of the simile of two clocks chiming harmoniously. The harmonious relation between the two clocks is possible in three different ways:

1. The two clocks may be so connected with each other by a joint mechanism that the motion in one may be communicated to the other for the corresponding movement. This is the kind of relation, according to Descartes, in which the mind and body interact on each other. However, Leibnitz rejects the explanation in terms of inter-action, for mind and body, being windowless monads cannot inter-act.

2. Two clocks may work harmoniously if a skilled mechanic keeps on regulating the two from time to time. This constant miracle or interference by God to keep the harmonious relation between mind and body was taught by the Occasionalists. However, Leibnitz rejected this explanation for, according to him, constant interference by God is unworthy of His divine power.

3. Lastly, the two clocks may be constructed with so much skill and perfection that they may always work harmoniously. This conception alone is worthy, says Leibnitz, of the creator. The one miracle is to be preferred to constant miracles.

Thus the doctrine of the pre-established harmony teaches that the "bodies act as if (to suppose the impossible) there were no souls, and souls act as if there were no bodies, and both act as if each influenced the other."

4.07. Mechanism and Teleology

Mechanical relation involves the factors of space, time and interaction between material bodies. In strict sense, then, Leibnitz does not admit the presence of mechanism. First, matter does not exist in reality but is only an appearance having its real basis in the passivity of the monads. Then there can be no inter-action, for monads are windowless. Space and time, again, do not exist but are abstraction from the relations existing between monads. In the moderate sense, however, according to Leibnitz mechanism simply means the mutual relation between objects in reference to magnitude, figure and motion. Like Descartes and Newton, he wanted to push the mechanical explanation to the farthest limit but he subordinated it to teleology. First, the striving in lower monads does not appear in conscious form but appears in the forms of mechanical movement. As such the inorganic world can be explained quite adequately in terms of mechanism. Besides, even in the higher monads, the conscious movement is due to preceding state and as such any action can be explained in terms of the past. Besides, the pre-established harmony has so arranged the monads that the change in one is followed into the other. This arrangement also gives rise to the appearance of mechanical causation. Hence mechanism is defensible and quite intelligible.

But mechanism is really based on teleology. No matter however mechanical may be the appearance of movement in any monad, it always works for some end within it. Besides, the inorganic world may appear to be determined mechanically but ultimately the arrangement of these monads serves some end in the mind of the creator. The mechanism serves the end in the same way in which the motor car or cycle serves the purpose involved in human movement.

Hence, mechanism is valid and legitimate but it has its ground in teleology.

4.08. Theory of Knowledge

There are two kinds of truth involved in knowledge, namely, necessary and contingent. Necessary truths follow with logical and mathematical certainty. Their opposite is inconceivable. They are self-evident, self-consistent and based on the law of contradiction. They are so eternal and unchangeable that even the will of God cannot alter them. Such truths no doubt may be complex but they can be analysed into simple identical propositions. Leibnitz did not agree with Locke in disparaging identical propositions. In the last resort the truths of reason can be analysed into ideas so simple as to be indefinable, axioms so simple as to be indemonstrable, and postulates which neither need nor admit of proof. Leibnitz himself pointed out that the axioms of Geometry are very near examples of what he aims at expressing by necessary truths.

Descartes laid down that there is only one kind of truth, namely, necessary. However, there is another kind of truth called contingent or truth of fact. We can always think the opposite of any contingent truth. For example, it is fact that the table is before me, but I can always think the possibility of something else instead of the table just now and here. As the necessary truth depends on the law of contradiction, so, the contingent truth depends on the law of sufficient reason. Leibnitz makes very great use of Sufficient Reason which he expresses thus. It is that "by which we believe that no fact can be true or real, no statement trustworthy, unless there is a sufficient reason why it should be so and not otherwise although in a greater number of cases we cannot know these reason." For example we can analyse the reasons for the presence of the table just here with reference to its purpose, its relation to the doors, windows, light, arrangement of seats etc. But we can never totally exhaust all the reasons which explain the presence of the table just here, though we believe that there must be adequate reasons for it.

The law of sufficient reason teaches the harmony theory of truth. In this connection Leibnitz makes a distinction between possible and compossible. To say that a thing is free from contradiction is to maintain that it is possible, but that alone is actual which is compossible or that which is in conformity with the actual system of things. Thus the reason for the existence of a particular thing is the system of the actual things. This system is the sole sufficient reason which explains a particular thing. This doctrine comes very near to the harmony theory of truth according to which a statement is true which harmonises with all other things known.

But can we not say that we, being limited beings, cannot know all the reason for the existence of any particular thing, but cannot God know all the reasons for the existence of a thing? Surely God knows that given a certain arrangement of doors, windows, light etc., the table must be here and nowhere else. Thus for God it is unthinkable that a certain table be somewhere else. In His case then the law of sufficient reason becomes identical with the law of contradiction? Leibnitz is not very clear here. In spite of his strong tendency for compromise he has not been able to harmonise between these two kinds of truth. In one sense, we can say, that the law of sufficient reason is wide enough to include the law of contradiction for there must be some reason why the necessary truths are clear and self-evident. But Leibnitz rather makes a sharp distinction between them. The necessary truths are abstract but the contingent ones are concrete. The knowledge of facts cannot, according to Leibnitz, be reduced to the knowledge of necessary truths. Even for God the contingent truth cannot be reduced to the necessary truth. God cannot think of a particular thing otherwise than what it is in a system of facts, but the whole system itself can be otherwise. God has chosen this world out of all the infinite possibilities because it is the best possible world for achieving the moral value in His mind. Hence contingent truth is dictated by moral necessity but truths of reason have absolute, compelling and metaphysical necessity.

The further nature of knowledge, according to Leibnitz, will be clear from the ontological status of the monads. It is not right to interpret the metaphysics of Leibnitz as following from his epistemology but it is valid to deduce his theory of knowledge from his monadology.

Now every monad contains in it the possibility of everything that will ever happen to it. "From the moment when my existence began, it could be said of me (i.e.truly) that this or that would happen to me; we must grant that these attributes were involved in my nature in its completeness, which is the basis of the connexion of all my varying inner states, and which God has known perfectly from all eternity." Similarly, if one could get an adequate idea of the nature of Adam, then he could have known everything that happened to him or through him. This relationship between the monad and its varying states is, according to Leibnitz, of the nature of the subject-predicate relationship. In every affirmative proposition the predicate describes some quality or activity belonging to the subject. The predicate may be variously modified about the same subject like 'Ram is intelligent' or 'Ram is a first year student' and so on. But the subject seems to contain all the possible predicates (as each monad is windowless and self-contained) though actually we know very few of them. Hence Leibnitz maintains: "I find that in all true propositions, in every necessary or contingent one, predicate . . . is included." Here he comes very near to the doctrine of Spinoza in which everything follows from divine necessity and nothing can ever happen otherwise. Leibnitz wants to modify the doctrine of absolute determinism by introducing the law of sufficient Reason: God foresees what will happen to any individual not because everything is mathematically determined but because He knows that in a certain setting of all other things only a particular kind of conduct will follow in a certain monad. This doctrine of fatalism differs from the determinism of Spinoza only by a slender thread. Externally determined teleology of the monads is scarcely different from the mechanistic determinism. The past, present and future of each monad, according to Leibnitz, have been decreed in the very nature of the monad, in its compossibility with all other monads. It is this kind of teleology which hardly differs from mechanical necessity. For this reason, Bergson rejected both teleology and mechanism. But Leibnitz did not think it so. However, this point requires further elaboration.

According to Leibnitz, there were many possibilities concerning this universe. But God as if weighed these possibilities in the light of goodness which the universe had to subserve. Out of these numerous possibilities, this world has been created by God as the best possible world, in accordance with moral necessity. Given all the possible conditions in which moral excellence has to be safeguarded, could this world be different from what it is? If God is all perfect, as Leibnitz supposes Him to be then the perfect calculator God could not have chosen any other possible world. Further, the past, present and future of this world, along with every monad in it, are just like an open book in the eternal 'now' of God. Hence, for God all things follow from the possibilities and potentialities of each monad, according to the pre-established Harmony subserving moral necessity. How does this scheme in Leibnitz's philosophy differ from the abstract monism of Spinoza? Leibnitz did think about this and yet he felt that he had avoided the blank and mechanical necessity of Spinozism. For Leibnitz, mechanical necessity is the same as logical necessity in a deductive system. This kind of necessity, according to him, is found in mathematical system. Such a system is independent of any final causes. Besides, this is found in regard to abstract truths. But the necessity which rules the world is dependent on the will of God who is guided by the purpose of moral excellence. Further, though this universe is the best possible world, we can always imagine it to be otherwise. Hence, the universe is not regulated, according to Leibnitz, by blind necessity, but by moral necessity.

As noted earlier, the solution is not satisfactory. Could God imagine this world to be otherwise? Given all the monads, as they are, could he have willed otherwise? Yes, under one proviso. If all the monads could have been created otherwise, and if the same moral excellence could be achieved in many other alternative ways, then alone this world is one of the many best possible worlds. But under these circumstances, God becomes responsible for evils in the world and one can always argue that these evils could have been otherwise in other possible worlds. Thus the problem of evil would remain unsolved. And yet it was this problem which Leibnitz had in mind in the construction of his system. So we find that Leibnitz has not been able to escape from Spinozism.

4.09. The Criticism of Lockean Empiricism

At the present time the epistemological problem is stated with a great deal of precision. This was not so in Modern philosophy. A proper epistemological problem is concerned with *truth and meaning*. Unfortunately, the modern epistemological problem is also mixed up with the *source* or origin of knowledge. Now the problem, how does knowledge arise? is really psychological. The empiricists were contending that knowledge arises *from* experience, and there is nothing in knowledge which could not be traced to experience. For this reason, John Locke criticised the doctrine of innate ideas. In relation to this doctrine we can summarise the views of main contenders thus:

According to Descartes *some* (e.g. the idea of God), according to Locke *none*, and according to Leibnitz, all ideas are innate.

But here, as elsewhere, Leibnitz seeks a compromise between Descartes and Locke. True, the innateness of all ideas, both of the ideas of sense and of reason, follows from the doctrine of windowless monads. But in relation to his criticism of Locke's empiricism, Leibnitz uses the term in guarded ways. It is not very clear how he uses the term perception. But to begin with by virtue of his doctrine of appetition and development he tends to compromise between Locke and Descartes.

Now both Descartes and Locke took mind to be purely conscious. Hence, if by 'innate ideas' meant that certain ideas are in the mind, then for Locke, it meant that they are in the Cs of each individual. Hence, for him it was contradictory to hold that there are innate ideas of which the individual is unaware. Here, Leibnitz holds that the mind could have unconscious states as well. There are states in many stages of awareness for they can be arranged in a series from the most obscure to the clearest. There are minute perceptions, so small that in themselves they are hardly noticeable. But when they are combined together would they become noticeable?[1] If the mind could be unconscious then there be no contradiction in holding that there may be innate ideas of which the child, the idiot etc., may be quite unaware.

Again, Descartes has laid emphasis on clear and distinct ideas alone, and Locke, according to Leibnitz, on confused perceptions alone, as constitutive of knowledge. But in a way knowledge consists of both. Knowledge begins with perception and ends in clear and distinct ideas by way of gradual development. Every perception because of development has to pass from obscure states to clear ones. So perception, in due course, has to give rise to apperception. So knowledge begins with perception and ends in reason, which alone gives us clear and distinct ideas and necessary propositions. Here we are reminded of Kant's statement:

> Knowledge begins with the senses, proceeds thence to the understanding and ends in reason.

Leibnitz has not fully explained the theory of innateness with regard to the whole realm of knowledge. His object in criticizing Locke was limited. His aim was to show that knowledge does not consist in experience alone, as many elements in it are not derived from experience. Hence, he thought that Locke's thesis could be shown to be false if it could be shown that there are elements in knowledge which could not be derived from experience. Leibnitz could achieve this easy refutation of Locke's empiricism very easily. Let us take the general statement of Locke.

The general statement of Locke is that there is nothing in intellect (knowledge) which was not previously given in the senses. In a general we can accept this. If one has not heard, then he cannot have any knowledge of sound, and, similarly, for a man born blind there could be no knowledge of colour. But Leibnitz went much deeper. *Nibil est intellectu quod non Feurit sensu of* Locke, Leibnitz added *nisi ipse intellectus.* Before we experience the sensation of blue or yellow or of sound and heat, at best the capacity of so experiencing the sensation must be granted to be *innate.* And this contention of Leibnitz has to be conceded. Seeing or hearing is innate, though its content depends on experience. The capacity of seeing is there, though one has to depend on experience with regard to what is green or red or white. Hence, the very capacity of having experience is innate. So the very root of empiricism, according to Leibnitz, lies in rationalism or innateness.

If the intellect itself is innate, then it has certain ideas which are innate. Some of these innate ideas are listed as being, unity, cause, substance, identity etc. These are all involved in any knowledge whatsoever. Hence, there is much in knowledge which cannot be derived from experience.

Here some reference to the term 'substance' appears desirable. Locke had expressed doubts concerning 'substance'. According to Locke, the primary bricks of knowledge are so many simple ideas. But where are these ideas? Locke points

---

1. For arguments against limiting 'mind' to 'conscious states only', see A. Russell, *The Monadology of Leibnitz,* pp. 156-57.

out that we suppose some *substratum* which supports these ideas or qualities. Now the notion of 'substance' is fundamental for Leibnitz. Therefore, he criticised Locke's account of it. Leibnitz points out that Locke begins with attributes or qualities or simple ideas. But they are abstractions. But if we begin with concrete experience dealing with concrete entities like a table or an orange, then we from the start hold that diverse qualities of brown, hard etc., being to one subject or substance called a table.

Some of these ideas which are at the basis of any knowledge whatsoever, according to Leibnitz, are not different from the 'categories' of the *understanding* of Kant. Hence, once again, there is much in the epistemology of Leibnitz which may be regarded as the anticipation of Kant. For Kant, knowledge proper is a joint product of percept and concept. So let us see in which sense Leibnitz uses the term 'perception'.

Locke had used the term perception in relation to having ideas of external objects. But for Leibnitz there is nothing external which a monad can perceive. So by perception is not meant any modification of consciousness by any external object. But there are passive states in the monads. So perception means the passive states in each monad which being in the undeveloped stage remain confused. Hence by perception is meant those passive states which are the confused states of the mind with regard to space, figure, motion and extension.

Hence, according to Leibnitz, knowledge begins with confused perceptions and gradually rises to clear and distinct ideas. The mind is neither conscious alone, nor is it purely a blank tablet. The mind may better be compared to a block of marble in whose veins the outlines of the statue are prefigured. Experience serves the occasion of making these veins prominent. The ideas of *being,* of *possibility* and of *identity* are wholly innate and experience tends to make them explicit from their being implicit.

It is not the place for assessing the full value of Leibnitz's criticism of Locke's empiricism. We shall satisfy ourselves with a few comments only.

Leibnitz does not fully realise the criticism of knowledge for its own sake. His epistemology is wedded to his monadology. Besides, he does not really go to the very root of the discussion raised by Locke. Though Locke was superficial yet his problem was perennial. Leibnitz could answer Locke but could not solve the problem raised by him. We might grant that senses give rise to reason but the question still remains, how do the confused sensations give rise to the knowledge of the universal and necessary ? This problem is unanswered by Leibnitz.

The theory of Leibnitz seems to suffer from absolute relativity. The essence of each monad consists in representing the other monads. If A mirrors B and B mirrors C, then A's perception does not simply include B but also B's perception of C. Hence we are landed in interminable series. Thus considered the philosophy of

---

1. For a detailed discussion, the reader is advised to consult. H.W.B. Joseph, *Philosophy of Leibnitz.* Clarendon Press, Oxford.

Leibnitz gives us no escape from the relativity of knowledge. But most probably he aimed at explaining the degrees of knowledge. The human knowledge even when it falls short of absolute certainty is gradually approximating it in the course of development.

Besides, the relativity of knowledge Leibnitz has to explain its objectivity. Each monad mirrors the other monads, but each monad is nothing but a series of representations. "Even an infinity of little mirrors with nothing but each other to reflect must at once collapse into absolute vacuity." This is important for according to Leibnitz space, time and matter are all illusory. This hopeless state of the monads may be compared to the unhappy state of certain ·islanders who maintained themselves by washing one anohter's clothes.

Finally, the theory of knowledge of Leibnitz appears to solipsistic. If every monad is windowless, how can it go outside itself to posit the existence of other monads? This objection has been answered in the same way in which the concept of the unknowable has been answered by Kant. Kant defended his unknowable by pointing out that we know *that* there is something unknown but we do not know *what* it is. Similarly, the knowledge even when it is encased in one single monad contains in it the implication of outward reference to other monads. In other words knowledge by its very nature must make reference to other monads though it has is locus in one monad alone.

4.10. Theodicee

Theology and Monadology: Leibnitz like Descartes closes his system of thought by making God the centre of his monadology. In his Theodicee he tries to reconcile science with theology, monadology with the dogmas of faith. It seems certain that Leibnitz was a confirmed theist, but then his theism is not so intimately connected with his monadology. Sometimes by God he understands not the creator but the very harmony of the monads. In this sense his conception would have been the same as that of Spinoza, i.e., the nature itself would have become God. At times, he thinks God to be the very crown in the series of monads. But in many places he also thinks God to be the creator of the monads. If the monads be created, then they cease to be eternal and if the monads be uncreated then God becomes unnecessary. Hence monadology and theology go ill together in the system of Leibnitz. Again, if the monads proceed from God, then how are they related to Him? He describes the monads as proceeding from God by constant radiations. But if the metaphor means that monads emanate from God as light emanates from the sun or as thought is the fulguration from the mind, then the monads are reduced just to the status of 'the modes' of Spinoza. Even when Leibnitz consciously tries to recoil from Spinoza, his ghost seems to haunt his monadology.

Ontological Proof: Leibnitz gives various proofs for the existence of God. The most important proof is ontological which he expresses thus. Every monad has two aspects, namely, actual and possible, activity and passivity. The less developed monad is more passive and less active, the more developed monad is more active and actual and less passive and possible. In the hierarchical series God is the most developed monad the *actus purus,* i.e. every possibility of which has become actual and fully existent. Now his proof runs thus : 'If God is possible, He exists, for His Existence is a necessary consequence of His possibility. If He did not exist, He would not be possible, nor would any thing outside of Him be possible.' In other words, every monad has both actuality and possibility, but in the case of God what is possible is also actual. Hence the existence of God follows from the very possibility of Him.

However, the ontological proof of Leibnitz suffers from the same Cartesian fallacy of treating existence as a quality. The possibility and actuality cannot be identical. Even the highest possibility need not be actual.

Cosmological Proof: To the above proof Leibnitz adds the cosmological argument. Every particular thing is contingent for we can always think its non-existence. Not only particular things but the universe as a whole can be easily imagined to be non-existent. As such it is contingent. But every contingent truth is based on sufficient reason. Hence the universe as a whole, being contingent must have a sufficient reason outside the universe. This sufficient reason is God. This proof depends on the validity of the law of sufficient reason which is rather unclear. Besides, it depends on the ontological proof for it assumes the existence of a necessary Being who can be the sufficient reason.

Again, Leibnitz adds a third proof based on eternal truths. There are certain propositions which are always true like 2+2=4. The basis of eternal truths cannot be contingent but must be found in eternal truths. But a reason for what exists must itself exist. Therefore, the eternal truths must exist and they can exist as thoughts in the mind of God.

Lastly, from the monadology it is clear that there is a Harmony in the monads. This harmony supposes that there is a Being who has regulated and introduced this harmony from outside and this is God.

Leibnitz believes in the existence of a good, just and loving God. Man differs from other souls not only in being a clear image of the universe but in being a conscious image of God. By virtue of being a conscious image of God, man can know and imitate Him. It is this higher knowledge which tells him that 'he is not only what an inventor is to his machine, but also what a prince is to his subjects, or indeed, what a father is to his children.' Here he emphasizes the conscious devotion and participation in the divine mind, but then his doctrine of self-contained, windowless monads is greatly stretched to meet the logic of the case.

God has chosen this world out of an infinity of possibilities. "But since He has chosen, it must be admitted that everything is comprised under His choice, and that nothing can be changed because He has foreseen all and ruled for all times." If God is good and he has also foreseen everything, then how are evils and sufferings to be explained? Here his sturdy optimism grows most marked. The world is the result of the wisest and best choice and so it must be the best possible world. There is evil but then it contributes to the greater perfection of the universe as a whole. Evil is a foil to the good and enhances its beauty by contrast in the same way as the shading increases the beauty of a picture. Leibnitz divides evils into three classes and suggests their respective importance. *Metaphysical evil*—Every monad is limited and cannot but suffer from this physical and intellectual limitation. *Physical evil*—This kind of evil God wills though for the good of man. Physical pain educates and corrects him.

Moral evil—God wanted a world to be peopled by free men and the award of freedom of will was absolutely necessary. But with the granting of the will to choose freely God had to allow the possibility of wrong choice. Thus moral evil God has not willed but has allowed it in order to create moral beings. No doubt God could have created men always to do rightly but they would have been machines. But machines, howsoever good they may be, are less perfect. Hence the road to perfection is through sin and suffering.

Leibnitz's explanation is more suggestive than logical. Evil appears so from the viewpoint of individuals or from a human viewpoint. But it has to be viewed from the viewpoint of the whole universe. Thus looked at, Leibnitz points out, the sum of good preponderates over the aggregate of evils, in the life of each individual as well as in the universe as a whole. Besides, a little bitter is often more pleasing than sugar. However, the metaphor cannot take the place of logical proof. Pain does not become less painful by being told that it is necessary for the greater perfection of the universe.

4.11. Morality—Freedom and Necessity

Man, according to Leibnitz, is free to pursue his perfection. This perfection consists in the enlightened benevolence of all. But the free action does not mean an action without determinism. Nothing can start *de novo*. Every action has its root in antecedent movements. A purely undetermined action means an abrupt action. But this will break the law of continuity. Hence every action is determined by the past antecedents. The more ignorant we are of past antecedents, the more determined is our action. The more we act from clear ideas or distinct perceptions, the freer we are. This freedom consists in self-determinism. The clear ideas or eternal truths have their special seat in the mind and the more we act according to them, the more self-determined and freer we are. Besides, the clearer we are about the goal, the more rationally we will have to decide between the various possibilities and the choice will be guided more by the law of sufficient reason.

Thus true freedom consists neither in necessity nor in strict spontaneity but in the spontaneous unfolding of the action guided by clear perception. Thus God is most free not because He can do whatever He pleases, nor because His action is dictated by His rational nature; but because His every act is determined by infinite wisdom for the best possible end.

4.12. Leibnitz and Spinoza

Leibnitz began with the opposite end of the philosophy of Spinoza but then he remained far more Spinozistic than what he was ever prepared to acknowledge publicly. In his previous topic of freedom, he has really denied freedom. First, every monad is only a cog in the great machine of pre-established harmony. Secondly, everything is determined in advance in each monad. It makes really no difference when every act in the monad is determined internally instead of externally. Necessity as much rules the philosophy of Leibnitz as it does Spinozism. Real freedom in Leibnitz as also in Spinoza consists in acting according to rational motives. Besides, the pre-established harmony is simply an extension of the parallelism of Spinoza. But the great paradox is that the system of Leibnitz is as much nihilistic, deterministic and pantheistic as that of Spinoza. It is nihilistic if we emphasize that the universe is nothing but the representation of each monad. But the perception of what? Leibnitz denies the reality of space, time and matter. The plurality of monad is nothing but an assumption, for we can be sure of only one monad. We are left with nothing tangible and real. Reality, according to Leibnitz, is the series of perceptions in a monad. But then there is nothing to perceive. Interpreted in this way Leibnitzian system is nihilistic. Again, it is deterministic. We have already pointed out before that everything in the monad is due to the past and the past with the full potentialities for the future has been implanted by God. For God, then, every activity in the monad is foreseen. There is, then, determinism. Besides, in the esoteric philosophy which he did not publish during his life time, he even dispenses with the creator. Everything which is self-consistent is possible. But a great many possibilities compete with one another to be existent. That only becomes existent which is compassible with the system of things. Here the existence is not brought about by God but by the fitness of each thing in the total system. Lastly, Leibnitzian system is also pantheistic if we take his theism seriously. Every monad tries to progress in the line of Godhood. Each, therefore, is a gradual approximation towards one and the same reality. Hence each monad is a focalisation of one absolute monad called God. At times, he even says that the monads perpetually emanate from God in the same way as thought emanates from the mind. The monads, then, become nothing but the modes of Spinoza.

4.13. Concluding Remarks

The system of Leibnitz remains unequalled in modern philosophy on account of its many-sidedness and of its rich suggestiveness. He brought together a number of conflicting tendencies of his age into focus and tried to strike a compromise between them. We have already maintained that no philosophy can equally illumine all the facts of all the fields of enquiry. But we attempt at synthesis of a large number of facts in a meaningful whole. This synthesis depends on some vision, aided very much by a key-notion. This is true of Leibnitz's system no less. Though Russell would not accept our account of philosophy, yet his observation concerning Leibnitz supports the viewpoint of this book.

> Leibnitz, in his private thinking (i.e. esoteric philosophy) is the best example of a philosopher who uses logic as a key to metaphysics. This type of philosophy begins with Parmenides and is carried further in Plato's use of the theory of ideas . . . . Spinoza belongs to the same type, and so does Hegel.[1]

In other words, he means that Leibnitz builds up his metaphysics on the basis of his notion of subject and predicate. According to Leibnitz, as also according to most philosophers from the time of Parmenides to Bradley, it was held that every proposition must have a subject and predicate and no other relation. Even, the philosophy of Vedantic Absolutism, according to Prof. G. Misra, is based on the same subject-predicate view of proposition.[2] But key-notions aim at supporting our philosophical vision intellectually. The role of arguments in favour of vision is secondary. If Leibnitz had consistently held to the subject-predicate notion of propositions, then he would have come to the conclusion that there is only one subject of which all other modes and attributes are predicates. This was the view of Spinoza and Bradley. In the case of latter philosophers, logic fitted very well into their vision. As Leibnitz recoiled from Spinozism, so his logic could not fully support his vision. The 'many' somehow prevents one from attaining to the vision of unity or harmony. Later on James Ward tried to follow the monadology of Leibnitz, but without much success. God, in Spinoza and Leibnitz is the very principle of unity. Leibnitz tries to preserve both God and monads in his system, without bringing them into organic relation. We have already noted that the monadology of Leibnitz goes ill with his Theodicee. In James Ward, we find that the eternity and infinitude of God is suppressed in favour of the reality of the monads. God becomes finite for Ward and such a God fails metaphysically.

After a perusal of rationalistic systems of Descartes, Spinoza and Leibnitz one gets the impression that they are trying to 'know' the Absolute Reality without a prior study of the nature, function and limit of knowledge itself. This was the task which was taken up by British Empiricists. It is this kind of empirical study which has assumed the exclusive pre-occupation of philosophers at the present time. So we turn now to the classical empiricism of the moderners.

---

1. *History of Western Philosoph,* p. 575.
2. This is found in his address at 'All India Philosophical Congress', Cuttuck, 1959.

5

John Locke (1632-1704)

5.01. Introduction

John Locke was born at Somerset on the 29th August, 1632 and was educated at Oxford. He practised medicine and was mostly concerned with political activities. He made lasting friendship with the notable men of his time. Locke wrote very little in his early years. His chief work is *Essay Concerning Human Understanding* which was probably finished by 1679, but was actually published in 1690. He died on the 28th October, 1704.

It was Locke who raised the question of epistemology in most clear terms. He was more concerned with knowing than with the things known. In this he did not entertain any ambitious project but called himself 'an under-labourer in clearing the ground a little, and removing of the rubbish that lies in the way to knowledge'. Besides, he was concerned with the origin of the furniture of the mind. As such he has given us psychology as an empirical science and has introduced historical method in philosophy. Both contributions were of very great importance in philosophy. The historical method led him to explain everything in terms of experience and he may be justly regarded to have developed the Baconian ideal of Empiricism. In Locke the British thought begins to be crystallized in its distinctive way.

5.02. The Problem of Locke

Knowledge Proper is certain, instructive and real: Locke was not a sceptic. He believed in knowledge which he took to be certain. "With me" he says, "to know and to be certain is the same thing, what I know that I am certain of . . . and what comes short of certainty, I think cannot be called knowledge." Besides certainty, knowledge should be instructive as opposed to trifling information. Lastly, Locke always believed in the existence of an independent world of tables, houses and mountains. Now any knowledge must be real for it must refer to and hold good of this actual state of affairs.

Locke lived in an age in which mathematics had made a deep impression on thinking minds. It conformed to the definition of knowledge laid down by him. But he believed in the importance of moral and religious ideas as is clear from his following expressions. "Our business here is not to know all things but those which concern our conduct." "Morality is the proper business and science of mankind in general." "Morality and Divinity are those parts of knowledge that men are most concerned to be clear in." Unfortunately, to these ideas mathematical reasoning cannot be applied for they are non-quantitative. Thus mathematics gives us valid knowledge but it has its own limitation. Hence Locke wanted to give an explanation of knowledge which will give us certainty of God and moral ideas. Thus the problem of Locke was of determining the nature and possible extent of human knowledge. As such he wrote, "If I have done anything new, it has been to describe to others more particularly than had been done before, what is they do, when they perform that action which they call knowing."

5.03. Meaning of 'Ideas'

Locke tries to determine the nature, function, origin and limit of knowledge. He defined it as the perception of the connection or repugnance of ideas. Hence the use of the term 'idea' is very important both for understanding his philosophy and that of his successors Berkeley and Hume. The idea has two distinct meanings.

(1) It may mean a mode of individual consciousness. As such it becomes a subjective modification without any necessary reference to objective things.

(2) Or else, an idea may mean a representation of something other than itself.

Locke does not make any such clear distinction and continues to use the term in both senses. When we say that we have an idea or thought of the table, then ordinarily we mean that we are conscious of something before us. If we further analyse this then we find that the idea of table consists of some images, sensations and feeling standing for something independent of the mind. Thus each idea is a modification of an individual's consciousness pointing out and representing something in the extra-mental world.

Again, idea as an event in individual's consciousness can be studied in two ways.

Logical and Psychological study of idea as an individual's consciousness

(a) We may just analyse and describe any idea in one's consciousness in terms of sensation, images and feeling. It turns out to be a purely psychological study.

(b) Again, we may just try to discover the fundamental, timeless and logical content involved in it. This kind of content is known as categories which are formed in all ideas.

Locke uses the term 'idea' in all these senses and as such nothing but confusion arose in his and subsequent philosophy. Nonetheless there is little doubt that Locke was a realist and believed in an extramental world to which our ideas refer. Thus an idea for him 'is at once the apprehension of a content and the content apprehended; it is both a psychical existent and a logical meaning'. He never ignored the representative character of an idea for it refers to something really existent. But the confining of knowledge to ideas led to the development of epistemological explanation of knowledge in terms of subjective process in the philosophy of Berkeley.

5.04. Refutation of Innate Ideas

In his polemic against the doctrine of innate ideas Locke was not refuting any particular author. No doubt Descartes had made use of the term 'innate ideas' but he used them for a natural bias or predisposition to their formation like an inherited tendency to certain diseases. Now Locke admits the presence of natural faculties but not of innate ideas. Thus he refuted a doctrine of innate ideas only to make his own position clear by contrast.

By innate ideas, Locke understands, ideas which the mind simply finds in itself, as distinguished from those ideas which it receives from outside or those which it creates within itself. Such ideas were supposed to have a mysterious origin. They were supposed to be directly imprinted on the mind by God and as such enjoyed certainty and authority which no other ideas could claim. Thus they put forth their claims on the extraneous support of an incomprehensible source. They also rested on universality as the indubitable test of their innateness. The doctrine of innate ideas tended to make an appeal to authority instead of making an appeal to reason. Hence the doctrine, according to Locke, formed a hindrance in the path of free inquiry. In his refutation of innate ideas he relied on the assumption that true knowledge is found by the active employment of human faculties, in the consideration of things.

The supporters of the innate ideas never made a catalogue of innate ideas, nor could give any satisfactory criterion of noting them. However they refer to the universality as the mark of innateness. We see that, first, it cannot be proved and secondly, universality can be explained in other ways besides innateness.

If by innate ideas are meant, says Locke, that certain principles are present in the mind from birth, then no such principles are found. The laws of contradiction and identity and the like are supposed to be innate but no such ideas are found in the mind of the insane, idiots and children. Instead of being present from the very beginning, they are the last fruit of knowledge. But the defenders of the innate ideas may point out that the ideas may be in the mind of children, the insane or idiot but they may not be recognised by them. Locke held with Descartes that the essence of mind is consciousness and nothing in the mind can be unconscious. Therefore, he replied to this possible objection thus. It seems "to me near a contradiction to say, that there are truths imprinted on the soul which it perceives or understands not. . . .To say, a notion is imprinted on the mind, and yet at the same time to say that the mind is ignorant of it, and never yet took notice of it, is to make this impression nothing".

The criticism of the innate principles of cognition can be easily extended to moral and religious ideas. There is hardly one single moral principle which is universally admitted by all nations. On the other hand, there is hardly any moral principle the contrary of which has not been regarded as virtue. Stealing and murder have been regarded as virtues by the Spartans, the head-hunters and others. Besides, even amongst the civilized people, 'Robberies, murders, rapes are the sports of men set at liberty from punishment and censure". Again, the so-called morals require proof and are not self-evident innate principles.

At this juncture, it might be held that the idea of God must be innate. But the idea of God is no more universal than other ideas just now examined. Besides, this idea is just as relative, various and conflicting as others. And, again, what to speak of single individuals there are whole tribes without the idea of God.

Thus Locke concludes that no ideas are innate as none are universal. But again, from the universality of any idea we cannot prove its innateness. Ideas may be universal without being innate. For example, everybody has the idea of the sun, fire and heat and yet nobody regards them innate.

Locke's dilemmatic argument: If the upholders of the innate ideas maintain that innate ideas are only implicitly present in the mind and become explicit in the course of time, then this is true of all other ideas and as such innate ideas cease to be unique. "I think nobody who reads my book can doubt that I spoke only of innate ideas and not of innate powers." In this sense all ideas are innate for even the ideas of fire, sun and heat are acquired only because we have the innate capacity of acquiring them. Thus Locke submits this dilemma? "Either the theory signifies that certain ideas and principles are explicitly present from the earliest period of consciousness, or it merely asserts the existence of a general capacity for knowledge. In the former case, it is admittedly false. In the latter case, it is totally unable to support the theory of certainty which has been reared upon it."

Innate ideas are really acquired: The denial of the innate ideas does not mean the denial of the truths of science, morals and religion. Only he wanted to give them a basis sounder than that of the mystical belief in innate ideas. Locke believes in the universal knowledge which he thinks, can be explained by his thesis of empiricism. Knowledge, like two and two are equal to four or sweet is not bitter, is not gained by having innate ideas but by having clear and distinct ideas through experience. In the last resort he wants to emphasize the Baconian ideal according to which knowledge of the world around us comes from actual observation of it and not from any introspective analysis of the furniture of the mind. The so-called innate principles of the Laws of Identity, contradiction, or the idea of one single, infinite and perfect Being appear almost meaningless except to persons of wide experience with disciplined intellect, cultivated for years.

5.05. The Origin and Formation of Ideas

We have seen that there are no innate ideas and therefore, they are all acquired. Hence we have to study the way they are acquired. Of course, Locke believed that real knowledge is composed of propositions but these propositions themselves are composed of simple ideas. As such we have to find out the origin of ideas which are the real materials of knowledge.

An enquiry into the origin of ideas implies several things, namely,

1. Tracing the history of the ideas.
2. Or, it may mean finding out the causes, which though themselves may not be ideas yet may originate ideas.
3. It may also mean those ultimate logical formations on which all ideas and knowledge depend.

Locke uses all these three methods in his study of ideas which produce nothing but confusion. Nonetheless he calls his enquiry 'plain historical method' and that primarily it is. Locke's method is primarily psychological for he wants to analyse the processes in which we do come to have our actual experience. This historical or psychological method he confuses with the logical method, for he believes that the validity of knowledge depends or the way in which we might entertain it.

Psychological method is not logical: However, the history or origin of ideas may deepen our insight into them but it does not explain them or determine their truth. Lotus has its origin in the mud but from this it does not follow that it is itself muddy. One may arrive at a true proposition in a very incomplete and doubtful way but the uncertain history of that proposition will not make it doubtful. For example, children, the savage and fanatics may learn of God in a very defective way but from this it does not follow that the idea of God is itself defective. Or else, we might have a complete history of knowledge and yet may fail to understand its significance. For instance, we may gather a complete history of the different ideas in morals of different races at different times and yet may not understand the true ideal of morality. This confusion between the psychological and logical method has been the main cause of the failure of the empirical and hedonist school in philosophy and Ethics respectively.

Principles of knowledge are logically prior but psychologically are the last to develop: Most probably, in his own imperfect way, Locke was trying to find out those ultimate principles on which all knowledge depends. These principles or categories of thought are put into operation as soon as experience begins. But they are not subsequent to but really are prior to experience. Experience as experience ceases to be as soon as the categories are removed. They are, thus, logically first but as a matter of history may be the last to reach consciousness. Locke recognizes such principles in the form of the ideas of relations and general ideas, but calls them derivative for they are the result of later and secondary activity.

5.06. Simple Ideas

Locke lived in an age of composition theory according to which a complex whole is only a sum-total of simple parts. This ignored the fact that the whole itself may have a characteristic by virtue of its being a whole and, again, a part is greatly changed by the whole of which it becomes a part. Nonetheless, Locke believed that he could explain knowledge by reducing it to simple ideas.

A *simple idea* is one which 'being in itself uncompounded, contains in it nothing but one uniform appearance or conception in the mind and is not distinguishable into different ideas.' In other words it is an unanalysable simple datum of knowledge. However, Locke does not explain how an idea is to be regarded as unanalysable. He points out that the ideas of extension and duration are simple, 'yet none of the distinct ideas we have of either is without all manner of composition; it is the very nature of both of them to consist of parts. He once more confuses logical simplicity of conception with the simplicity of sensible presentation. His simple ideas are not the sensation or feeling of the present-day psychologies nor are they elements of logical empiricism. Besides unanalysability Locke mentions two other marks of simple ideas, namely,

1. The mind is *passive* in the reception of simple ideas and when the mind becomes active, then we get complex ideas.

2. Simple ideas are *directly known* as the contents of actual experience. For example, we at once know the colour, heat, extensity through sensation. Again the simple ideas enter the mind one by one, though the qualities to which they refer are found together. For instance, we get the ideas of colour, smell, taste, touch of the apple one by one.[1]

---

1. At this stage we would also mention that ideas are not regarded by Locke as mere subjective modifications. They are appearance of really existent things. This uncritical assumption leads him into confusion. "Ideas of the qualities of external things come to be treated as ideas received from them, and the experience in which the simple ideas originate is treated as depending for its existence upon the operation on the mind of an extramental material cause." Thus in the *Essay* the existence of ideas is taken for granted and their function is being examined 'without' entering upon the questions which may be raised concerning their nature as elements of reality, or their relation to the mind as a substance.

After destroying the doctrine of innate ideas and after a due analysis of ideas, Locke advances his positive theory of the origin of knowledge.

Mind is passive: All ideas originate with and from experience. Mind at birth is a clean slate or *tabula rasa* and all the character of knowledge are acquired through experience. Experience is found in two forms of sensation and reflection. By sensation the mind acquires all knowledge about the determinations of the external world and by reflection it receives information about the operations of its own process.

5.07. Sensation

Sensation arises by bodily affection and it is representative of real things: A sensation arises by the affection of the body by external material things. This bodily affection is conveyed to the brain which gives rise to sensation. Locke mentions all these distinctions but how bodily motion gives rise to consciousness, he tells us, is unintelligible though the fact is undeniable. Again, as a realist he maintained that a sensation always represents or stands for something in the real world.

5.08. Reflection

As sensation tells us about the external world, so likewise reflection tells us about the internal world. We can also characterise it as an internal sense by which the mind becomes aware of its own action. It differs from sensation, not only in having a distinct sphere of its own but also in two other respects, namely,

(a) A sensation performs a representative function by standing as a symbol of external things. However, in reflection the mind is present directly without being represented by an idea as a sign.

(b) Secondly, noticing or attention is necessary in the reception of all simple ideas but in reflection there is greater attention needed than in sensation.

We might note with Kant that knowledge begins with experience but it does not originate from it. Experience may simply afford an opportunity for the full exercise of the mental activity. In many places Locke himself seems to point to this theory of active mind but he suffered from the assumption of his own times in regarding knowledge as purely receptive and representative. Any recognition of constructiveness in knowledge, according to this view, will reduce knowledge to invention. Thus the copy-theory of knowledge, is responsible for his rejection of the theory of an active mind. Thus he likened the mind to a mirror. But even this Baconian nature of mind does determine the nature of images reflected by it. Therefore, like all pre-Kantians he held the passivity of the mind to save knowledge from becoming arbitrary and fictitious.

5.09. Mental Operations in Complex Ideas

Compounding: In forming ideas, the operation of mind is essential. Locke seemed to be too much occupied with the composition theory of complex ideas, though he saw its limitation. Once we have got the simple ideas through sensation and reflection we can compound them in infinite number of ways to get complex ideas. Compounding is that operation of the mind upon its ideas by which it "puts together several of those simple ones it has received from sensation and reflection, and combines them into complex ones." But even in compounding there is something which is not supplied by sensation or reflection. There is the *unity* in the complex ideas which is truly a mental contribution to the formation of complex idea. Besides, compounding is possible with simple elements which we can get by decompounding. Hence decompounding is also admitted by Locke to complete his account of complex ideas. Besides compounding, Locke is obliged to admit two other mental processes of comparing and abstraction and indeed towards his advanced years he pays greater attention to them. The product of comparing and abstracting cannot be called as the composition of simple ideas. It is quite different from the elements of sensation and reflection. Thus Locke seems to depart from the purely sensationalistic account of knowledge, though theoretically he still holds that there is nothing in the intellect which was not previously given in the senses.

Comparing: Comparing consists 'in bringing two ideas, whether simple or complex, together, and setting them by one another, so as to take a view of them at once, without uniting them into one.' This process at once gives rise to the apprehension of relations between the terms compared. This seeing of the relations of difference or similarity is itself not a sensation or reflection. However, Locke maintains that no comparison is possible without the simple ideas to be compared and in this sense it may be said to be ultimately founded upon them.

Abstraction: Locke rightly points out that all scientific knowledge is based on general ideas which we gain through abstraction. General ideas, however, are never given in sensation or reflection. The object given in experience is always concrete and particular. In abstraction we perform two processes.

(a) First, the content to be generalised must be considered apart from its original setting, and

(b) Secondly, the content so considered must be thought of as standing for or representing all other particulars of the same kind.

In order to form the abstract ideas of a triangle, we first of all take out the common content of three-sidedness apart from the shape, size, and colour of particular, experienced triangles and secondly, the content so considered is made to stand for all triangles. The universality or generality of abstract ideas consists not in having an abstracted content but in its signifyingness to represent all particulars of the same kind. This account of abstract ideas, however, was misrepresented by Berkeley. Berkeley supposed that Locke had taken an idea for a psychological image and the general idea for a composite image of many inconsistent contents of sense-perception.

Berkeley's mis-interpretation of Lockean abstract ideas: By general ideas Locke understood the same thing as 'notion' which Berkeley himself was obliged to use. Besides, Locke by abstractions did not understand of separating the inseparable elements and the taking of them as really existent. By considering apart of a certain content, he understood its partial, feasible separation i.e. we can consider the light of the sun without its heat. In spite of certain vagueness in explaining abstract ideas, most probably he tried 'to recognise the necessity of a relating activity, by which the abstracted content is thought of in distinction from and at the same time in relation to its particular exemplifications.'

Thus, we can say that according to Locke, knowledge may be about a great many ideas. Some of these ideas may be very sublime and very complex. But all of them ultimately are reducible to simple ideas. True, complex ideas require the activity of mind, but this activity deals with the *relations* of ideas. However, the processes of comparing, compounding and contrasting the ideas are secondary, and subsequent to the formation of simple ideas. Further, these activities of comparing, contrasting and so on do not create one single simple idea. Hence, Locke did admit the functioning, may even the synthesizing activity of the mind in the form of noting agreement and difference in the formation of knowledge. But his contention lay in holding that knowledge is solely confined to simple ideas, in the ultimate analysis.

> All those sublime thoughts which tower above the clouds, and reach as high as heaven itself, take their rise and footing here; in all that great extent wherein the mind wanders in those remote speculations it may seem to be elevated with, it stirs not one jot beyond those ideas which sense or reflection have offered for its contemplation.[1]

We shall examine latter whether this sensationism of Locke has been successful.

5.10. Division of Complex ideas

The number of complex ideas formed by compounding, comparing and abstracting is almost infinite, but they can be classified into Modes, Substance and Relation. We shall deal with each one of them separately.

---

1. B.K. II. 1.24.

5.11. Modes

Mixed Modes: Modes are those 'complex ideas which however compounded contain not in them the supposition of subsisting by themselves but are considered as dependences on or affections of substances' e.g., the ideas of number, duration, triangle and gratitude. Modes have been further sub-divided into simple and mixed. Locke says very little about the mixed modes which consist of simple ideas of different ends, combined by the mind, and considered as forming a single complex idea, which is consolidated and fixed by means of a name. However, we should be careful in being consistent in forming mixed modes. Under this, he gives the instances of obligation, drunkenness and lies. Again, let us take the example of beauty which consists of certain composition of colour and figure, causing delight in the beholder.

Simple Modes: Simple modes are 'variations, or different combinations of the same simple idea, without the mixture of any other.'

Here there is the repetition or combination of the same kind of ideas. This is best illustrated in the counting of dozen or score. In the case of number of conception of the combination of identical elements to form the complex ideas of simple modes, seems to work most smoothly. Here the idea of one unit is simple and can be added into any increasing number. Similarly, in spatial forms we can get simple modes. If we settle about some determinate length as our unit, then we can variously repeat the units to arrive at the mixed mode of a mile or any such distance. In all combinations, it is necessary that they should be fixed for the mind, by means of a name. But this adding unit to unit and the fixing of the whole by means of a name, goes beyond the mechanical composition to which Locke drew our attention.

Of simple modes two are worthy of note. First, according to Locke, the idea of infinite is a purely negative simple mode. Starting with numerical unit or with spatial unit of finite space, we can repeat the same kind of ideas to form larger wholes. But we find that there is no reasonable limits to the enlarging of the ideas. Hence we arrive at the infinite, in a purely quantitative, comparative and negative way.

Locke observes one difference when he comes to explain the simple modes of qualities. When we repeat the simple ideas of one kind say of whiteness or warmth, then there seems to be no increase in the quantity. We can only combine the ideas of the same kind varying in different degrees, like the shades of the same colour or the pitch of the same kind of sound. This would have led Locke to reject the composition of simple qualities, but inconsistently enough he retains it

5.12. Substance

In explaining the complex ideas of Substance and Relations, Locke departs from the purely sensationistic account of knowledge. They are not given by sensation or reflection, but they appear after the simple ideas are supplied to the mind. Hence they are derivative or secondary rather than complex.

In his account of Substance, Locke seems to be confused between the logical, metaphysical and empirical account of it. A substance is not any simple idea but is implied by it. It is the idea of a substratum or support underlying a number of simple qualities experienced together. For example, greenness, a certain size, weight, smell, taste, etc., go to make an apple.

Different viewpoints about substance: But these qualities cannot exist by themselves. There must be something in which they inhere. Nor can we think that an experienced thing like an apple or mango is simply a sum-total of these qualities. Hence all simple ideas, all sensible qualities, carry with them a supposition of a *substratum* to exist in.' Apart from this common sense view of substance, he points out, that it rests upon the necessity of thought. We apply the idea of substance to simple qualities because we cannot conceive of the simple qualities existing by themselves. Sometimes like Hume he tries to explain the origin of substance in terms of custom or habit. When a certain number of these simple ideas go constantly together, we accustom ourselves to suppose some *substratum* of the qualities we experience.

The logical consideration of substance as a category of thought causes Locke great difficulty. A substance is not given in sensation or reflection. As such it is not experienced by us. Hence it is an unknown substratum of qualities. . . .,'a supposed I-Know-Not-What.' (He failed to realise that a substance apart from the qualities is an abstraction. We cannot know any abstraction through our senses though we can grasp it by our intellect. The very fact that a substance was contrasted with the qualities, it could not be something definite and determinate like the qualities).[1] As the idea of the substance is I-know-not-what, so material as well as spiritual substances are equally unknown to us.

The above view is tantamount to scepticism but Locke was not a sceptic though his empiricism contained the germ of it. When he comes to the existence of God, then he does not apply this notion of 'I-know-not-what' to Him. Besides, he had another doctrine of substance too, which he derived from the scientific view of his time. In this sense, a substance is that which remains permanent in the midst of changes. In the history of Philosophy, it is this sense in which the doctrine of substance has been largely held. In this usage Locke believed in the reality of atoms. But the scientists do not regard the reality of atoms as unknowable. Hence we find that Locke from his logical viewpoint regarded substance as unknowable but from

---

1. Somewhat like this was the comment of Leibnitz with regard to Locke's view of substance. See H.W.B. Joseph, *Philosophy of Leibnitz*, p. 74.

the scientific standpoint held it to be knowable. Thus in his account of matter he comes to hold that it is partially knowable and partially unknowable. Even when he regarded substance unknowable, he held it to be real. Hence he was not a sceptic but a critic of the commonsense view of substance.

Matter: When Locke comes to give an account of the qualities of matter he comes to take the help of the scientific theory of his day. Besides, here he quite definitely takes the copy-theory of ideas.

Locke believes that there are two kinds of qualities, namely, primary and secondary. The Cartesian dualism of qualities was maintained by a criticism of matter regarded as pure extension. According to Locke, the real quality of matter is not extension but solidity which really depends on the insensible, minute particles of matter called atoms.

Primary and Secondary qualities: Now the primary qualities are utterly inseparable from the material bodies, in all their different sizes and various changes. There are six such original or primary qualities, namely, solidity, extension, figure, motion, rest and number. They are constantly found in the bodies. The secondary qualities, 'which in truth are nothing in the objects themselves, but powers to produce various sensations *in us by their primary qualities*'.[1] They include colour, sounds, tastes etc. Again, 'primary qualities of bodies are resemblances of them and their patterns do really exist in the bodies themselves; but the ideas produced in us by the secondary qualities have no resemblance of them at all.' Closely following this distinction, Locke points out that primary qualities of solidity, extension etc., are found in their objective right. They are really existent whether there be any person to perceive them or not. But secondary qualities are totally dependent on human subjects and their various sense-organs. Without eyes, there are no colours, without ears there are no sounds. Besides, secondary qualities are relative for the same bucket of water may be cold or hot, according to different arrangements. Finally, secondary qualities are produced by the primary qualities of bulk, solidity etc.

As pointed out before, Locke pointed out that the material substance is unknown. But his account of the primary and secondary qualities points out that the matter is much more than 'I-know-not-what'.

Mind: We get the knowledge of mind through reflection. We know that it has the qualities of perceiving, thinking, memory and willing with the idea of an unknown *Substratum.* Hence the real nature of mind is unknown, though its qualities are known. The primary qualities of mind are (i) thinking and (ii) the ability to initiate movement willing. How does the mind move the body by willing? This remains a mystery, but the fact is undeniable.

God: In relation to God, Locke does not apply the conclusion of the unknowability of substance. He seems to tell us that God is knowable and his nature

---

1.   Italics ours.

is purely immaterial. The content of the idea of God consists of those qualities and powers which we experience in ourselves by reflection and which it is "better to have than to be without", each enlarged by the idea of infinity.

5.13. Relation

Causality and Identity: The simple ideas of sensation and reflection suggested the idea of substance; similarly, the experienced data of change imply the necessary ideas of power, causality and active efficiency. The power or causality is an idea of relation for it implies the capacity of producing changes in another body. However, it seems clear that the ideas of power and causality are subordinate to that of active initiation of changes.

Causality derived from voluntary action: How do we derive this idea of active initiative? Do we get it from the examination of impact and motion between external bodies? The idea is not derived from the examination of the movement of external bodies for we never experience the activity in one leading to changes in the other, though we observe the impact and consequent movement in the bodies. The idea of active efficiency is really derived from our experience of willing in producing movements or controlling thought.

Though the idea of active efficiency involved in causality has been derived from voluntary action, the idea becomes necessary in understanding all kinds of changes. Thus we derive the proposition *"Everything that has a beginning must have a cause. . . . .by contemplating our ideas, and perceiving that the idea of beginning to be, is necessarily connected with the idea of some operation, and the idea of operation with the idea of something operating, which we call a cause."*

No necessary connection in object: The idea of causality, for Locke, is not necessarily connected with uniformity. The law in nature is essentially a thing of divine pleasure. Hence we do not see any real or intrinsic connection between the phenomena of nature. The experienced regularity in nature depends on laws implanted by God which we must not be too presumptuous to penetrate.

. . . . though causes work steadily, and effects constantly flow from them, yet their connection and dependencies being not discoverable in our ideas, we can have but an experimental knowledge of them.

This experimental knowledge is only probably in character.

This view of Locke led Berkeley to hold that there is no causality in things. This led to the further denial of causal connection in the objects by Hume.

Thus Locke concludes that one thing causes change in another is undeniable, but the fact is most unintelligible.

Identity: In general by identity is meant nothing but a continuity of existence. "That, therefore, that had one beginning is the same thing; and that which had a different beginning in time and place from that, is not the same but diverse." However, in the treatment of identity, Locke shows that its idea varies with the nature of different objects. A material thing is identical with itself when it exists at a particular place, at a particular time, excluding all other things from occupying that particular place or time. But this consideration of identity seems to be appropriate in the case of individual atoms. A material object is said to be identical with itself when the mass of atoms remains to be in the same order and number.

Identity of atoms, plants and men: A living thing, however, has its atoms constantly changed and still we call it the same Oak or tree. Here identity consists in the sameness of the organisation of the parts in one coherent body, partaking of one common life. The identity of man as a living creature is 'nothing but a participation of the same continued life by constantly fleeting particles of matter, in succession of vitally united to the same organised body.' However when he comes to personal identity, then he thinks that it depends upon the sameness of consciousness. This immediacy of the same self does not depend on the immediacy of feeling but of judgment of the same consciousness involving past and present consciousness for it is by the consciousness it has of its present thoughts and actions that it is self to itself now, and so will be the same self, as far as the same consciousness can extend to actions past or to come."

Locke did not co-ordinate all these different ideas of Identity. He, without disbelieving in the existence of substance, causality and identity, declared that they are not intelligible to us.

5.14. General Nature of Knowledge

So far Locke has finished the account of all kinds of ideas which are the materials and instruments of knowledge. As pointed out before, according to Locke, knowledge as against opinion is certain, instructive, agreeing with the reality of things. Thus there are three important problems in relation to knowledge.

1. Objective certainty as against the probability of opinions,
2. Reality and validity of knowledge, and
3. Instructiveness. Knowledge proper must be instructive as against trifling knowledge in tautological propositions.

Locke's definition of knowledge: Knowledge, according to Locke consists in 'perception of the connection and agreement, or disagreement and repugnancy of any of our ideas."[1] First, knowledge depends on the mental power to perceive or apprehend ideas and not in the mere receptivity of ideas. Secondly, knowledge is *rational* for it consists in seeing the agreement or disagreement between ideas. Further, he confined knowledge to ideas alone without reference to real things.

---

1. B.K IV. 12.

5.15. Degrees of Knowledge

"Sometimes the mind perceives the agreement or disagreement of two ideas immediately by themselves, without the intervention of any other and this, I think, we may call *intuitive* knowledge." Here we see the agreement or disagreement as directly as we see the light with our eyes. Thus we at once see that white is not black, that a circle is not a triangle.

Intuitive knowledge : This knowledge is most clear and certain and is the highest kind of knowledge which human faculty is capable of achieving.

Next in the degree of knowledge comes the *demonstrative Knowledge,* in which we perceive the agreement or disagreement between two ideas by the *mediation or intervention of other* ideas. For example, we see that. A and B are equal to one another because each is equal to C. We express the reasoning like this :

$$A = C$$
$$C = B, \qquad \text{Therefore } A=B.$$

The separate steps in the reasoning, however, should be immediately clear. Thus demonstrative knowledge consists in a series or chain of intuitions.

The knowledge gained by demonstrative method is certain but it is indirect, requiring proof depending on the quickness and sagacity of the mind. It is not very easy either, for it involves many steps in which a steady application and pursuit is required to this discovery. Again, in intuitive knowledge there is no doubt anywhere but in the demonstrative knowledge, before a demonstration takes place, there is doubt. Besides, demonstrative knowledge is not so clear for it passes through different stages. Lastly, it requires the memory of the previous steps or intuitions. However, memory opens the door to the possibilities of errors and mistakes. Thus, we conclude that the demonstrative knowledge is inferior to intuitive knowledge in degree of certainty.

Locke thought that demonstrative knowledge is not confined to mathematics alone but could be applied to Ethics as well. However, in spite of repeated requests he never carried a demonstration of ethical principles.

Sensitive knowledge: Anything that comes to acquire the certainty of intuitive or demonstrative knowledge is knowledge and anything which comes short of it is not knowledge but is an opinion. "There is, indeed, another perception of the mind employed about the particular existence of finite beings without us; which, going beyond bare probability, and yet not reaching perfectly to either of the foregoing degrees of certainty, passes under the name of knowledge."[1] This knowledge regarding the particular external objects is called *sensitive knowledge.* Locke does not find the element of certainty in sensitive knowledge but could not deny the name of knowledge to it. Though it may not be knowledge proper, still it guides our

---

1.   B.K. IV. 2.14.

happiness or misery, 'beyond which we have no concernment to know or to be.¹

5.16. Validity or Reality of Knowledge

We know that a Centaur or a Pegasus is not an elephant. This is intuitively certain, but Locke does not recognize it to be real knowledge. In order that knowledge be real it must agree with the reality of things. If we take ideas as existing in human minds and real objects be considered extramental, then the reality of knowledge .is difficult to establish. Locke did not raise the question of the reality of knowledge in the form of correspondence of the ideas to real objects. By the reality of knowledge he understood a tacit reference to the real world. Such a reference is involved even in imaginary ideas of a centaur or a pegasus of knowledge is guaranteed. The reality of knowledge is guaranted if the ideas which it coptains can be known to be ideas of possible existents. With this view of reality he takes the different ideas one by one and established their reality separately.

Simple ideas: The reality of simple ideas is guaranteed by their simplicity. Our very inability of producing them like the ideas of heat, fire, light shows that they are not fictions of our fancies, but are natural and regular productions if things without us, really operating upon us; and so carry with them all the conformity which is intended, or which our statement requires.

Complex ideas: Granted that simple ideas are real, what can be done to guarantee the reality of complex ideas? Now the ideas of modes and relations are formed by the free activity of the mind without reference to their archetypes.

Complex ideas of modes and relations: As such their reality does not depend on their correspondence with real objects. They should be consistent and 'so framed that there be a possibility of existing conformable to them.' Is mathematics and morals we deal with abstract ideas and reach demonstrative certainty in them. But knowledge in them is also said to be real for they refer to things capable of existing. The mathematicians may never have experienced a perfect circle or a triangle but any one of them can exist. Similarly, the moralist might not have experienced a case of murder still his knowledge will be said to be real for murder is an act capable of being performed. Thus the knowledge of the mathematician is real for "he is sure what he knows concerning those figures when they have barely an ideal existence in his mind, will hold true of them also when they have a real existence in matter."

5.17. Reality of Substance

Mere possibility of existence cannot explain the reality of substance for substance claims to represent an actual constitution of the reality. Its reality is derived from its being actually experienced, i.e., the combination of qualities, which constitutes

---

1.   The confinement of knowledge to ideas proper sounds like subjectivism which is foreign to his system of thought. First, ideas are regarded by him as the objects of understanding. Hence, a relation between ideas is a relation between objects. Secondly, the connection is rooted in the very nature of the ideas themselves. "In some of our ideas there are certain relations, habitudes and connections, so visibly included in nature of the ideas themselves, that we cannot conceive them separate from them by any power whatsoever." Thus knowledge amongst ideas is determined by their nature, without being influenced by the subject himself. The perception of agreement or disagreement between ideas is an objective intellectual necessity.

the specific content of a particular substance called a mango or an apple, is being actually presented in experience. This test of actual experience is most necessary for each material substance possesses a real constitution consisting of primary qualities caused by the minute particles ; and again, these minute particles and primary qualities produce secondary qualities. Now without actual experience we cannot say which qualitiesare found in any substance, for without actual experience we cannot say which primary qualities are found in any substance and which secondary qualities are produced by which primary qualities.

5.18. Instructiveness of Knowledge

Locke, further makes a distinction between Trifling and Instructive propositions, a distinction which was later emphasized by Kant in the form of Analytic and Synthetic propositions.

First, trifling propositions are those which do not add to our knowledge. Under this heading he found identical propositions like A is A or Substance is Substance. No doubt such propositions are certain but are tautologous. Again, the so-called analytic propositions in which a part of the connotation of the subject is predicated, also come under trifling propositions, e.g., 'Lead is a metal' or 'men are animals'. Hence in an instructive proposition, which adds to our knowledge, there must be something more than the relation the whole and part. In an instructive proposition we may affirm something which is not contained in the subject.

5.19. Kinds and Limits of Knowledge

Knowledge, according to Locke is universal, certain, instructive and real. Now let us see how far we can know. He divides knowledge into four sorts, namely, (i) Identity or diversity, (ii) Relation, (iii) Co-existence or necessary connection, and (iv) Real existence.

Knowledge of Identity: By identity is meant the identity of the content of an idea and its distinction from the content of every other idea. Though the power of perceiving similarity of difference is fundamental yet knowledge of mere identity, can give only a trifling proposition. If each idea is absolutely distinct from every other, then how can we unite the ideas in real knowledge? According to Locke, any "significant predication involves the assertion, not of bare identity or diversity, but of other and more determinate relations between the contents of our ideas." Thus the proposition 'a man is white' means that the thing which has the quality of man has also the quality of whiteness. Thus he advances the relational nature of knowledge.

The consideration to identity gives rise to the knowledge of relations, which is really important in the epistemology of Locke. This kind of knowledge consists of a perception of relations between the content of one idea and that of another after abstracting them from the spatial, temporal and other circumstances of sensible existence.

Knowledge of Relations: This is the fundamental assumption of Locke for explaining the universal and necessary knowledge in science. The perception of these relations between abstracted contents adds to Knowledge. Besides, the perception of the relation of agreement or disagreement is necessary for it arises from the very nature of the ideas. For example, 2+2=4 follows from the very nature of the ideas. Knowledge thus gained is *universal* for it is true of ideas which are timeless and free from concrete details. The knowledge being necessary in the abstract ideas will be true in all cases where they will be embodied in some concrete setting. Such knowledge also may be said to be *eternal* for it is based on ideas abstracted from all time-relations.

The best kind of knowledge in sciences is best seen in mathematics. This is possible because it does not deal with concrete or sensible experience but with ideal construction. The knowledge of mathematics is not due to any innate ideas but because the least difference between different ideas is clearly perceptible. The demonstrative character of mathematics depends on the perfect determination or precision of the ideas with which it is concerned. Besides, the subject-matter of mathematics is formed of discrete ideas. The same thing may be shown in Geometry. Here the subject-matter is continuous, instead of discrete extension, but the value of Geometry depends, like Arithmetic, on the ideal construction.

Besides, it has been able to discover the just equality of two angles or ideal elements of extension or figures. Lastly, it has been able to make use of visible and lasting marks in the form of diagrams. The great merit of diagrams lies in checking the tendency towards variation and thereby in securing a common understanding with others.

Demonstration of Mathematics due to (1) Ideal construction. (2) Precision of ideas. (3) Use of visible lasting marks: Locke does not confine demonstrative knowledge to the science of number or space alone but extends it to Ethics also. In order that Ethics be a demonstrative science it must be shown to have all the important marks of the science of mathematics. Now Ethics, like mathematics, is an abstract science concerned with relations between the contents of certain abstracted ideas without being complicated by the necessity of referring to the actual concrete existence. Further, if we could entertain the concepts in Ethics with precision then it would be possible to see intuitive relation between them giving rise to mathematical certainty in knowledge.

Ethics is Demonstrative: However, Locke mentions a point of difference between Ethics and mathematics. The moral laws possess no ethical significance until they are shown to be the expression of the divine will. Hence ultimately. Ethics is based on an existential proposition which is lacking in the case of mathematics. In spite of this he treated Ethics as demonstrative as is clear from the following extract.

The idea of a Supreme Being, infinite in power, goodness, and wisdom, whose workmanship we are, and on whom we depend ; and the idea of ourselves, as understanding, rational beings, being such as are clear in us, would, I suppose, if duly considered and pursued, afford such foundations of our duty and rules of action as might place morality amongst the sciences capable of demonstration ; wherein I doubt not, but from self-evident propositions, by necessary consequences, as incontestable as those in mathematics, the measures of right and wrong might be made out, to any one that will apply himself with the same indifference and attention to the one as he does to the other of these sciences.[1]

5.20. Knowledge of Co-existence

Locke gradually now makes transition from the abstract ideas to ideas referring to the reality. He turns to the knowledge of co-existence and necessary connection. Now any knowledge worthy of the name must have necessary connection. Let us see whether we can know substance involving co-existence of several qualities. In coming to the knowledge of co-existence "what Locke has in mind is really a distinction between the relations which our thought discovers between the contents of our ideas, when abstraction is made from the coditions of actual existence, and the special relations which are involved in the fact of concrete existence itself."[2] Here he points out that the most part of the material knowledge consists of the knowledge of co-existence, namely, our idea of fire is a body hot, luminous and moving upward ; of gold, our idea is a body heavy, yellow, malleable and fusible. But this kind of knowledge is inadequate for the majority of such propositions are lacking intellectual necessity. No doubt we frame such necessary propositions regarding co-existence as 'figure necessarily supposes extension', 'two bodies cannot be in the same place' etc. Unfortunately, such propositions are trifling. The knowledge of actual substance is confined to particular instances and this cannot be raised to the status of the universal and certain knowledge for the following reasons.

1. Such knowledge of actual co-existence is one of fact and not of intellectual necessity. We know that food nourishes men, but we cannot guarantee that it cannot be otherwise. On this ground Locke doubts the possibility of a science of physical nature.

2. Secondly, the connexion between the simple ideas which compose the complex ideas is unknown. We cannot say that heat must be luminous or yellow must be malleable gold.

3. Besides, our knowledge of co-existent things always involves reference to the secondary qualities of colour, heat, warmth etc. But we do not know how they are caused by the primary qualities.

1. BK. IV Chap. 3-18.
2. Gibson. J., *Ibid.*, p. 160.

4. Again, the chief bar to knowledge, according to Locke, consists in the inability of our senses to convey ideas to us in regard to the minute constitution of matter. This inability of the senses does not allow us to know the manner in which heterogeneous qualities are made to co-exist.

5. Lastly, the difficulty of knowing the co-existent, things depends on the incomprehensible inter-action of mind and matter.

Locke was not a sceptic for he believed that there is necessary connection depending on the nature of the minute constitution of things but our limited understanding fails us to inform about it. The more he thought about the knowledge of existent material things, the greater difficulty he experienced. When he comes to the last division of knowledge, then his treatment of the subject becomes slight.

Knowledge of existence: All the while Locke believes that there is a real objective world existing in its own right but he confines knowledge to ideas alone. This dualism he could not overcome. He finds that knowledge about existential things is not possible, in general. There are only two things whose existence we know with perfect transparency of knowledge. First, we have the intuitive knowledge of our own self. The unique nature of self-knowledge depends on the fact that the mind and mind alone is present to the understanding.

Intuitive knowledge of self-existence: However, the intuitive knowledge of self differs from the intuitive knowledge about abstract ideas in one important respect. The immediate apprehension of abstract ideas is possible because our abstraction from concrete settings makes it independent of the intervention of many other ideas ; whilst the intuitive self-judgment is so perceived because it is self-sufficient, without needing any idea.

The existence of the material world is possible: The existence of God is also known to be real because His existence can be demonstrated. But apart from the existence of self and God, the existence of particular substances cannot be known with certainty. Should we deny, then, the existence of the material world? Locke was not a subjective idealist like Berkeley for he believed that ideas are mere signs, pointing something real beyond themselves. He also granted that the knowledge of the primary qualities is possible. He could not deny the existence of the material world because of the following reasons :

1. There is a peculiar tang of reality found in sense-perception for any one will be able to make a difference between an actual taste and imagined taste.

2. Besides, there is a certain amount of coerciveness or forcefulness in actual sensation pointing out to something real as their cause. "If I turn my eyes at noon towards the sun I cannot avoid the ideas which the light or sun then produces in me." This independence of the subjective control is not found concerning an imaginal product.

3. Lastly, our sense-organs are not the instruments of creating ideas but only of receiving them. If a person has no eyes, then he can have no ideas of colour or light. Thus the dependence of sensation on our sense-organs points to the existence

of something actually existing outside of us.

We know the existence of particular substances with the help of sensitive knowledge. However, sensitive knowledge lacks certainty for it has no intellectual necessity about it. We know that an apple in soft, yellow, sweet, fragrant but we cannot say that it *must be so*. But such knowledge is sufficient to ensure us happiness and is thus fit for guiding us to action. Besides, sensitive knowledge cannot guarantee the material world as a whole nor can ensure us the existence of spirits in animals.

Underlying the four divisions of knowledge, there is the fundamental opposition between the universal knowledge in science and the knowledge of actual experience. This opposition appears in the very definition of knowledge which consists in the perception of connection and repugnancy of any ideas only, without reference to real things. Besides, he always implies the existence of the material world but this he never proves from the mere presence of ideas, as is clear from the following: "For, the having of the idea of any thing in our mind no more proves the existence of that thing than the picture of a man evidences his being in the world, or the visions of a dream make thereby a true history." The real existence is known only by actual contact but this can never yield certain and universal knowledge. The universal and certain knowledge found in sciences deals with 'abstract ideas which are imperfect, which cannot exist.' This emphasis on ideas as the constituents of knowledge makes him almost a Platonic idealist and yet he hoped to be a consistent empiricist. In order to be a pure empiricist he ought to have confined knowledge to experience alone but he denies the name, to sensitive knowledge based on pure sensations. Instead of basing knowledge on sensation, he thinks, the real knowledge is based on the abstract ideas, divorced from the concrete setting. The rationalistic edifice contradicts the sensationalistic foundation. Instead of calling him a Bacon or an inconsistent empiricist, it is better to call him a Cartesian influenced by Bacon. With Falckenberg we can summarise the conflicting tendencies in Locke : "The remarkable spectacle is presented of a philosopher who admits no other sources of ideas than perception and the voluntary combination of perceptions, transcending the limits of experience with proofs of the divine existence, viewing with suspicion the ideas of substance formed at the instance of experience, and reducing natural science to the sphere of mere opinion ; while on the other hand, he ascribes reality and eternal validity to the combinations of ideas formed independently of perception, which are employed by mathematics and ethics, and completely abandons the individualistic position in his native faith in the impregnable validity of the relations of ideas, which is evident to all who turn their attention to them." However, Locke hopes that perfect knowledge will consist in having the fullness of concrete reality which will have also perfect intellectual transparency. Thus he leaves the problem to Kant who tries to give us knowledge which will be instructive without being abstract, and should be universal without being confined to abstract ideas alone.

5.21. Extent or Limit of Knowledge

Our knowledge can reach only to the ideas and any thing beyond the possibility of ideas is also beyond knowledge. Besides, our knowledge is narrower than ideas for there are things too big, too remote or minute to give us the clear ideas (e.g., Planets are too big, too remote and atoms are too minute to be perceived clearly). Even if there be ideas we cannot perceive any necessary connection between them e.g., we do not see any necessary connection between the secondary and primary qualities. Knowledge proper is confined to the abstract ideas in mathematics and Ethics but there is no proper knowledge in Physics. Even in the case of mathematics and Ethics the ideas are purely abstract which are imperfect for they do not exist. We are certain of the intuitive knowledge of the self and the demonstrative knowledge of God. Thus our knowledge is very small in extent. Indeed our ignorance is much greater than our knowledge.

5.22. The Estimate of Locke's Philosophy

Locke was neither consistent nor profound. However, a lack of these excellent virtues of philosophising has not robbed him of his immense influence on his successors. Partly this is due to the ability of the ensuing generations of Berkeley, Hume, Mill, Russell, Wittgenstein, Austin and Ryle who have carried on this British tradition of empiricism. It would be too much to read current development in the works of Locke, but, equally it would be idle to deny the historical continuity of current *analysis philosophy* with his aims and purposes. Prof. Ryle remarks that the current revolution in philosophy is largely associated with the 'notion of sense or meaning'.[1] It would be absurd to suppose that Locke could have done what Quine, Carnap, Austin and Ryle have succeeded in doing now. But it would not be too wild to hold that the current enquiry could not have taken its present shape if Locke and his empiricist successors had not busied themselves with the problem concerning knowledge. On the whole it might be said that Locke wanted to make clear, what we do when we are said to *know*. True, he defined knowledge in terms of 'certainty'[2] which could not be possible with regard to propositions of facts. Yet these very empirical propositions formed the main subject-matter of his enquiry. Here Locke was inconsistent with regard to his initial problem itself. But in any analytic movement of thought these muddles and inconsistencies provide food for further research and provoke thereby new results. In connection with Locke, Russell remarks.[3]

> The most fruitful philosophies have contained glaring inconsistencies but for that very reason have been partially true.

1.   Ayer, A.J. & others, *The Revolution in Philosophy,* p. 8.
2.   Bk. IV 16.3.
3.   *History of Western Philosophy,* p. 592 (1961).

We shall see now the fruitfulness of Locke's inconsistencies.

To begin with Locke holds that mind at birth is a clean slate and contains nothing but what experience writes on it. But at the very next moment he adds that there are innate *powers*. It was at this point that Leibnitz had shown that if mind be credited with innate powers of receiving ideas, then it cannot be described as *tabula rasa* or a white piece of paper. In the same context, Locke tells us that the mind is passive in receiving simple ideas but becomes active in comparing, contrasting and compounding them in diverse ways. But does not Locke observe that we at once know that black is not white, or hot is not cold? This means that whilst receiving simple ideas, the mind also is noting agreement or difference between them. As such the mind does not remain passive, but also active at the same time with regard to simple ideas. This point is conceded by Locke with regard to simple ideas of reflection, since mind has to attend to the ideas of reflection by *attending* and *reflecting* on simple ideas obtained by sensation.[1] This inconsistency of Locke was shown with a great deal of effectiveness by Kant, who showed that there cannot be ideas which are not tampered with the nature of mind. Even simple ideas, according to Kant, are transformed and moulded by the two *a priori* forms of sensibility.

Further, Locke grants that after receiving the simple ideas, the mind becomes *active* in the formation of complex ideas. Here the mind is said to *relate* the simple ideas by comparing, contrasting and compounding them. And by seeing the, agreement or repugnance between them, the mind reaches knowledge. Here we ask, are the simple ideas distinct and separate? If they are so, how are they related? Locke did not note that the assumption of atomic simple ideas would create trouble with regard to their synthesis. It was this difficulty which was later on raised by the idealists. But there is another problem which is immediately connected with Locke's assumption of atomic simple ideas. We connect ideas with the help of such general notions as substance, causality and so on. Locke simply pointed out that such general notions are obtained by comparing, contrasting and compounding activities of the mind. But it is one thing to maintain that they are obtained immediately after simple ideas are received and quite another thing to maintain that they can be reduced to simple ideas. Can the notion of substance or causality be said to be compounded of simple ideas? We shall presently find that Locke does not think that such notions can be obtained by sensation. Then he should have maintained that these notions cannot be empirically obtained, even when psychologically they seem to be subsequent to simple ideas. Here, Kant criticising the whole empirical tradition held that substance or causality is an *a priori* category of the understanding which cannot be obtained by sensibility, but is at the basis of any empirical knowledge whatsoever. This aspect of Locke's contention led to important result in philosophy and even at the present time powerfully moves the philosophers.

---

1. Bk. II. 1.24.

As an empirical philosopher Locke has to show that there is nothing in the intellect which was not previously given in the senses. For this reason he had to explain the notions of substance and causality empirically. But Locke has not done so. He simply states that the notion of substance is of an *unknown* substratum. Similarly, he holds that the notion of causality is unintelligible. We know only this much, according to Locke, that one thing causes change in another. But we do not know how one thing causes change in another. With these confessions Locke had only two options left to him. Either he should have rejected these two notions outright as idle figments of imagination, or he should have admitted their non-empirical explanation. Locke was followed in both of these suggestions. Barkeley and Hume carried out the denunciation of material and mental substances respectively. Similarly, Berkeley did not accept causality with regard to natural phenomena and Hume most thoroughly examined and refuted the notion of causality. In this sense, the germ of Humean scepticism lay in the writings of Locke himself. Kant, on the other hand, maintained ; since the notions of substance and causality cannot be empirically explained, therefore, they should be regarded as *a priori* or non-empirical.

Besides, Locke's purpose was 'to enquire into the origin, certainty, and extent of *human knowledge*'. He thought that he would be able to do so by a study of 'ideas' of which it is composed. However, ideas are artificial units and a study of them would disclose the nature of 'knowing'. This defect was shown by Kant, according to whom 'judgments; and not 'ideas are the real units of knowledge. The challenge continued to be made by the idealist, notably by Bradley and Bosanquet and very recently was taken up by Russell, Wittgenstein and other logical positivists and empiricists. Here once again Locke in spite of his superficialities has become influential, both in idealistic and empirical traditions.

We may grant for the time being that knowledge is constituted by 'ideas'. But, are the ideas mental or do they stand for *objects* of knowledge? Berkeley emphasized the former aspect of ideas which led to *subjective* idealism. This led to objective idealism in due course. Later on in 1903 it was G. E. Moore who in his celebrated 'Refutation of idealism' showed that the term 'idea' stands for two elements, namely, psychical process and the object to which this process refers. The 'idea' of blue stands both for *sensing* blue and for the blue *sensed*. In other words, the ambiguous word 'idea' led to further analysis and elucidation and in fullness of time paved the way for sense-data theory and also for the theory of verifiability.

As noted earlier, Locke instead of occupying himself with purely philosophical problem concerning 'knowing' confused it with the psychological problem of the origin of knowledge. Besides, we have pointed out several times that Locke held inconsistently the rationalistic ideas of certainty in knowledge alone with his emphasis on experience. Only now Russell has tried to make Locke consistent by making his empiricism logical. But of course no empirical proposition can have the certainty of analytic propositions.

Locke began as an empiricist to account for knowledge in terms of experience. But the task proved too much for him. He left a final dichotomy in the theory of knowledge. The psychological origin of ideas could give only probably knowledge and the universal knowledge could be found in abstract ideas alone (excepting self and God). He, after all, found out that the important element in knowledge is the *perception of necessary connection*, but this cannot be supplied by experience. In such a case the experience serves, only as the *occasion* for the exercise of the mental power and does not, therefore become the constituent of knowledge. Besides, he is led to believe that the rational elements of knowledge, like substance and causality, are such as men cannot help in reading into their experience. Ultimately, then knowledge cannot be explained in terms of the ideas through experience alone. This insistence on the fixed orders of ideas which men must supply to experience in order to get knowledge makes him really a precursor of Kant.

The importance of Locke lies in the fact that he laid down the foundation of the great problem of the theory of knowledge. He is, as such, to be regarded as the beginner of the theory of knowledge and he himself truly styled himself as 'an under-labour engaged in cleaning the rubbish on the road to knowledge.' The final estimate of Locke has been thus summed up beautifully by the poet philosopher Santayana.[1]

...I had Locke's mind been more profound, it might have been less influential. He was in sympathy with the coming age, and was able to guide it, an age that confided in easy, eloquent reasoning...Locke played in the eighteenth century very much the part that fell to Kant in the nineteenth...his opinions became a point of departure for universal developments. The more we look into the matter the more we are impressed by the patriarchal dignity of Locke's mind. Father of psychology, father of the criticism of knowledge, father of theoretical liberalism,.....was the ancestor of that whole school of polite, moderate opinion which can unite liberal Christianity with the mechanical science and psychological idealism.

---

1. *Five Essays*, p. 3.

6

George Berkeley (1685-1753)

George Berkeley was the Bishop of Cloyne and a native of Ireland. He was born in 1685 and after his schooling at Kilkenny entered Trinity College, Dublin in 1700. After graduating he remained there as a tutor and fellow for about thirteen years. Towards the end of his life in 1752 he left Cloyne for Oxford and died in 1753 in this land of letters. Berkeley with all his scholarship lived a chaste life of childlike beauty and innocence and by Pope was ascribed to have every virtue under heaven. Again Atterbury is reported to have said to Berkeley 'so much understanding, so much knowledge, so much innocence, and such humility, I did not think had been the portion of any but angels till I saw this gentleman.'

Berkeley wrote many books but the chief works were finished at the age of 29 and the next 40 years did not add much to them. His chief works are *Commonplace Book* (1706-8), *New Theory of Vision* (1709), *Principles of Human Knowledge* (1710), *Three Dialogues* (1713), *Alciphron* (1732), and *Siris* (1744).

6.01. The Problem of Berkeley

Problems of Berkeley: Berkeley lived in an age in which materialism and atheism were slowly making themselves establ3ished. These tendencies were very much strengthened by the sciences of the time. Against them Berkeley holds that the reality of the physical world is essentially spiritual for it manifests the activity of spirit and the goodness of God's will. Towards the end of his life in *Siris* he maintains : "All things are made for the supreme Good, all things tend to that end; and we may be said to account for a thing when we show that it is so best."[1] This spiritualism appeared so obvious to him that he hardly cared to defend it. The main philosophical ingenuity he, therefore, showed in the refutation of materialism. This negative task itself should be based on some philosophy and the philosophy which Berkeley inherited was mainly that of Locke. However, Locke had tacitly assumed the existence of matter, abstract ideas etc. These Berkeley holds to be inconsistent with Lockean empiricism and, therefore, he tried to be a more consistent Locke.

Main tenets of his empirical philosophy were :

1. We always begin with the exclusively particular and distinct sense qualities of heat, colour, smell etc.

    (a) These sense qualities are either directly presented to us, or,

    (b) They may be at once represented to us by way of images.

---

1. *Siris*, iii—247.

2. The same positive thesis may be expressed negatively by saying *nibil est in intellect quod non prius fuerit in sensu*. Thus there is no knowledge that cannot be reduced to sensation.

3. The things like tables or chairs are collections of ideas which often go together and are marked by their specific names.

4. Apart from the ideas, there are spirits that perceive the ideas.

5. Things cannot exist without some mind to perceive them. When there are no human minds, things are sustained by the divine mind.

Finally, then, the reality consists of spirits and their ideas only. This is known as Berkeley's *spiritualism*. The main tenets of Berkeley's philosophy can be stated in his own language.[1]

The *objects* of human knowledge are either

(a) *"ideas* actually imprinted on the senses; or else

(b) *ideas* perceived by attending to the passions and operations of the mind; or lastly

(c) *ideas* formed by help of memory and imagination, either compounding, dividing, or barely representing those originally perceived in the aforesaid ways. . . .

"And as several of those are observed to accompany each other, they come to be marked by one name, and so to be reputed as one *THING*. Thus, for example, a certain colour, taste, smell, figure and consistence having been observed to go together, are accounted one distinct thing, signified by the name *apple;* other collections of idea constitute a stone, a tree, a book, and the like sensible things. . . .

"But besides all that endless variety of ideas or objects of knowledge, there is likewise *something which knows or perceives them, and exercises diverse operations,*—as willing, imagining, remembering,—about them. This perceiving, active being is what I call Mind, spirit, soul, or myself. . . .

"That neither our thoughts nor passions, nor ideas formed by the imagination, exist without the mind, is what everybody will allow.

"And to me it is no less evident that the various *sensations,* or *ideas imprinted in the sense,* however blended or combined together (that is, whatever, *objects* they compose), cannot exist otherwise than in and perceiving them. . . .

"Some truths there are so near and obvious to the mind that a man need only open his eyes to see them. Such I take this important one to be, viz. that all the choir of heaven and furniture of the earth, in a word all those bodies which compose the mighty frame of the world, have not any subsistence without a mind—that their *being* is *to be perceived or known*; that consequently so long as they are not actually perceived by me, or do not exist in my mind or that of any other created spirit, they must either have no existence at all, or else subsist in the mind of some Eternal Spirit."

---

2. Fraser, A.C. 'Selections from Berkeley', Rationale of the principles Sec. 1-7.

6.02. The Refutation of Abstract Ideas

The reality of God was a theme for which Barkeley felt most deeply. His logic is subordinate to that very sovereign interest of his life. He, a therefore, had to contend against materialism which was opposed to spiritualism. For Berkeley, two things indirectly at least supported the cause of materialism, namely, (i) Locke's doctrine of abstract ideas, and, (ii) Science. Berkeley tried to refute the primacy of both of them. And in both cases, he relied on his doctrine of *sensationism*. According to this doctrine, thought is nothing but an image, and an image is simply a reproduction of a past sensation. Thus, sensation is the alpha and omega of any knowledge whatsoever. As sensation deals with particulars, so Berkeley denies the reality of concepts, universal ideas or the essences of things. His doctrine is known as nominalism. Of course, sensationism is too crude a doctrine to account for knowledge and Berkeley himself felt insecure, but inconsistently he persisted in sensationism. He first undertakes to refute the doctrine of abstract ideas.

The chief error of Locke according to Berkeley lies in his doctrine of the abstract ideas. As long as the people will believe in the reality of abstract ideas, they will also believe in the abstract idea of matter. Now Berkeley in criticising Locke really misinterpreted him but his understanding of Locke's idea of abstraction is important in estimating his refutation of abstract ideas. The following process of abstraction is given by Berkeley.[1]

Abstract Ideas: 1. First, we start with particular things as the mixture of different qualities like colour, heat, smell etc.

2. We arbitrarily select any one quality from the other qualities with which in the concrete it was inextricably mixed. For example, we isolate the redness of the rose from its smell, smoothness, softness etc. Thus we form the abstract idea of red colour.

3. The process of abstraction can go farther. We can compare the different abstracted colours like red, green, yellow etc. and can select the quality common to all of them. In this way we frame the more general abstract idea of colour.

4. We can also frame the 'abstract ideas of the more compounded beings which include several co-existent qualities.' In order to get the abstract idea of man we compare several particular men and take out the common qualities of colour-in-general, size-in-general and so on.

Criticism of abstract ideas: Berkeley refutes this doctrine of abstract ideas on logical and psychological grounds. His first point may be called the fallacy of vicious abstraction[2] concerning abstract ideas. Any perceived quality is found inseparably mixed with other qualities. Now what is the guarantee that any quality isolated from the rest can also exist in separation from them? The redness of the

---

1. Introduction to principle; Sec. 7-9. Readers will do well by comparing this account with the real view of Locke given in Sec. 5.09.
2. Introduction, Sec. 7. *Principles,* Secs. 5 and 97.

rose is always found with other qualities of smell, softness, smoothness etc., of the rose. How can we think of the redness existing apart from the other qualities of the rose? This is too arbitrary an assumption to be accepted.

Again, Locke points out that the abstract general idea of a triangle is one "which must be neither oblique nor rectangle, neither equilateral, equicrural, nor scalenon, but all and none of these at once. . . .It is an idea, wherein some parts of several different and inconsistent ideas are put together."[1] But how can we accept to be real something which is at once a congery of inconsistent ideas? The abstract idea of man will be one which is tall and short, fair and dark, dull and intelligent and so on. But how one and the same idea will contain *all* and yet *none* of these? To believe in abstract ideas, is clearly to accept a manifest contradiction.

Lastly, Berkeley takes the help of the psychological method of Introspection.[2] We have no faculty for framing abstract ideas. "For myself, I find I have indeed a faculty of imagining, or representing to myself the idea of those *particular* things I have perceived. . . .But then whatever hand or eye I imagine, it must have some particular shape and colour. Likewise the idea of man that I frame to myself must be either of a white, or a black, or a tawny, a straight, or a croocked, a tall, or a low, or a middle-sized man." Thus we think only of the particular and not of any general man. "And it is equally impossible for me to form the abstract idea of motion distinct from the body moving, and which is neither swift nor slow, curvilinear nor rectilinear; and the like may be said of all abstract ideas whatsoever."

The real aim in the refutation of abstract ideas was to establish *immaterialism*. Matter is an abstract idea for it means something which is moving and stationary, hard and soft etc., all and yet none of these. Besides, it means something *existing* apart from its being perceived. But this is a vicious abstraction for what right have we to maintain that there can be something independent of our perception when everything in our actual experience is always in our perception? Thus matter is an abstract idea but an abstract idea does not exist. Hence matter does not exist. This is the general refutation of matter. Meanwhile, we shall scrutinise his refutation of the abstract ideas.

Note 1. [3]**Abstract ideas are really inconsistent with the empricism of Locke.**[4]

According to Locke, ideas are particular, distinct and unique and they are rendered universal by the operations of thought. But in the *principles* Berkeley does not admit any activity of thought independently of perception. Thus as there are no thoughts there can be no universal element in knowledge. Berkeley himself could not accept this, though it is the real consistent view of the empiricism of Locke. He saw that real knowledge must be general but he himself could not give any real explanation for the thesis of empiricism of the type of Locke which

1. Introduction of Principles, Sec. 13.
2. Introduction to Principles, Sec. 10, 11, 13
3. This along with Note 2 may be omitted in the first reading of the book.
4. Lindsay, A., in *Introduction to New Theory of Vision and Principles.*

precludes its possibility. Anyway once we grant that there is nothing in intellect which was not given in sense, we have to grant further that there could be no abstract universal ideas.

If the ideas are particular and unique with nothing in common with other ideas then, how can there be any common element between them? And without common quality we cannot form the universal abstract ideas. If the ideas of blue, yellow etc., have nothing in common, how can we form a common general idea of colour?

Even if we grant that the common element can be found by comparing the ideas, the question still remains, how can we do it? In order to abstract certain elements we have to notice the points of similarity and difference between them. For example, in order to form the abstract idea of man we retain the common elements found in particular men, by ignoring the elements in which they differ. But this seeing of difference or similarity, say between the sensations of red and blue, is itself not a sensation. This capacity of noting likeness or difference can be given by no sense-organs, but really is due to the functioning of the intellect. If, like Berkeley, we do not admit the function of intellect and confine ourselves to sensations alone, then there can be no seeing of likeness and difference between the ideas and as such there can be no abstract ideas.

Thus consistently speaking abstract ideas do not follow from the sensationism of Locke and Berkeley. But this very point should have led to the departure from the Lockean sensationism, for it does not explain the general element in knowledge. Knowledge of its very nature is conceptual. What we say should be clear to others; but this means that there is something common between our words and the words of others. Thus without some common and universal elements there is no possibility of knowledge. Seeing this Berkeley writes :[1] "And here it is to be noted that I do not deny absolutely there are general ideas, but only there are any *abstract* general ideas." And, again, in sec. 15 of the *introduction*, he notes : "It is, I know, a point much insisted on, that all knowledge and demonstration are about universal notion, to which I fully agree." Now Berkeley taking his stand on sensationism had to grapple all his life to explain the possibility of general ideas. But his solution could not take a final shape for he had taken his stand on the questionable assumption of sensationism for explaining knowledge.

Note 2. **General notions according to Berkeley.**[2]

There are general ideas but they can be anything but abstract ideas. The ideas of their very nature, whether given in perception or imagination, Berkeley points out, are concrete and therefore, '*abstract* ideas' is a contradiction in terms. Hence Berkeley is obliged to give various accounts of general ideas. There are six possible views which he expresses about them, namely,— the function of the universality in knowledge may be carried by (1) Particular things, (2) Particular images, or (3)

---

1.   Introduction to principles, Sec. 12, also see Sec. 15.
2.   Johnston, G.A., *Development of Berkeley's Philosophy*, pp. 124-41. Also see Morris, C.S., *Lock, Berkeley, Hume*, pp. 86-96.

names, or (4) Meanings, or (5) signs, or (6) notions. Berkeley makes use of all these views and towards his matured years prefers (6) to all others. The function of notions *looms* large when he comes to account for our knowledge of spirits, operations of spirits and relations. The last element concerning notion, we shall consider in relation to the knowledge of spirits. In the remaining five views of universality in knowledge a certain development of Berkeley's thought may be traced. In *Commonplace Book* (1706-1708) the predominant views are primarily (3) and also (1). In *Principles* (1710) he makes a further development. Here he discards (3) and adheres to (1), (2), and (4). In *Alciphron* (1732) the doctrine of signs is most clearly stated.

I. *A particular thing or image becomes general by standing for all similar particulars.*[1] For example we draw a triangle and prove that all its <s=2 rt. angles. Here the idea is of a particular triangle but it becomes general by standing for of representing all other particular triangles. Similarly, an image of a line or a triangle may serve the purpose of Geometrical demonstration. Only the image is doubly representative. First, an image stands for a sensible figure and thus a sensible figure stands for all other particular sensible figures of the same sort. Thus "An idea, which considered itself is particular becomes general by being made to represent or stand for all other particular ideas of the same sort." (Sec. 12 of Introduction to Principles).

II. *Universality may be considered not to belong to things but to the* **names** *which designate them.* Berkeley in his early work of Commonplace Book thought that every word has a regular and uniform signification. By virtue of this the same name applies to a large number of similar things. However, this extreme nominalism he discards even at the stage of the *Principles* for he soon saw that "There is no such thing as one precise and definite signification annexed to any general name."

6.03. The Refutation of Matter

A. *The refutation of matter as an abstract idea:* Berkeley's whole aim was religious. He refuted the doctrine of abstract ideas not so much because it was inconsistent with empiricism but because it supported matter. He believed in sensationism because it at once gave him a weapon of attack against the sciences which supported the reality of matter and motion. Thus Berkeley believed in spiritualism, for which he hardly adduced any real proof, but this necessitated the refutation of materialism. This negative task was the most serious thing he ever undertook to prove. We have already seen the general refutation of matter on the ground that it is an abstract idea. But he attempts this refutation most systematically.

---

1. Principles sec. 12, 15 and 16
2. Introduction Sec. 18 For details see Johnston, *Ibid.*

B. No matter besides ideas. THE REFUTATION BY A CRITICISM OF THE DISTINCTION BETWEEN PRIMARY AND SECONDARY QUALITIES : There is some justification for the vulgar, says Berkeley, in wrongly clinging to the existence of matter, but philosophers ought to have been wiser. However, both Descartes and Locke believed in an independent material world which our ideas somehow copy. Berkeley criticises this representative theory of ideas in acquiring knowledge, with great success. If we are merely confined to ideas alone, how can 'we know whether our ideas are true or false copies? This we could have judged if we were allowed to compare the copy with its original. But *ex hypothesi* we are so made that we can know the ideas and not the things directly. Thus Berkeley points out that as long as we believe in an external world, we are eternally condemned to scepticism. Here, again, Berkeley tries to make Locke consistent by simplifying perception. According to Locke perception is due to the affecting of the sense-organs by the external world. Berkeley refutes this external world and retains mind only, as the cause and source of ideas.

Again, Berkeley with great acumen pointed out that Locke had wrongly followed Descartes in holding the distinction between *primary* and *secondary* qualities.[1] According to Locke and Descartes, the primary qualities of extension, figure, solidity, motion, rest and number are supposed to be really in things and the secondary qualities of colour, heat, cold etc., are supposed to be in the perceiver and not in the things. But obviously the so-called primary qualities are also ideas. Ideas are mental. Therefore, even the primary qualities are mental.

The distinction of primary and secondary qualities is unjustified: Again, primary qualities of extension, solidity etc., never exist apart from the secondary ones. Who can imagine extension without its being coloured etc. What right have we to say, then, that primary qualities can also exist in things apart from the secondary ones? This is nothing but vicious abstraction. Hence we must conclude that both must have the same kind of existence. As the secondary qualities are taken to be mental, so the so-called primary should also be regarded as mental.

Besides, the experiment of Locke showed that the same bucket of water may seem hot or hotter, cold or colder by suitably interchanging one's hands in buckets of cold and hot water. Therefore, he held that the secondary qualities are *relative*. But this relativity is true of the primary qualities as well. Against Newton, he holds that every motion is relative. The same man on the boat is said to be stationary in relation to the moving steamer and, again, moving in relation to the man standing on the bank. The same relativity is true of number as well. The same yardstick may be called either three feet long or thirtysix inches long. Thus if the secondary qualities are said to be subjective because they are relative, then the primary ones should also be regarded as subjective for they are also relative.

---

1.   Principles IX XV.

Lastly, the primary qualities can no more be perceived without the sense-organs than the secondary ones. Extension, as he shows in *The New Theory of Vision*, is entirely dependent on our touch and vision.

Thus all qualities are really subjective and mind-dependent and there is no necessity of assuming matter in which the primary qualities are wrongly supposed to be existing.

C. A systematic refutation: Now Berkeley undertakes to refute the existence of matter on any doctrine whatsoever. If there is matter then it can be shown to have the following alternatives.

1. Matter is directly perceptible.

2. If it be not immediately perceptible, then its existence is inferred either on the strength of the

      (i)   Likeness of our ideas, or,

      (ii)   As the cause of the ideas, or

      (iii)   As the instrument of our ideas, or

      (iv)   As the occasion of the ideas.

3. If matter be shown to be neither perceived nor inferred, then it must be shown to have some use, either religious, moral or practical.

Now Berkeley takes up all these alternatives one by one and shows that matter is neither perceived nor inferred nor has any use. Thus it does not exist at all.

(i) *Matter is not perceived*: If matter be perceived at all, it must be perceived either by the eye or ear or nose etc. But if it be perceived by the nose then it is smell; and if by the eye, then it is some colour and so on. But *ex hypothesi* matter is not any quality but is the supporter of it. But Locke himself points out that the supporter of the qualities is 'I-know-not-what'. Thus matter as the substratum of the qualities is not perceived.[1] Again, if matter were really perceptible, then it will be as variable as our perceptions. But matter is supposed to be invariable, permanent and stable. Therefore it cannot be our variable perception. Lastly, even if it be perception, it is an idea. An idea is mental. Therefore, matter is really mental. If a thing is mental, then it cannot be material.

Therefore, we conclude that there is no perceived matter.

(ii) *The existence of matter is not based on Inference*: If matter be not perceived, we may say that its existence is inferred. We may suppose that it is *like* our ideas. But we have just seen that matter is supposed to be permanent but our ideas are variable. How can matter be like dissimilar ideas? Again, matter we have seen to be insensible but ideas are all sensible. But an insensible matter can no more be like the sensible ideas than colour be like something invisible.[2]

Thus matter cannot be inferred to be like our ideas. But it may be taken as the *cause* of the ideas. Our ideas are independent of our will, may not therefore matter be the cause of our inactive, fleeting and variable ideas? Even this cannot be

---

1. Principles, sec. 18.
2. Principles, sec. 8 and 25.

granted. First, if there be matter, how can it act upon the mind? This has been considered to be unintelligible. Besides, Berkeley following the contemporary thought, looked upon matter as purely inert, passive and inactive. Now, how something inactive should be regarded as the active agent of the ideas? This is contradiction in terms. Again the cause and effect are of the same nature. Now the unthinking matter can produce only an unthinking effect but it cannot produce the thinking ideas, i.e., ideas dependent on the spirits who think.

Now the materialist may hit upon a third expedient. "Though matter may not be a cause", says Hylas, "yet what hinders its being an instrument, subservient to the supreme Agent in the production of our ideas?" Now an instrument is necessary only when thing cannot be achieved by an act of will. But God's will is sufficient to produce any effect. Hence there can be no need of an instrument called matter in the hands of God.

Lastly, however, the materialist may point out that though matter cannot be regarded as the copy, cause or instrument, yet it may mean "an inert, senseless substance, that exists without the mind or unperceived, which is the *occasion* of our ideas, or at the presence whereof God is pleased to excite ideas in us."[1] First, a substance without qualities is as impossible as the qualities without the substance are inconceivable. Besides, if a substance is purely inert, inactive etc., then is it not purely nothing? Again, the word 'occasion' may mean either (a) a causal agent, or (b) something which accompanies or precedes the events. Now we have seen that matter being insensible can neither precede nor accompany any event. Thus the matter cannot be the occasion of ideas.

Thus we conclude that the existence of matter cannot be inferred on any ground.

(iii) *The existence of matter serves no useful purpose:* Now the materialist is forced to withdraw to his last ditch. He may choose to use the word 'matter' as unknown somewhat—a something purely inert, thoughtless, indivisible, unmovable, inextended, existing in no place.[2] Thus he ultimately rests his laurels on the grandeur of an empty name. But even this cannot be conceded. First, an unknown somewhat is scarcely different from pure *nothing*. Again, pure existence as somewhat apart from other qualities is the wildest of abstract ideas and therefore is open to the worst objections against abstract ideas. Lastly, it involves the fallacy of *regress ad infinitum*. If the concept of the unknown substratum is necessary to support the sensible thing, then this unknown substratum also needs a further support leading to infinite regress.

Hence we conclude that the existence of matter cannot be held for it involves a contradiction and serves no useful purpose. Instead of doing any good, it leads to atheism and materialism which shut us from the very source of life and light, according to Berkeley. Philosophically speaking, the notion of matter serves no

---

1.   Principles, Sec. 67-70.
2.   Principles, Sec. 80-81.

useful purpose since it gives rise to the knotty problem of mind-body relation. Further, it would lead to scepticism. If matter exists unsensed and unknown by the mind, then no knowledge concerning it is possible. We will not only know its real nature, but we will not know even this much that it exists, For we have, *per* supposition, no ideas of it.

With regard to the refutation of matter a problem has been posed. Was Berkeley a metaphysician or an idealist or an analytic philosopher? Prof. A. J. Ayer maintained that Locke and Berkeley were not metaphysicians so much as they were analytic philosophers.

> Nor is it fair to regard Berkeley as a metaphysician. For did not in fact deny the reality of material things, as we are still too commonly told. What he denied was the adequacy of Locke's analysis of the notion of a material thing.[1]

Against this observation of Prof. A.J. Ayer, we are holding that Berkeley was essentially a metaphysician. He did take the help of analysis but only in subservience to his idealistic vision. He was full of the vision of God and the finite spirits. He analysed away matter, because the existence of matter did not fit into his metaphysical vision. For this reason Berkeley did not carry his empiricism to its logical conclusion with regard to the reality of God and the knowledge of selves. Here both Russell and Ayer remark that Berkeley has committed error in accepting the reality of God and spirits. If Berkeley were primarily an empirical analyst, then his error in accepting God and spirits were indefensible. But a metaphysician takes the central things in his vision to be real and subordinates all cognitive prepositions to that end.

Berkeley was in favour of using precise language, for he wanted us to 'draw the curtain of words to behold the fairest tree of knowledge'[2] But he also knew that "......the communicating of ideas marked by words is not the chief and only end of language, as is commonly supposed. There are other ends as the raising of some passion, the exciting to or deterring from an action, the putting the mind in some particular disposition—to which the former is in many cases subservient".[3]

Hence, Berkeley has analytic method and cognitive statements as subservient to his vision of God. For him the whole of nature is the language of God. Hence, we think that Berkeley was a metaphysician and that he has used 'analysis' in the service of his metaphysics.

6.04. The Theory of Knowledge

Berkeley based his theory of knowledge on that of Locke. He no doubt criticised

---

1. *Language, Truth and Logic*, p. 53. See also pp. 139-40.
2. Selections, p. 26.
3. Supra 03(B).

it and even simplified it but did not sufficiently analyse it. From this lack of adequate analysis his system looked too unconvincing even to his own contemporaries.

According to Berkeley knowledge may be reduced to two heads of ideas and of spirits. The so-called ideas are also of two kinds, namely, (a) the ideas imprinted on the senses, and (b) the ideas formed by memory and imagination. The ideas of senses are either ideas of particular sensible qualities like heat, colour, smell or else they may be a collection of suh qualities called a thing. The different kinds of knowledge, according to Berkeley, may be thus expressed.

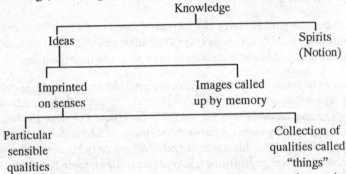

The ideas of imagination differ from those of the senses in certain important respects.[1] The sensible ideas are strong, lively and distinct but their images are faint and sketchy. Besides, the ideas of sense have a certain steadiness, order and coherence, but the ideas of imagination are jumbled together. Lastly, the ideas of sense have certain forcefulness by virtue of which they are independent of the will. But the ideas of imagination depend on one's fancy.

His system further shows the following characteristics of ideas. We get the ideas *directly* and *immediately*. This directness of knowledge is an important contribution as was realised by the new realists of the twentieth century. He arriveed at this by a criticism of the representative function of ideas. To this we have already alluded.[2] Consistently following the criticism of representative status of ideas he points out that the images too are directly received. Thus in the early phase of *principles* he holds that thinking=imaging=sensing. Later on Berkeley had to modify his position and accepted almost its opposite thesis.

Again, Berkeley simplified Locke by denying the extramental world of material things. Locke believed that in perception there are three elements, namely; (i) Percipient, (ii) the external objects and (iii) the ideas within the percipient, standing for the objects. We have now seen that Berkeley refutes the existence of the external objects and we have also seen that the copy-theory of ideas does not explain

1.   Selections, p. 26
2.   Principles, Sec. 29-30.

knowledge. Therefore, according to Berkeley ideas are themselves things, known directly and immediately. Thus instead of three, according to Berkeley, there are only two elements in perception, namely (i) and (ii).

Berkeley tried to base his whole theory of knowledge on the basis of perception alone. Curiously enough Berkeley in the last resort always appeals to the uncorrupted commonsense and unprejudiced observation and yet the ordinary man always believes that his perception is not the thing but is representative of the thing. For example, we get the sensation of sound on the ringing of the bell but the sound itself is not the bell. His theory of direct perception is at the root of his difficulty. But his own important analysis of the perception of distance shows that perception need not be direct. He himself shows that we judge the tangible distance with the help of visible signs. The present-day thinkers are agreed that in perception at least there are two elements, namely the psychical process and the real object to which it refers.

"Presentation are always contents of immediate experience; but they are not themselves the things that they present. They perform the function of presenting objects that are not themselves contents of immediate experience. . .What he calls ideas bear much resemblance to presentions, but in distinction from them they are presentative of nothing apart from themselves. Ideas for Berkeley are both presentations and what presentations are presentative of."[1] Thus his 'idea' suffers from want of adequate analysis.

Again, Berkeley like Locke takes mind to be purely passive in the reception of ideas. We may grant that the mind is passive in the reception of simple ideas, but the formation of complex ideas 'requires mental activity', as Locke held. But Berkeley seems to hold that the complex ideas of things are due to the passivity of the mind. Yet even in the *Dialogues* he has to admit that we construct and not merely receive the idea of the 'same' object. "Strictly speaking, Hylas, we do not see the same object that we feel;. . .Therefore. . .men combine together several ideas apprehended by diverse senses or by the same sense at different times. . ."[2]

Knowledge of spirits: The knowledge of spirits is not through ideas. This special distinction which he introduced is of great importance. Ideas are variable, fleeting and momentary. Had he held mind to be a collection of ideas, as Hume later on did, then there would have been no reality except of the succession of ideas. This would have meant complete scepticism. Berkeley refers to this in the *dialogues* (i, 449.51). But he retained mind on the ground of its expediency. If there be no permanent minds, then no knowledge is possible. Besides, there is nothing inconsistent in its existence. Again, Berkeley felt that religious and moral values could be safeguarded by believing in the existence of spirits. For all these reasons Berkkeley believed in the exiistence of spirits. But the question is, if we have no

1. Johnston, G.A., *Berkeley*, p. 153-54.
2. Dialogues i. 463-64 and again 469.

302 A Critical History of Western Philosophy

ideas of spirits, then how do we know them? Berkeley relies that we know the spirits by having notion of them. What is 'notion', then?

The word 'notion' has not been cleared by Berkeley. It is a great pity that the philosopher who wrote 'we need only draw the curtain of words, to behold the fairest tree of knowledge' should have lost himself in a pure verbal subtlety. Following Sergeant, he seems to have used notions and ideas in the following ways:

(1) Ideas are sensible, but notions are intelligible and conceptual, (2) Ideas are particular but notions are universal, (3) Brutes have ideas in common with man but notions are found in man alone.

Notions are very much like reflection of Locke but they differ from reflection in scope and nature. Reflection is essentially sensible for there seems to be an internal sense which tells us about the operations of the soul. But notions are intellectual. Besides, reflection is concerned about ideas as well, but the notions have three objects only, namely, (a) Spirit, (b) Mental operations, and (c) Relation. The objects of a notion then are mental or spiritual. Ideas may be described as the objects of the objects of notions, for all the objects of notion are concerned with ideas. The very essence of *spirits* consists in the causing and perceiving ideas; *mental operations*, are essentially 'acts about ideas'; and *relations* are found 'between ideas'.

The more Berkeley thought, the more he was inclined to emphasize the conceptual element in knowledge. However, this was the antithesis of what he held in the *Principles., Commonplace Book* and *Dialogues*. The thing is that he began against sciences because they supported materialism. The sciences were essentially conceptual in character, therefore, he first denounced the sciences on the ground that the real knowledge is sensationalistic. This would have made the knowledge of spirits impossible. But the refutation of matter was undertaken to support spiritualism, somehow then the spirits must be known by means other than that of ideas. This led to the doctrine of spirits. The more he thought about the existence of spirits and the methods of sciences in the light of his later Platonic readings, the more inclined he was towards the intellect, concept and thought.[1] Following Platonic distinction of sense and understanding he comes very nearly to the Kantian division of sensibility and understanding in *Siris*. "Strictly the sense knows nothing . . . .As understanding perceiveth not, that is, doth not hear, or see, or feel, so sense knoweth not: and although the mind may use both sense and fancy, as means whereby to arrive at knowledge, yet sense or soul, so far forth as sensitive, knoweth nothing."[2] This admission was really a revolution rather than evolution in his thought. But Berkeley never undertook to reconstruct his philosophy on this new foundation.

---

1. *Siris* iii. 243-49.
2. *Ibid.,* p. 271.

6.05. The Existence of Spirits

The essence of a thing, as distinguished from that of spirits, consists in being perceived. But the essence of spirits consists in their being *perceived* or perceiving. If spirits were nothing but ideas, then everything would have been reduced to mere succession of ideas and no permanence could be established. Thus in order to explain the permanence of things, the existence of spirits must be granted. The very essence of a spirit consists in activity,— in its active principle of producing motion and change. Now there are three kinds of spirits, namely, (i) Myself, (ii) Other finite spirits like myself, and (iii) The infinite spirit or God.

I am intuitively aware of my own existence. First, I am aware of the happening of the ideas of colour, heat etc., as *mine*. Besides, I am immediately aware of myself in my activity of (a) calling up mental images, and (b) of producing changes in my body and other things through volition. Thus perceptually and volitionally I am convinced of my existence.

The existence of other spirits is based on inference by analogy. The finite spirits are passive in the reception of presentations but they are active in the reproduction of images and in exciting changes in their own bodies or in the bodies of others and other things to a limited extent. Now we can know the presence of other finite spirits by virtue of their exciting changes in things. We know our own activities in causing changes and when we find that similar changes are taking place, then we can infer the existence of other finite spirits like ourselves. For example, we have made a table and when we find a similar table, then we can infer that there are similar beings like ourselves who have made the table.

The existence of the infinite spirit can be known in the following way[1] : I am aware of a succession of ideas in me. 2. There must be some cause of them which is either, (a) matter, or (b) some other idea or (c) spirit. Now (a) and (b) being passive cannot be active agents or causes. 3. Now the causes must be a spirit, but the finite spirits are incapable of producing ideas of fixed order on such a vast scale. Besides, many of the ideas which compose nature like the rivers, mountains and falls are independent of their will. 4. Therefore, God alone is the cause of all ideas. Besides, the surprising magnificence, beauty and perfection of nature confirm us in this belief. Thus if we know other spirits by their operations in us, through finite and narrow assemblage of ideas they excite in us, then the existence of God is more manifest to us. We know God "withersoever we direct our view, we do at all times and in all places perceive manifest tokens of the Divinity…everything we see, hear, feel, or any wise perceive by Sense, being a *sign* or *effect* of the power of God."[2] The whole of Nature is the living language of God be-speaking of His Goodness, Wisdom and Presence to all.

---

1. Principles, Sec. 145-150. Also see Johnston G.A. Berkeley, p. 194.
2. Principles, Sec. 148.

This insistence on activity as the essence of spirits has important conclusion with regard to causation. According to Berkeley, God is the real cause of spirits and things. In nature there is nothing like cause and effect. God arranges the succession of events according to His own fiat of will. Of course God, chooses the ideas to take place in regular and uniform order, known as the laws of nature. This fixed character of events follows from the Will of God, though it is arbitrary yet it is not whimsical. God could have produced any thing in order, different from what it is. He might arrange the sun to give us cold instead of heat and He might change the whole gradual process of nature. He does not do this in our own interest. From the regular order we can gain an insight into the working of nature and the knowledge so gained is beneficial to us for the wise regulation of life. Besides, the complex machinery of nature serves the function of educating mankind in learning to reproduce the machines on smaller scales.[1] Berkeley clearly lays down that everything in nature being passive cannot be the cause of another. They are conjoined but not connected. One idea is not the cause of the other but is the sign or the prognostic of the other. "The fire which I see is not the cause of the pain I suffer upon approaching it, but the *mark* that forewarns me of it."[2]

Criticism of the proof concerning spirits: Berkeley is not very careful in relation to spirits. As a matter of fact he simply assumes their existence. Here he encounters difficulties almost at every step. First, he departs from his strict empiricism or sensationalism in as much as he resorts to 'notion' to justify the existence of spirits. Now we have seen that notion may be anything but cannot be sense-perception. Besides, do we really know the self ? Is not the self-certainty of Descartes an illusion? Kant who grappled with this difficulty had to declare that self-knowledge is only a transcendental illusion called *the paralogism* of reason. Again, how can we know the existence of the other finite selves ? Berkeley points out that we know the existence of other spirits by the effects which they excite in us. But are not these effect the passive ideas? How from *passive* ideas can we know the existence of the *active* spirits? Can we not hurl back the arguments for the nonexistence of matter, against the existence of spirits?[3] Lastly, what can be said about the finite spirits can be repeated in relation to God. The knowledge of God as He is for Himself is as impossible for us to know, as is the case with matter. Berkeley then resorts to the existence of spirits on extralogical grounds of morality and religion. Thus with Morris[4] we conclude thus: "It is clear that Berkeley's views about our apprehension of spirit are a mass of half-articulated dogmas. Even the dogma is only half-hearted, for while Berkeley seems bravely to assume that spiritual causation and spiritual activity generally are wholly intelligible, as contrasted with matter, he knows, and admits, that the ways of God, who is pure spirit, are unknowable by us."

---

1. Principles, sec. 60-64.
2. *Ibid.,* 65.
3. Indeed Berkeley was aware of this, ". . . .to me it seems that according to your own way of thinking, and in consequence of your own principles, it should follow that you are only a system of floating ideas, without any substance to support them. . . and as there is no more meaning in *spiritual substance* than in *material* substance, the one is to be explored as well as the other" (see, p. 163).
4. *Ibid.,* p. 101.

6.06. The Idealism of Berkeley

Berkeley has contributed in a significant manner both to epistemology and idealism. His epistemology has been considered to be a chain in the development of thought from Locke to Hume through Berkeley. But Berkeley himself considered his theory of knowledge to be secondary to his idealism. Hence that which is of abiding interest in observation of Prof. A.J. Ayer, we have maintained that empirical analysis of matter and substance, causation etc., in the system of Berkeley remains subservient to his idealistic aim and purpose. We would attempt to show this in the following way.

Idealism is that systematic philosophy which teaches the supremacy of spirits over matter. Berkeley's system is idealistic, since it teaches that reality consists of spirits and their ideas only. However, he establishes this idealistic conclusion as the implication of his famous maxim *esse est percipi* and of *percipere*. We may ignore for the present his theory concerning 'spirit', and may concentrate on *esse est percipi*. With regard to esse est percipi, Berkeley shows that the essence of anything in principle consists of ideas. As he uses the term 'ideas' both in the sense of mental *states* or activities and of *objects*, so he quietly ignores the latter sense in favour of their being mental content or states in order to establish his idealistic conclusion. His arguments can be stated thus.

Berkeley takes for granted that any sensation which is relative must be mental. If heat or cold or sweet were objective, then they would be felt to be the same by all persons and by the same person at different times. As the perceptions of heat, cold, colour, motion, extension are all variable and relative to human perceivers, so they are all, according to Berkeley, mind-dependent, subjective states or mental.

Again, it is proved that sweetness is not really in the sapid thing, because the thing remaining unaltered the sweetness is changed into bitter, as in case of fever or otherwise vitiated palate. It is not as reasonable to say that motion is without the mind, since if the succession of ideas in the mind become swifter, the motion, it is acknowledged, shall appear slower without any alternation in any external object ?[1]

Again, in '*A dialogue concerning the principles*', the same teaching concerning the ideas of colour, heat etc., to be mental is elaborated. Here also Berkeley maintains:

And, nothing can be plainer than that diverse persons perceive different tastes in the same food, since that which one man delights in, another abhors. And how could this be, if the taste was something really inherent in the food?[2]

---

1. Selections, pp. 42-43, Principles, sec. 14.
2. Selections, p. 129.

Further, Berkeley takes the instance of 'pain'. Pain being a state of affective feeling is subjective and mental. So heat, the most intense form of which is pain, is also mental.

Hence, Berkeley concludes that it is absurd to suppose that perception can exist without the mind. However, according to Berkeley, from the ideality of all things it cannot be inferred that things are shadows or evanescent etc.

If everything is an idea, then have we not reduced everything to shadows and fancy ? No, says Berkeley, we fully make the distinction, between the real and fanciful ideas. The real world has in it clear, distinct coherent, orderly and objective ideas. The world of fancy is full of vague, transitory and incoherent ideas. The real world is coherent enough to have the eternal laws in it. According to the *principles*, the world becomes all the more real, for we point out that alone is real which we feel, taste and smell.

Externality of things. If everything is an idea or a group of ideas 'in' the mind then the question will arise, are there no things external to the mind ? In order to answer this question we have to make clear the meanings of 'ideas' and 'in the mind'. First, the things are ideal but the are real. It may sound rather harsh if we say that we eat and drink ideas. But we should think with the learned and speak with the vulgar. The things, as opposed to spirits, are nothing but ideas. Secondly, the phrase, 'in the mind' need not exclude the externality of things. 'In the mind' need not mean that things have their locus within the ego. It really means that a thing has entered into the knowledge-relationship with the subject. When we say that nothing can be outside the mind, it means that the subject-object relationship is so universal and pervading that nothing can escape it. Thus having explained the prejudice we can point out the externality of things in the following ways.

1. First, things are said to be external in the sense that they are the objects for human subjects or perceivers. So Berkeley instead of subjectifying things tries to objectify ideas. "I am not for changing things into ideas but rather ideas into things."[1]

2. Again, things are said to be external in the sense that they are independent of the will of the individual perceiver. If we open our eyes, then it is not up to us whether there be hot or cold, red or green sensations for us.

3. Things are said to be external to us in the sense that they are caused by the supreme spirit or God who is external to any finite spirits.

4. Most probably there are real archetypes or original ideas in the mind of God which our ideas somehow copy and reproduce. Thus the real ideas are external to the human perception.

5. Lastly, ideas are external in the sense that the reality of things is not fully exhausted by my perception. A thing may not be in the mind of an individual spirit

---

1. Dialogues i : 463.

but it may be in the mind of other finite spirits.

Another question regarding the permanence of things may crop up. If things are ideas then they will be fleeting and transitory like ideas.[1] First, Berkeley points out that it is not so absurd for the schoolmen and even the Minute Philosophers have taught the doctrine of the prepetual creation and annihilation of things. But things need not be transitory like the ideas for they are not exhausted by the perception of any one individual. Things may exist even when we may not be perceiving at a particular moment. They may exist as the *permanent possibility of perception,* as determined by the sure and well grounded predictions. For example, we have not seen the motion of the Earth and yet it exists as a possibility of perception. If the well calculated disadvantages of time and distance be removed, then we will be able to perceive it.

Permanence of things: Besides, even when one finite spirit is not perceiving, the things may be sustained in their existence by the perception of other finite spirits. For example, I may not be looking at the table, yet it may exist for other spirtis like myself may be perceiving it. Lastly, even when no finite spirits are perceiving, the things exist for they are constantly perceived by God. Ultimately, the permanence of things is explained by the eternal divine thoughts. Things are not only perceived but they are willed or caused by God. The divine will creates things according to a fixed and uniform order and thus gives the character of self-existence and permanence to things. Berkeley favoured the creation of the archetypes in the mind of God in which afterwards, they exist as permanent perception. Thus from a human viewpoint things are constantly changing but they are really permanent.

6.07. Is Berkeley's Idealism Subjective?
The term 'subjective' is rather vague. Most probably it means that only 'subjects' are real and 'objects' as independent of the mind are not real. Hence, nature, which is considered to be 'the other' of mind, according to subjective idealism is not real. Therefore, subjective idealism holds that Nature is merely the projection of some minds and has no existence of its own. In this sense, Berkeley's idealism is subjective, since according to it nothing exists of consciousness, then this interpretation would reduce subjective idealism to *solipsism,* according to which theory all things and other spirits are so many states of consciousness of a single individual thinker. For simple, we say that this blade of grass is green. Now how can we be certain that A or B is not enough, for we know that to the colour-blind nothing appears red or green. Yet he learns to call a certain patch as 'green' which really appears to him as a shade of grey or brown. Similarly, nobody can ever verify that a certain shade of colour or a certain degree of sweetness or warmth

---

1. Principles, sec. 45-48.

is actually exprienced by another individual. If it is so, then what appears to me is real for me and has no validity for others. But who are others ? How can we be sure of the existence of other spirits ? According to Berkeley, we know the existence of other spirits by the effects they produce on the perceiver and other objects. But certainly those effects are ideas and ideas are the furniture of an individual mind at the time they are entertained. In dreams also we perceive many individuals and many objects, though all of them are the projections of the dreamer's mind alone, who knows we are dreaming all the time ? Most probably there can be no way out of solipsism, if we accept the subjectivity of an idea. The sense-data theory is a way out of solipsism. This supposes that our sense data are neither mental nor material. They are the simples, rockbottom, primary elements of knowledge. But the whole sense-data theory is only a procedural presupposition, a mere convention or recommendation in epistemology. Berkeley did not suspect that his 'idealism' would lead to solipsism. He assumed the reality of other finite spirits besides himself and certainly of God. Hence, Berkeley was not a solipsist. Was he a subjectivist only? Against subjectivist, Berkeley maintained:

"Many things, for aught I know, may exist, whereof neither I nor any other man hath or can have any idea or notion whatsoever."[1]

Further, Berkeley maintained that there is a real world, independent of any human subject. The distinction between the real world and the world of fancy is as follows:

1. The objective world is characterised by strong, lively and vivid ideas: whereas the world of fancy is characterised by fleeting ideas.

2. Again, the ideas of the real world are orderly and coherent, and are knit together by the so-called laws of nature; whereas, the world of fancy is loosely connected and has an arbitrary order of ideas.

3. Lastly, the real world is independent of the will of individual perceivers; but the world of fancy or fiction is dependent on the will of human subjects.

Now if Berkeley grants that there is an objective world, independently existing of the human mind, then why should his system be called subjective idealism? Well, the objectivity of the world does not logically follow from Berkeley's theory of ideas. Berkeley held the reality, externality and permanence of the real world on the basis of divine perception. Does not this admission mean a departure from *esse est percipi*? Is it not a fact that the reality of things cannot be maintained on the basis of *human* perception, since it is relative, transitory and arbitrary? Can divine perception, which eternally sustains all things be called perception at all? Have we not lumped together two distinct elements of knowledge by a common name? Divine perception is eternal and permanent, creative and productive;

---

1.   Selections-p. 162.

whereas, human perception is variable and transitory and at most is only recreative or re-productive. Besides, we perceive with the senses but "God perceives nothing by sense as we do. . . .God knows, or hath ideas, but his ideas are not conveyed to him by sense, as ours are."[1] If the distinction is so great then the divine perception is no human perception. Thus *esse est percipi* is no longer true in the original sense of 'perception.'

Berkeley points out that when an idea is not perceived by me then *it* is perceived by God. But the it perceived by God is eternal, archetypal and original and the *it* perceived by me is temporal and derivative. The question will arise, how on earth are we to know that there is an archetypal and eternal perception in the mind of God, for *ex hypothesi* we are shut up in our temporal perception? Even the divine perception as perceived by human beings is humanised perception and is no longer divine. Thus three possibilities follow from the distinction between human and divine perception.

(a) The divine perception as it is really in the mind of God is not known by human perception.

(b) The divine perception is the same as human perception.

(c) The divine perception is much fuller than ours but is essentially of the same nature as ours.

The first admission would amount to scepticism, the second will give rise to subjective idealism or *Solipsism* and the third position is of objective idealism. Berkeley does not work out these possibilities and has left his position very vague. From his point of view there are three-degrees of the reality of things :

1. The archetypal and eternal ideas in the mind of God.

2. The ectypal or secondary ideas as are perceived by human subjects and are the reproductions of divine perceptions.

3. Mental ideas which are framed by human imagination.

The first type of ideas, according to Berkeley, has the most, and, the third kind has the least reality.

2. There is another reason why Berkeley's idealism could not remain objective.

According to Berkeley the things are nothing but our perception of them. But perceptions are always relative and changeable. No two perceptions of A and B can be the same. Therefore, no two persons will have the same world. This will reduce us to the sceptical maxim of Protagoras 'Homo mensura', - so many worlds as many minds. It cuts the very root of universality and objectivity. Objectivity in philosophy means an identical reference for all minds. The objective idealists hold that the world is a system of thoughts or reason. We human beings are so made that we know things through certain categories or concepts of substance, causality, Space, Time etc. These are the same for all. We have the same objective

2. Dialogues i. 459.

world for we have the same concepts or thoughts which constitute the universe. As long as we believe in the constituents of thoughts which go to make the world and are shared equally by all subjects we will have true objective world. Thus the rationality of the universe alone explains inter-subjective and trans-subjective reference to the same thing.

3. Further, if the *esse* of a thing is not its *percipi* but its *intelligi*, as Kant and the Kantians have held, then they have to remain as an organic system. It was the genius of Hegel which showed that the categories that constitute the reality of things are found in a logical system. The categories are so arranged that we can proceed, step by step, from the poorest category of 'Being' to the most concrete and the rich category of the 'Absolute' through a dialectical order of thesis, antithesis and synthesis. Thus, the reality of things is constituted by the categories and these categories are logically or rationally related. Hence, for Hegel, the most prominent objective idealist, the real is rational. There is no arbitrariness, according to Hegel, anywhere., Berkeley did not go so far. He maintained that the world is sustained by the will of God and the order and system formed in it can change. Hence, the subjective will of God is real, according to Berkeley. As against this, Hegel holds that the logical order is the same for all. Hence, the world being logical or rational is objective for all, according to the objective idealists. Therefore, Berkeley's idealism, being based on God's subjective will is subjective and not objective.

4. Besides we have already noted earlier that Berkeley made a sharp distinction between human and divine perceptions. This would have led to disagreeable conclusions for Berkeley if he had the will to do so. The objective idealists do not cut the worlds of human and divine with a hatchet. The human categories of thinking are also the divine way of thinking, for human beings are nothing but the focalisations of the divine omnipresence and immanence. Human thought is too fragmentary and will have to be transmuted and transformed in the fuller reality of divine thought, but then it is not opposed to it. In the final analysis human and divine categories differ only in *degree*.

5. Further, objective idealism holds that divine thought, no less than human thought, works according to certain inherent law and order. The world, therefore, is a necessary elaboration of God's existence and thought; and also the infinite potentiality of God works and realises itself through the world. Hence the world cannot exist apart from God, but God also cannot exist apart from the world. The relation between God and world may be compared to the relaion between the artist and his art. The art cannot exist apart from the artist but the artist as an artist cannot exist without continually creating the art. Hence God and world are inseparable. Now Berkeley does not go so far. According to him the world cannot exist without God but God can exist without the world. But Berkeley is not right. As long as we hold that the world can be different from what it is that it can even cease to be, then it has no reality of its own. Hence, Berkeleian idealism, in a real sense,

simply assumes but does not explain the reality of the trans-subjective world.

6. Lastly, Berkeley had mintained that the *esse* of a thing is its *percipi* and that *percipi* must be found in some mind. But objective idealism holds the essence of a thing consists of thoughts and that these thoughts are not my thoughts or your thoughts or even God's thoughts. These thoughts are real, in themselves, without any actual existence in any existing mind at all. In contrast with this teaching, the 'perception' of Berkeley is subjective, for it cannot exist without some mind. For this reason, Berkeley concludes that there is an actually existing personal God whose perceptions for ever sustain the world. Whereas objective idealism holds that the absolute reality is neither actual nor personal. It is super-personal, infinite potentiality which is progressively realised through nature, life and mind. Hence, Berkeley's reality is personal God as an infinite *Subject*; whereas the absolute of objective idealist is not any personal, existent mind at all. It is real but not an existent in any spatiotemporal order.

Hence, we conclude that Berkeley's idealism remains subjective in spite of its attempt to be objective.

6.08. The estimate of Berkeley's Philosophy

Berkeley was a great man and a great philosopher. He made significant contributions to the psychology of space-perception. It must also be conceded that he made important contributions to British empiricism. But it would be a great mistake to suppose that his philosophy is just a chain in the development of empiricism, or that he practised 'analysis' for the sake of philosophical precision of language. He was primarily a metaphysician with a world-view of theocentric phenomenalism. This view was also accompanied with a denial of matter.

The above estimate of Berkeley's philosophy would be accepted by Prof. J.O. Wisdom.[1] And then his conclusion is that Berkeley's metaphysics taken as a whole is a fantasy.[2] But for him this is true of philosophy in general which is the last and, we may be permitted to add, a lasting refuge of myths. However, according to Wisdom, this remark about philosophy does not rob its value and sense. Should be further comment that philosophy owes its charm and its appeal because of its capacity of fulfilling some undying urge within some intellectual men ? Wisdom tries to lay bare the unconscious motivation which formed the basis of Berkeley's metaphysics. If by a number of such studies of different philosophers one could find out the predictive value of psychical processes for the formation of philosophy, then such a conclusion would be of lasting value. But such studies do not contribute to the cognitive understanding of philosophy. Berkeley's arguments cannot be treated as the verbal gymnastics of a schizophreniac. He took the help of logical arguments which were recognised to be valid by other contemporaries and even by successive philosophers including Hume. But it is

1. The unconscious origin of Berkeley's philosophy (The Hogarth Press, 1953).
2. *Ibid.,* pp. 3, 230.

a fact that no logical arguments can establish the vision on which alone a metaphysic rests. Berkeley's arguments too, whose acuteness can never be doubted, fall short of his vision of a theocentric immaterialism or idealism. But arguments are the means of conveying to other thinkers the vision by which a philosopher lives. A philosophy is petty or great precisely by the vision it portrays or evokes. When the arguments are adequate, then the persuasive value of a philosophy gains in depth, richness and appeal. It is for this reason that idealist thinkers, after Berkeley, did not discard his vision, but tried to refine, amplify and broaden the arguments for idealism. The appeal of idealism does not lie so much in the arguments, but in its vision. And this vision is great and grand. If idealism has not been smashed by its critics, then it is not due to any lack of their critical powers or of weighty arguments. Berkeley's arguments in favour of idealism are not convincing, but the world-picture his idealism gives continues to be as important today as it was during his time. Berkeley's idealism would become obsolete only when it is superseded by a vision of greater range, depths and richness of experience.

Even when the argument of Berkeley in favour of idealism is not satisfactory, it remains central and epochal in the history of post-Berkeleyan idealism. We have already noted that the subsequent philosophers have accepted objective idealism in place of the subjective idealism of Berkeley. They have done so by transforming the maxim *esse est percipi* into *esse est intelligi*. This acceptance of concepts or the categories in place of perception as the essence of things is not the substitution of *esse est percipi*, but is merely its refinement or modification,. Even in the epistemological argument of Hegel, Green, Bradley and others, the central theme of Berkeley's contention remains unchanged and that is that thinking, perceiving and conceiving are constitutive of things. For this reason, the critics of idealism have chosen to attack *esse est percipi*, for they think that its refutation alone matters in the refutation of idealism. The following arguments have been offered against the doctrine of *esse est percipi*.

6.09. The criticism of *esse est percipi*

1. According to Moore, the theory of *esse est percipi* is based on an insuffcient analysis. Thus Moore observes that the term 'perception' includes two things, namely (i) the act of perceiving and (ii) the object perceived or perception. For instance, the sensation of blue includes the sensing blue and the sensed blue. The sensing act is no doubt mental but the sensum blue exists in its own rights and is non-mental. Similarly, the perceiving of a table is mental; but the table perceived is nonmental. As the term 'perception' refers to both, so Berkeley one-sidedly concludes that perception is mental.

2. Later on, the theory of *esse est percipi* was subjected to a great deal of criticism by the realist amongst whom the name of Prof. R.B. Perry deserves special mention. First, according to Perry, the theory of *esse est percipi* is open

to the charge of *exclusive particularity*. This fallaciously means that a thing is said to belong to one relationship only. Because it is related to mind as an idea, therefore, it is falsely supposed that it cannot stand in any other relationship. However, a thing stands in *multiple* relationship. For example, Ram is the husband of Sita and a son of Dasaratha, and a killer of Ravana. Hence, a table becomes an idea when it stands in relation to a knowing mind. But it is a thing amongst other things in relation to a chair or a desk. Viewed in this light instead of an idea being the essence of a thing may be just an accident which may happen to a thing.

No doubt Berkeley sought to prove *esse est percipi* by throwing a challenge: 'Show me anything which exists and which at the same time is not an idea'. Now at the first glance it becomes very difficult to meet the challenge. As soon as one says that a miser's treasure exists hidden in a field, he does not succeed in showing that the treasure exists without being an idea. Obviously it is not hidden or unperceived for the objector. It is there in his mind as an idea. It appears that Berkeley's contention is irrefutable.

"No *thinker to whom one may appeal is able to mention a thing that is not an idea,* for the obvious and simple reason that *in mentioning it be makes it an idea.*"[1]

However, this is only a predicament for any thinker to show that a thing exists unknown. But from the fact that a thing when known cannot be shown to remain unknown it does not follow that it cannot exist as unknown. All that can be established from the fact of egocentric predicament is that a known thing is known. This is simply tautology and from this tautology no factual statement can be proved.

However, from the nature of the challenge, with regard to ego-centric predicament one gets the impression that *esse est percipi* is as inductive conclusion. In that case it would be only probably and then Berkeley could not have held it with so much dogmatism. Even if it were an inductive conclusion, it could be arrived at only by the method of agreement for *exhypothesi* there could be no negative instance of it. However, the conclusion of the method of agreement is extremely precarious and no idealistic system could be reared up on this shaky foundation.

Conclusion : Not only Berkeley has persuaded us to see the universe through the lenses of idealism, but he has also raised a great many observations which were later on developed by Hume. The denial of causality and substance, which Berkeley maintained half-heartedly, was held by Hume with a great deal of logical vigour. So if Berkeley's empiricism is that of Locke made consistent, then in several respects the same remark is perhaps, truer of Hume's empiricism in relation to Berkeleism also. So now we turn to Hume whose philosophy is the culmination of classical empiricism and whose analysis of knowledge has contributed much to contemporary logical empiricism, positivism, pragmatism and so on.

---

1. R.B. Perry, *Present Philosophical Tendencies*, p. 129.

7

David Hume (1711-1776)[1]

7.01. Introduction

Hume may be regarded as Locke and Berkeley made consistent. His criticism of
Berkeley showed that the certainty in knowledge is inexplicable on the basis of
empiricism. It has been said, following Hume, that scepticism is the logical
outcome of the empiricism of Locke. We find that Hume may be regarded to be
a critic rather than a sceptic. At the present time Hume is taken to be a logical
positivist. He was a sceptic in relation to the belief in the possibility of reason to
solve all problems but then he was not a total sceptic for he allowed the possibility
of knowledge on the basis of custom and imagination. He had also a constructive
philosophy of empiricism, but this proved too weak to remove the weighty doubts
which he himself had introduced into his speculation.

Whatever may be the just estimate of Hume at the present time, in the history
of modern philosophy he was taken to be a sceptic and as a sceptic he has been
influential in rousing Kant from his dogmatic slumber. Now what could be the
reason for his scepticism? Kant who tried to answer Hume pointed out that
empiricism, confined to the psychological method, cannot but be sceptical. Even
up to the present time many who differ from Hume think that this is the real reason
of Hume's scepticism. However, British and American empiricists think that
though Lockean empiricism with its inadequate analysis of knowledge may lead
to scepticism, yet empiricism itself need not be sceptical. It is difficult to decide
between the two for ultimately it is an issue between the two tempers of the
philosophising mind. Certainly, the problem raised by him are critical, crucial and
acute and we have to understand them well.

At present Hume is regarded as the most important empirical philosopher.
Hume's theory of morals and religion is treated as highly significant in
contemporary philosophy. Hume's criticism of the ontological and teleological
arguments for the existence of God is certainly more lucid and devastating than
that of Kant's criticism of rational theology.

In France, Hume was honoured as a historian for writing *History of England*.
However, Hume himself wanted to be known for his contributions in Ethics and
Political Science. In order to establish morals and political science, Hume laid
down the science of man, which meant psychology. Principal works of Hume are
the following:

---

1. The page reference in the margin has been taken from Selby-Bigge's 'Hume's Treatise' E. means
   Essays.

1. A Treatise of Human Nature, 1739.
2. Essays, Moral and Political, 1741-42.
3. An Enquiry Concerning the Human Understanding, 1748.
4. Three Essays Moral and Political, 1748.
5. An Enquiry Concerning the Principles of Morals, 1751.
6. Political Discourses, 1752.
7. Dialogues Concerning Natural Religion, 1750, but was posthumously published in 1779.
8. History of England, 6 Vols. 1754-62.

The writings of Hume have been subdivided into the following heads :

1. Epistemology : *Treatise,* Book I, *An Enquiry Concerning Human Understanding.*
2. Psychology : *Treatise,* Book II, *A Dissertation on the Passions.*
3. Morals : *Treatise,* Book III, *An Enquiry Concerning the Principles of Morals.*
4. Religion : An Enquiry Concerning Human Understanding, The Natural History of Religion, Dialogues Concerning Natural Religion, Of the Immortality of the Soul.

Hume is a good subject for dissertation, so a few books of and on Hume are worth mentioning.

1. Hume's Enquiries, L.A. Selby-Bigge, Oxford, 1963.
2. A Treatise of Human Nature, L.A. Selby-Bigge, Oxford, 1968.
3. The Philosophical Works of David Hume, ed. T.H. Green & T.H. Gross, 4 Vols. (Reprinted, London, 1964).
4. Flew, A., *David Hume,* Collier Books, N. Y. 1962.
5. Hendel, C.W., *Hume,* Liberal Arts Press, N. Y. 1955. *Studies on Hume*:
1. Basson, A. H., *David Hume,* A Pelican Book, 1958.
2. Chappell, V. C. (ed.) *Hume,* Macmillan, 1966.

This is a *must* for every Hume scholar. It contains excellent articles and a good bibliography.

3. Hendel, C.W., *Studies in the Philosophy of Hume,* Indianapolis, Ind. 1963.
4. Pears, D.F. (ed.) *A Symposium,* Macmillan, 1963.
5. Seasonske, A./Noel Fleming, *Human Understanding*, Belmonet, Calf., 1965.
6. Smith, N.K., *The Philosophy of David Hume,* London, 1941.

Hume himself regarded *An Enquiry Concerning Human Understanding* as his authoritative work. But Treatise is regarded by Hume-scholars to be much more important of the two.

David Hume was born on the 26th April, and died on the 25th August, 1776. He himself has described his character thus : "I was a man of mild dispositions, of command of temper, of an open, social and cheerful humour . . . . Even my love of literary fame, my ruling passion, never soured my temper, notwithstanding my frequent disappointments." Historians agree in this just estimate of Hume about himself.

7.02. Fundamentals of Human Philosophy

Locke and Berkeley employed the psychological method in philosophy and Hume quietly inherits it. This consists in the careful analysis of the contents of experience in order to discover the original elements of knowledge. Of necessity it had to rely on introspection and Hume always appeals to unprejudiced searching of the mind as the last court of appeal. He clarifying Locke points out that there are two kinds of contents of the mind, namely, impressions and their ideas. These are the only perceptions which compose the human mind. First, impressions and ideas have been divided into simple and complex. All ideas or impressions are those which admit of no separation or distinction, like the sensation of red or cold or smell. Complex ideas or impressions are those which are composed of simple parts like the idea of an apple, having the parts of colour, taste, smell etc. Again, impressions may be divided into sensation and reflection. Sensations seem to arise from unknown causes but the reflection of passions, desires, emotions and the felt inclination of the mind is 'derived in a great measure from our ideas." (7 and 8) Thus reflection is secondary and sensation is primary. But reflection though secondary is not the copy of the sensation because like all other true elements the impressions of reflection are original facts and realities, complete in themselves, and implying no reference to other passions, volitions and actions." (415)

Now let us turn to the important distinction between impressions and ideas. Simple impressions are the originals of which the simple ideas are the copies. Thus impressions are prior and the ideas are posterior. There can be no simple ideas without their corresponding original impressions. The complex ideas however, compounded in fancy need not correspond to their impressions but their elements do correspond to the impression. For example, we may fancy a new Jerusalem whose pavements are made of gold and whose walls are built of rubies. However, the elements of pavement, gold, wall etc., are all derived from simple impressions. Further, the impressions have superiority in force, liveliness and vivacity; but the ideas, for the most part, are weak and faint. (9) Thirdly, the simple ideas are representative and the simple impressions are represented, but the simple impressions themselves are not representative of anything else. We cannot say that the perceptions are the copies of the extra-mental thing. The cause of the sense-impressions is inexplicable by human reason for we do not know whether they arise immediately from the object, or are produced by the creative power of the mind or are derived from 'the author of our being'. (84) However, the simple ideas are the copies of the original impressions. Lastly, the impressions, strictly speaking, are always simple but the ideas can be both simple and complex.

Ideas, again, may appear either in the form of memory or imagination. The distinction between the memorial and imaginal ideas is not well marked. To a certain extent memorial ideas are strong and lively, and the imaginal ideas are weak and faint. Secondly, in imagination we are freer to produce complex ideas, though not so much the simple ones which are tied to their original impressions; but memory is tied down to their corresponding impressions. **(8, 9, 85)**

In determining the simple elements of which the mind is composed, Hume takes the help of his famous dogma: *what is distinguishable is separable.* All impressions as such are distinct and separate with no logical connection between them. This is known as Humean atomism. As such the impressions are neither related amongst themselves nor are they connected with the objects or the mind. But knowledge is a unified whole and a connected system. Hence, Hume supplements his atomism with the Principles of 'union and cohesion' amongst the separate impressions. He points out that there is a gentle force which attracts the separate impressions into union. This gentle force is nothing but the law of association working according to the principles of resemblance and continuity. Because of these bonds 'one idea naturally introduces another', and even the product of fancy cannot be arbitrary. This law of association is the all-pervasive principle which binds the separate ideas in every sphere of imagination and science. In the sequel it will be shown that the so-called disciplined reasoning of science does not show any logical or necessary connection. In the last resort the necessary connection will be shown to be one of the association of ideas. Hence there is connection amongst the impressions which is not rational but is effected through custom and imagination.

Later on we shall try to give the details of Hume's criticism of causality and substance, the so-called rational connections, but at present let us see whether his fundamentals are such as can stand the stress the arguments.

7.03. Evaluation of Human Fundamentals

Hume agrees with Locke in the rejection of innate ideas. Every idea is acquired, according to him, and can be traced to its corresponding impression. Let us chase our imagination, says he, to the farthest limit but we will not be able to escape from the narrow compass of impressions. However, Hume differs from Berkeley and Locke in the use of the term perception. Impressions are separate and are neither mental nor are they caused by something extramental. By this use of the term he tries to avoid the epistemological dualism of Descartes and Locke. As long as we believe that ideas are the copies of the objects outside the mind, we will not be able to explain the knowledge of objects. This was shown by Berkeley. But Hume goes beyond even Berkeley and does not recognise the *mental* status of the impressions. Perceptions of Hume are no more mental than physical. We may call them neutral stuff. They are not the states of mind, but then they are the contents and the what of the human knowledge. This comes very near to the sense-data theory of Bertrand Russell.

Hume is consistent in developing empirical atomism. But his perceptual units though clear are not as we would like them to be. Perception of its very nature refers to something or an object and includes much more than mere sense-impressions. Hume does not seem to make clear these points. He wants to make his position clear in this way: 'By the term of impression I would not be understood to express the manner in which our lively perceptions are produced in the soul, but merely the perceptions themselves.'

This failure to mark out the simple is also seen in another place also. About the complex impression of Paris, he uses the term 'I have seen Paris'. But this seeing is far more complex than simple impression of seeing. Hume no doubt is most acute in his psychology to philosophy, but then he is not so acute in his psychology. A few difficulties of his system he himself points out. He takes great pains to establish that all simple ideas are, without exception, derived from their corresponding impressions. He himself, however, shows an exception to this exceptionless principle. Suppose a man be presented with a graded series of all blue shades except one, then, Hume points out, that this one shade can be supplied through imagination. Hence there can be an idea without its corresponding impression. This would have refuted his whole philosophy. But Hume brushes aside this observation by saying that it is 'so particular and singular, that 'tis scarce worth our observing, and does not merit that, for it alone, we should alter our general maxim.' **(5 and 6)**

Even if we grant that the ideas are derived from impressions, can we show that the ideas are the copies? If we call up an image of a certain shade of red, then this same image will fit into several closely similar shades and we cannot point out its corresponding impression. When Hume says that the ideas are the copies of the impressions which they *exactly* and quite distinctly represent, he asserts something which is no psychologically true.

If the ideas cannot be shown to copy impressions exactly in any particular case, then can we establish the general statement that any idea is the copy of an impression? The vivacity and force cannot serve as a criterion. In fever, in madness or violent emotions ideas may become as strong, lively and vivid as the actual impressions; and on many occasions the impressions themselves may be weak and faint. **(2)** The other important criterion of priority also fails to show that ideas are always derived from impressions. The priority is judged by memory and really no memory prototype can be given. "It being impossible to recall the past impressions, in order to compare them with our present ideas, and see whether their arrangement be exactly similar." **(35)** As we cannot recall the primary impression we cannot prove that a particular idea is a copy. In the absence of any satisfactory criterion between impression and idea we cannot say that every idea must be derived from an impression. Hence, against Hume's thesis of empiricism we can still hold that there may be ideas without having their corresponding impressions.

Locke became an inconsistent empiricist for he held that the mind as *tabula rasa* or as a clean slate could yet compare, contrast, compound the ideas in diverse ways. He made two important omissions. First, simple perceptions in the complex compound get greatly modified and really are created anew. The simple perception of red becomes altered in the many-qualitied rose. Thus the mind by its activity of compounding etc., creates ideas not given in impressions. Secondly, he did not notice that seeing of difference between yellow and blue is not visual seeing but is purely an intellectual process. A similar mistake is committed by Hume. He regards impressions as absolutely unrelated, distinct and separable and then turns to find the principle of union and cohesion in the association of ideas.

7.04. Kinds of Meaningful Propositions and Knowledge

Hume has presented a very careful analysis of knowledge-situation. Philosophers had taken mathematics to be the paradigm case of knowledge and had derived philosophical methodology from their study of mathematics. At least two things can be said about mathematics. Firstly, the discovery of axioms and, secondly the process of deducing theorems and other conclusions are said to be intuitively certain and self-validating. Philosophers by patterning empirical knowledge of matters of fact hoped to obtain scientific principles from intellectual vision. However, factual propositions are based on experiments and are not obtained by sheer thinking alone (as is the case with mathematics), then how can factual propositions be explained in terms of intellectual intuition?

Well, experimental data may be taken to be the occasion for the rise of an intellectual insight into the laws of Uniformity of Nature and the Principle of Causation, which in turn guarantee the indubitable truth of external facts. As against this some philosophers contended that observed experimental data and scientific methodology themselves provided indubitable truth. In both the cases mathematicising consisted in holding that intuitive insight into the fundamental principles of nature guaranteed certainty in knowledge.

Against these mathematicising attempts of philosophers, Hume contended the following :

1. Propositions of mathematics differ in kind from propositions concerning matters of fact. Naturally factual propositions cannot be confused with mathematical propositions. In other words, mathematical certainty with regard to factual propositions cannot be obtained or demonstrated.

2. No amount of observation or experiment can guarantee the truth of future events. Nay, every rational attempt to base factual proposition on uniformity of nature did the law of causation is bound to fail.

3. Even the certainty of mathematical reasoning cannot be ultimately guaranteed because of the frailty of the judging powers of man.

4. However, Hume holds that man is not guided by reason alone. Nature, custom and habits determine human thinking. This natural propensity in man

leads him to believe in causal relation, external world moral principles and God.

We shall be very brief about Hume's theory of mathematics and shall take up (2) concerning Hume's theory of substance, causality and external world. Points (3), and (4) will be included under *Hume's scepticism.*

Hume so far has established the proposition that real knowledge is based on ideas and their impressions. "Let us chase our imagination to the heavens or to the utmost limits of the universe; we never really advance a step beyond utmost limits of the universe; we never really advance a step beyond ourselves, nor can conceive any kind of existence, but those perceptions, which have appeared in that narrow compass." **(67)** But then the perceptions and their ideas are unrelated and knowledge is essentially connected. Hence, we have to enquire into the nature of relations involved in knowledge. Hume mentions seven kinds of relations:

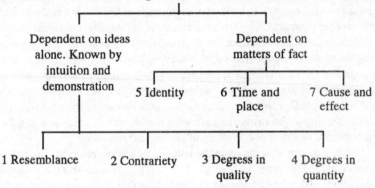

Hume has little to say about relations dependent on ideas alone. Ideas are all copies from impressions. Hence real knowledge is to be decided by matters of fact. For this reason Hume is concerned with the second class of relations of identity, space and time, and cause and effect. He pays scant attention to identity and we may omit here his reference to space and time. All reasonings of matters of fact are founded, according to Hume, on the relation of cause and effect. To this Hume pays his greatest care. Geometry, Algebra and Arithmetic are based on **relation of Ideas,** and propositions concerning them are intuitively or demonstrably certain. For example, three and four are together equal to seven. This proposition is certain and it is concerned with a relation between numbers. **[E. 321-22]**

> Propositions of this kind are discoverable by the mere operation of thought, without dependence on what is anywhere existent in the universe. Though there never were a circle or triangle in nature, the truths demonstrated by Euclid would for ever retain their certainty and evidence. (Enquiry, 1962, Sec. IV, p. 25)

Finally, for Hume only two kinds of propositions are literally meaningful, which is clear from the following oft-quoted line:

> If we take in our hand any volume; of divinity or school metaphysics, for instance; let us ask, *Does it contain any abstract reasoning concerning quantity or number? No. Does it contain any experimental reasoning concerning matter of fact and existence?* No. Commit it then to the flames: for it can contain nothing but sophistry and illusion. (Enquiry, sec. XII, pt. III, last para)

Substance an idle fiction of imagination: It would be better, however, if we begin with Hume's idea of substance. According to him any knowledge in order to be real must have elements corresponding to some impressions. Now if there is something permanent, as the supporter of qualities, then it must be traced to some sensation or reflection. If it is a sensation, then it must be either a sensation of colour or heat or cold. But then it is regarded as none of these. Again, if it comes from reflection, then it must be either an emotion or some passions. But a substance is derived neither from sensation nor from reflection. Thus a substance as understood by philosophers is an 'unintelligible chimera'. The idea of substance, for Hume means, a collection of simple ideas, united by imagination, which have a common name assigned to it.

Hume seems to accept the refutation of material substance by Berkeley, but he goes beyond Berkeley in refuting the spiritual substance also. Hume asked the same question regarding the self which Berkeley had raised with regard to 'matter'. Please show me any impression from which the idea of permanent self is derived, "For my part, when I enter most intimately into what I call *myself,* I always stumble on some particular perception or other, of heat or cold, light or shade, love or hatred, pain or pleasure. I never can catch *myself* at any time without a perception, and never can observe anything but the perception. When my perceptions are removed for any time, as by sound sleep; so long am I insensible of myself, and may truly he said not to exist. . . .If any one upon serious and unprejudiced reflection, thinks he has a different notion of himself, I must confess I can reason no longer with him." **(252)**

If the identity of the self is purely fictitious, then how does it arise at all? According to Hume, the fiction of personal identity is the work of imagination. The succession of pleasure, pain, sensations and images are connected together by resemblance, contiguity and causation. Our notion of personal identity, for Hume, proceeds entirely from the smooth and uninterrupted progress of the thought along a train of connected ideas, according to the principles of resemblance, contiguity and causation (260T). This resemblance is sustained by our memory. Again, causation also produces the notion of personal identity. The human mind, according to Hume, is

> a system of different perceptions or different existences, which are linked together by the relation of cause and effect, and mutually produce, destroy,

influence, and modify each other. Our impressions rise to their correspondent ideas; and these ideas in their turn produce other impressions. (261)

Thus, the subject, self or mind, for Hume, is just a construct of sensations, feeling and images.

The so-called self, according to Hume, "is nothing but a heap or collection" of passing sensations. About this refutation of self, Russell writes very approvingly thus : This conclusion is important in metaphysics for it takes away the last vestige of substance; it is important in theology and morality as it abolishes the doctrine of the permanent and immortal soul. In epistemology it is important for it shows that the category of subject and object is not fundamental.

7.05. The Idea of Cause

Causation is the most important category for Hume. On this according to him, depends our knowledge of the matters of fact. Secondly, on its strength we pass from the immediate impressions to something not immediately presented in senses. On the basis of the causal principle we bind together the passing impressions into universal laws. If this principle is valid then there is rational justification for the science, otherwise, Hume points out, we have no reason to accept their claim to certain knowledge.

In order to show that the idea of cause be true and real, it must be, according to Hume, traced to some impressions. Now let us see whether there are any common *qualities* found in objects by virtue of which any one of them becomes the cause of the other. But the things named as causes are so various that there is no quality by virtue of which a thing may be called a cause. The idea of cause, therefore, must be derived from the *relations* among objects. First, the objects regarded as cause and effect are always *contiguous* like fire and heat, food and nourishment etc. Again, there is the relation of *priority,* i.e., the cause is always antecedent to the effect. Thus contiguity and succession are the two relations from which the idea of causation might have been derived. But there is a third and the most important element in causation called the element of *power or necessary connection.* It is said that a cause *produces* an effect, or, the effect is necessarily connected with the cause. Let us see from what impressions it is derived. It seems that impression cannot yield the relation of necessary connection. All that we see is that one billiard ball strikes the other and the other moves. But we never perceive any power in one passing to the other. Most probably the clue to the understanding of the necessary connection will be found if we answer two questions :

   (1) For what reason we pronounce it *necessary*, that everything whose existence has a beginning, should also have a cause?
   (2) Why do we conclude, that such particular causes must *necessarily* have such particular effects? 78

Replying to the first question Hume refutes the proofs of causality given *a priori* by Hobbes, Clarke and Locke. According to him every demonstration which has been produced for the necessity of cause is fallacious and sophistical, instead of proving causality, really presupposes it. He does not regard the necessity of necessary connection. ". . . .as all distinct ideas are separable from each other, and as the ideas of cause and effect are evidently distinct it will be easy for us to conceive any object to be non-existent this moment, and existent the next, without conjoining to it the distinct idea of cause or productive principle." **(80-81)**

As every rational account has failed to demonstrate the necessity of cause and effect, let us see how *experience* helps us to regard particular causes necessarily leading to particular effects. "The nature of experience is this. We remember to have had frequent instances of the existence of one species of objects; and also remember, that the individuals of another species of objects have always attended them, and have existed in a regular order of contiguity and succession with regard to them. Thus we remember to have seen that species of object we call *flame*, and to have felt that species of sensation we call *heat*. We likewise call to mind their constant conjunction in all past instances. Without any further ceremony, we call the one *cause* and the other *effect,* and infer the existence of the one form that of the other." **(87)** Thus contiguity and succession are not sufficient. It is the relation of the **constant conjunction** which produces the mental habits of regarding things necessarily connected. Now on the basis of past experience and on our remembrance of the constant conjunction we make transition to necessary connection.

Is this transition based on reasoning or imagination? If reason determined the course, then it would take the help of the principle, "that instances, of which we have had no experience, must resemble those, of which we have had experience, and that the course of nature continues always uniformly the same." Clearly this cannot be the rational principle. For experience cannot guarantee that which has not been experienced. Then the idea of necessary connection through experience is due to imagination.

At first it seems difficult to accept that imagination plays the trick in producing the idea of necessity. If one experience cannot discover the connection between objects, then many repetitions cannot produce any. At this stage Hume introduces his theory of beliefs. A belief, as distinguished from fancy, is a lively idea related or associated with a present impression. No constant conjunction can ever produce an impression of a new quality *in the object* but it produces an effect on the mind. The mind, after a repetition of similar instances, is carried by habit, upon the appearance of one event to expect its usual attendant. The utmost search in the objects would indicate that they are *conjoined* but never connected. "After he has observed several instances of this nature, he then pronounces them to be connected. What alteration has happened to give rise to this new idea of *connection*? **(E. 353)** Nothing but he now feels these events to be connected in his imagination, and can readily foretell the existence of one from the apearance of the other. Whenever we pass, says Hume, from the impression of one to the idea or belief of another, we are not determined by reason but by custom or principle of association. Thus there is no necessity in objects but there is a subjective necessity in the form of mental propensity by virtue of which we read causality into objects.

Thus the idea of causation, according to Hume, has two elements. First, there is the human nature in the form of imagination and its principle of association. Secondly, the past experience of constant conjunction. The latter determines a certain sequence of ideas. Even sometime one instance may associate one as the cause of the other. But this is, due to the allied habit of reading causality into the objects.

This reduction of causality to connection conjured up by imagination as a convenient device for dealing with things, takes away the last hope of scientific knowledge. If there is no causality, then there is no real connection between things. Naturally Hume's inquiry ends in the denial of knowledge. Hume is said to be consistent empiricist but we can make here two important observations. First, Hume nowhere tells us how the successive ideas can be co-existent or even contiguous. Besides, if we have no guarantee to believe that things of the future will be like the things of the past, then we cannot believe in the mental habit as well. If fire and heat cannot be connected but are only conjoined then how can we say that the mental habit will always be the same for all men? Mental habit itself becomes a causal principle,—a universal law to explain causality.

Hume appears to be describing causal relationship, and, in this description psychology and philosophical analysis are interwoven. This is clear from the fact that Hume gives two definitions of cause on the same page 170 of his **Treatise**

(a) We may define a cause to be 'An object precedent and contiguous to another, and where all the objects resembling the former are placed in like relations of precedency and contiguity to those objects that resemble the latter'.

(b) 'A cause is an object precedent and contiguous to another, and so united with it that the **idea** of the one **determines the mind** to form the idea of the other, and the impression of the one to form a more lively idea of the other.'

The definition of cause given in (a) is based on philosophical analysis, and, in (b) it is based on psychological analysis. According to the philosophical analysis causal relation is found in two events or objects, when they are contiguous, successive and in constant conjunction. But constant conjunction is not enough to account for the necessity in causality. Constant conjunction must also at the same time create a mental habit of expectation. If A and B be causally related, then the necessary and sufficient condition of A becoming the cause of B are

1. A be precedent and contiguous to B
2. Events resembling A be precedent and contiguous to events resembling B
3. Due to constant conjunction, the idea of A be associated with the events

or idea of B.

4. A mental habit of expectation be produced in the mind so that the idea of A be followed by the idea of B.

Thus for Hume, the psychological analysis of causation in terms of imagination (being the product of resemblance, contiguity and custom, i.e., causal relation based on associative inference) is relevant for philosophical analysis, though not a justification of causal relationship. In other words for Hume genetic consideration is relevant for epistemological analysis of causation.

7.06. Belief in the Existence of the External World

Ordinarily we believe that there is an independent and permanent world outside of us which we can easily discover by the sense. However, Hume's enquiry into the furniture of the mind has shown that the passing impressions are the only reality. How, then, can we know about the existence of permanent and independent external world from the fleeting, perishing and interrupted perceptions? We might have proved this with the help of causation but then this has been shown to be an affair of imagination. Now we will further see that the belief in the external world is not an affair of reason but is entirely owing to **imagination**. "The belief in the external world is neither on account of the involuntariness of certain impressions, as is commonly supposed, nor of their superior force and violence, that we attribute to them a reality, and continued existence, which we refuse to others, that there are voluntary and feeble. For it is evident our pains and pleasures, our passions and affections, which we never suppose to have any existence beyond our perception, operate with greater violence, and are equally involuntary, as the impressions of figure and extension, colour and sound which we suppose to be permanent beings." **(194)**

The continued, distinct and independent existence of the external world is derived from the *constancy* and *coherence* of the external world is derived from the constancy and coherence of the impressions. The mountains, the houses, the table, the bed "have always appeared to me in the same order; and when I lose sight of them by shutting my eyes or turning my head, I soon after find them return upon me without the least alteration. . .(They) present themselves in the same uniform manner, and change not on account of any interruption in my seeing or perceiving them." And whenever these impressions change there is coherence and regular dependence on each other. "When I return to my chamber after an hour's absence, I find not my fire in the same situation, in which I left it : But then I am accustomed in other instances to see a like alteration produced in a like time, whether I am present or absent, near or remote." **(194-95)**

Just as the objective factors of contiguity and succession had to be coupled with the mental or subjective factor of custom to account for causality; in like manner, the coherence and constancy have to be combined with mental propensity to account for the belief in the external world. The constancy and coherence engender in the mind the habit of finding uniformity as complete as possible. The mental habit of finding coherence and constancy is best fulfilled by the supposition of the continued, distinct and independent world. This supposition, based on mental propensity, makes the closely resembling impression as identical.

"The thought glides along the succession with equal facility, as if it considered only one object; and therefore confounds the succession with the identity...I shut my eyes, and afterwards open them; and find the new perceptions to resemble perfectly those, which formerly struck my senses." **(264)** At first the supposition of a distinct, independent and contined existence of the external world is purely hypothetical. But it gains in strength by its success in harmonising many contradictory impressions.[1] The belief in the continuous existence is generated, then, by imaginational one which ignores the gaps or interruptions and fuses the succession of similar impressions into one identical and continuous object.

Reason easily shows that the belief in the continued existence is illusory, for our own reality is of the passing and interrupted impressions only. "This propensity to bestow an identity on our resembling perceptions, produces the fiction of a continued existence; since that fiction, as well as the identity, is really false, as is acknowledged by all philosophers, and has no other effect than to remedy the interruption of our perceptions, which is the only circumstance that is contrary to their identity". But instead of discarding the fiction of the continued existence, human beings inconsistently enough form the hypothesis of double existence. The perceptions are supposed to be interrupted, perishing and different at every different return. But the objects are uninterrupted and preserve a continued existence and identity. Thus both the contradictory verdicts of reason and imagination are inconsistently retained by us. **(211)**

7.07. Was Hume a Sceptic?

Hume analysed the furniture of the mind in terms of fleeting impressions. Anything called knowledge not derived from impressions, according to him, could not be based on reason. Taking impression as his touchstone he called in question the validity of the concepts of substance, causality etc., which make up knowledge proper. He after a careful analysis of the main categories of thought came to the conclusion that there is no substance, neither matter nor self. We are left with passing impressions only. Is there any necessary connection between the impressions so that we could pass with certainty from the one to the other? His most careful search into causation showed that there could be no necessary connection between the impressions. Nothing remains,—the vast structure of philosophy crumbles to dust. In Hume philosophy finds itself in the midst of ruins of its own making. Yes, the result of Humean inquiry appears to us sceptical. Yet lived in an age in which men entertained the highest hope in the possibility of

---

1.   Here we can easily note the pragmatic nature of Hume's argument.

knowledge. Paradoxical it may sound but it is quite true that Hume's too much faith in the science of psychology, the science of his own making, was the main cause of his scepticism.

However, it may be held that Hume could not be regarded as a sceptic for he allowed the possibility of mathematical knowledge. Hume rejected the demonstrations of geometry because they are based on the absurd principle of infinite divisibility of extension. But the algebraic and arithmetical demonstration, according to him, maintains 'a perfect exactness and certainty'. Unfortunately he does not tell us, 'how are these ideas of algebra and arithmetic derived ?' **(72)** For an inquiry into them might have revealed that they too, like other ideas, are not derived from any impressions. Any way he maintains that the rules of the demonstrative sciences are 'certain and infallible' but due to our frail faculties our application of them is notoriously fallible. So even here knowledge is only probable. Therefore "having thus found in every probability, beside the original uncertainty inherent in the subject, a new uncertainty derived from the weakness of that faculty, which judges, and having adjusted these two together, we are obliged by our reason to add a new doubt derived from the possibility of error in the estimation we make of the truth and fidelity of our faculties." **(180, E. 344)** This quotation shows that Hume was a total sceptic. But the total scepticism is self-contradictory. The doubting of everything leads also to the doubt of that theory which doubts everything, i.e., scepticism itself becomes doubtful. Hume himself was aware of this and points out, "Whoever has taken the pains to refute the cavils of this *total* scepticism, has really, disputed without an antagonist." A few lines earlier he writes, "should it here be asked. . . .whether I be really one of those sceptics, who hold that all is uncertain, and that our judgment is not in *any* thing possessed of *any* measures of truth and falsehood; I should reply, that this question is entirely superfluous, and that neither I, nor any other person was ever sincerely and constantly of that opinion." **(183)**

In the light of the last quotation we have to modify our judgment about Hume. No doubt he was, to a certain extent, sceptic and as such he became a potent force in the history of thought. But in recent years, the careful analysis of the writings of Hume by Laing, Laird, Kemp Smith and Church shows that he was a 'moderate sceptic' and not a total sceptic. Besides, his scepticism, as is popularly held, is not the logical outcome of empiricism. It is not empiricism, but reason which fails to dispel the dark clouds of scepticism.

Hume was moderate in his scepticism for he maintained that reason apart from imagination cannot solve our doubts but then there could be, he hoped and partly advanced, a system of thought based on our natural propensities. It is the Cartesian abstract reason which falls into doubts and difficulties but a sound basis of valid philosophy can be raised on the 'established habits of the mind'. He had a positive philosophy too about which he writes, "We might hope to establish a system or of opinions, which, if not true (for that, perhaps, is too much to be hoped for), might at least be satisfactory to the human mind, and might stand the test of the most critical examination." His display of the sceptical arguments purports to show that truth lies in the custom or habit of imagination and not in reason. True thinking, according to him, is really sensitive and not cogitative in nature, "Nature, by an absolute and uncontrollable necessity has determined us to judge as well as to breathe and feel." Again, he writes, "Most fortunately it happens, that since reason is incapable of dispelling these clouds, nature herself suffices to that purpose, and curse me of this philosophical melancholy and delirium...I dine, I play a game of backgammon, I converse, and am merry with my friends; and when after three or four hours' amusement, I return to these speculations, they appear so cold and strained, and ridiculous that I cannot find in my heart to enter in them any father." Thus we are constrained to maintain that Hume was not a total sceptic but then he used scepticism as a powerful weapon of attack against rationalism. The sceptical arguments are by no means his original property. They derive their source from the Greek scepticism. Empiricism based on naturalistic psychology is not the cause of scepticism but really according to him, is a way of escape out of the difficulties in which reason falls. Thus Hume had a constructive empirical philosophy but due to the following reasons he has been interpreted as a sceptic.

1. First, Hume makes a full display of the sceptical arguments. Thus critical and negative element is so widespread throughout the discussion that one gets the impression that he is *merely* negative and destructive.

2. Hume makes scepticism the background of his own philosophy. It provides him with a convenient weapon of attack against rationalism and dogmatism.

3. From the rationalistic point of view (which prevailed for a long time in the universities) his philosophy is really sceptical for he maintains that reason is not capable of making our knowledge intelligible. He gives us almost a counsel of despair, "Carelessness and in attention alone can afford us any remedy." He maintains that reason is really sensitive and no rationalist can ever accept this thesis.

4. Lastly, his own constructive philosophy is weak and powerless to deal adequately with the doubts which he himself had raised.

Yes, there are valid grounds for treating Hume as a sceptic. But really he is not one. He had a constructive philosophy of empiricism with these four principles. (i) The doctrine of impressions and ideas, (ii) The laws of association, (iii) The imagination and (iv) His theory of relations. By these principles he wants to show that real knowledge is habitual and not cogitative.

First, the impressions must be admitted even by the sceptics and so Hume regards them to be the basic touchstone of knowledge. Further, what logic cannot explain, psychology does. With the help of the law of association he shows that in causation there is no logical but psychological necessity, power and substance are not to be discovered in objects but are really in subjects. The law of association explains the mental world, according to him, as the law of Gravitation explains the phenomena of the physical world.

Similarly, Hume takes the help of imagination in constructing knowledge. No rational ground can be given to explain the connectedness of impressions in knowledge. The real ground lies in the power of imagination to fill up a gap.

Thus Hume's philosophy is sceptical with regard to dogmatism and rationalism but not so in relation to sceptism itself. Of course, the reply which he supplied to sceptical doubts was unsatisfactory but then it shows that he could not remain in scepticism. Really he hoped to encourage philosophers to think better and never wanted to induce them to remain in despair. Apart from the constructive empirical philosophy he accepted the validity of mathematics and the experimental truths concerning matters of fact. In view of his limitation of knowledge to that which is capable of exact measurement and to that which is present in experience, coupled with his rejection of the suprasensible entities like God or soul, may justly entitle him to be called a positivist rather than a sceptic. Again, in view of his arguments against the capacity of reason to solve our problems, he may be justly styled a pragmatist, an anti-intellectual rather than a sceptic.

Thus, Hume had two aspects, one of philosophical empiricism and another of psychologism. His philosophical empiricism could provide no rational basis for the indubitable knowledge of substance, God, external world and soul. Even causality for Hume can have no rational basis for passing from the given to the future events. But for Hume, man is much more than reason. He has to live, grow and gain stability in life. On the level of philosophy, Hume has advised us to accept probabilities. For living naturally, one has to accept habit, custom and social culture. This is exactly what Pyrrhonism stands for. For natural guidance in one's life

1. One has to accept sense-impressions,
2. One has to give oneself to one's appetites of hunger, thirst and other such biological drives.
3. One has to be guided by one's tradition of custom and laws.
4. On has to give oneself to the life of culture of one's age.

If we emphasize Hume's views with regard to his philosophical empiricism, then Hume's acceptance of impressions as the indubitable touchstone of knowledge, coupled with his denial of permanent substance, self and God, then we would place him among the positivists. If, however, we emphasize his doctrine of naturalism, imagination based on associative inference, then Hume would be regarded as a pragmatist. In the history of philosophy, Hume has become famous for his positivism with its negative conclusions and that is how he is viewed even now.

8

Immanuel Kant (1724-1804)

Kant has been regarded as the most important modern philosopher. In him meet the cross currents of modern philosophy and then again pass out many more tendencies in the contemporary thought. Kant was not only a philosopher but also was essentially a moralist, a theologian and a natural scientist. In him the German thought with its characteristics of thoroughness, profundity and obscure terminology began to show themselves.

8.01. Introduction

Kant began his philosophical career as a rationalist of the Wolffian school, but he soon saw its inadequacy. According to it, we can begin with innate ideas, but how can we say that they are also true of the external world? Like spiders we cannot weave out fancies and regard them to be valid of the real world. After rejecting rationalism as a natural scientist, he began to look upon experience to explain knowledge. However, he was roused from his dogmatic slumber by the sceptical writings of Hume. Thus he was dissatisfied with both rationalism and empiricism. For the time being he tried to take refuge in *Nouveaux Essais* of Leibnitz. But the whole system of Leibnitz was based on the doctrine of the pre-established harmony, which is only an uncritical assumption, incapable of supporting a scientific system.

In this hopeless state of philosophical progress a lesser man would have succumbed to despair. But Kant believed in the validity of scientific knowledge and his faith in moral goodness never failed to enkindle his spirits. His problem, therefore, was to find out the conditions which would make knowledge possible. There is knowledge, according to Kant, in Mathematics and Physics and if this cannot be explained by rationalism or empiricism then so much worse for the theories. The failure of empiricism and rationalism should open a new avenue of approach to the understanding of knowledge. Kant attributes the failure of metaphysics to the uncritical use of reason itself. Before we trust ourselves to the guidance of reason, we should examine its nature, limit and competence. Thus in general the problem of Kant is the same as that of Locke, namely, "If, by this inquiry into the nature of the understanding I can discover the powers thereof; how far they reach, to what things they are in any degree proportionate, and where they fail us; I suppose it may be of use to prevail with the busy mind of man, to be more cautious in meddling with things exceeding its comprehension, to stop when it is at the utmost extent of its tether; and to sit down in a quite ignorance of those things, which, upon examination, are found to be beyond reach of our capacities." (*Essay-I*, 1,2,4)

8.02. Kant's Problem and its Solution

Like other moderners, viz., Descartes and Locke, Kant answered that knowledge means certain knowledge. Such knowledge according to him, is found in mathematics and physics. Both of these sciences were making good progress. So scepticism appeared to him to be unwarranted. If, therefore, empiricism and rationalism had failed to explain knowledge, then their failure would not be reflecting any actual state of affairs in the world of science. Their failure would be entirely the consequence of their improper analysis of knowledge.

The failure of empiricism—Kant agreed with Hume and the perceding classical empiricists in holding that the manifold of sense-data or the sense-impressions are passing events. However, knowledge proper is obtained by ordering, connecting and synthesizing them into some system. Ordinarily, we systematise the discrete sensory data with the help of the categories of substance, causality etc. However, following the hints of scepticism concerning 'substance' made by Locke and Berkeley, Hume had come to the conclusion that there could be no intelligible account of substance, either material or spiritual. In the long run, the notion of substance, according to Hume, was an idle figment of imagination and of the association of ideas. In the same strain, Hume demonstrated that no intelligible account of universality and necessity involved in causality would be given on the basis of 'impressions and their ideas'. Like substance, therefore, 'causality' according to Hume, was a figment of imagination. Now if substance and causality, not to speak of other lesser categories, were mere fictions, and then certainly there could be no intelligible way in which the discrete and passing manifold of sense-impressions could be ordered. Without the order, there could be no knowledge. Therefore, scepticism is a necessary outcome of classical empiricism, according to Kant.

Again, as noted earlier,[1] on the basis of experience, strict universality and necessity cannot be obtained. So empiricism can never guarantee universal and necessary elements in empirical propositions. And, for Kant, knowledge proper must have universal and necessary factors along with factuality. So, on the very face of it, according to Kant, empiricism cannot explain knowledge as is found in mathematics and physics.

The failure of rationalism—According to rationalism there is a universal faculty of reason by virtue of which each individual has certain *innate ideas*.

---

1. Supra § 0.09, p. 23.

Knowledge proper, according to it, is exclusively constituted of such ideas. This theory successfully explains universality and necessity, according to Kant. All men have the same innate ideas because of their possessing a common faculty of reason. Naturally, being constituted of them cognitive proposition must be the same for all men. Again, all persons cannot but perceive the truth as their rational faculty directs them. Hence, cognitive propositions constituted by innate ideas must be necessary as a result of inner compulsion or constraint.

But the difficulty of rationalism lies in another direction. Innate ideas are subjective, being in the mind of human knowers. What is the guarantee that they will also be true of facts? Here Descartes and Leibnitz take recourse to *deus ex machina*. According to Descartes, God's veracity is the ultimate guarantee for the factual truth of *clear and distinct* ideas. Quite obviously, clear and distinct ideas by themselves do not explain their factual guarantee. This is most patent with regard to Descartes' explanation of our knowledge of the external world. But if clearness and distinctness of ideas by themselves cannot explain factual propositions, then the magic term 'God' cannot do this miracle. Similarly, according to Leibnitz, all ideas are innate. He has, therefore, to answer the question concerning their factuality. Here he takes recourse to the doctrine of *Pre-established Harmony*. According to Leibnitz, God has so created the monads that the order and development in one is reflected in those of all other monads. As such a thought of a table in a soul-monad called Ram is actually reflected in a bare monad called 'table'. But, how can Ram verify this correspondence? Obviously, he cannot, since being a windowless monad, he can never put himself outside his own cocoon-like monadic existence. Therefore, the doctrine of pre-established harmony is *a priori* assumption, which ordinarily cannot explain actual states of affairs. Hence, the doctrine of pre-established harmony remains an unverifiable and a fictional explanation of knowledge proper.

There is yet another difficulty of rationalism. Rationalism starts from certain clear and distinct concepts, and proceeds to other ideas systematically and gradually as a result of deductions from them. Thus, Descartes started with a definition of substance as that which is in itself and conceived through itself without depending on anything else for its existence. Of course, Descartes inconsistently enough had accepted the reality of mind and body as two relative substances. Spinoza tried to correct this inconsistency of Descartes. Spinoza through his rigorous logic concluded that there could be only one substance. Other things of our daily experience, including the thinker himself, according to Spinoza, are mere modes 'which never are'. As such plurality stands negated, and, yet this has to be included in any philosophy. Leibnitz saw this inconsistency of Spinoza. He, therefore, began with the plurality of monads. His difficulty lay in nor reaching any unity in plurality, to which reference has already been made.

Thus, rationalism has given rise to the two contrasted systems of Spinoza and Leibnitz. Both of them have the same starting point, namely, a self-evident definition of substance as appeared to them. Yet their conclusions taken singly are highly unsatisfactory, and, taken together are mutually contradictory. The upshot of the review is that reason, unaided by experience, can build castle in the air only, and, by no stretch of imagination can it lay claim to actuality. Therefore, Kant rejected rationalism on the ground that it dealt with airy structures without correspondence with facts.

8.03. Copernican Revolution

According to Kant, empiricism and rationalism both had failed to explain knowledge because both of them were based on a common assumption concerning the status of objects. According to both of them, things as objects of knowledge exist external to the mind. The mind therefore, has to approach them in order to know them. But on this assumption concerning the status of objects, how can knowledge be explained?

If objects be external to mind, then we can know them only by having experience of them. On the basis of experience alone we can never be certain concerning the objects. All that we can say about them is that such objects are such and such, and, we can never say that these are *all* the objects which *must be* such and such. In other words, if objects be external to the human mind which it has to approach to know, then universal and necessary propositions concerning objects are not possible.

Seeing the failure of rationalism and empiricism concerning objects, one requires a bold step. This situation of philosophy reminded Kant of Ptolemy and Copernicus. Copernicus was faced with a complete stalemate in astronomy which was at that time based on Ptolemaic assumptions. Copernicus, therefore, by a bold thrust of thought effected a revolution in that branch of science. Instead of assuming the earth to be the centre, he assumed the sun to be the centre of the universe. With this complete reversal in the standpoint, astronomy since then has registered advance by leaps and bounds. A similar reversal in the ordinary standpoint concerning the status of objects would make philosophy progressive, according to Kant. Accordingly, Kant stated that instead of the mind approaching objects, we have to assume that the objects must approach the mind to be known at all. 'Reason must approach nature not as a pupil but as a judge.' We have to assume that the mind lays down the conditions for the objects to become objects for knowledge. Unless objects conform to these preconditions, they will not be objects for human knowing. Later on, we shall find that these preconditions for objects are the two forms of sensibility (space and time) and twelve categories of the understanding (substance, causality etc.). Suppose there are a number of holes of various shapes and sizes in a surface of a table. Similarly, suppose that there are a number of pebbles of various shapes and sizes. Let these pebbles roll down the surface. Only those pebbles will be caught up that fit into their holes.

In the same way the mind lays down the conditions for the objects to be known. Only those objects which fit into these conditions are known; those which do not fit, are not known at all.

Only on this basis of Copernican revolution regarding the status of objects in relation to the knowing process, we can explain knowledge. Because the conditions which the mind puts forth for objects are the common properties of all minds, therefore, all minds as knowers will view objects under these very conditions. This would explain uniformity and *universality* in cognitive propositions concerning any objects whatsoever. Besides, these conditions are not the conditions under which the mind knows objects, but are those conditions under which the mind as mind *must* know them. The mind cannot help seeing things but in accordance with its own native constitution. The most important thing for Kant, therefore, is to show that there are certain *a priori* forms as pre-conditions for knowing any objects. Without this the Copernican revolution which Kant sought to introduce in philosophy could have not been effected. Many critics of Kant have raised objections against the use of the terms 'Copernican revolution'. It is pointed out that instead of establishing a heliocentric standpoint, Kant has really tried to re-establish a Ptolemaic way of thinking. We shall find that it is a fact that Kant sought to show that the mind 'maketh nature' or is a law-giver to all objects. Thus instead of showing the unimportance of the earth and its dwellers (men), Kant has sought to enhance the worth of man. However, Kant, by the phrase 'Copernican revolution', is not seeking to emphasise the dethronement of man or to wound the Narcissism of man, as Freud termed it, but is simply emphasising a proposal for a revolution in human thinking as was done by Copernicus.

8.04. The Critical, Transcendental and Agnostic Philosophy of Kant

General solution: Kant did not reject empiricism and rationalism outright. He tried to retain all that appeared to be valuable in them. His statement was that both empiricism and rationalism are right in what they *affirm*, but wrong in what they *deny*. Empiricism affirms that knowledge is constituted by experience, and, rationalism affirms that knowledge is constituted by innate or *a priori* ideas. Empiricism is right inasmuch as it points out that propositions of facts can be derived from experience. But rationalism is also right inasmuch as it points out that knowledge is constituted of *a priori* elements also. Again, empiricism is wrong inasmuch as it denies the presence of *a priori* elements involved in knowledge. In the same way, rationalism wrongly denies that sense-experience also constitutes knowledge. The proper view, according to Kant is "knowledge *begins with* experience, but does not necessarily *originate from* it." As soon as sense-experience registers its impressions on the mind, the mind at once is stirred into its own activity and contributes its own ordering activity into discrete impressions. The ordering activity is discharged by *a priori* elements. Knowledge proper is a joint venture of *sense* and *understanding*. But we shall also find in due course that the mind does not remain satisfied with scientific knowledge of the phenomena only. It also tries to *know* the suprasensible, and, this is not possible. Apart from sense and understanding there is *reason* which uselessly tries to constitute knowledge. However, the *Ideas* of reason are not constitutive but regulative principles of knowledge. Hence, according to Kant, *knowledge begins with sense, proceeds thence to understanding and ends in reason.*

That a factual proposition is based on experience is quite obvious and Kant did accept this contention of the empiricist. However, that there are *a priori* or universal and necessary elements involved in any empirical knowledge is a crucial point raised by Kant. According to Kant, any epistemology should have occupied itself with the enquiry of *a priori* elements involved in knowledge. These elements are independent of any experience whatsoever. Nay, indeed they are the pre-conditions of any cognitive experience whatsoever. Unless these *a priori* elements be operative, no experience of any object would arise at all. So Kant is not so much concerned with any specific objects of knowledge as with the universal or *a priori* ways of knowing any object. Hence, Kant has called his epistemological enquiry **Transcendental.** "I entitle *transcendental* all knowledge which is occupied not so much with objects as with the *mode* of our knowledge of objects insofar as this mode of knowledge is to be possible *a priori*." There are three modes in which the mind proceeds for ordering any empirical knowledge. In the first instance, discrete sensations have to be organised into space and time to give rise to *percepts*. These percepts have to be organised further still by the twelve categories of the understanding in order to give rise to judgments. Percepts and concepts joined together yield empirical knowledge proper. A further process of synthesis is effected *a priori* by the three *ideas* of reason, namely, the world, soul and God. However, these ideas are regulative only and concerning them no knowledge is possible. This conclusion of Kant, concerning supersensible and metaphysical entities is known as Agnosticism.

Agnosticism is that branch of philosophy according to which it is claimed that human beings have no faculty for knowing certain ultimate realities. We know *that they are*, but we do know *that they are*. Kant maintains that there are things-in-themselves which are unknown and unknowable. This doctrine of the unknowable follows from his transcendental philosophy. According to the transcendental philosophy of Kant only those objects are known which lend themselves to human forms of knowing. Naturally objects of knowledge would be transfigured and transformed by these *a priori* forms of human knowing. Therefore, Kant maintains that we can know objects only as they *appear* to us, coloured and transformed by our ways of knowing. What these objects are in themselves apart from our ways of knowing, of course, can never be ascertained by us. Hence, according to Kant, knowledge of the phenomena alone is possible; *noumena* or the things-in-themselves remain unknown and unknowable. Later on,

Kant has maintained, although they are not objects of knowledge, they are yet proper objects of *faith*. After all he was a deeply religious man and so he demolished knowledge in order to make room for faith.

Kant's major works comprise three *critiques* of pure reason, practical reason and judgment. Hence, his philosophy is known as criticism, as opposed to dogmatism. *Dogmatism*, according to Kant, is the presumption that it is possible to make progress with pure knowledge from concepts alone, without having first investigated in what way and by what right reason has come into possession of these concepts. Dogmatism is thus an uncritical procedure in philosophy without previous criticism of human powers of knowing itself. Hence, according to Kant, both empiricism and rationalism were dogmatic systems. The empiricists dogmatically maintained that experience exclusively constituted knowledge, and, in the end fell into the scepticism of Hume. Similarly, the rationalist, with equal dogmatism held that innate ideas alone constituted knowledge. They too ultimately became the architects of many a world of thought without correspondence with reality. The dogmatist set no limit to knowledge, and, the sceptic set no limit to ignorance. Thus, the one-sided and exaggerated claims of dogmatic philosophers earned nothing but ridicule. However, before we trust ourselves to reason, prudence demands that we subject this organ of knowledge to the strictest possible scrutiny. 'It is a call of reason to undertake anew the most difficult to all its tasks, namely, that of self-knowledge, and to institute a tribunal which will assure to reason its lawful claims'. Religion on the ground of its sanctity and *Law* on the ground of its majesty cannot escape this criticism.

A critique of pure reason, according to Kant, is concerned with the faculty of reason in general, in respect of all knowledge after which it may strive *independently of all experience*. In other words, Kant's enquiry is transcendental in which he seeks to lay bare the *a priori* elements which the mind brings to bear upon knowing any objects whatsoever. *A critical philosophy*, in the sense of Kant, goes beyond any dogmatic systems insofar as it is an attempt to reach principles, which are prior not only to a particular controversy but to all controversy.[1] The enquiry of Kant is almost exclusively concerned with *a priori* contributions of mind. The subject of the present enquiry is the question, how much we can hope to achieve reason, when all the materials and assistance of experience are taken away.[2]

8.05. Relation of Criticism with Empiricism and Rationalism

Kant's philosophy is known as a reconciliation between empiricism and rationalism. The points of difference and similarity between them can be stated in the following manner:

---

1. Caird, E., *Critical Philosophy of Kant,* Vol. I. pp. 7-8.
2. N.K. Smith, *Immanuel Kant's Critique of Pure Reason*, p. 8.

Empiricism	Rationalism	Transcendentalism
1. The mind at birth, according to Empiricism, is a clean slate or a *tabula rasa*. All the characters of knowledge are inscribed on it by experience only. Thus knowledge begins *with* and *ends* in experience.	According to it, mind is active and creative. As soon as we begin to reflect, we become conscious of certain innate ideas. Knowledge is constituted exclusively of innate ideas.	Knowledge begins with experience but experience stirs mind to become creative as well. Hence, in knowledge sense-experience is at one moulded and transformed by the *a priori* elements contributed by the mind.
2. Empiricism over-estimates sense and under-estimates reason. The intellect, according to Locke, can function only after simple ideas have been supplied to it. Similarly, according to Hume, intellect cannot create one single simple idea of sense. The place of intellect is at most secondary.	Real knowledge, according to rationalism, consists in clear and distinct ideas which are given by reason alone. Sense-experience can neither constitute knowledge nor can it ever confirm-disconfirm proposition given by reason. Sense provides only with an occasion for thinking about innate ideas.	Knowledge proper is a joint product of sense and understanding. The material is supplied by the sense are ordered and synthesized into cognitive statements by the *a priori* from of the mind.
3. Empiricism holds that sense and understanding differ in degree only. This is at least very clear in sensationism according to which thinking is perceiving or imagining.	Rationalism too did not make any sharp distinction between sensing and thinking. According to Descartes, and clear *ideas* and clear *perceptions* (e.g. of the external world) have the same status. But it was Leibnitz who regarded the distinction between sensation and thought as of *degree only*.	Kant makes a sharp distinction between sensing and thinking or understanding. Sensing is *passive*; understanding is *active* or spontaneous. Sense supplies the matter and understanding connects the discrete data into judgments.
4. Empiricism holds tht the data supplied by experience are discrete, distinct and unconnected. Any connection is introduced by the process of	Rationalism starts with clear and distinct ideas and connects them with the help of logical rules. But innate ideas by themselves have no correspon-	True, data by themselves are discrete. But the connection introduced into them by *a priori* forms is the same for all persons. Hence, though the

association and *imagination*. As these connecting processes are considered to be purely relative and subjective, so knowledge based on them is taken to be lacking in certainty.

dence with facts. Therefore, knowledge, according to rationalism, becomes purely conceptual and airy nothing.

connection depends on the *subjective* constitution of the human mind, yet it is valid for all, for all human knowers have the same constitution. But of course, knowledge is confined to phenomena only.

5. Empiricism is dogmatic, for it is uncritically assumes the constitutive role of experience, without reference to *a priori* elements. In the end it sets no limit to ignorance which finally terminates in scepticism.

Rationalism is also dogmatic since it confines knowledge to innate ideas only, ignoring the claims of sense-experience. In the end, it terminates in the inconsistent systems of Spinoza and Leibnitz.

Transcendentalism points out the importance of *a priori* elements in knowledge. However, it points out that without sense-materials, they alone cannot constitute knowledge. It successfully reconciles the rival claims of empiricism and rationalism and maintains a golden mean between the exaggerated scepticism and excessive claims of knowledge.

8.06. The Problem of Synthetic Judgments *a priori*

Kant held that Hume and others went wrong simply because they did not analyse cognitive statements sufficiently enough. Since the time of Kant, it is now accepted that a good deal of successful solution depends on a precise and meaningful statement of the question. Kant, therefore, stated that knowledge for his always meant scientific knowledge, the clearest examples of which are found in mathematics and physics. An analysis of knowledge in mathematics and physics reveals that it consists of *synthetic judgments a priori*. Now this important phrase, in relation to which Kant's epistemology has been developed, requires very careful explanation.

A proposition is said to be *analytic* when its predicate is already contained in the connotation of the subject. For example, "All bodies are extended". If we understand the meaning of the term 'material body' whose connotation was taken by Descartes, Spinoza and Leibnitz to be *extension*, then certainly the predicate 'extended' is already contained in the subject. Parkinson[1] has stated Kant's containment-theory concerning analytic proposition thus: "To all X to which there

---

1. G.H.R. Parkinson, Mind 1960, July LXIX. p. 397.

belongs the concept body $(a + b)$, there belongs also extension, (b)". So in spite of the unsatisfactoriness of the containment-theory, in relation to Leibnitzian formulation, Kant's statement is intelligible enough. Analytic propositions simple explicate the meaning of the terms involved and do not add anything to our knowledge. A *synthetic* proposition is one in which the predicate does not belong to the subject either as its parts or whole, e.g., 'Material bodies are heavy'. Whether a body is heavy or not is known through experience.

Again, a proposition is said to be *a priori* when it is independent of any experience whatever. *Necessity* and strict *universality* are the two criteria of *a priori* propositions and both of these criteria are inseparable. By 'strict universality' is meant 'true in all possible worlds'. *A posteriori* propositions are those which are possible through experience.

Kant does not take pains to distinguish an analytic from *a priori* proposition. However, it is clear that for him *a priori* necessity is different from analytic necessity. Again, *a posteriori* propositions are all synthetic. But Kant would not maintain that all synthetic propositions are *a posteriori*. According to Kant there are propositions which are *a priori* and yet which add to knowledge. Again, *a priori* proposition may have a predicate which is not contained in the connotation of the subject.

For a critical and highly informative study of analytic-synthetic and *a priori* and *a posteriori* propositions the reader is directed to consult *Experience and the Analytic* by Alan Pasch (The University of Chicago Press 1958). Here this much I hope, would suffice. The distinction between the analytic and the synthetic is based on the *content* of propositions. Here the question is, 'Does the proposition add or does not add to cognition or knowledge?" If it does, it is called synthetic; if it does not, it is called analytic. However, the distinction of *a priori* and *a posteriori* propositions has reference to the *sources* of cognition. *A priori* propositions stem from *pure reason* or pure understanding. As such they are valid independently of any experience whatsoever. *A posteriori* propositions, on the other hand, are derived from experience They, therefore, require experience for their validation.

For most of the empiricists *a priori* and the analytic propositions, and, *a posteriori* and the synthetic propositions are identical. For Kant, as noted earlier, synthetic propositions instead of being *a posteriori* may be *a priori*. For the empiricists in general, they are absurd and self-contradictory, and consequently nonsense. For Kant, however, synthetic propositions *a priori* are most significant in scientific cognition and are found in mathematics and in physics.

8.07. Synthetic Judgments *a priori* in Mathematics

Propositions of mathematics are universal and necessary. For example, 5+7 are together equal to 12. Being universal and necessary such propositions will be called *a priori*. But doubt would arise with regard to their synthetic character.

In order to show that 7+5 are together equal to 12, all that we have to do is to demonstrate that 12 is not already contained in the subject '7+5'. This would be regarded now as false. Most probably Kant's explanation is not correct, and, this will adversely affect the formulation of the problem which he has tried to solve in the *Critique of Pure Reason*. However, we shall confine ourselves to the explanation of Kant. According to him the subject '7+5' contains nothing over and above the uniting of both these two numbers into one, and in this no thought is being taken as to what that single number may be which combines both.[1] According to Kant, the subject '7+5' simply connotes a *process of adding* and in itself it does not refer to the *product*. Here, according to Kant, the predicate or the product 12 is very easy to calculate. This obviousness of the product gives one the impression that the predicate is already contained in the subject '7+5'. However, if we take sufficiently large numbers of six or seven digits each, then of course by adding on fingers we cannot reach the product.[1]

Obviously the explanation offered by Kant is not satisfactory. Indirectly he appears to be referring to the *psychological* process of adding, since he refers to 'larger numbers' to support his case. In the case of 'larger numbers' in the subject the actual process of counting them on fingers would not be possible to find out the sum-total or the aggregate. However, the consideration is logical. We have to decide, whether the predicate '12' is not already contained in the subject '7+5'. It is immaterial whether one is able or not to add the numbers on one's fingers. Here Kant should not have confused logical issue with a psychological one. It appears that Kant was aware of the difficulty and if he had not been prepossessed with the creative notions of his 'transcendental' philosophy, he would not have resorted to the poor explanation regarding arithmetical judgments as synthetic. Kant fares no better with regard to geometrical judgments.

A Geometrical judgment is synthetic, according to Kant, for example 'The straight line between two points is the shortest, Here the predicate 'the shortest' could not be contained in the subject 'the straight line between two points', since, according to him, *the straight* is a qualitative notion, while *the shortest* is a quantitative concept. Therefore, the quantitative predicate cannot be contained in the qualitative subject. Therefore, according to Kant, Geometrical propositions are synthetic. Nobody now would accept the explanation of Kant, since 'the straight line between two points is the shortest' is a primitive proposition of geometry and as such will never be taken as synthetic.

8.08. Synthetic Judgments *a priori* in Physics

Pure physics, according to Kant, contains synthetic judgments *a priori*. For example, 'everything that happens or every event has its cause.'

---

1. N.K. Smith, *Ibid.*, p. 33.

In order to hold that it is synthetic, we have to show that the predicate here is not already contained in the subject, either in part or whole, explicitly or covertly. Now by 'event' is meant any succession of two or more happenings. By 'cause' on the other hand is meant a *necessary* connection between two or more successive happenings. Consequently the element of *necessary connection* is not contained in the subject 'event' which means mere successive happenings. Thus the predicate 'cause' is not contained in the subject 'event' or 'things that happen'.

'Every event has a cause',

Hence, according to Kant, is a synthetic judgment.

Most probably there is not much difficulty now in taking factual judgment of physics as synthetic. At present, however, they are regarded as probable. Kant, on the other hand, regards such a judgment to have an *a priori* necessity. In other words, he thinks that a physicist undoubtedly takes recourse to sense-experience. But the data of sense-experience are discrete and chaotic. And they have to be organised and ordered into scientific judgments. However, here Kant would emphasize with all his might that no scientific judgment which is valid for all persons can ever be produced without resorting to the principle for causality. So 'causality' for Kant is a *must* for every physicist. The notion of causality no doubt cannot be derived from chaotic and discrete sense-data, yet this notion does help in ordering the sense-data. So causality being non-empirical can yet be indispensable for ordering sense-data or organising them into factual knowledge proper. So Kant regards 'causality' as an *a priori* necessity in physics.

Hence, for his 'Every event has a cause' is also *a priori*.

First, 'everything that happens has a cause' will no longer be regarded as universal and necessary. In physics the law of causal determinism has become outmoded. Therefore, it will not be called *a priori*. But in the days of Kant, without accepting the law of causal determinism no physicist would have proceeded in his investigation. Hence, Kant had taken this law to be universal and necessary.

For Kant knowledge means scientific knowledge which is found in mathematics and physics. An analysis of scientific knowledge of physics and mathematics shows that they are constituted by synthetic judgments *a priori*. And Kant in his *Critique of Pure Reason* tried to solve the problem, how synthetic judgments *a priori* are possible. But as indicated above, if such a judgment is not logically possible in mathematics and physics, then the problem of Kant turns out to be a pseudo-problem, and, his solution turns out to be equally fictitious and meaningless. In this sense the harsh judgment of Russell concerning Kant becomes justifiable.[1]

Hume, by his criticism of the concept of causality awakened him from his dogmatic slumbers so at least he says, but the awakening was only temporary, and he soon invented soporific which enabled him to sleep again.

---

1. *Ibid.,* p. 678.

However, we do not agree with Russell. First, Kant's philosophy is to be judged not in terms of logic and statements of science alone. They remain subordinate to his philosophical vision. And the vision of Kant is as living today as it was to him and to his contemporaries. Besides, the nature *of synthetic judgment a priori* was first stated by Kant and today its logical analysis is itself a fruitful enquiry. We think that the contention of Kant concerning synthetic judgments *a priori* can be formulated afresh to remain valid and significant even now.

8.09. Synthetic Judgments *a priori* in Metaphysics

Kant was most anxious to show that there are *a priori* elements in knowledge which are not derived from experience and yet which help in increasing empirical knowledge. This is the real meaning of the synthetic judgment *a priori*, that is, according to Kant, there are elements which increase our knowledge (i.e., synthetic) without being empirical (i.e., *a priori*), or, there are universal and necessary cognitions without being analytic. However, the central point of Kant lies that *a priori* elements serve to increase *empirical* knowledge. So some elements in knowledge have to be derived from experience. This condition is not observed in metaphysics, according to Kant. In metaphysics we deal with the supersensible entities like God, immortal self, the cosmos etc. None of these objects can be experienced. So the *a priori* principles are not applicable to them. Therefore, according to Kant, metaphysics as a science is not possible. The attempt at extending knowledge with the help of *a priori* elements alone, without reference to empirical objects, land us, according to him, into hopeless illusions. However, though we realize the illusory nature of metaphysical objects, yet we can never completely shake them off. Hence metaphysics, according to Kant, is not a science but is supported by a natural disposition in man.

> For human reason. . . .proceeds impetuously, driven on by an inward need, to questions such as cannot be answered by any empirical employment of reason, or by principles thence drived.[1]

8.10. Main Divisions of Kant's System

Kant was meditative and methodical. A desire for thoroughness has made him highly analytic. As such Kant divides and sub-divides his subject into indefinite details. So one is likely to lose the thread of the main argument. In the midst of leaves and branches, one gets a glimpse of the wood with some difficulty. Hence the remark of Wallace:

> There is a great parade of logical sub-divisions, and yet a great abruptness often to be felt in the succession of paragraphs. It is only gradually and with

---

1. N.K. Smith, *Ibid.*, p. 36.

labour that one can shake off the feeling of drowsiness induced by the multiplicity of currents which murmer here and there over the ground; only after several attempts that one is able to grasp the general drift and direction of the stream.[1]

It was Kant who has introduced the tripartite division of mental processes into cognition, cognation and affection. Corresponding to these three divisions. There are three *Critiques*, namely, *Critique of Pure Reason, Critique of Practical Reason* and *Critique of Judgement*. In the history of philosophy Critique of Pure Reason has played more important part than the other *Critiques*. Therefore, we too shall pay more, if not exclusive attention to it.

The *Critique of Pure Reason* is really a treatise on epistemology with special reference to science. But even here the cognitive process has been subdivided into three, namely, **sensing, understanding** and **reasoning**. But of course Kant is concerned with *a priori* sensing, understanding and reasoning. So Kant's enquiry is of the *a priori* forms of sensing, understanding etc., and not so much of the objects of sensing, understanding and so on. So in the first instance, Kant divides his Critique in the following way.

Critique of Pure Reason

Transcendental Aeshetic
Here Kant shows that there are *a priori* forms of sensibility. Everything to be perceived must be spaced and timed as the very condition of its being perceived at all. Propositions of mathematics can be synthetic *a priori* only when space (on which Geometry is based) and time (on which successive numbers are based) are *a priori* percepts.

Transcendental Logic

Transcendental Analytic
(In this central section of his work, Kant shows that just as there are *a priori* forms of sensing, so there are *a priori* forms of thinking also. Here he deduces and proves twelve concepts of the understanding. Scientific knowledge, as in physics, according to Kant, results from interpreting and combining the discrete manifold of sensibility in judgments with the help of the twelve categories of the understanding. This section contains metaphysical, transcendental deduction of the categories, the Schematism and the Principles of pure understanding).

Transcendental Dialectic
(In this final division of his work, Kant shows that without precepts, with the help of the twelve categories of the understanding alone, one cannot *know* the supersensible entities called the World, Soul and God. Attempts to know these three Ideas of Reason lead to three transcendental illusions called *paralogisms* (concerning Soul), *antinomies* (with regard to the World) and *Ideals* of reason (in relation to God). Though these Ideas are not constitutive they are yet *regulative* of scientific knowledge.

8.11. Transcendental Aesthetic

Here Kant tries to answer the question, how are synthetic judgments *a priori*

---

1. W. Wallace, *Kant*, p. 159 (Blackwood Series).

possible? Of course, according to Kant, knowledge proper is a joint product of percepts and concepts. But in this section, he is dealing with *a priori* percepts. The reason is that Hume had agreed that the proposition of mathematics were universal and necessary. But then he added that they were so because they were only analytic and did not described any actual state of affairs. In other words, they were purely conceptual. On the contrary, Kant was convinced that they were synthetic. Hence he tried to show that mathematical propositions were really derived from perceptual experience, put he also added that they were based on *a priori perception* of Space and Time. As such they were synthetic, according to Kant.

Now a percept can be either empirical or pure. An empirical percept is one which has been derived from some sense-experience. For example, the table before me or the black blackboard in front of the students is an empirical percept. A pure percept, on the other hand, is not the sense-experience of this or that object given in our present consciousness, but is at the basis of *any perception whatsoever.* Further, Kant regards this *pure* percept as also *a priori,* that is, the percept which has not been derived from any sense experience, but which is *presupposed* by any sense experience.

In order to show, therefore, that mathematics is based on perception, Kant is concerned to show that it is based not on any empirical percept, but on *a priori* or pure percepts, i.e., on those percepts which have not been derived from any sense-experience, but are presupposed by any and every sense-experience. According to Kant, space and time are the *a priori* percepts on which all other empirical perceptions are based. Hence, for him the statements that judgments of mathematics are synthetic means that ultimately they are based on the *a priori* percepts of space and time.

Further, for Kant space meant primarily Euclidean space, which according to him was unalterable and all-pervasive feature of any perception of outer things. Keeping these things in mind, Kant proceeds to show that:

1. Space and time are *not* concepts, but are *percepts.*
2. They are not empirical percepts, but are *a priori* or pure percepts.

Secondly, he has to show that not only Space and Time are *a priori* percepts, but also that unless they are so regarded the synthetic *a priori* character of mathematical propositions cannot be explained. The first part is known as the **Metaphysical**, and, the second part is known as the **Transcendental** exposition of Space and Time.

Metaphysical Exposition: Space and the corresponding notion of Time for Kant are percepts, i.e., are particulars and are not concepts or universals. We shall confine ourselves to space, supposing that the same argument can be applied to Time as well.

1. Concepts are formed by comparing the various *instances* and by concentrating on common and essential qualities found in them after ignoring their inessential factors. If space were a concept, then it would also be reached by

having instances of space. But are there *instances* of space of the same kind as are individual instances of the concept cow or man ? Three feet long or ten yards of length are not really instances, but are *parts* of a single space. Hence space is really one and has no instances. Therefore, it can only be a percept or one particular or an individual entity.

2. Again, the same contention can be supported by a slightly different statement. A concept *subsumes* a number of instances coming *under* it. For example, the concept 'cow' subsumes a number of particular cows of various builds, colours and kinds. But certainly all the particular cows are not lumped up together to yield the construction of a gigantic cow. Even if it could be done, the gigantic cow will not be known as the concept 'cow'. However, in the case of space, all the so-called instances of space come *within* it and go to make or constitute it. So really Space is not a concept but is a percept which is constituted by a number of its parts called spaces.

812. Space and Time Are *a priori* Percepts

It is not enough to show that Space or Time is a percept and not a concept. Rather the important thing is to prove that it is *a priori*. If Space or Time is not *a priori*, then it is *a posteriori*. If it is derived from experience, then two views are possible, namely,

(a) Space or Time is really objective, existing in its own rights. This was the view of Newton according to which Space is an objective receptacle of outer objects. Kant refutes this view of Newton, but we shall refer to it in connection with Transcendental Exposition.[1]

(b) Space or Time is not an objective receptacle, but is an appearance and is relative. However, it is derived from experience. Kant tries to refute this view of Leibnitz, to which we may turn now.

For Leibnitz only the monads which are spiritual, exist. As such there could be no space or time as real. However, Space or Time has been derived from experience of things as near and far, above and below etc. But Kant asks, if there was no notion of Space for the beginning then certainly there could be no experience of things as outside or alongside one another. The very experience of objects as outside or alongside of one another presupposes, the notion of Space. Therefore, instead of taking the experiences of objects (as near and far, outside and alongside) as explaining the notion of Space, we have to maintain that the notion of space is *presupposed* for explaining such experiences themselves. Therefore, experience cannot explain the notion of Space. The idea of space is prior to any perceptual experience. Hence it is *a priori*.

If the idea of space or time were derived empirically, then it could be imagined to be non-existing as is the case with colour, taste or smell etc. But though we

---

1. N.K. Smith, PR, pp. 44, 48.

can imagine a particular object not to have this colour or that, or not to have this smell or that, or even not to have any colour at all, yet we can never think of an object not to have spatial characters at all.[1]

We can never represent to ourselves the absence of space, though we can quite well think it as empty of object.[2]

Because space can never be thought away, therefore, for Kant, it is an *a priori* form of perception, without which there can be no perception whatsoever.

8.13. Transcendental Exposition

In metaphysical exposition Kant has shown only this much that Space and Time are *actually* given to *a priori*. Space is an *a priori* form of all outer perception, and time is an *a priori* form of all perceptions, whether outer or inner. The reason for this claim in favour of time is that even outer perception is a form of mental process which is always found in succession. Now by a transcendental exposition is meant 'the explanation of a concept, as a principle from which the possibility of other *a priori* synthetic knowledge can be understood.' (P.R. 45)

Therefore, a transcendental exposition of Space and Time consists in showing that the propositions of mathematics as synthetic judgments *a priori* are possible if and only if space and time are *a priori* percepts. Secondly, this possibility of synthetic judgments *a priori* can follow only if space and time are taken as the *a priori* forms of all perceptions.

If Space is not *a priori*, then it can be derived from experience. If it is derived from experience, then it is either an appearance, as Leibnitz supposed, or it is an objective receptacle of outer objects. We have already refuted the view of Leibnitz concerning the empirical origin of the idea of space, so let us see now whether Newton's idea of space as an objective receptacle, existing in its own rights can be taken as satisfactory. If space were an objective entity, having an independent reality of the perceiving mind, then it can be known only by being experienced. But if it be derived from experience, then the empirical notion of space cannot have strict universality or true necessity.

Thus the idea of space cannot be empirically derived. Therefore, it is prior to experience. Only by taking this as such we can explain the synthetic *a priori* character of mathematical judgments. Because space and time on which mathematics is based are *a priori* forms of sensibility, so they would be felt to be the same by all persons, since they are the subjective conditions of perceiving for all persons.

---

1. Here Kant seems to ignore the observation of Berkeley who pointed out that extension without secondary qualities is as difficult to perceive, as secondary qualities without extension are difficult to be perceived.
2. N.K. Smith, *Ibid.,* p. 44.

Again, since space and time are entrenched in the human constitution itself of perceiving any object at all, so human mind cannot help perceiving objects except as spaced and timed. Mind cannot help perceiving except in its own way. A child can perceive objects only in his own childish ways, and a dog in his own canine way by smelling them, so man can perceive object only by spacing and timing them. Space and time are the two glasses through which we can perceive the world of objects. If we do not use them, then we cannot perceive at all; and if we do make use of them then objects cannot but be coloured by the colour of the glasses. So human minds cannot but perceive objects in space and time.

Thus mathematical judgments being based on Space and Time can be strictly universal and necessary, only if space and time are *a priori forms* of all perceptions or pure intuitions. They will also be synthetic since they are based on pure perception or intuition of space and time.

8.14. Conclusions of Transcendental Aesthetic

First, we are not in space and time, but space and time are *in us*. This paradox simply means that space and time are the subjective forms of perceiving any object for all human beings. Because they are subjective in the same way for all human beings, therefore, they are truly objective. Ordinarily in the terminology of commonsense realism and science 'objective' is that which is free from any subjective involvement that is, in the cognition of which no desire, passion or any condition of the subject or knower should enter. This is, however, not Kant's or even the idealist's definition of the term objective. By 'objective' is meant for them that which is the same for me, for you and for all at all times and places. In this sense and time are objective, for they are public and the same and must be (necessarily following from the very necessity of human constitution of perceiving objects) the same for all.

> Objectivity is universal validity. . . .a dream all men dream together, and which all must dream, is not a dream, but reality.[1]

Kant at once hastens to add that space and time having universal validity, are certainly *empirically real*, but are no less *transcendentally ideal*. This means in simple language that space and time are real for practical concerns of life. They are not real absolutely. In the language of the *Vedanta*, they have *vyavaharika satta*, but do not have *paramarthika satta*. So far as the world of science and commonsense is concerned, they would be experienced alike as spatially and temporarily real. But in the final analysis, they are simply subjective *forms* of knowing.

---

1. One wonders whether *a priori* forms of space and time can be called pure *perceptions* at all. It has created linguistic confusion for Kant.

Kant later on makes an important distinction of *phenomena* and *noumena*. In the light of this distinction we can say that space and time can yield knowledge of phenomena only. This admission follows from the fact that whatever we perceive, we colour them, modify and transform them by spacing and timing them. Without doing this we cannot perceive them at all. But what things, apart from our modes of perceiving them, are in themselves, we have no means of knowing. Might be that objects are really spaced and timed, or might be they are not at all in space and time. For example, a fish can know what life in water is, but it cannot know what life in any other media could be. We do not know how angels or Gods perceive objects. We know only this much that we perceive objects only by spacing and timing them. But within this world of phenomena scientific knowledge is possible. Everybody perceives objects in the same way and must perceive them in space and time. Hence, universal and necessary knowledge of phenomenal percepts is possible for Kant.

Is there then no distinction between facts and fiction? Of course, this absurd conclusion does not follow from the doctrine of Kant. According to the view of Kant there is a great deal of contrast between the transcendental subjectivity of space and time and the subjectivity of the so-called secondary qualities. The so-called secondary qualities are called subjective because they vary from persons to persons; are relative to the perceiver and are contingent. On the other, space and time are universal, uniform and the same for all persons. The secondary qualities are subjective because they are variable; but space and time are transcendentally subjective because they are universal. Further, the secondary qualities are qualitative could not be reduced to quantitative precision. But space and time are at the very basis of mathematical precision. However, Kant would say that the distinction of secondary and primary qualities is applicable to the world of phenomena and even the primary qualities do not, according to Kant, belong to the noumena. Again, ordinary illusions like seeing a rope as snake can disappear after being checked. But this does not happen with regard to space and time which remain permanent and ubiquitous. The illusions of everyday life are like dreams which vary from persons to persons. Kant would call them as *mere appearances* corresponding to the dream-reality of Shankara.

From the *Aesthetic* one is likely to judge that knowledge is possible from mere percepts. This of course is false. Percepts are mere materials. They have to be further combined to yield knowledge proper. The work of combination is done by the faculty of understanding. But Kant was anxious to explain the synthetic character of mathematical judgments. Therefore, he has exclusively limited himself to showing the intuitive character of mathematical perception. Pure intuitions of space and time do not deal with the empirical properties of objects. Yet they do help in perceiving them. Hence Kant has shown that some contributions of mind are non-empirical, which yet help in the acquiring of empirical knowledge. Therefore, Kant has shown that there are cognitions in mathematics which increase our knowledge without being empirical. This is the same thing as saying that there are synthetic judgments *a priori* in mathematics.

One of the reasons for regarding space and time *a priori* is that one can never empirically perceive any object without finding it spaced or timed. One question can be asked? Is this inability logical or psychological? Kant himself is not very clear on this point. He tells us that this is the subjective condition of our sensibility. He also suggests that they are 'subjective constitution of the senses in general'[1]. Hence, in this aspect the subjective necessity of perceiving all things in space and time are psychological. But if it is so, then it is a matter for the psychologist to decide and not for philosophers. The main function of philosophy is to clarify concepts in use and to pursue an empirical enquiry. If this be so, then Kant's enquiry ceases to be philosophical or even meta-psychological.[2]

If on the other hand, space and time are logical modes of perceiving things, then they cannot be empirical. Most probably Kant never meant his enquiry to be psychological. When he calls space and time *pure* intuitions, then he certainly means that they are not sensuous. But if space and time are not empirical, then no judgment based upon them can ever be called synthetic. Had Kant been clear, much confusion of his system would have been avoided.

8.15. Transcendental Logic

Kant makes a sharp distinction between *sensing* and *understanding*. In sensing an object, the mind remains passive, as Locke's view of the mind as *tabula rasa* had represented. But this is not enough for the explanation of the knowing process. The manifold of sense are discrete and passing impressions. Obviously a proposition is a combination of two or more ideas. This knowledge consists of judgments which are the combinations of two ideas. Hence, the knowing process consists in *combining* the ideas.

Here the two terms 'thinking' and 'knowing' have to be distinguished. By 'knowing' is meant the thinking process validly applied to percepts.

∴ Knowing = Thought × Percept.

But Kant holds that thinking, being an active and spontaneous activity, unlike the passive sensibility, can continue to combine and synthesize pure concepts alone, even in the absence of appropriate percepts. This might give us the semblance of knowing, but which really can yield no knowledge proper. We shall find that in metaphysics we *think* about God, Soul and the World, though we can never *know* them. Hence thinking is much wider than knowing, and, the limit of knowing is not the limit of thinking.

Now we can say, according to Kant, that knowing consists in thinking about percepts. To think means to combine the percepts into judgments with the help of

1. Falckenberg, R., *History of Modern Philosophy,* p. 350.
2. PR, pp. 54, 56.

concepts. Ordinarily, we combine the ideas in judgments which have been empirically acquired and associated. For example, this grass is green. We have already acquired the empirical concepts of 'grass' and 'green'. Further, this combination of 'grass' and 'green' appears to us to be objective, that is, the same for all persons. The question is, how can this objectivity of empirical judgments be explained? There are only two ways in which we can explain this: (*i*) The combination involved in objective empirical judgments is really so in its own right in nature, independent of any human knower; or, (*ii*) this combination is *a priori*, being introduced by the faculty of thinking called understanding.

If the combination between ideas, as in the greenness of the grass, were objective in its rights, apart from human knowers, then it can be known only by being experienced. But experience can never bestow strict universality and necessity. But natural science, which for Kant meant physics, does contain synthetic judgments *a priori*. Obviously then the objective combination of ideas in judgments cannot be empirically explained.

Hence, as we have already seen in the case of space and time, the objectivity of empirical judgments can ultimately be explained only if we could show that there are *a priori* forms of thinking which are also termed as *categories*. Unfortunately, as observed just before, thinking need not be confined to percepts and may be applied to concepts also; and when it does so it leads to transcendental illusions. Hence the transcendental logic has two parts:

I. Transcendental Analytic Dealing witht the *discovery* and *proof* of the *a priori* categories of the under- standing	A.(i) Discovery of the 12 concepts of the understanding by reflecting upon the 12 kinds of formal judgments given in Logic. (ii) Transcendental proof of these 12 concepts showing that by their means alone an object can be thought to be empirically and objectively actual.
II. Transcendental Dialectic	B. Use and application of the concepts. This deals with the illegitimate use of the concepts with regard to the supersensible objects yielding the transcendental illu- sions of paralogisms, antinomies and Ideals of reason.

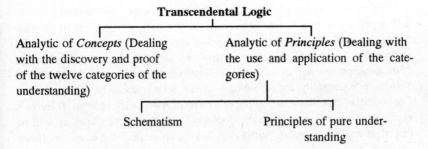

Transcendental Logic

Analytic of *Concepts* (Dealing with the discovery and proof of the twelve categories of the understanding)

Analytic of *Principles* (Dealing with the use and application of the categories)

Schematism

Principles of pure understanding

8.16 Discovery of Pure Concepts or Categories

Just as sensibility yields percepts, so understanding makes judgments possible. So let us take a judgment, 'This stone is heavy as it appears to me' or, 'It seems to me that the sun heats this stone'. These are instances of empirical judgments which are true to one subject only, as is clear from the phrase 'It appears to me', or, 'it seems to me'. This bringing together or the synthesis of 'stone' and 'heavy' is for my private, momentary and relative consciousness only. As soon as my consciousness lapses the heaviness of the stone will cease for me. Kant is not interested in explaining such transitory, subject-dependent and relative judgments. He wants to concentrate on judgments of science which are true for all persons in the same public way. In other words, he wants to explain judgments which are empirically real for all persons, which may also be called objective in the sense already defined. The example of Kant of such judgment is: 'This stone is heavy', or, 'The sun heats the stone'. If the statement is true, then it is so for all persons. Now Kant undertakes this problem in his *Transcendental Analytic*: What should be the nature of this synthesis or the concepts which help such a synthesis in order that such judgments be universally and necessarily true for all persons? One again the necessity which Kant has in mind is *a priori* necessity and not *analytic* necessity. In general, Kant thinks that an objective judgment, that is, a judgment which is empirically true for all human subjects, consists in a synthesis between two ideas through an appropriate concept. Hence, in order to lay bare the objective synthesis involved in an objective judgment, one should be sure of the underlying concepts.

Further, concepts may be empirical or *a priori*. An empirical concept is one which has been derived from sense-experience. For example, concepts of cow, colour or table have been derived from our experience of them. But such concepts cannot help an objective synthesis. The reason is that empirical concepts of cow, dog, or colour differ from persons to persons, depending on the varying sense-experience of the people. Hence, Kant is in search of *pure* concepts which have not been derived from any sense-experience whatsoever. He calls such pure concepts also *a priori*, i.e., concepts which are prior to or independent of any experience whatsoever. And yet without which no objective judgments concerning matters of fact are possible.

Now in an objective judgment like 'This stone is heavy', there must be some such *a priori* concepts which alone render such a judgment true for all persons. According to Kant, the underlying *a priori* concept in 'This stone is heavy' is substance-accident. Similarly, 'The sun heats the stone' has been possible because of the concepts or category of causality. Kant rejected the humean explanation of Substance or Causality, for according to Hume, such concepts have been derived from constant experience, according to the law of Association of Ideas. If Hume's explanation were correct, then the concepts of Substance or Causality will be empirical and not *a priori*. But if causality be an empirical concept, as Hume contends, then no objective knowledge based on it will be true for all. This is supposed to be the sceptical conclusion of Hume. But Kant would hold that such a sceptical conclusion is not warranted by scientific knowledge. Science, according to Kant, invariably uses the concept of causality and by doing so yields an objective knowledge of facts. So against Hume, Kant would say that Substance and Causality are not empirical, but are *a priori* or pure concepts.

Granted that there are *a priori* concepts like those of Substance, Causality and so on, without which no objective judgments concerning facts are possible. The further task is to find them out and also to demonstrate their number. How are we going to discover the concepts and fix their number? Well, the position of Kant is that knowledge or an objective judgment is a joint product of percepts and concepts. That is, as soon as percepts are supplied by the sensibility, the understanding which is the faculty of thinking out concepts, at once becomes active. Hence, the concepts of the understanding have not been derived from any or any number of perceptual experience, yet they are found in any objective judgment concerning perceptual knowledge. If it is so, then such concepts can be discovered and their number determined by analysing, scrutinising and examining all possible judgments in their pure form, without being mixed up with any empirical matter. Fortunately as Kant thought formal logic had established already all the possible forms of pure judgments, so the task of Kant lies in analysing such formal judgments by which alone, according to Kant, both the concepts and their number can be conclusively established.

8.17. Discovery of the Pure Concepts

Understanding thinks or conceives. To think is to judge. Therefore, in order to find out all the possible modes of thinking we have to establish all the possible forms of judgment. Kant took for granted that all the possible forms of judgments were exhausted in Aristotle's fourfold classification of judgments. In the light of recent developments in logic it would not be correct to say that these are all the possible forms of judgments. But at present we have to ascertain the nature of deduction or the discovery of the concepts. Kant has to discover not all kinds of concepts. Of course, there are empirical concepts. But empirical concepts cannot confer true universality and objectivity upon judgments. We have to confine ourselves to judgments from which matters of thinking have been abstracted. The process is analogous to the proof of space and time as *a priori*. We have to abstract everything empirical in the hope of discovering what is not derived from experience at all. In formal logic we deal with forms alone apart from matter. Therefore, Kant finds it easy to find out the pure form of thinking by reflecting on the forms of all judgments as given by formal logic.

Formal logic has classified all the possible judgments according to *quantity, quality, relation* and *modality*. Corresponding to each form of judgments, Kant deduces a particular concept:

Kinds of judgments	Table of Categories
I. *Quantity*	
1. Universal All S/is/P	1. Unity
2. Particular Some S/is/P	2. Plurality
3. Singular This S/is/P	3. Totality
II. *Quality*	
1. Affirmative S is P	1. Reality
2. Negative S/is not/P	2. Negation
3. Infinite S/is/not-P	3. Limitation
III. *Relation*	
1. Categorical S is P	1. Substance—Accident
2. Hypothetical if S, then P	2. Cause—effect
3. Disjunctive S is either P or Q	3. Reciprocity or Action-reaction
IV. *Modality*	
1. Problematic S *may be* P	1. Possibility—Impossibility
2. Assertory S is P	2. Existence—Non-existence
3. Necessary S *must be* P	3. Necessity—Contingency

In the first instance, readers may be confused by the terms 'concepts or categories' and 'judgments'. But there need be no confusion. We have defined a judgment as a *synthesis* between two or more ideas. How is this synthesis possible? The synthesis is achieved through concepts. Even an empirical concept brings together a number of observed particular instances under a general idea. For example, the concept 'green' clips together a large number of different shades of green. The same is true of 'cow' which pins up together all the observed and possible instances of black, brown, white cows and so on. Again, let us take a judgment 'grass is green'. Here the synthesis between 'grass' and 'green' has been achieved through the concept of 'green grass'. Further, the relation of green and grass has been possible because of their being experienced together for a number of times. The synthesis between 'green' and 'grass' has been brought together through the association of ideas. According to Hume a concept does synthesize, but then he would add, the synthesis is always empirical, being based on the psychological law of the association of ideas. Kant does not deny that there are empirical syntheses through concepts which have been derived from experience. He would, however, hold that such empirical judgments cannot be regarded as scientific or objectively true. Men have different associations and they will vary from persons to persons. On the other hand, scientific judgments, and what is the same things as saying that the concepts through which they are possible, are the same for all persons. Now Kant takes it for granted that there are such objectively valid scientific judgments, consequently for him there are again concepts through which judgmental syntheses are carried out that are true for all persons. Hence, Kant tries to lay bare those universal and necessary concepts without which there can be no objective judgments. Such concepts, of course, following the termi-nology of Kant, must be regarded *a priori*.

Those concepts that underlie all possible judgmental synthesis have been called categories since the time of Aristotle. Hence, the *a priori* or pure concepts can also be called categories. The most important categories for Kant, categories that lie at the basis of scientific judgments, are substance and causality. For Kant, unless such categories be regarded *a priori* no scientific judgments can be rendered explicable. The empiricist Hume, as a consistent empiricist, cannot accept anything *a priori*. Hence, this is the most vital difference between Hume and Kant. In any case, we can now understand as to why Kant is concerned with the discovery of the *a priori* concepts or a categories.

Kant has called the first six categories, derived from formal judgments according to quantity and quality, as *mathematical*. The remaining six were called *dynamical*. Mathematical categories are concerned with all objects, whether pure or empirical. The dynamical categories are concerned with the existence of these objects, in their relation either to each other or to the understanding. Again, the former have no correlates; but the dynamical categories always go in pairs.

Kant uses the term 'category' for describing *a priori* concepts. The term was used by Aristotle for all the modes of predicates in any judgment whatsoever. But the list of the ten categories given by Aristotle, according to Kant was neither exhaustive nor systematic. Further, Kant holds that the third category under each heading is a synthesis of the second category with the first. Thus, *totality* is plurality considered as unity; *limitation* is simply reality combined with negation; *action-reaction* is the causality of substances in reciprocal relationship; and, *necessity* is just the existence given through the possibility itself. Thus, this observation of Kant[1] might have thrown out hints for the triad of *thesis, anti-thesis* and *synthesis* of Hegel's famous dialectical method.

Thus, according to Kant, knowledge begins with discrete and passing impressions. If mind were not stirred into its own activity of forming and combining these manifold of sensory data, then there would be no knowledge at all. Fortunately,

---

1.   PR, p. 74.

mind at once is thrown into activity as soon as impressions are imprinted on it. First, the mind moulds the sensations by the forms of space and time to yield percepts. But these percepts too have to be further actively combined into judgments under *a priori* concepts of Substance, Causality, Affirmation, Negation etc. The underlying assumption of Kant is that the *a priori* concepts of the understanding have their legitimate sphere of the percepts alone. Hence, his oft-quoted statement is that *percepts without concepts are blind, and, concepts without percepts are empty*. Percepts may be compared to soft clay and concepts to moulds. Soft clay without being put into proper moulds have no specific forms. It is like Aristotle's 'matter' without any shape. Similarly, moulds without the soft clay is empty and by themselves cannot produce any image or earthenwares. However, only when the soft clay is put into moulds then we get earthen articles. Thus, Kant agrees with the empiricists that without the matter supplied by sense-experience there would be no knowledge whatsoever. However, he was equally convinced that without *a priori* forms of sensibility and *a priori* concepts of the understanding there could be no true objectivity in knowledge. So he agrees with the rationalists no less. Wallace has put this into the following picturesque style:

The spark of fire which runs along the line of sensations and sets them in a blaze; the string which gather the single beads into a necklace; the glass which collects the beams of sentient life into a focus,—is what we call intellect. Synthetic unity is the one function of thought—the one architectonic idea which lays sense-brick to sense-brick, and builds the house of knowledge.[1]

The metaphorical way of putting the relation between percepts and concepts can be replaced by a clearer statement. Obviously, mere ideas by themselves, as in fiction, cannot yield knowledge of any empirical object. So concepts without percepts are blank and airy nothing. In the same way whatsoever cannot be thought cannot be known either. For example, square circle is not an existing thing. Even if there were experiences, say the mystic vision of God which cannot be expressed or thought, then it would not lead to any knowledge at all. So any intuition which could not be conceived is infra-cognition.

Of course, moulds are meant for the clay. In the same way we can say with Kant that the concepts of the understanding have their legitimate sphere of percepts alone. But the understanding has spontaneous activity of its own. It works even when there are no percepts, with the result that we get pseudo-knowledge concerning metaphysical entities of God or Soul. Further, in the absence of percepts, concepts have the other function of arousing *reason* in the service of *faith* and *morality*. Thus, we have to determine now the following with regard to the *a priori* concepts of the understanding:

1. W. Wallace, *Kant*, p. 195.

1. The legitimate use of concepts in the service of knowledge. Further, the most important thing we have to do is to show that without the synthetic activity of the understanding there can be no objective empirical statements.

2. The limit of the useful employment of the concepts, the transgression of which leads to Transcendental Illusions.

3. The transition from the realm of knowledge to the sphere of faith and morality, that is, to the activity of *practical reason.*

We shall now take up the first part which Kant has discussed in *Transcendental Deducation of the Categories.*

8.18. Transcendental Deduction

First, the deduction is transcendental which means that it deals not with this or that instance of thinking but with the general condition of thinking. In other words, the enquiry is conerned with *a priori* mode of judging or thinking or connecting the matters of perception in judgments. We have to show that there are certain *a priori* conditions without which there could be no possible experience at all. Again, following the meaning of the term 'deduction' as used by eighteenth-century jurists, Kant means the establishing of the logical right of these categories in constituting empirical knowledge. The earlier enquiry has shown that there are categories which are involved in any judgment. But it is not enough to show that the categories are found in all judgments as a matter of fact. We have to further show that unless they are granted as the sole means of determining objectivity in empirical knowledge, our enqury would not be complete. Hence, *ranscendental deduction* means that there are *a priori* categories of the understanding which determine the objectivity of empirical statements and that by their means alone such statements can ever be obtained.[1]

At the outset a warning is necessary. Though the explanation which Kant offers is couched in psychological terms, its purpose is strictly logical. Kant agrees with the empiricists in holding that sense-impressions are discrete and separate. However, knowledge consists in connecting them into judgments. Of course, space and time are the first steps in synthesizing the discrete data into percepts. But this passive synthesis is not complete. Even Locke had noted that the complex ideas are formed by the greater activity of the mind. This activity, according to Locke, lay 'in comparing, contrasting and compounding the simple ideas in diverse ways'. Obviously, this activity of comparing and connecting is not derived from experience. Therefore, Kant argued that these connecting activities are introduced into the discrete data of experience by the understanding.

Again, from the *Transcendental Aesthetic* one might get the false impression that percepts do not involve any other synthesizing process over and above those

---

1. PR, p. 82.

provided for by space and time. Now we see that the perception of even a 'line' requires the synthesizing activity of the understanding. In other words, without the synthesizing activity of the understanding there can be no object of any empirical knowledge. This spontaneous activity of the understanding in synthesizing the discrete data is the *a priori* ground of any empirical knowledge, and is expressed in threefold syntheses, namely,

1. The synthesis of apprehension in intuition.
2. The synthesis of reproduction in imagination.
3. The synthesis of recognition in a concept.

The synthesis of apprehension in intuitution: Ultimatley any perception, whether of outer objects or of inner process, is given in time. Now suppose there is aline A B having various parts. Unless the divisions of A B are held together in one single apprehension, we cannot have the idea of A B as a whole. If we could

$$X \qquad X^1 \qquad X^2$$
$$A -- + -- + -- + -- + -- + -- B$$

perceive the parts alone, say, AX, AX^1, AX^2 etc., then we would perceive separate parts AX, AX^1, AX^2 etc., but not a complete line composed by these parts as A B. Hence, the multiplicity of parts must first be run through and grasped together in one whole. This is known as 'the synthesis of apprehension in intuition.'

The explanation given here reminds one of the Gestalt theory of perception. But Kant is not emphasizing the psychological phenomenology in perception. He is pointing out the logical condition of perceiving an object as one whole.

The synthesis of reproduction in imagination: Again, when we look at the line A B, we successively perceive the parts AX, AX^1, AX^2 etc. This observation would be clearer still if we take for example the perception of a building or a long wall. When we have to perceive the whole line A B or the whole long wall, then at the time we are perceiving the part $A X^2$, then the image of the previous parts AX and AX^1 must be faithfully reproduced and must fuse into AX^2 and other successive parts. If we drop out AX, AX^1 at the moment of perceiving AX^2 and other successive parts and do not faithfully reproduce them in our further successive perceptions, then no obejct can ever be correctly perceived as one whole thing. According to Kant, if this condition be not granted then even the most elementary perception of objects in space and time would not be possible.

Kant of course is referring here to the absolete fusion-theory of perception, according to which the past experience of an object is reproduced and fuses into the presentative factors of perception. For example, we are just receiving only the visual data of a tree. But we perceive a tree as hard, fragrant, solid etc., as a result of past experiences of touching, smelling, pressing it and so on. These past experiences are reproduced in image-forms and fuse into the presentative visual data to yield one synthetic perception of a tree. Now this fusion-theory is not supported by empirical evidence at least in the light of perceptual Gestalten. But once again, the explanation of Kant is not affected by the fate of the fusion-theory of perception. Kant is advancing a logical condition of perceiving the line A B or a tree as one object if each one of them is perceived part by part. And every object involving more than one moment of perception would certainly involve the perception of various successive parts severally. In order that an object be perceived to be the same for me at all times and for others the various elements of the manifold must be correctly reproduced as parts of a necessarily related whole.

8.19. The Synthesis of Recognition in a Concept

Not only the past perceptions AX, AX[1] are correctly reproduced but I must be aware of the fact that it was 'I' who perceived AX and, AX[1]. By this statement concerning 'I' is meant that there is the same consciousness which reproduces the various past images and fuses them into one unitary experience of an object.

> If we were not conscious that what we think is the same as what we thought a moment before, all reproduction in the series of representations would be useless.[1]

Suppose that the line AB is twelve yards long. If I perceive the fifth yard and forget that I have already perceived its parts consisting of four yards, then I shall not know the line as twelve yards long. But how would the past perception of four yards form part of the same line? Only if I be aware of the fact that I who am perceiving the fifth and the sixth yards of the line, did also perceive its previous parts of four yards. The consciousness which in perceive the part of the fifth and sixth yards is the same as that which severally perceived its preceding parts. Further, implicitly there is the possibility of my being aware of my own past experiences in relation to the present consciousness of the line or a tree or a building. There is an underlying unity or sameness of a self-consciousness. In some cases at least I can explicitly be aware of the fact that it was 'I' who perceived the parts and it is the same 'I' who am recognizing my past experience to be the same which had occurred to me in the past. Thus 'I think' must accompany every perception as its most fundamental condition of objectivity.

In other words, the consciousness which *apprehends* the parts severally which later *reproduces* the various images of its past and which finally *recognizes* them as one and the same parts belonging to one related whole must be the one and the same all through.[2] If we, like Miss Lucy or Beauchamp, what we perceive a moment before forget in the next, then we can have no knowledge at all. This can be

---

1. PR, p. 84.

2. "There must, therefore, be a transcendental ground of the unity of consciousness in the synthesis of the manifold of all our intuitions, consequently also of the concepts of objects in general, and so of all objects of experience, a ground without which it would be impossible to think any object for our intuitions; for this object is no more than that something, the concept of which expresses such a necessity of synthesis." (PR, p. 85).

illustrated thus with the help of a story.

A drunkard in a state of intoxication challenged a nawab saheb who was riding on an elephant and asked, 'what is the price of the elephant?' This infuriated the nawab and he ordered his courtiers to put him in the hajat to be produced the next morning in the court. The man was produced in the morning in the court and was asked: 'Are you going to buy the elephant?' The man with folded arms answered: 'The man who wanted to buy is not present here'. Phillip the drunk is not the same as Phillip the sober. But in order that there be a whole of interrelated parts there should be one and the same Phillip the sober.

The synthetic unity of apperception which is the final condition of connecting percepts objectively into judgments is not empirical. Descartes, according to Kant, in vain sought to find out the permanent self on the basis of 'cogito'. *Cogito* at most can say that there is thinking, but not there is a permanent thinker. Here Kant agrees with Hume that on the basis of empirical introspection nobody can 'catch the permanent self'. If one enters most intimately into what one calls one's self, then one stumbles but on some passing feelings of pleasure or pain, but one never catches one's self. But because one does not discover permanent self, therefore, one cannot argue that it is not implied in knowledge. The synthetic unity of apperception is *a priori.*

> There must, therefore, be a transcendental ground of the unity of consciousness in the synthesis of the manifold of all our intuitions and consequently also of the concepts of objects in general, and so of all objects of experience, a ground without which it would be impossible to think any object for our intuitions; for this object is no more than that something, the concept of which expresses such a necessity of synthesis.[1]

Of course, the synthetic unity of apperception is *a priori,* that is, it is a ground of any objective connection at all, without which there can be no knowledge whatsoever. The connection which is introduced is the same for me at all times for there is one and the same consciousness which carries on the diverse operations of sensing, imaging and conceiving. This unity being *a priori* is the same for all persons. Hence it is the absolute condition of objective empirical knowledge. But Kant would not agree that synthetic unity be raised to the status of one Absolute Mind. For Kant the *a priori* synthetic unity of apperception is only a logical presupposition of any objective empirical knowledge. However, Hegel and the Hegelians have transformed this logical presupposition of Kant to the status of a metaphysical reality. This is very clearly seen in Green's idealism where there is an easy transition from 'relating consciousness' to the existence of an Absolute Mind.

---

1. PR, p. 85.

This part, as also the main contention of the *critique*, assumes that sense-impressions are discrete and separate and the cognition of the object as one whole thing is a later work of construction and elaboration by the Mind. Kant would emphasize the essentially *a priori* forms of sensibility and *categories* of the understanding as the combining principles of the discrete, sensory impressions into the cognition of an object. But if we discard this assumption and accept that an object is a given Gestalt then the whole Kantian explanation would fall to the ground. Where will there be the necessity of the synthetic unity of apperception for synthesizing apprehension in intuition, reproduction in imagination and recognition in conception? Thus the rise of Gestalt psychology of perception has rendered much of Kant's Transcendental Aesthetics and Logic obsolete.

8.20. The Synthetic Unity of Apperception and the Categories •

In order that there be objects of knowledge, they must be presented as necessarily inter-related wholes. Further, to be inter-related wholes, they must be connected by means of certain fixed rules. These fixed fules of combining the percepts into objective judgments are known as the categories. Finally, in order that the rules be the same and identical for all, they must be grounded in the same unity of consciousness. This consciousness to be the same for all must be *a priori*. Hence, we can say that the combining functions of the categories are all derived from the fundamental unity of apperception.[1] We can also say that the peculiarity of our understanding is that it can produce *a priori* unity of apperception by means of the categories.[2] Summarising the result we can state the whole thing thus:

(I) First, we receive the discrete, disconnected manifold of impressions through our Sensibility. As soon as discrete impressions are received, the mind is at once stirred into activity and the passing manifold are arranged into percepts through the two forms of Space and Time. The combination of discrete impressions into *percepts* arises automatically. In any case the combination found in sense-impressions is not there in them, but is introduced into them by the sensibility which works only by spacing and timing them.

> But the combination (*conjunction*) of a manifold in general can never come to us through the senses, and cannot, therefore, be already contained in the pure form of sensible intuition.[3]

(II) But percepts turn do not constitute knowledge. For example, when we utter the word 'tree'. Is it a piece of information? No. Only when we give some information which can be rejected, accepted or modified *in principle*, then alone it can be given the name of 'knowledge'. For example, 'This tree is green'. This

1. *Ibid.*, pp. 92, 97.
2. *Ibid.*, p. 98
3. PR, p. 91.

can be rejected or accepted or modified *in principle*. Hence, it does constitute knowledge. But then it is no longer a percept 'tree': it has bacome a judgment. A judgment alone is a constituent of knowledge and is a true unit of knowledge. In this sense, a percept is an implicit judgment. Now a judgement is a relation between two or more percepts. How are the percepts combined into a judgment? All combination of percepts, empirical or non-empirical, conscious or unconscious, is an act of the understanding.[1] This combination of percepts into judgments is done through the concepts or categories.

(III) But the unity or the synthesis as a whole, at both the levels of sensibility and understanding is not itself derived from either sensibility or understanding, but is prior of and basic to both of them.

> This unity which precedes *a priori* all concepts of combination, is not the category of unity; for all categories are grounded in logical functions of judgment, and in these functions combination, and therefore, unity of given concepts, is already thought. Thus category already presupposes combination. We must, therefore, look yet higher for this unity, namely in that which itself contains the ground of the unity of diverse concepts in judgment, and therefore of the possibility of the understanding, even as regards its logical employment.[2]

This supreme condition of any combination at any level is the *synthetic unity of apperception*. Now all the principles of combination of the understanding are derived from this fundamental principle of the transcendental unity of apperception.[3]

This transcendental unity of self-consciousness is neither empirical (as Descartes supposed) : nor ontological (as later on Hegel supposed) : but is wholly logical.

8.21. Understanding Makes Nature Out of the Materials it Does Not Make

There can be no knowledge without some system and order. But obviously there must be materials to be ordered. Understanding is the sole faculty, according to Kant, which produces connection, order and synthesis into the discrete data obtained from sensibility. So far as human beings are concerned, according to Kant, they can think or systematise the data only when they are supplied to the intellect. Only through our sensibility can we receive our data. Thinking or understanding cannot sense, and sensibility cannot think. Of course, there can be an intuitive intellect, possibly of God, which produces objects by thinking about them. However, human beings have to wait for sensory data to be supplied to their understanding. For example, however hard we think of snow during summer heat

---

1. PR, p. 91.
2. PR, p. 92.
3. PR, p. 97.

we cannot produce any low temperature at all. Similarly, in our hunger pangs we cannot enjoy even a morsel of food if we think very intensely of a feast. We have to remain dependent hopelessly on sensibility for the materials of our thought. Only when the materials are given by our senses, concerning colour, whiteness, hardness etc., then alone understanding in conformity with the *a priori* unity of apperception can combine them into objective empirical judgments like 'this sugar is white'. Thus, understanding can make judgments out of sense materials which it cannot produce, but which it has to receive from sensibility.

Kant of course was very keenly conscious of the inadequacy of understanding when it functions with the help of concepts exclusively. By means of concepts, empirical or pure or both, not only we dream, imagine and produce fiction, but we think about the supersensible also. In the latter case we fall into the illusion of having knowledge with the help of the understanding alone. However, factual knowledge proper can never be obtained through concept alone. Therefore, Kant was of the opinion that understanding can rightfully function only when materials are supplied to it by sensibility. This follows from the very nature of the case in which synthetic unity of apperception comes into operation. We become conscious of the synthetic unity when there is an internal process within us, say the sensing or feeling pleasure. But this is possible 'only through the existence of actual things which I perceive outside me'[1]. Hence, the supreme condition of the objectivity in knowledge is based on the supply of data by our sensibility. Hence understanding can produce connected knowledge only when the materials are given to it. Thus far Kant would agree with the principle of verifiability.

However, here the first part of the sentence under discussion requires a greater elaboration, namely, *understanding makes nature*. According to Kant, understanding alone is the sole faculty of introducing connection, order and laws. Any system which we find in nature is not there in its objective right. If it were so, we would know it only by having sense-experience which can never give universality and consequent objectivity (i.e., universal validity). Hence, understanding alone gives laws to nature. But the question is, how can subjective conditions of understanding or thinking have objective validity? Why would nature respect the laws which our understanding prescribes to it?

In the first instance, by 'nature' we do not mean here 'nature over and above human mind, existing by itself as a thing-in-itself'. By nature is meant here 'a sum-total of interrelated appearances'. Naturally, nature for us is only a system of phenomena bound by certain laws or order of connections. So understanding gives laws to nature which is only a sum of phenomena, and not a noumenon. As we have already posited that there can be no connection anywhere except what understanding produces, so the system in nature can be the work of understanding only. In this

---

1. PR, p. 138.
   From such statements one can easily draw the Hegelian conclusion that the Absolute realizes itself as concrete consciousness by positing its 'other' called nature or matter.

sense, understanding gives laws to nature which nature cannot but accept. This follows from the fact that nature is only a sum of phenomena. A phenomenon is one which is moulded, transformed and coloured by our two forms of sensibility, namely, space and time. Secondly, it is further ordered and systematised by being conceptualised. If any connection has to be derived from understanding then nature in its *inter-connected* system of phenomena can derive it solely from the understanding. Thus, however exaggerated or absurd it may sound that understanding makes nature, that is, produces an ordered system of appearances according to its categories, nonetheless such an assertion is correct, says Kant, and is in conformity with experience.

> Accordingly, the order and conformity to law in the phenomena which we call *nature* we ourselves introduce and we could never find it there if we, or the nature of our mind had not originally placed it there.

Just as percepts cannot but be transformed by our forms of sensibility, so phenomena cannot but get connected, according to the laws which our understanding gives to them. If they do not get connected as our understanding would mould them, then we shall never have them connected. And if they be not connected, then they would be too transitory to be objects of any knowledge at all. Hence, nature as a system of phenomena cannot but obey the laws which our understanding prescribes to it. In this sense understanding makes nature.

8.22. Has Kant Faced the Scepticism of Hume?

Both Hume and Kant had agreed in tacitly maintaining that empirical knowledge can be universal, certain and objectively valid. Then again both of them were equally aware of the fact that empirical knowledge to be objectively valid has to be a connected system which is being built out of perceptual data. For both of them perceptual data were discrete and separate, so connection between them had to be introduced by the categories of substance, causality etc. But Hume was a thoroughgoing empiricist. If substance, causality etc., are at the basis of ordering the discrete sensory data, then, they in the last resort have to be empirically derived. He tried to do so on the basis of association of ideas and imagination. Kant did not pay attention to the part which, according to Hume, imagination played in the formation of the ideas of substance and causality. If the 'imagination' of Hume be very akin to the 'understanding-faculty' of Kant, then the difference between Hume and Kant would be greatly narrowed down.[1] But from the viewpoint of the history

---

1. Hume had pointed out that imagination as a faculty of producing belief works according to principles which are permanent, irresistable and universal. Again, as a faculty of producing fancies, imagination works according to principles which are changeable, weak and irregular (*Treatise*, pp. 225-26, ed. Selby-Bigge). Inasmuch as Hume tried to explain objective thinking with the help of 'permanent, irresistable and permanent principles' he came very near to Kantian solution (W.H. Walsh, *Reason and Experience*, pp. 181ff. Clarendon Press, 1947).

of philosophy we can say that the explanation of Substance or Causality by Hume on the basis of the association of ideas was not acceptable to Kant. The reason is that an empirical derivation of substance and specially of causality showed that they were idle figments of imagination. Any knowledge based on these fictions would be equally fictitious. For this reason Hume denied the possibility of empirical knowledge, and, in the history of philosophy this has been called the scepticism of Hume.

To-day the denial of necessary or certain knowledge about matters of fact will not be termed as scepticism. As a matter of fact no empirical statement can have the certainty of logically necessary propositions. Factual propositions can be probable only and it would be an illogical demand to ask for certainty, beyond reasonable probability, of factual propositions. However, Kant did not give this reply to Hume's scepticism. He wanted to defend the possibility of synthetic judgments *a priori* in physics. In other words, at least ostensively Kant sought to show that universal and necessary propositions are possible in physics. For doing so Kant attacked the empirical explanation of substance or causality given by Hume.

If causality were based on experience, then of necessity it could be only contingent, relative and variable like all other products of experience. Therefore, according to Kant, Hume had correctly shown that on the basis of experience all that we can maintain is that causal connection consists of *sequence* of events but not of any necessary *consequence*. On the basis of experience we can say that in the case of so-called causal relation there is *contiguity*, but there is neither *continuity* nor *connection* between the two events. But if mustness or necessity cannot be obtained from experience, then how can mere association create it with regard to mental expectation? In other words, according to Hume, if fire and heat go together for a number of times, then due to custom or association a mental habit is formed by which mind is forced to expect one (heat) when the other (fire) is presented. How can we ascribe necessity to the rule of association itself? Any law whether of association or of mental habit of expectation has universality about it, and, how is this universality to be explained on the basis of experience?

> How is this association itself possible? The ground of the possibility of the association of the manifold, so far as it lies in the object, is named the *affinity* of the manifold. I therefore ask, how are we to make comprehensible to ourselves the thoroughgoing affinity of appearances, whereby they stand and *must* stand under unchanging laws?[1]

We have already seen that strict universality and necessity cannot be obtained by experience. Should we deny like Hume that causality or substance is a figment of imagination? Kant agreed with Hume that the 'necessity' of causal connection is not empirical. For this reason it would also be a mistake to obtain 'necessity of causal connection' from experience.[2] But causality cannot be denied for with the

---

1. *Ibid.*, p. 27.
2. PR, p. 35.

denial of causal necessity, according to Kant, pure philosophy will be destroyed. Further, Kant held that mathematics contains synthetic judgments *a priori*. And with the denial of causality mathematics will also be denied,[1] along with general science of nature.[2] According to Kant, the correct approach should be that causality or substance is an *a priori* function of the understanding. They are born out of subjective necessity. But this 'subjective necessity' as a result of *a priori* endowments of the understanding is quite different from the subjective necessity resulting from the psychological law of association. As association is likely to differ from persons to persons, so the subjective necessity will also differ from persons to persons. Hence because Hume's causality is based on subjective necessity created by custom or association, therefore, there can be no universality and objectivity in knowledge based on this kind of causality. But *a priori* subjectivity is the same for all, because it comes out of a uniform mental constitution of any human knower whatsoever. Hence, *a priori* subjective necessity alone ensures strict universality and objectivity, according to Kant.

Therefore, Kant held that the scepticism of Hume was ill-founded. If knowledge is based on causality and, if causality is not fictitious, then certainly knowledge is possible. However, this possibility of knowledge is accompanied with certain limitations. Knowledge is confined to percepts alone which have to be moulded by the *a priori* forms of space and time and further synthesized by the categories of substance and causality and so on. These *a priori* forms of sensibility and understanding so transmute and transform all objects of knowledge that we cannot be sure of their real nature. We know only the phenomena. We have no means of knowing at all what things-in-themselves are. But within the realm of phenomena, we have knowledge proper. Hence, Kant's agnosticism is considered to be a sufficient answer to the scepticism of Hume. But is it acceptable to us?

Has Kant really directly dealt with the problem of Hume? Hume was concerned with regard to the universality and objectivity of such empirical laws as 'bread nourishes the bdoy' or, 'all material bodies gravitate.' His patent enquiry is, is there any necessary connection between fire and heat? According to Hume the relation is contingent, for we always imagine that fire instead of giving us heat may be followed by cold. Before we determine of nature of Kant's reply to Hume, we should analyse the problem of Hume.

In the light of current analysis of empirical laws we can say that in the roughest outline it has two parts, namely

(i) The protocol statements in relation to the theoretical construction in the respective science in question.

(ii) The connection between them through the help of the rules of logic and mathematics.

Both Kant and Hume would agree with regard to the first part involved in empirical laws. Hume like all other classical empiricists had imperfect notion

---

1. *Ibid*, p. 80.
2. As was understood by the scientists at the time of Kant and even much after until the establishment of the principle of indeterminacy in microscopic universe.

concerning the laws of logic and mathematics which go to connect the protocol statements, which in the language of Hume were called 'impressions'. The rationalists felt the importance of the rules of logic and mathematics. They, however, were wrong in holding that these rules by themselves can constitute empirical knowledge. Only in recent times a satisfactory relationship has been established between sensory data and the rules of logic and mathematics. True, Kant's explanation of these rules in terms of *a priori* elements in knowledge would be considered vague, inaccurate and even confusing. But it must be accepted that it was Kant who effectively pointed out to Hume that empirical knowledge is a joint product of senses and intellect (to which even Leibnitz had hinted in his criticism of Locke). Kant again was right in maintaining that the rules which connect the sensory data are not themselves impressions or their derivatives. What is called *a priori* by Kant is treated to-day as 'convention'. So in current language, Kant's terminology would be considered unsatisfactory. And it is so, but inas-much as Kant pointed out the importance of logical rules in the formation of empirical laws, he must be considered to have answered Hume.

But it is not enough to say that there are logical laws in the formation of empirical knowledge. One should have shown this in detail. Kant has not done it. His sketchy reply to Hume is that in general 'impressions' alone cannot constitute knowledge. Secondly, the rules of logic are necessary. This observation of Kant would be regarded as a meta-scientific statement. Such meta-scientific statements are too general. Unless rules of application are laid down for deducing specific empirical statements, they would be regarded as too speculative. And Kant also takes it in the same light. So, what about the specific empirical laws like 'all things gravitate'? Kant does not conceal this problem here. He points out that all empirical laws stand under the categories of understanding, but their content has to be obtained from experience.

> Special laws, as concerning those appearances which are empirically deter-mined, cannot in their specific character be *derived* from the categories, although they are one and all subject to them.[1]

But the important thing is to show that one and all of such specific laws are subject to the categories. And this Kant has not done. So his reply to Hume is only partial. Secondly, can any specific *empirical* law be taken as universal and necessary, even when it is guided and constituted by the categories? Hume would say that it is *probable* only. Can Kant go beyond this? Most probably not. Kant's observation here is that the *a priori* laws alone which constitute experience *in general* can be universal and necessary. Specific laws being dependent upon experience can only be probable in character. Kant should have said this much only that empirical laws can be probable in character and might have added that no reasonable scientist

---

1.　PR, P. 103

should demand more than this. Kant really remained content with showing that in the formation of empirical knowledge there are rules of logic which within their framework can be taken to be universal and necessary. But, of course, the time was not ripe for saying so. It was enough for Kant to have shown the place of the rules of logic or the categories of understanding in the formation of scientific laws. Thus, Kant's reply to Hume is not sufficient, but is certainly a step forward towards meeting Hume's scepticism.

However, if we analyse the whole problem then it comes to this. Kant replied to Hume by accepting the possibility of synthetic judgments *a priori*. Hume would not accept this. Therefore, we should pay a little more attention to the problems Kant raised and the solution he offered with regard to them.

8.23. Are There Synthetic Judgments *a priori* in Mathematics and Physics?

Many objections have been raised concerning Kant's distinction between Analytic and Synthetic judgments. In the first instance, it is pointed out that Kant's distinction is not logical but metaphorical. He thinks of subject and predicate as containers and contained. How can precise relation be stated by means of metaphors? Secondly, Kant refers to the distinction only when judgments can be expressed in terms of subject-predicate theory. However, since the time of Frege, Russell and others logic of relation has increasingly come to acquire more attention. Can we treat the judgment

'*A* is greater than *B*'

in the form of subject-predicate relationship? Obviously not. Should we say then that Kant's distinction is true for a very narrow range to judgments? Well, this can be said.

However, none of these two objections could be considered too formidable. By suitable modifications Kant's distinction between the Analytic and Synthetic can yet be upheld. But there is a third objection of considerable importance for Kant's philosophy. In the light of the definition of *Analytic* judgments, we can say that the predicate here is *necessarily* contained in the subject. Nobody can deny 'redness' of 'red rose' without involving himself in self-contradiction. So there is an analytic necessity. But Kant so defines *a priori* judgments that they also appear to be necessary.

Necessity and strict universality are thus sure criteria of *a priori* knowledge, and are inseparable from one another.[1]

Hence we can formulate the syllogism thus:
All necessary judgments are *a priori*.

---

1. N.K. Smith, PR, p. 27.

All analytical judgments are necessary.

∴ All analytic judgments are *a priori*.

In other words, in the light of the criterion of necessity analytic and *a priori* judgments can be just identical. If it is so, then the synthetic judgments *a priori* may come to be the same or synthetic judgments analytic. And this is a manifest contradiction. How can a synthetic judgment which is merely probably be also called *necessary*? This self-contradiction, according to the logical empiricist, cannot be removed, since for him necessity always means analytic necessity and as distinct from it there is nothing like *a priori* necessity.

Certainly Kant would most emphatically reject the contention that *a priori* necessity is the same as anlytic necessity. He would maintain that analytic necessity may yield *clearness* but can never help to *amplify* our knowledge. An *a priori* necessity helps us to do that. According to Kant, substance, causality etc., do help to synthesize and amplify our knowledge purely *a priori*. And this cannot be done by analytic necessity.

> Upon such synthetic, that is, ampliative principles, all our *a priori* speculative knowledge must ultimately rest; analytic judgments are very important, and indeed necessary, but only for obtaining that clearness in the concepts which is requisite for such a sure and wide synthesis and will lead to a genuinely new addition to all previous knowledge.[1]

A second point in this connection is that analytic necessity is quite clear to anybody by a mere inspection at the terms employed. For example, 'A rainy day is a wet day' is necessarily true by a mere inspection at the terms 'rainy day' and 'wet day'. In contrast, *a priori* necessity of causality, substance or of the two forms of sensibility require a very detailed demonstration and even then it may not be above doubt and further discussion.

How is it then that the empiricist fails to see this distinction in the writings of Kant? Of course, prejudice is one factor. But apart from this, Kant has interpreted the mathematical necessity which is merely analytic necessity as *a priori* necessity. For example, Kant explains

'7+5' are equal to '12'

as *a priori* synthesis. Nobody now will regard such judgments as synthetic. They are purely analytic, since in principle the predicate is already contained in the subject. Today we will say that this judgment is analytic since it is based on a consistent employment of the stipulated terms seven, five, plus, equivalence, twelve and so forth. But why has Kant called judgments of mathematics *a priori*?

Well, Kant thinks that the notion of number is acquired from counting and counting depends on succession of time. But the ultimate notion of time, according

---

1. N.K. Smith, PR, p. 32.

to Kant, has not been derived from any experience. Similarly Kant thinks that ultimately the whole of geometry is derived from the notion of Euclidean space. Kant most emphatically repudiates the contention that Space and Time are concepts which have been derived from our experience of relations between things. Yet, according to Kant, nobody can frame any judgments in mathematics without the notion of Space and Time. They are a *must* for any mathematician. Hence, he called such necessity *a priori*.

We might say now that Kant had some reason for regarding Space and Time *a priori* since in his days nobody could imagine that there could be mathematics without employing the notion of Euclidean Space and Time. But have we any reason now for regarding them as necessary? Of course, with the possibility of many types of Geometries, it is no longer proper to say that every geometrician must think in terms of Euclidean Space and the same thing is true about Time in the light of recent developments in algebra. Should we not say then that Kant's contention that Space and Time are necessary for all mathematicians and so are *a priori* in his sense false? Well, it might be so. Euclidean Space and Time are no longer necessary and so are not *a priori*. This only means that Kant's theory is not correctly illustrated. But this does not show that *a priori* necessity is the same as analytic necessity. All that we can say that Kant's contention is no longer tenable. But we cannot say that his problem of synthetic judgments *a priori* are self-contradictory. However, the empiricist may raise two more objections. In the first instance he may say that if Space and Time are not *a priori*, then any judgment in mathematics is only analytic and so, why call it *a priori* at all? Secondly, he might urge, has not Kant called space and time *a priori* what is not really *a priori*? It was a mere matter of historical development of mathematics that up to his time, Space and Time were regarded as necessary for the mathematicians, why should we take a historical accident for a logical must? We shall take up the latter question afterwards. Let us take the first question first.

True, by *a priori* Kant means that which is necessary and in the light of recent developments in mathematics the notion of Space and Time cannot be regarded as *must* for a mathematician. Should we not say, since the Euclidean Space and Time are no longer *a priori*, and so there is no longer *a priori* necessity for the mathematician, therefore, any intelligible sense of 'necessity' is analytic necessity. If it is so, should we not drop out the term *'a priori'*? True in the light of the present analysis of mathematical propositions, one would deny their synthetic character and would accept the view that the judgments of mathematics are analytic only. Yet with some suitable emendation, the Kantian notions of *a priori* can be saved. Kant can yet ask: Granted that the notion of Euclidean Space and Time be discarded, but can we altogether dispense with any notion of Space and Time? As we cannot; as some notion of Space and Time is still a must, so the notion of Space and Time can yet be regarded *a priori*. The only difference is this. The Space and Time of Kant's *Critique of Pure Reason* are fixed, invariable and *a priori*. The emended notion of

Space and Time will be variable, but yet *a priori*.

Most probably the notion of *a priori* too will have to be emended. Kant vaguely maintains that certain mental forms or ways of sensing or perceiving are embedded in the very mental constitution. At times his explanation of the *a priori* tends to be psychological: Whereas what he really means is logical. Hence, by *a priori* is meant 'psychological necessity' then it would be tantamout to Humean notion according to which there is a psychological necessity born out of the laws of association with regard to notions of causality etc. But a psychological necessity is just a fact, a matter of inner experience; and so cannot be called logical necessity. But if we regard *a priori* as logical necessity, even then we have to accept that this is purely a matter of convention. Some conventions may be more useful than others and we may grant that Space and Time are very useful conventions. But no longer by *a priori* necessity can we mean anything which is fixed and invariable for all persons at all times.

But after introducing these emendations in the philosophy of Kant, will there be any significant difference between the empiricist and Kant? I do not think so. Do we not then denude Kant's philosophy of its distinctive features? Well in the first instance Kant's contributions will remain disinctive in its own proper historical perspective. Secondly, Kant's logic and epistemology are mere subordinate elements in his total philosophy. The vision, the world-view of Kant remains as distinctive, as illuminating and as instructive as it was in his own times and even afterwards. As the synoptic world-view is the very soul of Kant's philosophy, so the distinctiveness of Kant's philosophy, so far as it relates to the most essential feature of philosophy, remains as the most rewarding adventure of human thought. Most probably there can be no higher tribute to Kant's thought if we could show that his vision can be yet defended in the light of modern logic and recent advances of scientific knowledge. We shall take up the second objection in our consideration of synthetic judgments *a priori* in physics.

8.24. Are There Synthetic Judgments *a priori* in Physics or Science?

Kant took for granted the Newtonian view of science, according to which Space and Time were regarded as the absolute receptacles of events and causality as the fixed and unalterable law of Nature. From this view Kant derived the conclusion that Space, Time and Causality are the *a priori* and fixed ways of ordering the discrete data of sensibility. These *a priori* forms of *sensing* and of *understanding*, for Kant were also synthetic in as much as they applied to matters of facts. Now in the spirit of Hume, the contemporary empiricist asks : Granted that there are certain fixed and unalterable modes according to which the mind orders the data. Is this conclusion concerning the ordering function of the mind analytic or synthetic, deductive or inductive? If the conclusion is inductive, then this is only probable in character. If so, then, these ordering principles of the mind cannot be called *a priori* (i.e., necessary). If, on the other hand, these principles be deductive, then we shall be simply explicating what we have already put into the stipulated definition of Space, Time and Causality. As such the conclusion concerning them can only be analytic and would not be applicable to matters of fact, and, so will cease to be *synthetic*.

The same dilemma can be put more pungently with regard to causality.

If the principle of causality makes an assertion concerning the matters of facts, then it is not *necessary* and is open to doubt; and, if it is necessary, then it does not apply to matters of fact.

For Feigl, Kant could not have escaped from this situation.[1]

We are now more clear about the nature of scientific knowledge than what people knew about the time of Newton and Kant. No longer we would maintain the fixity of laws either in Nature or in Mind. Even the laws of logic are no longer regarded eternal. They are all relative and some of them still rule the roost because of their usefulness, efficacy and convenience in our dealing with the world around us. If by *a priori* is meant that there are such laws of the human mind, then Kant's theory of the *a priori* would not be acceptable. Again, if by *a priori* is meant *the analytic* then the whole phrase *synthetic judgments a priori* would be self-contradictory. But did Kant mean anything so self-contradictory?

First, as has been suggested earlier already, Kant was just concerned with the problem of exhibiting the indispensable presence of the *a priori* factors involved in empirical knowledge proper. If sense-impressions be discrete and empirical knowledge be an ordered whole and also universal and necessary, then there must be non-empirical principles to account for strict universality and necessity. Of course, as we now know largely due to the Gestaltists that sense-impressions need not be discrete and due to the empiricist that scientific statements need not be universal and necessary. But Kant could not have gone beyond the intellectual horizon of his time and this is no reflection on him.

In the context of Kant's *Weltanschauung*, the order involved in scientific knowledge is not to be found in sense-impressions. Hence, it has to be traced to the faculty of reason which prescribes *a priori* rules of order and system. But does *a priori* mean for Kant analytic necessity? Of course, there are passages in the *Critique of Pure Reason* where *a priori* may mean analytic necessity. In the first place, both have the characteristics of universality and necessity and Kant makes no explicit distinction between analytic and *a priori* necessity. At times he equates the two. For example, with regard to Geometrical necessity he writes:

If he (a geometrician) is to know anything with *a priori* certainty he must not ascribe to the figure anything save what necessarily follows from what he has

1. H. Feigl, what Hume might have said to Kant in *The Critical Approach to Science and Philosophy*,, Edited by Mario Bunge, Free Press 1964, pp. 46-47.

himself set into it in accordance with his concept.[1]

But the two necessities are quite different for Kant. Analytic judgments, says Kant, do *clarify* concepts, but do not *amplify* them. On the other hand, *a priori* elements our empirical knowledge by synthesizing the separate and discrete items of judgments,[2] and Kant's sole aim was to lay bare 'the principles of *a priori* synthesis'.[3] So far as laws of nature are concerned the most important *a priori* principles of synthesis for Kant are the categories of causality and substance. Hence, his problem is:

> How categories can determine *a priori* the combination of the manifold of nature, while yet they are not derived from it?[4]

For Kant, all representations, i.e., percepts get connected through the faculty of understanding alone.[5] To-day the meta-scientist would not agree with Kant. He will not accept causality as the fundamental category, not even a category at all for sub-atomic events. Further, when causality is regarded as a category for gross material events it is not regarded as the product of a mysterious faculty. It will be regarded as a useful convention for describing the events concerning gross material bodies. Besides, laws would be regarded more as a matter of functional dependence between two events or even as a thing of statistical relationship. Hence the question of explaining *necessary* connection between events would not arise for the moderners. Should we, then, discard the contributions of Kant?

Well, the language of Kant is obsolete, but his statements can be easily emended. In a broad sense Kant was trying to bring out the truth that without the help of human language and its grammar it is not possible to have scientific knowledge. In his times, the rules of scientific language in the form of Space, Time, Substance, Causality and so on, were considered fixed and unalterable; to-day they are regarded as flexible and changeable conventions. There is no difference in the outlook for both Kant and the contemporary scientist agree in holding that in order to understand knowledge proper one should study the language of science. If Kant had known Quantum Mechanics, the theory of Relativity and the possibility of multi-dimensional geometries, then certainly his teaching would have been different. But he would still maintain that no knowledge proper is possible without the varying conventions of language and that these conventions arise out of the creative insight of the scientist. Kant would hold that no experiment is possible without some hypothesis in the mind of the scientist and finally any hypothesis ultimately rests on the scientific world-view. To the primitive man the world of

1. N.K. Smith, PR, p. 13.
2. PR, p. 32.
3. PR, p. 38.
4. PR, p. 102.
5. PR, p. 103.

magic was in the background in relation to which he would undertake to explain any phenomena at all. The contemporary scientist, as a result of much groping, has discarded every reference to the supernatral. Thus in science we do not observe or experiment upon phenomena at random. There are always some specific theories and far more specific hypothesis which we aim at confirming-disconfirming. The highly pervasive theories and the nebulous background of world-view may be termd *a priori* in the language of Kant. These theories and the world-view are not derived or are not empirically verifiable, but are relevant for any empirical knowledge whatsoever. Kant had this kind of function of the *a priori* in his mind which is reflected in the following:

> Accidental observations, made in obedience to no previously thought-out plan, can never be made to yield a necessary law, which alone reason is concerned to discover. . . . .Even physics. . . . .if learnt at all, only from nature, it must adopt as its guide, in so seeking, that which it has itself put into a nature. It is thus that the study of nature has entered on the secure path of a science, after having for so many centuries been nothing but a process of merely random groping.[1]

Therefore, for Kant the conventions at the root of scientific pursuit arise from the creative insight of man and without such creative froms there can be no knowledge proper. Emended thus the teaching of Kant with regard to *a priori* forms is as pertinent today as it was in the days of Kant.

8.25. Schematism

Kant makes a sharp distinction between sense and intellect but then the concepts must be applied to the sensible in order to constitute knowledge. However, the concepts are universal, involving no element of time; but the sensible is essentially temporal. For example, the concept of causality being a logical category is timeless and yet being applied to the sensible something is necessary succession in time. Now there is the need for something which will mediate between the heterogeneous elements of sense and understanding. It is the form of time which is the form of all perceptions, whether external or internal. Time is pure like the concepts and is yet at the same time sensuous. Every concept then to be applicable to the sensible must be cast in the form of time, i.e., the abstract concept is to be imaged in the time-form. Every universal has to be pictured, i.e., a concept has to be exemplified by an instance of it. As soon as we think of man, we at once think of an imaged man. Now each concept requires a general picture, an ideal particular. For instance the category of substance is the idea of something which is always a subject and never a predicate. When it is schematized then it stands for something permanent in time. "A secret art in the depths of the human soul' translates the intangible conception into a schema—a sort of generalised image, a universal which is withal

---

1. PR, pp. 14-15.

sensuous: not so much a picture itself, as a general formula or recipe for drawing pictures." Different kinds of categories are thus schematised:

1. *Quantity:* Time-series. One moment of time expresses *singularity;* general moments express *particularity* and all moments denote universality.

2. *Quality:* Time content. *Reality* is that which fills time, i.e., when a certain length of time is filled with uniform and continuous sensations. *Negation* is empty time, i.e. when the same length of time is characterised by the absence of sensations. *Limitation* is that in which we pass from the absence of sensation to some particular degree of sensation with a certain length of time.

3. *Relation:* Time-Order. *Substance* is that which remains permanent when everything else changes. *Causality* is that upon which something else invariably follows in time. *Reciprocal action* is that in which the qualities of substance and those of another are seen invariably appearing together in time.

4. *Modality:* sum-total of time or time-comprehension. *Possibility* is something existing at any time, *actuality* is that which exists at a definite time and *necessity* is that which exists at all times.

Thus the concepts come to be applied to the sensible throgh the time-schema. Our real thinking in science is pictorial,—always tinged with imagination. Thus the need for schematism ties down the intellect to a sensuous form, but then for the limitation to the sensible alone the schematism clothes the concepts in reality.

8.26. Transcendental Dialectic

Kant has so far shown that both physics and mathematics are possible. Now his enquiry enters the final stage. He has to answer, is metaphysics possible? There is scientific knowledge according to Kant, but then it is of the phenomena alone. We have no means of knowing the supersensible or noumena. We have all the certainty and objectivity of knowledge so far as phenomena are given. But this demands that the concepts be applied to the sensible. Beyond the sensible we can *think* but then we cannot *know*. Knowledge is, then, highly limited but the human mind cannot rest content with the limited sphere of phenomena. It craves for absolute spontaneity, necessity, originally and finality. That faculty which leads the human intellect to the unconditioned, the totality or the whole of knowledge is called *Reason*. "All our knowledge begins with the senses, proceeds thence to the understanding, and ends with reason." As the understanding illumines the sense, so the reason extends and guides the understanding. Just as the understanding unifies the sensible, so the reason instead of unifying the objects, unifies the operations of the understanding itself. We *infer* with the reason, just as we think with the understanding.

Physical knowledge is partial and conditioned. For example, nebula is the earlier stuff of the solar system which in turn is the origin of the earth. The earth with certain conditions gives rise to life and so on. The series can never be complete. But reason aims at giving us the totality of all conditions, the completion of the whole series. Certainly such unconditioned totality can never be an experienced fact. Thus reason aims at knowing the non-experienced or the supersensible. Reason unifies the understanding with the three ideas of God, soul and world in the same way in which the understanding unifies the objects with the help of the twelve categories. But we shall soon see that corresponding to these three ideas of reason there is nothing in the reality. They do not *constitute* knowledge but *regulate* it, by presenting us the kind of ideal knowledge. If we treat the regulative ideas of reason for the constitutive elements of knowledge then we fall into many illusions called paralogisms, antinomies and Ideals of reason. These illusions are called transcendental, for by knowing them to be illusory, we cannot shake them off. Though they are illusory, yet they are not phantastic. They arise from the very nature of the reason itself. Ultimately they show the farthest limit of knowledge and prepare the room for faith.

Reason is the faculty inference and as there are three kinds of inference, so corresponding to them there are three ideas. From the categorical syllogism has been derived the idea of an absolute subject which can be identified with an immortal *Soul*. The hypothetical syllogism yields the idea of the final synthesis of all phenomena called the *World*. From the disjunctive syllogism is derived the idea of an absolute unity of all phenomena called *God*. As said above these ideas only regulate and guide our intellect in the pursuit of knowledge but they do not constitute knowledge, for knowledge proper is confined to the perceptible alone. However, these ideas are so captivating that we treat them to be real objects of knowledge and so they give rise to the transcendental illusions.

8.27. Paralogisms of Reason

Psychology may be empirical or rational. An empirical psychology deals with the processes of feeling, emotion, thinking etc., which are given to us in our introspection. But these processes are all phenomena and are within the scope of the legitimate employment of the categories of the understanding. However, empirical psychology can never give us any knowledge of the permanent self or ego. In the language of Hume, when we enter most intimately into what we call our own selves, we never catch the permanent self at any time. But the human mind does not rest with the limited knowledge of the phenomenal self. It wants to know the permanent, eternal, free and the essential self. Inasmuch as this kind of self is not given in experience, so rational psychology (as opposed to empirical psychology) seeks to know the soul or self with the help of pure reason alone. However, there can be no knowledge proper without sense-experience or empirical data. Therefore, the bold bid of reason to know the supersensible 'self' is bound to yield invalid conclusions. These are termed by Kant *'paralogisms'*. 'A transcendental paralogism is one in which there is transcendental ground, constraining us to draw a formally invalid conclusion.'

As we think, according to quality, quantity, relation and modality, so transcendentally there are four kinds of illusory statements, concerning the self.

1. **Quantity:** The soul is *substance.* I am aware of myself as a subject and never as a predicate.
2. **Quality:** As regards its quality, it is *simple*, but nothing by way of its content can be asserted.
3. **Relation:** The self continues to be the same *identical unity* through the different times in which it exists.
4. **Modality:** Self is in relation to *possible* objects in space. It means that self alone is immediately given in our consciousness and all other things are mere inferences from perceptions in our consciousness. Hence, self is independent of all material things.

The conclusion of the *transcendental analytic* is that there cannot be any proper knowledge of anything unless it is given to us by perception. Of course, Kant has referred to the presence of the *synthetic unity of apperception* as the indispensable *a priori* condition of knowing anything. But is the synthetic unity of self an empirical fact? There can be no greater blunder to treat it as such. The pure self-consciousness involved in any knowledge is only a logical condition and is not itself an object of knowledge. The self is pre-supposed in knowing anything, but in turn is not an object which is known.

Now it is, indeed, very evident that I cannot know as an object that which I must presuppose in order to know any object. . . .[1]

In our current language we can say that the language of 'synthetic unity of apperception' is the highest language known to us. With its help we can know about all forms of language below its level, but it cannot throw any light on itself. In order to know it we have to find out a language of still higher order of generality. As we have not found as yet any higher level of language, so no clear and precise statement can be made concerning *a priori* synthetic unity of apperception. This is a rule of procedue or a linguistic proposal which prescribes the way in which we can talk meaningfully about knowledge. But in its turn is not an object or a statement about which we can talk meaningfully.

There can be no knowledge proper concerning the permanent self. Whatever statement we make concerning it being purely conceptual, may be either tautologous or analytic, or even meaningless and fanciful but not synthetic and empirical. Here we shall be dealing with the shadowy and chimercial concepts alone without the percepts. But with the help of mere 'bloodless' or empty concepts, we cannot attain to knowledge proper. For example, Descartes through his formula *cogito ergo sum* hoped to establish the reality of a permanent ego. But this is really a tautology, according to Kant, 'since the *cogito* (*sum cogitans*) asserts my existence immedi-

---

1. PR, p. 201. The reader is advised to consult a few pages more.

ately'.[1] As noted earlier, the *cogito* simply means that some thinking thinks.

Later on, we shall find that Kant has demolished the knowledge of a permanent, eternal and 'free' soul in order to make room for faith. We shall meet again these 'ideas' of soul in the *Critique of Practical Reason*. Meanwhile Kant has noted two important negative gains from paralogisms.

1. At least as long as one can *think* about these paralogisms of reason, one can free oneself from materialism. This shows that for thinking about self, one need not refer to material objects. So at least the thought concerning soul is possible without matter.

2. Of course, there is no knowledge concerning the immortal self. But paralogisms give me the right

to hope for an independent and continuing existence of my thinking nature, throughout all possible change of my state. . . .[2]

8.28. Parlogisms and Idealism

In § 6.07 we have already mentioned some of the characteristics of objective idealism. The contributions of Kant in the development of idealism are considered by many competent critics to be heavy. According to idealism there is an absolute mind with infinite potentialities which it realizes through matter, life and human minds. This form of idealism was greatly helped by the teaching of Kant in his *Transcendental Analytic*. First, according to Kant, 'understanding maketh nature'. This means that the categories determine the laws of phenomena in general. This transforms the *esse est percipi* of Berkeley into *esse est intelligi*. But more, in the final analysis, the concepts of the understanding can determine the objective knowledge of things only when the mind which perceives and variously conceives the percepts is one and same throughout the mental operations. Hence, the conclusions are:

(*a*) The synthetic unity of apperception is the absolute presupposition of any objective knowledge whatsoever.

(*b*) This self-consciousness works through the various concepts which determine objects.

Thus objects are thoughts or concepts, as determined by pure self-consciousness. Later on, at the hands of the successors of Kant, the logical condition of the synthetic unity of apperception was raised to the status of an ontological entity in the form of an Absolute Mind. Hence, the transcendental idealism of Kant was transformed into the objective idealism of Hegel and the Hegelians. Now this form of idealism held that the absolute mind actualizes self through the various objects which constitute nature. These objects are not only phenomenal, as Kant would

---

1. PR, p. 185.
2. PR, 197.

hold, but also real. Now the reality of the Absolute Mind directly follows from Kant's paralogisms. As a matter of fact Kant clearly states that transcendental idealism, which he holds, shows that nature or matter is but a product of mind. His statements can be briefly outlined thus.

According to Kant's transcendental idealism, no objects as things-in-themselves can be known. Whatever is known, is known as filtered through space and time which are the universal forms of perception, and later on is conceptualised by the twelve categories of the understanding. However, phenomenal objects alone are known. Matter or material objects do appear to us to be external to us and to be independent of our minds. But all objects, being phenomenal are *formed* by the mind. Even when they appear to be external they do so by virtue of being spatial. But certainly space itself is in us.

> Matter, therefore, does not mean a kind of substance quite distinct and heterogeneous from the object of inner sense (of the soul),. . . .the representations of which we call outer as compared with those which we count as belonging to inner sense, although like other thoughts these outer representations belong only to the thinking subject. They have, indeed, this deceptive property that, representing objects in space, they detach themselves as it were from the soul and appear to hover outside.[1]

Hence, Kant has cleverly hinted that nature is the 'other' of mind and is not as such refractory to the mind. Thus, the fourth paralogism, concerning the ideality of self, contains pregnant statements for the development of subsequent idealism.

8.29. The Antinomies

Just as the immortal soul cannot be *known,* so the world as a whole or as an ultimate reality, being suprasensible, is not known. Nonetheless the mind attempts to know all the objects comprising nature. This is simply a pseudo-problem and leads to mere transcendental illusions. The illusions may be called antinomies which have their 'content the unconditioned unity of the objective conditions in the field of appearance'. There are four antinomies according to quantity, quality, relation and modality which respectively refer to fourfold problems of *composition, division, origination* and *dependence of existence.* Both the thesis and anti-thesis are formally valid and can be proved with equal show of reason. None-theless they are opposed and inconsistent with each other. Here, again, Kant shows that there are only four antinomies:

---

1. PR, p. 198 vide p. 194f.

QUANTITY-THESIS
The world is limited in time and space

If the world was not created then it will become eternal. If it is eternal, then it means that an infinite time has already elapsed which is impossible. Time is a flowing series and as such at no stage it can be said that the series has attained infinity which would mean the end of the series.

Hence the world has been created.

Again, if the space is not finite, then it is infinite. But space being perception, infinite space would mean that an infinite number of things can be perceived at once. But this is absurd.

Hence the world is limited both in space and time.

QUALITY-THESIS

Nothing exists but the simple

If composite substances do not consist of simple parts then with the destruction of the composite substance, everything will be destroyed. This would go against the tested law of the conservation of matter and energy. Hence there can be a change of forms, but no destruction of all things. But composition is only accidental and the elements alone are real.

RELATION-THESIS
There is a free cause and everything is not determined.

If everything has a cause then we will go on backwards till infinity. But if everything is determined, then there can be no *first beginning*. But without the first beginning there can be no

ANTI-THESIS
The world has no beginning and is not limited in space

If the world is limited in space, then it is limited by something other than space, i.e., vacuum. But an empty space can limit nothing. Hence the world is not limited.

Again, if the world had a beginning then it means that there was a time when the world was not. But a time in which there is nothing is void. But the void is non-existent and in it nothing can originate.

Hence the world is not limited in time or space.

ANTI-THESIS
There exists nowhere in the world anything simple

If there is anything simple then it must exist in space. But anything in space contains parts external to each other. Hence there can be nothing partless or simple in the world.

ANTI-THESIS
There is no free cause and everything is determined

If there be a free cause then anything will produce anything. This will make everything impossible. Thus there can be no free cause and everything is determined.

sufficient cause for anything and this contradicts the law of causality itself.

Hence there must be a free cause to originate the world-series.

<table>
<tr><td>

MODALITY-THESIS

There is a necessary being in the world

The world contains a series of changes. The existence of every change presupposes a complete series of conditions up to the unconditioned. Hence something unconditioned or necessary must exist in order to explain any change.

Further, this necessary being must be in the world for only a being in time can originate a temporal series.

</td><td>

ANTI-THESIS

There is no necessary being in the world

Everything in the world is in time and being phenomenal is conditioned. Hence there cannot be anything unconditioned.

If the necessary being be out of the world and time, then being a non-temporal entity cannot originate a temporal series.

Hence there is no necessary being.

</td></tr>
</table>

In the antinomies there is no formal fallacy and yet there is an opposition between them. This shows that human understanding trespasses its limitation and ventures beyond into the unknowable. This proves that valid knowledge is confined to the phenomena and must not be extended beyond into the noumena. Again, the first two antinomies, called mathematical, are too inadequate. Either they are too wide or too narrow. Hence they are false. But the dynamical antinomies arising from relation and modality can both be true, in different contexts. The phenomenal world is determined but the noumenal world may be free. "Without unbroken causal connection, there is no nature; without freedom, no morality; without a Deity, no religion."

Antinomies show that nothing in the empirical discovery can be regarded final. The idea of the world constrains the understanding to find out the further term in the series.

8.30. Functions of the Cosmological Ideas

As both thesis and anti-thesis, according to Kant, are formally valid, so we cannot decide in favour of either side. All that can be inferred is that in relation to our speculation concerning cosmological matters, we seem to be at the end of the tether. They mark the limit of our knowledge. However they have also some regulative functions to serve and they can be thus noted:

(a) These together may form a dogmatic side of our philosophy. Dogmatism in this sense has importance, for guarding, sustaining and furthering the *practical interest* of man. In general theses maintain that there is a *primordial* being who has created the universe with a design for evolving creatures worthy of his fellowship. These dogmatic affirmations uphold the foundations of morals and religion.

(b) These have the function of furthering *speculative interest* as well. By postulating the beginning of the universe, along with eternal (simple) creatures (men) by a primordial being.

> The entire chain of conditions and the derivation of the conditioned can be grasped completely *a priori.*

Hence, the cosmological enquiries escape from fruitless *regressus ad infinitum.*

(c) These are supported to a great extent by commonsense and has the advantage of *popularity.* Hence, they guide the practical and theoretical interests of ordinary men and afford philosophical comfort and religious consolation to them.

Therefore, the theses serve an architectonic interest of philosophy by yielding *a priori* unity of reason.

Anti-theses arise from an empirical temper of the mind, according to Kant. They hold that there is no primordial being as distinct from the world, that there is no beginning of the world and that man's soul is perishable and determined. Such views *do not support the practical interest of* men.

However, the anti-theses fully compensate for the above-mentioned disadvantage with regard to morals and religious values. They offer far greater advantages concerning the *speculative interest* of man. They limit knowledge proper to genuinely possible experiences, investigating their laws and afford indefinite extension to sure and comprehensible knowledge. They encourage the study of nature and discourage deviations into supernatural investigation and specious forms of knowledge with regard to supernatural laws.

If the empiricist, holding anti-theses, is satisfied with this important task of urging moderation in our pretensions, of maintaining modesty in assertion and of encouraging empirical investigations of nature, then nothing but good would result. If kept within restraint, the antitheses would maintain only this much that there is *no scientific knowledge* of the creator of the world or of the eternal soul. But this cautious assertion does not cut off the ground of *faith* with regard to these entities. However, empiricism is likely to develop into a dogmatic temper and as such may confidently deny the reality of the supersensible. In doing so empiricism would lack the same modesty which the theses seem to encourage and would also do harm to the cause of morals and religion.

8.31. Antinomies and Hegel's Dialectic Method

Hegel is as much indebted to Socrates and Plato for getting hints for his dialectic method as he is to Kant. First a careful scrutiny of Kant's list of the categories would show that the third category in each of the fourfold classifications is a synthesis of the former two categories. For example, totality is plurality regarded as unity. Thus, the first two categories may be treated as thesis and anti-thesis, inviting a synthesis. Secondly, the antinomies give another hint in relation to the development of the dialectic method. Here the thesis and anti-thesis are strongly contrasted, yet they appear to be true as well. Kant did not think that any synthesis is possible. Here

Hegel was itched into thinking. According to Hegel, so we surmise, Kant could not reconcile the antithetical claims of the antinomies, since Kant confined himself to the *understanding* which deals with the static laws of non-contradiction. However, Hegel urged that *speculative reason* can proceed ahead, because of the contradictions, towards an all-harmonious and all-inclusive Absolute through a dialectic advance.

8.32. The Ideal of Pure Reason

The ideal of reason is not a mere idea, but is an ideal. It contains the sum of all possibility. The ideal seems to be farther removed from objective reality than the ideas of the world and soul. Further, this ideal refers to an individual, popularly known as a personal God.

> By the ideal I understand the idea, not merely *in concrete*, but *in individuo*, that is, as an individual thing, determinable or even determined by the idea alone.[1]

In other words, the transcendental ideal seeks to prove the existence of God with the help of pure concepts alone. Kant states that there are three and three proofs only for proving the existence of God, namely, ontological, physico-theological and cosmological. However, later on, he shows that physico-theological[2] proof tests upon the cosmological which in turn leans upon the ontological proof.[3] Hence, Kant pays special attention to the ontological proof and his refutation is even now repeated by standard authors of theology.

8.33. Ontological Proof

'Ontos' means essence. Hence, by the ontological proof is meant that 'existence' is the very essence of the idea of God. In other words we cannot think of God except as an existing being. The existence of God follows necessarily from his idea in the same way in which the three sidedness follows from the very definition of a triangle.

The ontological proof was fully developed by Anselm, Descartes and Leibnitz. We have already referred to the Cartesian treatment of the ontological proof. We would now follow Kant's refutation of the ontological argument.

First, there is a transgression here of linguistic usage. God is said to be an absolutely *necessary being*. But 'necessary' is used with reference to propositions and not with reference to 'things' or 'beings'.

> All the alleged examples are, without exception, taken for *judgements*, not from *things* and their existence. But the unconditioned necessity of judgments is not

---

1. PR, p. 269.
2. Popularly known a 'Teleological.'
3. PR, p. 298.

the same as an absolute necessity of things.[1]

Again, a proposition is necessary if its predicate cannot be denied without involving us in self-contradiction. For example, 'A triangle is a plane rectilineal figure bounded by three straight lines'. But in contrast to it, a synthetic proposition is that whose predicate can be denied without contradiction. This is true of every empirical proposition e.g., 'This table is brown'. We can always imagine this table to be of a different colour from what it is. Now if 'existence' is a predicate of God in an empirical proposition, then we can always imagine it to be different from what it is. Hence, the concepts concerning a "necessary being" are self-contradictory.

> But if, on the other hand, we admit as every reasonable person must, that all existential propositions are synthetic, how can we profess to maintain that the predicate of existence cannot be rejected without contradiction? This is a feature which is found only analytic propositions, and is indeed precisely what constitutes their analytic character.[2]

Besides, Kant holds that 'existence' is not a real predicate. It is a mere sign of the copula in a judgment. The word 'is' adds no new predicate.[3] By mere 'thought' or 'concepts' we cannot bring anything into existence. If thoughts were things, beggars would ride horses, nay, all will be kings and there would be no serfs. The concept of God remains a concept, no matter how hard we think about it.

Later on Caird wanted to rehabilitate the ontological proof by holding to the Hegelian doctrine of the inseparability of thought and things. He pointed out that God is such an idea that it guarantees its own existence. If it were not so, every possibility of thinking would cease. Kant seems to have anticipated this defence of the argument.[4] His reply to this plea is:

> My answer is as follows. There is already a contradiction introducing the concept of existence—no matter under what title it may be disguised—into the concept of a thing which we profess to be thinking solely in reference to its possibility."[5]

8.34. Cosmological Proof

Often it is maintained that the ontological proof fails simply because it is *a priori* proof for the existence of a being. However, existence is given in our experience. So it is argued that only proof which starts at least from experience can succeed

---

1. PR, p. 279.
2. PR, p. 281.
3. PR, p. 282.
4. PR, p. 280f.
5. PR, p. 281.

in yielding the existence of God. Now the cosmological argument in this relation proposes to make good the deficiency of the ontological proof.

The cosmological proof has its starting point in the contingency of the world. Every phenomenon is conditioned by its antecedents and they in turn by their own antecedents. The chain extends to infinity. But no matter how far we extend backward, we can never catch the total causes or antecedents of phenomena of the world. Hence, in order to explain this contingency of the world we are forced to assume the reality of an uncaused cause or a necessary being at the basis of the world.

Criticisim: Though the proof proposes to start from experience, yet its claim in favour of experience is spurious. The proof is concerned with only one characteristic of the world in general, namely, its contingency. It is not concerned seriously even with the aspect of the world. Its sole aim is to conclude the existence of a necessary being. But the contention concerning the necessary existence of God in ontological argument is repeated once again. Hence, the appeal to experience concerning the contingency of the world is merely a show of empirical proof. It is as much conceptual as the ontological argument.

Again, the contingency of the world is sought to be shown with the help of the principle of causality. However, the principle has no meaning to the supersensible world. The concept of a first cause, which in itself cannot be explained in terms of causality at all. From the premises forming a causal series (or caused causes), we cannot infer the existence of an uncaused cause. It appears that the conclusion is not at all contained in the premises. From contingency we can infer contingency, and not its opposite, namely, necessary being.

Conclusion: The truth is that it is legitimate to *admit* the existence of an all-sufficient cause or Being to assist reason in its quest for final unity, yet we cannot *assert* the existence of such a Being.

8.35. Physico-theological Proof (Teleological Proof)
The cosmological proof has only an empirical touch. It appeals to highly abstracted quality of contingency of the empirical world. In contrast to this, the physico-theological proof refers to a specific characteristic of the world, namely, its order. The argument starts from the variety, order, purposiveness and beauty which are found in nature in general as well as in its infinite details. From this it is inferred that there is a design and therefore there is a supreme Designer or Intelligence who has created the world. The several steps in the argument can be thus outlined.

(a) There is order in the universe, indescribably varied in content and unlimited in extent.

(b) This order is quite alien to the world and has been introduced into it contingently, for the fulfilment of determinate final purposes.

(c) The whole of the infinite order can be explained with reference to a design.

As the order is infinite, so the cause or author of this design must be an infinite intelligence.

Kant considers this physico-theological proof to be as untenable as the other two previous ones. However, he thinks that this proof strengthens the belief in the supreme Author with an irresistable force.

This proof always deserves to be mentioned with respect. It is the oldest, the clearest, and the most accordant with the common reason of mankind.

It also encourages the scientist to study the details of nature with enlivened interest. But in spite of these practical and theoretical advantages, the proof fails to establish the existence of God.

8.36. Criticism

1. This proof at most is *analogical*. It is based on the analogy of a mechanic in relation to its machine or of a pot in relation to a potter. This, therefore, has no force of demonstration.

What is the guarantee that the world in its infinite wealth of details is not full of blemishes, ugliness and disorder? Who can speak of the world as a whole?

Since the time of Kant such questions have multiplied and thinkers have not been slow in pointing out many cases of imperfection in the world. John S. Mill, J. Laird, J. Mackie, McCloskey have elaborated the objection against the argument from design on account of unaccountable evil in the world.

2. This proof at most shows that there is an *Author of* the world, but it does not show that there is a *Creator* of the universe. An architect is one who shapes and moulds something out of some pre-existing material.[1]

For example, a potter makes a pot out of pre-existing clay. An architect, therefore, co-exists with his material. Therefore, even an infinite architect presupposes the reality of matter which he, by his intelligence, fashions into an orderly universe. This means that God becomes *limited by matter*. However, creator God must be infinite and must create matter also out of himself.

3. This proof is really a disguised form of cosmological argument.[2] The second step in the argument assumes that the world of itself cannot give rise to the order that we behold with speechless wonder. Hence, the argument assumes that the order is contingent and requires therefore an external machinery to account for it. But who knows that the world by itself as given rise to this order by mere fortuitous combinations and permutations of its various elements?

---

1. PR. p. 296.
2. PR, p. 294, 297

Kant could have not been aware of Hume's argument in favour of self-regulating and self-ordering universe. But since the time of Hume and Kant, the view of a self-regulating universe has gained ground, largely under the influence of the theory of Cosmic Evolution. The theory of mechanical and *natural* selection in nature is supposed to be sufficient to account for the adaptation of means and ends. Anything that will not be adapted, of itself in the struggle of existence for the survival of the fittest would go out of existence.

Now if the order in the universe be not contingent, but implanted in it, then the question concerning the author of this orderly universe does not arise. Like Laplace, we can say, we have no need of an hypothesis concerning author of the universe. The universe by itself is self-explanatory. Hence, we have to add that any order in the universe is contingent and ultimately is grounded in an infinite Intelligence or Mind. But then it becomes a form of cosmological proof.

> Thus the physico-theological proof, failing in its undertaking, has in the face of this difficulty suddenly fallen back upon the cosmological proof; and since the latter is only a disguised ontological proof, it has really achieved its purpose by pure reason alone. . . .[1]

8.37. The Value of Transcendental Theology

The transcendental theology has a great deal of negative value. It rebuffs all attempts to know anything with the help of empty concepts alone. No idea can validate its own existence.

But if God cannot be proved, it cannot be disproved either. So the reality of God is safe in the ivory tower of faith, against all attacks of atheism, deism and anthropomorphism. If positive assertion concerning God is not possible, then counter-assertion against the reality of God is equally futile.

God, therefore, has a rightful claim for being an object of faith, the justification for which comes from moral life. Apart from this practical gain, it affords speculative satisfaction to our intellectual needs. True, God is a mere *ideal*, it is yet an ideal, without a flaw which completes and crowns the whole of human knowledge. (PR, p. 299)

8.38. Functions of the Three Ideas of Pure Reason

The *transcendental dialectic* has shown the impossibility of knowing the three regulative ideas of soul, World and God. If he were to dramatise his statements, he would say:

---

2.   PR, p. 297.

Thinkers! Some of you are just like the mariners. You know that as long as you are on the island, you are safe from wind, storms, fogs, icebergs and ship-wrecks. But you are the sailors. You have drunk of the sea. You know that the storm is raging and the sea is befogged and the lurking icebergs are beneath. Ship-wreck is certain. But you have smelt the sea. You cannot but unfurl the sail of your ship. Should I congratulate you on your venture for the unknown? Lo! I am silencing the sirens, but I cannot cure you of their charms. Now bush and speak no more.

The Transcendental Illusions have shown that there is nothing real corresponding to the ideas of reason. But then these ideas have certain functions to perform:

1. They point out the model knowledge, the highest unity of which our reason is capable. Their use is not immanent for they do not constiute knowledge; but they are transcendent inasmuch as they guide the understanding to clearer and wider knowledge.

2. They are the limiting concepts pointing out the utmost reaches of knowledge beyond which we must not venture.

3. They regulate the understanding by pointing out the ideal of knowledge. Sense and understanding can guarantee the actual, i.e., *what is*; but reason points out the existence of what *ought to be*.

4. Quite true, the reality of God, the immortality of soul and the freedom of will cannot be proved and known but they cannot be disproved either. They are unknowable and the doubt about their reality is as indefensible as the dogmatic assertion about them. Kant thus speaks about the dogmatists and the sceptics: "Both parties to the dispute beat the air; they worry their own shadow for they pass beyond nature to a region where their dogmatic grips find nothing to lay hold of." Thus where the ideas of religion and morality, Kant throws the magic fog of invisibility. Therefore, the sword of the sceptic and battering-ram of the materialist fall harmless on vacuity.

5. Lastly, the ideas pave the way for faith in morality and religion. As a matter of fact it is the need for morality that keeps the transcendental illusions.

8.39. The Critique of Practical Reason

Kant was above all a moralist and a theist. He knew that people believed in God and moral goodness because they have faith in them and not because of any abstruse arguments of the philosophers. No doubt *The Ciritique of Pure Reason* has shown that any knowledge of the suprasensible is impossible, but then any disbelief in them is equally untenable. On the other hand the demand of the will shows that we are justified in having belief in them. Hence the critical point of Kant puts three questions : What can I know? What ought I to do? What may I hope for? Of course, we cannot know the existence of God or the immortality of soul but we can fairly hope for both of them.

The Kantian doctrine of morality depends upon the examination of the moral consciousness of 'ought'. For example, what is implied in such proposition, we ought to repay the debt or we should be honest? Now 'ought' or 'should' implies that we can do otherwise than repaying debt or becoming honest. This means that there are alternatives which we are free to choose. But this freedom in moral consciousness implies that we are not the phenomenal self only, for the phenomenal self of sensibility is always determined. This freedom to choose indicates that as far as we are moral we belong to the noumenal self. In morality, therefore, there should be nothing of the sensibility or phenomenal self but it should be guided by the noumenal self or the rational self alone. Hence in morality the individual is guided by nothing except by his rational self and as such he is autonomous. As in the determination of objects the understanding gives laws to nature, so in morality the reason prescribes laws to itself alone.

Kant tries to find out the universal and necessary objects as the motive of will. Universal and necessary objects simply mean the *a priori* forms of determining the will. Hence Kant tries to find out the purely formal motive of moral consciousness. He finds out the good will as the only *a priori* motive of action. Nothing in the world, or even outside the world, can be regarded as good except a good will. Honour, wealth or even health can be prostituted to base ends if the will to use them be not itself good. Hence only a good will, without any qualification, is good and like a jewel shines by its own light. A good will coming from the rational self should have nothing of desire and pleasure. A good will is good not because of consequences for it might be that a niggardly provision of a step-motherly nature may frustrate the result. It is absolutely good in itself.

Again, being purely *a priori* not only a good will should be independent of all desires and pleasurable consequences but then it should also be universal. As such Kant lays down the maxim that "so act as if the maxim from which you act were to become through you will a universal law of nature." Hence any action which cannot be universalised is not *a priori* moral action.

Good will is an end in itself for it comes from the noumenal self of which the phenomena are. But everything in the phenomenal self is only an instrumental good. Name or fame or even health is not good in itself. As such the moral consciousness tells us to obey it unconditionally or categorically. Again, the demand from the noumenal self being *a priori* is of the nature of command or imperative. Hence morality lies in the obedience to the categorical imperative. Thus we have to surrender ourselves unconditionally to the dictates of the categorical imperative, without any hope of reward or fear of punishment. There should be no consideration for sensibility or the desire for pleasure. Any consideration for the phenomenal self will take away the moral worth of the actions. Hence Kant illustrates moral actions by examples which show that they are independent of and may even go against sensibility. The action out of the pure regard for the moral law, independent of any desires, but which is valid for all persons is known as duty. Now Kant points out that we should act for the sake of duty only. Pure duty is unmistakably seen in actions against impulses. If a man lives because it is natural in him to do so, then duty is not well marked out. But if a man keeps himself alive even when despair and misfortune have taken away all zest for life, then we can say that in his self-preservation he is following duty. One gets the impression here that Kant is teaching that duty is necessarily disagreeable. But this cannot be the meaning of Kant. Kant holds that man, being both phenomenal and noumenal is guided both by impulses and reason. Insofar as an act is determined by impulses yielding pleasure, it is not moral at all. Only when an act is motivated by reason, then alone it can be said to be moral. Here, in the above instance, Kant is trying to bring out the nature of pure morality, untarnished by sensibility.

It would be wrong to maintain that any act actuated by impulses, desires and feelings become immoral. Here the critics of Kant quote the sarcastic lines of Schiller:

> Willingly serve I my friends all, but do it,
> > alas, with affection;
> And so I am plagued with doubts, that
> > virtue have I not attained.

Kant would not regard an act promoted by affection to be immoral. As a matter of fact, an act can be motivated by sensibility as well as by reason. Charity may be prompted by friendship as well as by a sense of duty towards needy fellowmen. However, the moral excellence of an act, according to Kant, is determined by reason alone, and, not by passion.

If Kant had taught duty to be bereft of pleasure, then he would not have thought of the ultimate reconciliation of happiness and duty. Ultimately, according to Kant, impulses have to be made holy being transformed by reason.

Of course, Kant was trying to find out the *a priori* conditions which determine morality, irrespective of the material circumstances of the situation. Naturally Kant's enquiry was transcendental and formal. It would be, therefore, out of the mark to hold that Kant has not taught us what our specific duties are under particular circumstances. Kant has thought us this much that if the will or character has been hallowed and made rational, then a person can very well perform his duties.

> There is nothing in the world, nay, even beyond the world; nothing conceivable which can be regarded as good without qualification, saving alone a good will. . . .A good will is good, not because of the consequences which may be frustrated by a niggardly provision of a step-motherly nature. A good will is good in itself, and like a jewel shines by its own light.

In spite of the formal and rigorous character of Kant's morality there are points of lasting contributions to Ethics. First, Kant teaches that each man is an end in himself. As long as we act out of the pure regard for the moral law we are acting from the viewpoint of the noumenal self. But the noumenal self is the highest self, the supreme end for which the phenomena are. Hence each moral person is a true end in himself. Thus he lays down: "Act so that you treat humanity, in your own person and in the person of everyone else, always as an end as well as means but never merely as a means." Thus on this principle slavery in any form is inacceptable moral law.

Secondly, Kant teaches universal brotherhood. So far as we are moral we belong to the noumenal or ideal kingdom and not to the phenomena. The phenomenon is a kingdom of means for nothing here is its own end; but a noumenon really is the kingdom of its own end. So we are all fellow citizens of the intelligible kingdom of ends.

8.40. Primacy of Practical Reason

The critique of Pure Reason shows that the scientific knowledge of God, World and Soul is not possible. *Paralogisms* show that soul cannot be said to exist independently of the body; *antinomies* show that the freedom of will cannot be discursively established; and *Ideals* of Reason make it clear that God's existence cannot be demonstrated. From these negative conclusions it does not follow that there are no noumena. Kant did not deny their existence and so he was not a sceptic. However, he held that there are noumena: only we cannot have empirical knowledge of them. Hence, Kant is said to be *agnostic*. Now, Kant goes a step forward. He states that the problems concerning the supersensible at least can partly be solved through practical reason. For him, the freedom of will, the immortality of soul and the existence of God are moral postulates. As morality has to be accepted, so these postulates which alone guarantee its possibility have to be taken as plausible objects of faith. He also gives reason for not treating this supersensible objects as illusory. He would maintain that to the extent a person is moral he belongs to the kingdom of ends or *noumena*. But the theoretical reason at most can establish the validity of phenomena alone. Hence, Practical Reason dealing with noumena is to be considered higher than theoretical reason. It is the demand of practical reason which makes theoretical reason think of them. Besides, the existence of moral postulates is compatible with phenomenal existence and the two need not be opposed. Again, morality has to be accepted as a fact and therefore all the conditions which make morality possible, must be granted as valid. God, soul etc., are precisely the conditions which make morality possible. Hence, instead of being treated as useless phantasies, they have to be granted as valid possibilities. Therefore, Kant points out: "I was obliged to destroy knowledge in order to make room for faith."

'Faith', for Kant has a moral and a pietistic suggestion. It shows that Kant used the term 'reason' in a much broader sense than mere cognition. The importance of Practical Reason and Judgment implied for. Kant the recognition of non-discursive mode of apprehension.[1] Further, Practical Reason gives one the apprehension of the self as 'free', which cannot be scientifically cognised.[2]

First, the freedom of will is the most important and direct postulate of morality. The categorical imperative or 'ought' implies that we are free to choose between two possible courses of action. If we are not free to choose, then any act becomes absolutely determined. And if I cannot act otherwise than what I do, then there will be no room for blame or praise and consequently there will be no meaning of 'ought.'

Immortality of soul and the existence of God are only indirect postulates of morality. Kant makes a distinction between Supreme Good and Complete Good. Virtue indeed is the chief good but it does not contain any element of happiness. However, the complete good should also include happiness and this is not a dogmatic statement but results from the moral demand itself. It is a moral demand that the just must not remain in miseries. But happiness arises from the satisfaction of desires and as such it belongs to the phenomenal self. Hence virtue and happiness are heterogeneous and they cannot be related analytically. A synthetic connection is possible if we believe that one is the cause of the other. But in actual life we find that the virtuous are not rewarded with happiness. Hence, they are united together only by the author of our being, an author of both of our phenomenal and noumenal nature. Hence, we must postulate the existence of "a Being who is quite distinct from nature, and at the same time the cause of it and who contains in himself the ground of the realisation, i.e., of the realisation of the combination of happiness with virtue." Kant, however, is careful in pointing out that the existence of a moral governor or judge is only a moral necessity and is not an objective fact. We must so act as if there is a moral governor who will unite virtue with happiness in the noumenal world.

Lastly, holiness is the supreme end of moral will. But in this life we can never be holy for our action is never out of pure reason only. The struggle of reason continues with the senses and the struggle is only partially won. We must postulate an infinite series of life in which the senses are completely overcome and perfect holiness results. Hence there must be an immortality of soul to give meaning to our moral struggle. Hence we must so act as if there is a life beyond. Of course, 'the immoratality of soul' can now be demonstrated but is "an inseparable corollary of an *a priori* unconditionally valid practical law."

Immortality and God are only indirect postulates of morality, for moral law is autonomous. They are only objects of faith. Thus we find that the metaphysical

1. *Masterpieces of World Philosophy*, edited by F.N. Magill, p. 549, Col. I.
2. *Ibid.*, p. 549, Col. 2.

A Critical History of Western Philosophy

problems of God, soul and immortality were raised in *The Critique of Pure Reason* but only *the practical reason* partially solves by showing them to be the necessary postulates of morality.

8.41. Phenomena and Noumena

Kant emphasises the role of *a periori* activities of the mind in having knowledge proper from the manifold of sense-impressions. He accepts the assumptions of the moderners concerning the discreteness of the manifold data of the sensibility. There is little doubt then that without the transcendental synthesizing activities, according to Kant, there can be no knowledge proper. But Kant never leaves behind him the firm ground of empiricism in order to build a rationalistic edifice in the air. According to him by the employment of mere synthetic unity of apperception through the twelve categories of the understanding there can be no knowledge. Concepts without percepts are empty. Percepts must be supplied to the understanding in order that they may become *objects* proper. Here he adds also that space and time are pure percepts. They are not empirical intuitions or perceptions. For him the presence of empirical intuitions are necessary to constitute knowledge.

But because understanding gives laws to nature, therefore, there is the danger of speculating that there can be knowledge by the understanding alone. We have already seen now that this is not the case. At least the transcendental illusions are there to remind us of this danger. But there might be an opposite mistake. True, all that we can say that knowledge must *begin with* experience, but should any experience be of the same type as ours? Is there not the possibility of another kind of intellect, which instead of waiting for the sensible matter being supplied to it, may create its own? Here Kant holds that so far as human beings are concerned, they have an active intellect or understanding but a passive sensibility. But there might be an *intuitive intellect* possibly of God that creates its own matter. Here mere thought of a thing is enough for the intuitive intellect to create a real objects for it. For example, according to the Bible God said, 'Let there be light, and there was light'. But for human being mere wishing, even a hard one, is not enough to have objects. So without sensibility there can be no knowledge.

Now the question arises, Do we perceive the objects as they are? Not at all. Here we have to guard ourselves, according to Kant, both against materialistic realism and subjective idealism. According to Kant, the manifold of sensory data are discrete. But whatever we know is at once ordered and organised. First, the manifold data are at once brought under the forms of space and time. Unless we time and space the discrete manifold of sensory data we cannot empirically perceive any object at all. However, this *a priori* condition of perceiving the manifold for ever shuts us from knowing the sensory data as they are in themselves, in their naked forms, without being clothed by space and time.

We do not stop at two *a priori* forms of space and Time. We place the spaced and timed sensory data called percepts into another operation chamber of the understanding. Here the twelve categories of the understanding further order and synthesize the percepts into judgments. The net result is that without the concepts there can be no objects, for percepts as percepts become objects of knowledge when they are subjected to the categories. But these operations, so alien to the sensory data themselves, disguise the real nature of the objects. Objects of knowledge, therefore, are objects to us as they *appear* to us. Of course, what their real nature is, apart from *a priori* forms of sensibility and the twelve categories of the understanding, we have to means of knowing. Should be way: Things are as they appear to us and there are no things-in-themselves apart from the phenomena?

This is what Berkeley, according to Kant, had taught. According to Berkeley things are but our ideas. In other words, ideas within the consciousness of a thinker are alone objects, and there are no objects besides the ideas. Kant offers two kinds of refutation of this form of subjective idealism.

(*a*) First, pure perceptions, also called *a priori* forms of perception (space and time) by themselves though precede all objects yet even this intuition of space and time is not objective. It can acquire its object and objective validity only through *empirical* intuition. Hence, for Kant, the data must be given and no empirical objects can be created by intellect alone.

(*b*) Secondly, Kant states that all instances of temporal succession require something relatively permanent. For example, the movement of the sun is perceived in relation to some relatively permanent objects of this earth. Now our own selves are perceived as an aggregate of successive changes. Here Hume and Kant both agree that the empirical self is a bundle of passing mental processes. If the self is perceived as a bundle of successive changes, then there must be something relatively permanent in relation to which it is felt to be in a temporal flow. This relatively permanent something is bound up with the existence of outer things. Unless there be something relatively permanent outside of us, with which to compare and contrast our passing sensations, we shall not experience ourselves as bundles of successive changes.

In other words, the consciousness of my existence is at the same time an immediate consciousness of the existence of other things outside me.[1]

In the above contention, Kant has turned the table against idealism. According to subjective idealism, the immediate exeeperience is inner experience and outer objects are merely constructed out of it. Against subjective idealism and even against realism, Kant points out that immediate states of consciousness themselves are not possible without the consciousness of outer things. Here Kant shows

1. PR, p. 138.

the immediateness of outer experience and only in relation to it, according to him, inner experience is possible.

Of course, the consciousness of 'I am' or the synthetic unity of apperception which accompanies every item of our knowledge of objects is only an *a priori* logical condition. This is never *known*. So the only empirical self which we know is a bundle of successive changes. And this kind of self is not possible without reference to outer things. In this contention of Kant much food for thought is contained, which was fully exploited by Fichte, Schelling and Hegel.

If the forms of sensibility and the concepts of the understanding be constitutive of objects, as objects of knowledge, then this view supports what Kant has termed Transcendental Idealism. According to this view subjects are objects within phenomena and we can never style them as things-in-themselves. Of course, we have full scientific knowledge of the phenomena. Yet we cannot assert that only phenomena are and noumena are not, or that any talk of noumena is self-contradictory.

'Noumenon' for Kant has purely *negative* sense. The term means a thing so far as it is *not an object of our sensible intuition*. The term may acquire a positive sense when it refers to an object of a non-sensible intuition. It may mean that a noumenon is an object of knowledge, possibly for an intuitive intellect. However, the notion of an intuitive intellect is only problematic and human intellect can say nothing about it. Human knowledge cannot know non-sensible objects. We cannot legitimately apply to them the concepts of existence, causation or even of 'non-existence'. Hence, for Kant 'noumenon' stands in *negative sense only*.

Since no category of our understanding can apply to 'noumenon', should be discard the term? Kant would say 'no'. The notion of a noumenon is necessary to prevent sensible intuition from being extended to things-in-themselves. But the limit of knowledge is not the limit of thought. We can think about the noumenon for marking out a possible limit to knowledge proper. Therefore, for Kant, noumenon is an *empty* or a limiting concept with a view to curbing the extension of sensible knowledge and it can admit of negative employment only.

Thus, the concept of noumena, for Kant, served the purpose of guarding philosophy from the errors of subjective idealism, materialism and even realism. But in due course there were many things in Kant's philosophy which paved the ground for *objective* Idealism.

8.42. The Hegelian Criticism of 'the Unknowable'

Hegel was not satisfied with the limiting of knowledge to phenomena only. With his 'unearthly ballet of bloodless categories', he hoped to know the *things-in-themselves* too. He could achieve this by removing the distinction between

---

1.   PR, p. 138.

phenomena and noumena. For him noumena are as much objects of knowledge as phenomena. For reaching this result, Hegel has tried to show that the concept of the unknowable is self-contradictory.

For Kant, 'noumenon' is only an empty concept. We know *that it is*, but we do not know *what it is*. 'The what' is matter or content of a concept, which (matter) is supplied by sense alone. As a noumenon is beyond sensibility, so it is beyond knowledge proper. However, even Kant could not confine himself to the negative sense of the noumenon. At times he spoke as if the unknowable things-in-themselves were the causes of sensibility and understanding.[1] Further, though, according to Kant, no knowledge of noumena is possible, yet they are the proper objects of faith. Therefore, for Kant the notion of a noumenon is not merely negative, nor is it purely empty. Hence, his doctrine of the unknowable came to be criticised by Hegel.

Hegel observed, if the unknowable is beyond every kind of knowledge and, if it is beyond the legitimate use of the concepts of the understanding, then we cannot apply the concepts of causation, reality and existence to it. Inasmuch as we say that a noumenon *is*, we are applying the concept of 'existence' to it. And inasmuch as this statement is true, we are knowing it to that extent. Might be that our knowledge of the noumenon is scanty, but we cannot say that there is no knowledge at all.

Again, Hegel proceeded, we cannot escape from our responsibility of knowing by stating that the term 'noumenon' is a limiting concept. To be aware of a limit is to go beyond it. No one could be aware of the end of the edge of a table without getting aware of an empty space surrounding it. Hence to say that we know that noumena form the limit of knowledge is to *know* this limitation. If we know nothing about the noumena, then we would not say even this much that they exist. Total nescience implies total unawareness. Hence, to say that a noumenon is and yet not to know anything about it, for Hegel is self-contradictory.

Hegel's criticism appears to be unjustified. Hegel did not seem to take seriously Kant's distinction between *knowing* and *thinking*. The unknowable can be thought, but without being given in sensibility cannot be known. Further, objects of *faith* are not necessarily objects of *knowledge*. In current language, we can say that for Kant, the unknowable does not form part of any cognitive meaning. But it may have emotive, persuasive, numinous or imperative meaning. In our language we have stated that metaphysical statements have holistic meaning. So Kant's doctrine of the unknowable has important implication and is not as self-cointradictory as Hegel and Hegelians have contended.

8.43. Kant and Current Empiricism

Much in the writings of Kant reminds us of current empiricism having various forms, called logical empiricism, logical positivism, linguistics etc. Like

---

1. PR, p. 38.

contemporary analytic philosophers, Kant makes a distinction between philosophy and metaphysics. He too would regard metaphysics, as the science of the supersensible, as impossible. Kant too limits knowledge to the observable or the perceptible. He too maintains that the function of philosophy, which he called 'transcendental critique' is not to *extend* knowledge, but only to *correct* it.[1] And yet there is hardly any contemporary logical positivist or logical empiricist who would not take Kant to task. For example, Russell doubts whether Kant was really roused from his slumber by the writings of Hume. And if he was so roused, so Russell continues, he took to soporific again, of his invention.[2] Similarly, a great many positivists contend that Kant's problem, which was centred round the possibility of *synthetic judgments a priori*, is a pseudoproblem.[3]

Strictly speaking Kant does commit a great many mistake. But in a history of philosophy a thinker is to be judged by his intent and not so much by his literal statements. Kant is to be judged not so much by what he has said, but by what he intended saying. There is hardly any great thinker whose statements do not contain much more than what he could have clearly stated. In the same way, Kant has to be interpreted sympathetically with the help of a great many emendations. However, these emendations are not so many thoughts alien to Kant, but are really present in his writings which the philosophical language of his times could not permit to be clearly stated.

True, Kant has to be given credit for drawing a clear distinction between analytic and synthetic statements which were vaguely held both by Locke and Hume. But it must be confessed that his treatment is often defective and confused. His treatment is based on the containment theory of the subject-predicate relationship in a proposition. This theory besides being metaphorical, often takes recourse to the familiarity of the connotation. Hence, this introduces a psychological element, when the distinction should be strictly logical. We have already referred to the presence of psychological elements in the synthetic judgments *a priori* in mathematics (**8.07**). However, these defects are comparatively minor. In the days of Kant, propositions meant those that could be explained in terms of subject-predicate relationship. Mathematical logic had not captured the imagination of the logicians. So Kant does not refer to propositions based on relations. With some modification the distinction between the analytic and synthetic propositions can be made adequate to meet the requirement of precise statement.

Again, before the Riemannian type of Geometry had been invented, it was considered that Euclidean Geometry was the only form of it. Kant shared the same view. He, therefore, thought that the Euclidean space was fixed and unalterable

---

1. PR, p. 38.
2. *History of Western Philosophy*, p. 678.
3. Richard von Mises, *Positivism*, p. 6 is only one out of many such criticisms.

for all human beings. The same thing may be said about the categories. He took certain forms of propositions to be fixed and unalterable. Naturally he took them to be *a priori*. To-day we would consider the views of *a priori* forms of perceiving and thinking as ill-conceived and erroneous, simply because we are heir to the researches and wisdom of scholars of many decades after Kant. But we would not have reached the conclusion concerning the categories or even about 'space and time' if Kant had not directed the thoughts of thinkers for all these days. The important thing was that Kant pointed out that without the categories mere empirical account of knowledge would not explain scientific knowledge. As Kant had taken the fixity of thought-patterns for granted, so he could not explain the nature of the categories except by assuming them to be *a priori*. To-day the empiricist explains the categories as conventions. Of course, there is a great gain in treating the categories as useful conventions and there is an escape from psychological mysticism in which Kant's account of *a priori* elements appear to be heavily enmeshed. Kant, in the last resort would fall on the sameness of the human constitution of thinking in order to explain the nature of *a priori* elements. But if we by emendations substitute the mental constitution by 'conventions', then Kant's account of knowledge can be suitably and easily reconstructed.

Most probably many such emendations can be introduced to show that Kant's thoughts are still living. However, the most central point of difference between the contemporary empiricists and Kant would be that for the former metaphysical propositions are nonsense, whereas for Kant they are not cognitive and yet are significant in a non-cognitive way.

8.44. The Meaning of Metaphysics for Kant

For Kant, 'knowledge' meant 'scientific knowledge'[1] as was contained for him in mathematics and physics. His analysis of knowledge revealed that mataphysics is not capable of yielding scientific knowledge of God, soul and the world. Therefore, for Kant metaphysics as a science is not possible. But he laid down that metaphysics actually exists, if not as a science, yet still as *natural disposition*.[2] A thinker is driven to metaphysical problems by virtue of some inward need within him. In our current language, we would say that there is some extra-logical, often called psychological motivation by which metaphysics is initiated and sustained. As yet people have not fully stated the problem concerning the nature of that inner need by virtue of which some sort of metaphysics becomes a necessity for philosophers. What is important here to state is that at the beginning of the movement of logical postivism, Schlick, Carnap, and Ayer dismissed metaphysics as nonsense. Now Kant had as much reason for discarding metaphysics as these positivists had. But he did not. That does show a greater appreciation of the

---

1. PR, p. 36f.
2. PR, p. 36.

problem by Kant than by these empiricists. Later development has shown that
after all metaphysics may have some non-cognitive sense, and, therefore,
empiricists are trying to ascertain emotive, persuasive or some such meaning of
a metaphysical statement. But unfortunately empiricists are not recognizing the
lead of Kant in this direction.

Kant frankly stated that metaphysical entities have some practical interests
and religious needs of man to fulfil. Metaphysical statements, therefore, have
moral and religious meanings. But what are they? This problem is being discussed
very much in recent years and the present author has expressed his views in three
articles.[1] But probably the view is not much different from that of Kant.

Kant hoped to achieve a truce between science and religion by demarcating
their respective regions. Science is a region of knowledge and religion is a realm
of faith. Naturally the two have sovereign rights within their jurisdiction. But in
the ultimate analysis, knowledge has a subordinate place in relation to the primacy
of practical reason. This conclusion can be established in the following way.

Kant distinguished between phenomena and noumena. Human beings can
know but their knowledge is confined to the phenomena alone. However, insofar
as men are moral, they cease to be phenomenal. Now an act proceeding from a
phenomenal self is causally determined. But insofar as we are moral, we act as
if we are free, that is, we act as if we are not phenomenal, but are noumenal. Again,
a noumenal self is a self in itself, an end in itself, for which the phenomena are.
Hence, a moral act proceeds from a higher realm than scientific knowledge which
is confined to the phenomenal world.

Besides, we have to act out of the pure regard for the national or noumenal
law, if we want to attain to morality. In doing so we belong to the kingdom of
ends, the realm of noumena. Hence, in morality we do not *know* God or the
immortality of soul. But we *become* the higher self. Indeed we require persistent
efforts of a number of endless lives to achieve a state in which our wills will
become as holy as of God. Hence, the practical interest of man lies in making
himself a thing of moral worth and value.

Is this demand of morality alien to the speculative interest of man? No, these
metaphysical entities, the transcendental ideas of the supersensible are not alien
to scientific interest, since they regulate knowledge and point out the farthest
limits to which knowledge may extend. Further, the so-called transcendental
illusions arise from the very nature of the cognitive structure in man. He has an
active and spontaneous faculty of understanding, which however, he can use
legitimately only with reference to the limited scope which sensibility prescribes.
Consequently man *thinks* about a great many more things than can be grasped
securely in scientific knowledge. Surely, therefore, metaphysical problems arise

1. 'The psychology of the metaphysicians' *Darshana*, January 1962: 'The reality of God', **Souvenir Volume presented to Dr. S. Radhkrishnan on his 75th birthday** 'An empirical study of theological statements', **Contemporary Indian Thought,** Edited by Prof. K.S. Murty, 1961.

from cognitive achievements to which they are geared. Grant scientific knowledge, and, one will have to grant the possibility of metaphysics as a realm of possible knowledge, a realm of faith. Hence, metaphysical and ethical life appears to be welded on intellectual life and follows from it as a promise and fulfilment of a larger life of values.

Therefore, we can conclude that, according to Kant, metaphysics is driven by an inner need of man which consists in so manipulating his thinking that in the end a life of moral value and religious piety results. In the final analysis, the inner spirit of Kant's transcendental idealism lies in holding that scientific knowledge is subservient to a life in which metaphysical values are realised. 'So think and so know all things that in the long run you may become a thing of moral excellence. Finally, you so temper your spirit by constant commitment and dedication to moral values that ultimately you may become as holy as God is.' This appears to the author as the metaphysical exhortation of Kant.

We can win for ourselves a permanent lesson from Kant's philosophical meditations with regard to the possibility of metaphysics. Metaphysics is sustained by a 'natural disposition' in man, because there is something in him which tells him to fulfil his ultimate destiny. This consists in becoming a whole or a self which gives him meaning to his intellectual restlessness and practical struggles of life. A thoughtless man in due course would also ripen, decay and die, but he would do so without becoming a citizen of the kingdom of ends. His journey in the next life would start de *novo* for becoming a thing of value. However, a thoughtful man, knowing fully well that on earth virtue is not rewarded would continue still to hear the voice of the categorical imperative of his good will, for he knows that there is nothing higher than this, either in this life or in the next. Is there any fundamental distinction then between Kant and Spinoza? Is not the life of intellectual love of God the same submission to a life of categorical imperative? Spinoza tells us to love without the prospect of being recompensed and Kant teaches a life of virtue independently of any prospect of happiness. The still small voice of the spiritual in man keeps on dinning in his ears. Those who have ears let them hear. Leonardo Da Vinci, according to Freud, heard it and so did Freud himself, say Hopkins and Jones. Philosophy uses its descriptive statements in the interest of prescriptive and exhortative statements and they are all welded together for inducing man to follow his vocation of becoming a thing of value, a thing of beauty. And a thing of beauty is a joy forever and it would never pass into nothingness. In this, all the teachings of philosophy are fulfilled.

9

George Wilhelm Friedrich Hegel (1770-1831)

9.00 Transition to Hegel

I. We have already stated in § 8.40 that for Kant Metaphysics is not science, but it deals with values. Metaphysical entities for Kant are not objects of scientific enquiry, but of faith. Faith for Kant lacks evidence sufficient for cognitive certainty, but is sufficient for action. Faith therefore is belief even in the face of contrary evidence which leads to devoted acts for the realization of values. Thus, for Kant metaphysics leads to all-pervasive orientation to life. Secondly, Metaphysics is prompted by *a natural disposition* in Man. Hence, Kant would opt for metaphysics *a priori*. The problems of metaphysics, even though declared as transcendental illusions, can never be shaken off. Therefore, in a very large measure, Kant leads to idealistic metaphysics.

II. True, Hegel was very much indebted to Aristotle, but he was greatly prompted into his philosophical construction by the specualations of Kant. By calling his philosophy Critical, Transcendental and Copernican Revolution, Kant has shown the primacy of mind in constituting knowledge proper (§ 9.01). Kant in various ways wants to show that the nature of the human mind is the main factor in any knowledge whatsoever. No matter whichever be the object of knowledge, it has to be moulded, transformed and coloured by the organ of knowledge, namely, the human mind. But the most central statement of Kant is,

'Understanding maketh nature out of the materials it does not make.'

Well, it means whenever we think about empirical laws of nature, we have to observe the laws of thinking, which are laws of logic or rules of language. This is an innocent observation. However, Kant also adds that these laws determine the empirical laws of *phenomenal' nature*. This does not mean beyond the statement that the rules of logic are indispensable even for science. But apart from logical order, there is *conjunction* of facts and science discovers this conjunction. For Kant this conjunction is not strictly universal and logically necessary. Here Kant wrongly took empirical laws to be *necessary*. Nor can scientific statement could be necessary. Even laws of logic, at least now, would not be regarded as valid for all human beings at all times. But Kant thought them to be binding on all human beings. Therefore, faulty analysis of knowledge for Kant, made him say that scientific knowledge is human knowledge of humanised objects. Of course, the human knowledge is human knowledge, but this is *of* things. Things remain extra-linguistic, extra-logical and extra-human even when they are brought in the human sphere of influence.

In any case Kant maintains that the human understanding constitutes the laws of phenomenal nature and within this limitation man can secure certain and necessary knowledge. In the last resort, for Kant, mind is essentially a combining principle, a principle of synthesis. At the level of perception, sensibility unites the passing and discrete sensations into percepts with the two *a priori* forms of Space and Time. Later, these percepts are further combined into judgments with the help of the twelve categories of understanding. But all the modes of combination must be one and the same for all human beings. This sameness of combination can be achieved if there be one and the same unity of consciousness for all human beings. Now Kant supposed that there is one and the same synthetic unity of apperception for all acts of combination for all human beings. This synthetic unity of self-consciousness is only a logical condition, for Kant, for explaining one uniform and objective knowledge for all human beings. But in due course it proved to be a powerful factor for supporting the reality of one Supreme and Absolute Mind.

Kant's doctrine of 'Understanding maketh nature' directly paved the way for idealism. True, Kant meant that the human understanding gives *a priori* laws to *phenomenal* nature. But Hegel did away with the distinction of 'phenomena and noumena' by declaring the doctrine of the unknowable as self-contradictory. Thus it meant that understanding constitutes the laws of nature, for nature is essentially a system of thoughts. Secondly, the synthetic unity of apperception became the ontological Reality. Human mind was considered to be a finite reproduction of the Absolute Mind. So the human thought of God is at the same time the thought of God as expressed through its human vehicle. Hence, Kant's teaching was transformed into an idealistic system according to which there is an Absolute Mind which progressively expresses itself in Nature, Life and Human Mind.

Kant held that the three Ideas of Reason are not *constitutive,* but *regulative* of knowledge. These ideas are of God, Soul and the World. According to Kant these metaphysical entities are not objects of knowledge, but of faith and largely may be regarded as postulates of Practical Reason. Practical Reason does not yield knowledge, but is higher than Pure Reason, since moral imperatives arise from the free and noumenal self of man. Thus, belief in metaphysical entities for Kant is not irrational, but super-rational. Secondly, man is prompted to think about the World, Soul and God by his natural disposition. So metaphysics comes from the higher reason of man and so Kant indirectly accepted the idealistic thesis of metaphysics *a priori*.

However, Hegel's idealism is justly famous for its dialectic method, according to which the Absolute unfolds itself through the triple steps of thesis, antithesis and synthesis. Kant's philosophy abounds in triads and this might have suggested the dialectic method. In the first instance Kant wrote three *Critiques*. Critique of Pure Reason ends in scepticism concerning metaphysical entities called the World, Soul and God. But this scepticism is considerably modified in the *Critique of Practical Reason*. Metaphysical entities are called as legitimate objects of faith and postulates of the higher self of man. In the *Critique of Judgment* Reality is held with far greater assurance. It appears then that the third *Critique of Judgment* holds the key and is the synthesis of the earlier two critiques. Even the *Critique of Pure Reason* accepts the three faculties of Sensibility, Understanding and Reason. Knowledge begins with *sense*, proceeds thence to *Understanding* and ends in *Reason*. Sensibility is *passive*, Understanding is *active* and Reason limits active understanding to the materials supplied by Sensibility. Here again Reason is a synthesis and regulative of Sense and Understanding. But the triad of thesis, antithesis and synthesis is most clearly demonstrated in the metaphysical deduction of categories. The first three concepts are unity, plurality and totality. Here Unity is the thesis, plurality is antithesis and totality is plurality considered as unity, i.e., the synthesis of the first two categories. This is true for both mathematical and dynamical triads of categories (§ 8.15). Further, the doctrine of Antinomies presented a challenge for Hegel and Hegel perused long over the antinomies. Hegel held that Kant could not solve the contradictions involved in antinomies, for he remained at the level of abstract reasoning or understanding only. The solution lies in going beyond understanding and reaching the stage of speculative Reason. The antinomies are certainly arranged in the form of thesis and anti-thesis (§ 8.25) and nobody can accept them to be true together at the same time. The solution of the problem lies in their synthesis.

The dialectic method is based on the assumption of the identity of thought and things. It is the thought itself which passes from the abstract to the concrete, from the empty to the fuller ideas. Ultimately things are nothing but a system of thoughts. This identity of thought and thing could be reached only by a criticism of Kant's doctrine of the unknowable (§ 8.38).

Hence Kant's teaching directly and indirectly has contributed to the rise of Hegelian idealism through Fichte and Schelling.

9.01. Idealistic Metaphysics
Idealism is a metaphysical doctrine which teaches the supremacy of the spirit over matter. The most important kind of idealism is known as the Absolute Idealism. And the absolute idealism holds that matter is not mind, but mind remains foundational to matter and is the key to the understanding of matter. The word 'Spirit' is vague and cannot be precisely stated. For all practical purposes it means 'self-conscious mind' which becomes articulate in its gradual manifestations and graded creation through matter, life and the human mind. For the absolute idealism matter is the *other* of the mind, but matter has been posited by the mind so that by 'a struggle with and opposition of the matter, mind may become aware of itself'. Again the story of the material world is unfolded by the scientist. But

the scientist is a conscious mind. So matter is unintelligible without a mind. Again, the matter ultimately is regulated by scientific laws. But laws are ultimately thoughts. Thus matter consists of thoughts and cannot be understood without the thoughts of the conscious mind called the scientist. So mind remains the foundation of and key to the understanding of matter.

The word 'idealism' is ambiguous : it may, mean 'idea-ism' or 'ideal-ism'. The term 'idealism' is used in both senses. The message of idealism was given in the most finished form in language most appropriate for its expression by Plato (427 B.C.-347 B.C.). According to Plato, ideas alone are real and they are hierarchically arranged with the idea of the good at the apex : The idea of the good draws all things unto itself in the same way in which a thing of beauty attracts its admirers. As the idea of the good can be interpreted as value and Ideal, so the idealism of Plato is both idea-ism and ideal-ism. Following the thoughts of Plato, Aristotle has called the idea at the apex as Actus Purus, the Form of forms. For Aristotle the highest form is the indwelling spirit and reason of the world which moulds all things. Hence, in the Philosophy of Aristotle, the idea-istic and ideal-istic trends have been intimately welded together. Hegel, who has presented absolute idealism, was greatly influenced by Aristotle.

Ever since the time of Plato and Aristotle, idealism has been a most important stream of thought in the Western world. It was propounded afresh by Spinoza, Leibnitz and Berkeley. But Hegel himself remains indebted to Kant for deriving the key-concepts of his idealism. Kant himself never accepted idealism and called idealism as 'ghost-seeing'. However, Kant's speculation has contributed to the rise of idealism much more than the philosophy of any other modern thinkers. Kant called his philosophy critical, Copernican revolution and Transcendental, and, in all these forms Kant has taught that the human mind is the law-giver to nature. The *critical* philosophy of Kant teaches that the knowing faculty of mind is the supreme organ and it has to be understood first as the prior condition of any critique of epistemology. The same emphasis on the knowing mind is made out by the claim of *Copernican Revolution*. The Copernican revolution for Kant means that instead of the mind going to the objects to know them, the objects have to conform to the conditions laid down by the human mind in order to be the objects of knowledge at all. Lastly, the *Transcendental* philosophy of Kant holds that any philosophical enquiry is not concerned with this or that or any object at all, but with *the mode or manner in which the mind* knows any object whatsoever. Hence, for Kant the human mind is the key to the analysis of scientific knowledge. Later on Kant was led to posit one supreme self-consciousness or the synthetic unity of apperception as the ultimate condition of there being any objective knowledge, alike for all human beings. This synthetic unity of apperception is the logical condition and is the implication of scientific knowledge. Thus the human mind in the first instance and the synthetic unity of apperception in the final form is the key to the understanding of nature, for Kant. Since the time of Kant, the self-conscious mind has become the basal category of Idealism, in maintaining the primacy of the spirit over matter. Viewed in the historical perspective, the idealism of Hegel is as much Greek (Aristotelian) as it is Kantian (German). But German idealism in the Anglo-American thought was assisted by its native philosophy of empiricism. British empiricism was given an idealistic turn by Berkeley. Later on Bradley rears up his idealistic metaphysics on the Berkeleyan foundation of *esse est percipi*.

Berkeley's doctrine of *esse est percipi* has been found to be unsatisfactory, both by idealists and realists. Nevertheless this formula has proved central for British idealism. Idealist thinkers substituted *intellegi* for *percipi* since percipi is subjective, relative and is open to the charge of solipsism. However, concepts are universals, nay, the ideas of Plato do not require any mind or thinker at all. So the ideas of Plato are not mind-dependent as percipi is dependent on the percipient. Hence, the substitution of Ideas for percipi has made idealism objective by going beyond the subjective idealism of Berkeley. We have already explained the idealism of Berkeley (§ 6.06) and have also explained the distinction between subjective and objective idealism (§ 6.07). However, we have defined idealism as a form of metaphysics and the nature of this metaphysics accounts for some of the tenets of the idealism of Hegel and Bradley. So we shall explain it a little before proceeding further.

9.02. The Nature of Idealistic Metaphysics

As idealism is found in its classical form in the philosophy of Plato and Aristotle and in its final shape in Hegel and Bradley, so we shall explain the nature of metaphysics, first, according to Plato and Aristotle and afterwards as it was understood by Hegel and Bradley. According to Plato and Aristotle, metaphysics consists in *contemplating*[1] on eternal and unchangeable entities[2] leading to the attainment of wisdom.[3] Aristotle defined metaphysics also as the science of Being as being, of first principles.[4] Of course both Aristotle and Plato distinguished metaphysics from special science.[5] Knowing things in general, according to Aristotle, is quite distinct from knowing things individually.[6] Again, special sciences are cultivated for success by furthering the means of adjustment to practical concerns in life. According to Plato and Aristotle metaphysics appears to be useless[7] and cannot be evaluated in terms of money.[8] Further, both Plato and Aristotle have arranged their metaphysics in an hierarchical system with the Idea of the Good (Plato) or God (Aristotle) at the apex. This shows that for Plato and

---

1. Aristotle Dictionary, ed. Thomas P. Kiernan, Philosophical Library, Ny 1962 p. 388.
2. *Ibid.*, pp. 343, 388.
3. Aristotle's Metaphysics H.G. Apostle, Indian University, 1966, p. 14.
4. Metaphysics, 982(b).
5. Plato Dictionary, Morris Stockhammer, p. 196.
6. Aristotle's Meta, p. 14.
7. Plato Dictionary, pp. 196-97.
8. Ari. Met. p. 14, Dictionary, p. 388.

Aristotle metaphysics was taken to be an all-comprehensive study. Nay, Being, essence, first principles, all such terms indicate that Aristotle was trying to reach that by knowing which everything gets illuminated. The same conclusion can be reached with regard to the Ideas of Plato. However, the ideas, forms, essences, eternal entities and so on are to be grasped with the help of reflective intuition.[1] Plato used the highly metaphorical terms like reminiscence to have the glimpse of ideas. Though Plato banished poets from his *Republic*, yet his whole philosophy is a vision and is communicated through myths, parables, allegories and metaphors.

Plato and Aristotle have not explained the use of metaphysics. If it is useless, why should it be studied at all? Secondly, what is the nature of knowledge conerning Ideas or Essence or Forms ? Certainly it is not empirical knowledge, then what is it? Even if there be the *intuitive* grasp of ideas, then how can we test its validity? Most probably the key-words 'contemplation' and 'Wisdom' would put us into a proper perspective to appraise the questions which have been raised here. Contemplation on eternal ideas or forms gives us satisfaction for its own sake and is self-rewarding. From this follows peace of mind and emotional stability. Though Hegel and Bradley do not explicitly say, but they too in some way mean this, to which we shall make reference a little later. Secondly, metaphysical contemplation gives us 'Wisdom' and not 'knowledge'. We cannot say with certainty, but wisdom means perhaps the art of living based on comprehensive and shrewd observation of human behaviour. One thing is certain that metaphysics is not science, metaphysical illumination is not scientific knowledge, and, metaphysics deals with the reality as a whole and contributes to human peace of mind and emotional stability. There is the theory that metaphysics is as natural as breathing and the question of having no metaphysics does not arise. The choice is not between metaphysics or no metaphysics, but between good and critical metaphysics or bad and dogmatic metaphysics. This is the doctrine of metaphysics *a priori,* i.e., man cannot do without some sort of metaphysics. And Bradley and Hegel have accepted this doctrine of metaphysics *a priori.*

For Bradley metaphysics means an attempt to 'comprehend the universe not simply piecemeal or by fragments, but somehow as a whole'.[2] For Bradley at least some men cannot abstain from thinking about the universe and, adds, that perhaps most men cannot cease from reflecting and pondering on ultimate truth.[3] Again, for Bradley, some people are in touch with something higher, which both chastens and subdues, supports and humbles us. Such people experience the Deity by means of such intellectual efforts, i.e., as their ultimate satisfaction.[4] According to

1. For Aristotle 'Intuitive Reason', Arist. Meta., p. 14
2. Appearance and Reality (Clarendon Press, 1959) p. 1.
3. *Ibid.,* p. 3.
4. *Ibid.,* p. 5, 401-02.

Bradley metaphysical knowledge cannot be assimilated to scientific knowledge.[1] Finally, metaphysics is prompted by human nature. For Bradley, as also for Hegel, metaphysics deals with the Reality as a whole and Bradley describes the Absolute Reality as all-inclusive, all-harmonious sentient whole.

Hegel regards philosophy[2] as the work of *reflective reason* in order to have an *insight* into the idea which 'is the true, the eternal, the absolutely potent, that it reveals itself in the world, and that nothing is revealed in the world except this idea, its grandeur and its honour'.[3] Philosophy is a rational insight which follows from *reflection* on the whole happenings. History and Science are concerned with accidental and temporal processes. In contrast, "philosophy is the science of necessary thoughts, of their essential connection and system, the knowledge of what is true and therefore eternal and imperishable,. . ."[4] Hegel distinguishes science and philosophy very sharply. Science for Hegel is the work of *Understanding*, but philosophy works through reflective intuition and speculative reason. Hegel is also fully conscious of the holistic nature of philosophy and propounds the doctrine of concrete universal without which the later doctrine of Internal Relations cannot be understood.

9.03. The Hegelian Theory of Concrete Universal

Both Plato and Aristotle visualised Reality as one. True, their doctrine of 'matter' was not fully assimilated into the elucidation of their monistic system. But there is little doubt that Plato and Aristotle have maintained the sole reality of Ideas and Forms and that these ideas are found in a system. Hegel has made this theory of ideas consistent by advancing the doctrine of *concvrete Universal*. The doctrine follows from the viewpoint of metaphysics as an all-comprehensive study of Reality as a whole. The 'form' of Aristotle is for all practical purposes the same as the Idea of Plato. And the Idea of Plato has to be sharply distinguished from the *concept* of Socrates from which it was initially derived.

1. The concept of Socrates depends on the mind of a thinker who wants to go beyond the transitory, momentary, relative *perceptions* of things. According to Socrates knowledge cannot remain confined to perception if knowledge is to be regarded as objective and universal for all men. However, the conception of cow is derived from many perceptions of various cows. By abstracting *cowness* from the accidental and variable qualities of size, colour etc., we reach the common and essential quality of cowness. So cowness is the concept of cow, humanity is the concept of human beings, redness is the concept of different shades of colour and so on. The concept goes beyond *particular* things and embraces the whole class which comprises a number of particular instances coming under it to each

---

1. *Ibid.,* pp. 401-02, 439-441, 502.
2. Which for him is metaphysics.
3. Carl J. Friedrich, *The Philosophy of Hegel* (Modern Library Book), p. 5.
4. *The History of Philosophy* in HEGEL, ed. C.J. Friedrich, p. 162.

of which the concept is applicable in the same sense. In this way a concept comes to acquire universal applicability which leads to universal and objective knowledge of things. But a concept is a *human device* to gain universal knowledge and cannot be imagined independently of the human mind.

2. Plato has transformed the Socratic theory of epistemology into an ontology. For Plato concepts are human but they are the means to disclose to us the essence of things, which essence was called 'Idea'. Ideas are objective entities which we know through conceiving them. This is not a chance by virtue of which the theory of concept has led to the theory of Ideas. Greek thought did not separate *knowing* from *known objects*. For it even perception reveals a thing, only the thing revealed is transitory and relative. For the Greek perceiving could not be imagined to be subjective and solipsistic. So according to this realistic thinking corresponding to the process of conceiving there is an objective essence of things which is revealed to the conceiving mind. Hence, for Plato, Ideas exist independently of human thinking. Once again this should not sound strange, for ordinarily we think that redness is not exhausted in any number of red shades. Even Russell, Meinong and others at one time taught that universals have their independent subsistence and contrasted with actually sensed objects (existences), they were called *subsistences* (i.e., some sort of shadowy realities). Plato too was conscious of picturing the independent realities of Ideas and so he called Ideas to have heavenly existences only. This is only a metaphorical statement and Plato by using the metaphor of 'heavenly abode' wanted to say that Ideas are real even though they are not sensible existences. Aristotle's criticism of his master is unnecessary.

3. Even if the reality of Ideas be granted, two further questions become important.

(i) How are the Ideas related to things?

(ii) How are the ideas related amongst themselves?

The first question will be taken up shortly. Only this much can be said here that, according to Plato things are the copies and that they remind us of the Ideas which they imperfectly try to imitate. Aristotle has made the relation between forms and things much closer by holding that forms are not found independently of things, but always *in* them. Further, Aristotle regarded forms as the *reason* of things, their inmost pervasive principle which controls all possible movements in them. Without further discussing this relationship between forms or Ideas and things, we can pass on to the second question, namely, the relationship between the ideas themselves.

Plato seemed to have thought of the ideas arranged hierarchically in a system, beginning with ideas of least generality at the base, the ideas of intermediate generality in the middle and the Idea of the Good at the apex. The following table would help us:

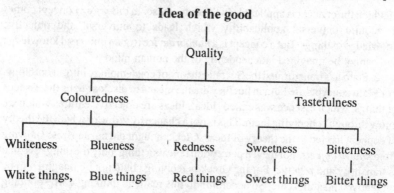

The difficulty about the mutual relationship between the Ideas is that one cannot be organically related with the rest. Plato tells us that white things imitate the Idea of white, but how do white things follow from their essence of whiteness? In the same way Hegel would ask, how do whiteness, bluesness and tastefulness follow from the Idea of quality? Again, how do all other Ideas follow from the Idea of the Good? Plato has not derived the lower ideas from the higher ideas, and, according to Hegel, Plato could not have succeeded in deducing the lower from the higher even if he had attempted to do so. The reason is that the Ideas of Plato, according to Hegel are so many empty *abstractions*. They have been reached by explaining away or ignoring the particular qualities, accidental features and other details from the objects. For example, the idea of whiteness has been abstracted from white lilies, white roses, white milk, white snow and so on. Here in order to reach the idea of whiteness we ignore the smell, smoothness, the green leaves of lilies and roses, and, in the same way we pay no attention to the other concrete details of white milk and snow. But any concrete thing consists of numerous details. Once you omit the details to reach the idea of whiteness, you can no longer deduce the white things characterised by a number of particularising qualities which constitute them. In other words, qualities which constitute white things cannot be deduced from the idea of whiteness, for the simple reason that the idea of whiteness has been formed by emptying all other characteristics of white things. From the empty husk of whiteness one cannot deduce any thing. For this reason, according to Hegel, Plato failed to relate the Ideas themselves. In order to arrange the ideas in a system, ideas must be much more than empty abstractions. Ideas must be concrete.

In the first instance a concrete universal is *not*

(a) a concept which depends on human intellect, without which it cannot be found anywhere.

(b) Nor is it the Idea of Plato, since the idea of Plato, according to Hegel, is an *abstract* universal.

Hegel calls the concept of Socrates Gedanke and the Idea of Plato Gattung; whereas a concrete universal is called Begriffe (translated rather vaguely as notion). The Begriffe is not an abstract generalisation obtained by classifying mind through abstraction. It has been called by John Caird as an organic universality. A concrete universal is not reached by stripping away the differences and details which constitute particular things. In forming a concrete universal we do not think first of particulars. On the contrary, particulars follow from the universal. A concrete universal is a whole or system. Once we know the whole, its parts follow automatically from it. Members of an organism, i.e., their form, place, structure, function are directly determined by the idea of the organism of which they are the parts. As soon as we say 'Cat' we at once know the kind of teeth, paws, tail and the structure of the organism concerned. It is the whole which determines the parts or particulars. Here the notion of the concrete universal is logically prior of the particulars.

Here, then, we have a kind of universality which is altogether different from the barren and formal universality of generalisation, and the indication of a movement of thought corresponding to an inner relation of things which the asbtracting, generalizing understanding is altogether inadequate to grasp.[1]

A concrete universal has been described as a living organism where the particulars derive their meaning and function from the whole, and, the whole is also sustained by its parts. An organic system is to be distinguished from a machine. A *machine* is a whole of parts, but parts can exist apart from the whole. For instance, the spring, the dial, the balance staff etc., are all parts of a watch, but they all can exist apart from a complete watch. In a mechanical whole the relation between the parts and the whole is not very close. In comparison, in a *chemical compound,* the inter-relation between parts and the whole is less abstract. Chemicals in their inter-relation are often transformed and give rise to the whole which is quite different from the parts. For example, hydrogen and oxygen, when they are suitably combined, then elements lose their gaseous form and become liquid water. Here the inter-relation is achieved by the affinities of chemicals themselves. However, in an *organism* the inter-relation between the parts and the whole is very much deeper, since the parts live through the whole, and, the whole is sustained by the parts. There is an immanent teleology which combines the parts in an integrated whole.

Keeping in mind the doctrine of Aristotle's forms which are the immanent and informing principle of things, their inmost essence and reason, Hegel looks at the whole world as one Reality which is guided and sustained by the Absolute Idea. The Absolute Idea is a system of all ideas and is the indwelling spirit of the whole

---

1. John Caird, *Philosophy of Religion*, p. 229f; See also J. Royce, *The Spirit of Modern Philosophy*, Houghton Miflin Co., 23rd Impression, 1931, p. 497.

universe, from the dust up to the distant stars and works itself out in Matter, Life and Mind. Nay, the whole human society is one single organism and only by treating it as such that the whole human history gains in intelligibility. Looked at thus, an isolated individual is a myth and ceases to be truly human. An individual becomes human by learning language, practising morality and becoming a product and bearer of the cultural heritage of the people. All these things are not possible without becoming an indispensable part of the society. Again, the individual has to develop his moral and spiritual powers which he can attain by living in a family belonging to a society. Here we must not think that individuals exist prior of the family. On the contrary, the family comes first in which the individual is found as its indispensable part. "Here, as elsewhere, the universal is the *prius* of the particular". Nay, the whole humanity is a totality of inter-related individuals, families, groups, tribes and nations, making manifest the law lodged in them. The concrete universal or the Absolute Idea, according to Hegel, is a system of which the individual, the tribe and nation are so many inter-related parts.

Man too is not an isolated accident. Nature and life have been conspiring for billions of years to give birth to man. Man is organic to Nature and Life. Not only man embodies in himself physical processes and vital forces, but the working of the dead matter and living organisms become articulate in his scientific pursuits and attainments. Hence, the separateness, independence and cocoon-like isolation of man and nature have to be denied.

> The principle that solves the difference between Nature and finite Mind is, that their isolated reality and exclusiveness is a figment, and that the organic life of reason is the truth or reality of both.[1]

Here, one is reminded of the famous statement of Hegel,

> 'The real is rational, and, the rational is real.'

The formula of Hegel means that the whole universe consists of ideas which are interrelated in a coherent, rational system. Only in this system one has to understand the relation of one element with one another and the whole. Bradley would call this relation 'internal' and Hegel calls it 'logical'. No matter how we interpret the relation which an element has to other parts and whole, it has to be explained only in a whole of organically interrelated parts. Later idealists have preferred to picture this whole as a work of Art in which a part is most intimately and consciously found interlaced into the whole. Without this notion of the concrete universal, the idealistic metaphysics and its main tenets would be inexplicable.

---

1. J. Caird, *Ibid.*, p. 240.

9.04. The Function of Philosophy

We have already discussed in §.9.02 the nature of idealistic metaphysics and we can derive the function of philosophy from the idealistic metaphysics. The function of philosophy for the idealist is to *explain the universe*, to have an intuitive insight into the happenings of the world after a close observation of events in the world. From the viewpoint of analytic philosophy the whole idealistic enterprise is nonsense. For the analytic philosopher

1. The world as a whole is not an object of scientific enquiry; nor, can it admit of any explanation.

2. Secondly, explanation simply means scientific explanation, which predominantly has been causal explanation.

3. The world consists of simple elements which we know through our perception or sensation of them. So the sentient experience, in the most indubitable form, may be described as the *simple* which may be most nearly illustrated in the form of sense-data.

As against Russell, Ayer, Reichenbach and many other analytic philosophers, idealists have maintained that the subject-matter of philosophy is the world as a whole. However, idealists do hold that this is not an object of scientific enquiry. Philosophical wisdom comes in the form of an *attitude* to the whole world. . . .in regarding the world as the progressive revelation and manifestation of the personalised spirit which in itself is eternal and timeless. Thus, idealists maintain that the temporal is the expression of the eternal. Certainly any intuition of the eternal cannot be called scientific. For this reason Aristotle, Plato, Spinoza, Hegel and Bradley looked upon philosophy as something distinct from special sciences.

Idealists, also hold that the philosophical insight is gained by a perusal of the events of the world. So *experience* is quite relevant for philosophy and whichever be the attitude towards the world, it has to be sustained throughout by facts revealed by the sciences. However, idealists, specially Bradley would maintain that we should have our starting-point in the uncorruptible, primordial experience, uninterpreted by any philosophical view. According to Bradley, the starting-point of philosophy is 'a blur, as yet unparted by thought.' Bradley would not accept sensation or sense-datum as primordial. He would treat it as 'an abstraction' from actual primordial experience. Bosanquet, would say that the starting-point of philosophising is not any experience, but the most important and significant experience of the human being. Thus, idealists do not disregard experience, but they differ from the analyst with regard to the *kind* of experience, relevant for philosophy.

But the most important difference lies in standpoints. For the idealist the world has to be taken as one whole and all our experiences have to be studied, not in piecemeal, but as a totalised whole. Of course, the world as a whole cannot be the object of any observation or experimentation. So no scientific study of the world as a whole is feasible. Science is always compartmental and this nature of science is getting more accentuated with the trend towards specialisation. No philosopher also can claim the knowledge of the whole world. He means one or more the following things:

(i)   There is some underlying stuff, may be called the essence or being or primordial entity. By having an apprehension of this primary Being it might be possible to know all things in general. This seems to be the view of Aristotle.

(ii) We cannot know all the fields of knowledge, but we can know one or more of these fields better than the rest. The concepts drawn from the favoured field of enquiry may serve as key-concepts for understanding all other fields of enquiry. Here the key-concepts of necessity have to be strained and stretched to cover facts belonging to fields removed far away from the original field. This appears to be true of Spencer, Bergson and Whitehead. This is known as the root-metaphor theory of philosophy to which reference has already been made in §.0.02.

(iii) Most probably the nature of the Absolute Reality can never be known in detail. But this knowledge gains in solidity with progress in knowledge of things in general. At most we can have glimpses of this Reality. This appears to be the view of Hegel and Bradley. For Hegel, a study of human history, will give us an intuition into the nature of the Absolute. This intuition reveals that the Absolute unfolds itself in a dialectic march of thesis, anti-thesis and synthesis. Similarly for Bradley we know only, this much that the Absolute is all-inclusive, all-harmonious sentient experience. But we can never know this in detail.

Whichever be the view of the Absolute Reality, for the idealist unless our quest is for total reality, it is no philosophical quest at all. The quest appears to be prompted by a desire for intellectual satisfaction or rational illumination. For Bradley, the quest aims at the satisfaction of all sides and aspects of man. Hegel calls it 'rational satisfaction'. However, this satisfaction can never be limited to intellectual processes alone. For Hegel, philosophical revelation comes only after we have reflected on all the events that have taken place. By means of all-comprehensive *retrospect*, we understand the ways in which the Absolute has revealed itself in the course of world events. Unless the retrospective deliberation gives us sure, certain and satisfying illumination, our grasp will not be satisfactory. By 'sure and certain' is understood here, inescapable. Just as the conclusion follows from the premises, apprehension of parts follows from the nature of the whole, so the world-events should follow from our understanding of the Absolute. This understanding has its reference to the general modes or manner in which world-events take place. By knowing a particular triad in a certain sector of life, we cannot deduce any particular fact in that area. Philosophy is concerned with knowledge *in general*, in contrast with science which deals with events in their *individuality*. This has been expressed by Aristotle in his statement that philosophy is the science of *First Principles*. If we keep this in mind, then we should not make any predictive use of the dialectical advance in nature. The dialectic method of Hegel is only a philosophical key which throws light on the world as it is experienced by us. It should not be misinterpreted as a scientific law which is not only postdictive, but also *predictive*.

'Illumination' is not a mystical term. In any scientific enquiry there are roughly four stages, collection of data, formation of hypothesis, illumination and verification. The third stage is one in which the scientist feels that he has discovered what he wanted to know. This is known as 'hunch', creative synthesis, sudden flash, an 'aha-experience' and so on. For a scientist this is a very important stage, but unless the result of sudden flash is verified by means of laboratory tests, it is not considered important for scientific purposes. For philosophers, poets and creative artists illumination is the most important stage of their quest. Here no verification is possible, because the Absolute Reality does not admit of being confirmed-disconfirmed by any series of tests. Besides, the subjective element is most pronounced, since satisfaction (emotional satisfaction) also. Thirdly, the end purpose is to get an insight into the meaning of life, a hang of the on-goings of world-events.

The meaning or ideals of life are posited by the free decision of man in the light of the data collected pertaining to the total field of experience but any free decision is always open to fresh negotiation, protests and also confirmation by the accumulation of newer facts or by the newer patterning of old facts in favour or against the previous decision of man. But a philosopher is guided more by it conviction than by the truth about facts. The subjective certainty born of creative joy is the mastering key for the evaluation of any philosophy. Philosophical explanation has to be understood as an illumination concerning the total experience of man, which includes experiences called scientific, moral, social, logical and so on. That which appeals to the whole man cannot be called irrational or non-rational or anti-rational. So it is a *rational* reconstruction of experience. Philosophy is akin to poetry and religion, where illumination is brought about by logical skill and masterful marshalling of facts in favour of a certain point of view. In this sense philosophical explanation has been understood. Hegel protests against the view of explanation which is popularly known as scientific.

Usually by the 'explanation' of events, people mean causation. In the days of Hegel, as also in the days of Kant, scientists could not proceed in their task of establishing laws, without taking recourse to causation. But can causation explain the world as a whole? Of course, in explaining a particular event like the theft of a car, we do take the help of causation. As soon as the thief is caught, the theft of the car is said to be explained. But the whole world consists of a series of unending events. The search for causes would lead us to an interminable series. The cause of A is B, of B is C, of C is D, of D is E and so on. The search of its very nature can never end. It leads to infinite regress and the search is bound to end in fiasco. Should we then dogmatically posit a first cause? This arbitrary decision will not do. If there is no event without a cause, then there is not even the first cause about which logically we cannot ask. What is the cause of this particular cause?

The point is that analytic philosophers have correctly pointed out that no intelligible question can be asked about the world as a whole, which is a series of events. Even before Russell, Ayer and Reichenbach, Kant had pointed out that the principle of causation is valid only with regard to the explanation of phenomena, but causation cannot be used for explaining the world as a whole or noumena. In current language the attempt of explaining the world as a whole in terms of causation will be called a category-mistake, i.e., we shall be wrongly using a category (causation) for noumena where it is not applicable at all.

Hegel has gone one step further. Hegel tells us that causation is an unsound principle from the viewpoint of philosophy. It is alright to say that cold solidifies and heat expands. For practical purposes of life, this is acceptable along with many such statements concerning particular events of everyday life. For philosophical purposes, we should not simply state that cold contracts, but we should also be in a position to hold as to *why* cold contracts. Science is not concerned so much with *why*, as it is concerned with *how*. Science can tell us that this *is so and so,* and not that this *must* be so. Any factual law is a description of brute facts. In everyday life we bow down before facts with *natural piety*, as Samuel Alexander has beautifully described, but, in philosophy, we ask, why this fact and not any other fact, why this fact in this way and not in any other way? We may ask, why is grass green? From the viewpoint of man in the street, this question will be deemed unaskable, —a mere childish curiosity. But what is clear for commonsense, need not be so for philosophy. Commonsense accepts many things without realising that they raise a host of questions. The commonsense view is riddled with contradiction, as Bradley has pointed. For Bradley in science we bring together cold and contraction. But this is a mere *conjunction*, without connection, and for Bradley this is self-contradictory. Philosophical explanation for Hegel and Bradley must be self-explanatory, self-consistent and rational.

To be self-explanatory we should be able to find out the *reason* of things and not their causes. We cannot ask of reason, what is its own reason? There is no point of asking reason of reason, since reason is the reason of things and explains the movement and direction of all events (as Aristotle would say about his forms). It is final and wholly self-explanatory. Cause refers to temporal events individually; in contrast, reason has its locus in the world as a whole. According to Spinoza, a philosopher in an intuitive glance sees the place and part which an event plays in the world, viewed *sub specie aeternitatis*. Reason is a-temporal and holistic. Only in a whole, a part can have meaning and function. Rational explanation follows from the whole, of necessity. This holistic necessity should not be interpreted as logical necessity. We can summarise the result in a tabular form.

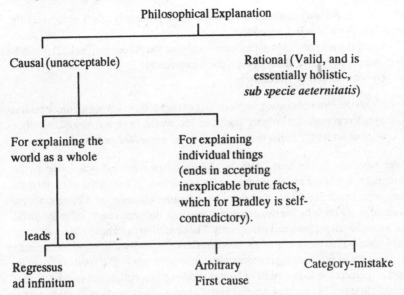

This philosophical explanation in terms of reason can be explained only gradually by showing that *Ideas* are the reason of things and their inmost essence. This will come under the heading of 'Idea-ism'. Later on, we shall find that rational explanation can only be holistic.

9.05. Idealism as Idea-ism

In § 9.03 we have already distinguished an Idea from a percept or concept. We have also held that the Idea of Plato means the *essence* and is regarded as timeless or eternal. For Hegel and Bradley, Idea means concrete universal. Now we shall try to explain idealism as idea-lism in its most persuasive way, which was presented by Berkeley. For the detail of Berkeleyan thesis, the reader is to consult § 6.06 and 6.07. We can summarise the result thus.

1. A thing is its *percipi*.

In the form of challenge, which has been called as egocentric predicament, Berkeley says,

Show me anything which exists which is not an idea.

A table is a congeries of colour, shape, weight and so on, and, these are all percipi or ideas.

2. An idea (perception) depends on the human percipient. For example, the sweetness of tea is in the taker of tea and the burning pain is in the experiencer and not in the fire.

3. From (2) it can be generalised that all perceptions are equally relative and dependent on the percipient, even extension, solidity and motion (which had been

alleged to be primary qualities and *in things*, independently of any perceiver) are all subjective and mind-dependent.

4. A thing is a congeries of perceived qualities and perception (as in 2) is mind-dependent. So finally all things are mind-dependent.

The conclusion of Berkeley is :

> . . . .all the choir of heaven and furniture of the earth, in a word all those bodies which compose the mighty frame of the world have not any subsistence without a mind. . . .that their *being* is *to be perceived* or known.

Like Socrates in the past, Berkeley himself had regarded perception to be momentary, relative and dependent on the percipient. The same tea does not taste the same to all tea-takers and even to the same tea-taker at different times. Naturally, if a thing be a series of perceptions, then the same object will not remain the same for all persons and percipients. The objectivity of knowledge cannot be explained on the basis of *esse est percipi*. Berkeley realised this and hastened to add that the *esse* of a thing is ultimately divine perception. But whatever may be said of perception in the mind of God, the divine perception is a matter of pure speculation and beyond any rational verification and justification. For this reason later idealists did not regard the *esse* of a thing its *percipi* but its *intelligi* as its *esse*. According to the idealist a thing is a series, congeries or an aggregate of universals. For example, a piece of stone is hard, coloured, cold, heavy and so on. Hardness, colouredness, coldness, heaviness etc. are all universals. A universal is the same for me, for you, and for all human beings. So if a thing is to be known, then we have to know the universals of which it is constituted, and, by treating a thing as an aggregate of universals we can explain objectivity of knowledge concerning any object whatsoever.

A universal is obtained by detecting a common essence by ignoring accidental accompaniments of particular things. For instance, by ignoring variable colour, size, eyes, nose and so on, and by concentrating on the common feature we obtain the abstract essence of cowness and horseness. So a universal is in thought and *is* thought. In the same way we can say that universal is an abstraction by thought, for thought, so a universal is thought. Again, a universal is not *temporally prior* of a thing. Things and universals constituting them are found together, but when we think, we think first of universals and afterwards of objects which are constituted of universals. So universals are only *logically prior* of things. Besides, a thing is sensible, but a universal has only a logical *being* which can be grasped by intellect alone. But a logical being will be called thought. So a universal is thought in the last analysis. So a thing constituted of universals, is ultimately constituted of thought. Thus, the doctrine of *esse est percipi* finally, leads to the cardinal tenet of idealism, according to which a thing is nothing but thought, or, thing and thought are identical. Here a question crops us. Things and thoughts are so different in kind that we can never imagine them to be identical. This question was raised by Berkeley, but he answered the question by regarding a thing as an aggregate of sensible qualities. But the idealists regard a thing as an aggregate universals which are not sensible. How can sensible thing be explained in terms of thought? Plato also saw a great gulf between an *Idea* and the thing and for this reason the argument of the *third man* is considered a great objection against the theory of ideas. Kant would not subscribe to idealism, for he would hold that *concepts* without percepts are *empty*. At this juncture we turn to Aristotle's theory of forms to explain the efficacy of thought in moulding things.

According to Aristotle, a thing is a combination of matter and form. By 'matter' is understood the physical stuff of which a thing is made, namely, the wood, gold, or any such thing. A formal cause comprises three kinds of cause coming under it, namely, efficient, formal and final. An *efficient cause* is the cause of every type of change in a thing; formal cause is the very *essence* of a thing, which is explicated in a definition of that thing. But a definition lays bare the concept or Idea of the thing. So formal cause is the Idea of that thing. A final cause is the end or purpose in the mind of the man who wants to bring about a change for a thing. Thus the final cause in general is the very thing itself. For example, a carpenter makes a chair out of wood (matter) with his skilled labour (efficient cause) for the office use (final cause) which when finished is the completed Idea of (formal cause) of the chair itself. Aristotle finally reduces efficient, formal and final causes into one, namely, formal cause. A formal and a final cause are one, since the final cause aims at the realisation of the essence or idea of the thing itself. Again, the efficient cause is the cause of becoming or making the desired thing. Thus, it is the end for which there is the efficient functioning. Thus, the essence or what the completed thing is going to be is the real cause of any efficient handling. Hence, for Aristotle, the essence or form is the real cause and also the reason of any movement in a thing or for becoming a thing.

For Aristotle matter and form are *distinct* but *not separate*. We can distinguish them in thought, but they are inseparable in reality. In other words, the distinction in matter and form is purely logical. Form means the qualities which a thing has, but above all it means the relationship in which a part stands with regard to other parts and the whole. Form also stands for the function which a thing has and the function of a thing is to become its very essence. For example, a knife has its essence of cutting a thing. So a knife functions well only when it does the cutting which is its essence. That the form is the moulding principle within a thing by virtue of which a thing becomes its essence is best understood in terms of the related notion of potentiality and actuality.

Matter for Aristotle is without any form, i.e., without any quality. But a thing is matter with some specific quality. For instance, gold is matter with the qualities of yellowness, malleableness and so on. However matter without quality is not anything in particular. But it may become anything according to the form put upon it. For example, melted gold has no very specific form of its own. But it may become any piece of ornament according to the form put upon it. So matter by itself is pure possibility by virtue of which a matter becomes an *individual thing*. Similarly, we can say that acorn is relatively matter and back is the form or end towards which the acorn is driven. But form is also the end or essence. So we can say that the form is the reason by virtue of which a thing becomes what it ultimately is. Here also the end to which a thing is driven is said to be logically prior, since it is this which drives potential matter to become an actual thing. In the same way Aristotle held that God, as pure actuality, the form of forms is the driving force of the whole world. Thus prime mover does not move the world mechanically, but ideally. Just as in a svayamvara ceremony princes are drawn towards the beauty queen, similarly the whole world is pulled up and attracted by the Idea of the Good (Plato) or the matterless form.

Thus, for Aristotle the form (same as the Idea of Plato) is the *reason* why a thing is what it is, for a form is the very *essence* of the thing. Again it is the indwelling or immanent principle in the thing and drives the thing to become its essential nature. For example, there is the form of a chick, implanted in the egg itself which moulds the changes in the egg to give rise to a chick. Thus, the idea is the meaning, reason and the immanent principle of a thing. Of course, both Plato and Aristotle assumed the reality of matter along with form, but the driving principle that explains the thing is not matter, but form or Idea. In this sense, the Idea is the essence and its explanatory principle of the thing. Matter by itself does not exist, it is pure potentiality, waiting to be transformed into any specific thing, according to the impress of the form. Matter is not the Form, but the form is its very meaning and essence. And in this sense, form or Idea is that which *constitutes* the thing. In this sense, we can now understand the contributions of Kant for Hegelian Idealism.

'Understanding maketh nature', but this phrase does not mean that nature is mind. It means, however, that nature is for the emergence of mind and the meaning of nature is unfolded by the mind of the scientist. Though nature is other than mind yet the mind is the key to the understanding of the workings of Nature and is its real end towards which the whole of nature is drawn up.

But if we understand the message of idealism as Idea-ism through the philosophy of Aristotle, then somehow the reality of matter remains as distinct as that of thought (Idea or form). However, Hegel has reduced matter not as something over and above, and independent of thought. Matter is also an implicit thought, something to be informed by thought. We can remember now that for Leibnitz everything, even the so-called dead matter is spiritual, only mind implanted within it is in stuperous or sleeping state. Some such view of matter is also found in Hegel. A thing then is an aggregate of thought, and, a table or chair is an aggregate of thoughts which are not fully conscious, not fully within the orbit of the organic wholeness of which all constituent thoughts are the parts.

Somethings have more degrees of reality than other things, depending upon the nature of the explicitness of thoughts constituting them. Later on, Bradley has posited the criteria of all-inclusiveness and self-consistency of the concrete universal or whole for determining the degrees of Reality of a thing. Thus, for Hegel and Hegelians a thing is nothing but an aggregate of Ideas, but no idea is to be taken in isolation. The aggregate really means a whole and, each smaller whole is a unit of a larger whole as its inseparable element. Thus, the whole world is an organic whole, or a system of hierarchically ordered ideas. This was clearly stated both by Plato and Aristotle, but this has been most fully hinted by Hegel in his statements.

'The actual is rational, and, the rational is actual'. That the actual, i.e., nature, life and Mind are regulated by values and ideals has been beautifully worked out in detail by Josiah Royce, Bernard Bosanquet and A.S. Pringle-Pattison. However, if there is still some doubt left with regard to treating a thing as thought, then it really rests on the doctrine of the unknowable to which doctrine we can make brief reference.

Ordinarily people think that thought and thing are distinct and opposed. But if they be really so different in kind, then how can an object be known at all? This was the doctrine of Kant. According to Kant, there is scientific knowledge which is quite reliable, universal and necessary. But this knowledge is of phenomena alone. Things-in-themselves are unknown and unknowable. There are two aspects of this doctrine of the unknowable.

(i) If things-in-themselves are unknown and unknowable, then there can be no way out of scepticism.

(ii) Secondly, the whole doctrine is self-contradictory and absurd. Hegel has raised objections to both aspects of the doctrine and we have already explained Hegel's refutation of the doctrine of the unknowable in § 8.38. Other idealists have followed this lead of Hegel, including Bradley. However, in the writings of Bosanquet and Pringle-Pattison there is a more positive reference with regard to the doctrine of the identity of thought and thing. These writers have fully assimilated the evolutionary view of the world. According to these idealist authors, life has emerged from matter, and mind has emerged from life. Naturally, mind is implanted in matter and life, and in a way mind is the higher form of matter and life, and, so discloses the story of matter and life in a clearer way than what is possible for matter and life themselves. Again, if mind were not adjusted to the demands of matter and life, then mind could not have survived in the matter and life struggle of existence. So mind is most fitted to disclose the in most secrets of matter and life. So mind is organic to nature. Nay, the Hegelian thesis that thought and things are opposed and yet identical, has been given a richer orientation by Bosanquet and Pringle-Pattison. According to these authors matter and life are other than mind and yet matter and life in due course have given birth to mind. Further, mind is sustained into its being by matter and life. Thus, matter and life are not only opposed, but are also in close partnership with mind. Nay, if mind were not in some form already in matter and life, then it could not have come out of matter and life at all.

If we take the various senses in which idea-ism has been used, then the thesis of the identity of thought and thing will appear to be fairly intelligible. But many things which have not been made clear will become intelligible after we have learnt the philosophy of Hegel and Bradley.

GEORG WILHELM FRIEDRICH HEGEL (1770-1831)

Georg Hegel was born on August 27, 1770 and died on November 14, 1831. Hegel may be regarded as the national philosopher of Germany, for according to him, the Absolute Spirit has been unfolding itself through ages and is speaking most clearly in the hopes and aspirations of German people. In contrast Kant was an internationalist, since he regarded each person as a citizen of the kingdom of ends. Hegel wrote at a time when the French Revolution had made a powerful impression on all thoughtful persons. Hence, for Hegel freedom remained a central key-concept of his philosophy. However, for Hegel, a loyal German citizen participating in the German state enjoyed his freedom most. It was this teaching which ultimately paved the way for the rise of German Nazism. Hegel has presented a monistic philosophy, according to which the Absolute Reality is progressively manifesting itself dialectically in the form of thesis, antithesis and synthesis. Some Marxists have interpreted this dialectical advance for predicting the future course of history. However, Hegel has remained true to his Aristotelian vision of Philosophy. Hegel was not concerned with what has been, nor what will be, but through history he is concerned to know what *is* and *is eternally*.

Kant is a philosopher of science. In contrast, Hegel is a Speculative Philosopher and delights in painting his vision through the scenes of history of events and thoughts. No doubt in his creative stride he has thrown new light on logic, but his logic remained always subordinate to his metaphysics. The important works of Hegel are :

1. The History of Philosophy (1805)
2. The Phenomenology of the Spirit (1807)
3. The Science of Logic (1812-1816)
4. Encyclopaedia of the Philosophical Sciences (1817)
5. Philosophy of Right and Law (1821)
6. Lectures on Aesthetics (1818)   Based on
7. The Philosophy of History (1822)   classes-notes
8. Lectures on the Philosophy of Religion of students.

9.06. The Outline of Hegel's Idealism

From Plato to Bradley, idealists have made a distinction between appearance and reality. Things as they appear to a man in the street are actual and do exist. They are true as far as they go for everyday life. But they are mere appearance on the level of philosophical reflection. The reason is that philosophy views things in one monistic system and things of daily life like tables, chairs, beautiful objects, Gods and charms and even scientific entities like electrons and genes cannot be put together in one system. Therefore, idealism seeks to go deep into things to discover their underlying essence in order to view them together. In contemporary analytic philosophy the search for any essence and an all-inclusive system is said to be a pseudo-search and any talk about Reality is said to be nonsense. Most probably the criticism of analytic philosophy is irrelevant, but even it makes distinction between different levels of language. According to analytic writers the language used for dealing with things may be called first-order language. However, we may also talk about the first-order language in the same way in which the first-order language is used for directly dealing with things. We can imagine even the third and fourth levels of language. The first-order language ordinarily is quite satisfactory for dealing with things but very often it uses terms which are vague, imprecise and gives rise to pseudo-problems. For this purpose, philosophy is needed to analyse and elucidate concepts used in first-order language. This task of analysis and elucidating concepts is difficult. In the words of Ryle, we think alright *with* categories in dealing with objects, but not so in relation to concepts themselves. Well analysts may and may not be correct with regard to the task of philosophy, but the point is that they also make a distinction between ordinary and philosophical talking. So we can say that idealists are on sound grounds when they distinguish between appearance and reality.

Reality for Hegel is that which is eternal, unchangeable and a systematic whole. Anything which comes short of this is only an appearance and not Reality. However, things of daily life are short-lived, changeable and have their beginning and end. So quite obviously, things of daily life like tables and chairs and even the yonder mountain and planets are not real *per definition* of Reality. But things do exist and are actual. A thing is said to exist if it can be known through the senses and located in spatio-temporal frame of reference. We can certainly sense a table or tree and can locate it in space and time. But an actual thing cannot be said to be real for

(i) Things are shot through with illusions. A rope appears as a snake, and a plane or a kite appears to be a tiny bit in the sky.

(ii) There are ordinary, abnormal and dream delusions. We often hear voices when there are none in actuality.

(iii) Things too far or too small are beyond the ken of human senses.

(iv) Actual things do not endure and have their beginning and end.

But actual things have punch and sting and have to be accepted as things to which we have to adjust ourselves. Fire burns and too much of cold kills. We cannot brush them aside by calling them as not absolutely real. In that case they cannot be called absolutely unreal. Hence, things have both reality and unreality. Things are not as unreal as barren mothers or square circles. Nor are they as unreal as sky-flowers or horns of a hare. Every puff of existence, no matter however, ephemeral has some reality about it. It was maintained even by Plato. No doubt for Plato ideas alone are real, but things are mere *copies* and they also remind us of Ideas. So there is the *participation* of things in Ideas. For Hegel, a thing is an aggregate of universals which are the same thing as ideas. For example, a table is an aggregate of solidity, heaviness, hardness, colouredness etc. But we might be landed up in another difficulty. A universal is not a spatio-temporal entity which can be sensed. We can sense a heavy thing, but not heaviness; a hard object, but not hardness and so on. But if a universal cannot be sensed in a spatio-temporal frame, then it *cannot be said to exist* either, according to the definition of the term 'existence'. Hence the paradox,

> That which exists is not real,
> And the Real does not exist.

True, Hegel would maintain, and so does Bradley that existence and reality, appearance and reality cannot be separated. They are opposed and yet identical. The key-concept of Hegel is identity-in-difference, or, difference-in-identity. Existence and reality are opposed inasmuch as existence is ephemeral and Reality is eternal. But they have something in common too. Both existence and Reality have *Being*. A thing may be illusory, even a delusion or a mere fiction, but it has some sort of *isness*. A centaur, is a thing of fiction, but even a centaur has being in a world of fiction. In the same way heaviness, solidity and other universals have also being. As opposed to existence, they were credited with shadowy subsistence and Plato expressed the same thing metaphysically by saying that Ideas have *heavenly* existence. Existence and Reality both have Being, but they do not have being in the same way. Reality is said to have an *independent* being. In contrast, existence has *dependent* being. Ideas as real, according to Plato, are eternal and self-existent. Hegel too would regard universals as thoughts, but not *your* thoughts or *my* thoughts or thoughts *of any mind* at all. But things are said to follow from thoughts in the same way as the conclusion follows from its premises. This is easy to understand in terms of Aristotle's Forms, as the immanent and moulding principle of things. Thoughts are the causes and reasons of things and constitute their inmost essence. The forms of Aristotle become *explicit* in individual things, but without being actualised in things they remain implicit. So we can say that the Ideas of Hegel pass from the implicit to the explicit or from bare possibilities to their actualities. Of course, for Hegel ideas are not isolated. He subscribes to the doctrine of concrete universals, i.e., an organic whole of universals as their constituent elements. This whole is called the *Absolute*. We can summarise the views of Hegel by saying that each thing is an aggregate of universals in the first instance, and, all the things are organised in an all-inclusive self-consistent whole. This picture of Reality as an all-inclusive whole of Ideas or universals may give us a static view of things. However, for Hegel, the Absolute is pictured as a system of changing entities. To say this we can say that the Absolute is a storehouse of infinite possibilities which are progressively and gradually realised in history and actual happenings of the world.

We can once more repeat here that thoughts which constitute things are not the abstract ideas of Plato; much less the concepts of Socrates. These thoughts are very much akin to Kant's pure or *a priori* concepts of the understanding. However, the concrete universals of Hegel are not only valid for human thought, But are independent of any mind, whatsoever.

9.07. Hegelian Monism
According to the Absolute Idealism of Hegel there is only one Reality. If there were more than one Reality, then each would be limited by the rest. But a limited reality cannot be eternal, self-dependent and all-inclusive. The other thing is that according to Hegel this one Reality is an all-inclusive and self-consistent whole. If there be more than one reality, as in the system of Leibnitz, then one will have to posit some other supreme Reality that will unify, combine and harmonize all realities into one. We have already seen that the monadism and theodicee of Leibnitz do not go together (§ 4.10 first para). Therefore, pluralism cannot be harmonised with monism, i.e., with order, system and unity of things. This point concerning monism has been further elaborated by Bradley. According to Bradley mere juxtaposition of two or more reals without any apparent harmony, i.e., without being reduced to its being parts of one whole, will lead to self-contradiction. However, we shall refer to this point in due place. Thus, at this point we can conclude that monism cannot be reconciled with pluralism.

Even if we grant that Reality is one, this monism will be either abstract or concrete. According to Hegel, Spinoza's idealism will be called *abstract* monism, i.e., according to Spinoza, Reality is one without the many. In Spinozism manyness disappears. All the things, including human beings, are mere passing waves that never are. Therefore, Hegel has called Spinozism as a black night in which all cows are equally black, or, Spinoza's Substance is just like the lion's den to which all foot-prints point, but from which nothing returns. But the things of daily life are our premises and the things are there to be explained. They give us the starting point of our enquiry. No explanation can be deemed satisfactory if they are *explained away*. Reality instead of swallowing up the things to be explained, somehow must conserve them in it. The principle of Hegel is *not one or many,* but *Many-in-one* or *One-in-Many*. Hence the abstract idealism of Spinoza has to be rejected, as it emphasizes the *One* at the cost of *Many*; in the same way, the system of Leibnitz has to be rejected because it accepts *the Many* at the cost of One. Reality is one of which the Many are its integral parts. That Reality is one organic whole consisting of the Many was explicitly hinted at by Plato.[1]

Plato, in his dialogue called *Parmenides* explicitly stated that one and many imply each other. One without many is unreal and many without one is only a juxtaposition of various units. So Reality has to be pictured as one organic whole with many things as its members. Plato has presented Reality as a hierarchical system in which the individual objects are at the base and the more general ideas are towards the apex. All red things are subsumed under the idea of redness, and white things are brought under the idea of whiteness and so on. Further, all the ideas of different colours are further subsumed under a still higher idea of colouredness. In the same way the higher and more general ideas of colour, taste, smell, temperature and so on, can be classed under a still higher Idea of Quality. For Plato the Idea of the Good is at the apex, drawing all other ideas towards itself. What has been just said can be put into a tabular form:

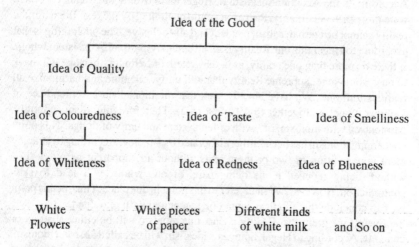

Plato's monism is both axiological and teleological. And Plato's explanation or his teleological system has been accepted by Hegel. According to both Aristotle and Plato the whole system of things is regulated by an Ideal entity, say, God (or the form of forms, Aristotle) or the Idea of the Good (Plato). The Idea of the Good causes change in all other things ideally without any change in it. For example, the beauty of a princess causes a good deal of movement among her suitors, but she herself remains unmoved. Following the teleological system of Plato, Hegel too would say that the Absolute contains many histories, but has no history of its own. The Idea of the Good, as also the Absolute of Hegel, remains eternal,

---

1. Plato discussed the relation of One and Many in the *Parmenides*. Refer, I.M. Crombie, *Plato's Doctrines*, Vol. II, pp. 326-52, specially p. 327 and 352.

changeless and timeless embodiment of eternal truths. Hegel agrees with Plato in regarding the Absolute Reality as the system of Ideas, but he tries to advance upon Plato both by further analysing the notion of Ideas and by clarifying the notion of inter-relation between the Ideas. Plato was not clear about the nature of those ideas which constitute Reality. Plato appeared sure about the Ideas of beauty, justice and goodness. Hesitatingly he also allowed that there are ideas of man, fire and water. But he doubted whether there are ideas of hair, mud and dirt. However, Plato has not clarified the notion of Ideas which constitute Reality. Secondly, Plato has not analysed the notion of Relation, both among Ideas themselves and of Ideas with the perceptual things of the world. Plato simply said that the things *participate* in Ideas, or that the things remind us of the Ideas. Is this relationship of Ideas and things the same as the resemblance of the copy with the original? Many puzzles have been found in the dialogues of Plato himself concerning this inter-relationship. Hegel, by criticising the hierarchical system of Ideas, presented by Plato, prepares the ground for his own system.

1. Hegel does subscribe to the thesis that Reality is a system of Ideas, arranged hierarchically according to the degree of generality or reality. The most general Idea certainly lies at the apex. But, according to Hegel, Plato's hierarchical system does not tell us as to why the Idea of the Good is at the apex. Plato has only dogmatically assumed that the idea of the Good is the highest Idea. But in any philosophical account of the world we must give reasons for holding any particular Idea to be the highest Idea at the apex.

2. Secondly, according to Hegel there should be a rational relation between the Ideas themselves. So far as Plato is concerned he has not logically related the Ideas amongst themselves, nor has he rationally related the Idea with the things. We would like to know as to how white things follow from the idea of white, or red things from redness. In the same way, Plato has not shown as to how the idea of white or red follows from the higher Idea of colour. Nor has Plato shown us as to how in due course the idea of Quality follows from the Idea of the Good.

3. It appears from the various Dialogues of Plato that he thought that along with Ideas there is also Matter, at least this is clearly visible in his conception of Demiurge who has fashioned this world out of pre-existing chaotic matter (Timaeus). According to Hegel there is no matter at all. There is the sole reality of Ideas. For example, a table is a congeries of Ideas like heaviness, hardness, brownness and so on. Over and above there is nothing like non-Idea or matter. What appears as non-mental, in the analysis, is nothing but an aggregate of Ideas.

Hegel is not satisfied with showing that Reality is Idea-l, but also adds that the Ideas are organically related. It is possible to deduce all other Ideas from any one given Idea, and, in this system of Ideas, there is always a logical reason as to why the first Idea is *first* and the *Last* Idea is last. And thus system can be developed from seeing the shortcomings of Plato's hierarchical system itself.

Plato has not succeeded in showing that Reality is one organic whole, for he has not shown as to how particular things follow from their corresponding ideas. Even if Plato had attempted to do so, he would not have succeeded in deducing the less general from the more general ideas, for the Ideas of Plato are *abstract Ideas* and not concrete Ideas. Secondly, the Ideas of Plato are as much empirical as they are also pure or non-empirical. Empirical Ideas are really formed from the admixture of matter and form (to use the terminology of Aristotle) or percepts and form (Plato). But we have already seen that Reality is One and there is no place in it of Matter or any other kind of reality apart from Mind or Ideas. For this reason the idea of white is not a pure idea at all. How can then white things be deduced from the Idea of white? The Idea of white is an abstract idea. We have seen many white flowers, white pieces of paper, milk of various shades of whiteness. From many such things we have found out the common quality of whiteness by arbitrarily excluding all other characteristics of white flowers, white pieces of paper or the various features of different kinds of milk. But what right is there in supposing that whiteness, so divorced from all other qualities of various white things, will continue to be the same? Any part of the body cannot be living limb apart from the whole body. Similarly, any universal idea which has been abstracted by the method of exclusion of so-called arbitrarily declared inessential details of particular things cannot be regarded as real.

Thus the Ideas which constitute Reality are concrete and not abstract, are non-empirical and not empirical and the system of concrete Ideas constituting Reality is logical and not arbitrary.

A concrete idea is a whole which includes all particular instances under it as its essential parts. For example, a cycle is a mechanical whole which includes spokes, rims, freewheel, chain, handles and so on, as its essential parts. A concrete idea therefore is not reached by excluding, but by including the details. We can illustrate this kind of concrete Idea even in the case of First Idea. As the Idea is non-empirical, so we can also call it *a category*, following Kant. Kant held that understanding maketh nature and understanding works through its twelve categories which are *a priori* and wholly independent of any experience. So the non-empirical Ideas are also the categories or *a priori* notions. Again, the procedure should be logical and not dogmatic. In other words, unlike Plato, we should be able to say that a certain category is first and it *must* be the first if we follow a certain rational principle in presenting the hierarchical system of thoughts, constitutive of Reality.

9.08. The First Category and First Triad
If we look at the hierarchical system of Plato, then we find that the whole scheme is based on the principle of generality, i.e., the more general idea is towards the apex and the less general idea is towards the base. Naturally therefore the most general idea should be at the apex. And why? The reason is that the less general

idea always presupposes its proximate more general idea. For illustrating this we can take the following table :

Creature

|

Animal

|

Man

We cannot think of man without supposing him to be an animal at the same time. But its converse is not true. We can think of an animal without making any reference to man. In the same way we cannot think of an animal without presupposing the notion of a creature, but certainly we can think of a creature without presupposing it to be an animal.[1] Following the table presented here we can say that the most general Idea is the presupposition of each and every idea below it and so the most general Idea will be called the first category, since it is this category or idea on which all other ideas depend. So the search for the first category really means the search for the most general Idea. Now the most abstract and most general category is the category of Being. How?

An object may not be material, may not be heavy, may not be round but it is always true to say of it that it is. A thing may not be an existing thing, nay, it may be wholly fictional like a centaur, or a pegasus. But it will still have some sort of Being. So whatever any object, real or unreal, be said to be it must have *being* or the quality of *isness*. Therefore Being is that most general category which is presupposed by any object whatsoever.[2] Therefore, Being, being the ultimate presupposition of every thing is the first category. Substance, cause or any such general notions also presuppose the category of Being, for whatever be called as cause, it must have some sort of being. At least we can always say of cause that it is. Hence, Being is the first category because all other ideas or categories depend on it, or, is logically presupposed by all other ideas. Because Being is the first Category and is the ultimate presupposition of every other category, so all other categories can be deduced from this category of Being.

Being means the most general being or isness. It does not mean any specific kind of being. It certainly does not directly donate material being or spiritual being or human being or wise being or wicked being. Every kind of being certainly, comes out of Being in general, but Being does not refer to any specific or particular being. For example, every kind of gold ornaments depends on gold, but gold does not directly mean, either an ear-ring or a bangle or a chain. So Being is without any feature. It is absolutely indeterminate, empty and without any specific content. We can always describe pure being as not this, nor that, nor anything.

1. A creature is much wider than an animal, for birds, insects and many such living beings are included in the notion of being a creature.
2. C.J. Friedrich, *The Science of Logic* in The Philosophy of Hegel, p. 207. ". . . .and the actual *'Prius'* for thought is also to be first in the logical thought-process" (*Ibid.*, p. 204).

In the Vedantic terminology we can say only this much that it is not this, it is not that, it is not man, it is not god and so on. The language is *neti, neti* (not this, not this). So featureless pure being is just emptiness, pure vacancy and is just as good as nothing. Hence, Being is non-Being, i.e., it is not any kind of specific thing. So non-Being is the second category and has been shown through simple analysis of the concept of Being that Being contains non-Being. This showing of non-Being as contained in Being means that non-Being has been *deduced* from Being.[3]

Being and non-Being are opposed and yet are *identical*. On the face of it Being and non-Being are contradictory terms and so are instances of the extreme form of opposition. Yet they are identical, because non-Being has been deduced from Being and it could have not been deduced from Being if non-Being was not there in it at least implicitly. Again, Being and non-Being, both are empty and vacant and in this sense they are identical. Because Being and non-Being are identical, so Being passes into non-Being, and, Nothing (non-Being) passes into Being; for, the thought of nothing is the thought of emptiness, and emptiness is what pure Being is. This passing from Being into non-Being, or, of non-Being into Being is known as Becoming, which is the third category of the entire system of thoughts constitutive of Reality. Thus, Being, non-Being and Becoming form the first three categories, and by reflecting upon them we shall find the general nature of Reality and also the Dialectic process through which Reality manifests itself in the things of the world.

We found that Plato could not deduce the world of things from general Ideas, or, even the less general from the more general Ideas. The reason of this failure lies in the method of abstraction by which Plato sought to ascend from the lower to the higher. Take the table again :

Creature
|
Animal
|
Man

The definition of 'Man' is rational animal. 'Animal' is the genus and 'rational' is the differentium which differentiates man from all other animals. Now the method of abstraction lies in excluding the differentia and by exclusive attention to the genus in order to reach an idea having higher generality. In this way we ascend to the next higher Idea of animal, by excluding 'rationality'. Similarly, the next higher idea of creature is reached by excluding animality from the definition of animal for the definition of an animal is created being (genus) and animality (differentium). But this process of abstraction will not do. No doubt by this method of systematic and careful abstraction we can reach even the highest

1. C.J. Firedrich, *The Science of Logic, Ibid.*, p. 21.

general Idea, Being. But can we descend from Being to 'Rational mammal'? We cannot deduce the lower from the higher for a very simple reason. In ascending to the higher we exclude differentia, at each stage. By excluding 'rationality' we reach 'mammal', again, by excluding 'mammality' we reach the higher idea of Vertebrate. And in this way by systematic exclusion of differentia, we are left with the *genus* alone at each stage. For descending or deducing the lower from the higher we require the necessary differentium. For example, in order to deduce 'man' from 'animal', we need the differentium 'rationality'. But how can we get this differentium from 'animal', seeing that we have excluded 'rationality' from 'animal'. 'Animal' is bare and empty of 'rationality' and so rationality cannot be obtained by analysing 'animal' in any way we like. In other words, Plato failed to deduce the world of things from Ideas, because the ideas which he used were *abstract* ideas. They are called abstract in the sense that they lacked details, lacked differentia. Whereas the idea should be concrete, that is, it should contain differentia. And this point can be seen if we concentrate on the first triad of Being, non-Being and Becoming. By a little reflection on them we find that they can be recognised as Genus, Differentia and Species.

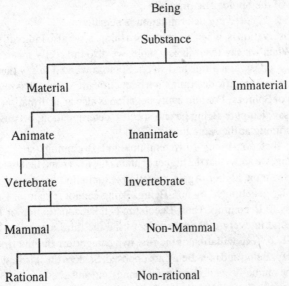

The positive category of Being invites its anti-thesis non-Being. This opposite category of non-Being serves as the differentium. Now by combining the genus Being with the differentium non-Being we get the species Becoming.

$$\text{Being} + \text{non-Being} = \text{Becoming}$$
$$\text{(Genus)} + \text{(Differentium)} = \text{(Species)}$$

Becoming is also a kind or species of Being, for we can say of Becoming that it *is*; only Becoming here means pure motion, i.e., a being in motion, which simply means a being which constantly denies itself. But if Being is genus and Becoming is its species, then it means that Becoming (species) has been deduced from Being (Genus), i.e., the higher (Being) has been shown to contain the lower (Becoming). Thus, the Being of Hegel, instead of excluding the lower contains the lower. In this sense this is a concrete idea. But how have we got the species? Of course by combining the genus with the differentium which in this case is non-Being. This non-Being is contained in Being itself and is the negation of Being. By combining non-Being with Being we get the species Becoming. Thus, negation is the principle of movement from one category to another. Negation is never bare negation. It becomes a new determination,— a new quality. Hence, Hegel propounds a very famous principle, *Every negation is determination.*[1] By negating the higher Idea we get the lower Idea. By negating Being, we get the species Becoming. Thus, the higher Idea contains the germ of its own negation and this negation serves as the differentium leading to the next lower idea. Hence, negation is a potent force of movement from the higher to the lower. This principle is the complementary of the Spinozistic principle.

'Every determination is negation.

Spinoza's observation is, when we say what a thing is, we also indirectly state what it is not. When we say that this is a table, we also indirectly mean that it is not a chair, not a desk, not a tree and so on. Spinoza wanted to say that pure Being cannot have any specific determination or qualification. Hegel has reversed this observation of Spinoza. For him every negation is also an affirmation at the same time. We say that pure Being has no specific determination, because it is a process or becoming at the same time.

By showing that non-Being (differentium) and Becoming (species) are contained in Being, we show that the higher contains the lower and that the lower can be deduced from the higher. Again, negation is limitation or determination inasmuch as Being gets limited by non-Being. Being cannot remain in Being : it has to give way to Becoming. Thus, Becoming is the reconciliation of Being and non-Being, and in every other subsequent triad the third category always serves as the unity or reconciliation of the first two categories. But the first two categories, namely, Being and non-Being are opposed. So does the third category by reconciling the mutually exclusive thesis (Being) and anti-thesis (non-Being) deny the law of contradiction. We shall take up this issue again shortly. At this stage we can say this much that the third category known as the synthesis does not deny the law of contradiction. One is driven to the synthesis because one cannot rest in the contradiction of Being and non-Being. Becoming does not simply contain both Being and non-Being and is a reconciliation of them, but is

1. C.J. Friedrich, *The Philosophy of Hegel*, p. 191.

also something new or rather is the transformation of Being and non-Being. Later or, Llyod Morgan talked of resultant and emergent. The synthesis contains both Being and non-Being, but Becoming is not only a summation of Being and non-Being (resultant), it is also an emergent.

Hence, we can conclude that Reality is an organic system of thoughts which can be arranged in triads and triads are so related that we pass from one idea to another, and, from one triad to others logically. This logical process is known as the Dialectic Method and now we shall try to explain this famous method.

9.09. The Dialectic Method

Both Plato and Aristotle tried to explain the world of change through eternal Ideas. Following the idealistic lead of Plato and Aristotle, Hegel also regards the Absolute as eternal and changeless. Nonetheless the Absolute is a system in which all changes are hushed and silenced in the eternal symphony of the Absolute. Hegel does recognize that the world contains many changes and these changes are neither chaotic nor accidental. They all are logically guided and are regulated by the dialectic advance of thesis, anti-thesis and synthesis.[1] Before Hegel, the idealistic world of Spinoza was just static. True, Hegel appeared on the Western scene before the advent of organic evolution propounded powerfully by Charles Darwin. Nonetheless the talk of a dynamic and evolving Reality was quite familiar at the time of Hegel and Hegel took evolutionary process seriously. Whatever be the shortcomings of the Dialectic Method, it has to be interpreted as a philosophical method to explain a dynamic and evolving world, according to some rational plan. The dialectic method tries to explain this world of change and evolution in terms of unchangeable Ideas. Hegel would explain the logical transition from the Abstract to the concrete, from the more general to the less general Idea. The nerve of the dialectic process is that logical unfoldment can be read off from empirical events, but the dialectic steps do not become empirical on that account. Empirical events are merely illustrative guide of the dialectic advance. The significance of this observation will become clear in the light of the critical appraisal of the Dialectic Method.

To understand the Dialectic Method we have to reflect upon the first triad of Being—non-Being—Becoming. We have already said that the dialectic advance traces logical transitions from the abstract to the concrete. Being is most abstract: it is abstract from all determinations, beyond being itself it has no other, qualities. In comparison with Being, Becoming is more concrete since it includes both Being and non-Being within itself. But of course, Becoming in comparison with other succeeding categories, is terribly abstract. Becoming simply means a process without being any specific process. It is bare change which again has to be negatively described that it is not mechanical, nor chemical nor organic, nor any such special kind of change. Naturally it has to grow more specific. It will

---

* C.J. Friedrich, *Ibid.,* p. 191.

invite its anti-thesis which in turn would lead to a second synthesis. And this second synthesis will be more concrete than Becoming itself. Thus, as the dialectic advances, the succeeding categories become more and more concrete till we reach the Absolute which is the fullest and richest and the most concrete of all the categories. In the last or highest category all the previous categories are preserved and nothing is lost. In this sense, Hegel's system is known as concrete monism in contrast with Spinozism which is called abstract Monism.

The higher and the more concrete categories contain the lower or the more abstract. For example, Becoming does contain Being and non-Being. But the reverse is also true : the lower category also contains the higher. For example, Being does contain Becoming and if it were not so, Becoming could not be deduced from it. With a view to elucidating this paradoxical position we can say,

> The higher categories contain the lower (i.e., the abstract) *explicitly*, but the lower categories also contain the higher (the more concrete) *implicitly*.

Being implicitly contains Becoming and without Becoming, Being could not be Being. Becoming is therefore an explicit condition on which Being depends. Becoming explicitly contains Being, since Becoming is certainly a kind of Being. Becoming (being a kind of Being) presupposes Being, but Becoming in turn is also the foundation of Being. By 'foundation' is meant that Being is logically deduced from Becoming. True, Becoming comes later than Being, it is also the logical beginning and foundation of the first category 'Being'. In the most sketchy manner we shall show that Being not only contains non-Being and Becoming, but also all other categories, including the final category, the Absolute. But it is also true to say that the Absolute is the foundation of Being in the sense that Being can be explicitly deduced from it, for the Absolute, the final category contains all previous categories and so Being is naturally contained in it. Thus, the first category is also the last and the last contains all the first and all other previous categories quite explicitly.

> What is essential for the science (of logic) is not so much that a pure immediate is the beginning, but that itself in its totality forms a cycle returning upon itself, wherein the first is also last, and the last first.[1]

For example, in a drama the first scene contains the last scene, and, the last scene contains the meaning of the first and all other scenes. That the last is also the first category is very important for the Hegelian philosophy and put in the form of Aristotelian philosophy it forms the very nerve of the logical idealism of Hegel.

In Aristotle's philosophy the form is the reason behind all the changes of an individual thing. Therefore, *actus purus* (corresponding to the Absolute of Hegel),

---

1. C.J. Friedrich, *The Philosophy of Hegel*, p. 208.

the Prime Mover is the Absolute Reason or the foundation of all that exists. It is the end (the form in the thing) which is the meaning of the beginning or of a thing and should be said to be logically prior of the actual thing. So in Hegel's terminology, the Absolute is the logical foundation of all that exists. As the category or the form is the *reason* of the thing, so the Absolute is the absolute reason of the whole world. Understood thus we can quote from Hegel's *Philosophy of Right and Law*

"The rational is actual (real)
And the actual is rational."[1]

The whole world is really a system of categories, inter-related dialectically in such a way that the Absolute is the reason of Being and all other previous categories, and, Being too is implicitly the reason of the Absolute. The whole system of categories returns into itself and is self-explanatory. This is tantamount to saying that reason is its own reason, and, is self-determined, wholly rational or logical.

For Hegel, logic is not purely formal which does not contain any material content. For Hegel, logic is ontology : things and thoughts are one and the same. This is easily seen in many statements of Hegel, but is clearly, supported by the following quotation from *The Science of Logic.*

Thus this older metaphysic stands for the view that thinking and the determinations of thinking are not something foreign to the objects of thought, but are rather of them very essence of those objects; in other words that *things* and the *thinking* of them are in harmony in and for themselves. . . .indeed language itself expresses an affinity between them. . . .that thought in its immanent determinations, and the true nature of things, are one and the same content.[2]

Therefore, in order to evaluate the dialectic method of Hegel, we have to see its working in its myriad forms from abstract logic to the history of the mankind.

9.10. The Dialectic Advance of the World-Spirit
Or
Hegel's Idealistic Interpretation of the World

Geist or Spirit is the key notion of Hegel. The Absolute is the world-spirit at work in the form of dialectic process. The world-spirit is some sort of Personal Mind, but for Hegel, the personal God of Christianity is not the Absolute Reality. It is the Absolute Reality which unfolds itself in the dialectic process in Nature, Life and Mind, and becomes articulate in the self-consciousness of the final philosophy of the age. Quoting Hegel, Friedrich writes in his *Introduction* to Hegel's works :

---

1. *Ibid.,* p. 224.
2. C.J. Friedrich, *Ibid.,* p. 180

Man knows about God only insofar as God knows about himself *in man* : this knowledge is self-consciousness of God, but this knowledge is at the same time God's knowledge of Man, and this God's knowledge of man is man's knowledge of God; the spirit of man knowing God is only God's own spirit.[1]

Thus, we can say that the Absolute's knowledge of itself and philosophers' knowledge of the Absolute are aspects of the same reality. In his great work, *the phenomenology of the spirit,* Hegel writes,

Reason is spirit, when its certainty of being all reality has been raised to the level of truth, and reason is consciously aware of itself as its own world, and of the world as itself.[2]

In other words, the world-spirit rises to self-consciousness in man through his science, morality, religion and philosophy. And man has become aware of the reason, which is the essence of the various processes, as a result of the struggle of man with nature and life. However, the laws embedded in the workings of nature are nothing but thought. So the objective nature, when revealed to man in his scientific knowledge, is the supreme spirit itself. So, for Hegel, the supreme spirit alone is real. This spirit for Hegel is consciousness-in-itself andd in-and-for-itself. Consciousness-in-itself is abstract and becomes concrete in relation to appropriate objects of Nature and Life. The objects in Nature and Life appear as *the other* of Mind. This otherness of objects has to be overcome by being mentalised (i.e. secrets of Nature, have to be disclosed as thoughts) and spiritualised (i.e., when human history has to be shown as the progressive realisation of Spiritual freedom of man through many struggles and failures). This notion of Spirit is best seen in its triple movement.

1. *Thesis* : The spirit-in-itself is undisturbed identity or unity within itself, which as yet is oblivious of its object.
2. *Anti-thesis* : The spirit posits its other, in the form of Nature and Life. On the surface, Nature, with organic and inorganic elements appears to be opposed to the Spirit.
3. *Synthesis* : There is the final movement in which the Spirit reduces Nature to the inwardness, which the Spirit itself is. Only at this stage the spirit rises to self-consciousness in man.

The life of spirit is not mere contemplation, but essentially is an activity in which the dump and mute Nature is subjugated to yield reason or thought hidden within its bosom. Consciousness, for Hegel, is not like a searchlight which reveals an object out there. It is rather a process through which the universal meaning or underlying pattern is disengaged from the object where it lies in a petrified form.

The detailed exposition of spirit-in-itself comes under abstract category or Logic. Its anti-thesis is known as Nature and the synthesis is called Spirit. We might have given the impression that triads of thesis, anti-thesis and synthesis run into simple, linear series alone. On the contrary, the whole series of triads may

---

1. *Ibid.,* p. XXXV—Italics mine.
2. C.J. Friedrich, *Ibid.,* p. 410.

fall within larger series of triads. Further, the series as a whole may form as thesis, inviting another series as its antithesis, leading to a third kind of series as synthesis. In this sense, Logic deals with pure reason with its series of abstract categories. Nature is the anti-thesis of Logic and is supposed to include within it space, time, inorganic matter, plants and animals. Spirit is the Synthesis which harmonizes the contradiction of Logic and Nature. In other words, Logic is the Idea, Nature is the Idea in its otherness. But Idea and Nature, though opposed are yet identical, because both of them are *Idea*. Spirit is the unity of Nature and the Idea. The Idea is Reason and spirit is the self-conscious and rational human spirit. So Spirit is the *existent* Reason. As Reason, the Spirit is Idea, and, as *existent* Reason, spirit is a part of Nature. The spirit therefore is the final category and is the ultimate foundation of both Logic and Nature. Though the Absolute is spirit, it is not an existent, particular human spirit. The Absolute Reality is the Absolute Spirit of which human spirits are finite reproductions.

The Absolute has been described as a system of categories arranged dialectically in triads. The scheme has been exemplified both by W.T. Stace[1] and J.N. Findlay.[2] Here a very sketchy scheme is given below by way of illustration

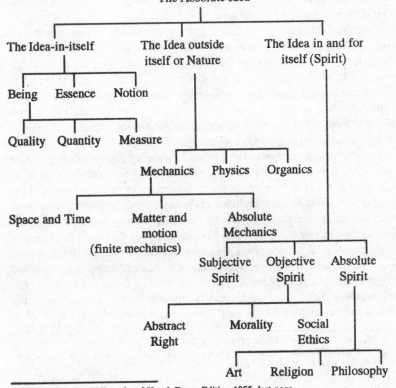

The Absolute Idea

- The Idea-in-itself
  - Being Essence Notion
    - Quality Quantity Measure
- The Idea outside itself or Nature
  - Mechanics Physics Organics
    - Space and Time Matter and motion (finite mechanics) Absolute Mechanics
- The Idea in and for itself (Spirit)
  - Subjective Spirit Objective Spirit Absolute Spirit
    - Abstract Right Morality Social Ethics
    - Art Religion Philosophy

1. W.T. Stace, *The Philosophy of Hegel,* Dover Edition 1955, last page.
2. J.N. Findlay, *Hegel: A Re-examination,* Macmillan 1958, last pages.

The Absolute, for Hegel, is the Idea, concrete in itself and unfolding itself, an organic system, a totality which contains a rich set of levels and aspects.[1] This all-inclusive Reality attains to self-consciousness by subjugating Nature and Life. The key-notion here is Kant's 'synthetic unity of Apperception' which is the ultimate basis of the synthetic function of each and every category and universal[2]. Thus by showing that all objects are ultimately pervaded by universals, we show that they are finally brought under the self-conscious world-spirit. It is the dynamic, active and self-revealing activity of the Spirit which realizes itself in all objects of Nature and in human histories. However, in philosophy alone the world-spirit reaches its full self-realization.

> The history with which we are concerned is the history of thought finding itself. Thought only finds itself by creating itself—indeed it only exists and is actual by finding itself. The creations are the philosophies.

Thus, the world-spirit is a universality-discovering process in things which appear to be its negation, because they seem to be particular and also many. Hence, the Spirit is the self-knowing actual Idea.

It is essential for Hegel's notion of Spirit that it should be encompassed by *objects or* things, which appear as *other, distinct* and *opposed* to the Spirit. Only in relation to and by overcoming the otherness of objects, Spirit becomes self-conscious. It is a fact that animate and inanimate objects in Nature are brought under their laws and explanatory thoughts by individual minds. Again, it has to be conceded that individual minds have emerged out of the inanimate nature which antedated both Life and Mind. Yet, for Hegel, the opposition between mind and nature is illusory. The Spirit overcomes Nature by bringing its material process under Ideas, thoughts or universals. In knowing and remoulding Nature under thought-pattern, Nature is made to assume the mirror-image of the spirit itself. After all the *ideal* laws are not alien to nature, but are its very essence. These thoughts were there already implicitly in the functioning of Nature. Only these implicit thoughts are made explicit by the toils, sweats and suffering of the scientists by successfully wrestling with material things. So Nature is ultimately Spirit inasmuch as Nature is *ideal* or law-abiding or rational. For the self-realisation of Spirit, it is essential that there be objects of Nature totally opposed to it. Only by coming in grip with something opposed, Spirit can come to self-consciousness. Spirit, for Hegel, requires "the seriousness, the suffering, the patience and the labour of the negative". Hence, Spirit inasmuch as it is confronted

---

1. C.J. Friedrich, *The history of Philosophy, Ibid.,* p. 164.

2. Hegel's idealism isasmuch German as it certainly is Greek. Hegel's statement is remarkable here.
    "It is to be remembered that I frequently take the Kantian philosophy into consideration in this work (i.e., the science of Logic)—and elsewhere, it still remains the basis and beginning of modern German philosophy; whatever faults we may find with it, this must be set down undiminished to its credit." (Friedrich, *Ibid.,* p. 200n).

with nature, deals with something which is involved in, and necessary to, its own being. In dealing with Nature in a sense, Spirit refinds itself or deals with itself. Hence, the activities of Spirit are no more, than the various ways of reducing external objects to the inwardness which Spirit itself is, and only through this reduction, this idealization of things in Nature, Spirit realizes itself. This necessity of the 'other than Spirit' and its subjugation is best seen in relation to individuals in society.

Spirit is not only universality-finding activity, but is also free. So this may also be described as self-conscious activity in which freedom is realised. Only by struggle with something opposed to Spirit, that Spirit refinds its freedom. Spirit is opposed by Nature in which this freedom appears buried and is seen as mechanical necessity. This mechanical necessity is said to be overcome when the mechanical laws are made to serve the ends of self-conscious man. However, this re-finding of freedom is also a slow process in man in his social setting. Man finds himself confronted by other men and only by mutual struggle in which each man seeks to treat others as external to him and seeks to cancel and annihilate each other's freedom. Through a long struggle each man realises his freedom in terms of *universal* purposes and aims in a State. By 'subjugation of the other in society' is meant here a cooperative understanding of 'the other' as a necessary condition of one's own self-consciousness. Hegel has beautiful mentioned many *moments* in the life of man by which he has passed through to reach his present status of a free being in a well governed State. In a general way the rise of self-conscious freedom has been well illustrated in Master-Slave relationship in his *Phenomenolohgy*.

The rise of self-consciousness can be illustrated in a setting of primitive society. Here one man may be said to be an independent being whose essential nature is to be for himself. He may be called the Master. In relation to the Master there is a dependent being whose essence is to live for another man, his Master. Both the Master and Slave rise to self-consciousness through the medium of material objects. The Master employs the Slave because he wants the enjoyment of material things. In this relationship the slave has more advantage than the Master, for rising into self-consciousness. First, the Slave stands in fear and trembling before the Master. The Slave has to carry out the orders of his Master and the fear of the Master makes him aware of his own state. Again, the slave sees material objects as external to him but he has to know them; he has to work and labour on the objects. And by shaping and labouring upon the objects, the slave comes to bend the objects as his Master wants them. Thus, the slave inwardises the objects, and becomes aware of his being by virtue of his fear of the Master. However, the Master exists only for himself. Hence, for Hegel, this relationship of Master-Slave is not satisfactory. Indeed through labour and

---

1. C.J. Friedrich, *Ibid.*, p. 163n.

obedient service the slave discovers himself by himself, but the Master does not rise to his full self-consciousness. Hegel calls the consciousness of the Master 'the negative power'. Only when the Master does to himself what he does to his slave, then alone this negation will be negated and this will give rise to higher self-consciousness.

Hegel, in this context, has beautifully traced the gradual and progressive enrichment of self-consciousness through the various stages of stoicism, scepticism and unhappy consciousness. As our purpose is only expository of the system in bare outline, so we now proceed further to Social Ethics where this rise of self-consciousness and freedom is well marked. Here there is the triad again :

1. First, there is the subjective spirit in itself.
2. Second, other persons are also recognized as external and independent of the subjective spirit.
3. Finally, the subject rises to universal self-consciousness in which other persons are recognized both distinct *from* and *one* with itself.

As has been noted earlier, the subjective spirit can never remain in a cocoon-like existence. It has to issue out from its inwardness and subjectivity into the external world of institutions. 'Institution' includes not only law, society and the State, but also customs, manners, morality and so forth. One can easily see that the institution spoken of is the product of human beings themselves. Therefore, the institution is the spirit externalised and solidified and may be called objective spirit. The society and the State are not alien to man, but are spiritual, being the embodiment of laws which spirit itself has projected into the institution.

We have already posited that Spirit is free and is governed by universal principles. Hence, to the extent the spirit is governed by universal law, it finds its essential self fulfilled. But if the institution enacts laws in the interest of *particular* class and private individuals, then the spirit remains in bondage and is unfree. As only the universal is real, so, for Hegel, any society and State working for a particular class and individuals will be superseded by that State which embodies universal norms and interests. Therefore, for Hegel, nothing has come about in Social Evolution which is not necessary in the dialectic advance of the World-Spirit. The watch-word of Hegel is

'Reason rules the world.'

Here also again there is the advance from the *abstract* rights to concrete rights of persons in a State. Here there is the dialectic triad of family, Civil Society and the State.

For Hegel only persons matter. By a person is meant here a self-conscious individual who has rights to material things, say property. A slave or a table is not a person, for neither the slave nor the table has any right. A person not only

---

1. C.J. Friedrich, *Ibid.*, pp. 404-09.

owns a property, but he rises to self-consciousness by effectively appropriating it. But a person can enjoy his property as long as other persons do not violate the contract amongst themselves. However, there might be other persons who may wrongfully take possession of another's property. Here there is a crime and a violation of the contract based on the union of wills. This incidence of wrong brings into focus the opposition of particular and universal will, i.e., wrong (which is a particular will) and the principle of rightness (the universal will). This opposition is resolved when the wrong is punished and thereby the particular will is harmonised with the universal will. In other words, wrong negates the right. Punishment negates the wrong, or, this is the same thing as the negation of the right (wrong) is itself negated leading to a synthesis of the particular and universal will.

This synthesis, or harmony of the particular and universal will is still at the level of abstract right. It rises into the next higher phase of morality. The abstract right is confined to the laws and consequent punishment with regard to their violation as something external to the man. However, when the opposition is inwardised in the subject, then it is known as morality. In morality the conflict is felt between *what is* and *what ought to be*. The law to be obeyed has to be felt as the law of one's conscience. This is nothing but Kant's doctrine of 'the categorical imperative'. A moral man feels that he is obliged to obey only those laws which issue forth from his rational self. So Hegel describes morality as the law of one's conscience.

> Conscience expresses the absolute right of subjective self-consciousness to know *in itself* and *through itself* what is right and duty, and to recognize nothing as good other than what it knows to be good, at the same time asserting that what it knows and wills as good is in truth right and duty.[1]

However, Hegel does not subscribe to Kant's formalism. For Hegel, Kant's doctrine of Duty, for the sake of Duty is empty and formal. Duty comes from society and without society there is no duty. To know what one's duty is, i.e., the content of duty, has to be found out in an organised society. This Hegelian doctrine was later elaborated by Bradley in his famous teaching of *Station and its duties*. Thus, for Hegel, the inwardness of moral law has to be taken up and unified at the higher movement of Ethical Life.

The abstract right is *external* and morality is *inward*. Their synthesis is found in Social Ethics in the form of the State. Man is the universal will. The State is the universal will in the concrete. In other words, the individual is *implicitly* universal will. In the State this implicit universal will is actualised : the State is the individual fully actualised and made articulate. For Hegel, the State is no alien

1. Quoted by F.C. Copleston in *A history of Philosophy*, Vol. VIII, p. 251 (Image Book).

authority over and above the individual. The State is the true self of each individual. The State lays down laws which are the laws of the individual himself. Hence, by observing the laws of the State the individual is obeying laws which he himself has projected into the State. So in following Social Ethics, the individual is not determined by something alien to him, but is determined by his own laws, and, so he is self-determined which means his true freedom. The State is not a chance product, but has arisen as a necessary moment in the dialectic advance of the World-Spirit. This advance passes through the triadic march of family, civil Society and the State.

Family presupposes an institution. Members of the family are united primarily by the feeling of love. But feeling is not thought. So it has to undergo dissolution in the stage of civil Society. In the state of family life children do not attain their independence. However, when they have been educated and come of age, then the family life dissolves into independent individuals. Each individual now looks upon himself as an end and treats other individuals as meant to his end. But individuals for realising their own particular ends remain dependent on one another. This mutual inter-dependence of individuals for the satisfaction of their particular needs gives rise to *Civil Society*. Civil society works through economic classes and corporations, giving rise to the division of labour and capital, law-courts, judiciary and police. But ultimately, Civil Society can rest on the State for without it there can be no enforcement of law and punishment of crimes. The family is the stage of undifferentiated unity of members. Civil Society represents the particular interests of individuals who issue forth from the dissolution of their family-membership. The State represents the unity of particular interests in the interest of universal will, subserving the in-most essence of each individual. The State is a true organic unity, existing in and through particulars, subserving the universal end of Welt-Geist (the World-Spirit).

As the State is the highest end in which the true universality of an individual life finds fulfilment, so it may demand the sacrifice of *particular* individuals for furthering its higher end. Indeed the State is considered by Hegel to be 'this actual God'. From this it does not follow that Hegel has taught the doctrine of State-dictatorship or totalitarianism. Through Hegel's teaching of the State and his insistence on the German State as the highest development of the World-Spirit and his eulogising war, along with the doctrine of the Superman by Nietszche, did contribute to Nazism. But Hegel never visualised that Prussian Militarism would degenerate into a mighty organ of suppressing individual liberty. Indeed Hegel would regard Nazism as a degenerate form of the Ideal State he had in mind. The Nazi German would be regarded as an ugly pseudo-State for furthering a highly private and megalomaniac interest of Hitler. The State of which Hegel speaks, is an evolving Ideal Republic of Plato, which will progressively realize the highest aspirations and culture of the people. It is the ethical idea which is realized by the participating community. As such it is a self-realized consciousness of a cultural complex of art, religion, morality and technology of committed people for giving free expression to their deepest value.[1] The State should not be interpreted as a bureaucratic political organization headed by a despotic individual.

The State in actuality does not reach the Ideal stage. In actuality it may come short of allowing full liberties to each individual for his highest development. But each national State is a rational stage in the march of the World-Spirit for its self-realization. Individuals, specially the great heroes of history, Caesar, Alexander, Napoleon and Hitler are the instruments through which the necessary landmarks in world-history are progressively realized. Human history with its tales of woes and empty glories ultimately reveals the eternal and rational hidden in the depth of Reality. Tracing the course of history, Hegel expresses his key-notion with regard to his idealistic interpretation of history,

> . . . .reason rules the world and that things have happened reasonably in world history.[2]

The goal of history is to attain freedom which each spirit is and this is progressively realised from ancient times to the present age. The world-spirit becomes self-conscious in man and the whole process is also mediated through men. The attainment of self-consciousness or the awareness of the idealisation of the whole historical process is the real end of the World-Spirit, but men, again, serve as instruments for this final realisation of the Absolute End. Men with their private interests, aims and purposes are energised to put forth efforts which lead to the realisation of the Absolute End. Men are endowed with passions which goad them to do this and avoid that. So all things are achieved because of the great energy of passions. So Hegel wrote,

> We are obliged to state that nothing great happens in the world without passion.[3]

But in the final analysis, individuals are mere means, pawns and cannon fodder who are sacrificed for the end of world-history,

> The infinite mass of wills, interests and activities, are the tools and means of the world spirit to accomplish its end. . . . That those living processes of

---

1. This interpretation is now in fashion in evaluating the teaching of Hegel.
    - (1) F. Copleston, Vol. 7, pp. 254-55.
    - (2) W.T. Stace, *Hegel,* pp. 406, 427.
    - (3) F.N. Magill, Masterpieces of World Philosophy p. 598.
    - (4) C.J. Friedrich, *Ibid.,* Introduction, p. XLVI.
    - (5) J.N. Findlay, Hegel, pp. 322-23.
2. C.J. Friedrich, *Ibid.,* p. 4.
3. *Ibid.,* p. 15.

individuals and nations, by seeking and satisfying their own limited ends, serve at the same time as the means and tools of something higher of which they know nothing. . . .[1]

The passions and interests of men have been called by Hegel as the 'cunning of history'. These individuals who unconsciously serve as instrument of the world-spirit have been classified into *citizen, person, hero* and the *victim*. The citizen is the individual who observes customary morality. He has not become aware of himself as his own *genuine* self. The *person* becomes aware of the ethos of the people and can even transcend it. The person becomes conscious of his freedom. Socrates has been called as an example of person. He knew the thought of what was right and wrong involved in customary morality. However, Hegel lavishes his highest praise on *heroes* of world-history. World-historical individuals, namely, Alexander, Caesar, Napoleon are the decisive figures. No doubt they are motivated by their private interests and ambitions, but these interests unconsciously remain, attuned to the end of the World-Spirit. Through their achievements, they introduce higher goals and achieve new landmarks of human progress. But one must not forget that the heroes bring into focus the prevailing forces of their time and by evoking passions of men, achieve the historical task assigned to them. Seeing Napoleon riding on the street of Jena, remarked Hegel

Today I saw the World-Spirit riding on horse-back.

But Napoleon, used by the cunning of history was just a tool in the march of history. Amidst the clash of steel and din of battle there goes the *victim*. His goal is private success and happiness. Hegel and later on his adversary Kierkegaard, have expressed their contempt of the victim who really promotes no historical progress, but by large forms the bulk of the population. After all in the philosophy of history, for Hegel, the hero and the victim, both are the victim of the World-Spirit. The victim is the victim of the hero and the age and the hero, in turn, serves as the mere tool of the World-Spirit.

After all, the march of history affords opportunities for the rise of the State. The individual is for the State. But it is the function of the State to make individuals aware of their destiny, the destiny of becoming aware of Reason and Eternal ends involved in the affairs of men. It is the State which has become the carrier and progressive vehicle of the World-Spirit. In his gigantic sweep Hegel observes that the State moves from the freedom of *One* (oriental despot) to the freedom of *Some* (for the Greeks and Romans denied freedom to slaves in the Greeco-Roman State) to the freedom of *all* (the German State). Without commenting on the verdict of Hegel, we can pass on to the next question. The verdict of Hegel is not of a historian, but of a philosopher who is seized with a vision of the rise and fall of

---

1. *Ibid.,* p. 16.

empires. One may ask, should be say,

What has been is really reasonable?

Are the destructions of Chengez Khan and Nadir Shah, necessitated by events? Are the two global wars justified? Have they, paved the way for new awareness and vision? Has Hitler with his gaschamber and heartless destruction of men contributed to any new landmark in history? Most probably as yet we are too much involved if not in hot at least, in cold wars of the world. Men have become aware of the dire necessity of a world-federation of nations. Oil crises and power-shortage along with the vast engine of mass-destruction are going to infuse, new spirit into world-politicians. In the midst of changes India remains in the hands of despots and feudal lords. However, the time for Hegel was not ripe for visualising a world-federation of nations. Hegel saw only this much that through clash of ideals and ideologies amongst national spirits, the World-Spirit will fulfil itself. But even if world-federation becomes an accomplished fact, the further march of the World-Spirit will not cease. The world-federation will continue to be as finite as national states obviously are.

So far we have traced in bare outline the dialectic march of the Absolute Spirit as it issues itself out into objective Spirit comprised of the triad of Abstract Right, Morality and Social Ethics. However, the World-Spirit has to experience itself as the Absolute Spirit in which the World-Spirit rises into full self-consciousness. Of course, the Absolute's knowledge of itself is the same as man's knowledge of the Absolute. After all, the Absolute is not beyond the sky or beyond the ken of human experience. The Absolute is omnipresent and exists in all spirits. After all God's own knowledge is man's knowledge of God. Hence, the Absolute Spirit becomes self-conscious in human beings when they apprehend the Absolute in Art, Religion and Philosophy. In Art, Religion and Philosophy the Absolute actualises itself in finite spirits as Thought becoming conscious of itself. In Art, the absolute is apprehended under the sensuous form of beauty, in Religion in pictorial form or image-thinking, and in Philosophy the Absolute is apprehended in the purest form, namely, conceptually.

Hegel does not think much of Natural beauty, for the simple reason that he has gone now beyond the sphere of Nature, nay even beyond the stage of subjective and Objective Spirit. In the higher realm of the Absolute, the manifestation of the spirit alone counts. In pure form the Idea creates the form of unity in difference: it is the Spirit manifesting itself to the Spirit. Art is the apprehension of the Infinite through its sensuous veil. Now the moments of Art are to be evaluated in terms of the intermixture of the sensuous element with the ideal content. Hegel mentions the three moments of Art, namely, Symbolic, Classical and Romantic. In *symbolic* art the Absolute does not shine through the sensuous veil. This is best seen in Egyptian art, and Architecture is its best medium. Here the sensuous matter over whelms the spiritual manifestation with the result that the infinite is expressed ambiguously and even mysteriously. The Sphinx is considered to be a symbol of the symbolic art. However in *Classical* art there is a harmonious unity of the sensuous and spiritual. The best example of classical art is the Greek Sculpture where human body itself embodies a perfect union of matter and form. As unity is the true expression of the spirit, so through sculpture the classical art not only suggests but truly expresses the Infinite. However, the free expression of the Spirit is possible only in *Romantic* art where in words in the form of poetry the Infinite is seen in movement, conflict and triumph. However, poetry through its medium of words, finds even imagery as inadequate for the fullest expression of the Infinite Spirit, pointing to Religion in which the Absolute can be better apprehended than in Art.

Religion is the manifestation of the Absolute in pictorial thinking which in the contemporary theology will be called *mythological* thinking. Here also there are three phases, namely, Nature-religion, the religion of spiritual individuality and the Absolute Religion (Christianity). By nature-religion, Hegel does not mean, Naturalism nor even religion guided by the natural light in man (as opposed to revealed religion). By nature-religion is meant that religion in which spirit has not gained full mastery over nature, or, where the object of worship called deity is conceived as less than Spirit. Under this heading are included the three moments of magic religion, religion of substance (which comprises Hinduism and Buddhism) and Zoroastrianism in which some glimmering of spirit is seen in the form of Light. Next is the stage of spiritual Individuality in which there is the worship of a personal God. However, the highest from the religion, for Hegel, is Christianity where the Absolute Spirit is perfectly expressed in the image (mythology) of. God-Man, namely, Jesus Christ. However, only thought can be the true witness of Spirit. Therefore, Philosophy alone can express spirit most adequately.

According to Hegel, philosophy is the science of necessary thoughts, of their essential connection and system, the knowledge of what is true and therefore eternal and imperishable.[1] Of course the philosophical truth is one[2] which unfolds itself slowly and gradually from Thales to the present time. In the beginning philosophy consisted of the poorest, the most abstract and indistinct thought, "whereas the most recent philosophy is the most concrete and the deepest".[3]

Dwelling upon the theme that the newest philosophy (i.e., his own) is the most developed, the richest and most profound, Hegel writes,

In this latest philosophy all that appears at first as past must be preserved and contained: it must be a mirror of the entire history (of philosophy).[4]

1. C.J. Friedrich, *The History of Philosophy,* p. 162.
2. *Ibid.,* p. 163.
3. *Ibid.,* p. 171.
4. *Ibid.,* p 172.

Hegel could regard philosophy as the culmination of knowledge for he saw his idealistic system illustrated in the wide range of sciences of his day. Secondly, he could, with some justification, call his philosophy as the final fruit, for in it was included and preserved all that was best and living in Plato-Aristotle, Spinoza-Leibnitz-Kant, Schelling and Fichte, and, he could imagine his evaluation to be sound because it was based on the irrefutable dialectic method. But a philosophy which is based on the dialectic advance cannot claim finality. Its very truth implies that in due course, dust must settle on its achievements.

9.11. An appraisal of the Dialectic Method
The dialectic method has justly been regarded as the contribution of Hegel *par excellence*. The whole philosophy of Hegel is its detailed illustration and its aptness is the justification of the method. It is this method which has cast so much light on the evolutionary processes themselves that since the time of Hegel it has been adopted as a valid method of evaluating history, philosophy, art, religion through the ages. According to the dialectic process nothing is accidental and so even the dialectic method itself has emerged in philosophy when the time was ripe for its conscious recognition. 'Dialectic' was sufficiently used in the *Dialogues* of Plato and even the Hegelian type of Dialectic was foreshadowed in the *Paramenides*, and *Symposium* of Plato. But it appears that Hegel got substantial hints from Kant whose philosophy was the starting-point of Hegel's philosophy in more respects than one.

Kant has used triple division throughout his system.

1. First, Kant divided mind into three faculties of Pure Reason (cognition), Practical Reason (conation) and Judgment (affection). Corresponding to these faculties Kant wrote three *Critiques* of Pure Reason, Practical Reason and Judgment. In Pure Reason, Kant gives an account of the phenomenal world; in Practical Reason, Kant deals with *Noumenal* self and in Judgment, phenomenal and noumenal Reality is synthesized in the doctrine of the Sublime. In the eyes of many commentators the critique of Judgment holds the key to the previous two *Critiques* of Kant, and, in this sense, the *Judgment* may be taken to be the synthesis of Pure Reason (thesis) and Practical Reason (anti-thesis).

2. Further, even the Critique of Pure Reason has three sub-divisions of Transcendental Aesthetic, Transcendental Analytic and Transcendental Dialectic. Transcendental Dialectic in the form of the three of Ideas of God, World and Soul, serving as *regulative* principles appear to reconcile the *passive* forms (of Space and Time) of Transcendental Aesthetics with the *active* understanding of transcendental Analytic.

3. Certainly the three Ideas of Reason, namely, the world (outer world), Soul (inner world) and God (as the synthesis of the outer and inner worlds) may be taken as three moments in the dialectic inner-relationship between pure

categories. But this triple inter-relationship is most marked in Kant's treatment of the categories of the understanding, where the third category is invariably the synthesis of the first two categories taken as thesis and anti-thesis of each other (§.8.15)

4. Kant's doctrine of *antinomies* posed a challenge to Hegel. Certainly one cannot remain in the paradoxical position of thesis and anti-thesis of antinomies. Kant comforted himself by regarding the three Ideals of Reason as limiting concepts. Well, the doctrine of limitation of knowledge to phenomena alone could have satisfied Kant, but the bold and intrepid spirit of Hegel challenged the doctrine of *the unknowable* itself. Hegel found the key to his solution of Kant's riddle in his philosophy of the Dialectic. The synthesis of Kant's paradox could be found in the creative thrust of Speculative Reason which alone reconciles the opposed notions of phenomena and noumena, and the antithetical character of the antinomies.

5. But there is little doubt that the glimmering of the dialectic advance is clearly visible in the writings of Fichte and Schelling.

Hence, the Dialectic Method of Hegel is the ripened fruit of the search for the philosophical method which will take philosophy beyond the arena of warring opinions to the certitude of philosophical knowledge. True, Descartes, before Hegel was pre-occupied with the search of the correct method which will ensure certainty to philosophical conclusions. Descartes found the mathematical method as the method of philosophy for attaining indubitable truth. Since the time of *Principle Mathematica* mathematics has been reduced to Deductive Logic. So the Dialectic Method of Hegel has to be evaluated in terms of mathematico-deductive method.

Mathematical Deduction and the Dialectic Method: In a deductive system there are a few simple and undefined concepts whose content is clear and fixed. From a few self-evident axioms, other concepts are deduced with the help of rules of deduction. In pure mathematics or mathematical logic, reasoning is supposed to be a game of symbols without reference to any actual state of affairs. But through *interpretation*, a logician believes that he touches concrete experience and thinking at vital points. However, a logician is aware that he cannot do full justice to the complexities of ordinary thinking. Hegel realised both the value and limitation of the deductive method. According to Hegel, the deductive method is quite appropriate at the level of understanding, but has to be superseded by the dialectic method at the level of the Speculative Reason. The deductive method, according to Hegel, with its axioms and rules of deduction, is well calculated to yield precision, fixity and definiteness of notions. But it is not a suitable method to deal with change, process and evolution, going on in the world.

The deductive method of mathematics, according to Hegel, is useful at the beginning of philosophy.[1] The nebulous and vague experience is analysed by the understanding into abstract concepts. The clearness gained by abstraction is highly commendable. However, these clear concepts often come into violent collision. The Eleatic doctrine of One Being comes into headlong conflict with the Becoming of Heracleitus. Similarly, opposed ideas of materialism and panpsychism, mechanism and teleology remain unreconciled at the level of understanding. These opposed notions are taken up and reconciled by the Speculative Reason in a higher synthesis in which the opposed moments are shown to be invitable complementaries. Again, for Hegel, the deductive method of mathematics is suitable for dealing with a static world, which is best illustrated in the pantheistic 'philosophy of Spinoza'. The reason is that thoughts become petrified as soon as they are locked up in precise thought. For example, a triangle once defined and drawn up on paper would not become anything else and would not grow. This Staticism leads to unprogressiveness and statement of empiricism and rationalism in pre-Kantian philosophy. This static nature of the mathematical method follows from the fact that it proceeds on the principle of Identity or Difference. For Mathematics A is A, and A can never grow into not-A. If A is A, then how can Spinoza consistently deduce finite Modes from the Infinite Substance? Modes and Infinite Substance remain unreconciled in the philosophy of Spinoza which is based on the inflexible 'either-or'. However, this limitation of *the Understanding* is transcended in Speculative Reason. For Speculative Reason the principle is not Identity or Difference, but Identity-in-Difference or Difference-in-Identity. A does not remain A, but has to give way to Not-A. A seed does not remain a seed, but has to sprout forth into a plant or a tree. Thus, the dialectic method arising from Speculative Reason is necessary to do full justice to an evolving world.

Again, for Hegel, Mathematical deduction is valid provided its axioms, pressupositions, primaries and rules of deduction are taken for granted. But why should they be taken for granted? Well the reason is that they appear to be self-evident. However, self-evidence is not a self-explanatory or rational principle. If a thing is self-evident, then at most it can be taken as a brute fact or, as an ultimate mystery. It will be said to be explained only when we further show, why *this* axiom and not any other axiom, why only *so many* axioms and no other axioms are to be taken up. And this is not possible for the mathematical deductive method.

Further, the mathematical method is not only dogmatic, but is also partial and one-sided. It keeps to one standpoint and rejects all other standpoints. By attending to one single aspect of a total situation, understanding reaches precision and clearness. But onesidedness ultimately paves the way for conflicting stands and warring views and finally such opposites are taken up and resolved by Speculative Reason with the help of its dialectic method.

---

1. C.J. Friedrich, *Ibid.*, pp. 194, 196.

The meaning of Dialectic Necessity: If the dialectic method is not mathematical method, then what is the meaning of the phrase *'deducing* the higher from the lower', or, *'deriving'* one category from the other category? Is the dialectic necessity the same as deductive or mathematical necessity or is it different from it? Hegel was a speculative philosopher and he could not have patience for linguistic analysis. He found that there is some sort of necessity if we pass from Being to non-Being and Becoming. It appeared to be quite a conscious and rational activity. But his rational activity is some sort of creative illumination which one acquires in passing from one position to another. For example, when Hegel characterised the antinomies of Kant as the product of Understanding and saw their resolution as the work of Speculative Reason, then this recourse to 'speculative Reason' and all that it stands for is not a logical transition from a premise to a conclusion. This is a product of a creative drive within Hegel himself. The dialective necessity may be compared to the illumination which one experiences in the sudden shift of attention from the usual to the unusual patterming of facts in a new configuration, as can be demonstrated in the case of puzzle-pictures or ambiguous figures. This is what Wisdom thinks about the philosophical activity in which we do not discover new facts, but we see old facts in a new way. Certainly the whole dialectic method illustrated in human history, art and religion is an important altered way of viewing things. But the re-arranged way of looking at things will not entitle any one to regard the various arrangements of facts as logical entailment. A very sympathetic commentator of Hegel (J.N. Findlay) thinks that Hegel was wrong in suggesting dialectic necessity as deductive necessity. And we think that this is also a mistake in the exposition of W.T. Stace in his otherwise very lucid and systematic work on 'Hegel'. Findlay correctly observed that dialectic illumination should not be interpreted as logical rigour. Dialectic transition is only necessary and inevitable in an indefinite sense, i.e., in the sense in which there is necessity and inevitable transition in a work of art.[1] The inter-relation between the three moments of a triad is found in a wide variety. At times the relation is of an *inner contradiction* which the other term is going to remove, sometimes there is *incompleteness* which the other term as the complement of the other exhibits it. At other times the relation may be of parts and whole, or, obscurity and explicitness.

The devices by which the Dialectic is made to work are, in fact, inexhaustible in their subtlety and variety.[2]

As a matter of fact even Stace has observed that the triadic relationship in many places is forced and arbitrary. For example, the deduction of family[3] and the triadic

1. J.N. Findlay, *Hegel : A Re-examination*, p. 74.
2. J.N. Findlay, *Ibid.,* p. 73.
3. W.T. Stace, *Hegel*, p. 408.

moments in Art,[1] according to Stace cannot be said to be satisfactory. The truth is that the eternal truth, according to Hegel, has to be realized through contingent events. Passions of men cannot be reduced to thought and the 'cunning of history' cannot be styled as logical moments. Hegel never meant that each and everything in the world follows from the Absolute in a logical sense. Then what is the meaning of the dialectic advance in the world-process? Is the dialectic also historical?

The Dialectic and the Historical: Hegel has pointed out that there is nothing arbitrary, accident or chance product in history. According to him, reason rules the world. But is the historical also the dialectical? Hegel himself contrasts the knowledge of philosophy and history :

> Philosophy is the science of necessary thoughts. . .the knowledge of what is true and therefore eternal and imperishable; history on the other hand is concerned in the common view with past events, that is, with accidental, passing and past affairs.[2]

Even if the common view of history be regarded as false, the historical is also the empirical. Can we say that the dialectic process is also empirical? The dialectic process is empirical, only in the sense of Aristotle. In other words, by an empirical study of history, art, religion and philosophy one can be said to become aware of the conceptual frame in which events are said to take place. The dialectic frame is not *a priori*, a kind of Procrustean bed to which all facts somehow are forced to fit, but by means of reflective intuition one discovers them as true of world-events. Here the observation of Friedrich is very apt :

> Dialectics is descriptive : descriptive of the process of thought which one must have experienced in order to be able to understand it. Dialectic in this sense shares something of the intuitive quality of all direct experience.[3]

The word 'descriptive' simply means that the dialectic triads are obtained through intuition by reflecting on actual events in the first instance, and, then, triads are seen to fit the description of events very appropriately. But by 'empirical' and 'descriptive' we cannot mean that the dialectic triads are empirical concepts which have been obtained by controlling and varying the experiential data. Experience cannot be said to be *constitutive* of dialectic knowledge. In other words, dialectic is not scientific and it has no predictive role to play. It is a big mistake of Karl Popper to take the dialectic to be empirical, descriptive and predictive of actual events.[4]

---

1. *Ibid.*, pp. 452-53. His point has been also accepted by F. Copleston, *A History of Philosophy*, Vol. VII, pp. 278-79.
2. C.J. Friedrich, *Ibid.*, p. 162.
3. C.J. Friedrich, Introduction, *Ibid.*, p. XL.
4. Karl Popper, What is Dialectic? MIND, 1940 pp. 407, 411, 418.

The dialectic is the general orientation of world-events and through it one can win illumination or the hang of the world. In his famous utterance, Hegel can be interpreted in this fashion. In one paragraph in his *Preface to Philosophy of Right and Law*, Hegel has most precisely stated the nature of the dialectic.

> When philosophy paints its gray in gray, a form of life has become old, and this gray in gray cannot rejuvenate it, only, understand it. The owl of Minerva begins its flight when dusk is falling.[1]

First, philosophical vision is not predictive, but retrospective. It is backward looking, but not in principle verifiable, since, according to Hegel, the past cannot be 'rejuvenated'. However, it is 'understanding' of what has gone past. This understanding has been called 'wisdom' and that it is. It comes only in the evening of life and is not the vision in the morn for the guidance of the whole day. Nay, Hegel holds that dialectic understanding does not serve even the purpose of exhortation.

> To say one more word about preaching what the world ought to be like, philosophy arrives always too late for that.[2]

Then what purpose does 'understanding' of world-events subserve? Copleston has raised an important issue in connection with the dialectic understanding of history. If Hegel's statement is correct that history is rational, then whatever has happened, the ugly, the mean as well as the glorious, is equally rational.[3] Might is just as much right, as right is might. Here philosophy not only paints gray on gray, but paints all colours as equally gray. Hegel's night is the same as Spinoza's dark night in which all cows are equally gray. Philosophy for Hegel is neither preaching nor predictive of future events. Here we are taught to view all things taking place with dialectic necessity. In my opinion, seeing things, *sub specie aeternitatis* and viewing things with dialectic necessity are one and the same thing. Words of Spinoza can be profitably quoted again,

> The wicked, knowing not God, are but as instruments in the hands of a workman, serving unconscioulsy, and perishing in the using: the good, on the other hand, serve conscioulsy and in serving become more perfect.

What Spinoza has said of the wicked that Hegel has said of the hero and the victim. Then the dialectic perspective may be said to be the eternal spirit of man brooding over the events that have gone past. This is the supreme consolation of philosophy.

---

1. C.J. Friedrich, *Ibid.*, p. 227.
2. The opening words of the paragraph already just quoted immediately, i.e., C.J. Friedrich, *Ibid.*, p. 227.
3. F. Copleston, *Ibid.*, pp. 267-68.

The dialectic process is, strictly speaking, neither empirical nor descriptive nor prescriptive nor predictive. It portrays a life of intellectual contemplation and looks upon its perspective as a thing of highest value because it includes within its grasp all that is highest and noblest for man down the ages.

The Dialectic Method and the law of Contradiction: Hegel has admitted that Being *is* non-Being: There is the identity of the opposites. How can two contradictories be combined and be made consistent? So many commentators think that Hegel does not accept the law of contradiction. Of course, Hegel has accepted that negation, and contradiction form the mighty instrument of progress. For this reason, Karl Popper is very critical of Hegel and thinks that Hegel's Dialectic, if it be accepted, would make nonsense of every kind of reasoning and scientific progress.[1] But this bitter criticism is irrelevant. Negation is a potent source of conceptual movement, because nobody can remain at the level of contradiction. Hegel himself could not accept the antithetical character of Kant's antinomies. So he was prompted to seek their resolution. Hence, Hegel, accepts the validity of the law of Contradiction. However, if Hegel accepts the validity of the law of contradiction, then how can one say, that A must become not-A? Well, A must become not-A, not for abstract thought or understanding. Hegel is maintaining the dialectical growth ontologically. From the viewpoint of Speculative Reason (which is higher than abstract understanding) everything is infected with growth and development. Nothing remains what it is for bringing out this intuition of ontological growth, Hegel has established the principle of Dialectic advance. Dialectic contains the principle of universal growth and evolution. So the dialectic has its context metaphysical vision of things and it should not be confused with the laws of abstract thought, i.e., thought apart from any matter, any reference to the world of things. Further, dialectic deduction has not to be assimilated to formal deduction of Aristotelian Logic. Dialectic is a description of world-events recollected in the contemplation of the evening hour, undisturbed by the heat, murmur and task of living of the day.

The third category of the triad is obtained by intuition and creative flash and this can never be reduced to the white heat of analytic thinking. So the Dialectic is based on creative drive and this cannot be the product of Abstract understanding or formal thinking of ordinary logic. Besides, the third category seeks to resolve the contradiction, and the third, category is very often a 'transformation' of the earlier categories. Hence, it is not true to say that Hegel disregards the law of contradiction.

In resolving the liar's paradox, Russell has propounded the theory of types or levels of language. According to this theory of type, we should think that only at the higher level of language liar's paradox can be resolved. Let us illustrate it.

All Cretans tell lies (Level I)

---

1. Karl R. Popper, *The Open Society and its Enemies*, Vol. II (Routledge, 1962), p. 39.

A Cretan says that all Cretans are liars (Level II)

Now Level II should not be confused with Level I, otherwise the paradox cannot be resolved. We have to maintain that L_2 throws light on L_1, but its reflexive use should not be allowed. In the same way Hegel was faced with the antinomies. He wanted to solve this. He could do so by speaking in a higher language than that of the antinomies. For Hegel, the language in which paradoxes appear, is of the *understanding*. In order to resolve the paradox, one has to go beyond this level into the language of the Speculative Reason. Hence, Dialectic is meta-language and should not be confused with the lower orders of language. It is a higher-order-comment on all past thinking[1].

Hence, Hegel does not disregard the law of contradiction, but presents his *Dialectic* as true of an evolving world, a world infected with change and development. This observation of Hegel has been more clearly expressed by Bosanquet's doctrine of 'the Spirit of totality' and by Bradley's view of 'self-transcendence.'

---

1.   J.N. Findlay, *Language, Mind and Value*, George Allen, 1964, pp. 219-21;
      J.N. Findlay, *Hegel's use of teleology* in Hegel's PHILOSOPHY, ed. W.E. Steinkraus, p. 94.

10

FRANCIS HERBERT BRADLEY (1846-1924)

10.00. Introduction

Francis Herbert Bradley was born on January 30, 1846 and died on September 18, 1924. In 1870 Bradley was awarded a fellowship at Merton College, Oxford, which could be terminated only by marriage. As Bradley remained unmarried, so he enjoyed this Fellowship till his death. It appears that Bradley remained wedded,to philosophy all his life. He was acclaimed as the greatest idealist thinker which England has ever produced. Indeed, Bradley's metaphysics is the ripened fruit, of idealistic speculations of Coleridge and Carlyle, Ferrier, J.H. Stirling, W. Wallace, T.H. Green, Edward Caird and John Caird. Bradley was a master of phrases and at times his polemic writings are full of satires. Bradley remained a consistent and an untiring critic of British empiricism, hedonism, psychologism and pluralism. His denial of God and Self as the highest reality known to human beings brought him in disfavour of Scottish idealists. His subtle and hair-splitting logic did much to usher in an era of Analytic Philosophy in Anglo-Saxon World. Both Moore and Russell are the pioneers of analytic movement in philosophy and both of them started their career under the idealistic tutelage of Bradley. Without understanding Bradley's metaphysics it would be difficult to understand the revolt of Moore and Russell. Bradley remained in the thick of philosophical battle against empiricism, pragmatism and Hedonism. His observations and criticism of these movements are still worth studying.

Bradley's writings are not too many, but they have proved influential in the history of philosophy. The following writings can be mentioned :

1. The Presuppositions of Critical History, 1874 (Reproduced in *Collected Essays*).
2. Ethical Studies, London, 1876 (Second Edition, 1927).
3. Mr. Sidgwick's Hedonism, 1877 (Reproduced in *Collected Essays*).
4. The Principles of Logic, 1883 (Second Edition with Terminal Essays in 2 Vols., 1922).
   References in this book are from 1958 impression, Oxford University Press, Oxford.
5. Appearance and Reality (Second Edition with Appendix, 1897).
   References in this book are from 1959 impression, Clarendon Press,

London.
6. Essays on Truth and Reality, 1914.
   References in this book are from 1968 impression, Clarendon Press, London.
7. Collected Essays in Two Volumes in 1935. Now Collected Essays have been produced in a single volume by Clarendon Press, London, in 1969.

Studies

1. Campbell, C.A., *Septicism and Construction*, London, 1931.
2. Church, R.W., *Bradley's Dialectic*, London, 1942.
3. Cunningham, G. Watts, *The Idealist Argument in Recent British and American Philosophy* (The Century Co. 1933).
4. Haldar, Hiralal, *Neo-Hegelianism*, London, 1927.
5. Kagey, R., *The Growth of Bradley's Logic*, London, 1931.
6. Lofthouse, W. F., *F. H. Bradely*, Epworth, London, 1949.
7. Muirhead, J. H., *The Platonic Tradition in Anglo-Saxon Philosophy*, Allen & Unwin 1931.
8. Ross, G. R., *Scepticism and Dogma: A Study in the Philosophy of F. H. Bradley*, New York, 1945.
9. Segerstedt, T.T., *Value and Reality in Bradley's Philosophy*, Lund, 1934.
10. Taylor, A.E., *Francis Herbert Bradley* (1896-1924).
    Proceedings of the British Academy 11, 1925.
11. Garrett L. Van der Veer, *Bradley's Metaphysics and the Self*, Yale University Press, 1970.
12. Wollheim, R., *F. H. Bradleys in 'Revolution in Philosophy'*, Ed. A.J. Ayer, Macmillan, 1956.
13. Wollheim, *F. H. Bradley*, A Pelican Book, 1959.
14. *Mind* 1925, Articles on Bradley by G.D. Hicks, J.H. Muirhead, G.F. Stout, F.C.S. Schiller, A.E. Taylor and J. Ward.
15. MASIH, Y., *Hegel Aur Bradley Ka Pratyayavada*, Bihar Hindi Granth, Akademi, Patna, 1974.

Abbreviations

AR—Appearance and Reality
ETR—Essays on Truth and Reality
PL—The Principles of Logic

10.01. Philosophical Assumptions and Problems of Bradley

Bradley is essentially Hegelian inasmuch as he believes that philosophy is a search of Reality and this search is essentially intellectual. Again, Bradley takes Reality as one organic whole which expresses itself immanently in all its appearances. It is this spirit of totality which does not allow any experience to be what it is, but impels each experience to transcend itself to become complete in the Absolute. True, Bradley does not make use of the Dialectic, but it is present in an attenuated form in the doctrine of the Degrees of Reality.

Though Bradley is essentially Hegelian yet his views about God, Self and Morality are much sharper than what they are in Hegel himself. For Bradley, God is a religious object and as such is the highest appearance. Nonetheless God is only an appearance and cannot be taken as the Absolute. Hegel almost means the same thing, but Hegel has not expressed himself in such unequivocal terms. Secondly, British Hegelians, notably T.H. Green and Caird brothers had taken Self as the key-concept for explaining idealistic metaphysics. Bradley thinks that the knowledge of self is not the clearest or paradigm of knowledge. The concept of self is riddled with contradictions and so this cannot serve as the model of knowing Reality. Again, for Bradley morality is not a matter of good will (or motive) alone (or subjectivity as Hegel put it), but also is a social concern. His doctrine of 'Station and its duties' not only goes beyond the formalism of Kant, but also renders precise the social ethics of Hegel.

However, Bradley develops his idealism in the context of British Empiricism, with the weapons manufactured in German armoury. Bradley carried out a relentless struggle against empirical epistemology, pluralism, hedonism, pragmatism and psychologism. This struggle has given a peculiarly polemical tinge to his writings punctured hither and thither with bitter sarcasm of his opponents. By the way his polemic enabled him to develop an analytic approach to the problem and much of his criticism is deep and subtle.

Bradley is never dogmatic, though he never lacked deep conviction. But there is healthy scepticism with regard to the knowledge of Reality. Even Truth for Bradley is not wholly true. Truth is only an aspect of Reality, but for philosophy this alone counts. Bradley's philosophy of Reality is also an appearance, and, there is no truth which in the long run has no prospect of being superseded by higher vision. Every epoch has its close and the owl of Minerva takes reckoning of things in the cool of its evening. Philosophers pass from vision to vision to have not only a closer, but also a more comprehensive view of Reality. This observation brings us to the starting assumptions of Bradley's philosophy.

It is better to begin the philosophy of Bradley in his own words :

Reality for me. . .is one individual Experience. It is a higher unity above our immediate experience, and above all ideality and relations.[1]

Following the terminology of Hegel, Bradley calls Reality 'Spirit':

Outside of spirit there is not, and there cannot be, any reality, and the more that anything is spiritual, so much the more is it veritably real.[2]

---

1. ETR, p. 343.
2. AR, p. 498.

For Bradley Spirit is an organic whole, where the whole is immanent in each of its parts.

> The ideal of spirit, we may say, is directly, opposite to mechanism. Spirit is a unity of the manifold in which externality of the manifold has utterly ceased. The universal here is immanent in the parts, and its system does not lie somewhere outside and in the relations between them. It is above the relational form and has absorbed it in a higher unity, a whole in which there is no division between elements and laws.[1]

These quotations might confuse the reader if he is reading Bradley for the first time. Before analysing the elements of Bradley's statements, we have to state his underlying logical assumptions on which his whole metaphysics is based.

> I have assumed first that truth has to satisfy the intellect, and what does not do this is neither true nor real.[2]

Nobody can deny this; otherwise the would-be objector has to say that the discordant, chaotic and self-contradictory is the truth. And the statement of the objector will be recognised as incoherent and unintelligible. That truth alone will satisfy the intellect which realizes the idea of a systematic whole. And such a whole possesses essentially the two characters of coherence and comprehensiveness.[3] Any partical element is characterised by self-transcendence, inviting complementary opposite towards a wider unity.[4] Any part without the whole, for Bradley, is jarring and self-contradictory, and harmony is incompatible with restriction and finitude. For Bradley, analysis always distorts, and, so a part from the whole cannot but be false. Therefore, the partial is also self-contradictory and false.[5]

> Hence the two principles of coherence and comprehensiveness are one. And not only are they one but they include also the principle of non-contradiction.[6]

Ordinarily in logic self-contradiction may be compared to the process of rubbing off what was written on the board. So ultimately nothing remains written on the board. However, for Bradley Reality is an organic whole and in this context any external relation, a mere juxtaposition of diverse elements or objects has been called self-contradiction. For Bradley, scientific laws, considered metaphysically are self-contradictory. For example, cold solidifies water. But Why? Science assumes the togetherness of things without answering the question Why (AR, p.

---

1. AR, p. 441.
2. AR, p. 509.
3. ETR, p. 223.
4. *Ibid.,* p. 223.
5. AR, pp. 321-22.

469). We shall explain and further deal with this meaning of self-contradictoriness. Bradley defines contradiction.

> But the simple identification of the diverse is precisely that which one means by contradiction.[1]

Again,

> But, I reply at once, the intellect is very far from, being satisfied by a 'scientific explanation', for that in the end is never consistent. In the end it connects particulars unintelligibly with an unintelligible law, and such an external connexion is not a real harmony.[2]

For Bradley, then, Reality is an all-comprehensive and harmonious sentient experience, above all ideality and relations, whether external or internal. Ideas are universal and for Bradley Reality is much more than 'impalpable abstractions, or unearthly ballet of bloodless categories'.[3] Bradley would agree with William James and Henri Bergson in treating sense-experience as having the bite and pungency of reality. So Bradley calls Reality as 'Sentient experience', or simply, Individual. However, Bradley does not take Reality to be personal. Reality, for Bradley, is both supra-relational and supra-personal. But Reality, is given in sense-experience which is foundational starting-point in our philosophical sojourn.

> And experience means something much the same as given and present fact .... Sentient experience, in short, is reality and what is not this is not real ...Find any piece of existence, take up anything that any one could possibly call a fact, or could in any sense assert to have being, and then judge if it does not consist in sentient experience.[4]

For Bradley, Reality is given in sense-experience, which remains basal even when it later comes to be supplemented, elaborated and expanded by Thought. We shall be taking up the problems of the given soon, but let us first explain the stand of Bradley with regard to the Reality taken as One.

The Absolute Reality for Bradley must be one, "because anything is experienced in or as a whole, and because anything like independent plurality or external relations cannot satisfy the intellect"[5]. That Reality is one is more a matter of conviction than a reasoned out belief or knowledge, for Bradley.[6] This is first based on the assumption that Reality must satisfy the intellect.

> It is after all an enormous assumption that what satisfies us is real, and that reality has got to satisfy us.[7]

1. ETR, p. 223.
2. ERT, p. 228; Also AR, p. 501.
3. AR, p. 553; Also pp. 504-05.
4. PL II, p. 591.
5. AR, p. 127.
6. AR, p. 495.
7. ETR, pp. 15, 242, 344.

And plurality and external relations between independent reals are self-contradictory, and so cannot satisfy the intellect.

> But on the other hand the character of the absolute Reality is everywhere manifest, and we can possess no other possible criterion of truth.[1]

The whole of the Absolute reality cannot be given in any experience, but in the immediate experience which is the most unalloyed and basal starting-point gives a foretaste and hint of what Reality is, because Reality is given in immediate experience. Immediate experience is a positive non-relational non-objective whole of feeling.[2] No doubt later on many distinctions of subject-object, one-many, substance-attribute and relations between such distinctions arise, but the felt unity of immediate experience is never overcome or obliterated. This basal unity remains foundational and gives us the hint that Reality is one supra relational whole.

> Every distinction and relation still rests on an immediate background of which we are aware, and every distinction and relation. . .is also felt, and felt in a sense to belong to an immediate totality. Thus in all experience we still have feeling which is not an object and at all our moments the entirety of what comes to us, however much distinguished and relational is felt as comprised within a unity which itself is not relational.[3]

Immediate experience certainly cannot serve as the rational criterion, but, Bradley wants to tell us that the criterion is not entirely *a priori*. Bradley nowhere tells us but we can say that the doctrine of Reality as one all-comprehensive, all-harmonious sentient whole is based on reflective intuition of our most incorrigible, basal experience called *immediate feeling*. Hence, Bradley's view concerning immediate experience is very important for understanding his entire system. However before proceeding with the task of giving the exposition of 'Immediate experience', it would be better to state at the outset some of the implications of 'monistic idealism'.

That reality is one organic whole is the primary key-notion of Bradley's idealism and from this many other secondary principles follow. This key-notion runs through his whole system. For instance, Bradley starts with 'Immediate experience' as his starting-point. His description of it as 'one blur, without being parted as yet by any relation' is not the rock-bottom rawest experience. It is as much a theory about' 'simple, primary and elemental experience' as the doctrine of atomistic sensationism is of the empiricist. One wonders whether Bradley would describe *Immediate Experience* as he does if he had not accepted the doctrine of

---

1. ETR, p. 344.
2. ETR, p. 178.
3. ETR, p. 178.
   Bradley holds that this immediate experiencee sugggests or points to the general idea of a total experience which Reality is (AR, p. 141).

Monism. As Bradley was committed to monistic idealism, so he tried to refute atomistic empiricism. Bradley has successfully criticised the theory of pluralistic sensationism and its atomism. He has shown that the whole theory of atomistic sensationism fails to account for the system, order and universality in knowledge on the basis of Associationism. In this book very little will be said about this refutation of atomistic sensation. However, atomistic sensationism leads to the ontological doctrine of the plurality of reals, According to this pluralism the truthh consiists in faithful *correspondence with facts*. Bradley rejects pluralism on the ground that it is not supported by

(*a*) Primary sense-experience.

(*b*) Besides juxtaposition of independent reals is philosophically unintelligible.

(*c*) There can be no independent fact, for any talk of an independent fact is really a talk about an unreal abstraction.

(*d*) Gone with the doctrine of independent facts is the correspondence-theory of truth. Bradley lays a good deal of stress on these points in his *Logic*. Not only he dwells at length in refuting the theory of independent reals, but he also energetically refutes the subject-predicate theory of judgments. In this refutation of S-P formula, the subject is taken as the *grammatical* subject. But Bradley does accept the S-P formula if the subject is taken as one Ultimate Subject which underlies each and every judgment. Against atomistic sensationism and pluralism Bradley maintains

(A) That immediate experience is one unitary experience with implicit and nascent distinctions.

(B) So-called independent reals are not externally related, but are *internally* related in such a way that the story of one part logically leads to all the other parts pointing to a super-relational whole.

(C) Not correspondence, but Harmony Theory is the correct account of truth involved in knowledge.

(Of course, at present the analysts tell us that truth is a property of propositions and not of knowledge. But this is a later development and requires a good deal of discussion. Bradley talks of *judgments* and not of propositions. A judgment is mental, unexpressed in language and admits of degrees. For example, 'The sun rises and sets', is not understood in the same way by a child, an adult and an astronomer. Whereas a proposition once true is always true. So the whole context of Bradley is different from that of analytic philosophers. Bradley can consistently talk of 'Degrees of Reality and Truth', but analysts cannot talk of Reality and certainly cannot talk of *degrees* in Truth).

(D) Bradley rejects the S-P formula and for him there is one ultimate subject and all other ordinary judgments are mere predicates of this ultimate subject. For example, 'This bird is yellow', or, 'All men are mortal' can be reduced to

(i) Reality/is such/that this bird is yellow.

(ii) Reality/is such/that men are mortal.

But the most contrasted views of Bradley and other empiricists, notably Moore and Russell (who were once his pupils) hovers round the doctrine of Relations. Moore and Russell, favouring pluralism of facts of daily life speak of *external* relation between facts. Bradley rejects the doctrine of *external relation* in favour of internal relations. Ultimately, Bradley rejects both external and internal relation, since the Absolute Reality, for Bradley, is super-relational.

Bradley grants that common sense is not wrong in accepting the plurality of facts in daily life. For practical convenience this is absolutely necessary, but Bradley contends that in philosophy this is not an intelligible doctrine. Chairs and tables and all the furniture of the earth are really *appearances* of Reality. As appearances, things of daily life are not as unreal as sky-flowers, but they are only partially true. Reality is unintelligible without appearances. So appearances do belong to Reality. Only appearances are higher and lower. There are *degress* of Reality in appearances.

Thus, Bradley weaves his whole system to demonstrate to us that Reality is one all-comprehensive, all-harmonious, sentient whole. His whole system is one artistic whole and cannot be rejected in piece-meals. Underlying notion about metaphysics is that it is an artistic construction of the world as a whole, through arguments, based on facts, specially psychological facts about man. For this reason Bradley had to brush shoulders with stalwart psychologists like Ward, Stout and William James. In any critical appraisal of Bradley one should not ignore the vastness, grandeur and reanosableness of his system. Critical, often sarcastic, arguments are many in the writings of Bradley. But they are so many pleas which aim at evoking a holistic attitude to Reality, from a perspective which is at once advantageous, adequate and satisfying. However, the starting point of Bradley is the doctrine of immediate experience, which we should now take up.

10.02. The Immediate Experience

Both empiricist and Bradley accept immediate experience as their starting point. This is most clear in Berkeley and Bradley, for in the foregoing quotation from Bradley we have noted that for Bradley sentient experience is real (AR, p. 127) and what is not this, is not real. But the empiricist and Bradley differ a lot about the nature of this, immediate experience. For the empiricist, sense-impressions are distinct separate and independent units. Bradley would never subscribe to this view. According to him the view of the empiricist is not a faithful description of what we find in immediate experience. The empiricist furnishes a view of immediate experience under the influence of his preconceived notion of philosophy. The uncorrupted version of immediate experience has been given by William James as 'One big, buzzing blooming confusion'. For Bradley it is felt unity, not yet parted by any relation and distinction.[1]

> It is all one blur with differences   that work and that are felt, but not
> discriminated.

This kind of immediate experience is the source of the knowledge of the Absolute
Reality and is the starting point.

> First, in mere feeling, or immediate presentation, we have the experience of a
> whole. This whole contains diversity, and, on the other hand, is not parted by
> relations.[2]

> As a fact and given we have in feeling diversity and unity in one whole, a whole
> implicit and not yet broken up into terms and relations. This immediate union
> of the one and many is an 'ultimate fact' from which we start; and to hold that
> feeling, because immediate, must be simple and without diversity is, in my
> view, a doctrine quite untenable.[3]

In other words, we do not start with distinct and independent reals either in the form
of sensations or objects or simples. Immediate experience *has* incipient or implicit
diversity. This gestalt experience suggests to us an experience which is total and
all at once inclusive of thought, feeling and will. At the same time each immediate
experience is imperfect, unstable and its inconsistencies within itself impel it to
transcend itself.[4] As a result of this self-transcendence implicit diversities work out
in the distinctions of substance-attribute, qualities-relations, subject-object and so
on. All these distinctions can be conveniently lumped together as Terms-and-
Relations. But no matter how far we proceed with the process of making explicit
the distinction of terms and relations, the immediate experience lurks beneath and
forms the basal foundation on which any distinction can rest.[5]

> "Every distinction and relation still rests on an immediate background of
> which we are aware, and every distinction and relation (so far as
> experienced) is also felt, and felt in a sense to belong to an immediate
> totality. Thus in all experience we still have feeling which is not an object,
> and at all our moments, the entirety of what comes to us, however much
> distinguished and relational, is felt as comprised within a unity which itself
> is not relational."[6]

The immediate experience is not only unstable because of nascent diversities within
it, but also it is at once continuous with our experience. It has ragged edges,
beckoning it backward and forward in the direction of the Absolute. To illustrate
this point Bradley takes the help of an imagery of a flowing stream (standing for
the Absolute Reality) and a searchlight illuminating a spot on it (standing for the

1. AR, p. 141.   2. AR, p. 141.
3. AR, p. 508 (Appendix). 4. AR, p. 141.
5. ETR, pp. 160, 161, 177, 190.
6. Bradley's discussion of Immediate Experience in Chapter VI, Appendix and Supplementary note
   in ETR is very important—ETR, p. 178.

sentients, immediate experience). This imagery should never be lost sight of if we are to understand Bradley's doctrine of immediate experience and its place in his system.

> Let us fancy ourselves in total darkness hung over a stream and looking down on it.[1] The stream has no banks, and its current is covered and filled continuously with floating things. Right under our faces is a bright illuminated spot on the water, which ceaselessly widens and narrows its area, and shows what passes away on the current. And this spot that is light is our now, our present.

> . . . We have not only an illuminated place, and the rest of the stream in total darkness. There is a paler light which, both up and down stream, is shed on what comes before, and after now. And this paler light is the offspring of the present. Behind our heads there is something perhaps which reflects the rays from the lit-up now, and throws them more dimly upon past and future. Outside this reflection is utter darkness; within it is gradual increase of brightness, until we reach the illumination immediately below us.[2]

This imagery of the stream and searchlight describes to us, the importance of immediate experience without which we can never know reality (which without illuminated spot is in total darkness) and also at the same time tells us about its limitations. No immediate experience can have the whole of the flowing stream. Again, no immediate experience is insulated. It is always a part of the whole, and each immediate experience is continuous and is given in the whole, immersed in the whole and pointing to the whole. When the empiricist talks about an insulated real, then, according to Bradley, he talks of an abstracted part taken away from the whole. But a part, taken away from the whole is unreal, mutilated and vicious. Empirical plurality of independent units and parts, for Bradley, is based on the doctrine of vicious abstraction. On the doctrine of immediate experience, Bradley bases his idealism in the following way.

10.03. The Idealism of Bradley

By a careful scrutiny of pages 127-29 (AR, Chapter XIV), one would see three positions, namely,

1. Reality must be experienced insofar as it is experienced (a tautology).
2. Reality must be experienced.
3. Reality *is* experience.

Richard Wollheim[3] may or not be correct, but in my opinion the argument of Bradley is very akin to that of Berkeley, with some notable difference. The

---

1. We can also add 'through a window' which stands for the limitation of any sense-experience.
2. PL, I, pp. 54-55.
3. F.H. Bradley, p. 202.

argument of Bradley has the following conjectured steps:

1. 'I urge that reality is sentient experience.'[1]
2. Find any piece of existence, which can possibly be called a fact, consists in being a sentient experience.[2] Again, Bradley tells us that the Other is also 'some mode of experience'. He puts it in the form of a Berkeleyan challenge: "Show me your idea of an Other, not a part of experience, and I will show you at once that it is, throughout and wholly, nothing else at all." (AR, p. 463)
3. To be real is to be indissolubly one thing with sentience. In this integral sentience there is no separation of subject and object, self and not-self.

But to be utterly indivisible from feeling or perception, to be an integral element in a whole which is experienced, this surely is itself to be experience. Being and reality are, in brief, one thing with sentience; they can neither be opposed to, nor even in the end distinguished from it[3].

The quotation appears to contain the very nerve of the argument which is fully stated in pages 128-29. Ordinarily it is held that any experience implies an experiencer (as we find in cogito-ergo-sum of Descartes) and that every experience is *of* something out there which may be called *ex-experienced*. We shall take up the first part of the contention a little later. About the second point, the contention of Bradley is that in primary experience, which is the starting-point and for Bradley incorrigible, there is no distinction between experienced thing and experience. The whole of primary experience is to be accepted. If so, then we cannot hold to the independence of the experienced from the whole of experience. This would be indefensible abstraction.

For if, seeking for reality, we go to experience, what we certainly do *not* find is a subject or an object or indeed any other thing whatever, standing separate and on its own bottom. What we discover rather is a whole in which distinctions can be made, but in which divisions do not exist.[4]

Bradley would contend that *experienced facts* are carved out later by thought out of the whole of sentience. But a part, abstracted from the whole is unreal. So experienced is really an indissolubly one with sentient whole. Only the sentient whole is real. Richard Wollheim reduced, the argument of Bardley into the Berkeleyan form.[5] Berkeley's argument is:

1. AR, p. 128.
2. AR, p. 127.
3. AR, p. 129.
4. AR, p. 129.
5. F.H. Bradley, p. 203. For Berkeley's Argument refer to § 6.01 and 6.06.

1. "Show me anything which exists and which is not an idea." Here 'idea' simply means an image or a concept in a *subject.*
2. Again, an idea, as of pain in approaching fire, is in the subject and not in fire. So an idea is always mind-dependent.
3. Hence, All things, being ideas are mind-dependent, or mental.

Berkeley's ideas are later products of immediate experience. Certainly *perceptions* of Berkeley always refer to objects perceived. This implies the distinction of subject and object, as Moore has clearly stated and criticised. *Perception* of Berkeley has two aspects of *perceiving act* and *object perceived.* When this distinction of subject and object, self and not-self has already been drawn up, then Berkeley further holds that experienced objects are mental. This conclusion is indefensible, for objects by any logical trick cannot be reduced now to perceiving acts. If they be so reduced, then the choir of heaven and furniture of the earth become mind-dependent. In order to get out of solipsistic conclusion, Berkeley takes recourse to divine perception. Each and every move of Berkeley is open too objection. But it is not so with regard to the argument of Bradley. For Bradley there is no solipsism.

Solipsism is a doctrine in philosophy according to which everything is a mental state of a solitary thinker. This presupposes that in this state of affairs there is a subject where all objects are his mental states. But Bradley contends that this is found at a level higher than immediate experience. At the level of *pure* experience, which immediate experience is, there is no distinction of subject and object. If there is no subject, then how can we say that things are *objects* of one single *subject*? Experience, for Bradley means, immediate experience, whereas yet there is no distinction of subject and object. We cannot say at this stage that experience is of *objects* for human or divine subject. If, however, the distinction is made of subject and object, then in this later and more developed scale of reflection, there is no possibility of solipsism. For there is no moral, aesthetic or cognitive experience where non-ego is not experienced along with the ego. Hence, whenever I become conscious of myself as an experiencer of a table or chair, then other selves are felt as palpably as myself. Therefore, the charge of solipsism cannot be attributed to Bradley's idealism, according to which reality is experience. However, there is one important question: Does experience imply, an experiencer? Or, can there be experience without a mind which owns it?

We shall be dealing with the problem of Self in Bradley's Metaphysics, where this question can be indirectly answered. Here we can state the position of Bradley directly, though briefly. According to Ward, experience implies an ego which has the experience. Bradley refutes the doctrine of Ward. According to Bradley, permanent or essential self or subject is not given in experience. Hence on the basis of experience, we cannot say that any Self is an object of empirical observation. On the other hand, Bradley maintains that the notion of Self is a construct out of experiential content.[1] Keeping in mind the imagery of the flowing stream, we can say that for Bradley this whole stream *is* experience and immediate experience in finite centres (i.e., any finite individual) is inseparably continuous with Absolute Experience, backward and forward, above and below it.

> Finite experience never, and as an inseparable aspect of its own nature, the all-penetrating reality. And there never is, and there never was, any time when in experience the world and self were quite indentical.[2]

The finite self is infected with self-transcendence but then it is impelled to proceed towards fuller Absolute Experience itself. The whole is one experience, above all ideality and relation.

> But this unity of all experiences, if itself not experience, would be meaningless.[3]

Again,

> That Reality is one system which contains in itself all experience, and, again, that this system itself is experience—so far we may be said to know absolutely and unconditionally.[4]

For Bradley the absolute reality is experience, and a further question, whether the Absolute is Mind or a Person which has this experience, is perhaps not important. Now Bradley tells us that the absolute is not personal, because it is personal *and more*. It is super-personal.

> If by calling it personal you mean only that it is nothing but experience, then it contains all the highest that we possibly can know and feel, and is a unity in which the details are utterly pervaded and embraced—then in this conclusion I am with you.[5]

But 'person' also means something finite, with feelings and thoughts limited and mutable in the process of time. In this sense, a person is a finite self which is moved by personal relations and feelings towards others. According to Bradley, the Absolute is personal, for it is not a finite being. Again, for Bradley, the Absolute is not personal, nor is it moral, nor is it beautiful or true. But the Absolute is not less than these distinctions: it is not below but above its internal distinctions. The net result of Bradley's view has been thus stated:

---

1. AR, p. 75-77, 464-65, 468.
2. AR, p. 464.
3. AR, p. 470.
4. AR, p. 475.
5. AR, p. 471.

The Whole is one experience then, and such a unity higher than all relations, a unity which contains and transforms them, has positive meaning. Of the manner of its being in detail we are utterly ignorant . . . . .[1]

The absolute then is Experience and we know Reality by having immediate experience of it and which remains as foundational even when thought-structure emerges later on. In terms of his imagery of the flowing stream, Bradley writes,

My way of contact with Reality is through a limited aperture. For I cannot get at it directly except through the felt 'this', and our immediate interchange and transfluence takes place through one small opening. Everything beyond, though not less real, is an expansion of the common essence which we feel burningly in this one focus. And so, in the end, to know the universe, we must fall back upon our personal experience and sensation.[2]

The immediate experience is diversity and unity in one whole, and it is an experience *of* the whole insofar as it appears through that small aperture. But this immediate experience can never capture the Whole Reality. Because of its narrowness, it is imperfect; because of its implicit diversity within it, it is unstable; and, because of its being a focus in a vaster show which Reality is, it is infected with self-transcendence.[3] Immediate experience has to be taken up by thought which breaks the unity into its diversities. Though in on sense our experience is enriched yet the unity can never be recaptured by thought. The result is that thought can give us appearance, and not reality. This is our next task to detail and explain.

10.04. Terms and Relations

Berkeley is supposed to have laid down the foundation of modern idealism by holding on to the formula of *esse est percipi*. Later idealists found percipi to be too relative, too momentary and changeable for becoming the solid foundation of Objective Idealism. They, therefore, changed the formula into *esse est intelligi*. Hegel, John Caird, Edward Caird, T.H. Green all held that Reality is a system of thought. Bradley clinging to his maxim that 'Reality is *experience*' rejects *esse est intelligi*. For Bradley thought is universal and Reality is immanent and pervasive in all particular things. Universal thought, therefore, misses the particular things. For this reason, for Bradley, thought is floating in the air without its footing on the solid ground of particulars. Hegel's Absolute, for Bradley, is an 'unearthly ballet of bloodless categories'. Therefore, for Bradley, thought no doubt is an improvement on and elaboration of immediate experience, but in the end it can offer only an appearance and not Reality. Of course, Bradley uses the term 'appearance' in

---

1. AR, p. 470.
2. AR, p. 229.
3. AR, pp. 141, 508.

a very special sense. For him appearance is not totally unreal: it is incomplete, fragmentary and inharmonious. However, appearance belongs to Reality and without it Reality will be empty and unintelligible. Thus, thought for Bradley, gives us something which is rooted in Reality and yet comes short of Reality. And we have now to study the machinery of thought to understand this paradoxical character of thought.

We start with immediate experience, which is unstable from within, because of internal implicit diversities, and unstable from without because of the surrounding flowing stream which infects it with the spirit of self-transcendence. Every immediate experience has its ragged edges which push and pull it in different directions. Though immediate experience is a whole, a unity; yet one cannot remain in it. Its incipient diversity has to break forth into explicit distinction. The first distinction is of 'that' and 'what'. Immediate experience is divided into something which *is* and also *what it is*. For instance, we have at first a vague blur, an indefinite nebulosity. By becoming aware and attending to it, we become conscious *that it is something* and after further attending to it we say it is a 'table'. We may further differentiate 'this table' by noting that it is hard, brown and wooden and so on. In the first instance, mere 'this' is the *That* and 'table' becomes its *What*. *That* means the givenness, the actual existence, the bite and pungency of reality disclosed in immediate experience. *What* means the quality or qualities which characterise the given thing. Here 'that' becomes the subject and 'what' becomes the predicate. Immediate experience is expanded into the judgment

This/is/a table. (i)

Later on, as a result of greater distinction more qualities appear and *what* becomes clearer. There is then another richer judgment,

This table/is/brown, hard, wooden etc. (ii)

Now thought works through judgments and a judgment works by making a distinction of subject and predicate. A subject is that about which we say something, and a predicate is that which says something about the subject or describes the subject. For example, 'This' is the subject in (i), and 'a table' is its predicate. In judgment (ii), 'this table' is the subject and the predicate tells us about this table, namely, that it is brown or hard. Such distinctions are very useful in daily life. But, are they defensible? "This' or 'this table' is said to be a subject. Is it an independent fact? Well, ordinarily people think so. But how can it be? It is only a part cut out of the whole. For example, 'this table' is found along with colour, weight, woodenness and other characteristics. Besides, a table has been carved out of the bigger surrounding of which it is a part. The table is found on a floor, beneath a ceiling in a room and that room in its turn is a part of the building and so on. Now can a part exist without the whole, of which it is a part? Certainly a hand cut off from a living body would rot and would not be a hand at all. So a table taken out of the whole surrounding cannot be said to be real. Bradley would detail this point much further in his discussion on analytic Judgment of Sense. But there is also a principle unsolved. According to Bradley everything is connected with everything else internally, i.e., a thing is what it is because of its relationship with other things. So, according to this principle, a table is a table because of the whole surrounding, and it will cease to be a table as soon as it is taken out from this surrounding. Hence for the sake of convenience we may treat a table as an independent subject but philosophically considered it cannot be said to have any independent status. Bradley takes up this issue again with regard to the status of a grammatical subject in S-P formula in his theory of a judgment.

If the issue with regard to 'subject' is bristled with difficulty, then the distinction of 'predicate' is no less free from difficulties. For example we say that 'This table' is brown. But what shade of brown? Is it the shade of brown leaf or of brown coffee? Even if we grant that the shade characterising brown leaf is meant by brown in this context, we shall not be out of trouble. Should we say brown mango leaf or lemon tree-leaf? If we say brown leaf of a mango tree, even then there is no way out of the impasse. Which kind of mango tree is meant and how much dryness is required? No matter however much we detail brownness we shall never succeed in catching the actual existing brown of sense-experience. But why? Because in judgment we use concepts and concepts are universal. They describe what a thing has in common with other things, but fails to give us what is unique and particular. The term 'brown' tells us what this table has in common, with all other brown things, but it cannot pin down the unique shade of brown that this table is. When we use the concept brown to describe the given table, then 'brown' is not totally false of immediate experience. It was there and thought has simply made it explicit; only thought fails to give us what is sensed. No matter how well we describe, 'brown' by piling adjectives on adjectives, we never *experience* brown through description. In other words, by mere description, no matter however detailed, we never get the actual thing. No matter however vividly we describe a rasagulla, we never can get the taste of an actual rasagulla. So thought cannot yield the bite and pungency which an actual experience of a table or rasagulla has. So much and so far there is loss in the elaboration of immediate experience through thought. But there is also gain. Thought connects the immediately given with a great many things not present here and now. Thus immediate experience is widened by thought. Secondly, immediate experience is unstable, but thought by virtue of its distinctions make, immediate experience as clear and stable as a concept is. Thus thought helps the transcendence of immediate experience, but it fails to restore its sting, the punch, its flesh and blood of immediate experience. Once the distinctions are made they can never be brought into their former unity of immediate experience. No doubt we do take the help of certain terms of individuation, like 'now', 'here', 'this', 'mine' and so on. For instance, we point out finger to the brown table and say, 'this brown, just now and here which I am seeing'. But do these terms 'now' or 'here' really help? 'Now' refers to many nows, and 'here' stands for many heres. Anybody can point to a thing and say 'Look, I mean this brown, now and here and in front of me'. So 'now' and 'here' are as much universal as any adjectival term, nay, it is more universal. Hence, no matter whay you do to concepts, you can never squeeze the unique, particular thing of immediate presentation. Therefore, thought extends immediate experience beyond its presentation, stabilizes its instability and makes it distinct, but it can never give the unity of immediate feeling. Bradley dwells on showing at length that thought makes distinct the differences which were only implicit in immediate experience, but these distinctions once made can never be made harmonious and consistent with themselves. Thought works by parting the hidden diversities of immediate experience into subject and object, substance and qualities, space and time, self and not-self and so on. But Bradley shows that the breach once made between subject and object, substance and qualities etc., can never be healed up. Let us illustrate this.

We say 'This table is brown'. Here this table is said to be the substance in which the quality of brown inheres. Similarly, taking the example given by Bradley we say this sugar crystal is sweet, hard and white. Here this lump of sugar is the substance and whiteness, sweetness and hardness are its qualities. The question arises, how is the substance related to its qualities of sweetness, hardness and whiteness? Can we say with Locke that substance is an unknown substratum which somehow supports these qualities? Obviously the admission of 'unknown' and 'somehow' does not satisfy the criterion of intelligibility. Can we say then that 'substance' is an empty name and qualities somehow cohere together? Even if we suppose that qualities alone count, how are they related? Here lies the rub, the real crux of the problem. We cannot say,

Sweetness/is/hardness.

If we interpret 'is' as a sign of equivalence, then the statement becomes tautologous, and, later on we will see that Bradley a tautologous statement is no statement at all. But even if the statement be not tautologous, it is most false to hold that sweetness and hardness are one and the same quality. But if we do not interpret 'is' as a sign of equivalence: instead we treat it as a copula,—a sign of predication, then the above statement means that sweetness is the subject and hardness is its predicate. Here the meaning of the statement is

Sweetness/has/ hardness.

Once again the subject has been treated as a substance which owns hardness as its quality. But the notion of substance is unintelligible. So even if 'is' is interpreted as a sign of predication, we do not solve the problem of relating the qualities themselves. However, so matter how we express a judgment, it is always caught up in the following dilemma:

If you predicate what is different, you ascribe to the subject what is *not*: and if you predicate what is not different, you say nothing at all.[1]

---

1. AR, p. 17.

Take the proposition

S/is/P

If P is the same as S, then the above proposition will be

S/is/S

And this is a tautology, and for Bradley tautology asserts nothing. If on the contrary, P be different from S, then the proposition will become

S/is/S

which is self-contradictory. This dilemma shows that the qualities cannot be consistently related.

If the qualities of whiteness, hardness, sweetness cannot stand related, then they have to be supposed to be independent units without any intrinsic or internal relation.[1] Of course, even if qualities be supposed to be independent units, they, cannot remain without relations. For to be different from one another, implies distinction and distinction is also a kind of relation. Hence, there must be qualities and they *also must be related*. Relation, here can be only external, that is, which does not change the character of the qualities to be related. Suppose now that qualities are externally related. Sweetness is externally related to hardness. But how is this external relation R related to S (sweetness) and H (hardness)? As R is an external relation, so R has is to be related to S and H with the help of another external relation R_1. But this relation R_1, is as much externnal to R, as R was to S and H. So in order to relate R_1, with R and S-H, we need a fresh relation R_2. This process of relating the qualities will lead to an infinite labyrinth of relations without relating the qualities at all.

> . . . . we are hurried off into the eddy of a hopeless process, since we are forced to go on finding new relations without end. The links are united by a link, and his bond of union is a link which also has two ends; and they require each a fresh link to connect them with the old.[2]

But the question will arise, external relations might fail to relate the qualities, cannot internal relations relate? We shall find that relational way of thinking is shot through with contradiction. Unfortunately thought cannot but work through the machinery, of terms and relations and in the end cannot give us anything but *appearance* and not Reality. Readers might object here. They might say, that surely we do think in terms of substance and qualities, and in daily life we do not discover any discrepancy. So the wholesale debunking of relational way of thinking is

---

1. Relations are either internal or external. An external relation makes no difference to terms. For example, the pen is on the table. This relation of being on the table is said to make no difference to the essence of the pen. An internal relation is one which makes a difference to the terms related. For instance, the relation of being a husband makes a difference to a bachelor man. In this context Bradley talks of *external relation*.

2. AR, p. 28.

unjustified. Bradley would grant that in daily life, in ordinary speech we deal with appearance and so we are justified in making use of substance-qualities and other thought-distinctions. But in metaphysics we deal with Reality and on this higher plane of deeper analysis we find that the machinery of terms and relations.

> . . . . is a makeshift, a device, a mere practical compromise, most necessary, but in the end most indefensible.[1]

This conclusion of Bradley has been re-echoed by G. Ryle when he says that in ordinary thinking we talk *with* concepts without experiencing any disturbance; but we cannot talk *about* them without experiencing difficulty.

Bradley hammers his conclusion about the incapacity of thought in dealing with Reality, with relentless consistency. He takes up, one by one, the distinctions of primary and secondary qualities, space and time, motion, causation, self and not-self and comes to the same conclusion about the shortcoming of the relational way of thinking. By way of illustrating further, we shall take up the distinctions of Space, Time and Self.

10.05. Space and Time

We do use the concepts of Space and Time to describe our experience. They are highly useful in our mutual practical commerce with one another . But are they self-consistent? Bradley takes up space and time as separate concepts[2] and so let us take them one by one.

Space is and yet can be mere relation between units of space. Leibnitz had pointed out that space is an abstraction formed by relations between things as near and far, above and below, small and big and so on. Certainly in most cases we take space as a relational property of things. Hence, space, whether taken as big or small, is a *relation* between spaces which it (space) unites. Quite obviously spaces between which relation exists, must be solids or real units, otherwise relation will vanish into nothing which relation cannot unite. But are there independent units of Space?

Space cannot be taken as a whole or in smaller parts. Let us take space as a whole. For Bradley this is a search for an illusory whole. The very essence of space is that it must be enclosed by a bigger whole. 'A space limited, and yet without space that is outside, is a self-contradiction.'[3] But no matter how big be the space

---

1. AR, p. 28.
2. Samuel Alexander thinks that Bradley has not been able to make space *and* time self-consistent, for he has taken them separately. For Alexander, Reality is not space *and* time, but Space-Time or Spatio-temporal.

   Bergson thinks that Bradley has taken space as real as Time. But for Bergson, Time alone is real and Space is unreal. Besides, for Bergson, Bradley's Time divided into units is not real, but spatialised time. Bastard times, therefore, cannot but be mere appearance.
3. AR, p. 32.

we imagine, logically. There must be a bigger space to enclose it, and so the process of going beyond can never end. Hence, the search for space as a whole is illusory. But can there be hard, solid and independent units of space into which space can be subdivided?

Of course, space is extended. Any extended thing is divisible into smaller units. Hence, space is composed of parts. But parts must be real if they are going to explain space. Now no matter however small be the unit of space, in principle it is still divisible into smaller parts.

> Anything extended is a collection, a relation of extendeds, which again are relations of extendeds, and so on indefinitely. . . . It is lengths of lengths of—nothing that we can find.[1]

Therefore, there can be no real units of space. A solid part of space is not space; and,

> in trying to find space beyond it, we can find only that which passes away into a relation. Space is a relation between terms, which can never be found.[2]

Hence, space is self-contradictory: it is and it is not a relation between terms, because there can be no units of space, either within or without it. Let us see whether the concept of time fares better.

Like Space, Time is infected with the same dilemma. Time is a relation and yet it is not a relation. Time is a relation between events called before and after. But is there any real event or unit of time? We find that there can be no real unit of time. So relation is not a unity because its units are non-entities. Time as a whole cannot be a unit because it is an unending stream. No matter how long the stretch of time be taken, it has always a beyond, something in the end not discoverable. If time, on the other hand, is broken into smaller bits, then each bit in order to be a unit of time must have duration within it. Otherwise paradoxically duration-less and stationary unit of time will be said to explain duration, an everflowing stream which time is. If every 'now' has duration within it, then it has the internal fission of before and after, past-present-future. Every *now* then consists of nows. So we never catch the now, the so-called self-contained unit of time.

> If they are not duration, they do not contain an after and before, and are by themselves outside of time.[3]

---

1. AR, p. 32.
   Of course, space is only logically, infinitely divisible, but in practice, we do take same arbitrary units for our convenience. We must not confuse analytical with factual use of the term 'space', which confusion was caused by Zeno.
2. AR, p. 32.
3. AR, p. 35.

Thus, time is a relation between events and yet there can be no self-contained, durationless units of time between which relation can be established. So time is and yet is not a relation. Hence, both space and time are self-contradictory and are at most appearance and not reality.

10.06. Relation: External and Internal

Bradley remained occupied with the problem of relation to the end[1], but he never clearly stated his problem or its solution. In all his discussion he kept to his monistic idealism, namely, that Reality is an organic whole. This whole appears in immediate experience which itself is a whole, though unstable with incipient diversity and is continuous with experience of before and after it, always pointing to the larger whole beyond it. Immediate experience is at once a pointer to and a description of reality as far as it goes, namely, unity beyond relation. No doubt immediate experience, being unstable and fragmentary can never be the whole Reality. So it invites thought for its self-transcendence towards the larger whole. But immediate experience is infra-relational because at this stage diversity has not become distinct. Of course, literally speaking we cannot say that diversity is a part of the whole of immediate experience.

> If we may permit ourselves to speak here prematurely of a whole and parts, then in immediate experience the whole qualifies every part while the parts qualify all and each both one another and the whole.[2]

Almost in same words Bradley writes again about immediate experience.

> You have here a whole which at the same time is each and all of its parts, and you have parts each of which makes a difference to all the rest and to the whole.[3]

When the fragmentary immediate experience is being transcended with the help of thought in the direction of Absolute Reality, it breaks forth into relational differences. For Bradley relational thinking is valid as far as it goes, for daily life and practical convenience, but it cannot give us the whole which is Absolute Reality. This relational thought-construction ultimately must give way to supra-relational whole, the details of which can never be clear for relational thinking, which is the only instrument of knowing for philosophy. In this dialectic of infra-relational (also called non-relational) immediate experience, relational thinking and supra-relational Reality, we have to discuss the nature of relation which characterises every mode of thinking.

---

1. Bradley himself has expressed the problem in AR Chapters II, III, appendix, Note B (Relation and Quality). Last and unfinished article on Relation in CE-XXXI (Relations), ETR-Chapter. VIII. Excellent commenatry of R. W. Wollheim and G.L. Vander Veer with critical discussions can also be consulted.
2. CE, pp. 631.
3. ETR, p. 231

Bradley discusses two kinds of relation, namely, external and internal. For Bradley external relation is found only if we grant the plurality of independent reals. As it goes against Bradley's vision of Absolute Reality, so he rejects the doctrine of external relation. But even internal relation, for Bradley is in the end self-contradictory. Ultimately reality is above all ideality and relation and may be termed super-relational.

If Reality is supra-relational then no relation whether external or internal can be said to be valid. But if we take up the problem of relation independently of the Whole, then Bradley fails to do full justice to the doctrine and fails to reply to the objections raised by Russell, Moore, C.D. Broad, William James, Cook Wilson and others. We shall take up the case of Relation from the viewpoint of Bradley's monistic vision of Reality. From this viewpoint we shall show that relation cannot be understood without terms, and terms too cannot be understood without relation. But relation either with or without the term is unintelligible, and terms too either with or without the relation are equally self-contradictory. But let us try to explain external and internal relation first.

For Bradley any distinction of terms and relation has only a limited or relative validity. In the end, for Bradley, relational mode of thinking is riddled with contradiction. With this proviso, Bradley has defined external and internal relation thus:

> Wherever that part of your term which you select as its essence remains outside of some relation, in which the individual term enters, the relation so far is extrinsic. And on the other hand, where the entrance of the term includes, and carries into the relation, the essence also as in one with the whole term, the relation here is intrinsic.[1]

In other words, if the relation makes a difference to the essence of the term, then the relation is called Internal. If the relation makes no difference to the essence of the term, then the relation is called *External*. The external relation can be conveniently illustrated by cases of spatial relation and the relation born of comparison. For instance, the book is on the table. This spatial relation of the book with the table is said to make no difference to the essence of the book, that is, the book continues to be the book when it is placed on the table or the floor or the bed. Again, Shyama is taller than Veena. This comparison does not make any difference to the height either of Shyama or Veena. Therefore, the relation of being 'taller or shorter than' makes no difference to the height of persons concerned. On the contrary an internal relation makes a difference to the terms related. Terms would cease to be the terms under reference without their internal relation. For example, being a husband makes a difference to Rama, or being a father makes a difference

---

1. CE, pp. 645-46.

to Dasaratha. If Rama were not the husband of Sita, then the whole story of Ramayana, at least of Tulsidas, would become vitiated. For Bradley, any relation between terms is ultimately based on the distinction of terms *and* relation and this is indefensible. Further, internal relations are found *in* wholes and are the characteristics *of* wholes. Now Bradley undertakes to show that external relations are not possible. For Bradley, even external relations make a difference to the terms related.

Bradley has stated the dilemma of terms and relations in the following manner:

> Relation presupposes quality, and quality relation. Each can be something neither together with, nor apart from, the other,. . . . . .[1]

Again, relations

> are nothing intelligible, either with or without their qualities.[2]

For Bradley no relation whatever cannot be merely external, for it does make a difference to its terms,[3] and external relations by themselves are mere abstractions.[4] If a relation makes no difference to its terms, then why should it be called relation at all. If however a relation is merely external then it will require another relation to relate it with its terms. Suppose there is the relation R which relates A and B. But R is as external to A and B, as A and B are themselves external to each other. But if we get another relation R, to connect R with A and B, then R_1 will require in turn another relation R_2 to relate R_1 with R and A and B. And this leads to an infinite regression of links.[5]

But if a relation makes a difference to its terms, then the relation becomes an adjective of terms. But if it becomes an adjective of one term only, then the other term stands unrelated. If on the other hand, the relation becomes a common property of both the terms, then they are not *two* terms, but become parts of one whole.[3] Hence,

> "all relations imply a whole to which the terms contribute and by which the terms are qualified.[6]

So far the criticism of external relations is rather too abstract. But the same point can be made good in concrete instances. It is supposed that the book is the same book whether it is placed on the table or bookshelf. Indira Gandhi is the same person

---

1. AR, p. 21.
2. AR, p. 27.
3. AR, pp. 513, 514.
4. CE, p. 643.
5. AR, p. 28
6. AR, p. 27n.

whether she goes to Madras or Calcutta. Bradley would not admit this. For Bradley every relation makes a difference to the terms related. Only when relations and terms are taken in abstraction, then alone the theory of external relation can be maintained

> For a thing my remain unaltered if you identify it with *a certain character*, while taken otherwise the thing is suffering change....But take them as *existing things* and take them without mutilation, and you must regard them as determined by their places and qualified by the whole material system into which they enter.[1]

If a thing is defined and taken as a series of universal character (quality), then of course spatial arrangement makes no difference. For example, the bookness of the book remains the same whether the book be on the table or shelf. Similarly, if Indira Gandhi is taken as a woman or the leader of a political party, then she continues to be a woman or leader of a political party, then she continues to be a woman or leader of the political party whether she goes to Madras or Calcutta. But certainly, any particular, existing book is much more than bookness. In the same way, Indira Gandhi is much more than a mere woman or leader of a political party. An existing book on the table matters much to the person who has to read the particular book. And certainly the book with an examinee on the desk means much to the invigilator, and this spatial arrangement does make a difference to the existing book. Similarly, spatial position does make a difference to Indira Gandhi when she goes to Madras or Calcutta. When Indira Gandhi goes to Madras, then her political manouvre becomes different from what it takes place in Calcutta. Certainly Indira Gandhi either as a person or as a leader of a political party does not remain to be the same person or leader when she is at Delhi, Moscow and London. Thus, for Bradley, even the most insignificant external relation does make a difference to the terms related if we take the terms in their particular setting in the concrete. Of course, for our practical convenience we abstract a thing from its concrete setting and treat the book as mere bookness. However, if we take a thing apart from its concrete setting then we mutilate and distort it. A part ceases to be a part as soon as it is taken out of its concrete setting. If a nose or an eye be taken out of its place on the face, then it ceases to be the nose or eye. Thus, external relation is true only in an abstract or unreal situation.

Even a spatial arrangement is a gestalt or configuration, and every such whole must qualify and be qualified by its terms. Of course, in science we make abstractions and we establish some law between abstract characters. For example, we say that heat expands, or cold contracts. But why should heat expand or cold contract? Why should not this arrangement or conjunction be otherwise than what it is? Bradley points out that this relation between heat and expansion or cold and contraction is not merely external. It is our ignorance of the wider whole in which heat, cold, expansion etc., are all found.

---

1. AR, p. 517. Italics mine.

Nothing in the whole and in the end can be external, and everything less than the Universe is an abstraction from the whole, an abstraction more or less empty, and the more empty the less self-dependent. Relations and qualities are abstractions, and depend for their being always on a whole, a whole which they inadequately express, and which remains always less or more in he background.[1]

We have shown so far that external relations apart from and together with qualities mean nothing. Let us see whether qualities apart from and together with relations are meaningful or not.

Bradley uses the term 'quality' in place of things or substances for he does not accept the reality of independent things. Wherever possible the world 'term' can be used in place of 'quality'. All along Bradley thinks that a thing is after all a bundle of qualities and qualities have meaning only in relation to a whole. Bradley raises four questions with regard to qualities.[2]

(i) Whether qualities exist apart from some whole.
(ii) Whether qualities can exist independently of relations.
(iii) Whether new qualities emerge whenever there are fresh relations.
(iv) Whether in the case of identity we can talk of any relations.

We shall not take up (iv). (i) will be the conclusion which will follow the discussion of (ii) and (iii). For Bradley qualities cannot exist without relation. At the stage of unbroken feeling there are no explicit relations and qualities. Whenever we pass beyond the state of feeling we have to compare and contrast the various aspects or diversities of feeling. But comparing, contrasting and differentiating qualities with one another and with the whole come under the process of relating the qualities. Qualities have to be different and distinct from one another and this means relating the qualities.

. . . .What is different must be distinct, and, in consequence, related.[3]

So without any further elaboration it can be maintained that according to Bradley there can be no quality without relation. However, once we admit that there can be no quality without relation, we fall into a dilemma:

Each (quality) has a double character, as both supporting and as being made by the relation.[4]

And this is the third question which has been raised by Bradley concerning qualities.

Suppose these are two qualities A and B which stand in relation R. Now a relation in order to be a relation must make a difference to the related, otherwise

1. AR, p. 521.
2. AR, p. 512.
3. AR, pp. 22-23.
4. AR, p. 26.

the relation R will become a mere external relation. And we have already seen that an external relation is meaningless. If the relation R makes a difference to the terms A and B, then what does this mean? It means that A or B does not remain as they were before they entered into the relation R. Now A has two aspects, one by virtue of which we can still talk of A as A and another aspect which being in relation to R has become different. The aspect which supports the relation R may be called *a* and the aspect which has been changed because of R may be called a_1. Clearly *a* and a_1 are distinct and so are now in a new relation R_1. But this R_1 will again make a difference to *a* and a_1, generating in *a* the two aspects of *x* and x_1, and in a_1 the two aspects of *Y* and Y_1. But this principle of fission has no end.

> This diversity is fatal to the internal unity of each; and it demands a new relation, and so on without limit. In short, qualities in a relation have turned out as unintelligible as were qualities without one.[1]

Of course, qualities cannot be reduced to relations, for relations must exist between the terms, and not between 'nothings'. How can we solve the dilemma? Of course, by holding that terms and relations do not exist by themselves. They are mere aspects or appearances of the whole.

> The terms, each as real by itself, are not actual facts; and the relation taken by itself is but one more abstraction.

And while we keep to our terms and relation as external, no introduction of a third factor could help us to anything better than an endless renewal of our failure.[2]

> The terms here once again are no more than abstractions. Taken each as real independently, and apart from some whole, they are things which cannot be found to exist in any actual experience.[3]

Many clever things have been said against Bradley's theory of terms and relation. However, in my opinion these criticisms are based on two mistakes. First, Bradley is not concerned with any actual chain and links. They are good enough for practical convenience of life. Distinctions of daily life, for Bradley are indispensable, but for philosophy they are indefensible. I wish that James, Broad and Russell should have kept this point in their mind. Secondly, for Bradley a monistic view of Reality is alone acceptable. Keeping to this stand, one has to decide whether Bradley is or is not consistent. The next thing could be whether the monistic stand is at all justifiable and further whether metaphysics itself is

---

1. AR, p. 27.
2. CE, p. 643.
3. CE, p. 644.

possible. All these points have been raised with regard to Bradley. Here I would mention one criticism of Russell in order to show both the weakness and strength of Bradley's theory of *Terms and Relation.*

The viewpoint of Bradley is that relations are unmeaning except within and on the basis of a substantial whole and that there can be no independent terms apart from the whole.[1]

> . . . .a relation is unmeaning, unless both itself and the related are the adjectives of a whole. And to find a solution of this discrepancy would be to pass entirely beyond the relational point of view.[2]

Russell keeping to his pluralistic stand classifies relation into *symmetrical, asymmetrical* and *non-symmetrical.* A symmetrical relation is reciprocal between *A* and *B* e.g. 'same as', 'equal to', 'close to' etc. An asymmetrical relation is not reciprocal. *A* stands in relation *R* to *B*, but *B* does not stand in the same, relation *R* to *A* e.g. 'father of', 'husband of', 'greater than' and so on. *A* non-symmetrical relation may or may not be non-symmetrical. *A* is a brother of *B*, but *B* may be a sister or brother. So B may or may not be a brother of *A*. Can the asymmetrical relation be clearly stated as belonging to a whole? can we say that the whole of *AB* is characterised by numerical diversity? How are we to reduce the relation '*A* is the husband of B'?[3] How would Bradley reply:

(a) First, when relation and terms are reduced as aspects of a whole, then they would lose their separateness. All appearances have to be modified in order to be accommodated in the whole. So the relation, whether symmetrical, asymmetrical or non-symmetrical, instead of being sharpened or rendered precise will lose their distinctness.

(b) Secondly, *A* and *B* are mere abstractions. They too will lose their separateness and distinctness.

(c) Spatial relation (as in 'greater than') is illusory, as has been already shown in § 10.05.

Thus, Bradley's theory of *Terms and Relations* can only be indirectly refuted by showing that no monistic idealism is possible. Or, that no metaphysics is possible. It is the latter position which has become fashionable in current streams of thought viz. analytic philosophy, linguistic philosophy, existentialism and so on. We need not take up this large issue. We shall instead proceed with Bradley's programme of dealing with the concept of Self, once more demonstrating that we think quite successfully *with* concepts, but not so *about them.* Bradley, dealing

---

1. AR, pp. 125, 201.
2. AR, p. 394.
3. R. Wollheim, Bradley, pp. 119-120. Bradley's reply, CE, p. 672.

with the concept of self not only further elaborates and elucidates his analysis of current metaphysical concepts, but shows his own unique sceptical stand in opposition to other idealists, notably T.H. Green and Edward brothers.

10.07. The Concept of Self

The concept of self has loomed large in philosophy from its very inception, both in the East and West. Socrates started his philosophical mission with the Delphic oracle 'Man! know thyself' and the burden of the Upanishadic teaching is 'Atmanam Viddhi' (know thyself). Descartes laid down his philosophical maxim *Cogito Ergo Sum*. Even the empiricist Locke maintained that we have an intuitive certainty of our own selves. It was Hume and Kant who denied any empirical certainty of our own selves. Bradley maintained this Humean and Kantian tradition in denying the empirical certainty of any eternal self. However, Kant had not only maintained that the self is not an object of any phenomenal knowledge, but he also held that the synthetic unity of apperception is the *logical* condition of any scientific knowledge whatsoever. Hegel went one step further and maintained that the logical or rational is also real. Hence, self-consciousness is Reality itself. We have already seen that for Hegel, the Absolute is the Geist which is the progressive self-consciousness through the whole process of Matter, Life and Mind. However, it was Green who holding to neo-Kantianism maintained that the Eternal Self is the sole guarantee of knowledge and morality. Human beings themselves are finite reproductions of this Eternal Self. So what we know of our own selves in knowledge and morality is surest intimation of Reality in its inmost nature. Caird brothers simply extended this thesis. For them human self is the best example of concrete universal. So the nature of self is the paradigm case of what is to be understood as Reality.

Bradley rejects this notion of self. Bradley grants that in daily life we do take the help of the concept of self and it may be taken to be indispensable for practical life, but metaphysically speaking, for Bradley, the notion of self is full of contradiction and cannot be defended. The denial of the unintelligibility of self takes away one of the best known key-concept of idealism, from Hegel to Edwards and gave a rude shock to morality and religion in which spheres the notion self plays an important part.

Our enquiry into the distinctions of Substance-attribute, Space and Time have led us to conclude that these distinctions or the categories are not self-consistent. This conclusion certainly can be extended to any machinery of thought which works through terms and relations. In this sense the notion of self is no less self-inconsistent. But this problem deserves to be examined on its own merits. Foreshadowing Freud, Ferenczi and other psychoanalysts, Bradley traced the origin of the distinction of self and not-self to the principle of pleasure-pain. Pleasurable experiences form a group of their own called as self and the unpleasant experiences are rejected to form the solid core of not-self. On this basis therefore an individual carves out the notion of self from the initial blur or what James calls as 'one big, buzzing, blooming confusion'. Even at the level of advanced reflection, the vague mass of organic sensations does constitute the notion of self at least in part, for certainly it includes else besides. At times one identifies oneself with one's body, on other occasions with his wife and children, and yet at other times his works, his country, his friends become one's self. In general, it will contain more or less of whatever in the environment has not been dissociated from itself.[1]

Different Meanings of 'self': It appears that the inter change between the self and not-self is never complete and never static. But for most of us the self is a felt *unity* of psychical existence.

> When I see, or perceive, or understand, I (my term of the relation) am palpably, and perhaps even painfully, concrete. And when I will or desire, it surely is ridiculous to take the self as not qualified by particular psychical fact.[2]

Average Self. But even if we grant that the self is a unity of psychical existence, can we catch it at any one moment? Surely whatever notion we may have of our momentary self, it never remains self-contained but leads to something beyond itself. Nobody can identify his self with his passing mood, passions, perception etc. Can we then take the average mass of what constitutes the self at different periods of man's life? The average self will be said to be constituted by a man's habits, enduring dispositions, character and so on. But even this average self is too fluctuating and so there is nothing by way of a self-contained average self. Hence, Bradley observes,

> And yet, when we look at the facts, and survey the man's self from the cradle to the coffin, we may be able to find no one average.[3]

Essential Self: At this stage it might be held that there is an *essential* self which remains unchanged. This was the view of Plato and is the dominant theory concerning the self in Indian philosophy. In relation to this view of the essential self, Bradley puts forward the following dilemma:

> If the essential self can change, then it is not essential, and if it does not change then it is not describable at all.[4]

Hence the self cannot be understood as a windowless monad, for its unity is sundered by diversities within itself.

---

1. AR, pp. 80-82.
2. AR, p. 77.
3. AR, p. 68.
4. AR, p. 68.

However, in the history of philosophy, specially in the idealistic epistemology of his predecessor T.H. Green, the self was dominantly conceived as the *subject* or knower. Against this view of self as subject, Bradley observes that certainly the concept of 'subject' without reference to 'object' is not possible because together they form an organic unity: one is the correlative of the other. And if we give up the abstraction of the subject apart from the object, then the two cannot be precisely demarcated. Much in the subject and object keeps on shifting their place and every feature of the self, sooner or later, passes into the not-self or object. So how can we pin down the subject and call it self? Besides, the notion of self is formed very early in life, but the notion of the 'subject-object' emerges very late in the individual consciousness. So this view of self is too sophisticated to be taken as a primary datum.

The Moral Self: It might be said that so far our treatment of 'self' has been very partial, since we have isolated the self from its social setting. Yet our self is social and every fibre of its being is interpenetrated by social nexus. An individual is bathed in the life of the whole, and as Hegel had said 'a pulse-beat of the whole system, and himself the whole system'. This social is best seen in our moral experience and so let us see whether moral self is not a self-consistent organic whole.

In morality we try to attain the Good in a perfected self. This consists in passing from the present inharmonious self of imperfection to a deeper and fuller self,— from what *is* to what an ideal self *ought to be*. The perpetual healing of the breach between the actual and ideal self is sought through a future, higher self. But no sooner we attain a higher self a further ideal looms ahead of us calling for a fresh effort for a more inclusive self. Morality then aims at a unattainable unity of what *is* and what *ought* to be. The two demands remain discrepant and the gulf between them remains unabridged. The task of reaching perfection for ever remains fruitless.

But surely it will be said that we are thinking of the moral ideal in an abstraction. We are taking too general a view of moral end. It is not enough to know that we have to perform our duties but we have also to know *what our duties are.* And we know what our duties are in a concrete 'station' of life in which we are placed. Every student has some specified duties to perform. So too every doctor, teacher, leader knows what is required of him in his station of life. For this reason in Indian social philosophy specific duties were detailed for every man according to his caste and Ashrama. If it is so, and if we fulfil all the duties in our station of life, then do we not attain perfection? No. First, it is a tall claim indeed to make that we can perform all our duties. But even if we do so, we know that we attain only a broken arc of what was proposed to be a complete rainbow. We become in our particular station of life either a perfect footballer, perfect leader of the Congress or perfect painter and so on. But the task of morality is to become perfect in every walk and every station of life. And this is not possible for any mortal. He can follow anyone ideal and even if the ideal of Goodness is attained, the other two ideals of truth and beauty remain unattained. Secondly, one may have attained perfection in a certain social setting e.g., a person may be a perfect athlete from an Indian standpoint, but he may not be so from the viewpoint of the world-standard. And even if he is a world-athlete, he is so at the present and he cannot claim to be so for the future. Every social setting itself is only transitory, inviting a higher and greater ideal in which it may be superseded or included. Every station of life has meaning only in reference to a social structure. But this social structure in its turn is only a passing phase in a higher and progressive social system. Therefore, even the doctrine of 'station and its duties', says Bradley, cannot yield us the goal of Goodness:

> Every separate aspect of the universe, if you insist on it, goes on to demand something higher than itself. And, like every other appearance, Goodness implies that which when carried out, must absorb it.[1]

But can we rest content with the inconsistency of our moral demand? No, we are led on to a still higher search towards super-morality, in which the ideal is supposed to be attained and the breach between the actual and ideal fully healed up. This is the promise which religious experience offer us. For Bradley, religious experience is the highest, and anybody who demands something still higher, according to him, knows not what he says. But do we reach the unified self in the ecstasy of religious experience?

Religious Experience: The essence of religion lies in having communion with God, who is the embodiment of all values to *afortiori* goodness. In religious experience one becomes one with God and so in that moment of union, we seem to attain to divine perfection. Hence, what we vainly seek in morality appears to be attained in religious communication. In that moment of union we feel as Perfect as God is. But do we attain to perfect unity? Here once again the old dilemma crops up. If the union with God is not complete the finite self does not become the absolute reality; and, if the union is complete, then the possibility of devotion also disappears, since the individuality of the worshipper is lost in the reality of God. So even in religious experience, either we do not attain perfection or else we go beyond religion into a stage of supra-religion.

Again, religious relationship requires that God should understand, will and love the worshipper. In other words, God is supposed to have personality. But any personality remains sundered internally by diverse demands of feeling, will and cognition. So God having personality becomes a finite being. Besides, God's personality will repel the impact of other finite personalities of worshippers, with the result that the total union with God never becomes possible. Hence, both God

---

1. AR; p. 386.

and the religious experience remain incomplete, inconsistent and so ultimately they are appearances and not the Absolute:

> If you identify the Absolute with God, that is not the God of religion. If again you separate them, God becomes a finite factor in the whole. And the effort of religion is to put and end to, and break down, this relation—relation which, nonetheless, it essentially presupposes. Hence, short of the Absolute, God cannot rest, and having reached that goal, he is lost and religion with him.[1]

Bradley did not lack religious conviction, but he did not share religious belief called popular christianity.[2] The highest reality is the Absolute, for Bradley. And the Absolute means that which in the end is related to nothing.[3] But in religion the worshipper is related to God. So the Absolute cannot be the God of religion. Nor can God be the highest reality, for God has will and personality and these are marks of imperfection and finitude for Bradley. Therefore, God cannot be the highest reality. But why should not religion be limited to a finite God, as was taught by Mill and William James? However, Bradley does not believe that 'with lowering of God religion tends to grow higher.'[4]

> And it is an illusion to suppose that imperfection, once admitted into the Deity, can be stopped precisely at that convenient limit which happens to suit our ideas.[5]

But Bradley grants that ideas which best express our highest needs and their satisfaction must certainly be true.[6] This highest religious need consists in realising the supremacy of goodness in worshipper's will.[7] This experiencing the presence of God's will in finite minds, for Bradley is far more than ascribing 'personality' to God.[8]

> The Supreme Will for good which is experienced within finite minds is an obvious fact, and it is the doubt as to anything in the whole world being more actual than this, which seems most to call for inquiry.[9]

But quite obviously it is pantheism and Bradley accepts this.

---

1. AR, pp. 395-96.
2. ETR, p. 443.
3. ETR, p. 428.
4. ETR, p. 429.
5. ETR, p. 430.
6. ETR, p. 431.
7. ETR, pp. 431, 433.
8. ETR, p. 433.
9. ETR, p. 435.

Banish all that is meant by the indwelling Spirit of God. . . .and what death and desolation has taken the place of God.[1]

Bradley, however, chooses to call the highest Reality super-personal and not impersonal.[2]

Bradley knew well that his Christian readers will not be satisfied. But he lays down the condition for any true account of religion and metaphysics. According to Bradley there is a deep-seated desire in human nature for truth, and for rational justification of our best instincts.[3] We want a creed to do full justice to all human interests and which can be also rationally defensible. Popular religion, having its assumption of individual worshippers and an External God cannot be rationally justified, according to Bradley.

Therefore a religious belief founded otherwise than on metaphysics, and a metaphysics able in some sense to justify that creed, seem to me what is required to fulfil our wishes.[4]

And an Absolute metaphysics, for Bradley does this job. However, the criticism of the God of religion aims at showing that no self, not even the highest self, called God can be considered as real. To quote again,

. . . .short of the Absolute, God cannot rest, and having reached that goal, he is lost and religion with him.[5]

10.08. Appearance and Reality

So far our search has failed to find out all-inclusive, all-harmonious sentient whole. Our own selves, no doubt stand very high as they include within themselves a great many things of the universe in an integrated whole. But they remain in the end disrupted from without and dissected from within. Even God cannot escape from contradiction. Thus, the net conclusion so far has been negative. We are left therefore with three alternatives:

I. Appearances alone are real and worth the human effort for knowing and controlling them scientifically.

II. If appearances cannot be held to be sufficient, then we can hold on to the doctrine of the unknowableness of Reality.

III. If the above two alternatives fail, then we can say that Appearances and

1. ETR, p. 437.
2. ETR, p. 436.
3. ETR, p. 446.
4. ETR, pp. 446-47.
5. AR, pp. 395-96.

Reality are intimately related, in spite of the difficulty of understanding this relation.

Science is concerned with phenomena and their laws. For it what appears grouped in a certain manner is a matter of fact. No matter whatever be the value of phenomenalism for practical life, for Bradley it is riddled with contradiction. Phenomenalism may disregard any reference to what is not sensible and it does accept certain elements and relations between them e.g., the relation between heat and expansion.

1. Phenomenalism cannot explain the relation, either external or internal, between the elements themselves, as has already been shown in § 10.04 and § 10.06.

2. Any scientific law has to take note of past and future events with their bearing on the present. But obviously, past and future are not sensible events. And this is the inconsistency of phenomenalism.[1]

3. Facts have to be taken as identical with themselves in spite of changes. If they remain the *same* throughout the changes, then they are universal (not particular facts); and if they differ, then there are no persisting facts to deal with.

Thus, Bradley rejects the case for phenomenalism. Should we subscribe to the thesis that Reality remains free and independent of appearances? This would be the thesis of the unknowable.

If appearances are all illusory, then the natural conclusion would be that Reality must be beyond them and beyond all human experience and thought. But this doctrine, for Bradley is untenable.

If Reality were not knowable, we could not know even this much that it existed.[2] Then, in the manner of Hegel, Bradley states:

If there were any Reality quite beyond our knowledge, we could in no sense be aware of it; and, if we were quite ignorant of it, we could hardly suggest that our ignorance conceals it. And thus, in the end, what we know and what is real must be coextensive, and assuredly outside of this area nothing is possible.[3]

Therefore, Reality cannot be considered, over and apart from appearances and cannot be regarded as unknowable. The position of Bradley is that we know Reality in its general nature, but as finite creatures, we do not know Reality in detail. In other words, we *apprehend*, but do not *comprehend* the nature of Reality. How do you apprehend, the nature of Reality? Through *its* appearances, which things of daily life are. Thus Reality is related to appearances, and appearances are appearances of Reality. But if Reality is related to appearances

1. AR, p. 107.
2. AR, p. 111.
3. AR, pp. 457-58.

we are once more impaled on the horns of a dilemma:

> If Reality is related to appearances, then they are adjectival to Reality and Reality becomes itself a changing appearance; and if Reality does not own the appearances, then Reality becomes qualityless and void.[1]

The thing-in-itself, apart from appearances, has no human interest, so appearances, no matter how poor they be must belong to Reality, and Reality cannot be less than appearance.[2]

> . . . .for the present we may keep a fast hold upon this, that appearances exist. That is absolutely certain, and to deny it is nonsense. And whatever exists must belong to reality. That is also quite certain, and its denial once more is self-contradictory. Our appearances no doubt may be a beggarly show, and their nature to an unknown extent may be something which, as it is, is not true of reality. . . . what appears, for that sole reason, most indubitably *is*; and there is no possibility of conjuring its being away from it.[3]

Is this conclusion a mere matter of convenience? No. Appearances are given by thought, and, thought itself is hidden in the depth of immediate experience, because immediate experience itself has those diversities, nascent within it, which thought renders explicit. Thought-products called appearances fall short of Reality. Reality is super-relational whole and thought is relational. We get a pointer to this Reality in immediate experience itself. But apart from it in our supreme moments of rapture and creative thrust we have a glimpse of what Reality can be in its unity and wholeness.

> The delights and pains of the flesh, the agonies and raptures of the soul, these are fragmentary meteors fallen from thought's harmonious system.[4]

There are two things about appearances, in relation to Reality. First, all appearances, from the lowest to the highest, have to be given a place in Reality. Secondly, when they are so housed, their distinctiveness is lost and merged. Let us elaborate these two points.

Reality is all-inclusive whole. Naturally nothing can remain outside this Reality. The emptiest of abstract thought and the wildest of fancies, somehow ideally qualify Reality[5] and as such belong to Reality. In this all-inclusive, all-harmonious sentient experience main wants for truth and life, beauty and goodness must all find satisfaction.[6]

---

1. AR, pp. 112-13.
2. AR, p. 119.
3. AR, p. 114.
4. AR, p. 150.
5. AR, pp. 324, 326, 328.
6. AR, pp. 130, 140.

Every flame of passion, chaste or carnal, would still burn in the Absolute unquenched and unabridged, a note absorbed in the harmony of its higher bliss.[1]

But no appearance, however fuller and higher, can be Reality. Every appearance is infected with its self-transcendence, on the road of indefinite expansion, leading to a goal where distinctions cease and thought commits a happy suicide. This means that every appearance is given a place in Reality, but not *as an appearance*. This appearance gets transformed, changed and transmuted in the Absolute, a note hushed and silenced in the deeper harmony of Reality. This means that Reality is beyond Truth, Goodness and Beauty.

But, once again, since the distinctive differences would now have disappeared, we should have gone beyond beauty or goodness or truth altogether.[2]

Again, Bradley holds truth and goodness as partial aspects of Reality.

Hence both goodness and truth contain the separation of idea and existence, and involve a process in time. And, therefore, each is appearance, and but a one-sided aspect of the Real.[3]

We have already seen (§ 10.07) that the Absolute is not personal, for personality belongs to the realm of appearance. But, for Bradley, Reality is not less than any appearance. So the Absolute is super-personal. But Reality is in every appearance no less. Thus, every appearance is preserved in some way in Reality, though not in its distinctiveness. Thus, truth, beauty, goodness, personality and all other appearances are found in Reality after they all have been transmuted and transformed. Naturally the question is,

Is Truth or God or Newton preserved in the end? No, then what is preserved? Bradley brushes aside this question. He maintains that *somehow* all are preserved. This question is raised with regard to time and changes no less.

Reality does enter the world of change, but itself is incapable of evolution and progress.

The Absolute has no history of its own, though it contains histories without number. These, with their tale of progress or decline, are constructions starting from and based on some one given piece of finitude. For nothing perfect, nothing genuinely real can move. The Absolute has no seasons, but all at once bears its leaves, fruit and blossoms.[4]

---

1. AR, p. 152.
2. AR, p. 414, the whole page contains the same thought.
3. AR, p. 356.
4. AR, p. 442.

No appearance, in its distinctive feature remains ultimate, yet every appearance, no matter how paltry and trite, fails to qualify Reality.[1] If each appearance is neutralized by complement and addition, then how is its *private* character preserved? Bradley carries this question, like all other idealists, including Hegel. The position of Hegel is that the Absolute progressively realizes itself through nature, life, mind, human history, through great men of science, religion, art and philosophical genius. The Absolute is all this and much more. At each epoch the Absolute Spirit becomes articulate in the self-consciousness of philosophers. Does Bradley mean anything different? In my opinion Spinoza, Hegel, Bradley and Bosanquet, all in their own way recommend to us a life of hard reflections and in becoming richer and fuller as a result of synoptic reviews, they tell us to realize the Delphic Oracle 'Man! know theyself'. The concluding lines of Bradley's *Appearance and Reality* are:

> But I will end with something not very different, something perhaps more certainly the essential message of Hegel. Outside of spirit there is not, and there cannot be, any reality, and, the more that anything is spiritual, so much the more is it veritably real.[2]

We must not forget that for Bradley Reality is *Individual* or Sentient Experience, eternal and yet must manifest itself through temporal events. Though Reality is found in all appearances, but not in the same degree.

10.09. Degrees of Reality

Reality is an all-inclusive and all-harmonious sentient whole. No appearance is all-inclusive, but some is relatively more inclusive than others. And in this sense one appearance may be said to be more real than others. Spinoza too had observed that a mouse and an angel are both modes, but an angel is more of the substance than the mouse is. Expansion and harmony are the two criteria of Reality.[3] Again, every truth, as also every error has to be given a place in Reality. However, error, ugliness and sin will undergo far greater modification and transmutation by addition and complement than truth, beauty and goodness. So negatively we can also say the more an appearance in being corrected or transmuted and destroyed, the less real it is. A stone is less inclusive than life, and mind is much more consistent and inclusive than life. So mind is more real than life or matter. Similarly, the abstract principles of mathematics, for Bradley, are more remote from fact, more empty and more incapable of self-existence than concrete connections of life or Mind.[4] The higher the principle and the more vitally it grips

---

1. AR, p. 453.
2. AR, p. 489.
3. AR, pp. 332-33.
4. AR, p. 328

the soul of things in wider proportion and so is more real than abstract principles. Of course, it would have been much better had Bradley hierarchically arranged appearances in their systematic order like Hegel or Plato. Bradley hints at this hierarchical system in many places.[1] Had he done so, his system would have taken the form of Hegelian system in a far greater degree than what Bradley has allowed. Bradley, has included in *Degrees of Appearances* the full substance of Concrete Universal and the dialectic march of world history.

Bradley admits that the building up of a rational system may appear hopeless, but he feels that Reality owns all appearances in varying degrees, even though Reality is beyond any change or degrees. In one place he frankly admits that finite creatures cannot know in detail how all appearances are preserved in transmuted forms.

> Fully to realize the existence of the Absolute is for finite being impossible. In order thus to know we should have to be, and then we should not exist.[2]

Bradley, in the end admits that on any metaphysical criterion one has to grant that the Absolute *must* be harmonious and the possibility of such a Reality alone admits of reasonableness.

> For what is *possible,* and what a general principle compels us to say *must be*, that certainly is.[3]

10.10. Truth and Reality

Ordinarily truth is a characteristic of propositions, and, logically once a proposition is true, it remains so timelessly. For instance, if it is true that it rained today (on 18.3.1974), then it remains true tomorrow, day after and always. Naturally this truth does not become false; nor does it admit a degree. However, for Bradley truth refers to a *judgment* and a judgment has a mental history. The same proposition of geometry may not be true in the same degree for a teacher and a student.

The truth of any geometrical statement is much richer for the teacher than for his students. In other words, judgmental truth pertains to the growth of knowledge. Even the greenness of grass is much richer for a botanist of grass than for the gardener, because a botanist judges the greenness of grass in the light of his wider knowledge and perspective. Russell and other realists talk of propositional truth and not of 'truth' as it is found in growing and developing knowledge. Naturally the two views will differ, but they hardly seem to collide. Of course, Bradley may

---

1.   AR, pp. 152, 332, 496.
2.   AR, p. 140.
3.   AR, p. 173.

be accused of using 'truth' in an unusual sense. But Bradley is quite clear about his use of the term 'truth'. Bradley tends to use the term 'truth' for Truth, i.e., the ultimate truth and no ordinary man or scientist aims at the ultimate Truth. As Bradley accepts that Reality is one, so for him every piece of information has reference to this ultimate Reality. For Bradley there are no facts, no plurality of facts, so Bradley would not ascribe to correspondence theory of truth. Each and every fact is an abstraction, for Bradley. Tables, chairs, rivers and mountains and all other so-called solid furniture of the earth are infected with their self-transcendence, pointing to an all-inclusive reality. So a judgment is true, if it can harmonise with the rest of other judgments. But can a harmonious fiction or story be true?

This objection is based on a misunderstanding of the nature of thought. Thought arises from sense-experience and divorced from sense-perception it travels far from Truth and Reality.

> . . . .the union in all perception of thought with sense, the copresence everywhere in all appearances of fact with ideality—this is the one foundation of truth.[1]

Thought divorced from sense is merely ideal and most incomplete. Therefore, a consistent fiction is not truer than a true tale, because ultimately a fiction in order to be true has to be grounded in facts. On the other hand, even the most imaginary idea has its root in reality and does ideally qualify reality. Only to be true of reality it will stand in need of much correction and modification. But every idea, no matter however abstract has its root in the Absolute.

> But to hold a thought, so to speak, in the air, without a relation of any kind to the Real, in any of its aspects or spheres, we should find in the end to be impossible.[2]

Therefore, any judgment in a work of fiction is not as true as a judgment with its root directly in sense-experience. Again, any fictional judgment is not entirely out of Reality, since it is true in an imaginary world. And this imaginary world is controlled by Reality somehow.

> We treat the imaginary as existing somehow in some world, or in some by-world, of the imagination. And, in spite of our denial, all such worlds are for us inevitably the appearances of that whole which we feel to be a single Reality.[3]

---

1. AR, p. 335.
2. AR, p. 324.
3. AR, pp. 325-26.

Thus, truth does belong to Reality. But truth given by thought is true relatively.

> There will be no truth which is entirely true, just as there will be no error which is totally false.[1]

Why is truth imperfect? For two reasons. First, truth given by thought is based on the distinction of subject and object, substance and quality, self and not-self and so on. These distinctions can never be made fully harmonious. So truth given by thought remains riddled through contradiction. Secondly Truth *and* Reality also form a conjunction without sufficient reason. So Truth ultimately must give up its distinctiveness in the higher symphony of the Absolute.

> To gain truth the condition of the predicate must be stated ideally and must be included within the subject. This is the goal of ideal truth, a goal at which truth never arrives completely; and hence every truth, so long as this end is not attained, remains more or less untrue.[2]

Truth may be relative, but the criterion of thought is absolute, for in denying it we presuppose it. The thing is that in thinking and judging we criticize and to criticize is to use a criterion. The absolute criterion is that the ultimate reality does not permit self-contradiction.

> And it is proved absolute by the fact that, either in endeavouring to deny it, or even in attempting to doubt it, we tacitly assume its validity.[3]

But cannot Truth with capital 'T' be the same as Reality. We have already seen that for Bradley this is not so. But have we not defined Reality as that which satisfies the intellect, and does not Truth satisfy the intellect? If so, then Truth is Reality.

> But then, on the other hand, can thought, however complete, be the same as reality, the same altogether, I mean, and with difference between them? This is a question to which, I could never give an affirmative reply.[4]

The one reason is that truth ceases to be truth once its distinctiveness is merged in the Absolute. Secondly, truth is given by thought and through works through the machinery of terms and relations which can never be made wholly consistent. Once these distinctions disappear in the whole, thought to be thought and with it Truth is dissolved in Reality. Lastly, Truth satisfies one side of life. Here feeling

---

1. AR, pp. 320-31.
2. ETR, p. 232.
3. AR, p. 120.
4. AR, p. 492.

and willing remain untouched. So Truth remains supreme for human intellect, and intellect is an inseparable aspect of Reality.

> Even absolute truth in the end seems thus to turn out erroneous. And it must be admitted that, in the end, no possible truth is quite true.[1]

Just as Wittgenstein found that his philosophy is nonsense, so in the same way Bradley comes to conclude that even the Absolute idealism must cease to be absolute.

> Truth is the whole world in one aspect, an aspect supreme in philosophy, and yet even in philosophy conscious of its own incompletness. . . .The absolute knowledge that we have claimed is no more than an outline. It is knowledge which seems sufficient, on one side, to secure the chief interests of our nature, and it abstains, on the other side, from pretensions which all must feel are not human.[2]

10.11. Introductory Remarks on Bradley's Logic

In philosophy vision counts. But this vision has to be communicated. And this can be done through the statements of logic, commonsense and science. Of necessity there is much pick and choose of factual judgments and a certain emphasis and even modification of logic have to be carried out if the philosophical vision has to be communicated in all its faithfulness. Bradley also has a vision of the world as one artistic whole. He shares this vision with other fellow thinkers and has to resort to factual statements of common sense and science. Yet again the vision he had was not only idealistic but of a certain unique type of idealistic philosophy. This could be expressed only through a certain shift in logical doctrines, statements and the traditional teaching. As the idealistic philosophy of Bradley stands opposed to empiricism, so Bradley often turns to empiricism for showing by contrast the peculiarities of his philosophy. So a short reference to the method, theory and facts on which empiricism was based have to be stated, for Bradley's idealism and the corresponding logic are in a large measure opposed to much in empiricism.

Empricisim of Bradley's time: The empricism with which Bradley had to deal was one of Locke, Berkeley, Hume, Mill and Bain.

First, for empiricism philosophy was just essentially epistemology and so one should not be surprised that in the contemporary Logical Empiricism the main function of philosophy has come to be regarded as the clarification of concepts involved in language. For Bradley philosophy is primarily metaphysics. Much of

---

1. AR, p. 482.
2. AR, p. 485.

the difference between the two schools in the past and present follows from this fundamental difference of standpoint.

For Locke and subsequently for the majority of empiricists philosophy deals with the origin, scope and limits of knowledge. Again, the underlying assumption of Locke and Hume was that human knowledge can be best studied from what is in the human mind.

Once we equate philosophy with epistemology and the subject-matter of epistemology with what is in the human mind then the natural consequence of this would be the acceptance of the 'plain historical method'. Philosophy, according to Locke must not refer to faith or even reason when the matter concerns simple ideas.

> All that is ever required of us, is the patient, accurate, detailed observation of the things that go on in our mind.[1]

This use of the historical method substitutes psychology for logic. And Bradley aimed at freeing logic from psychology and so the present emphasis on logic owes much to the polemics of Bradley against the empiricism of his time.

Assumptions of empiricism: Though the empiricists of Bradley's time claim that what they say about the simples or elements which constitute knowledge are given by their plain historical method, yet their doctrine about the simples is a theory and not a statement about facts. They assume that the mind in relation to simple impressions or primitive, raw elements is passive, 'a blank tablet', 'an empty chamber' and so on. Mind acquires its knowledge through sensation and reflection or more simply what Hume called 'impressions'. They also vaguely assumed that these impressions are caused by something external to them and these impressions somehow do give us knowledge of them. But they did not clarify the relation of impression with their causes.

Simple ideas as they come through sensation and reflection are discrete, distinct and separate or as Bradley expressed it by saying that ideas are distinct 'repellent units' without any elements of identity and universality.[2] No doubt mind becomes active after receiving the simple ideas and may compound them into complex ideas. But ideas are stored up not as complexes but as simple elements and mind can creatively associate and mould them variously in fancy, imagination and so on. We may for the time being ignore the empiricist's account of vivid and faint ideas to explain the difference between veridical and imaginary knowledge of things. The important point here is that there are universal elements in knowledge. And how are they to be explained by empiricism? Here a chance remark of Locke assumed importance in the development of empiricism.

---

1. Richard Wollheim, *F.H. Bradley*, p. 20.
2. PL, I, pp. 301-02.

Words are general, as has been said, when used for signs of general ideas, and so are applicable indifferently to many particular things; and ideas are general when they are set up as the representatives of many particular things; but universality belongs not to things themselves, which are all of them particular in their existence. . . .[1]

This associationism was fortified by the laws of contiguity and Resemblance, and confirmed the assumption that simple ideas are discrete and distinct and could be made complex by means of association. The same assumption concerning the reality of particulars was extended by Mill when he tried to show that we always argue from particulars to particulars.

Bradley's criticism of the Empiricist's view of 'Idea': As Bradley holds that we infer on the basis of universal and that judgements are constituted of universal ideas, so Bradley comes in clash with empiricism. As inference is an elaboration of judgments and a judgment at least must consist of ideas, so the doctrine concerning idea has to come first in discussion.

The idea for the empiricist is in the human mind. So it is equated either with the actual image entertained or the sensation experienced by the mind. Now Bradley contends that an idea cannot be equated with an image or sensation. He puts forth the following argument. In the first instance, he tells us that we must analyse the situation accurately. Of anything we can say *that* it is and *what* it is, that is, it has *existence* or presentation and *content*. But apart from these two elements in any idea there is a third element of signification and it is this which, according to Bradley, empiricism has ignored. And yet the most important thing of an idea is that it signifies or has meaning. Let us take the idea 'horse'.

When we think of of horse, we might have an image of a horse, and this image may have the various properties of colour, of possessing a mane or bushy tail and so on and so forth. But does this image with all its properties stand for the 'meaning' of horse? According to Bradley, empiricists erroneously identify meaning with the image because they do not pay sufficient attention to the two characteristics to an idea, namely, its *artificiality,* and *generality*.

Artificiality: The meaning of an idea is not an observable quality like redness or roughness. It is something which is given to it and is found in the use to which it is put (PL, p. 7). In thinking of horse we might have an image of a horse. But we never equate the meaning or the idea of horse with its image. The image is only the carrier or vehicle of meaning. The image is made to stand for or to refer to something other than itself.

Again, it is not necessary to have an image at all in having an idea. But even if we suppose that there is an image as the carrier of meaning of an idea, it is not the whole but only an arbitrary part of it which serves the meaning. At times the

---

1. John Locke, *An Essay Concerning Human Understanding*, Fontana Library, 1964, p 267.

mere mane, tail and head of the horse-image are enough to stand for the meaning. Here it is matter of arbitrary convention according to which a particular part or image comes to stand for the idea. Hence there is no natural relation between the image and idea. This is again clear from the fact that in having idea, meaning or thought of a red rose there might be the mental image of a lobster or in thinking of a white dog there might be the mental image of a black dog. We do not apply the whole of the lobster-image or black-dog-image to the meanings of these terms concerned. What we use in signifying general meaning is only a part of the image. And this relationship between a part of the total content of the image and general meaning is arbitrary and conventional. It is wrong, therefore, to say that an idea is an image. The idea is the universal meaning; and at times there might not be even the occasional imagery, and still less can it be said to constitute the whole psychical event. (PL, p. 10)

The mistaken notion that an idea is an image may have some justification in having an idea of a horse, where there might actually be an image of a horse, but this is unjustified when we turn to non-representational symbol, e.g. the language of flowers, where a red rose may stand for love, yellow for jealousy, white for innocence, pink for hope. Here there is no natural relationship between an image and meaning involved in an idea. This artificiality is still more marked when we come to ideas which are mediated through verbal imagery. What is the resemblance between the word 'dog' and the animal dog? Does the word 'dog' bark to represent the idea dog? Here the empiricist may say that the word 'dog' does not in the first instance arouse the image of a dog directly. At first, words are directly attached to dog-images in the mind which in their turn mean the animal dog. So after all verbal idea, according to the empiricists, work through the symbolism of images.

> But even if this account be true, it still of course leaves open the problem how word can be attached to mental images and so goes no way towards establishing a 'natural' theory of symbolism.[1]

In one place Bradley tells us that it is a matter of doubt whether in every idea some image has actually been noticed. Here we are reminded of the findings of the Wurzburg school which holds the possibility of imageless thinking. Bradley does not refer to that theory of imageless thinking, but tells us that the role of imagery in actual thinking has been greatly exaggerated.[2] But the more important point in the refutation of the doctrine that every idea is but an image lies in holding that an idea is universal and so cannot be a particular psychical existent.

Generality or Universality of an idea: The empiricist of Bradley's time held that an idea is but a particular image,

1.   Willheim, R., *Ibid.*, p. 30.
2.   PL, pp. 38-39.

and that generality occurs only when, in the interests of economy, this relation is extended to include similar images and similar objects.[1]

Bradley agrees that an idea refers to a number of instances coming under a class. The idea horse refers to a number of horses forming the class horse. The difference lies in this that according to empiricists the idea horse refers to '*a*' by way of association and this again to *b*, *c* and so on. In this associative arousal we pass from particulars to particulars. Bradley rejects this psychological explanation. According to Bradley the meaning involved in an idea is not the property of any *particular* image or sensation at all. It is possessed by the class and by each member insofar as it is a member of that class. This view of Bradley is most clear in the case of verbal symbols.

When we utter the word 'horse', do we attribute meaning to the particular noise 'horse'? If instead of Ram uttering the noise 'horse', Shyam speaks the word 'horse' then do we not understand the meaning involved in the idea?

> Our concern is rather with the class or universal of which the noise is or is thought to be an instance.[2]

Hence, the word-symbol is itself universal since it is that which is the same in its various utterances or writings. Further, it is doubly universal, since

> the relation of meaning runs not only *from* a class of objects but *to* a class of objects.[3]

The reference to a thing is never to a *particular* thing but to a *kind* of thing. When we say 'horse', the reference is to a horse having certain properties, commonly called connotation or intension by virtue of which the term 'horse' is applicable indifferently to any one horse in general. Even if as a matter of fact there is only one instance of an idea, e.g. 'the present prime minister of India is a short man', the idea in principle is applicable to a number of persons. So an idea always refers to a number of members of a class to each of which the idea is equally applicable.

However, it is not enough to say that an idea is universal as a symbol. It has to be shown that the empiricist account is erroneous. The empiricist holds that A applied to *a*, *b*, *c*, *d*, because of the association of A with, *a*, and of *a* with *b* etc., on the basis of resemblance and contiguity. For example, as soon as the word 'dog' is uttered, an image of a black-gray dog may crop up. Let us call this image A. A arouses the image of an another dog B, because of their resembling in both being grey. B, in turn arouses C because of their having similar bushy tails and

---

1. Wollheim, *Ibid.*, p. 31.
2. Wollheim, p. 31.
3. Wollheim, p. 31.

so on. Now Bradley tells us that the universal cannot be explained in terms of resemblance and contiguity. In order that two images convey the impression of resemblance, they must both be present before the mind. But A and a, or B and b as images or sensations are successive. If A is there then 'a' is not, or if B is there then 'b' is not.

> To talk of an association between psychical particulars is to utter nonsense. These particulars in the first place have got no permanence; their life endures for a fleeting moment.[1]

So now no two fleeting things can be presented together and so there can be no impresssion of resemblance. Therefore, a particular image cannot stand for a number of other particulars forming a class on the basis of the principle of resemblance.

So far we have maintained that no images or sensations being fleeting, once they occur, can ever *recur*; and, if they never recur, they can never be revived, nor can we then have any idea of them. And if there is no recurrence, then there can be no impression of resemblance either. Hence the fundamentals of the associationist stand refuted.

> What are we left with? 'Impressions' is gone: 'recurs' is gone: 'idea of it' is gone.[2]

This argument of Bradley is valid as far as it goes and this contention of Bradley is supported by psychological considerations and other views of James, Stump, Leibnitz and others. Therefore, it is better to dwell a little more on the logic of the argument. The previous argument is based on the principle of resemblance. Now let us see whether resemblance can explain the universality of ideas. Bradley tells us that resemblance instead of explaining universality really presupposes it.

> Resemblance, so far from being the creator of, becomes a mere parasite upon, universals: universals are prior to resemblance.[3]

Here the reasoning is simple. In order that two images or sensations resemble, they must have something in common. But that which is in common with two or more particulars is universal. So on two particulars can resemble unless they have some identical or universal element in them.

So far we have not made any reference to the principle of contiguity because, according to Bradley, ultimately it rests on resemblance. The empirical foundation of associations through contiguity has been thus made:

---

1. PL, p. 306.
2. PL, p. 314.
3. Wollheim R., 37.

"When two impressions have been frequently experienced (or even thought of) either simultaneously or in immediate succession, then whenever one of these impressions, or the idea of it, recurs, it tends to excite the idea of the other." But every impression is too fleeting and can occur only but once. Hence it can never *recur*. Again, the revival of the original idea is also a myth, for as stated already no idea can be brought back into consciousness with its original wealth of detail. Hence, what really is said to recur or what is said to be revived are ideas which resemble the original ones.

> There is, therefore, a suggestion by resemblance—a calling up of the idea of a past sensation by a present sensation like it—which not only does not depend on association by contiguity, but is itself the foundation which association by contiguity requires for its support.[1]

This admission of Mill that the ideas which were contiguous now (e.g. at the time of thinking them) are non-existent and the ideas said to be re-instated have never been contiguous proves fatal for associationism. So really there can be no association by contiguity. But even if we take the help of resemblance, as stated earlier, resemblance itself can work on the presence of identity (either partial or complete), what is found in a number of instances is universal. So the conclusion is that Association is never of the particulars. The true view, according to Bradley is that Association is and must always be of the universal.

> What works in the connection between the universals, and the basis of that working is the ideal identity of some element in what is present and in what is past.[2]

But before we close this point, we should also ascertain the nature of concrete universal to which Bradley subscribes.

CONCRETE UNIVERSALS

A universal, according to Bradley is *not*
1. a supersensuous form subsisting in a realm accessible to intellect alone (Platonic Realism).
2. a subjective concept in the mind of the thinker (Nominalism).[3]
3. an abstract property in things, though not identifiable or putative (Conceptualism).

---

1. Quoted by Bradley, pp. 316-17 from J.S. Mill, *On James Mill* , pp. 112-13.
2. PL, p. 307.
3. Nominalism holds that universals have no objective reality, and have no resemblance with individual members of their class.

A universal is a concrete object existing in nature and given to senses. It has elements or members. As space or time is illusory, so any members regarded distinct through the individuation of space and time cannot be really distinct. A universal is really a system of various parts in which the whole is more than the *sum* of the parts, but the parts are inseparably bound up with the whole. It means that each part is inseparably connected with the other and would not be what it is if others were not what they are. Similarly, if one could know the universal, then one can in principle, know all the instances that come under it. The so-called particular ideas of the empiricists are really the instances, or members or parts of the universal. As parts they must differ, but the important thing about them is that they are identical insofar as they belong to one whole. Of course, in isolation no idea of man or cow is a concrete universal. Logically and consistently there is only one concrete universal which includes all the instances as its indispensable parts. Hence for Bradley there is only one all-inclusive sentient whole, in which all our experiences are harmoniously related. Further, this notion of universal works from the very beginning and is not derived from the particulars.

Judgement: The conclusion of Bradley is that an idea is not a particular image or sensation. Again, a judgment is the first instance consists of ideas, and an idea is not a psychical existent, e.g., it is neither a sensation nor an image nor a fact. An idea, for Bradley, is an incipient judgment which always deals with the universal. Hence, a judgment consisting of *ideas* can never directly assert a fact. According to the empiricist's theory of psychological atomism each sensation or idea is a distinct entity and each judgment expresses one atomic fact. Bradley rejects this view and tries to show that no judgment can directly succeed in asserting a fact. There are three kinds of judgments according to relation, namely, categorical, hypothetical and disjunctive. In disjunctive propositions there is either-or, e.g. This is either a mouse or a mole. But no fact is of the nature of either-or. So a disjunctive proposition can never directly assert a fact. A hypothetical proposition has 'if-then' e.g. it deals with supposals and a supposal is not an actual state of affairs. So a hypothetical too does not assert a fact directly. Now a categorical proposition is either singular or universal, affirmative or negative. But a negative judgment, at least on the very face of it denies a fact and does not directly[1] assert a fact.

Further, we shall find that all universal judgments are really hypothetical. For example, 'All men *are* mortal' really means 'If men, then they are mortal'. But a hypothetical does not directly assert a fact, so a universal being really hypothetical cannot directly assert a fact. So we are left with one type of judgments, namely, categorical singular judgments.

(A) Singular judgment is of three kinds, namely,

---

1. Of course, Bradley maintains that every negation implies an affirmation. However, here the main contention is not refuted by this admission.

1. Analytic judgment of sense.
2. Synthetic judgment of sense.
3. A judgment which deals with a reality which is never a sensible event either in space or time e.g. 'God is a spirit'.

We can omit the third class of singular judgments, since they deal with an entity which is not in time or space. So obviously it is not a fact. Hence we can deal with the analytic and synthetic judgments of sense only. An analytic judgment of sense makes an assertion about that which we feel or perceive, e.g., 'I have a toothache' or 'this is a white wall'. A synthetic judgment of sense states either some fact of time or space or again some quality of the matter given, which we do not here and now directly perceive e.g. 'This road leads to Delhi'. Quite obviously if we have to show that a judgment directly asserts a fact then this claim is strongest in relation to the analytic judgement of sense. However, if we can show that even the analytic judgment of sense cannot directly assert a fact then we conclusively refute the empiricist's thesis that there are atomic facts which are asserted in atomic judgments.

Bradley takes up the case of analytic judgments of sense and shows that it never succeeds in asserting a fact. The so-called facts to which reference is made in Analytic judgments are no facts at all. They always refer to something which transcend them and ultimately to an all-inclusive, all-harmonious whole. So once again the empiricist's thesis of pluralistic atomism is rejected in favour of a monistic *Weltanschauung*. But no where the empiricist's thesis appears to be more reasonable than in explaining judgments in terms of subject, predicate and copula. Bradley rejects the thesis that a judgement is a relation between two ideas in which one idea is subject and the other is predicate. Bradley rejects the contention that there is a grammatical subject in every judgment because, the acceptance of such a view would logically support pluralism. As each grammatical subject is said to be a substance and as there are many grammatical subjects, so it would mean that there are many self-contained substances or things. Hence Bradley rejects the theory that in every judgement there is a grammatical subject.

> By the subject I mean here not the ultimate subject, to which the whole ideal content is referred, but the subject which lies within the content, in other words the *grammatical* subject.[1]

But he does not totally reject the subject-predicate view of judgments. According to him there is really only one ultimate subject of every judgment. As a matter of fact all ordinary judgments are adjectival to or are predicates of one subject called the Absolute Reality. Take the judgment 'This wall is white' or 'All horses are mammal'. Ultimately, according to Bradley, they mean, 'The Absolute reality

1. PL, p. 22.

is such that this wall is white. OR, The Absolute Reality is such that all horses are mammal.'

'Once again the upshot of Bradley's theory of judgment is monistic idealism. Hence, it is not logic which constitutes philosophy but it is the philosophy of philosophers which moulds logic. In this sense, the logic of Bradley is inseparable from his metaphysics, with this introduction let us deal with the Logic of Bradley.

Summary of the Introduction to the theory of Judgment : Bradley's idealism is monistic and monism cannot be established without the refutation of pluralism. As the most important pluralistic system of Bradley's time was empiricism, so Bradley rejects the pluralistic account of judgment and knowledge.

I. Empiricism is mainly based on two assumptions.

(*a*) All ideas are particular and distinct and the external connection between the ideas is achieved through association.

(*b*) In a judgment the predicate says something about a substantival subject. As there are many judgments, so there are many substantival subjects (Aristotle). Hence, there is a plurality of individual things.

Now any theory of knowledge and judgment should be able to explain scientific knowledge, the most important characteristic of which is universality. The empiricist explains universality in terms of Association which works according to the principles of Contiguity and Resemblance. As Contiguity ultimately rests on Resemblance, so resemblance should be able to explain the universal element in knowledge. Resemblance between two ideas is possible only when both the ideas are present together. However, mental processes are successive. Therefore, no two ideas can be found together simultaneously. Besides, once an idea occurs, it can never recur. So resemblance between two momentary ideas is absurd.

Further, instead of resemblance explaining universality, it is universality which explains resemblance. Again, contiguity depends ultimately on the resemblance of revived images. Therefore, if resemblance fails to account for universality and connection between ideas, then the empiricist assumption concerning plurality of discrete, separate and distinct impressions as their starting-points miserably fails.

II. Bradley's proposal is that ideas are universal, and the most distinctive feature of ideas is their meaning which is universal. This follows from the artificiality and generality of meaning which an idea has.

A judgment is the explicit elaboration of an idea. So like an idea a judgment is also universal and does not *directly* assert any particular fact. The judgment with the strongest claim to asserting fact is called the Analytic Judgment of Sense. Here Bradley shows that the analytic judgment of sense fails to assert any fact directly. Of course, like any other judgment, the analytic judgment of sense refers ultimately to the Supreme Reality which is really the implied and implicit subject of every kind of judgment.

III. It might be pointed out, against the view of Bradley that in every judgment there are three elements, namely, the subject, Predicate and the Copula. If subjects be there necessarily, then certainly corresponding to them there are so many independent facts.

Bradley rejects the view that the three elements of subject, predicate and copula are necessary for any judgment. According to Bradley, for the sake of convenience we can divide a complex idea into subject, predicate and copula, but strictly speaking, any grammatical subject is not the real subject of a judgment. The real subject of a judgment is the Supreme Reality, and the whole of the grammatical judgment is the predicate of, and is adjectival to the Supreme Reality. The valid form in every case is

Reality / is / such that S is P

IV. Bradley maintains that knowledge begins with vague universal given in immediate experience. This immediate experience itself is unstable and invites thought to transcend it in the larger whole of which the immed'ate experience is indicator and pointer. Thought comes in the form of a judgment making implicit distinction explicit in the form of subject and predicate. But thought of its very nature can give us only appearance and not reality, even though by its absolute criterion of all-inclusiveness and all-harmoniousness it points towards Reality in which all the distinctions made by thought are merged and silenced. So no judgment can assert any fact directly.

10.12. The Nature of Judgment

According to Bradley, a judgment is a synthesis of ideas claiming truth. Hence, it has two elements, namely,

(*a*) it consists of an ideal content.

(*b*) which has reference to reality. Therefore, Bradley defines it thus:

Judgment proper is the act which refers an ideal content (recognised as such) to a reality beyond the act.[1]

Now in explaining the nature of judgment, Bradley always has the empirical thesis in the background, in contrasting with which he wants to make his own theory clear. The empiricist tends to equate an idea or a thought with an image or a sense-impression. And an image of sense-impression is a psychical fact. Bradley is opposed to this view and tries to refute the empiricist's thesis and shows that the most important element in an idea is its meaning or signification and this is a universal and can never be any particular given fact, whether an image or a sense-impression.

Idea: In the first instance an idea should not be confused with a fact or a sensation or an image. True, in every idea there is an element which has been

---

1. PL, 10.

selected, taken and cut out of a fact or of even an image. But insofar as the element is a part of existence, it is not an idea. Only when it comes to stand for something or things beyond itself or when it is universal that it has meaning and then it becomes an idea. For example, everything of the green flag is not attended to by the driver. He ignores the holes, the texture, the material and even the faintness of the colour. All that matters to him is the *green* flag and that means for him the signal for starting the train. Certainly the element of green is a part of the fact. But that it is a part of an existing fact is immaterial for an idea having meaning. When we use the term 'rose', it may stand for many particular rose flowers and it may also signify hope and love. But the term 'rose' does not mean or stand for any particular rose is clear at least in those cases where it signifies love and hope. But even apart from this arbitrary meaning, the term 'rose' does not mean any particular rose. When it stands for all other roses, it leaves its particularity and individuality.

> . . . .it stands as an adjective, to be referred to some subject, but indifferent in itself to every special subject.[1]

When we say 'rose', we do not mean *this* rose just now in the hand. Even the particular sound 'rose' has nothing to do with the meaning which this term has. Hence, 'idea' when it is a symbol and has meaning is indifferent to any physical existence (e.g., the sound of the term rose) or any psychical image (e.g., the image of a rose). It does not exist. That is its loss. It loses the sting and the pungency of the reality. But

> by merging its own quality in a wider meaning, it can pass beyond itself and stand for others.[2]

That is its gain in width and breadth. The redness of the rose stands for a great many other red things like a book, a piece of paper, a garment and so on.

The idea, therefore, is not a fact, either physical or psychical; but is a part of the fact, considered apart from the existence.

> The idea is the fact with its existence disregarded, and its content mutilated. It is but a portion of the actual content cut off from its reality, and used with a reference to something else.[3]

Facts and ideas are related and yet are distinct.

> A fact is individual, an idea is universal; a fact is substantial, an idea is adjectival; a fact is self-existent, an idea is symbolical.[4]

1. PL, p. 6.
2. PL, p. 4.
3. PL, pp. 45-46.
4. PL, pp. 43-44.

Now if a judgment consists in an ideal content, then it refers to something beyond the given fact, for an idea transcends the immediately given. But a judgment must have reference to reality, otherwise it cannot be true or false. And unless a judgment be such which can be true or false, it cannot be a judgment at all. And truth and falsehood, according to Bradley, depend on the relation of ideas to reality.

> We not only must say something, but it must also be about something actual that we say it. For consider; a judgment must be true or false, and its truth or falsehood cannot lie in itself. The involve a reference to something beyond. And this, about which or of which we judge, if it is not fact, what else can it be?[1]

Though, Bradley interchangeably uses the terms 'fact' and 'reality', yet he does not mean that the two are identical. There is a vast difference between 'a fact' and reality. A fact is that which is given in our immediate experience. Though a fact reveals the reality, it is by itself too fragmentary to be taken as the whole of reality. But we contact the reality only through what is given to us in our immediate experience. Hence, the fragmentary element of the reality which is in our immediate contact is fact. Hence, in a judgment we refer an ideal content in the first instance to a fact, but in doing so we always make reference to the absolute reality. For instance, when we say 'All horses are mammal', we refer to individual horses which are mammal. We trust that the mammality of horses is true of the actual state of affairs. But the true reference, according to Bradley is to the reality as a whole. The implication of the above judgment is that the reality is such that horses are mammal. In other words, the whole of a judgment is an adjective which qualifies the reality. And, secondly, we think that the reality is so qualified, independently of and even apart from our way of judging it. In other words our thinking does not constitute the reality, though it takes cognizance of the reality. In our judgment 'Horses are mammal' we perceive

> that the relation (of the complex ideal content concerning the mammality of horses and the reality) thus set up is neither made by the act, nor merely holds within it, or by right of it, but is real both independent of and beyond it.[2]

So far we have interpreted the clause 'beyond the act' by holding that the judgment is not confined to ideas alone but refers to something independently of them, in relation to which a judgment may be called true or false. Secondly, by 'beyond the act' is meant that the nature of reality described by the judgment does not depend on our thinking. Later on we shall find that Bradley would maintain that

---

1. PL, p. 41.
2. PL, p. 10.

no ideal content, however exhaustive, can yield an individual fact. Further, the reference to an immediately given fact is never final, since the immediately given is extremely relative to and hopelessly dependent on the surrounding particular. The so-called perceptual fact invites its own self-transcendence. The nature of·the ideal content will become still more clear if we go through the various theories of judgment. Now we cannot ascertain the correct view as long as we do not expose the errors of false ones. So we shall take up some erroneous theories of judgment, according to Bradley.[1]

The erroneous theories of judgment have been roughly put under two heads, namely,

1. Those which in some sense hold that a judgment consists of subject, predicate and copula, and,
2. Those which labour under other defects.

Let us take the second first.

(I) Judgment is an association of an idea with a sensation or depends on liveliness or strength of an idea or ideas.

There are three points in the above-mentioned erroneous theory,

1. A judgment is an idea or a group of ideas.
2. Its truth depends on the liveliness or strength of an idea or ideas.
3. A judgment is an association of ideas.

Bradley rejects all these points.[2] First, the idea is universal and cannot be an existing psychical event, either as an image or a sensation or a complex of sensation and image. As long as anything *is*, it is not an assertion, and if there is an assertion, it always goes beyond the given fact. An image or a juxtaposition of an image and of a sensation is mere *is*, 'but does not stand for anything, and which exists, but by no possibility could be true.'[3]

In other words, a sensation is a felt existence and a judgment is the relation of an idea to a reality beyond the given fact. So a mere idea by itself is an existent, but no judgment at all. Later on, it was held by the empiricists and others that a sense-datum is a mere occurrence and by itself is incorrigible. In the same sense, Bradley means that only when an idea is related to something else, a fact or reality, then it can be alone true or false. Otherwise, it is a mere incorrigible occurrence.

Secondly a judgment is not an association, since there may be association, and yet there may be no judgment and where ideas become adequate for judgment there may be no association. Suppose two things like headache and a syllogism coexist, or are contiguous, but where is the judgment? Is syllogism the predicate of headache? The mere fact of coexistence of two phenomena is no assertion at all.

---

1. In refuting false theories here Bradley refers to the two characteristics of a judgment. First, that it goes beyond the act of judging itself. Secondly, in a judgment there is the question of truth and falsity.
2. Here we have to note that for the associationist the idea is a psychic particular, and for Bradley an idea is essentially meaning or universal.
3. PL., p.14.

Again, an association means the bringing together of particular, hard and distinct facts. For example, in an idea of an orange, there are sensations of coloured patches with images of softness, taste and so on. Now each of these sensations and images

is a hard particular, and qualified by relations which exclude it from all others. If you simply *associate* this bundle of facts who would take them as one fact?[1]

It would be mere juxtaposition of repellent particulars. But a judgment is the real unit of thinking and so is one unitary though a complex fact, according to Bradley.

And if you blend them by ignoring their particularities, then where is the association? Since the hard particularities and sensations and images are excluded, so really there are no sensations and images x, y, y^1, y^2. Besides, if sensations and images are blended together in a single presentation then where is the assertion of truth and falsehood? The given presentation is a mere fact, a mere *is*. However, in order to be true or false, the complex presentation has to be related to something else. There must be reference to something real and this reference is absent here.[2]

Does liveliness add anything? A belief, according to Hume, is based on living and vivid ideas and so liveliness contributes to truth. Let the image of a dead person yet strong enough to secure a hallucination, will this lively idea be called true? This hallucination

could not be judged to be outwardly real, any more than the fainter and normal images are judged to be anywhere but in our own minds.[3]

We turn now to another erroneous theory stated by Bain.

(II) A Judgment is a practical belief. (*Bain*)

According to Bradley, every mental process is both theoretical and practical. (Terminal Essay XII, Vol. II, P.L.) Therefore, even a judgment has a practical aspect. But the essence of a judgment lies in truth and falsity and this should not be confused with practical activity. Assume that an asserted idea, an idea believed in causes action and an idea merely suggested, not believed in, does not produce an act. From this does this follow that a judgment is nothing but its consequence?

Against this theory of Bain, Bradley maintains

(a) *The practical influence* may be absent from a judgment,

(b) that it may be present with other facts,

(c) that the fact of judgment contains *other* characteristics which are the true differentia,

---

1. PL, p. 14.
2. PL, p. 15.
3. PL, p. 16.

(d) these true differentia have a positive quality which excludes 'practical influence' as the criterion of truth and falsity.

(A) *Practical Influence is absent*: Let us take a judgment consisting of abstract ideas, e.g., All the angles of a triangles = 2 right angles. Where is an inducement for an action? If the reply is that there are no actions, but even here there are *tendencies* for drawing a figure of B and measuring its angles. But are tendencies ideas or movements? Obviously there are no ideas and no movements. So there are judgments without inducing practical influence.

(B) *Practical Influence may go with a false J:* Even if we do not believe that a worm bites or the cemetry has ghosts, yet the worm or cemetry may cause action in us.

Again, the absence of food may move us to act, precisely because at present the food is not real. Hence, there might be practical influence without the true belief or judgment.

(C) *Practical influence is irrelevant in many judgments:* An idea believed in may exert an activity in us and yet this may not be directed towards making a change in the world and in ourselves.

> Assertion and denial, together with the difference of truth and falsehood, are real phenomena, and there is something in them which falls outside the influence of ideas on the will. It is comic if the judgment. It will rain tomorrow, is the same as buying an umbrella today. . . . [1]

(D) *The real criterion excludes practical influence:* A judgment claims truth and truth is not a matter of degree. Either a judgment has truth or does not possess it. But the practical influence has degrees.

Practical influence is a matter of intellectual conviction. Its strength depends on the wide linkage which an idea makes with other ideas and impulses and the frequency with it is entertained by the mind. If an idea is seldom entertained and that also with hesitation, then the conviction is weak. However, if it makes wide remification and connections and occupies a place of persistent habit and ruling principle, then the conviction is quite strong.

Again, not only conviction is a matter of degree, but it also influences the will in more or less degrees. A strong, persistent and dominating desire influences the will more than a fleeting impulse.

If the very nature of intellectual conviction at the root of practical influence is quite different in nature from the truth involved in a judgment, then a judgment cannot be said to be practical influence. Hence Bradley concludes that

> . . . .the main logical mistake which Professor Bain has committed is to argue from the (false) promise 'Belief must induce action' to the inconsequent result 'Belief is that inducement. [2]

---

1. PL, p. 19.
2. PL, p. 20.

10.13. Subject-Predicate View of Judgment

Now we can deal with the erroneous view of judgment according to which a judgment consists of subject-predicate and copula.

A judgment is a relation between two ideas in which one idea is a predicate of another idea called its grammatical subject.

The whole of the judgment, with its grammatical subject and predicates characterizes the nature of reality. Well, the grammatical subject marks the place or the point at which the reality is in contact with us.

> The natural subject is concrete, and the predicate abstract; the Subject real, and the Predicate ideal, but pronounced to be real. The reason of this is that every judgment is the connection of parts in a whole and to be a whole is the characteristic of reality.[1]

So every judgment with a grammatical subject and a predicate refers to the larger whole of which the ordinary judgment becomes adjectival. Hence, we can conclude here that the relation between Subject and Predicate is within an idea, and not between ideas. Therefore, the whole explicit content, Subject and Predicate together can be regarded as predicate of the Absolute Reality.[2]

First, the explicit *predicate* is more necessary than the *explicit subject*. For instance, in one-worded judgments like 'wolf', or 'fire'; or, in impersonal propositions 'It is raining', 'It is hot', there is hardly any explicit subject.[3]

Of course, there are also such judgments as 'Matter exists', where there is subject but hardly any predicates. However, Bosanquet brushes aside such judgments on the ground of their highly artificial character.[4]

> Except, however, in the case of these peculiarly abstract and reflective assertions, it must be laid down that a predicated content is necessary to judgment, while an *explicit* subject of predication is unnecessary.[5]

Here two points may be mentioned. (a) In 'wolf-eating lamb' we may no doubt divide the ideas in such a way that 'wolf' becomes a subject and the other part becomes its predicate. But merely confined to the ideas, the relation is the same whether I affirm or deny or doubt or ask.

> The *differentia* will be found in what differences the content, as asserted, from the content as mereley suggested.[6]

---

1. Essentials, p. 108.
2. Essentials, pp. 109-10.
3. Essentials, p. 100.
4. Essential, p. 101.
5. Essentials, p. 101.
6. PL, p. 13.

And this cannot be done without reference to the reality beyond the ideal content. So not an idea treated as the grammatical subject is a subject, but the reality to which the whole ideal content is referred is the real subject. The implication of the above judgment is that the reality is such the the wolf eats the lamb.

(b) Further, the doctrine concerning the grammatical subject as the subject in a judgment can be refuted in the light of the following instances 'A and B are equal'. 'A is south of B'.

It is unnatural to take A or B as the subject and the residue as predicate.[1]

This difficulty of finding out the subject is great in relation to such a judgment as 'there is nothing here'. A few more consideration are also pertinent to the subject.

(i) At times it is pointed out that a judgment is inclusion in or exclusion from *a class.*

Bradley rejects this view because it is opposed to the fact. For example in saying 'this is my best coat', or '*B* is to the right of *C*', nobody is thinking of the class of best coats, or the class of B's.

(ii) Similarly, a judgment cannot be said to be inclusion in, or exclusion from, the *subject.*

In instances like '*A* is simultaneous with *B*', '*C* is to the east of *D*', or '*E* is equal to *F*' it is unnatural to think of *A, C,* or *E* as sole subjects. Here the position can be as easily reversed. Of course, artificially we can reduce the sentence to the form of subject-attribute relationship. We can say that 'Simultaneous with *B*' is the attribute of *A*. But even this artificiality is difficult to sustain in relation to such existential judgments as 'Nothing is here'.

(iii) The above-mentioned erroneous views have led to the equational theory of Jevons. According to it subject and predicate are identical or equal. This theory has both important elements of truth and error. So let us turn to it carefully.

Equational theory of Judgment: First, equality is a term which can legitimately be applied to cases of *quantity* only. It would be a mistake to talk of equality with reference to quality. So let us use the term equality for 'an identity in respect of quantity'. In this sense, at least in case of *some* judgments the equational theory becomes absurd. For instance, 'Hope is dead'. Does this mean that 'in hope and a fraction of dead things there is exactly the same sum of units'? But apart from this refutation, let us quantify the predicate and examine the equational theory more closely. Further, let us assume that equality means that the units of the subject and predicate are identical in *quantity*. Hence, the proposition

'All Negroes are men' really means

'All Negroes are some men', i.e.

All Negroes=Some men.

Now does identity in quantity here mean (a) likeness? No. Iron=Some metal' can hardly mean 'Some mental is similar to iron.' If 'similar' or 'like' means quantitative identity then 'A is *like* B' would mean that one can be written for

1. PL, p. 13.

the other. But this is absurd. We cannot use the term 'some metal' for 'iron'. For example, in relation to a building structure we cannot say 'use some metal' for 'iron'.

(*b*) If, however, equal means identity in some points of quality, then we have to specify these very points. We shall meet this point again.

(*c*) Suppose 'Negroes= Some men'. But does 'some men' always stand for the Negroes? Not at all. Certainly Indian, Chinese, Germans are as much 'some men'. So 'some men' quite certainly are not 'Negroes'. Will the matter improve if we use quantitative fraction? If we say $A=1/3$ of men. Hence, we cannot maintain the identity in quantity of subject and predicate.

> The quantification of the predicate is a half-hearted doctrine, which runs against facts, if "=" does mean *equal*, is ridiculous if '=' comes to be no more that plain 'is', and is downright false if '=' stands for '*is the same as*.'[1]

It might be retorted here that the point raised in that 'Negroes=Some men' becomes false because we quantify the predicate only. To be precise we must also *specify* it. Instead of 'All Negroes =Some men', we have to specify the predicate and say 'Negroes=Negro-men', 'iron=Iron=metal'. On the face of it the predicate is the same as the subject. However, is it true?

If 'iron-metal' is the same as 'iron', then it is misleading to set down the two terms as different. But, if the two terms are different, then it is false to put the sign '='. The difficulty may be put in the form of a dilemma :

> If you predicate what is different you ascribe to the subject what it is *not*; and if you predicate what is *not* different, you say nothing at all.[2]

Hence we can say that a judgment cannot be said to consist of two ideas, one of which is the subject.

> We take an ideal content, a complex totality of qualities and relations, and we then introduce divisions and distinctions, and we call these products separate ideas with relations between them.

> And this is quite unobjectionable. But what is objectionable, is our then proceeding to deny that the whole before our mind is a single idea. . . .the relations between the ideas are themselves ideal. . . .And the whole in which they subsist is ideal, and so one idea.[3]

(For another question relating to this topic please see the Questions.)
We have held so far that an ideal content is complex which admits of division and distinction. But can there not be a simple idea which asserts and expresses

1. PL, p. 24.
2. AR, p. 17.
3. AR, p. 11.

an individual thing? Here Bradley does not accept the empirical doctrine of simple impressions and departs from the sense-data language. Instead, he starts with the immediately given which though may be unparted by relations, yet is full of incipient diversities. Secondly Bradley rejects Hume's contention that an idea is a copy of a simple impression. An idea, according to Bradley, can never yield us any 'impression' or a perceived fact. The point will be discussed at great length with regard to what he calls *Analytic judgment of sense*. Now we have to discuss in detail that a judgment must consist of *universal ideal content* which at the same time must be true of reality. Bradley shows this by taking into account all the three kinds of singular judgments, namely,

    (i) Analytic judgements' of sense.

    (ii) Synthetic judgments of sense, and

    (iii) Judgments which deal with a reality which is never a sensible event in time.

We shall take up the first two classes of judgments in order to show the two elements of a judgments, namely, the ideal content as universal and the reference to reality. We shall find that the first point is being disputed with regard to analytic judgments of sense and the second point is not so obvious in relation to synthetic judgments of sense. So now we take up analytic judgments of sense where we shall show that they can never assert an individual thing.

An analytic judgment of sense makes an assertion about that which we now perceive, or feel, or about some portion of it. e.g., 'I have a toothache', or, 'this is a table'. This may be called a perceptive judgment.

10.14. Can an Analytic Judgment of Sense Assert a Fact?

The term 'analytic'

Is intended to imply that there is a breaking and reconstruction of what, in our usual loose way of talking, is said to be given in sense perception.[1]

A synthetic judgment of sense states either some fact of time or space, or again some quality of the given matter the whole of which we do not here and now directly perceive, e.g.; 'this road leads to Delhi', or 'To-morrow is Sunday'.

They are called synthetic because they extend the given through an ideal synthesis or construction.

We shall show that ultimately the distinction of analytic and distinction of analytic and synthetic judgments cannot be sustained, since all judgments transcend the given.[1] We can also note that Bradley has warned us that his terms 'analytic' and synthetic have nothing to do with Kant's distinction of judgments into analytic and synthetic. We can also add here that in current terminology Kant's use alone has gained in currency.

Analytic judgments of sense and the ideal content: True, every judgment refers to reality as its ultimate subject, but the reality cannot be identified with

---

1. Essential, p. 63.

that which appears in perception. The correct statement is that all judgments predicate their ideal content as an attribute of the absolute subject which appears in perception.

> . . .that all judgments predicate their ideal content as an attribute of the real which appears in presentation.[1]

Hence, Bosanquet defines a judgment "as predicating an ideal content of a subject indicated in present perception."[2] In the first instance no judgment can yield an individual thing because it consists of ideas.

> Ideas are universal, and, no matter what it is that we try to say and dimly mean, what we really express and succeed in asserting, is nothing individual.[3]

Let us take an analytic judgment of sense, 'I have a toothache'. The personal pronoun 'I' can be used by anybody Ram, Shyam or Jadu. What we want to express by the term 'I' is extremely unique, but what we succeed in saying is a term which is applicable to many persons. We fail to pin down the term to one *unique* person. In the same way the toothache I am experiencing now is unlike any other pain and in being an actual state in me just now it has an infinite number of particularities which constitute it what it is. This may be true of any experienced toothache of any thing given. However, as a given it is a 'blur' and when we begin to understand it we have to use concepts. And a concept is too general. Now the term 'toothache' is applicable to another man's toothache no less. No doubt we may pile more ideas, such as 'now' and 'here'. For example, we may say 'I have a toothache *just now*'. Will not the judgment be pinned down to what is a fact, just now and here? No, for time and space cannot serve as the principles of individuation. There is no instant of time and no point in space which can exist in their individuality, apart from other heres and nows.

> For time and extension seem continuous elements; the here is one space with the other heres round it; and the now flows ceaselessly and passes for ever from the present to the past.[4]

But can we not fix one moment of time which has neither past nor future?

> But here we fall into a hopeless dilemma. This moment which we take either has no duration, and in that case it turns out no time at all; or, if it has duration, it is a part of time and is found to have transition in itself.[5]

---

1. PL, p. 50.
2. Essential, p. 61.
3. PL, p. 49.
4. PL, p. 52.
5. PL, p. 52.

Ultimately every here is made up of heres and every now is resolvable into nows. There can be no bare position in the series of time or space. We can help ourselves with an image to illustrate what we are trying to express.

> Let us fancy ourselves in total darkness hung over a stream and looking down on it. The stream has no banks, and its current is covered and filled continuously with floating things. Right under our faces is a bright illuminated spot on the water, which ceaselessly widens and narrows its area, and shows us what passes away on the current. And this spot that is light is our now, our present.
>
> We may go still further and anticipate a little. We have not only an illuminated place, and the rest of the stream in total darkness. There is a paler light which, both up and down stream, is shed on what comes before and after our now. And this paler light is the offspring of the present. Behind our heads there is something perhaps which reflects the rays from the lit-up now, and throws them more dimly upon past and future. Outside this reflection is utter darkness; within it is gradual increase of brightness, until we reach the illumination immediately below us.[1]

Two things follow from this imagery, namely,

(i) Our now is the source of the light that falls on the past and future. Through it alone we know that there is a stream of floating things, and without its reflection past and future would vanish.

(ii) True, the now has greater brightness than the revelation of past and future. But we see that the stream is one continuous thing and see the continuity of the element in past, present and future.[2]

The now and here are not confined within simply discrete and resting moments. They are parts of a series. As the problem of asserting an immediately presented individual thing is most partinent in relation to analytic judgments of sense, so we shall take up the thread of our discussion again to ascertain whether a mere synthesis of ideas can ever yield us the presented fact. Now let us describe the different forms of analytic judgments of sense.

The essence of an analytic judgment of sense lies in holding on to what is present now and not to transcend the immediately given. It may or may not have a subject or a copula. So now let us take up analytic judgments which have neither subject nor coupla.

(A) Here the ideal reference is (*a*) to the whole sensible quality, or (*b*) to some part of it.

---

1. PL, pp. 54-55.
2. PL, p. 55.

(*a*) for example, looking at the whole presented reality one may cry out 'wolf' or 'Rain'. In spite of the fact that the subject is not given here there is some statement or some information which is conveyed to us.

> In the 'Wolf' or 'Rain' the subject is the unspecified present environment, and that is qualified by the attribution of the ideal content 'wolf' or 'Ran'. It is the *external* present that is here the subject.[1]

True, 'Wolf' or 'Rain' might not be truly a predicate but only an interjection. But Bradley says,

> An *habitual* interjection soon gets a meaning, and becomes the sign of a received idea, which, in reference to the context, may be an assertion of truth or falsehood.[2]

(B) Again, instead of referring to the whole of the presented reality, we may refer to one piece of the present. On seeing a wolf we may simply say 'asleep' or 'running'. Here too the genuine subject is not an idea, elided or expressed, but is the immediately sensed presentation.[2]

Quite obviously if no subject is there explicitly then there are no facts corresponding to the subjects. Hence, in such analytic J, no fact is directly asserted.

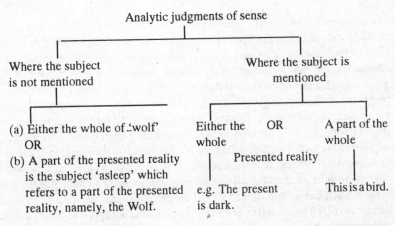

(C) We may now take up those analytic judgments in which a subject is expressed. Here too the real subject is not the grammatical subject, but is *the reality in presentation*. It is the absolute reality of which the synthesis of ideal

---

1. PL, p. 56.
2. PL, p. 57.

elements is predicated through either (*a*) of the whole, or (*b*) of a part, of that which appears.

(*a*) For example in 'the present is dark', or 'Now is the time' we cannot call 'the present', or 'Now' as the subject. These grammatical subjects are mere signs of a reference either simple or embodying implications, to the whole given reality.[1]

(*b*) The same thing is true when the grammatical subject refers to a part of the sensible presentation. For instance, 'this is a bird', 'There is a wolf'. Here too we make a reference to the reality as it is presented in the immediately given. The grammatical subject is no more than a sign of distinction and indication. In such cases too we are not directly asserting any fact, but are referring to the reality as it appears to us.

If we go a step forward and take such analytic judgment as 'this bird is yellow' or 'this leaf is brown', then even in such cases the grammatical subject is not the real subject.

It is not the bare idea, symbolized by 'this bird', of which we go on to affirm the predicate. It is the fact distinguished and qualified by `this bird', to which the adjective 'yellow' is really attributed. The genuine subject is the thing as perceived, the content of which our analysis has divided into 'this bird' and 'yellow', and of which we predicate indirectly those ideal elements in their union.[2]

In other words, 'this bird is yellow' means 'this yellow bird' which stands on par with (A) and (B) cases. For Bradley in principle the 'wolf' of (A) and 'this yellow bird' stand on par. But now we come to proper names which stand for individuals. Should we say that an analytic judgment of sense with a proper name as the grammatical subject directly asserts a fact ? Hence, here Bradley's theory that a judgment consists of universals has to deal with singular judgments with proper names because they tend to refute Bradley's theory. It might be pointed out that there are singular Judgments with proper names and proper names only mark out or point to the presented individuals without reference to the meaning or essence or connotation of these names. A proper name, it is held, is used to *designate a particular thing and no* idea with its meaning can do this (Essential, p. 92n). Any meaning is generic and universal and so proper names are said to be non-connotative (60) because they are meaningless marks put upon the individuals so that they may become object of discourse.

The view that a proper name is designative and has no connotation was held by Mill. According to Mill, a proper name is merely a conventional mark to distinguish an individual much more clearly than by pointing. Bradley rejects this

---

1. PL, p. 58.
2. PL, p. 58.

view of Mill. True, at the time of naming an object we might not have any special reason for calling a person 'Napoleon' or 'Remesh'. But certainly in due course even an arbitrary name gets associated through the usage of that name with some qualities and characters of that which it stands for. For example, the proper name 'Nehru' stands for certain characters and attributes which serve to distinguish the late Prime Minister of India from all other leaders. But in this case, says Bradley, the name does *mean* and stand for the qualities.

Against the view of Bosanquet, Bradley asks: It might be, however, pointed out that a proper Name has a connotation but not a fixed general connotation. Does the person designated remain the same? No, the person is never found in the same set of particularising circumstances. However, the proper name of a man is 'the name of an individual, which remains amid changing particulars'. The person indicated in this sense always transcends the given. So a judgment dealing with Proper Names is not analytic but synthetic. The person really makes reference to a whole series and can never remain shut up within any one presentation in that series.

And, when we take the proper names of 'objects which last and which reappear, then the given is transcended in a still higher sense. The meaning of such a name is universal, and its use implies a real universality, an identity which transcends particular moments. . . . . We could-not recognize anything unless it possessed an attribute, or attributes, which from time to time we are able to identify. The individual remains the same amid the change of appearance which we predicate as its quality. And this implies that it has real identity. Its proper name is the sign of the universal, of an ideal content which actually is in the real world.[1]

So far we have seen that a judgment is a synthesis of ideas and an idea can never yield us an individual fact.

Nothing in the world that you can do to ideas, no possible torture will get out of them an assertion that is not universal.[2]

No doubt we do take the help of ideas of 'this', and 'mine' to get at the particulars. But do we succeed?

It is an illusion to suppose that, by speaking of 'events' we get down to real 'and solid particulars, and leave the airy region of universal adjectives.[3]

The 'now' or 'this' gives us the illusion of getting down to the particular even in our immediate experience, because we think of a series in which one unit

1. PL, p. 61.
2. PL, p. 63.
3. PL, p. 63.

excludes all other units. But this exclusion by one unit of all other units cannot be absolute.

> There is nothing whatever in the idea of a series to hint that there may not be any number of series, internally all indistinguishable from the first. How can you, so long as you are not willing to transcend ideas, determine or in any way characterize your series, so as to get its difference from every possible series within your description?[1]

The designating terms 'this' and 'mine' do not help, for any other perceiver can use such terms with regard to his given events in a different series.

But at this stage, it might be said that the uniqueness of a presentation follows from its being given. The series becomes exclusive because of its appearing directly within this point of contact, or indirectly in the element continuous with this point. So we can distinguish here 'this' and 'thisness'. 'This' is the *that* and 'thisness' is its *what*.

Thisness belongs to the content and stands for the idea of particularity.

> Everything that is given us is given, in the first place, surrounded and immersed in a complex detail of innumerable relations to other phenomena in space or time.[2]

But the particularities coming under thisness are all general. They are parts of the *content* and not of existence. They mark 'the *sort* but miss the thing'.

> No amount of thisness which an event possesses will exclude the existence of self-same events in other like series. Such exclusiveness falls all within the description, and that which is only of this description is simply such and cannot be this.[3]

However, 'this' as distinguished from 'thisness' is a mere sign of our immediate relation, our direct encounter in sensible presentation with the real world. But, can we not proceed further and say that 'this' does not refer so much to thisness as 'the idea of immediate contact with the presented reality? and that

> It is that idea which is signified by 'this', and which qualifis the idea which stands as the subject of our analytic judgment.[4]

True, we are able to abstract an idea of presence from that direct presentation which is never absent. But surely it is recognized as the same and a change of

1. PL, p. 64.
2. PL, p. 65.
3. PL, p. 66.
4. PL, p. 66.

content is separable from thisness and makes a difference to it. Thus ideally fixed the 'this' certainly becomes a universal among universals.

However, a further attempt can be made where 'this' may be made to assert a fact. It may be said that apart from the 'that' and 'what', there is the element of symbolic reference by virtue of which an idea signifies and it is this which constitutes its essence. Now we may hold this distinctive feature of 'this' that it refers to the aspect of the presence of any perception or feeling disregarding the content. We contemplate 'this' ideally, without any reference to the content of that which is actually before us.[1]

But are we out of the wood ? We must not forget that we are judging and in judgment we go *beyond the* given. Can now 'this' refer to something else ? Suppose that A is used to mark not the whole sensibly present, but that only to which we specially attend. If so then it cannot apply to B or C. Now a 'this' must refer in order to be an idea at all, in order to judge in any sense of the term. Now in order that the idea of this be true, A must be present unique.

We have then either two unique presentations, nor one mush disappear. If the first one (A) goes, the idea goes it (the exclusive focus of presentation, i.e., that fact. Call it B) If the last one goes, there is now o fact for the idea to be referred to. In either case there can be no judgment. The idea, we see, is not the *true* idea of anything other than its own reality.[2]

If A and B be taken separately, then this does not apply to both of them, for no two elements can be in the same focus of presentation at the same time. And if A and B are to be taken together, then one cannot be predicate of the other. Both A and B belong to 'this' and there is nothing else to which the judgment refers and in the absence of nothing else besides A and B, thee is no judgment at all.

'This the presentation may be analysed into 'this', the that-aspect and thisness the aspect of its content, consisting of the particularising details. We first distinguish here between

1. 'This' and 'thisness' the content. But Bradley holds that every particularising detail in principle is applicable to other things as well. So thisness fails to describe the uniquely given.

2. But can not analyse 'this' by concentrating on the that-aspect by ignoring how thisness ? Yes, we are here near the given fact, the fact of the presentation.
   But even this meaning of 'this' as something present immediately before consciousness cannot be fixed down to what is uniquely presented, for there are many facts actually presented in relation to which 'this can be used for indicating the meaning of 'immediately given in consciousness'.

---

1. PL, p. 67.
2. PL, p. 68.

Thus interpreted far from describing uniquely given 'this' becomes the universal of universals.

3. But, can we not make a further attempt in such a way that 'this' may be used to apply to the uniquely given ? Can we not hold on to the meaning specified in such a manner that here 'idea' and 'fact', judgment and that of which it is the judgment may be made to coincide? Here might we not say that the idea of the uniquely given and the fact of being uniquely experienced become one? Bradley holds that this is not possible, for a judgment implies meaning and this means going beyond what is given. How can going beyond and yet being confined to the given be reconciled if the idea and fact be made to coincide with regard to 'this'? Further, can two presentations, one an idea and another an actual presentation, be facts of occurrence in the *same moment* of consciousness?

Thus, we conclude that mere ideas can never yield us individual facts. In analytic judgments of sense facts were supposed to be asserted directly. However, if this cannot be done here then Synthetic judgement of sense can do so much less. In synthetic judgments, we go beyond the presented given; we have ideas but no facts. And yet without reference to the reality no judgment can be true or false. So we have to ascertain this reference to the reality.

True, every judgment must refer to the reality and yet hardly any judgement, not even the analytic judgment, can assert a fact. Are these two characteristics contradictory? No, because reality is neither any one of the facts even all the facts taken together. The Reality is self-existent, substantial and individual, but a fact is none of these things.

The (presented) content throughout is infected with relativity, and, adjectivitself, the whole of its elements are also adjectival. Though given as fact every part is given as existing by reference to something else. The mere perpetual disappearance in time of the given appearance is itself the negation of its claim to self-existence.[1]

Yet the reality is presented to us through what appears in the focus. We see the stream through a hole. But what we see of it makes us almost certain that beyond this hole, it exists indefinitely. (This extension or 'beyond this hole' is either an empirical fact or not. If the former it must share its unstability and lack of security with all other presentations. If the latter, then it is a matter of mere blind faith). The Real, then, transcends the given and yet is known indirectly on the elaboration, extension and completion of the given. The notion of the reality is built up by intellectual construction which is based on inference. Reality which can *never be perceived* in its fulness and entirety

exists *for us* connected, by an inference through identity of quality, with the real that appears in present perception.[2]

1. PL, p. 71.
2. PL, p. 75.

That which is presented to us is 'this' which contains a complex detail of times, spaces in a series. This series may be called *c, d, e, f*. The idea by way of memory or imagination may contain the series *a, b, c, d*. The identity of a and in each extends the series in a bigger whole of *a, b, c, d, e, f*.

The whole series now is referred to the real, and by the connection with unique presentation, has become a series of events or spaces, itself unique and the same as no other series in the world. It is thus by inference that we transcend the given through synthetic judgments.[1]

Hence, all judgments, refer to the reality. In this sense, synthetic judgments are not merely adjectival. They are connected by inference with the presented fact.

They (the ideas involved) are attributed to the reality, which both shows itself there, and extends itself beyond. The content of our perceptions, and the content of our ideal constructions, are both the adjectives of one reality.[2]

Presentation and ideal constructions are both appearances, but they are valid and true of the reality. Hence, no judgments can assert facts and yet must refer to the reality. At this point the problem of universal propositions crops up. Universal propositions transcend what is singular or particular.

They are not 'concrete' but 'abstract' since, leaving things, they assert about qualities, alone or in synthesis.[3]

For example, in 'All equilateral triangles are equiangular' it is affirmed if there is the quality of being equilateral then there is also the quality of being equiangular. Here is also the quality of being equiangular. Here the existence of the subject or predicate is not affirmed but the connection between them. And this connection rests on a *supposal*. 'All *A* is *B*' really means 'Given *A*, then *B*' or 'If *A*, then *B*'.

In short, such judgments are always hypothetical and can never be categorical. And the proper terms by which to introduce them are 'given' or 'if' or 'whenever', or 'where', or etc.[4]

Of course, 'All' here does not mean enumerative all which is only a sum-total of singular judgments. For example, if by counting and examining each and every table in a class-room we say 'All tables of this class-room are made of mango wood', then it is really a collection of singular judgments like 'Table No. 1 is made of mango wood', (Table No. 2 is made of wood, and so on. However, barring the

---

1. PL, p. 73.   3. PL, p. 81.
2. PL, p. 75.   4. PL, p. 82.

case of spurious universal judgments, all genuinely universal judgments are all hypothetical. Here Mill has advanced an opposed view. He has pointed out that all hypothetical judgments can be reduced to and in the end *are* nothing but categorical.[1] For example, according to Mill, 'If A is B, then. C is D'can be reduced to 'All cases of A being B are cases of C being D'. Of course Mill, further holds that all categorical universal J's are ultimately reducible to particulars. So Mill's thesis is quite opposed to that of Bradley. But if we carefully analyse the meaning of 'all', then 'all cases' simply means '*suppose* any case'. When we say 'If butter is held to the fire it melts', we are not asserting about any actual packet of butter. 'All' means 'if'.

As a matter of fact, Mill himself holds that in 'All cases of A being B are cases of C being D' what is asserted is not the truth of either of the propositions but the *inferribility* of the one from the other.[2] Now 'inferribility' implies not what *is*, but what *might be*. There is a supposal. It means *suppose* you have A B, *then* you may legitimately get C D. So Mill succeeds in reducing hypotheticals to categoricals only as a result of verbal jugglery. The meaning continues to be hypothetical.

But the statement 'All universal judgments are hypothetical' cannot be easily understood unless we explain the meaning of 'supposal'. A supposition, in the first place, is known to be ideal and known perhaps to diverge from fact.[3] When we say 'suppose there be the sun', we do not mean that the Sun is actually shining now. The fact of there being the Sun is neither included nor excluded by the supposal. A supposal is an ideal experiment with a view to disclosing the latent content of the reality. We only want to know as to what would happen if a certain element were there.

> The connection of the consequence, of the 'then' with the 'if', of the result of our experiment with its conditions, is the fact that is asserted, and that is true or false of the reality itself.[4]

We ask our fried, 'what will you do id you be faced with this situation?' The test no doubt is a fiction and the answer is not a fact. Yet it is his *latent* character that is brought out by his reply. Similarly, the relation between antecedents and consequents of hypotheticals tries to bring out the quality of the reality.

> It is the ground of the sequence (i.e., between the antecedent and the consequent) that is true of the real, and it is this ground which exerts compulsion.[5]

There is a certain quality in the reality by virtue of which the relation between the sun and the light, humanity and morality is stated. When it is said 'If I had

---

1. PL, p. 83.   3. PL, p. 85.   5. PL, p. 88.
2. PL, p. 84.   4. PL, p. 86.

a toothache, I shall feel miserable', then certainly it does not mean that I am suffering from toothache. But it is trying to bring out the *general* connection between toothache and the feeling of miserableness. 'I', 'now', 'this', do not pass into the supposal, but they are so many points to which the ideal experiment is applied. Hence, Bradley concludes that hypotheticals do not refer to actualities or individuals so much as to general conditions which uphold the connection between antecedents and consequents, 'Ifs' and 'thens'. This is not only true of universals and hypotheticals, but of all judgments.

> The real judgment is concerned with nothing but the individual's *qualities*, and asserts no more than a connection of adjectives. In every case it is strictly universal as well as hypothetical.[1]

Now we have to show the truth of this remark not only with regard to universals but also with regard to singular judgments.

10.15. Singular Judgments too Are Hypothetical

(The main argument in outline is that all singular judgments assert conditional facts. So they are all hypothetical.)

It might be held that universal judgments assert qualities which by themselves do not exist. Hence, they are based on a supposal. In contrast, it might be stated that singular judgments claim to be wholly categorical and true of the reality. Of course, this claim has to be viewed with suspicion, since scientific laws are expressed, in universal propositions and nobody would think that scientific laws state less of truth than singular judgments. However, the matter cannot be settled in this general manner. So let us start with the claim of singular judgments as asserting the existence of this content.

Take a singular judgment, 'this bough is broken'. It is said to be categorical because its content is considered to be the given elements, and predicates of the real nothing but a content that is directly presented. The ideal content, namely, the broken bough is attributed to the reality which presents itself to us just now and here.[2]

The crux of the matter can be put thus. The 'broken bough' or any such ideal content is only a fraction of a richly presented whole. The broken bough does not exist by itself, but is found in the mass of outward and inward setting. If the mass of particulars be *a, b, c, d, e, f, g, h*, then our judgment concerning the broken bough is only *a b*. But certainly *a* does not exist by itself.

> It was *in* the fact and we have taken it out. It was *of* the fact and we have given it independence. We have separated, divided, abridged, dissected, we have mutilated the given.[3]

---

1. PL, p. 90.   3. PL, p. 94.
2. PL, p. 93.

But it is wholly unjustifiable, says Bradley, to predicate of the reality a mutilated fragment obtained through analysis of the given complex whole.

> The whole that is given us is a continuous mass of perception and feeling; and to say of this whole, that any one element would be what it is there, when apart from the rest, is a very grave assertion.[1]

But it might be retorted that the analysis does not distort the given inasmuch as it simply discloses the various elements which compose the whole. Bradley rejects this contention. According to him even perception is not wholly true, and cannot be said to copy any actual state of affairs, since it selects and selection cannot but distort. The whole argument of Bradley, so far as we view the matter now, is not an empirical supposition, but is a proposal for philosophers. Of course, the realist and the analyst are perfectly right in holding the proposal, that there are atomic facts. The two kinds of philosophy ultimately rest their case on two different visions of the reality. Their logical postulates too therefore are different. For Bradley reality cannot be anything less than an all-harmonious sentient whole. On this assumption Bradley proceeds thus.

The reality which appears within the given cannot remain encased within it. The given has its outer edges ragged in all directions. The given is infected with its own self-transcendence, backward and forward, for its own completion in the Absolute. Of course, the past and future do not come within the presented fact. But, although the past and future are not within the given, the given would vanish without them.

> If real with them, it would not be given; and, given without them, it is for ever incomplete and therefore unreal.[2]

Of course, if the whole series of temporal succession or spatial points be given, then alone we shall get the whole and entire of the presentation. But is it possible?

> No possible mind could represent to itself the completed series of space and time; since, for that no happen, the *infinite process must have come to an end, and be realized in a finite* result. And this cannot be. It is not merely inconceivable psychologically; it is metaphysically impossible.

Conditioned and conditional: All that has been said about the singular judgment is that it is *conditioned* by and because of a large number of particular details. But a proposition is *conditional* when there is a supposal or an 'if' However, this objection is not valid, for there is no question of *because* in relation to solid facts. Bradley here again refers to an imagery.

---

1.   PL, p. 95 and p. 77.
2.   PL, p. 98.

The given may be compared to a link in a vast chain. No doubt a given may be held fast by preceding and succeeding links. But can we find the last link which alone can guarantee the secureness of the chain and consequently of the given link in the chain ? The chain is such that every link begets another and we can never reach the last link.

> Our chain by its nature cannot have a support. Its essence excludes a fastening at the end. We do not merely fear that it hangs in the air, but we know it must do so. And when the end is unsupported, all the rest is unsupported. Hence our conditioned truth is only conditional. It avowedly depends on what is not fact, and it is not categorically true.[1]

Hence nothing which can be said to be given in sense can be seized fast. The given in the end disappears.

> It (the given) is not self-existent and is therefore unreal, and the reality transcends it, first in the infinite process of phenomena, and then altogether.[2]

Hence analytic judgments of sense are conditional because what they affirm of the reality is incomplete and requires any other things as complements to complete them.

Conclusion: Thus, all singular judgments of sense are hypothetical, because they are really universal. If it were not so, they could never be used as the basis of inference. The singular statement goes beyond the particular, but it must start from the given particular. No doubt inasmuch as the ideal content is ascribed to *this* reality, which appears to us just *now* and here, the judgment is singular. But inasmuch as the judgment asserts a synthesis *inside* the ideal content, it transcends perception :'. . . .The synthesis is true, not here and now, but universally'.

But of course, even hypotheticals are based on reality as it is given in sense. The reality is given and is present to sense. But the proposition cannot be converted into 'what is present and given in sense is real'. We feel the presence of the reality in the connection or synthesis between the elements of the ideal content and we take this ground of the synthesis as the quality of the reality. In science, therefore, says Bradley, the aim is not to record the complex of sensible phenomena, but to establish a connection between the elements of the ideal content. It tries to find out those abstract elements which could enable it to state, 'Given this or that element and something else universally holds good'. Hence, science, following Hegel, Bradley tells us is an idealizing instrument.

At the end Bradley summarises this discussion in the following paradoxical statements :

---

1. PL, p. 100.
2. PL, p. 101.

All judgments are categorical, for they all do affirm about the reality, and assert the existence of a quality in that. Again, all are hypothetical, for not one of them can ascribe to real existence its elements as such. All are individual, since the real which supports that quality which forms the ground of synthesis, is itself substantial. Again all are universal, since the synthesis they affirm holds out of and beyond the particular appearance. They are every one abstract, for they disregard content, they leave out the environment of the sensible complex, and they substantiate adjectives. And yet all are concrete, for they none of them are true of anything else than that individual reality which appears in the sensuous wealth of presentation.[1]

10.16. Negation

The suggestion of the real as qualified and determined in a certain way, and the exclusion of that suggestion by its application to actual reality, is the proper essence of the negative judgment.[2]

The analysis of the above definition will show the following characteristics of the negative judgment. First, the negative and affirmative judgment are not co-ordinate. Take the negative judgment 'A is not B'. Some logicians have tried to reduce a negative judgment into an affirmative form, namely, 'A is not-B'. This is likely to give the impression that affirmative and negative judgments are co-ordinate. Against this view it will be maintained that, 'A is not B' is not equivalent to 'A is not-B'., though negative judgments rest on affirmative judgments but they evolve later and as such may be considered of higher order than that of affirmative judgments.

Affirmative judgments refer to the reality directly; in contrast, negative judgments refer to the reality indirectly, through a rejected affirmative judgment. In an affirmative judgment 'the tree is green', we do not have first to ask, 'Is the tree green?' We note the reality as it is presented to us in perception and we immediately and directly affirm greenness of the perceived tree. But take a negative judgment 'The tree is not yellow ?'. We entertain the idea of the tree being below. This idea is rejected and then we maintain 'the tree is not yellow'.

That negation must begin with is the attempt on reality, the baffled approach of qualification .... Thus in the scale of reflection negation stands higher than mere affirmation. It is in one sense ore ideal, and it comes into existence at a later stage of the development of the soul.[3]

1.   PL, p. 106.
2.   PL, p. 114.
3.   PL, p. 115.

The second important contention of Bradley is that negative judgments *rest on* and *presuppose* some affirmative judgments as their basis. In 'the tree is not yellow' there is not bare denial. Really it rests on the fact that the tree is green or of some other positive colour. 'The tree is green' is the positive ground of the negative judgment 'the tree is not yellow'. Hence, a significant negative judgment '*A* is not *B*' Can safely be analysed into '*A* is not *B*, *C*', or '*A* is *C* which excludes *B*'. This analysis shows that every negation implies an affirmation.

However, there are two forms of negation, namely, negation by opposition and by privation. Privation refers to the present absence of a quality in a thing or object where it is intended to be. For example, this man is blind. Here at present this man has no eyesight, but at any other time, an eye may be grafted and he might see. Here there is no opposed quality which is excluding eye-sight. It is pure absence of a quality. If so then where is the positive quality which blindness implies ? In contrast, in a negative judgment based on opposition, it is said, a subject is denied the possession of a quality not just because of the absence of that quality, but because of the presence of an opposite quality. For instance, 'this tree is not yellow' because 'this tree is green'.

In the light of the distinction between privation and opposition, it might be said that Bradleian account of negation is applicable to *opposition, but not to cases of privation*. In case of negation by opposition every negation implies affirmation; but in privation there is no underlying affirmation, but pure absence. However, Bradley maintains that his account covers all cases including those of privation. Now privative judgments may be of two types, namely,

(a) 'This man has no blue eyes'. This is based on the fact that the man is eyeless. In such instances Bradley would maintain that it is not a case of bare denial or literal blankness. It has some quality, may be indeterminate and unspecified, and this quality is the real basis of negation.

You *must* represent the orbits as somehow occupied, by peaceful eyelids, or unnatural appearance. And so the content itself gets a quality, which, in contrast to the presence of eyes, may be nothing, but which by itself has a positive character, which serves to repel the suggestion of sight.[1]

(b) 'This stone does not see'. Here there is no space which could be filled up by the presence of an eye. It might be held with regard to this kind of privative judgments that there is no determination. There is an absolute blank. And this contention would go against the maxim, 'every negation implies affirmation'.

Bradley smells the difficulty here but tries to meet it courageously. When in such a case we refer to the reality, we know it must be qualified, though perhaps we cannot state the qualification. The stone is X which excludes the eyes and we

---

1. PL, p. 118.

may be quite ignorant of X.

'Ignorance' is privative and in itself cannot support any contention. Why is Bradley so much concerned with the maxim 'every negation is affirmation'? The reason is that he has to support the thesis that every appearance belongs to the reality. Ultimately everything has to be given a place, though it might be transformed in the Reality. Reality's a concrete universal.

> It is our ignorance, in short, and not the idea, which supports our exclusion of every suggestion.[1]

In this context the suggestion of sight is excluded. But ignorance, says Bradley, is never a bare defect, of knowledge.

> It is a positive psychological state. And it is by virtue of relation to this state, which is used as content to qualify the subject that the abstraction, or the ignorance, is able to become a subject of privation.[1]

Thus, the psychological state of ignorance is the positive ground of negation in the case of private judgment of the second type.

Is negation a form of affirmation? We have so much emphasized the affirmative ground of negation that it may wrongly be held that negation itself is a kind of affirmation. Of course, negation does imply an affirmation, but from this it does not follow that we can reduce a negation into an affirmation. In other words, we cannot reduce '*A* is not-*B*' into '*A* is not-*B*'. The reduction of '*A* is not-*B*' into '*A* is not-*B*' rests on several errors. First, according to it a proposition is affirmative when the copula is affirmative, and is negative when the copula is negative. Against this view it can be pointed out that copula is unnecessary. Mere term 'wolf' is a judgment and so is 'No wolf'. There is no need of any copula at all.

Secondly, the reduction supposes that not-*B* is some determinate quality which it is not. At one place Bradley considers not-*B* as mere void which as such cannot serve as a positive ground of negation. Here '*A* is not-*B*' means that *A* is not-*B*, because it is not-*B*. Bradley would reject this, for any infinite term like not-*B* or not-*A* for Bradley is nonsense.

> It is impossible for anything to be only not-A. It is impossible to realize Not-A in thought. It is less than nothing, for nothing itself is not wholly negative.[2]

If it is so, then *A* is not-*B* is a nonsensical judgment. In another place, Bradley, holds that not-*B* means every possible contrary of *B*. Let us take the concrete example 'this tree is not-yellow'. By 'not-yellow' is meant red, green, blue, white,

---

1. PL, p. 119.
2. PL, p. 123.

black etc. In other words, '*A* is not-*B*' means that there is some indeterminate ground for the rejection of *A* as *B*.

In yet another place Bradley asserts that '*A* is not *B*' never means '*A* is not-*B*'. Logical negation, says Bradley, always contradicts, but never asserts the existence of the contradictory. '*A* is not-*B*', according to him, can never assert that the contradictory of *B* i.e., not-*B* is real. The positive ground of negation is an opposite, incompatible quality either in the immediate or ultimate subject.

> But then this positive ground, which is the basis of negation, is not *contradictory*. It is merely discrepant, opposite, incompatible. It is only contrary.[1]

On the same page down below, Bradley holds that contradictory is the universal idea of the contrary or discrepant.

> It is a general name for any hypothetical discrepant; but we must never for a moment allow ourselves to think of it as the collection of discrepants.[1]

If not-*B* refers to some contrary, then it means that '*A* is not-*B*' always implies some determinate quality as the ground of negation.

But Bradley also maintains that negation implies an indeterminate affirmative judgment. In '*A* is nor-*B*' the discrepant ground is wholly unspecified. The basis of negation may be the assertion '*A* is *C*' or '*A* is *D*' or any one of a number of alternative possibilities. Again *A* itself may come to be excluded by the reality. For example, 'the King of Utopia is not dead'.[2]

Thus when Bradley does not reject not-*B* outright, he oscillates between two views, namely, determinate and indeterminate basis of negation. Hence, Mr. Richard Wollheim concludes :

> . . . .Bradley seems sometimes to be of the view that negative judgments loosely entail determinate affirmative judgments, and at other times of the view that they strictly entail indeterminate affirmative judgments, and at no moment to decide authoritatively between the two views.[3]

10.17. Contrary and Contradictory Opposition

At this stage we find that another problem has cropped up. Bradley appears to state that negation contradicts an assertion. But, according to him, whenever we try to assert the contradictory, in fact we assert the contrary. At least we have seen already that '*A* is not *B*' is based on '*A* is *C*'. But C is not the contradictory of *B*, but is its contrary.

1. PL, p. 123.
2. PL, pp. 123-24.
3. *F.H. Bradley*, A Pelican Book, p. 143.

Denial or contradiction is not the same thing as the assertion of the contrary; but in the end it can rest on nothing else.[1]

Then as noted earlier, Bradley maintains that logical negation always contradicts, but the basis of negation is not *contradictory*.

It is merely discrepant, opposite incompatible. It is only contrary.[1]

Now let us try to ascertain the meaning of his statement. It is significant to note that Bradley himself has not made his standpoint clear. Raising the issue concerning contrary and contradictory, he remarks

I do not find it necessary here to distinguish between these.[2]

Contrary and contradictory opposition between two propositions has been defined thus : Two propositions are said to be contradictory when the truth of one implies the falsity of the other and also *vice-versa*. Whereas two propositions are contrary when the truth of one implies the falsity of the other, but *not vice-versa*. Two propositions 'S is P', and 'S is P_2' are contradictories if it is impossible for both of them to be true or false together but are contraries if it is impossible for both to be true, but possible for both to be false. As the predicates in propositions determine the relation between them, so the distinction of contrary and contradictory opposition has been extended to predicate terms. For instance, not-white and white are contradictory terms, and white and blue are contrary terms. Now, according to Bradley, whenever we deny, this denial is based on the affirmation of a contrary quality. For example 'this tree is not yellow' is based on the presence of a quality blue or green or red. And these qualities are contraries of 'yellow'. Hence it turns out at least in the face of Bradley's argument that the contradictory is in reality no more than contrary. Is the traditional distinction between the contrary and contradictory baseless ? We shall find that Bradley does not really mean anything so sweeping.

It is significant to note now in this context that Bradley does not refer to propositions so much as he does to their derivative opposition which concerns the predicate terms. He seems to be suggesting that if 'S is not P' is the contradictory of 'S is P' in the traditional and the orthodox sense, then 'not-P' and 'P' must be contraries and not contradictories. This is clear from the fact that Bradley in the discussion of contraries occupies himself with properties and qualities and their relations, and does not make explicit reference to judgments. This interpretation of Bradley's treatment is also borne out by his treatment of Double negation, i.e., the negation of a negation as an affirmation.

1. PL, p. 123.
2. AR, p. 500.

10.18. Double Negation is Affirmation

According to the orthodox view if 'not-P' be the negation of P, then the negation of not-P is P. Hence the negation of negation is affirmation. But, according to the theory of Bradley, negation implies the affirmation of a contrary. But certainly the contrary of a proposition need not be that proposition. 'Yellow' and 'green' are co-contraries. Now we can say, 'this tree is not yellow', because 'this tree is green'. So far then the denial of yellow is based on its contrary 'green'. But is the negation of 'green' the same as 'Yellow'? Is the denial of 'this tree is green' the same as 'this tree is yellow'? Quite obviously this will be an invalid conclusion. 'This tree is not green' may be because it is white or black or grey. So the denial of the contrary 'green' need not be the proposition 'this tree is yellow'. If it is so, then either the case of 'Double Negation' refutes the contention of Bradley that the denial is based on the affirmation of its contraries or else the theory of 'double negation' is false. Well, Bradley is aware of this problem and states it thus :

> In judging A (The tree) not to be (yellow), I presuppose a quality (green) in A which is exclusive of b. Let us call this Y (green). I now desire to deny my judgment (this tree is not green), and need, as before, some quality on the ground of my new denial. Let us take some quality other than b. Let this quality Z (which may be black or grey or white) be exclusive of y (green), and let us see what we have. We have no AZ (white tree or grey tree or black tree or may be yellow and so on) with the exclusive of Y (green) which excluded b (yellow). But that leaves us nowhere. We cannot tell now if A is b (yellow), or is not b, because A itself, for anything we know, may also exclude b, just as much as Y did . . . . . The same result holds good with any other quality we can take, excepting b itself. The only certainty that b is not absent is got by showing that b is present.[1]

In other words, the denial is made on a positive basis, which is any property that is contrary to the negative assertion. In such circumstances the denial of the denial will not yield the required affirmation. For example, yellow is denied on the ground of green, and green may be denied on the basis of grey. Hence the denial of green does not yield yellow. Here Bradley proposes some restriction on the range of eligible contraries. Why does Bradley impose a restriction ? Why does he want to limit the range between not-B and b only ? Because he thinks that when we say 'this tree is not yellow', then we have only two statements in mind.

    (i) This tree is yellow

    (ii) This tree is not yellow.

If we have only two statements, then certainly the denial of one implies the falsity of the other and *vice-versa*. So when Bradley explains the *margin* of Double

---

1. PL, p. 159.

Negation, then he restricts the range of contraries and reduces them to a position of the orthodox-theory of contradiction.

So the whole of Bradley's treatment of Double Negation shows that, if he is anxious to equate the contradictory with the contrary on the level of predicates, this is on the understanding that contradictories are and remain contradictories on the level of propositions.[1]

We have to enquire into the metaphysical motive of Bradley as to why he has tried to reduce the contradictories, and, then again contraries to discrepants. Bradley assumes that the ultimate Reality is an all-inclusive all-harmonious, self-subsistent, individual whole. So there can be no opposites, no contraries and contradictions. There are only diversities united by internal relations. Of course thought or our discursive intellect can never reach this whole. The ultimate reality is beyond thought. Hensce, contraries and contradictories are for thought alone when it tries to unite discrepants by means of its machinery of external relations.

There are no native contraries, and we have found no reason to entertain such as idea. Things are contrary when, being diverse, they tend to be united in one point which in itself does not admit of internal diversity.[2]

Again, Bradley maintains :

Contradiction is appearance, everywhere removable by distinction and by further supplement, and removed actually, if not in and by the mere intellect, by the whole which transcends it.[2]

Now in the light of the above-mentioned metaphysical standpoint we can understand the logical reduction of the contradictories into contraries, and of the contraries into discrepants. We begin with the immediate experience which is feeling. This feeling is always 'diversity and unity in one whole and not yet broken up into terms and relations'. But by itself such an experience is 'self-transcendent and transitory'. In other words, contraries and contradictories appear to be so from a narrow standpoint only. For example, when we say that a thing cannot be both red and green at the same point and time, then we are treating the point or time-instant as a single self-contained unit. But we know there cannot be durationless instant nor indivisible point. The contraries are possible, therefore, in a world of abstraction only. The greater is the abstraction, the less opportunity there is for truth. If we widen our standpoint, then contraries are likely to be reconciled. For example, a thing is red during day, but dark at night. Here we have widened the time span and so both the contraries are true of the same thing.

1. R. Welheim, *Ibid.,* p. 147.
2. AR, p: 511.

Can this process of widening be restricted ? Now, in the metaphysics of Bradley the process of widening has no end. So there can be no pair of contraries or contradictories which cannot be reconciled. Hence within a narrow system there might be collision, but in a self-subsistent and self-contained system there can be no contraries. Contradiction therefore is everywhere and always removable by supplementation and widening of the standpoint. As the reality is always positive, so in it there can be no ultimate exclusion or negation.

> In a complete and perfect system, where all conditions were filled in, the real Universe would have all its determinations at once, all as connected and each as qualifying the others and the whole. And here negation would disappear except as one aspect of positive and complementary distinction.[1]

Thought steps into complete and supplement the deficiencies of the immediate feeling. But thought can proceed only by introducing external relations between the diversities which it discovers in the immediate experience. But external relations can never unite. Suppose thought discovers A and B as two diverse elements which being impelled by its own nature it has to unify by the relation R. R can be united with AB with the help of another relation R_1 and this again invites R_2 to relate R_1 and R, with A and B. This infinite chain of links within links can never be complete. The results is that thought can unite diversities with the help of external relations and the unities so attained are mere appearances and in the end are contradictories.

> For thought in its own nature has no 'together' and is forced to move by way of terms and relations, and the unity of these remains in the end external and, because external, inconsistent.[2]

Hence things are self-contrary when they are brought together as 'bare conjunctions'. Or, again, when there is ground of connection and distinction, then this is known as contradiction. Hence, contraries and contradictories are only for thought. They are artificial by-products.

> .... We have found that no intrinsics opposite exist, but that contraries, in a sense, are made. Hence in the end nothing is contrary nor is there any insoluble contradiction. Contradiction exists so far only as internal distinction seems impossible, only so far as diversities are attached to one unyielding point assumed, tacitly or expressly, to be incapable of internal diversity or external complement.[3]

---

1. PL, p. 138.
2. AR, p. 508.
3. AR, p. 505.

Of course this ultimate stage is only an ideal for human intellect and can never be attained.

10.19. The Disjunctive Judgment

A disjunctive proposition contains alternatives that are disjoined by 'either-or'. For examples, 'He is either wicked or foolish'. Usually a disjunctive proposition is not treated as an independent proposition, for it is supposed to be completely reducible to a combination or hypotheticals. For instance, the given disjunctive judgment can be reduced to

    (i) If he is not wicked then, he is foolish

    (ii) If he is not foolish then he is wicked

    (iii) If he is foolish, then he is not wicked.

    (iv) If he is wicked, then he is not foolish.

We have reduced a disjunctive judgment into four hypotheticals. But this is not acceptable to all logicians. According to Mill the alternatives in a disjunctive judgment need not be mutually exclusive. Therefore he does not allow the validity of (iii) and (iv). According to him a person can be both foolish and wicked. Hence from the affirmation of foolishness we cannot infer the denial of wickedness. In other words 'Or' in either foolish or wicked, according to Mill, can be interpreted conjunctively.

According to Ueberweg, on the other hand, alternatives are mutually exclusive. . . from the denial of one alternative, we can infer the affirmation of the other, and also *vice-versa*. Therefore, he grants all the four possible hypotheticals from either-or. Bradley favours the view of Ueberweg. However, everything depends on the *nature* of the alternatives used in disjunction. According to Bradley either-or always refers to incompatible alternatives. This leads to a controversy and Bradley raises the question.

Are alternatives always exclusive?

Again, with regard to the reduction of whatever may be the conclusion in terms of two or four hypotheticals, it might give one the impression that a disjunctive judgment can be reduced to a combination of hypotheticals. No doubt the meaning of a disjunctive proposition can be expressed hypothetically simply because

by an indirect process, and by making secret a categorical judgment, that hypotheticals hypotheticals can express disjunction.[1]

In other words a disjunctive proposition indirectly makes a categorical statement through the hypotheticals, i.e., a disjunctive judgment asserts a fact. Hence we have to explain now the remark of Bradley.

---

1.   PL, p. 128.

The basis of disjunction, the ground and foundation of your hypotheticals, is categorical.[1]

The metaphysical basis of Bradley's statement concerning a disjunctive judgment can be expressed by saying that the absolute reality is a unity of one and many. All Qualities belong to the reality and yet they are compatible and conjoined. So far as they are diverse, they are incompatible and disjoined.[2]

Bosanquet too very briefly states the point thus. In its perfect form, says. Bosanquet,

it is appropriate to the exposition of a content as a system, and it may be taken as returning to the categorical Judgment, and combining it with the Hypothetical, because its content is naturally taken as an individual, being necessarily concrete. [3]

With greater clarity he expresses the same point thus:

Taken all as a mass, they (systems of facts or qualities) are conjunctively connected, but taken in distinguishable relations they are disjunctively related.[4]

With the above-mentioned metaphysical background, let us try to ascertain the categorical basis of a disjunctive judgment.

Of course, a disjunctive judgment cannot be purely categorical, but by its categorical basis is meant that to some extent at least it is categorical. At least it means that *A is b* or *c*. By this is not meant that there is any object which has an ambiguous character '*b* or *c*'. No real fact can be 'either-or', except the mental state of hesitation or suspense. But a disjunctive judgment does not refer to this mental state so much as to some real fact. In the first instance, a disjunctive judgment states that *A* exists

If the subject of our predicate 'either-or' were proved not to exist, our statement could be false. It is clear not only that the subject has existence, but that it also possesses some further quality.[5]

Of course, the ultimate subject of every judgment is the absolute reality. In this context then *A* is *B* or *C* means that the quality *AB* or *AC* belongs to the reality

---

1. PL, p. 129.
2. PL, p. 138.
3. PL, pp. 123-24.
4. *Essentials of Logic*, p. 124.
5. PL, p. 129.

which can be asserted indirectly and in a concealed manner. Hence, by saying that the subject exists, is meant here 'the nature of things' which either accepts or rejects *AB* or *AC*. But what is the nature of this quality ? What does either *B* or *C* mean? Is it something that falls between them ? No, for that would be neither. For instance, grey is neither white nor black and it excludes both colour.

> It must then be a quality common to both, which is not yet either, but is further determinable as one or the other.[1]

This basis may be called x. Thus the categorical basis of '*A* is either *b* or *c*' is '*A* is *X*'. *X* may be explicit or implicit. For example in '*A* is either man or woman or child', the common basis *X* may be stated to be 'human being'. In '*A* is either white or black', it is the quality 'coloured'.

But *X*, the categorical basis of disjunctive alternatives is not any universal which is common to *b* and *c*. It is particularized. The *X* cannot be the negative of '*b* or *c*'.

> It is affirmed as fully determined not outside the region which is covered by *bc*. But since *b* and *c*, as predicated of *A*, are incompatible, it cannot be *both* of them. The conclusion remains that it must be *one*. 'One single element of the region enclosed by *bc*' is the predicate common to *b* and *c*. And this predicate it is which, in disjunction, we categorically assert of *A*.[2]

One single element within the region of bc' is a fact and no hypothesis, which is at the basis of a disjunctive judgment. But a disjunctive judgment is not wholly categorical; on the quality *X*, we erect hypothesis.

> We know that *b* and *c* are discrepant. We know that *A* is particularized within *b* and *c*, and therefore as one of *b* and *c*. It cannot be both, and it must be some one. . . .to complete the disjunction we add the supposal.[3]

'*A* is *b* or *c*' may express
   (i) If *A* is *b*, then it is not *c*, and
        if *A* is *C*, then it is not *b*,
   (ii) If *A* is not *b*, then it is *c*, and
        If *A* is not *C*, then it must be *b*.

The first two hypotheticals in (i) follow from the principle that *b* and *c* are incompatible predicates, or that *Abc* cannot be possible. The second pair in (ii) is based on the assumption that, because we do not find a predicate of *A* which excludes *b* or *c*, therefore there is none, i.e., cannot be the denial of both. In other words, within the limit of *A* there is no not-*b* but *c*, and no not-*c* but *b*: and *A* must have some further quality.

---

1. PL, p. 130.
2. PL, pp. 130-31.
3. PL, p. 131.

Therefore the essence of a disjunctive judgment is not a mere combination of supposals. It has a distinctive character of its own.

It first takes a predicate known within limits, and defined by exclusion, and then further defines it by hypothetical exclusion.[1]

Thus a disjunctive judgment is neither quite categorical nor quite hypothetical. It involves the elements of both. It is the union of hypotheticals on a categoric basis.

10.20. Are the Alternatives Always Exclusive?

We have already seen that logicians differ with regard to the nature of the alternatives involved in a disjunctive judgment. Some logicians like Carveth Read hold that either-or may have a conjunctive implication. For example, 'A is either b or c', according to this interpretation, may mean that A may be bc or b or c. In other words 'A is b or c' does not necessarily exclude 'A is both b *and* c'.

Bradley unequivocally rejects this interpretation. According to him 'Or' has no conjunctive implication. To express conjunction, we use 'and' and for expressing disjunction we use 'or'. Bradley states that he will despair of human language if the distinction between 'and' and 'or' be broken down. Under two conditions, however, Bradley admits that 'or' may mean 'and', namely,

(a) when there is a loose mode of common speech, and,
(b) when disjunction is incomplete i.e., when the qualifications under which a disjunctive judgment is made are not explicitly stated or ignored.

In the last analysis both conditions are one and the same. For example, Ram is either wicked or foolish. Ordinarily, the speaker may not *mean* to deny that Ram is both wicked *and* foolish. The speaker having no interest in showing that Ram is both, is satisfied with if Ram is found to have one of the alternatives only. The speaker ignores the possibility of Ram being both wicked and foolish. So ordinarily the speaker is right if he does not mention the alternative that Ram may be wicked and foolish as well. However, this is mere looseness in expression. Strictly speaking the speaker should logically express the disjunctive judgment as Ram is either wicked or foolish or both.

But the inaccuracy has a natural foundation. We use 'or' with an implication and at times we forget whether 'or' stands alone or with such implied qualifications. For example, when the number of tickets is *limited*, we say a person with either red or white ticket will get admittance. Here in the stated context red and white are incompatible. The implied qualification is that 'a ticket' means 'at *most* one'. But if the implied qualification is not stated then it may mean at least one'. Here a person holding both red and white tickets certainly will not be debarred. But Bradley holds that in itself 'or' is rigidly disjunctive. 'Or' is

---

1. PL, p. 137.

qualified by an unexpressed 'if not' or 'failing that'.

The alternatives offered are not red and white. Really then are firstly 'white', or 'red, white failing', or 'red without white'. These alternatives are certainly incompatible. However, 'or' is interpreted conjunctively, not because disjunction is faulty, but because it is incomplete.

> If 'white' really means 'white with or without red', and 'red' means 'red on the failure of white', and if the absence of both is fully provided for, then the disjunction is absolutely complete and exhaustive. And these alternatives (i) white with or without red, (ii) red without white, and (iii) failure of both, are absolutely incompatible.[1]

Bradley mentions the opposed view of Jevons here. According to Jevons 'Or' may be used conjunctively. For example, in 'wreath or anadem', or, 'unstained by gold or fee', 'or' is non-exclusive. By this Jevons means that the same thing may be both 'wreath and anadem', or 'gold and fee'. Here Jevons refers to the things named. Against this view of Jevons, Bradley observes that the alternatives are rigidly exclusive. The distinction here refers not to things but to the *names*. 'Wreath or anadem' means you may call it by either name you please. But can we use both names at once ? No. So the names are to be used exclusively. Take another instance, 'The greatest Roman poet is either Virgil or Vergilius. Can we say 'the greatest Roman Poet is Virgil-Vergilius? Hence Bradley concludes:

> In every instance that can be produced, we have either a loose mode of common speech, or else the 'or' denotes incompatibility, whether that lies in the simultaneous use of alternative names, or in the facts themselves.[2]

---

1. PL, p. 133.
2. PL, p. 135.

Questions for Exercise

Nobody can exhaust the possible number of questions. However, in preparation for examination critical and comparative questions have to be given special attention. For this reason a comparative knowledge concerning Substance, Innate Ideas, Causality, empiricism, rationalism and so on, is desirable. Some topics are important in themselves, for instance, the *cogito* of Descartes, the method of Spinoza, the monadology of Leibnitz, the idealism of Berkeley and Kant's doctrines of Space and Time, teachings of Transcendental Analytic etc. Somehow Locke's refutation of innate ideas, Berkeley's refutation of matter and Hume's refutation of causality have become classical. With these comments we can submit a list of the following questions:

1. What is philosophy? Is it linguistic analysis or also metaphysical? Discuss this in relation to Spinoza and Kant.

2. Point out the uses of studying 'a history of philosophy'.

3. State and explain the characteristics of 'Modern Philosophy'.

4. What are the tenets of rationalism? Why are Descartes, Spinoza and Leibniz called rationalist?

5. What is empiricism? Explain its fundamentals with special reference to Locke, Berkeley and Hume.

6. Explain the inductive method of Bacon. Can it be called a scientific method?

7. Expound the 'Idolas' of Bacon. Do they anticipate Kant's doctrine of understanding as a law-giver to nature?

8. Is Bacon the father of modern philosophy? Discuss.

9. Explain Descartes' method of doubt. Is it philosophical or scientific, deductive or inductive? (§ 2.01 and 2.02B)

10. Bring out the implications of *cogito ergo sum* for the Cartesian philosophy. Indicate its bearing for the philosophy of Hume and Kant. (§ 2.02, (A+B), 8.23)

11. Examine the proofs for the existence of God by Descartes.

The word 'examine' means here that after a careful exposition of proofs, they are to be weighed in the philosophical balance. (§ 2.04 and 2.05).

12. How does descartes establish the criterion of Truth? How does he apply the criterion in relation to the existence of the external world? (§ 2.03 and 2.07)

13. Expound Descartes' view of Substance. Does Descartes successfully establish the relation between Mind and Body? (§ 2.09)

14. Explain the doctrine of error, according to Descartes. (§ 2.0)

15. Are we justified in calling Descartes as the legislator of Modern Philosophy? (§ 2.10 A-D)

16. Describe the Geometrical Method of Spinoza and trace its effects upon his philosophy. (§ 3.03 and 3.04)

17. Explain the nature of Substance, according to Spinoza, and explain his dictum 'every determination is negation' with regard to it. (§ 3.05)

18. Explain the nature of attributes and modes, according to Spinoza. How are they related to Substance? (§ 3.07, 3.08, 3.09, 3.10)

19. What is meant by the phrases '*Natura naturans*' and '*Natura naturata*'? With reference to them discuss whether Spinozism is abstract or concrete monism. (§ 3.11)

20. Explain Spinoza's doctrine of Bondage and Liberation. Is it consistent with his pantheism?

21. What are the different stages of knowledge, according to Spinoza? Explain the nature and importance of '*amor intellectualis dei*' in Ethics. (§ 3.14)

22. Is it correct to say that Spinoza has cultivated certain seeds of Descartes' philosophy? Point out the special features of Spinoza's contributions to philosophy. (§ 3.02 and 3.17)

23. Distinguish between the 'finite' and 'infinite modes' of Spinoza. How are they related to his 'Substance'? (§ 3.09, 3.10 and 3.11)

24. Explain some of the salient features of Leibnitz's monadology. Does it reconcile the rival claims of Democritus and Plato? (§ 4.02 and 4.03)

25. Give a critical lestimate of the theory of Pre-established Harmony? Does it reconcile machanism with teleology? (§ 4.05 and 4.07)

26. Has Leibnitz explained the presence of evil by his doctrine of 'the best possible world'? (§ 4.10 Last four paras)

27. Compare Leibnitz's conception of God with that of Spinoza. Which do you prefer and why? (§4.10 (first para) and 4.12)

28. 'Monism must be pantheistic and monadism must be atheistic.' Discuss this statement with reference to the systems of Spinoza and Leibnitz. (§ 4.08 (Last para) and § 4.12)

Monism fails to do justice to the various facts of life and monadic pluralism fails to reach true unity. The Pre-established harmony of Leibnitz is an ingenious fiction. Afterwards Ward tried to give a consistent exposition of monadic pluralism. But he could at most offer a doctrine of a 'finite' God. But a finite God is no God at all. Hence, it is maintained that monadism must end in atheism.

29. 'Leibnitz abounds in ingenious distinctions but never succeeds in reconciling them.' Discuss this statement with reference to mechanism and teleology, determinism and freedom, and empiricism and rationalism. ((§ 4.07, 4.11, 4.09)

30. Give a clear exposition of Leibnitz's theory of knowledge. (§ 4.08 and 4.09)

31. Explain the relation of Mind and Body, according to Descartes, Spinoza and Leibnitz. Which one do you prefer and why? (§ 4.06)

32. Is the ultimate substance one or more? Discuss this with reference to the systems of Descartes, Spinoza and Leibnitz. (§ 4.05 will be helpful)

33. Examine Locke's refutation of innate ideas.

Here not only Lock'es refutation has to be given, but also this refutation itself has to be scrutinised. Therefore, once again the word 'examine' has to be kept in mind. (§ 5.04 and § 4.09)

34. 'There is nothing in intellect which was not previously in the senses'. Examine this statement in relation to Locke and Leibnitz. (Last para of § 5.04, 5.05 and 4.09)

35. Show how Locke received the problem of knowledge from Descartes and passed it on to Leibnitz. (§ 4.09)

This question mainly refers to the doctrine of innate ideas, though the answer should also refer to Leibnitz's attempted compromise between 'clear and distinct ideas' of Descartes and the vague sensations of Locke.

36. Explain that according to Descartes *some*, according to Locke *none*, and, according to Leibnitz *all* ideas are innate. (§ 4.0)

37. 'Locke was an empiricist, but not a consistent one'. Discuss. (§ 5.22)

1. The very conception of knowledge as consisting of universal, necessary and certain propositions is rationalistic. Experience can yield only *probable* conclusions.

2. Locke defined substance as an unknown substratum, but still retained the intuitive certainty of self and demonstrative knowledge of God. He also accepted the reality of atoms.

3. Without intelligibility of causality, he yet retained its notion in his philosophy.

4. Further, he inconsistently maintained that sensitive knowledge hardly deserves the name of knowledge, whereas intuitive and demonstrative knowledge consisting of bare tautologies, was accepted as the highest form of knowledge.

38. If the *esse* of a thing consists in its *percipi* then how does Berkeley explain the externality and permanence of things? (§ 6.06)

39. Give the refutation of matter by Berkeley. (§ 6.03)

40 Compare the view of Berkeley with that of Locke concerning abstract ideas. Which do you prefer and why? (§ 6.02)

41. To arrive at spiritualism all that Berkeley had to do was to efface the distinction between *primary* and *secondary* qualities. Elucidate. (§ 6.03B)

42. How does Berkeley establish the reality of finite spirits and God? Is he consistent with his maxim of *esse est percipi*? (§ 6.05)

43. Is Berkeley's idealism subjective or objective? Discuss. (§ 6.07)

44. Critically discuss the maxim *esse est percipi*. Is it the basis of objective idealism? (§ 6.0)

Percipi is the starting-point, but not the basis of objective idealism.

45. Explain the sensationistic atomism of Hume. Does it afford a sound basis of epistemology? (§ 7.02 and 703)

46. Show how Hume's analysis of experience leaves no ground for belief in any permanent reality, whether physical or psychical. (§ 7.04)

Here the answer mainly refers to the views of Hume, regarding substance. Here Hume's refutation of self should be elaborately given.

47. How has Hume criticized the *a priori* notion of causality? Is this account of causality adequate? Discuss. (§ 7.05)

The simple analysis is this.

(a) There are no *qualities* by virtue of which one event may be called a cause or another event (thing) be called an effect.

(b) There is no *empirical relation* either to qualify an event as cause or effect.

(c) No *a priori* decision can help, for cause and effect are *distinct* and so are separate, without any *necessary* connection between them.

(d) Observed relation between two events, regarded as cause and effect, viz., flame and heat, is one of *constant conjunction*. Events are *conjoined*, but not *connected*.

(e) Constant conjunction cannot create any new power in things or objects, but it produces an *association of ideas* and a mental habit of propensity. It is mind which forced by custom or habit of propensity. It is mind which forced by custom or habit is *forced* to take the antecedent event as cause, and the consequent event as effect. So causality is not in things, but *in mind*.

(f) Is this Human account adequate? For Kant and idealists this account is inadequate, because the mind of which Hume speaks is the individual mind of Ram, Shyam and Jadu. Individual minds differ. So no two events can be causally related logically minds differ. So no two events can be causally related logically speaking. For Kant, minds is the real source of causality, but *this mind is a priori, transcendent* and the same for all persons. There is one synthetic unity of apperception which is the ultimate ground of causality and all other categories, at the basis of scientific knowledge. As such for Kant causality is universal and necessary for the whole mankind.

Which of the two accounts are to be preferred? As causality is not necessary for sub-nuclear laws, so causality cannot be regarded as incorrigible, ubiquitous and pervasive feature of mind. At present any fundamental concept is treated as *human convention*. Causality is one of the human convention which is useful to us and as long as it is, it is to be accepted. So the transcendental and *a priori* nature of Causality has to be given up. But Hume is not correct either. No laws are incorrigible for man, either psychologically (Hume) or logically (Kant). They have originated from human endeavour to think about and control events.

48. 'The scepticism of Hume is the logical outcome of the empiricism of

Locke.' Elucidate.

§7.07 The following points

1. Knowledge is a construct of simple ideas which are supplied by sensation and reflection. End with quotation of § 5.09 lats para 'All those sublime thoughts . . . for its contemplation'.

2. What about things called tables or chairs? They are unknown substratum of qualities.

3. Causality, which help us to go beyond the given ideas. It is unintelligible concept for Locke.

Berkeley partially carries out the sceptical germs of Locke's finding concerning substance and causality. For Berkeley there is no *material* substance and there is no causality *in nature*. One event is only a sign of the other. Laws depend on the will of God. Berkeley retained selves, souls, spirits and God by calling them 'notion'. Is notion the same as ideas or not? If same, then soul is a mere stream of passing ideas without any permanent substance. If notion is not the same as ideas, then empiricism is given up.

Hume made both Locke and Berkeley consistent. Hume denied both material and spiritual substances. He also denied that *causality is in things*. Thus, there are no permanent things to know and there is no known way of causality of passing from one idea to another. So knowledge ultimately is a matter of human imaginal construction without any possible correspondence with actual state of affairs. This is known as Hume's scepticism, i.e. the denial of any universal, indubitable knowledge of things by human beings and historically it is the logical outcome of Locke's empiricism.

49. Must empiricism end in scepticism? Discuss this with reference to Hume.

If by 'empiricism' is meant Locke's empiricism, then logically and historically it does end in the scepticism of Hume.

(Give brief reference to Locke's germ of scepticism concerning substance and causality, and Berkeley's development of this sceptical conclusion. Then mention Hume's Scepticism. For details Q. 48.)

But if by empiricism is meant Logical empiricism, then it need not end in scepticism. Russell and Ayer would admit that *indubitable* knowledge is not possible. But in science we need reasonable certainty i.e. high probability. And this is granted by logical empiricism. Hence, contemporary empiricism need not end in scepticism.

50. Compare Hume's analysis of causality with that of Kant. Which do you prefer and why?

§ 8.20. Both Hume and Kant regard causality as not *in things* in their objective rights, but *in mind*. But the 'imagination' of Hume is too variable, too subjective and too psychological to account for objective and public tests. Kant's *a priori* and transcendental concept of causality accounts for scientific objectivity. But it is too mystical and does not account for corrigibility. Causality is no longer fixed and incorrigible. Modern explanation of causality is called conventionalism which combines the good points of both Hume and Kant. With Hume conventionalism holds that the concept of causality is a matter of experience of all mankind and is retained for explaining ordinary events because of its efficacy and usefulness. However, it is no longer useful in explaining nuclear events, and to that extent it is discardable and corrigible. With Kant, conventionalism agrees in maintaining that the concept of causality does not depend on an individual's will. As a matter of fact an individual is born into a certain convention, which for him appears to be incorrigible. However, against Kant, conventionalism holds that even the concept of causality is corrigible, as it is actually now in the world of neclear physics. Besides, it is not transcendental in the sense that man is not fated to make use of Causality for all times to come. True, the concept of causality has been found to be very useful for explaining and controlling gross things and events, and, it is still used in ordinary mechanical engineering or in building bridges. But being a convention, causality is no longer acceptable in nuclear physics.

51. Was Hume a Sceptic? Discuss and point out his positive contributions to philosophy.

§ 7.07. Hume was not a total sceptic, for total scepticism is self-contradictory. However, negative arguments are found in greater proportion than his positive conclusions. Hume believed that nature has given us sufficient instincts to accept what is proper for human beings. Further, his theory of imagination and association of ideas does seek a way out of this sceptical conclusions. (Last para of § 7.07 is important).

52. Has the critical philosophy of Kant succeeded in reconciling the rival claims of empiricism and rationalism?

§ 8.03 and 8.04. Bare points are as follow.

'Critical philosophy' of Kant seeks to reconcile the dogmatic and one-sided theories of empiricism and rationalism. Empiricism ends in the scepticism of Hume and rationalism ends in monadism. Rationalism not only leads to mutually contradictory conclusions of Spinozism (monism) and monadism (pluralism), but each is self-contradictory by itself. Monism of Spinoza fails to explain manyness of things and monadism fails to explain unity. Besides, rationalism cannot explain correspondence of *innate* ideas with external things.

53. What was the problem of Kant? How has he answered it?

The real problem for Kant was to explain scientific knowledge. Kant rejected empiricism as it led to the scepticism of Hume. He rejected rationalism for building castles in the air without any foundation in sense-experience. Yet his answer was the acceptance of what was right in both the systems. Empiricism and rationalism are right *in what they affirm*, and wrong *in what they deny*. In specific form Kant explained knowledge, in terms of synthetic judgments a priori in mathematics and physics.

(Bare summary of § 8.07 and § 8.08.)

54. How has Kant explained Synthetic judgments *a priori*? Point out its validity in mathematics and physics?

§ 8.06 and 8.07. For Physics § 8.08

55. Is the philosophy of Kant, Copernican or Ptolemaic? Discuss.

§ 8.03. By Ptolemaic is meant earth-centred i.e., man-centred, and by Copernican is meant sun-centred i.e., non-human reality as the centre of the universe. Kant called his philosophy 'Copernican' by which he meant revolutionary i.e. and entirely new way of looking at things. Here he held that for explaining knowledge, we must not take the externality of things first,— a postulate which has been assumed so far by the empiricist and rationalist. Kant reversed this common standpoint and instead, took the forms of mind as first and the real starting-point of epistemology. Only those things have the chance of being known which fit into the forms of mind. Thus Kant taught the priority and primacy of the *human* mind over things, by teaching the priority and primacy of the human mind over things. By teaching the priority and primacy of the human mind over things, Kant has really advanced the view of things in which man becomes the centre of the epistemological situation. Thus the *content* of Kant's critical philosophy is Polematic, though the spirit of Kant's philosophy is revolutionary and so Copernican.

56. How does Kant show that space and time are *a priori* forms of perception? § 8.11.

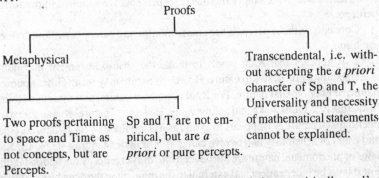

Proofs

Metaphysical

Transcendental, i.e. without accepting the *a priori* character of Sp and T, the Universality and necessity of mathematical statements cannot be explained.

Two proofs pertaining to space and Time as not concepts, but are Percepts.

Sp and T are not empirical, but are *a priori* or pure percepts.

57. 'Space and Time are transcendentally ideal, but empirically real' : Comment.

§ 8.13. For practical purposes things would appear *out there*. But the critical philosophy of Kant shows that space and time are really *in us*.

58. Give a metaphysical and transcendental deduction of the categories.

By *metaphysical* deduction is meant that from the fourfold classification of judgments, according to Quality, Quantity, Relation and Modality, twelve categories can be derived. And these categories can be classified into mathematical and dynamic categories. (§8.15)

By *Transcendental Deduction* is meant that any objective judgment requires (1) The synthesis of apprehension in intuition, (2) synthesis of reproduction in imagination and, (3) synthesis of recognition in a concept. Lastly, all these processes of apprehending, reproducing and recognising presuppose a synthetic unity of apperception. Thus, 'I think' or 'Self-consciousness' is the supreme condition of there being any objective knowledge possible. (§ 8.16 and § 8.17)

59. Give a gist of Kants' Transcendental Analytic.

(§ 8.14 and 8.15). Here Kant wants to show that without concepts, no knowledge is possible with the help of percepts alone. But ultimately the synthetic unity of apperception is the supreme condition of combining and synthesizing the discrete sensations into objective judgments.

60. "Understanding maketh nature out of the materials it does not make" : comment.

cp. § 8.19 and last two paras of § 8.20.

Knowledge proper for Kant is constituted by percepts and concepts. Percepts are obtained through sensibility and concepts are contributed by the understanding. Knowledge proper is constituted by judgments which are obtained by ordering the percepts through the concepts of the understanding. However, Sensibility is the faculty of *receiving* discrete sensations and the Understanding is the faculty of spontaneous ordering the materials supplied by Sensibility. But Understanding works even when no materials are supplied to it. It works through its concepts which are empty moulds if no percepts are supplied in the form of percepts.

Concepts without percepts are empty moulds and percepts without concepts are blind.

2. It appears that Kant wants to make the absurd statement that human understanding gives laws to nature. However, nature may mean either noumenal nature or phenomenal nature. For Kant noumenal nature, as a system of things-in-themselves is unknown and unknowable. Hence, by 'nature' Kant understands phenomenal nature as it appears to us and as it is moulded by the two forms (space and time) of sensibility and twelve categories of understanding. Thus, for Kant, laws of phenomenal nature are introduced into the percepts by the understanding. For if laws be independent and external to the mind, then they can be known only through experience. Experience for Kant, cannot explain *universality* and *necessity* involved in scientific knowledge. But if the laws be *a priori*, then they will be true for all human beings (being dependent on the very human constitution of the understanding) and so universal. Secondly, man cannot but use his *a priori* apparatus for knowing. This will explain *necessity* in scientific knowledge.

3. By 'laws' Kant does not mean 'empirical laws' but non-empirical, transcendental and *a priori* laws. Hence, Kant's explanation is metascientific (Cp the last two paras of § 8.21 and also § 8.22).

61. What is Schematism? Point out its place in relating the categories to the sensibility. (§8.21)

62. 'Kant read Leibnitz with the eyes of Hume, and Hume with the eyes of Leibnitz, and in doing this he went beyond both of them.' Comment.

(§ 8.03 and 8.04) This means that Kant criticised rationalism (represented by Leibnitz) with the help of Hume (empiricism), and criticized empiricism (Hume) with the help of Leibnitz (rationalism).

63. Knowledge must begin *with* experience, but does not necessarily originate *from* it. Elucidate.

Without experience we cannot get raw materials of knowledge. But knowledge also requires the moulding and combining these materials into judgments proper. This combining is possible by non-empirical, *a priori* forms of space and time and twelve categories of the understanding. Thus knowledge begins with sense-experience and also *originate from a priori* forms of the mind. (§ 8.03 and 8.04)

64. 'Empiricism and rationalism are right in what they *affirm*, but wrong in what they *deny*.' Explain and comment.

Empiricism and Rationalism are right in what they affirm, i.e. empiricism rightly affirms that knowledge must *begin with* experience, and rationalism rightly affirms that there are *a priori* forms which combine the discrete, separate and passing sense-impressions into judgments proper. (This part of the question is the same as Q. 63.)

Empiricism wrongly denies *a priori* elements, and rationalism wrongly denies the contributions of sense-experience (§ 8.03 and 8.04)

65. Explain Kant's distinction between phenomena and noumena. Is he justified in retaining the notion of things-in-themselves?

§ 8.37. Knowledge proper is concerned with phenomena alone. Noumena are beyond knowledge proper, for they are super-sensible. Hegel criticizes this concept of the unknowable. (§ 8.38)

For Hegel, to know a thing is to apply a category to it. In that sense we have maintained that the doctrine of the unknowable is self-contradictory inasmuch as we say that the unknowable *is*, but we do not know *what* it is. But another expedient can be suggested here in defence of the concept of the unknowable. Instead of holding that the unknowable exists, if we merely state that it *may* exist, then what possible objection can there be in saying this? Here we are not saying that the unknowable exists, nor that it does not exist. We have no ground for making any such definite statements, we have even no basis for maintaining whether it does or does not exist. But we suppose that the unknowable may or may not exist. What possible objection can Hegel bring against this position? Hegel would not accept even this last defence of the doctrine of the unknowable. Hegel would say that this defence *in principle* implies that the categories of existence-non-existence and also of possibility are applicable. Now inasmuch as categories are applicable, so the unknowable, according to Hegel, is *in principle* knowable. So according to Hegel there is no object which in principle can remain refractory to knowledge.

The position of Hegel is the same as that of Berkeley. We cannot think of anything without making it an object for thought. For this reason even the unknowable is an object *of thought* and to that extent Hegel has scored his point. But is the position of ego-centric predicament logically sound? We shall refer to this point later. There is one more point which Hegel has brought against Kant.

Hegel has pointed out that Kant did not go beyond the stage of understanding (Verstand) or abstract thinking. The abstract thinking is alright, for Hegel, for obtaining ordinary and even scientific knowledge. But this finds its limit and cannot go beyond antinomies. In order to transcend the limitation of the understanding, one has to take recourse to the higher faculty of *speculative reason* (Vernunft). At the level of speculative reason one would realise that thought and thing are identical. There may be many things unknown and they may remain unknown, but in principle no object can ever prove rebellious to thought. Things are thoughts and so no object can remain in principle beyond thought. No doubt there is the distinction of things and thought, but this distinction is at once *for* thought and is valid *within the sphere of thought.* So there can be no object absolutely independent of thought.

66. How has Kant shown that physics is, but metaphysics is not possible?

Kant holds that knowledge is limited to phenomena and physics, dealing with phenomena, is justified. But metaphysics deals with the supersensible. So no scientific knowledge of the supersensible is possible. (§ 8.08, 8.09 and 8.22)

67. Compare Kant's notion of synthetic unity of apperception with Descartes' *Cogito ergo sum.* Explain the paralogisms of reason, according to Kant. (§ 2.03 and 8.23)

68. Has Kant succeeded in showing that the so-called proofs of God are so many pleas for His existence? (§ 8.28-8.34)

69. Point out the function and place of the ideas of reason, according to Kant. (§ 8.34)

70. What are antinomies, according to Kant? What are the functions of theses and anti-theses according to him? (§ 8.25)

71. Give a gist of Kant's Critique of Pure Reason. Must duty be disagreeable, according to Kant? (§ 8.35)

72. "Like a juggler out of an empty hat, Kant draws out the concept of duty or God, immortality and freedom, to the great surprise of his readers." Comment and elucidate. (§ 8.36)

73. How has the Critique of Practical Reason modified the essentially sceptical conclusions of the Critique of Pure Reason? (§ 8.36)

74. What is idealism? What are the arguments on which it is based?

§ 9.02, 9.05 and 10.03. Idealism teaches the supremacy of mind over things. Idealism means both *ideal*-ism and *idea*-ism. As *idea*-ism, idealism is based on the epistemological argument, the first form of which is *esse est percipi*, and later on it was transformed into *esse est intellegi*. Finally in Bradley both forms have been combined for, according to Bradley idea is rooted in the immediate experience itself. (§ 10.08)

Idealism also holds that the Supreme Reality conserves values and in this form the argument is best termed *Contingentia Mundi*. In Hegel the principle is found in the form of the dialectic process of universality-finding. Bosanquet has called this as 'the spirit of totality' and in Bradley it may be called as the universal tendency of self-transcendence.

75. Mention the salient features of Hegel's idealism. (§ 9.06)

76. What is objective Idealism? Is the Idealism of Hegel Subjective or Objective? Discuss. (§ 6.07)

The essentials of objective idealism are that thought which constitute things are not dependent on any mind, whether human or divine. Secondly, these thoughts are concrete universals. Thirdly thoughts are rationally inter-related.

77. Distinguish between abstract and concrete universal. Is the idealism of Hegel based on the doctrine of concrete universal? (§ 9.03)

78. Is the idealism of Hegel, Hellenic or Kantian? Give reasons for the answer. (§ 9.00 and 9.01)

That things are ideas has been derived from Plato and Aristotle. That these ideas are reasons of things and their moulding spirit, has been derived from Aristotle. Again, that these ideas which constitute Reality are pure ideas, has been derived from Kant.

79. Explain the dialectic method of Hegel.

§ 9.11. A good answer should contain the following points:

(a) The historical background of the dialectic method
(b) Its relation to the law of contradiction
(c) Its relation to deductive and mathematical method
(d) The meaning of deductive necessity
(e) Discussion regarding the dialectic method as to whether it is logical or historical.

80. Give an outline of the dialectic advance of the World-Spirit, according to Hegel. (§ 9.10)

81. Comment: 'The real is rational and the rational is real.'

First, things of daily life are temporary, relative and dependent. Therefore they are mere appearance, and not Reality. Reality is permanent and eternal. So the reality of things consists in their being ideas which are eternal (Plato). As ideas are the reasons of things (Aristotle), so things being constituted of ideas are rational.

Secondly, ideas are concrete universals, for together they form an organic or an hierarchical system of ideas, in such a way that from any given idea, all other ideas can be deduced. In other words, ideas are logically related. That which is logical is called rational. So things being logically organized are said to be rational. Finally, Hegel has shown that Matter, Life, Mind and the whole human history are dialectically inter-related. The dialectical inter-relationship follows from the higher reasons of things. Thus, things being dialectically arranged are rational.

82. Explain the nature of philosophical explanation, according to Hegel. (§ 9.04)

83. What are the problems and assumptions of Bradley? (§ 10.01)

84. Explain the nature of Immediate Experience, according to Bradley. (§ 10.04)

85. Explain the idealism of Bradley. (§ 10.03)

86. State and critically explain Bradley's doctrine of 'Terms and Relations'. (§ 10.04)

87. How, according to Bradley, the concepts of Space and Time are self-contradictory? (§ 10.05)

88. Are relations external or internal, according to Bradley? What are the arguments of Bradley, according to which external relations are self-contradictory? (§ 10.06)

89. Explain the nature of Self, according to Bradley. How does he differ from Green and Cairds in this context? (§ 10.07)

90. How are appearances related to Reality, according to Bradley? (§ 10.08)

91. Is Time an appearance, according to Bradley? How is the Absolute related to Time? (§ 10.08)

92. What is meant by 'Degrees of Reality? (§ 10.09)

93. Explain the relation of Truth with Reality. (§ 10.10)

94. How is Bradley related to Hegel?

Bradley accepts Hegel's idealism, according to which things and thoughts are inseparable and that Reality is an organically related system of concrete universals. But Bradley lays emphasis on 'the immediate experience', and, for him no thought can be divorced from sense-experience. For this reason Bradley regards Hegel's system as an 'unearthly ballet of bloodless categories'. Again, Bradley does not accept the dialectic method as the key to idealism.

QUESTIONS

95. Explain *the nature of judgment,* according to Bradley.

I. Definition: Judgment proper is an act which refers an ideal content to a reality beyond the act. (PL I, p. 10)

II. Its analysis reveals four elements
   (a) There is an act of reference.
   (b) Of an ideal content.
   (c) To a reality independent of and apart from the ideal content.
   (d) In relation to the reality the judgment is either true or false.

These points can be made clear in the following manner.

III.   Relation between an ideal content and the reality.
- (a) Idea and fact
- (b) Fact and reality
- (c) The reference is to the reality.

IV.   Judgment can never be confined to ideas alone for in this case
- (a) Truth or falsity cannot be determined, but a judgment claims truth
- (b) Hence there is reference to a reality beyond the act of judging.

V. In order to support his contention Bradley shows that a judgment is not a relation between two ideas in which one idea is a predicate of another idea called a grammatical subject. Here he shows
- (a) Subject and predicate not always quite distinct e.g. A and B are equal
- (b) Of course, the ideal content may be complex in which case the various elements may be distinct and for the sake of convenience we can arrange them into subject and predicate. But in the final analysis the real subject is always the Absolute Reality in reference to which every judgment is said to be either true or false.

96.   Explain *the nature of Analytic Judgments* of sense.

Def.: An analytic Judgment of sense makes an assertion about that which I now perceive, or feel, or about some portion of it e.g. I have a toothache.

DOES AN ANALYTIC JUDGMENT OF SENSE ASSERT A FACT, ACCORDING TO BRADLEY? DISCUSS.

First, this has nothing to do with Kant's distinction of Judgments into Ana & Syn though at the present time, the term is used in Kant's sense only. We shall keep to Bradley's use of the term and would analyse it thus:

I.   Deals with the immediately given. But can we confine ourselves to the given?
- (a) Difficulty of 'I' the personal pronoun
- (b) The difficulty of confining ourselves to 'here' and 'now'.

II.   Imagery of the flowing stream. Two lessons from it
- (a) The focus is the only starting point.
- (b) The difficulty of confining ourselves to 'here' and 'now'.

III.   Now let us see the true meaning of analytic judgment. No subject is expressed

A. (a) Ideal reference to the whole unspecified sensible quality. 'Rain' or 'wolf'

    (b) 'asleep' or 'running', i.e. a part of the whole presentation.

B. Subject is expressed

    (a) Reference is to the whole that appears e.g. "The present is dark".

    (b) The reference is to a part of what appears e.g. This is a bird.

IV. Proper Names

V. We can never pin the ideal reference to the given.

97.   Hence the question:

Analytic judgments of sense are either false or conditioned.
(a) If one supposes that in analytic judgment we are confined to the given, then it is false, for
(b) What is given is always conditioned by other links in the chain. (pp. 100-101)

The underlying assumption of Bradley with regard to the two kinds of singular judgments *of sense* is that any knowledge must begin from what is immediately given. Hence, the starting-point of Bradley is empirical. His statement is:

"It is impossible, perhaps, to get directly at reality, except in the context of one presentation: We may never see it, so to speak, but through a hole." (PL, p. 70)

In relation to this view Bradley states that we are on surer ground in Analytic Judgment than in Synthetic Judgment of sense. But then we have to rely on inference in Synthetic Judgment much more than in Analytic Judgments. However, Bradley holds that both kinds of Judgments are descriptive and being descriptive cannot but be universal. Universals are not facts.

98.   WHAT DO YOU MEAN BY A SYNTHETIC JUDGEMENT OF SENSE? HOW DOES IT REFER TO REALITY?

Def. Judgments go beyond the given and yet must refer to the Absolute reality. Now we shall explain these two features of the synthetic judgment of sense.

A Synthetic Judgment of sense states either some fact of time or space or some quality of the given matter which we do not here and now directly perceive e.g., 'this road leads to Delhi' or 'To-morrow is Sunday'. So Synthetic judgments involve an element of inference

(49) Its analysis reveals two things in the first place

1. A Synthetic judgment starts from what is given.
2. Yet it also deals with that which transcends the given.

These two characteristics are found in all judgments, even in the singular judgments e.g. 'this bough is broken'.

(a) For what is given is only a small fraction of what is presented.
(b) And this given is only a link in the vast chain of what extends beyond the given, in all directions.

Hence, the ideal element in any judgment goes beyond the given. This is most clear in the case of universal and categorical judgments e.g. All men are mortal. The logical 'all' includes an infinite number of instances coming under it. Hence, universal judgments deal with Ideas which are not concrete but abstract. It means 'If humanity, then mortality', 'If-then' means that universals imply a supposal. Hence, All universal judgments are hypothetical, 'All' means 'If'. So a supposal. Naturally the Questions is, HOW THEN DO A UNIVERSAL AND A SYNTHETICAL JUDGMENT REFER TO THE REALITY?

True, supposal is not something given, but is an ideal experiment which lays bare the *latent* character of the reality. Ultimately the ideal experiments are applied to many given points of the reality and in this way bring out the ground or connection which holds between the elements of the ideal content. And this ground belongs to the reality. Hence Universal judgments too must refer to the reality.

Synthetic judgments refer to the reality in two-fold ways.

1. They start with the given and the given is rooted in the reality.

2. The element not given is an extension from what is given. But this ideal construction has its basis in the continuity between what is given in the focus and what surrounds the focus.

(Refer to the imagery of the stream down below the window.)

Now the given and the ideal constructions are both appearances and both of them belong to the reality. Hence, in spite of the fact that in synthetic judgments we affirm something of that which goes beyond the given, the reference is always to the reality or the total stream of our imagery. But no appearances can ever totally exhaust the reality.

99. DISCUSS THE CATEGORICAL NATURE OF A DISJUNCTIVE JUDGMENT.

or

Analyse a disjunctive judgment and discuss whether it is categorical or hypothetical.

In general a disjunctive judgment is reduced to hypotheticals. A hypothetical judgment or a supposal has its basis in the general condition of the reality. So a hypothetical is also categorical in as much as the supposal brings out the underlying inner connection in the reality. Hence a disjunctive judgment is finally categorical. We shall also show its distinctive feature towards the end of this question. Now we shall show in what particular sense a disjunctive judgment is categorical.

A disjunctive judgment is of the form 'A is B or C'. Of course, it cannot be purely categorical. It is so only indirectly and implicitly.

I. In the first instance, A *is* B or C, i.e. the fact exists about which we say ambiguously e.g. Ram of whom we say that he is '*either wicked or foolish*'.

II. (a) Of course, no quality is as ambiguous as B or C. Our knowledge may be vague and mentally we may be hesitant. But the quality is not of the form of B or C

(b) Hence 'B or C' is a quality which we may call 'X', i.e. a quality within the range of be

(i) X is *not a universal* which is common to B or C

(ii) X is not both *b* and *C*. Bradley rejects the possibility or B and C, for according to him 'or' can never mean 'and'. (A short reason to be given)

(iii) X cannot be either B or C

(iv) X is within the region of B or C and is particularized within it. This is a fact and no hypothesis.

III. Quotation, p.60

Quotation, p. 57-58

Metaphysical Basis, p. 57-58

Quotation-p. 58

Conclusion, Hence the...... p. 57

'the basis _____ is categorical'.

100. EXPLAIN, ACCORDING TO BRADLEY

(a) In the scale of reflection, negation stands higher than mere affirmation.

(b) Every negation implies an affirmation.

(c) Negation always contradicts, but never asserts the existence of the contradictories.

A. Negation and affirmation

In affirmation— There is a direct relation between an asserted quality and the reality.

In negation two phases :

(a) A quality is asserted and is expected in the reality.

(b) Expectation proves false or is rejected.

And this is negation.

Hence, Negation comes after, and evolves out of Affirmation. Negation *is not co-ordinate with* affirmation.

Some logicians by transferring 'not' from the copula to the predicate tend to reduce Negation into Affirmation, i.e.

A/is/not B

This reduction is rejected on the following grounds:

1. Copula is not necessary. Hence whether the particle 'not' be with or without copula does not matter. Only *sense* matters.

'Not wolf' is a negative judgment even when there is no copula; and 'wolf' alone is an affirmation J.

2. Bradley rejects the predicate 'not-B' in A/is/not-B on various grounds.

(a)   At times Bradley holds that not-B is mere void, nothing at all. Not-B can never be realized in thought.

(b)   At other places, he considers not-B as wholly indeterminate. For example, 'this tree is not-Yellow' means that it is either black or grey or green or any such discrepant quality which rejects 'the suggestion of yellow' with regard to this tree.

(c)   Yet in another place, Bradley rejects not-B on the ground that negation contradicts, but does not assert the existence of the contradictory. A is not B, does not mean that the contradictory of B, namely, not-B exists.

Hence, Bradley rejects the reduction of a negative judgment into an affirmative judgment.

B. But negation rests on an affirmative basis. *Every negation implies affirmation as its basis.*

'This tree is not yellow', because it is green. Again, A is not B, because it is C. Hence, the basis of denial is the presence of the positive quality 'green' or 'c'. Does this apply to both the cases of negation?

(a) Negation by opposite and
(b) Negation by privation.
(a) We deny because of the presence of the opposite quality. But in
(b) negation by privation there is bare denial, *mere absence* of a quality e.g. 'this man is blind: Bradley's theory is certainly based on the negation by opposition, but he says that it is applicable to all cases of privation as well.

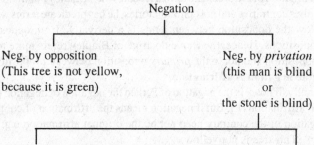

Negation

Neg. by opposition
(This tree is not yellow,
because it is green)

Neg. by *privation*
(this man is blind
or
the stone is blind)

(1) Where there is a present absence of an expected quality. 'This man has no blue eyes.' Even here there is the socket, filled or empty by peaceful eyelids. This basis is an indeterminate and an unspecified quality.

(2) Where there is no such expectation. 'This stone is blind.' Here there is some thing like ignorance of the positive quality X. But this ignorance is a positive psychological state. Hence, there is this psy. state which is the positive basis of the negation J. by privation.

C. Negation contradicts but does not assert the *existence of the contradictory.* The negative J. 'This tree is not yellow' contradicts or excludes the quality of yellow. But, Bradley tells us, it does not assert that this tree is not-yellow (because the contradictory of yellow is not-yellow). The reason is that we deny on the basis of some positive quality which is *contrary and not the contradictory* of the quality denied. 'This tree is not a yellow', because the tree is green or grey. Now 'green' or 'grey' is the contrary of 'yellow'. Hence, *neg. contradicts, but assert the existence of the contrary and not of the contradictory*

(a) This contrary may be difinite, or

Because the tree is known to be green or grey. Hence, the contrary may be determinate.

(b) This may be indeterminate

'This tree is not yellow', because it may be either green or grey or white or any such contrary. Hence, the contrary is there, but is indeterminate.

II. Negation contradicts but does not assert the existence of the contradictories, refers to the *predicate* terms or their derivatives and to the *propositions*. In traditional logic opposition refers to the two propositions having the same subject mostly. Hence, whether the opposition is one of contrariety or contradiction depends on the nature of the predicate terms. Hence, when Bradley maintains that negation implies contraries and not contradictories, he has predicate terms within his mind. Now the opposition between terms is a derivative from opposition between propositions. Hence, the above doctrine of Bradley refers more to the *derivative* opposition and not to the *primary* opposition between propositions.

III. **Double negation is affirmation.**

Traditionally, if not-P is the negation of P, then the negation of negation (not-P) is original affirmation (P). But if negation means the affirmation of contrary, then the negation of the contrary need not be the original affirmation e.g.

This tree is not yellow.

Because   This tree is green.

Now let us deny green —'This tree is not green'

Because 'this tree is grey'.

Hence, the denial of the denial is grey and not yellow.

Therefore, either Bradley's theory of negation in terms of contraries has to be given up, or, the traditional theory of 'Double Negation' has to be given up.

Bradley maintains both. In the case of double negation, he says the range of contraries has to be restricted between two qualities only, i.e.

1. This tree is yellow, and

2. This tree is not yellow.

Of course, by restricting the range between *two propositions* only, the T of one implies that of the other, and *also* vice-versa. So it becomes a case of traditional relation of contradiction.

Hence, Bradley confines himself to contrary terms with regard to his general theory of negation; but reverts to propositions when he comes to justify the theory of double negation.

101. Do we make predication of a grammatical subject *in a judgment*?

Traditionally a judgment has been divided into three parts, namely (i) subject (ii) predicate, and (iii) a copula. Bradley rejected the traditional view of judgment because of his monistic vision of the reality. According to the traditional view the subject of a judgment is a substance. As there are many grammatical subjects, so one will have to accept the existence of many substances. This will lead to pluralism. Hence, in the interest of monism, Bradley rejected the notion of 'grammatical subjects' in judgments. His reasons for the rejection of this traditional view are as follow:

1. In predication we assert, say, A is B.
2. However, this subject-predicate view of judgment leads to this dilemma 'If you predicate what is different you ascribe to the subject what it is *not;* and if you predicate what is *not* different, you say nothing at all'. (AR, p. 17)
3. If the predicate is not different from the subject then all subject-predicate statements are really identity statements.
    (a) All identity-statements are tautologous.
    (b) If tautologies are taken to be any *significant* assertion, then they are really empty assertion.

Subject-predicate statements are really identity-statements: The assertion that A is B is true if and only if B is not different from A, and false if and only if B is not different from A. Now if A is B is true, then it means that B is not different from A. This means that B is the same as A. So to assert that A is B, is to assert that a relation of identity holds between A and B.

If all judgments are subject-predicate judgments, then they are really identity-statements.

Identity-statements are tautologies

If A is the same as B, then there is no difference between A and B. And if there is no difference between A and B then it means that A is the same as B. Hence it means that A is B is the same as A is A. Hence the identity statement becomes a case of tautology.

All tautologies are really false

If A is B really means A is A, then the assertion is empty. When we assert that A is A, then there are no two things or elements so to hold that tautologies are *assertion* is false. But the subject-predicate view of judgments holds that there is an assertion, for we have started with 'A is B' where B is said to be asserted of A.

We conclude that the subject-predicate view concerning judgments is not tenable. Now we shall try to make clear these reasons of Bradley for rejecting the traditional view that a judgment makes a predication of a grammatical subject.

Does the judgment A is B mean that A is A?

Few people will think, that the judgment 'the day-star is bright' is a statement of identity, that is, 'the day-star is day-star'. Therefore, Bradley establishes this interpretation of A is B as identity-statement by eliminating various other possible interpretations of 'A is B'. *Nominalist* holds that A is B means that the name 'A' and the name 'B' are borne by the same individual. Here Bradley holds that some judgments may be about names, but certainly a majority of them, says Bradley, are assertion about *things* and not about names. In current language we can say that this nominalistic interpretation is based on a confusion between *use* and *mention* of a word. Thus Bradley indirectly refutes the nominalism of De Morgam.

Again, Jevons had advanced the *equational interpretation* of A is B as A being numerically equivalent to B (PL, pp. 22-23). Bradley rejects this. Let us take an example, namely, 'Hope is dead'. Now it is absurd to say, says Bradley that this judgment means that 'In hope and a fraction of dead things there is exactly the same sum of units. (PL, p. 23).

Thirdly, there is the view that 'A is B' asserts *likeness or similarity*, either partial or complete between A and B. Bradley rejects this view on the ground that facts go against this interpretation. Can the subject-predicate judgments be interpreted at stating 'inclusion in, or exclusion from, a class? Let us take this view in conjunction with Hamilton's theory of the quantification of predicates. According to class-inclusion theory, in the light of the quantification of predication 'All negroes are men' and 'All equilateral are equiangular' mean. All negroes are *some* men' and 'All equilateral Δs are all equiangular Δs'. But is the interpretation justifiable?

Here Bradley observes that 'negroes = some men' is not true for certainly, 'some men' may refer to Chinese, Japanese, Indians. In such a case 'some men' are not negroes. The matter will not improve, says Bradley, if qualitative fraction be substituted for 'some men'. The qualified adjective is universal, which can be applied to other men as well as to negroes. If one say 'negroes are 1/3 men do not cover negroes only, but is equally applicable to 2/3 men who are not negroes. (PL, p. 24)

Hence to be consistent, says Bradley, we must not merely quantify the predicate, we must actually specify it. Here we have to say that negroes are negromen. But in this case the proposition turns out to be an identity-statement. In this context it is worthy of note that the subject-predicate view of statements makes a sharp distinction between the functions of subject and predicate. The subject-term functions *referentially* for an object about which the assertion is made; the predicate-term functions descriptively, attributing a quality to an object. Bradley rejected this distinction, as is clear from his interpretation of subject and predicate in terms of extension and intension.

Bradley holds that both the subject and predicate have to be consistently interpreted, either extensionally or intensionally. And in either case, Bradley holds, the subject-predicate view of proposition will be reduced to identity-statements. In the first instance both the terms have to be interpreted referentially otherwise there will be nothing about which any predication can be made.

> If we keep to extension we must keep to the objects, and it is these we must try to predicate of the subject. In 'Dogs are mammals' we must try to assert some 'mammals' of dogs. What is affirmed must be identity. The dogs and dog-mammals are all the same thing. (PL, p. 177)

If extensional or referential interpretation leads to the identity of subject and predicate, then is the intensional interpretation any better? Well, if both the terms be interpreted intensionally, then both the terms become adjectives and then there is no object which can be the subject of assertion. And this is contrary of the traditional view of judgments. By the way this will pave the way for Bradley's theory according to which the subject of any judgment is not within it but is the reality itself.

Hence, if we interpret the subject and the predicate referentially, then judgments turn out to be identity-statements, and, if we interpret them intensionally, then the traditional view gives way to Bradley's theory of Judgment.

All identity-judgments are tautologies

There are two kinds of identity-statements, namely

    (a) The evening star is the evening star.

    (b) The evening star is the morning star.

Only the former type of statements can be tautologous, but not of the type (b). 'The evening star is the morning star', is not tautologous for it is not analytic. As a matter of fact the statement (b) is empirical. If Bradley had paid some attention of this type of identity-statements, he would not have regarded all identity-statements to be tautologous. There were two reasons for his committing the mistake.

I. First, Bradley had a very partial view concerning the meaning of a term. According to him the meaning of a term is to be identified with that to which it refers. Hence, if the two terms have the same reference then, according to him, they have the same meaning. It was Frege who analysed the notion of meaning and distinguished between the *sense* (Sinn) and the reference (Bedeutung) of an expression. The reference relates to the object to which an expression refers. The sense however depends on the mode or manner in which the object is presented. The truth-falsity of identity-statements depends on the referential objects. But whether an identity-statement is tautologous or not depends on the *sense* of the expression: Now (b) i.e. 'The evening star is the morning star' is true because the S and P refer to the same object. But is not tautologous because the 'evening star' has not the same sense as the 'morning star'. As Bradley failed to distinguish between the *sense* and *reference* of an expression, so he wrongly regarded all identity statements to be tautologous.

II. The second reason for his mistake lay in having a very inadequate symbolic, expression of his example. Keeping to the designatum-view of meaning, Bradley points out that the subject-predicate not only should be quantified, but also be specified. For example, 'Iron is some metal' is not correct expression of 'Iron is a metal'. It should be 'Iron is iron-metal'. Let 'Iron' be 'A' and 'non-metal' be AB. Now here we have to ascertain whether the identity-statement is tautologous.

> That A should be truly the same as AB, and AB entirely identical with A, is surely a somewhat startling result. If A=A, can it also be true to add B on one side leaves the equation where it was? If B does not mean O, one would be inclined to think it must make some difference. But, if it does make a difference, we can no longer believe that A=AB, and AB=A..... If there really is a difference between the two, then your statement is false when by your '=' you deny it. But if there is no difference, you are wrong in affirming it, and in opposing' 'iron' to iron-metal. (PL, p. 25)

But is the observation of Bradley correct? The identity-statement need not be tautologous and yet true. For example, 'The victor of Ramillies is (identical with) the victor of Ramillies and the victor of Blenheim'. Nobody would maintain that the victor of Blenheim is devoid of any meaning.

All tautologies are false
Bradley has gone wrong in holding that all identity-statements are tautologous. He has gone wrong further still in holding that all tautologies are false. In holding that all tautologies are false, Bradley appeals to Hegel Let us take the tautology A is A.

> As Hegel tells us, it sins against the very form of judgment: for, while professing to say something, it really says nothing. It does not even assert identity. For identity without difference is nothing at all. (PL, p. 141)

In other words, Bradley is maintaining that we cannot have a judgment without difference. Quite obviously, Bradley is maintaining something here which he tried to undo in reducing subject-predicate proposition to identity and in reducing further identity-statements into tautologies.

Concluding Summary
The upshot of the whole argument is that no predication is made in a judgment. There is something of which an assertion is made. As a matter of fact both S and P are to be taken together and taken together they are predicated of the reality. We should be able to write in every case "Reality is such that S is P". (ETR, p. 333)

But why not the dilemma concerning predication be applied to the Reality as a whole? If SP is the same as 'Reality then we say nothing and if SP is, different from Reality, then our assertion is false. This requires a careful consideration.

INDEX